HIDDEN ®

British Columbia

Including Vancouver, Victoria & Whistler

Eric Lucas

FOURTH EDITION

Ulysses Press ®
BERKELEY, CALIFORNIA

Published by: ULYSSES PRESS
           P.O. Box 3440
           Berkeley, CA 94703
           www.ulyssespress.com

ISSN 1523-5300
ISBN 1-56975-449-7

Printed in Canada by Transcontinental Printing

10 9 8 7 6 5 4

EXECUTIVE EDITOR: Leslie Henriques
MANAGING EDITOR: Claire Chun
EDITOR: Lily Chou
COPY EDITOR: Katherine Wright
EDITORIAL AND PRODUCTION: Steven Zah Schwartz, Lisa Kester, James Meetze, Leona Benten, Laura Brancella
CARTOGRAPHY: Pease Press
HIDDEN BOOKS DESIGN: Sarah Levin
COVER DESIGN: Leslie Henriques, Sarah Levin
INDEXER: Sayre Van Young
COVER PHOTOGRAPHY: Jupiterimages.com
ILLUSTRATOR: Doug McCarthy

Distributed in the United States by Publishers Group West and in Canada by Raincoast Books

HIDDEN®

British Columbia

"Bigger than Washington, Oregon and California combined—British Columbia has never been easier to navigate than with this guide."

San Francisco Chronicle

"This guide ferrets out off-the-beaten-track, lesser known or overlooked destinations, restaurants, lodgings and other phenomena that make for bona-fide travel."

The Vancouver Courier

"Armed with this book, our American guests should enjoy getting lost in B.C."

Victoria Times-Colonist

To Leslie Mae,

who has opened the door to
wondrous, unexpected journeys.

Acknowledgements

Writing a book about a region as large and varied as British Columbia and the Yukon would be impossible without the help of many wonderful people.

I've been aided by hundreds of Canadians whose love for the place they live is matched by their friendliness to travelers; their contributions ranged from opinions about local restaurants to directions along seemingly endless back roads. Chief among these helpers are Laura Serena and Lynda Trudeau, tourism media liaisons. Thanks also to Nora Weber, Heather Jeliazkov, Deirdre Campbell, Suzanne Girard, Brian Tate, Lee Morris, Tanis Fritz, Patricia Eyford, Glenda Patterson, Lena Canada, Kathy Cooper, Jayne Lloyd-Jones, Jill Killeen, Lise Magee, Leaf Escaravage, Wendy Cairns, Carson Schiffkorn, Larry Nagy and Jose Janssen, Carol Harper, Joanna Tsaparas, Richard Padmos, George and Rosemarie Greedy, Laura Street, Angela Murrills, Mark Nichiporuk, Norm and Nan Dove, and Anthony Everett; to Pat and Juanita Corbett, the fabulous hosts at Hills Health Ranch; and Nancy Peregrine.

What's Hidden?

At different points throughout this book, you'll find special listings marked with a hidden symbol:

◄ HIDDEN

This means that you have come upon a place off the beaten tourist track, a spot that will carry you a step closer to the local people and natural environment of British Columbia and the Yukon.

The goal of this guide is to lead you beyond the realm of everyday tourist facilities. While we include traditional sightseeing listings and popular attractions, we also offer alternative sights and adventure activities. Instead of filling this guide with reviews of standard hotels and chain restaurants, we concentrate on one-of-a-kind places and locally owned establishments.

Our authors seek out locales that are popular with residents but usually overlooked by visitors. Some are more hidden than others (and are marked accordingly), but all the listings in this book are intended to help you discover the true nature of British Columbia and the Yukon and put you on the path of adventure.

Write to us!

If in your travels you discover a spot that captures the spirit of British Columbia and the Yukon, or if you live in the region and have a favorite place to share, or if you just feel like expressing your views, write to us and we'll pass your note along to the author.

We can't guarantee that the author will add your personal find to the next edition, but if the writer does use the suggestion, we'll acknowledge you in the credits and send you a free copy of the new edition.

ULYSSES PRESS
P.O. Box 3440
Berkeley, CA 94703
e-mail: readermail@ulyssespress.com

Contents

Maps

OUTDOOR ADVENTURE SYMBOLS

The following symbols accompany national, provincial and regional park listings, as well as beach descriptions throughout the text.

▲	Camping			Snorkeling or Scuba Diving
	Hiking			Waterskiing
	Biking			Windsurfing
	Downhill Skiing			Canoeing or Kayaking
	Cross-country Skiing			Boating
	Horseback Riding			Boat Ramps
	Swimming			Fishing

ONE

British Columbia

The forces—human and natural—that made British Columbia spared nothing in the effort. The region is geographically, climatically, economically and culturally one of the most spectacular and varied in North America. The natural beauty of British Columbia is astounding. The people are friendly and diverse, and happy to live where they do. The rivers are broad and powerful, the mountains stunning snow-blanketed spires, the valleys green vales, the islands peaceful refuges. B.C.'s biggest city, Vancouver, is a world-class urban center. The province's natural resources hold immense wealth; its agriculture is famously bountiful; its seas are the source of fisheries that until recently seemed limitless. And B.C.'s wild lands harbor the greatest diversity of wildlife in North America, from desert species (rattlesnakes) to subarctic (caribou).

Vancouver and Victoria regularly show up in the top ten among polls of favorite travel destinations, and you don't have to look far to see why. Anglers the world over dream of B.C.'s lakes, rivers and salmon waters. Towering mountains, deep snowfalls, long seasons, and friendly resorts draw skiers from all over to Whistler; meanwhile, less than 100 miles away, the climate on the Sunshine Coast is balmy enough to grow palm trees.

Thousands of lakes (many reached by no road), hundreds of miles of coastal saltwater and thousands of miles of surging rivers are trafficked by millions of salmon and trout. And wilderness: several of the world's top backcountry treks await backpackers, who can wend their way along trackless ocean beaches, through stunning forested valleys, across gemlike lakes, down gaping canyons or across untrodden alpine tundra.

Urban pleasures abound as well: B.C. chefs have crafted the area's wide range of foodstuffs into a West Coast cooking style that melds Indian, Asian, European and coastal influences into a distinctive, savory whole. B.C.'s vineyard industry is coming into its own; its microbreweries are among the industry's originators; and Vancouver, like Seattle, is one of the top gourmet coffee cities on earth.

Canada's best theater, music, art and literature is born in or visits British Columbia. Vancouver is the center of a near-billion-dollar film industry, and not by accident: few places outside California offer so many options to filmmakers.

The province is equally varied socially and politically. Greenpeace was born in Vancouver, yet it's the capital of Canada's timber industry. Crime is low, by North American standards, yet social mores would seem quite lax to Southern Baptists visiting Wreck Beach, Vancouver's legendary nude showcase. Hunting and fishing are top tourist draws throughout the province, yet Vancouver residents voted to shut the Stanley Park Zoo in the early '90s, one of the first communities in the world to do such a thing.

Not surprisingly, such vast variety comes in a huge package. At 366,275 square miles (948,596 square kilometers), it's bigger than Washington, Oregon and California combined, and if you wanted you could squeeze Vermont in there, too. Drive north from the U.S./B.C. border at the 49th parallel, and you'd hit the end of the province almost 800 linear miles away at 60 degrees north. Start at the same spot and drive an equal distance south and you'd wind up halfway between Los Angeles and San Francisco.

▼▼▼▼▼▼▼▼▼▼▼▼▼▼▼▼▼▼▼

The British Columbia Story

GEOLOGY

Five major mountain ranges divide British Columbia into a peak-and-valley topography unlike any other in North America. Combined with the Pacific Coast climate, this topography is the key to the province's character and history; this is one place where *place* really matters.

Although the Rocky Mountains are what most people think of as the West's mountains, this range in fact only forms the eastern border of British Columbia. At the Rockies' foot, a remarkable geographic feature known as the Rocky Mountain Trench stretches from the U.S. border almost 700 miles north to the Liard River. Although quite narrow, this is North America's longest valley. The other mountain ranges are (from east to west, generally) the Columbia, Selkirk, Cariboo, Monashee and Chilcotin mountains, and finally the Coast Range, the forbidding granite wall of peaks that runs from the North Shore of Vancouver all the way to Alaska. Vancouver Island is also split by an imposing central range of mountains.

These mountains indelibly determine B.C.'s character. More than 75 percent of the province, for instance, lies above 3000 feet; among other things, this means most settlement is confined to the fairly narrow valleys between mountain ranges. The exception is the Interior Plateau, a vast escarpment between the Cariboo and Coast ranges.

The plateau, despite its name, is not flat; it's simply a less mountainous region, more than 200 miles wide and 300 miles long, in which elevations top out at about 3000 feet (1000 meters). There are really just two flat areas in all of B.C.—the fairly small Fraser

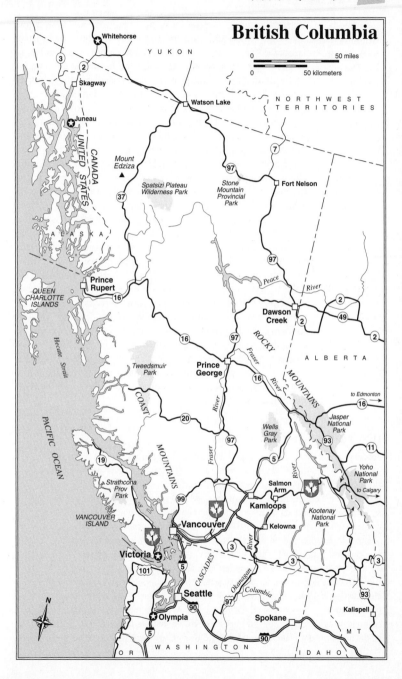

British Columbia

River delta that comprises the Vancouver metropolitan area and the Lower Mainland; and the Peace River plains northeast of Prince George, a small corner of the North American Great Plains.

Six major rivers cut through B.C. The Columbia arises in the southeastern corner of the province, heads north and then abruptly turns back south on its long journey into Washington state. The Fraser, B.C.'s longest river at 950 miles (1368 km), arises at the foot of the Rockies and like the Columbia also heads north, then swings back south in a wide arc through Prince George, carving a huge and fearsome canyon hundreds of miles long on its path to the coast. The Fraser is one of the largest undammed rivers on earth; it drains almost a quarter of the province. B.C. residents today are proud that there is not a single major dam on its mainstem—a distinction achieved only after many conservation battles earlier this century.

The Skeena and Stikine river systems arise in inland mountains in north B.C. and cut through the Coast Range to join the Pacific; they and the Fraser are the only major rivers to successfully breach the coastal mountain barrier. The Skeena traverses a wide valley ringed by mountains and splashed by showers and rainbows; the Stikine carves a massive canyon, at one point of which the entire river crashes through a seven-foot gap in the rocks. The Peace and the Liard rivers arise in the mountains north of Prince George, spill out onto the plain and head for the Arctic. The Peace and the Columbia both have been dammed on their upper reaches for large-scale hydroelectric projects. The dams on the Columbia and Peace are the foundation of B.C. Hydro's vast production of hydroelectric power, the surplus of which it sells to utilities as far south as Mexico.

NOT OUT OF THE WOODS YET

About 90 percent of B.C. is public land, and despite the traditional practice of awarding long-term leases to timber and cattle interests, ever-greater portions of it are being assigned preservation status. The government met its goal to have 12 percent of the land base (44,000 square miles) protected by 2000, and thousands of square miles of new parks were added by the outgoing government in late 2001. With all its natural wealth, however, the province has come under criticism for its lack of environmental protection; clearcuts (called "cutblocks" in B.C.) seem to be everywhere. As a result, a Greenpeace-led boycott of B.C. forest products prompted the province's largest timber company, MacMillan-Bloedel, to renounce clearcutting in 1998. MacBlo was bought by Weyerhaeuser in 1999; it remains to be seen whether the new owners will keep the company's commitment, although they did negotiate new, restrictive harvest guidelines with the Haida people of the Queen Charlotte Islands.

This complex terrain, carved by these rivers and by several ice ages, creates a complex environment. In the Fraser River canyon, 50 miles separates rainforest from desert; along the southern coast, winters are so mild that palms grow, while the Peace River country is subject to severe Arctic incursions during which temperatures reach 60 below. Rainfall ranges from 15 to 20 feet a year along the west-facing coastal slopes, to less than ten inches on the east side of the steepest mountains.

British Columbia's coastline, broken by as many fjords as Norway's, stretches a mind-boggling 16,780 miles (27,000 km) along a linear distance of about 1000 miles. Hundreds of islands add to the geographic confusion, including Vancouver Island, a massif 280 miles long that all by itself is slightly larger than Holland. Geologically distinct from Mainland B.C., Vancouver Island (along with the Alaska Panhandle) is suspected by some geophysicists to have migrated along the West Coast from Mexico over the past 90 million years.

Mountains mark the B.C. mainland. The province is bordered by two major chains, the Coast Range and the Rockies, with several notable ranges interspersed, such as the Kootenays, the Selkirks, the Monashee and the Cariboo. More than half the province is above 4000 feet. The sheerest, highest chain is the Coast Range, in which Mount Waddington near Ts'yl-os Park is, at 13,175 feet (4016 meters), the highest peak. It is because of this massive coastal mountain barrier that much of the province's interior is relatively dry and sunny. The only sizeable plain is in the northeast corner, along the Peace River.

There are ten separate ecological zones in B.C., ranging from coastal rainforest to Great Basin desert. As a result this is Canada's most ecologically rich area: of the country's 578 bird species, 454 are found in B.C. More than half the freshwater fish—100 of 191 —and 143 of Canada's 196 mammal species are in the province. There are 2500 different plant species—three-quarters of those in Canada—and 35,000 insects. Yes, that includes a few mosquitos.

The Yukon's topography is as rugged as B.C.'s, if not more so. The entire southern two-thirds of the territory consists of countless mountain ranges riven by powerful watercourses, including the Yukon River itself. Kluane National Park, in the extreme southwest corner, holds Canada's highest peak, Mount Logan; the sheer ramparts of Kluane's Coast Range account for the relatively dry interior climate. The MacKenzie Mountains, which form the eastern Yukon border, comprise one of the most forbidding wilderness areas in North America, crossed by zero roads and very few people. In the Yukon, as in B.C., roads and settlements hug the river valleys.

Mountains yield forests, especially in a land constantly struck by incoming Pacific weather systems. More than 60 percent of B.C.

FLORA

is forested; Douglas fir, cedar and spruce dominate the coastal forests, while pine, spruce and hemlock mark the interior. But local variation is considerable along such rugged mountains—the west sides of interior ranges hold lots of Douglas fir and cedar, and the dry east sides of coastal ranges harbor pine, chiefly lodgepole. Grasslands are common along the river valleys and on the vast interior plateau that holds the Cariboo and Chilcotin regions.

Pacific Coast forests bring to mind big trees—the coast of Vancouver Island holds Canada's tallest, a mammoth Sitka spruce (almost 300 feet tall); giant Douglas firs, Western red cedars, Western hemlocks and ponderosa pines are found throughout the province. A now-dead cedar right inside the Vancouver city limits (in Stanley Park) once was the largest in the world.

Those are the major timber species; Douglas fir is the most widely distributed and the most valuable timber tree in North America. Fir, cedar, hemlock and spruce can all potentially grow past 300 feet in height and 15 feet in diameter in ideal locations. Usually, however, ancient giants have had their tops broken off in storms. Ironically, Douglas fir is not a true fir, and red cedar is not cedar at all. (There are no true cedars native to the Western Hemisphere.) Preserved groves of big trees dot the province—one of the most accessible places to see some is Lighthouse Park on Vancouver's North Shore. However, big conifers are only part of the story.

With as many as 42 different First Nations dialects, B.C. is among the most linguistically diverse areas on earth.

B.C. is also home to bigleaf maple, a very large hardwood that has the biggest leaf of all northern hemisphere deciduous trees—sometimes as large as 18 inches across. Arbutus, a slow-growing hardwood called madrone or madrona in the United States, is a distinctive red-barked broadleaf evergreen found in dry sites near saltwater; most are on the Sunshine Coast and southern Vancouver Island. Red alder is a vigorous soft hardwood related to birch; it's found in damp locations, often alongside streams.

Inland, the forest shifts to pine—lodgepole and ponderosa, mostly, with Canada's largest specimens of the latter found in the Okanagan Valley. The high plateau forests of the Cariboo and Chilcotin regions are mostly Douglas fir and lodgepole pine.

Forests are not just trees. The coastal woods hold thick understories of salmonberry, salal (an evergreen broadleaf shrub that bears a dark blue berry) and a wicked thorny plant called devil's club. Trillium, lilies and other delicate flowers inhabit the forest floor.

The inland flora ranges from cactus, greasewood and sagebrush in hot desert valleys to vast rolling prairies of grass on higher plateaus. The cattle country of the Cariboo, Chilcotin and Okanagan are known for rich fields of bunchgrass, which amazed early settlers because it grew as high as a horse's belly.

Wildflowers range from coastal shrub roses—fragrant pink wonders—to the rare Pacific rhododendron (look for this in the lowlands of Manning Provincial Park) to columbines in the high country. Mushrooms are numerous, including the famed chanterelles and boletus that collectors fancy. However, B.C. fungi also include the deadliest species in North America—*do not pick any without expert guidance*. Even those familiar with mushrooms elsewhere should beware: some potentially poisonous coastal species are similar to benign species found in other places.

The same caveat obtains for other edible plants. Wild onion, for instance, was a staple pioneer food—and can be confused with death camas. Cow parsnip looks similar to poison hemlock. Wild raspberries, blueberries, huckleberries and strawberries are easy to identify and safe.

Despite its far-northern latitude, the Yukon's tree line extends almost all the way north to the Beaufort Sea. Its forests are mostly hardy lodgepole pine, spruce and cottonwood, with some aspen, confined to lower elevations along river valleys and the few low plateaus. The small size of the trees restricts commercial use, and hence there is little timber industry in the Yukon.

Mountains, lakes, rivers and forests yield wildlife; B.C. is an especially favorable habitat for predators. Eagles and bears, wildcats and salmon—condense B.C.'s wildlife to that little line of doggerel and you'd have captured about half of the most notable denizens of this geographic wonderland. B.C. is distinguished by special preeminence for all four of those animals. There are roughly 100,000 black bears and 10,000 grizzlies in British Columbia (though some environmentalists dispute those figures as overly optimistic); there may be as many as 15,000 cougars, and experts suspect Vancouver Island may have the world's highest density of mountain lions. B.C. is home to the largest populations in Canada (and North America, outside Alaska) of all these animals, plus vast herds of deer, elk, caribou and moose; and millions of birds, including hundreds of migratory species ranging from hummingbirds to bald eagles. For even broader perspective, naturalists point out that B.C. is home to 60 percent of the world's mountain goats, 25 percent of earth's grizzly bears, and 25 percent of the world's bald eagles. Among the bears is a rare race of white-coated black bears, called spirit bears or Kermode bears, that inhabit the central coast north of Vancouver Island.

There are also huge numbers of bald eagles—25,000 in the winter. As for salmon—the Fraser River system alone hosts runs reaching past 20 million fish in good years.

But these charismatic species are only the beginning. Moose and deer are common; so are elk in the southern sections and on Vancouver Island. Caribou roam northern B.C.; wolves are found

FAUNA

throughout the province. Tens of millions of migratory birds, including snow geese, white swans and other rare species, fly the coasts and inland waterways during their annual north–south journeys. Hawks, falcons, kites and owls, as well as bald and golden eagles, are common. The average B.C. visitor who ventures outside the two major cities is liable to see any of these animals, except for mountain lions. In fact, incautious visitors may see them under undesirable circumstances: the many moose crossing signs found in the Cariboo and north B.C. are to be taken quite seriously.

Dozens of other, lesser known species abound, ranging from martens to bats, from salamanders to rattlesnakes.

While bears are common in B.C., they are endemic in the Yukon, a daily fact of life for territory residents. Unlike B.C., though, here grizzlies (7000 to 8000) are in rough proportion to black bears (10,000). There are also a few hundred polar bears in the far north. The Yukon is prime habitat for caribou, both the woodland race (35,000) and the barren-ground Arctic type (180,000). The Porcupine barren-ground caribou herd, which roams northern Yukon into Alaska, is one of the largest of all. Currently healthy, it may be threatened by U.S. proposals to develop oil fields in northeast Alaska.

There are also smaller numbers of moose, elk and deer, and a healthy population of the wolves that prey on all these ungulates. The powerful presence of timber wolves (numbering 4500 in the Yukon) figured greatly in one of the most famous of all Yukon stories, Jack London's *To Build a Fire*.

The territory's far-northern Arctic wetlands are significant waterfowl breeding grounds in the summer, when insect numbers soar. Yes, those are the same insects that make life miserable for non-avian residents such as caribou, moose, bears and people.

HISTORY   **THE FIRST PEOPLE**   Natural riches are what have always drawn human beings to B.C. The area's first inhabitants arrived thousands of years ago—the oldest known site, Xa:ytem (east of Vancouver), shows signs of occupation 9000 years ago. These First Nations residents, who arrived on the Bering land bridge a millennium or so before reaching the Fraser Valley, probably came for the same things their descendants were enjoying 8800 years later, when European explorers arrived: bountiful salmon runs, dependable berry crops, cedar bark and wood. The area's profound geographic difficulties created numerous autonomous pockets of culture.

EXPLORATION AND SETTLEMENT   The mountains are what attracted European interest in British Columbia. First, around 1800, it was trappers seeking furs; little more than a half-century later, the discovery of gold precipitated a 50-year tide of exploration and development, with dozens of mountain towns undergoing the boom-to-bust syndrome in short periods of time. Considering the contrasts that typify B.C.'s geography, corresponding economic contrasts are little surprise.

The first recorded white explorers, Spanish sea captains, sailed around Vancouver Island and into the Strait of Georgia in 1792. They were followed in short order by British Captain George Vancouver, who not only surveyed the coastal territory much more extensively, but managed to talk the Spanish into ceding their northern interest, avoiding war, and concentrating on California. Meanwhile, an extremely determined overland trekker named Alexander Mackenzie crossed B.C. on foot, arriving at the Pacific near present-day Bella Coola in 1793—a journey as daunting and remarkable as that performed by Lewis and Clark farther south a decade later. Ironically, Mackenzie missed bumping into Vancouver by a few weeks.

> Recent historical research suggests Sir Francis Drake explored the Northwest Coast in 1579 while on a secret mission for Queen Elizabeth I; his discoveries were concealed by the British crown for two centuries.

Vancouver had encountered terrifying storms, Mackenzie mind-bogglingly difficult terrain. (The trail he followed from the Cariboo to the coast has recently been restored; it's one of the world's most challenging wilderness treks, taking up to a month.) Nonetheless, B.C.'s wealth was apparent. Furs drew the first settlers, Hudson's Bay Company trappers who established Fort St. James in north-central B.C. in 1806, a desperately remote outpost through which millions of dollars in beaver, lynx, marten, wolf, fox and other skins flowed. Fort Langley was built along the Fraser in 1827. It's worth noting that although the latter was also intended as a fur shipment point, salted salmon became its prime output within 20 years.

Changing fashions and collapsing beaver populations made fur old hat by the 1860s, but B.C. pioneers had only begun to plumb the region's treasure chest. The first timber shipment went outbound from Langley in 1832, and from Victoria in 1849. Victoria, established as a colonial port in 1843, became the region's capital in 1850 when it was declared a crown colony, following logically on the agreement between Britain and the United States to establish a border at 49 degrees north (excepting the southern spur of Vancouver Island).

When gold was discovered in the interior in 1856, B.C. attracted the acquisitive lust that had struck California a few years before. Many in America (and some in B.C.) believed the area's destiny still was to join the States, but the Civil War distracted American attention for a while. British interests seized the opportunity to solidify their hold; construction of the Cariboo Road into the interior from the lower Fraser Valley—a daunting task accomplished in inimitable British colonial fashion—assured that settlement of B.C. would pass through British territory. When coal was discovered north of Victoria in the 1860s, the province had all it needed to become a solid British community: trade and ports to serve it; coal to fuel industry; natural resources to exploit.

Meanwhile, the original inhabitants had been subjected to incredible oppression, both overt and subliminal. Smallpox killed more Natives than gunfire did—the disease wiped out the villages at Xa:ytem—and when outright killing became unacceptable, social repression took its place. Government suppression of the potlatch culture, including seizure of potlatch artifacts and materials, as well as language prohibitions, did as much to void the Native culture as warfare did. It's a testament to the strength and diversity of First Nations life—and to the region's legendary pockets of isolation—that most of these cultures have survived to the present, although some just barely.

Once eastern Canada had confederated and achieved autonomy, it turned its aspirations westward. B.C. told it, Send us a railroad, we'll send you a province.

This was no small demand. The mountains bisecting British Columbia are a monumental physical barrier, and construction of the Canadian Pacific railway was one of the 18th century's greatest engineering feats, the subject of countless tales and a part of the fabric of legend of the West. Importation of Chinese labor to help build the railroad cut the final facet of the social and economic face of B.C. today, establishing cultural ties to Asia that are more important than ever.

The first Canadian gold rush was in 1851 on the Queen Charlotte Islands.

The last spike was driven east of Sicamous, in the Monashee Mountains, November 7, 1885. The first transcontinental train left Montreal the next summer, and arrived at Port Moody July 4, 1886—one minute later than scheduled. When Vancouver was chosen to replace Port Moody as the railroad's ultimate terminus (dashing the hopes of Victoria interests who had hatched countless novel schemes to bring trains across the Strait of Georgia), the modern character of British Columbia was set. A year later, a ship arrived in Burrard Inlet from Asia with a cargo of tea and silk bound for London, to be shipped by rail and then steamer across the Atlantic.

THE 20TH CENTURY   Similar commerce persists today; the only difference might be that fine fabrics are often loaded onto planes using the eight-hour transpolar route to Europe, as Vancouver's airport is a major hub between Asia and Europe. The past century's history of B.C. has been one of consolidation of the forces that framed it before 1886—and attempts to repair the damage that was done along the way. The government is beginning the lengthy task of settling controversial land claims with dozens of First Nations communities that deserve redress. Fishing, timber, ranching and mining have all peaked and fallen back, and B.C.'s four million inhabitants are awarding ever greater significance to the characteristics that make it one of the world's top destinations for visitors—thus making tourism one of the province's strongest economic forces.

More than half of the yearly 25 million overnight visitors are B.C. residents traveling within their own province; of the rest, more than 3 million each come from elsewhere in Canada and from the United States. Less than 1 million arrive from overseas, although these travelers exert sufficient influence that Sprechen Deutsch signs are ubiquitous, and major resort hotels offer Asian breakfasts to Japanese, Chinese and Taiwanese tour groups. With European, Asian, North American and First Nations inhabitants and visitors, one hears literally dozens of languages in urban centers such as Vancouver and Victoria.

Vancouver's successful bid to host the 2010 Winter Olympics will further boost the area's presence on the world stage—and simultaneously challenge the province's ability to manage some of its problems, such as how to funnel traffic between Vancouver and Whistler on the narrow Sea to Sky Highway. Highway improvements are under way, though the most likely approach during the Olympics will be to shuttle most visitors back and forth on buses.

The prevailing policies on timber and fisheries management will undoubtedly receive closer inspection, too. World attention is bound to focus on a single place that holds three UNESCO World Heritage sites. Such a designation means that the territory is of global geographic, cultural and environmental significance—lending official weight to my own description of British Columbia: unsurpassed.

Where to Go

British Columbia offers the traveler virtually every possible non-tropical experience—cosmopolitan urban glitter, fun-filled family resorts, wild adventure. Most travelers hew to the main tourist itineraries—Victoria, Vancouver, the Okanagan—and while many hidden delights can be found in these areas, the visitor who wishes to experience less-crowded parts of the province should consider the Cariboo and Chilcotin, North B.C., and more distant parts of Vancouver Island and the Kootenays.

Vancouver is a world-class urban center with excellent dining and cultural happenings, diverse communities and a beautiful natural setting. Although most visitors come in the peak summer months, fall and winter are wonderful times, too: the city's cultural life is at its peak, and prices and crowds are low. The 2010 Olympics are bound to catapult the city to further prominence as a cultural destination.

The **Lower Mainland** surrounding Vancouver is the place to find hot-springs resorts, fresh-vegetable farms and historic fishing villages. The pastoral Fraser River Valley is still, as it has been for more than a century, a thoroughfare for commerce, and its delta is an important stopping point for migratory birds. The **Sunshine Coast** north of Vancouver, reached by ferry, is renowned for its balmy weather; sheltered by Vancouver Island to the west, it receives much less rain than the rest of coastal B.C. Its many small towns and hamlets hold delightful inns, cafés, shops and galleries.

Whistler is one of the top resorts in the world, and now that it will be sharing the Winter Olympics in 2010 (it is hosting alpine and Nordic events), its profile is rising even higher. In winter its one-mile vertical drop and copious snowfall afford excellent skiing, while its compact, visitor-friendly village design offers a distinctly European atmosphere. In summer, it offers lower rates and a myriad of recreational opportunities.

Victoria is a multifaceted small city whose veneer—colonial British—shouldn't obscure its more recent character as a diverse, dynamic urban center. It boasts a better climate than much of the rest of B.C., as it's somewhat sheltered from Pacific storms by the Olympic Mountains across the Strait of Juan de Fuca. The city features numerous parks and gardens, and one of the world's best-known hotels, the Empress. The rest of **Vancouver Island** offers, in microcosm, almost everything the entire province does: limitless recreation, ranging from swimming to wilderness trekking; towering mountains, sunny, sandy beaches, wildlife watching and great dining and accommodations.

The **Okanagan** region embraces a mostly dry, warm interior famed across Canada as a summer vacationland. With immense, warm lakes and hundreds of resorts, campgrounds, provincial parks and boating outfitters, these valleys fill with families in July and August, when they are literally the hottest travel spots in Canada. Fruit orchards and a burgeoning wine industry enhance the area's amenities; and the old cliche about the region, "beaches and peaches," remains true today.

Towering, snow-clad peaks, deep valleys, long sapphire lakes—**The Kootenays** are for many people B.C.'s favorite region. Stretching from the Okanagan east to Alberta, this area embraces a half-dozen spectacular mountain ranges, including B.C.'s Rockies, and a dozen small cities whose unusual flavor derives from the fierce independence of their residents. Nelson and Kimberley are the visitor capitals, with many small inns, galleries and cafés; Golden, at the foot of Yoho National Park, is the recreation center.

The **Cariboo** is an interior plateau where the Old West lives today. Vast cattle ranches, innumerable highland lakes, deep forests and a ring of mountains give it a distinct character much loved by adventurous travelers. In 1860, the Cariboo gold rush drew thousands of fortune-seekers here; today, its treasure is represented by the flash of fish on anglers' lines and the thunder of hooves on the upland prairie. The **Chilcotin**, west of the Fraser River, is perhaps the wildest section of B.C. today; just one road traverses this immense, beautiful plateau, and travelers seeking solitude will find a full share of it here.

Late September and early October frequently bring clear, delightful days with cool mornings, warm afternoons and starlit nights.

The **Queen Charlotte Islands**, wrapped in mist, colored by daily rainbows, inhabited by Native peoples whose artistic talents are known worldwide, are one of the most exotic travel destinations in North America. Here modern life has not forced all its hurry-up currents into the quiet villages that dot the islands; Gwaii Haanas National Park is a UNESCO World Heritage Site for both its wild beauty and the cultural significance of its abandoned Native villages.

All the regions above comprise a bit more than half of British Columbia; the remainder, **North B.C.**, is a vast and virtually undeveloped expanse of forest, mountain, wilderness and water in which wildlife abounds and the visitor can experience natural wonders like nowhere else. Grizzly bears, caribou, untracked spruce forests and nightless midsummers characterize this adventure-laden region. Simply driving it, on the Alaska or Cassiar highways, is considered a grand adventure—and it is.

The **Yukon**, still largely an undeveloped expanse of subarctic wilderness just as it was a century ago, offers travelers the chance to walk the paths of history, paddle down broad, unsettled rivers, trek untracked mountains and watch the midnight sun—or the aurora borealis. "Canada's True North," as this territory calls itself, is definitely true to its own nature.

When to Go

Two simple things determine the British Columbia climate— mountains and an ocean. The North Pacific Ocean sends almost constant surges of wet, moderate air southeastward toward the Pacific Northwest; the areas most exposed to these fronts receive huge torrents of rain. The areas most sheltered by the mountains—sometimes just 50 miles away—are much drier, often desert.

Conversely, the areas most exposed to coastal influence register milder temperatures; those most sheltered experience greater variation.

Generally speaking, most of B.C. is warm and dry in June, July and August, enjoying the benefits of a high pressure ridge that develops off Vancouver Island and blocks incoming weather.

The definition of "warm" ranges from an average high of about 68°F (22°C) in Tofino, on Vancouver Island's West Coast; to near 100°F (38°C) in interior valley locations such as Kamloops and Kelowna. Nighttime temperatures in the same locales are closer, from 50 to 60°F (10 to 15°C). Rain is rare, although fog is common in coastal locations, especially in the mornings.

These months, of course, are the peak travel periods, for two reasons: the good weather, and the Canadian custom of taking a family vacation between Canada Day (July 1) and Labor Day (first Monday in September). Accommodations and campgrounds book months ahead during these periods.

Travelers who dislike crowded conditions should strongly consider May, early June or September. The weather is often fine at these times, although not quite as warm. I have enjoyed superb weather in B.C. as early as April and as late as October, although it's less reliable then.

If you visit between November 1 and May 1, you *will* encounter rain. But so what? Part of B.C.'s world-class attraction is what that rain has wrought: spectacular forests, huge glaciers, snowy peaks and surging rivers. Personally, I find the cities—Vancouver and Victoria—just as enjoyable in rainy weather, and a stroll along a rainforest path with a soft rain sifting down through the conifers is an unmatched natural experience.

It doesn't often snow in the lowlands, but when it does, rain usually arrives within a day or two to melt it. It snows a lot—in some places, among the heaviest snowfalls in the world—in the upcountry from November through April. If you're skiing, that's great.

No matter what weather you favor, there's a place in B.C. that has it at some point in the year.

In the Yukon, summers are, amazingly enough, fairly warm and dry; most of the territory is sheltered from Pacific fronts by the Coast Mountains. Autumn comes early, though: late August in the far north and by early September everywhere else. Winters are undeniably cold, with temperatures dropping well below zero for weeks at a time.

Environment Canada offers frequently updated weather information for two dozen B.C. communities at its website: www. weatheroffice.com. You can also call, for a fee, and talk to an individual forecaster about the particular locations on your trip, at 900-565-5555.

CALENDAR OF EVENTS

Communities large and small across British Columbia and the Yukon have long embraced fairs and festivals—for many years, such events were all-important gatherings for local residents. Lately they have become important visitor attractions as well, ways for a city or region to show off what it has to offer. From sophisticated international wine and cuisine festivals to rodeos and log-rolling contests, it's not hard for the visitor to find an interesting event to attend.

Most communities have their own celebrations for Canada Day (July 1), Victoria Day (May 24) and B.C. Day (August 2) and the visitor should inquire locally for information on festivities. These are all high-traffic times, and reservations at popular tourist destinations should be made well in advance. Other recognized holidays in British Columbia are New Year's Day, Good Friday, Easter Monday, Labour Day (early September), Thanksgiving (mid-October), Remembrance Day (November), Christmas Day and Boxing Day (December 26). Oddly enough, although B.C. was once a British colony, only two B.C. communities still have a May Day (May 1) festival—New Westminster, east of Vancouver, and Sechelt on the Sunshine Coast.

The following list offers only the most notable and/or interesting annual happenings. Regional and local tourism offices can offer much more comprehensive information.

JANUARY

Lower Mainland & the Sunshine Coast   More than 2500 bald eagles roost along the Squamish River in midwinter, which occasions the **Bald Eagle Festival** in Brackendale.
Whistler   World-champion skiers visit Whistler during the World Cup Freestyle Skiing Competition.
Vancouver Island   The **Trumpeter Swan Festival** celebrates the restoration of these splendid birds in the Comox Valley.
Okanagan   Falkland's **International Sled Dog Races** take advantage of the area's bountiful winter snowfall.

FEBRUARY

Vancouver   Chinatown's **Chinese New Year Festival** (some years in late January) features parades, theater and lots of savory food.
Whistler   Whistler's **Gay Ski Week** is the largest gay and lesbian ski festival in North America.
Kootenays   **Winterfest** celebrates snow and skiing in Kimberley.
Yukon Territory   The Whitehorse annual **Yukon Quest** sled dog race, down the Yukon River to Fairbanks, is perhaps the world's toughest. Whitehorse's **Sourdough Rendezvous** is a winter carnival and all-around party.

MARCH

Vancouver Island   The annual spring migration of gray whales along the West Coast is the occasion for the **Pacific Rim Whale Festival** in the Tofino area.

APRIL

Whistler   The **World Ski and Snowboard Festival** brings thousands of boarders to Whistler.

Okanagan Okanagan Wine Industry Gala Fundraiser & Wine Auction focuses on B.C. wines to raise money for charitable causes in Kelowna. Later in the month, the Kelowna **Spring Festival** welcomes the arrival of blossom season.

Kootenays Every applicable form of human-powered locomotion must be used during Fernie's **Powder, Pedal, Paddle Relay Race.**

MAY

Vancouver Hundreds of world-class distance runners visit B.C. for the **Vancouver International Marathon.** At the end of the month, many of Canada's top rodeo professionals compete in the **Cloverdale Rodeo** outside Surrey.

Victoria The **Swiftsure International Yacht Race,** one of yachting's top events, winds up in Victoria. The **Victoria Harbour Festival** celebrates all forms of waterborne activity.

Okanagan First Nations culture is the focus at the **Cathedral Lakes Pow Wow** near Keremeos. Small-town rodeo comes to Falkland during the **Falkland Stampede.** The **Grebe Festival** honors the annual return of these dancing waterfowl to Salmon Arm.

Kootenays The **Wings Over the Rockies Bird Festival** takes place in Canada's largest inland wetland, a haven for migratory birds, between Golden and Invermere. The **Creston Valley Blossom Festival** honors the area's orchard heritage.

JUNE

Vancouver The **Vancouver International Jazz Festival** is one of the top music events in North America in Vancouver. The **International Dragon Boat Festival** honors Vancouver's Asian heritage. The **VanDusen Flower & Garden Show** showcases one of Canada's premier horticultural gardens.

Whistler The **Squamish Adventure Festival** is a nod to this town's new status as an outdoor activity center.

Victoria Dozens of major acts visit the island during **JazzFest International** in Victoria.

Kootenays Cranbrook's **Sam Steele Days** celebrates the area's frontier heritage. Summer thermals make Radium Hot Springs the perfect place for the **Kite Festival.**

Cariboo The **Williams Lake Stampede** is often considered Canada's best small-town rodeo.

North B.C. Stewart's **International Rodeo** has that appellation because of the remote town's location along the Alaska border. Night really never comes during the **Midsummer Festival** in Smithers. Boats, shipping and fishing are the focus during Prince Rupert's **Seafest.**

JULY

Vancouver The Canada Day weekend brings the **Steveston Salmon Festival** to The Gulf of Georgia Cannery National Historic Site. Later in the month, humor is the attraction at the **Vancouver International Comedy Festival.** Spectacular fireworks and stirring music fill the air over English Bay during Vancouver's **Symphony of Fire** at the end of the month (and into August). The **Molson Indy Vancouver** is one of the top street-course races in North America.

Lower Mainland & the Sunshine Coast   The **Abbotsford Berry Festival** celebrates one of the Lower Mainland's agricultural mainstays.

Whistler   Log rolling kicks off the **Squamish Loggers Days Sports Festival**.

Vancouver Island   The **World Championship Bathtub Race** puts hundreds of bizarre craft on the waters of Georgia Strait during Nanaimo's Marine Festival.

Okanagan   Participants saddle up in the high country and drive a herd to the lowlands during the popular **Kamloops Cattle Drive**. Working cowboys from nearby ranches ply their trade during old-time rodeo contests at the **Cowboy Festival** at O'Keefe Ranch near Vernon. The **Kelowna Regatta** takes advantage of the Okanagan capital's lakefront location. The **Merritt Mountain Music Festival** draws top Canadian and U.S. country acts to the Nicola Valley.

Kootenays   Spirited music fills the mountain air during the **Kimberley International Old Time Accordion Championships**. The **Elk Valley Jamboree** is an old-fashioned music, food and crafts festival in Fernie.

Cariboo   **Billy Barker Days** celebrates the Cariboo's rowdy past in Quesnel.

Yukon Territory   Musicians from across North America trek north for the **Dawson City Music Festival**.

Vancouver   The **Vancouver Folk Music Festival** features day and evening performances by local and international folk singers, songwriters and musicians at various outdoor venues. The **Greater Vancouver Open** is B.C.'s top professional golf event. The **Celebration of Light** is an elaborate competitive fireworks display pairing pyrotechnics and music.

AUGUST

Lower Mainland & the Sunshine Coast   Chilliwack's **Exhibition & Rodeo** is this Lower Mainland town's version of a county fair. The **Festival of the Written Arts** brings established authors and poets to Sechelt to mingle with up-and-coming writers. **Fur Brigade Days** is Fort Langley's chance to celebrate the heritage that put it on the map.

Whistler   Local First Nations culture and heritage is the focus of **Weetama**.

Victoria   Classical music is the order of the day during Victoria's **Symphony Splash**.

Vancouver Island   In Alert Bay, **Seafest** honors the tiny island's seafaring history, both Native and European.

Okanagan   The **Penticton Ironman Triathlon** is one of the top events on the international triathlon circuit. **Kamloopa Pow Wow Days** is a celebration of First Nations culture sponsored by the Secwepemc people who have inhabited the area for thousands of years.

Kootenays   Mount Seven near Golden is the launch point for the **Paragliding/Hang Gliding Championships**. Kaslo's splendid lakeside location is the setting for this small town's **Summer Music Festival**.

North B.C.   Hazelton's **Pioneer Days** celebrate the past in this Skeena River Valley town. Taylor's **World Invitational Gold Panning Championships** take place along the Peace River.

Yukon Territory   The event that put the Yukon on the map is marked in the **Discovery Days** annual festival in Dawson City.

SEPTEMBER   **Lower Mainland & the Sunshine Coast**   The **Bluegrass Festival** in Chilliwack brings dozens of Northwest, Canadian and U.S. acts to this Lower Mainland town during harvest season; everyone enjoys the free corn roast. The world **Sand Sculpture Championships** take place on the sandy lakefront at Harrison Hot Springs.

Victoria   Victoria's biggest annual music fair is the **Vancouver Island Blues Bash**. The **Victoria Fringe Theatre Festival** (which starts in late August) defies the city's stuffy stereotype.

Vancouver Island   The annual return of a coho salmon run spurs the **Port Alberni Salmon Festival**.

Okanagan   Local working cowboys compete at the **Top Ranch-hand Competition** at Hat Creek Ranch located near Cache Creek.

OCTOBER   **Vancouver**   The **Vancouver International Film Festival** brings thousands of cinema-industry figures and fanciers to town (sometimes in late September). The **Festival of Flavours** celebrates B.C. food and wine in Vancouver.

Okanagan   Every fourth year, the **Adams River Salmon Festival** near Salmon Arm celebrates one of the world's largest salmon runs; the next one is in 2006. Kelowna's **Apple Fair** honors the Okanagan's fall harvest. The **B.C. Rodeo Championship Finals** bring the province's top cowboys to Kamloops.

NOVEMBER   **Whistler**   The **Cornucopia Wine & Food Festival** in Whistler celebrates Northwest cuisine and wine-making.

Victoria   Victoria's **Great Canadian Beer Festival** focuses on a product for which Canadians are justifiably famous.

DECEMBER   **Lower Mainland & the Sunshine Coast**   During the **Candlelight Parade** in Mission, celebrants wend their way through town by candlelight.

Whistler   The **World Cup Downhill** brings the world's top ski racers to Whistler.

Vancouver Island   The **Festival of Lights** in Ladysmith is an extravagant holiday production.

There are more than 100 Visitor Info Centres throughout B.C. Some—Vancouver, Victoria, Whistler, major entry points—are open 365 days a year, staffed by tourism association employees. Some are operated by local Chambers of Commerce and are open during regular business hours. Others are simply roadside booths staffed by community volunteers, open afternoons only, or only in the summer, or sporadically as staff may be available. Whichever is the case, they are easy to find: signs guiding you to them are ubiquitous on major roads.

Before You Go

VISITORS CENTERS

Most visitor regions in B.C. publish their own guides to attractions. There are also province-wide guides to adventure vacations, guest ranches, winter vacations, freshwater fishing, and a travel industry guide listing tour promoters and packagers. The major tourism regions are:

Vancouver   604-683-2000; www.tourism-vancouver.org

Vancouver Coast (Lower Mainland) & Mountains   604-739-9011, 800-667-3306; www.coastandmountains.bc.ca

Whistler   604-905-4607, 800-905-4607; www.whistler-resort.com

Victoria   250-953-2033, 800-663-3883; www.tourismvictoria.com

Vancouver Island   250-754-3500; www.islands.bc.ca

Thompson-Okanagan   250-860-5999, 800-567-2275; www.thompsonokanagan.com

Kamloops   250-374-3377, 800-662-1994; www.adventurekamloops.com

ONE-STOP TOURISM

Canada's Visitor Info Centres are invaluable sources of visitor information. You'll find details on local lodging, restaurants, attractions and events, plus similar information for adjoining areas. The bigger the center, the broader the scope of the information in hand—Victoria's, for instance, has data on just about everything throughout Vancouver Island, plus quite a bit of the Lower Mainland and the rest of the province. The center in Vancouver, across the street from Canada Place, contains an encyclopedic array of pamphlets, catalogs, guides and maps, covering just about the entire province.

Rockies/Kootenays   250-427-4838,   800-661-6603;   www.bc
rockies.com

Cariboo-Chilcotin   250-392-2226, 800-663-5885; www.landwith
outlimits.com

North B.C.   250-561-0432,   800-663-8843;   www.nbctourism.
com

Yukon Territory   800-661-0494; www.touryukon.com

Overall tourist information for British Columbia is available
from the provincial tourism office at 800-435-5622; www.hello
bc.com. The B.C. provincial government operates **Enquiry BC**, a
universal information line for its services. ~ 800-663-7867.

PACKING   Most visitors to British Columbia will need significantly more
casual and outdoor wear than they will dress clothes. The province is a world-class recreation paradise—even if you're in the
heart of downtown Vancouver, be prepared to take advantage of
this. Activewear is essential; layering is highly advisable, since
conditions are not only changeable, but the province's often-steep
terrain takes visitors from lowlands to high country in a matter
of miles. Wool clothing is helpful in spring and fall, and necessary in winter. Jeans are standard everywhere. Have cowboy boots?
So do most B.C. residents, especially in the interior. Business suits
are expected and appropriate largely in Vancouver and Victoria,
but not for leisure travelers.

Good walking shoes are essential. Pack hiking boots if you
can; it'd be a shame to have to forego some of the fabulous half-
day hikes available no matter where you are. If you're a runner,
jogging is possible year-round in the Lower Mainland, Vancouver
Island, Kamloops and Okanagan areas—bring running gear. A
handy extra is a pair of lightweight tennis shoes that are somewhat expendable, for tidepool splashing and hiking muddy trails.

Swimsuits: absolutely. Even in the off-season—especially fall—
many beaches are quite swimmable. There are also a dozen notable
hot springs in B.C., and most B&Bs and small inns have hot tubs.
B.C. residents take outdoor living seriously.

Even in summer, prepare for cool evenings: nighttime lows in
Vancouver reach down into the 50s (15°C) most nights in July
and August; in the Okanagan and interior valleys, as hot as it
gets, nights cool considerably as well. With midsummer daylight
hours lasting well past 10 p.m., you'll want to be out and about,
but you'll need a windbreaker or long-sleeved shirt.

Bring a good camera—British Columbia is one of the most
scenic regions on earth.

Electric outlets and voltages are North American standard—
no need for adapters. Water supplies are safe. Vaccinations and
immunizations are not needed; it's okay to bring personal prescriptions, but simply for convenience, not because anything is

unavailable. *Make sure prescriptions are clearly labeled when crossing the border, and if it's a controlled substance, it's a good idea to have a doctor's note.*

British Columbia holds several of the world's finest and most fa- **LODGING** mous hotels—the Empress in Victoria, the Chateau Whistler and the Four Seasons in Vancouver—but there are also funky forest lodges, quiet small inns, sprawling resorts and bed and breakfasts that amount to a spare bedroom in the host's home. The province offers, all told, uncounted thousands of guest beds, and thousands more campsites. (See Camping, below.) I have generally avoided listing lodgings on or near major highways, as these are usually neither hidden, nor even quiet.

The prices for these range from US$20 (C$28) for excellent hostel dorm beds to more than US$1200 (C$1600) for the finest suite in Whistler. Generally speaking, rates drop 30 to 50 percent as you get farther from the major visitor centers; they also drop dramatically in the off-season.

Accommodations in this book are organized by region and classified by price. Rates referred to are for two people during high season, so if you are looking for low-season bargains, it's good to inquire. *Budget* lodgings are generally less than US$50 (about C$65) per night and are satisfactory and clean but modest. *Moderate*-priced lodgings run from US$50 to US$90 (C$65 to C$120); what they have to offer in the way of luxury will depend on where they are located, but they often offer larger rooms and more attractive surroundings. At a *deluxe* hotel or resort you can expect to spend between US$90 and US$130 (C$120 to C$170); you'll usually find spacious rooms, a fashionable lobby, a restaurant and a group of shops. *Ultra-deluxe* properties, priced above US$130 (C$170), are a region's finest, offering all the amenities of a deluxe hotel plus plenty of extras.

Many lodging chains have outlets in B.C.; these tend to offer clean, modern facilities with standard amenities and rates. In Vancouver, Victoria and Whistler, world-class, top-dollar luxury prop-

COMFY QUARTERS

Tourism B.C. maintains an accommodations guide that lists literally thousands of hotels, motels, campgrounds, small inns and B&Bs in the province. All have been inspected to meet the ministry's standards for cleanliness and conduct, and display an "Approved Accommodation" sign or decal at the establishment. The guide is available by calling 800-663-6000, or at Visitor Info Centres, travel agencies and the like. Visitor information outlets for the various regions, and in tourism centers, can also help.

erties are well worth a stay if your budget allows it. There are also dozens of unique small inns, hotels and lodges of all sorts throughout B.C.

Bed and Breakfasts   A word about bed and breakfasts in British Columbia: many of these are European style—that is, essentially a spare bedroom or two in the host's home, rental of which gets you the bed, use of a bath, breakfast, access to a sitting room and a cordial chat with your host if you wish. These are great bargains —but they're not quite the lavish, antique-filled accommodations U.S. B&B fanciers are accustomed to. Of course, there are also hundreds of B&Bs that do fit the more upscale profile. Two organizations offer further information about B&Bs, including contacts for regional bed-and-breakfast registries, of which there about two dozen, including: **British Columbia Bed & Breakfast Association**. ~ 604-734-3486. Or try **Western Canada Bed & Breakfast Innkeepers Association**. ~ 250-478-0588; www.wcbbia.com.

Hostels   There are 15 affiliates of **Hostelling International** in B.C., all of which offer extremely economical accommodation (less than US$20). It is not necessary to have an International Hostelling Association membership to stay at B.C. hostels, but members do receive preferential rates and other benefits. B.C. hostels all subscribe to policies designed to create a safe and civilized lodging environment; rowdy or illegal behavior is not desired. Some hostels observe lockout hours during part of the day, but this is becoming less typical than it once was. Each hostel is listed in the chapter that describes its locale, but general information about the hostels is available from the B.C. region HI office. ~ 134 Abbott Street #402, Vancouver, BC V6B 2K4, Canada; 604-684-7101, 800-664-0020; www. hihostels.ca. As is true for all lodging in British Columbia, reservations are strongly advised during peak travel months.

B.C. is also home to more than a dozen independent hostels not aligned with Hostelling International. The atmosphere is more relaxed, let's say, at these accommodations—curfews are rare, Friday beer busts are common. Although there's no central association for these, they do print a pamphlet you can find at most Visitor Info Centres.

Guest Ranches   British Columbia is the guest ranch capital of Canada—as it should be, with thousands of square miles of superlative riding country. Most of these are in the Cariboo, but there are also fine ranches in the Rockies, Kootenays, Chilcotin and North B.C.; many are listed in those individual chapters. The **BC Guest Ranches Association** includes many of these. ~ 250-374-6836; www.bcguestranches.com.

DINING   British Columbia's market basket is one of the world's most bountiful. Provincial farmers grow everything that doesn't require tropical weather, ranging from artichokes to zucchini. The best seafood imaginable comes from right offshore—six kinds of salmon, halibut, cod, crab, clams and oysters, squid. B.C. cattle growers produce superb beef, and specialty producers range from cheesemakers to the province's rapidly growing roster of wineries.

As a result of this abundance, a distinctive regional cuisine has arisen over the past decade. Usually called "West Coast," it relies on all those fresh local ingredients, seasoned with a hearty helping of the many ethnic influences that color B.C. society—Asian, Indian, Continental. Most of the province's best restaurants practice some version of West Coast cuisine, whether outright or as a coloration of some other approach. A Mediterranean restaurant, for instance, would use halibut and salmon in cioppino; Thai and Indian restaurants frequently offer salmon curries. One of Vancouver's best seafood restaurants has, as its signature soup, a tangy chowder combining Japanese, Thai and European influences. B.C. fruits are commonly the basis of desserts—huckleberry crème brûlée, say—and most wine lists feature B.C. vintages. Be sure to try ice wine, the unique dessert wine that originated in Okanagan vineyards and is now sought after internationally.

> Remember that, whether it's a top-tier restaurant or a neighborhood café, the currency exchange rate offers advantages to foreign travelers.

At the best restaurants the result of this approach is simply stupendous. Cooks the world over know that good local ingredients are the key to good food; West Coast cuisine in all its variations is never boring, always satisfying and constantly changing.

It would be silly to visit B.C. and not partake. Yes, Canadians have embraced fast-food chains as enthusiastically as Americans, and often they are the same old American chains; it's sometimes disappointing, frankly, to see just how many pizza parlors and frozen-patty burger flingers thrive. The traveler who believes it's best to rely on familiar brand names is missing out on one of the most delightful facets of travel in the first place—and in B.C., it's particularly worthwhile.

The very best restaurants are in Vancouver, Whistler and Victoria, with a few in isolated locales such as the Gulf Islands, Tofino and Nelson and Prince Rupert. Most of these are listed in their respective chapters; if there's a shortfall in *Hidden British Columbia*'s catalog of restaurants, it's in Vancouver: there are dozens and dozens of excellent ones, and not enough room for all in the book. The city is especially noted for its good Italian, Indian and seafood restaurants.

Second-tier restaurants—still good, but not of national caliber —are found in most of the major towns, such as Kelowna, Kamloops, Prince George and White Rock. Outside those areas, it's truly potluck: look for places that rely on local materials, even if it's just to make sandwiches, and you'll do all right. Major resorts, such as most guest ranches, offer good to excellent cuisine.

A full-scale gourmet dinner for two, with wine and dessert, can exceed US$100 (C$135) at the fanciest Vancouver and Whistler restaurants—pricey, but not enough to give New York or San Francisco any fiscal competition. (The food can be comparable, though, to the best restaurants in the world.) Prices decline according to the size of the city and renown of the restaurant—expect to pay $75 for the same meal in Victoria, $60 in Kelowna, and experience a slight decrease in quality. But even Vancouver diners can find exceptional meals for half that or less.

At the other end of the spectrum, economical restaurants in B.C. can offer excellent meals if you choose wisely: look for local ownership; ask area residents; avoid chains (even Canadian ones). My personal list of top five restaurants in B.C. would include two where a meal can be had for less than US$10. In most cities, Asian restaurants are quite a bargain: for instance, in the Okanagan, it's customary for Chinese restaurants to offer a fixed-price all-you-can-eat smorgasboard; that's what all the signs signifying "Smorg" mean.

Dinner entrées at *budget* restaurants usually cost under US$8 (C$10). The ambience is informal, service usually speedy and the crowd a local one. *Moderate*-priced restaurants range between US$8 and US$16 (C$10 to C$20) at dinner; surroundings are casual but pleasant, the menu offers more variety and the pace is usually slower. *Deluxe* establishments tab their entrées from US$16 to US$25 (C$20 to C$34); cuisines may be simple or sophisticated, depending on the location, but the decor is plusher and the service more personalized. *Ultra-deluxe* dining rooms, where entrées average US$25 (C$33) and above, are often gourmet places where the cooking and the service have become art forms. All restaurants serve lunch and dinner, unless otherwise noted.

Travelers really interested in budget provender should keep their eyes open for farmers' markets, produce stands and (common in B.C.) local independent bakers and butchers; the last invariably offer excellent handmade sausage. Fruit and vegetable stands are ubiquitous; local cheese-makers are less common but still available. Many times, on my journeys through B.C., dinner has consisted of a hunk of sausage, a chunk of cheese, and apples or peaches for dessert.

When all else fails, pizza is usually a safe fallback.

A few words about seafood: freshness is crucial to the quality of seafood, and only local products are fresh. These are coho (silver), chinook (king), pink, sockeye and chum salmon, and steel head; halibut; rockfish; sole and flounder; occasionally trout. Farm-raised salmon and trout are okay but hardly as good as wild fish; don't be shy about asking. A good restaurant respects such questions.

Lobster is not local. Neither is king crab or snow crab. The latter are from Alaska, and almost always frozen—not as bad as, say, gelatin. Dungeness crab is local, and it's scrumptious. Lobster is great—in Nova Scotia, where it's caught. Cross-continent travel doesn't help it.

Spot shrimp and prawns are native to the Northwest, and delicious, although sometimes hard to find; shrimp from elsewhere find wide use in restaurants. Again, ask your server. Oysters, clams, squid (calamari) and other novelties such as octopus, sea cucumber and sea urchin are also Northwest products. Give them a try; you only live once, and this isn't Alberta. Vancouver and Victoria have excellent sushi restaurants, too.

Dress standards throughout B.C. are quite informal, with the exception of the top-tier Vancouver restaurants. I can't think of one anywhere in which you'd have to wear a tie, although in several a jacket would be a good idea. Outside Vancouver, and in hundreds of Vancouver restaurants as well, jeans are acceptable even in the best places.

Oh, yes, coffee: Vancouver is coffee-crazed, every bit as much as Seattle. Decent coffee can be found on virtually every corner. Most (but not all) major cities in the interior—Kelowna, Kamloops, Nelson, Smithers—have a custom roaster where you can get palatable coffee. Outside those places, the situation, for those accustomed to good specialty coffee, is dire.

What better place to take your kids than a recreational paradise? B.C.'s thousands of lakes and hundreds of beaches are probably the top draw for families; alongside them are innumerable resorts

TRAVELING WITH CHILDREN

◆◆◆

NO KIDDING

Foreign travelers into Canada must bring ample documentation for all children traveling with the party. Let's say that again: Proof of identity and citizenship (a birth certificate or passport) is *required* for everyone. If the children in the car are not with adults who have legal custody of them, they must carry a letter from their parents or legal guardians expressing permission for the child to travel into Canada. A divorced parent traveling with children must have a copy of the custody agreement, as well as all the other above documentation. Canadian border officials consider child kidnapping a serious matter. No, you wouldn't dream of such a thing, but people do (usually in custody disputes). Sounds like a big hassle, but once you get across, you and your kids will delight in the wonders of B.C.'s recreation areas.

and commercial campgrounds, most of which have playgrounds, some of which have programs specifically designed to keep kids occupied while adults follow their own muse. We've listed some of the better ones in the lodging sections of each chapter.

Most of the larger B.C. parks are also expressly designed for families, with playgrounds, nature centers and trails and other amenities. Many have on-site naturalists during the peak summer travel months—making a B.C. park a remarkable bargain, actually, for family travel. That's one of the reasons campsite reservations are crucial. (See Camping, below.)

The major destinations for families are the Okanagan and Shuswap Lake areas; the east shore of Vancouver Island from Parksville to Campbell River; and the Sunshine Coast. The attractions here are obvious: sunny, sandy beaches, warm water to swim in, countless recreation facilities.

One thing to look for across B.C. is the fairly new system of water playgrounds, usually found in city and regional parks—Skaha Beach in Penticton is a notable example. These free facilities (built by local service clubs) will make adults wish such things had been around when we were young. Imagine grabbing a water cannon and blasting your dad! Well, it's never too late to act young.

A few lodgings in B.C.—probably less than 5 percent—are designed for adults and do not welcome children. These are small inns where quiet is at a premium; we've only listed a couple.

If you're traveling by air, try to reserve bulkhead seats where there is plenty of room. Take along extras you may need, such as diapers, changes of clothing, snacks, toys and books. When traveling by car, be sure to carry the extras, along with plenty of juice and water. And always allow extra time for getting places, especially on rural roads.

A first-aid kit is a must for any trip. Along with adhesive bandages, antiseptic cream and something to stop itching, include any medicines your pediatrician might recommend to treat allergies, colds, diarrhea or any chronic problems your child may have.

When spending time at the beach or on the snow, take extra care the first few days. Children's skin is especially sensitive to sun, and severe sunburn can happen before you realize it, even

IN CASE OF AN EMERGENCY . . .

Virtually all of B.C. is covered by 911 emergency phone service. In the Yukon, 911 is also in effect in Whitehorse and its surrounding area (Marsh Lake, for instance). In the rest of the Yukon, emergency calls should be made to the local RCMP office; the numbers for each community are listed on the back of official territorial road maps.

on overcast days. Hats for the kids are a good idea, along with liberal applications of sunblock. Be sure to keep a constant eye on children who are near the water or on the slopes, and never leave children unattended in a car on a hot day.

Even the smallest towns usually have stores that carry diapers, baby food, snacks and other essentials, but these may close early in the evening. Larger urban areas usually have all-night grocery or convenience stores that stock these necessities.

Many towns, parks and attractions offer special activities designed for children. Consult local newspapers and/or phone the numbers in this guide to see what's happening where you're going.

WOMEN TRAVELING ALONE

Traveling solo grants an independence and freedom different from that of traveling with a partner, but single travelers are more vulnerable to crime and must take additional precautions. In British Columbia, luckily, this warning is much less applicable than elsewhere; it's a low-crime place.

It's unwise to hitchhike and probably best to avoid inexpensive accommodations on the outskirts of town; the money saved does not outweigh the risk. Bed and breakfasts, hostels and YWCAs are generally your safest bet for lodging, and they also foster an environment ideal for bonding with fellow travelers.

Keep all valuables well-hidden and keep cameras and purses close to you. Avoid late-night treks or strolls through undesirable parts of town, but if you find yourself in this situation, continue walking with a confident air until you reach a safe haven. A fierce scowl never hurts.

These hints should by no means deter you from seeking out adventure. Wherever you go, stay alert, use your common sense and trust your instincts. If you are hassled or threatened in some way, never be afraid to scream for assistance. It's a good idea to carry change for a phone call and to know the number to call in case of emergency. For helpful hints, get a copy of *Safety and Security for Women Who Travel* (Travelers' Tales, 1998).

Dozens of major towns and cities in British Columbia maintain emergency shelters for women. The two major cities have hotlines for victims of rape and violent crime. In Vancouver contact 604-255-6344 or 604-872-8212. In Victoria, 250-383-3232.

GAY & LESBIAN TRAVELERS

Compared to most of the United States, British Columbians are quite progressive, especially when it comes to sex and sexuality. Gay and lesbian travelers thus find acceptance—in fact, almost indifference—throughout most of B.C. Open disdain or prejudice would be very difficult to find, even in the province's remote corners.

There are significant gay communities in Victoria and Vancouver, with many clubs and support groups. Vancouver's gay community is one of the largest in Canada, and came into its own when the city hosted the Gay Games in 1990. No other B.C. cities boast a distinct gay community, but quite a few contain gay-friendly visitor establishments. (Not that other areas have any anti-gay visitor establishments.) Whistler, Kelowna, the Gulf Islands, Prince George and Nelson offer gay-friendly inns.

Vancouver is the unquestioned gay capital of Western Canada. The area most often cited as the "gay neighborhood" is the West End, near Stanley Park, but many other areas contain establishments that cater to a gay and lesbian clientele, including Yaletown, the Broadway district, and Commercial Drive, which is sometimes reckoned the lesbian strip.

The city's **Gay and Lesbian Centre** (including a helpline available throughout B.C.) is in the West End. ~ 1170 Bute Street; 604-684-5307, helpline 604-684-6869 (Canada only). The **Gay and Lesbian Business Association** of Greater Vancouver is another resource. ~ 604-739-4522. The GLBA website is a notable resource for gay travelers to B.C., with a comprehensive listing of gay-friendly businesses throughout the province. ~ www.glba.org.

SENIOR TRAVELERS

Lest there be any doubt about the draw British Columbia exerts on senior travelers, the caravans of RVs on the Trans-Canada Highway in July and August speak volumes. With dependably mild weather, spectacular scenery and numerous opportunities for economical travel, B.C. is a delight for senior travelers. A well-developed network of heritage sites, museums and provincial parks affords plenty to do, and senior discounts are widespread.

It's important to make sure you have adequate insurance documentation when traveling in British Columbia—and, in the interior, to be aware that there are often vast distances between major towns that have advanced medical facilities. On the Alaska Highway, for instance, it can be a full day's drive between towns.

Thus it's important to make sure that prescriptions and other medical supplies are up to date and fully stocked, and that adequate documentation accompanies travelers crossing the border with medications.

There is a senior resource and activities center in most of B.C.'s cities and towns; look in the community services section of the local phone book.

The **American Association of Retired Persons** (AARP) offers membership to anyone over 50. Though based in the United States, AARP provides benefits that include travel discounts in (and to) Canada. ~ 601 E Street NW, Washington, DC 20049; 800-687-2277; www.aarp.org.

Elderhostel offers reasonably priced, all-inclusive educational programs in a variety of British Columbia locations throughout the year. ~ 11 Avenue de Lafayette, Boston, MA 02111; 877-426-8056, fax 877-426-2166; www.elderhostel.org; or Elderhostel

Canada, 4 Cataraqui Street, Kingston, ON K7K 1Z7, Canada; 613-530-2222, fax 613-530-2096.

A provincial senior citizen counselor can be found in every major town—they will be glad to assist travelers during weekday hours. In Vancouver, call 604-822-1350.

DISABLED TRAVELERS

Most public buildings and major visitor and commercial facilities in B.C. offer handicapped parking, wheelchair access and other aids for disabled travelers. This is less true as you leave the major cities, of course. Handicapped parking licenses and stickers valid in the States are equally valid in B.C. The provincial handicapped resource line is 800-465-4911 (Canada only). The **BC Coalition of People with Disabilities** maintains a helpline. ~ 604-875-0188; www.bccpd.bc.ca.

Detailed information about wheelchair accessibility is available from the **Canadian Paraplegic Association** in Vancouver. ~ 800-720-4933; www.canparaplegic.org. Information for those with speech or hearing impairments is available at the **Western Institute for Deaf and Hard of Hearing**. ~ 604-736-7391, TTY 604-736-2527; www.widhh.com. Travelers in need of a handicapped parking permit can contact SPARC. ~ 604-718-7744. Many hotels and other visitor facilities offering improved services display an "Access Canada" decal.

You can spend a whole day in Vancouver, one of the world's major urban centers, and not hear a car horn.

Twin Peaks Press in Vancouver, Washington, publishes a directory of travel agents who specialize in arranging trips for travelers with disabilities; the press also maintains a registry of nurses who specialize in accompanying travelers with disabilities. ~ 360-694-2462, 800-637-2256.

CUSTOMS

The U.S./Canadian border is often described as the longest undefended border in the world. That's true, but it doesn't mean crossing is carefree. In fact, in recent years it has become rather tedious in some spots—chiefly the main border crossing that serves Vancouver, at Blaine—and the enhanced security occasioned by 9/11 has exacerbated the problem to the point that some members of the U.S. Congress and Canadian Parliament have complained. Aside from hindering travelers, it slows trade to a crawl.

U.S. and Canadian citizens crossing back and forth need carry only proof of citizenship such as a birth certificate or passport. A visa is not necessary. A driver's license often used to suffice, but is no longer adequate.

Citizens of other countries do need a passport, although visas are not necessary for citizens of most European and Western Hemisphere countries if your stay will be less than two months.

Aside from illegal substances, there are two notable prohibitions at the U.S./Canada border: You *may not* bring weapons into Canada, especially firearms and Mace. Licensed to carry a firearm for personal defense? Makes absolutely no difference. Canadians do not want to experience the U.S. handgun problem. If you are going to be hunting, there are special procedures for importing registered hunting rifles.

U.S. regulations, for their part, bar import of the Cuban cigars that so many Americans relish while they're in B.C.

There may also be restrictions on agricultural products, sometimes depending on your ultimate destination in the U.S. or Canada. Huge amounts of cash are not a good idea to carry across the border; on the other hand, border officials on both sides will occasionally ask visitors to demonstrate their financial wherewithal.

For more information about crossing regulations and restrictions, contact **Canadian Customs & Immigration**. ~ 604-666-0545. Special regulations apply to children; see Traveling With Children, above.

About those border lineups: Traffic at Blaine, the major crossing between Seattle and Vancouver, sometimes becomes great enough to cause hours-long waits, chiefly for those coming back to the States. If you don't want to sit in a line that long, other crossings at Aldergrove and Sumas are sometimes much quicker. The best strategy is to cross at lower-traffic times, such as weekday mornings and late evenings.

About those border lineups: traffic at Blaine, the major crossing between Seattle and Vancouver, sometimes becomes great enough to cause waits of an hour or longer, chiefly for those coming back to the States. If you don't want to sit in a line that long, other crossings at Aldergrove and Sumas are often much quicker.

U.S. citizens flying back to the States through Vancouver International Airport need to allow some extra time at the airport, as passengers flying on certain airlines (especially to Seattle) must clear U.S. Customs and Immigration at the airport before they get on the plane. Here, too, lengthy lines sometimes build up— sufficiently long to make you miss a plane if you haven't allowed enough time. Customs officials are not particularly sympathetic to this problem, in my experience. You also have to take a few minutes to pay Vancouver's airport tax, which is C$5–$15, depending on your destination.

CULTURE Canadians are polite. This observation has become a stereotype, but like many stereotypes it's true. Visitors will find B.C. by and large a friendlier and more courteous place than most similar regions in the United States and Europe.

The surest way to brand yourself an outsider, then, is to act boorish. It's not okay in Canada to shove your way in line, ask invasive questions, make unwelcome observations or otherwise act obnoxious. It's also not acceptable to honk.

Some visitors from more frenetic places find all this unnerving. Hey, relax. Even if it wouldn't pass in Paris, say, it's quite pleasant when your surroundings are Stanley Park or Granville Island.

On the surface, driving in B.C. seems identical to driving in the United States. Driver's licenses and insurance policies apply in both countries; regulations are much the same; even local customs cross the border. (It's impolite to honk your horn in both Seattle and Vancouver, for instance.)

DRIVING

However, subtle changes distinguish driving north of the 49th parallel. Most notable is the difference in roads: Canadians simply haven't embraced superhighways as the United States and even most European countries have. There are no interstates, no autobahns. There are just a few multilane freeways in British Columbia—the Coquihalla Highway system leading to Kamloops and Kelowna; the Trans-Canada Highway from Hope to Vancouver; the Island Highway from Victoria to Parksville. That's about it.

Everywhere else, even the major routes are two-lane highways with periodic passing lanes thrown in where engineers could manage to build them. Summer travelers will thus spend some time in long caravans, especially on the Trans-Canada and Yellowhead highways in the interior. Patience is paramount here; the roads are not designed for Grand Prix driving or willy-nilly passing because it's not safe to do so. Highway engineers have installed many signs announcing that a passing lane is imminent (usually within a mile) to alert drivers and foster patience.

Finding your way in British Columbia, especially outside the major metropolitan areas, is a matter of watching carefully for signs. All the parks, lodgings and other sights in this book post signs on the major highways to direct travelers; on back roads, keep your eyes open for signs marking the way to towns such as

GET MOOOVING

Cattleguards are common on interior roads, even paved secondary routes. Signs alert drivers; try to steer for the tire strips most cattleguards have on each side. Yes, there are cattle along the road in many places. Much of B.C. is still open range; unlike in some U.S. states, though, a driver who hits a cow is not required to reimburse the cattle grower for the animal. It's still nothing you'd want to do. When you encounter cattle, remember this: They have not been bred for intelligence.

Bamfield, Telegraph Creek and so on. Usually green, these signs are posted at every place one must make a turn, and are unfailingly reliable. Less reliable is the business of road names. Not all roads are marked; many go by several names. The Bamfield Road, for instance, is also a Forest Service road with a different designation. Even the major highways have several names: Route 1 is also the Trans-Canada; Route 5 and Route 16 (and bits of Route 37) form the Yellowhead Highway. It's essential to obtain good provincial and local maps, which are widely available at Visitor Info Centres.

> Canadians take holidays seriously, and there is at least one three-day weekend in every month.

Canadian authorities also observe a stricter attitude on speeding—there's a practical reason all those B.C. drivers in front of you are hewing pretty much to the limit. The leeway drivers are accustomed to in the States is not the custom here. If you have one of the few cars left on the road that doesn't have an English/metric speedometer, 100 kph (the usual highway limit) is roughly 62 mph; stick to 60 and you'll be fine. Where the limit is 90 kph, 55 mph will do; at 80 kph, 50 mph is okay. The limit reaches 110 (about 67 mph) only on the Coquihalla, Island and Trans-Canada highways.

In other words: Don't speed. You *will* be stopped sooner or later.

Or you may have your picture taken. Actually, they're taking pictures of your license plate at the same time a radar device is registering your speed. This practice is becoming more common throughout B.C.; provincial officials aren't mailing these citations to the States, yet, but often there is a patrol car ready to go near a photo radar operation. If you're stopped, a citation will result. You can choose not to pay it, if you live elsewhere, but you'll be at risk of arrest if you return.

Other warnings and regulations are equally worth heeding. Once you get north of Kamloops, for instance, the deer crossing signs common throughout North America are replaced by similar warnings about moose. This is serious business: hitting a deer would be bad enough; a moose is an extremely large and solid creature (up to half a ton, some of them) and a vehicle that hits one is almost certainly going to be destroyed, with dire consequences for the occupants.

Once you get off the major numbered routes, much of B.C.'s road system is gravel—hundreds of miles of gravel road, sometimes, especially in the Cariboo, Chilcotin, Vancouver Island and north regions. These are the roads rural residents depend on, and they are well-maintained and plowed in winter. They can, however, become somewhat soft and sloppy when wet, no place for low-slung city cars. Most maps indicate roads that are likely to be in dubious condition; during wet weather it's a good idea to inquire locally before venturing onto any unpaved side road.

Many forest roads, and some major secondary roads, post signs warning that they are active logging routes. Although B.C. log truck drivers are not as reckless as those in the States (remember that Canadian courtesy) it's still wise to stay alert, ease your car to the right side of the road, and be prepared to cede the way to a log truck. It's not that they want to run you off the road; log trucks simply aren't as maneuverable as passenger cars. In some areas—the Queen Charlotte Islands, notably—log loads are carried by oversize trucks that use up just about all the roadway.

In the Yukon, highways are the arteries of life and thus well-maintained and passable year-round. The Alaska Highway and Klondike Highway, linking B.C., Whitehorse, Dawson City and Alaska, are paved throughout and kept clear through the winter. It's still a good idea, however, to make sure your car is in good mechanical condition; if nothing else, parts and repairs up here are not cheap. Gas is available at numerous way stations along the roads, as well as in all major towns. In the winter, carry chains.

In both north B.C. and the Yukon, wild animals are a common roadside sight. So are dunderheaded tourists stopped dead in the roadway. I know readers of this book would never make that mistake themselves (these roads are major international thoroughfares) but it's necessary to stay alert to what's in front of you. Sooner or later you'll round a curve and find an RV caravan parked in the road to roll video of a bear munching dandelion shoots.

Other things to note: Seat belt use is mandatory in Canada; radar detection devices are illegal in most places; right turn on red is allowed in B.C.

One last thing: *Do not* drink and drive. B.C. law enforcement officials have zero tolerance for this; potential penalties are severe, including immediate seizure of the vehicle. The threshold is .08 percent blood alcohol—two drinks within the hour for the average adult.

Railway travel is alive and well in Canada—entirely appropriate considering the role railroad construction played in the country's development. A number of excellent rail trips are available to B.C. travelers.

TRAIN

The **Rocky Mountaineer** follows the route of the original Canadian Pacific line, taking travelers through the Fraser Gorge, across the interior mountains and then across the Rockies into Calgary. Trips and excursions, including circle tours, of various lengths are available. ~ 604-606-7245, 877-460-3200; www.rky mtnrail.com.

VIA Rail Canada is the country's national passenger rail service; cross-country excursions beginning or ending in Vancouver range from a couple days up to a week. ~ 888-842-7245; www.viarail.ca.

METRIC SYSTEM

Yes, Canada switched to the metric system in 1975, abandoning the miles, feet, pounds and Fahrenheit degrees. However, this doesn't mean that metric configurations are as popularly uniform as they are officially prescribed. In fact, the vast majority of B.C. residents are what you might call bilingual when it comes to measurement systems, and can converse in miles or kilometers, feet or meters, Fahrenheit or Celsius. And most non-packaged items sold by weight, such as fresh fruit, are still measured in pounds.

"Actually, I like to use Fahrenheit for summer temperatures because it makes it sound warmer to say 90 degrees," one acquaintance explained to me on a warm June day in the Okanagan Valley. "In the winter, metrics make it sound not so cold."

Precise conversion charts are widely available. For the record, here are some rough guidelines to remember:

A kilometer is six-tenths of a mile. Five km are thus three miles; 10 km, a bit more than six miles. So 100 km is 60 miles, and so on. Remember, when you see highway distance signs, that it's not as far as your first reaction makes it, if you're used to thinking in miles.

Below 10° Celsius is chilly; below 20°, cool; 30° is warm, and 35° is hot. Past 40° is blistering; 110° Fahrenheit is 44° Celsius. Zero Celsius, of course, is freezing.

Three is the important factor for height and altitude. One meter is roughly three feet; thus 1000 meters is a bit more than 3000 feet—mountain country. As it happens, about 75 percent of British Columbia is above 1000 meters in elevation.

A liter is close to a quart. So when you're at the gas pump, four liters are comparable to a gallon.

Here is a useful metric conversion chart:

1 mile = 1.6 kilometers	1 kilometer = 3/5 mile
1 foot = 0.3 meter	1 meter = 3 1/3 feet
1 pound = 0.45 kilo	1 kilo = 2 1/5 pounds
1 gallon = 3.8 liters	1 liter = ¼ gallon (about a quart)

CURRENCY

Money is a dollars-and-cents matter in Canada. However, those dollars and cents are not worth the same as in the States (or Hong Kong); like almost all currencies in the global economy, the Canadian dollar is subject to commodity trading—and thus to the vicissitudes of commodity markets.

Over the past few years the exchange rate has favored the U.S. dollar over the Canadian, with the rate fluctuating in the 70 percent to 77 percent range most of the time. This offers obvious advantages to American citizens traveling in Canada; it's a wonder B.C. isn't overrun with Yanks, because when you factor in the general cost discount in B.C. along with the exchange rate, the whole province is in essence a half-price playground for those spending American dollars. The mark and pound sterling are usually stronger than the Canadian dollar, as well. (Money traders have taken a dim view of Canada's long history of deficit spending.)

ATMs (automatic teller machines) are ubiquitous throughout B.C. Since banks are also numerous (the Canadian banking industry is just beginning the merger madness that has swept U.S. banks) that means money machines can be found even in fairly small towns in out-of-the-way places. American visitors will appreciate the fact that Canadian banks are prohibited from charging an ATM fee. Most U.S. and European bank cards work in Canadian ATMs; you'll have to check your statement when you get back and see exactly what exchange rate your bank gave you—generally it's a better rate than you'll get for travelers' checks (and there's no commission), though your bank may assess a nominal fee for use of a non-affiliated ATM.

The advent of ATMs has made currency exchanges somewhat obsolete. However, they are still in operation in major visitor centers such as Vancouver, Victoria, Kelowna, Nanaimo and other entry points. If you have cash it makes sense for you to exchange; however, you'll get a slightly better rate if you use your bank card (or credit card) and you won't be giving a cut to the currency traders.

Canadian immigration officials occasionally ask travelers to demonstrate their financial viability at the border. A judicious amount of cash is one way to do this; however, too much is not a wise item to bring across, and regulations require declaration of sums greater than US$10,000 when crossing the U.S. border. I can't imagine what legitimate reason anyone would have for carrying that much cash across the border; neither can most customs officials.

LOONIE TOONS

After much initial resistance, Canadians have become rather fond of their high-denomination coins. The $1 version, with a depiction of Canada's national bird, the loon, is a solid piece about a third larger than a quarter, called a "loonie." The slightly larger $2 coin has brass in the middle, silver on the outer ring; it's called a "toonie." Canadian nickels, dimes and quarters are much like their U.S. counterparts.

Most Canadian businesses—especially those near the border—will happily accept U.S. currency, ringing up on their cash register whatever exchange rate you negotiate. The same is not true south of the border; most American businesses exhibit irritation if asked to accept Canadian currency (with the exception of a few shopping centers right along the border). For a nation constantly whining about its trade deficit, it's another example of the famous American insularity. I recommend Americans spend their Canadian dollars in B.C. before returning home.

One important thing to bring back is receipts. Visitors to B.C., like residents of the province, pay a goods and services tax (GST) of 7 percent on lodging and most retail sales (on top of various other local and provincial taxes). The GST is meant to apply only to residents; visitors are entitled to claim a refund if they wish by sending the appropriate form and supporting receipts to **Revenue Canada**. Forms and explanations are available at Visitor Info Centres, banks and other public outlets. ~ Revenue Canada/Visitor Rebate Program, Summerside Tax Centre, Summerside, PE C1N 6C6; 800-668-4748 in Canada; 902-432-5608.

Outdoor Adventures

CAMPING

British Columbia is an unparalleled paradise for campers. First of all, the landscape is matchless—scenic, mostly balmy (in the summer), wild, with endless recreation possibilities. Untracked wilderness beckons, as do friendly forests within minutes of major cities. There are deep blue lakes, snow-dappled peaks, clear, rushing streams, towering forests and peaceful meadows, and campsites next to all of those.

But just as important as the natural surroundings is the sheer breadth of campground development in the province. B.C. has more than 400 parks and provincial recreation areas encompassing more than 21 million acres—more land than *all* the state parks in the 48 continental United States. Add to that six national parks within B.C. and the total is almost 13,000 developed campsites.

Above and beyond all that is a much larger expanse of Crown land managed by the B.C. Forest Service (remember that 90 percent of B.C.'s land is owned by the provincial government, although much of that is under long-term lease), which lists another 1400 campsites, developed to some extent, on its lands. Add in the many commercial campgrounds, and all told, there are probably 20,000 separate campsites in British Columbia reachable by car.

And on certain nights almost every single one will be occupied.

It seems hard to believe, but not only are B.C. residents well aware of their home's outdoor virtues, so are many residents of the rest of Canada, plus a goodly number of European visitors

Please Bear with Us

"A fed bear is a dead bear." These cryptic signs appear throughout British Columbia, part of an intensive campaign to convince folks not to offer their Twinkies to the neighborhood ursine. Most of those folks are visitors. Although the semi-tame bears tourists encounter in B.C. and Yukon parks rarely turn on their culinary benefactors, it can happen. The results are not often fatal, but fatal attacks have occurred.

The most important problem is that bears accustomed to human beings, having lost their instinctive fear of people, become far more dangerous in general. B.C. and Yukon wildlife managers follow a policy of trapping and relocating, or simply killing, such habituated animals.

Naturally, no wild animals are "tame." Visitors who encounter bears, cougars, moose, even elk and raccoons, are best advised to keep their distance quietly. It's a special moment to see these wonderful creatures in the wild—and it happens a lot in B.C. and the Yukon. If it happens, there are several important distinctions to know:

- Black bears can climb trees. Grizzlies can't. If a grizzly is threatening you and you can get up a tall tree, it's not a bad idea. Otherwise, most experts consider playing dead (fetal position) the wisest tactic. Opinion is divided on whether to play dead or fight back when it's a black bear.

- Mountain lions are genetically programmed to chase small running creatures. Do not run. Instead, wave your arms to make yourself appear as large as you can. Speak loudly. In general, do everything you can to make yourself seem too large and threatening to be prey. If attacked, fight back; many people have driven off attacking cougars.

- Moose are temperamental. Keep your distance. They have the right of way on trails and roads, even if you're in a car. Why? Because they are much, much bigger than you.

- There are a few rattlesnakes to be found in the dry valleys of the southern interior, chiefly the Okanagan, Thompson and Fraser canyons. Don't step on them. More important, don't sit on them. And if you happen to be climbing in a rocky area in these regions, avoid putting your hands anywhere you can't see.

Encountering these animals, and numerous others, is part of the wonder of B.C. and the Yukon ... 99 percent of the time. The best advice is to be alert—which you should be anyway.

who rent camping vehicles and/or equipment. On some days the camper caravans along the Trans-Canada Highway stretch for miles; at 6 p.m. all those people are going to pull off and look for a spot to camp.

The crucial times are summer weekends, especially the holiday weekends. The keys to success, then, are either arriving early at your desired campground—on peak weekends, that can mean noon Friday—or reserving a spot at one of the 65 or so campgrounds listed with the **Discover BC Reservations** service. Reservations can be made starting March 1, covering the period from May 1 to September 15, and believe me for some of the most popular campgrounds at the most popular times, you'd best pick up the phone on March 1 and dial this number: 800-689-9025. They'll take your name, reserve a campsite, and collect a deposit. You'd best use your reservation, because the procedures for cancellation and refund of your money are just slightly less complicated than tax returns. ~ Discover BC Reservations, 800-689-9025, www.discovercamping.ca; BC Parks general information, w/apwww.gov.bc.ca/elp; additional B.C. camping info, www.camping.bc.ca.

High demand is usually not a problem on weekdays, with the exception of the week in which Canada Day (July 1) falls. June and September are quieter seasons at B.C. parks; I've had entire sections of gorgeous campground all to myself during the week in June. In the months of April and October the parks are practically deserted.

All BC Parks campgrounds are well-maintained, well-furnished, clean and attractive, with toilets, a picnic table and a fire ring at each site. Many campgrounds have resident hosts during summer months; a fee system is in force at most campgrounds during the same period. Fees range from C$12 to C$18.50 (US$8 to US$12; U.S. currency is not accepted). Water is supplied from pumps or faucets; firewood is for sale at most campgrounds. (The new 2002 government of Gordon Campbell abandoned the longstanding practice of offering free firewood at provincial park campgrounds.) Peace and quiet are another matter: the clatter and

HOW TO FIND A CAMPGROUND

All the B.C. parks are marked on the basic provincial travel map, which is available at all Visitor Info Centres; the map includes a catalog of the parks (yes, all 434—you'll need your reading glasses for the small print) listing their features, facilities and number of campsites, if any. It's an indispensable guide for camping travelers. The province also prints very useful regional map/parks guides, which are available at Info Centres as well.

rumble of arriving campers on Friday evening sometimes approaches urban noise levels. Quiet hours are enforced at most campgrounds, fortunately. Many of the individual sites have sand-base tent pads. Although most parks have sani-dumps, there are no hookups at BC Parks campgrounds.

The 210 **BC Forest Service campgrounds** are usually off the main road and generally consist of fewer than a dozen spots that may or may not have picnic tables, fire rings and other amenities. Sometimes access requires a four-wheel-drive vehicle; these locations are indicated on the Forest Service regional map/guides for the province's 23 forest districts. These maps, too, are available at Visitor Info Centres and at Forest Service district offices. ~ Forest Service regional centers: 2100 Labieux Road, Nanaimo (Vancouver Island), 250-751-7001; 3333 Tatlow Road, Smithers (northwest B.C.), 250-847-6300; 1011 4th Avenue, Prince George (north–central), 250-565-6100; 515 Columbia Street, Kamloops (Shuswap–Okanagan), 250-828-4154; 518 Lake Street, Nelson (Kootenays–Rockies), 250-354-6200; 640 Borland Street, #200, Williams Lake (Cariboo–Chilcotin), 250-398-4345; headquarters 595 Pandora Avenue, Victoria, 250-387-1300, www.gov.bc.ca/for.

The province's longstanding practice of offering free camping at its Forest Service sites was set aside—despite much public outcry—in 1999, when it became necessary to acquire an annual pass to use the Forest Service campgrounds. Annual passes cost C$27, and are available at the Forest Service offices listed above, Government Agent offices in most towns and cities, as well as at sporting goods stores, hunting and fishing outfitters and the like. One-night passes are C$8. A few Forest Service campgrounds are considered "enhanced" facilities and a C$10 per night surcharge obtains. The new Liberal government has been attempting to divest itself of these Forest Service campgrounds, hoping private operators will take them over. As of late 2002, this has not happened.

Commercial campgrounds are also common throughout the province. At least 300 of these—which are the best places to find campsites with hookups—are geared primarily to recreational vehicle campers, but offer some facilities for tents as well. Other amenities range from laundry rooms to rental refrigerators. Most of these campgrounds are along major highways, some stretches of which seem to have an RV park every five miles. Commercially produced guides to these are available at Info Centres, too.

A few general thoughts about camping in B.C.:

Be prepared for rain. Summers are dry and warm—most of the time. There's nothing more miserable than a wet sleeping bag. Tarps are great.

Heed the bear safety warnings. B.C. is home to a third of Canada's black bears and half its grizzlies. That's a lot of bears; encounters with humans are rare but inevitable. (See Please Bear with Us, above.) Wilderness campers in bear country must hang their food; car campers are admonished to keep their food in a secure cooler in the trunk of their car.

Campground rules are for real. Badly behaved campers can and do get thrown out of BC Parks campgrounds. Leave the boom box and beer keg at home.

The Yukon's three dozen roadside territorial campgrounds are almost all excellent places to spend the night, offering clean campsites with fire rings and firewood. A night's stay costs C$8; cash is not accepted, instead, you must buy coupon books that are widely available. Unlike in B.C., the campgrounds are not always associated with park facilities and they rarely fill up, with the exception of the two outside Dawson City.

Want to rent a camp trailer or full-scale recreational vehicle? You, too, can join the RV caravan on the Trans-Canada Highway —actually, it's a relaxing way to meander through B.C. Vancouver is the center for RV rentals, with dozens of operators, including several with airport locations. **WestCoast Mountain Campers** specializes in more compact models, van conversions and Volkswagen vans. ~ 11800 Voyageur Way, #150, Richmond; 604-279-0550; www.wcmcampers.com. **Candan RV Rentals** offers full-size motor homes. ~ 20257 Langley Bypass, Langley; 604-530-3645, 800-922-6326; www.candan.com. **Fraserway RV Centre** is one of the largest in Canada. ~ 31631 South Fraser Way, Abbotsford; 800-806-1976; www.fraserway-rv.com. Because **Ambassador Motorhomes** has locations in B.C., Alberta and the Yukon (and San Francisco), one-way rentals are its specialty. ~ 7973 River Road, Delta; 604-946-3696; www.ambassadorrv.com.

On Vancouver Island, **True North** RV is near the Victoria airport and the Swartz Bay ferry terminal. ~ 2078 Henry Avenue, Sidney; 250-656-5250; www.truenorthrv.com.

FISHING & HUNTING
B.C. is one of the premier fishing and hunting destinations in the world. Anglers can aspire to catch dozens of freshwater species, ranging from perch to bass to trout, plus all six of the Pacific salmon species, as well as halibut, rockfish and cod and other nearshore species.

The centerpiece of a B.C. fishing trip is usually angling for the province's famous Kamloops rainbow trout, or for coho and chinook salmon. There are thousands of lakes, hundreds of rivers and countless miles of bays and inlets in which to do so; B.C. truly has fish for all. However, declining stocks of certain salmon runs in recent years have caused some closures, notably for coho salmon in 1998. Conditions and regulations change regularly; it's imperative that would-be anglers acquaint themselves with the latest information before dropping a line in the water. For more

Mushing through the Yukon

In the Yukon, winter sports have really gone to the dogs—literally. While there is no alpine skiing, territory residents have revived a couple of activities their Gold Rush forebears favored, though what was once pragmatic necessity is now recreational amenity.

Dog-sledding is, of course, internationally known because of the famed Iditarod and Yukon Quest sled races. But the sport can also be pursued in a much more leisurely fashion, and it is a marvelously serene way to cruise the winter-bound forests and valleys of the Yukon. Most dog-sled courses follow snowed-in roads or flat river valleys.

Ski-joring, in which participants ride cross-country skis while being pulled by dogs, is a more exhilarating snow sport: experts often reach considerable speeds, blasting through woods and over ridges. Novices can use slower dogs on less demanding courses.

Visitors can enjoy these sports through guide services that offer dog-sledding and ski-joring excursions. There are also plenty of cross-country tracks near most towns, especially Whitehorse and Dawson City, and an entire territory of snowbound wilderness for experienced skiers to explore.

Yukon visitor information agents can supply references to guide services, and sporting goods stores in Whitehorse offer ski rentals and information.

The ultimate winter quest for many visitors is a night-time dog-sled trip into the country to see the Northern Lights—an experience no one ever forgets.

information on sportfishing in B.C., contact the **Sportfishing Institute** at 604-270-3439; www.sportfishing.bc.ca or www.bc fishing.com.

Separate licenses are required to fish in freshwater and saltwater; the nonresident annual fee for saltwater is C$110 (US$70); freshwater, C$40 (US$26). Weekly and daily licenses are available for reduced rates. In addition, a salmon stamp that costs C$20 (nonresident) is required to keep any salmon, and various other surcharges apply to several other specific races of fish.

Sea kayaking may be the ideal way to prowl the many bays, inlets and fjords of B.C.'s complex coast.

A truly byzantine array of regulations specific to individual areas and times of year is in effect for the various species of fish; the pamphlet describing these is available wherever licenses are sold, as well as at Visitor Info Centres, docks and marinas.

Freshwater fishing information, as well as information on licensed guides, is available from **BC Fish & Wildlife**. ~ 604-582-5200. Freshwater licenses are issued locally and can be bought at most sporting goods stores, which are also the best places to find out about local variations of the laws.

Saltwater fishing is regulated by **Fisheries & Oceans Canada**, which issues licenses for the entire province. ~ 555 West Hastings Street, Vancouver, BC V6B 5G3; 604-666-2828; www.pac.dfo-mpo.gc.ca.

Game species in B.C. include virtually all the major North American mammals, as well as ducks, geese, pheasants, grouse and other upland game. Specific licenses are required for all; there is no general open hunting season in B.C. For information visit the **BC Ministry of Water, Land and Air Protection** hunting website, wlapwww.gov.bc.ca/wld/hunting.htm. Remember that special regulations govern shipping personal firearms into Canada for hunting trips.

The Canadian Firearms Act that took effect October 1998 requires all persons owning or handling firearms to demonstrate firearms safety proficiency; more recent regulations have tightened licensing and registration requirements as well. For more information, call 800-731-4000 or visit the website at canada.justice.gc.ca.

There are dozens of excellent fishing and hunting lodges in B.C., ranging from luxurious full-scale resorts to fly-in wilderness cabins. For information and guide referrals, contact the **BC Fishing Resorts & Outfitters Association**. ~ 250-374-6836; www.bcfroa.com.

The Yukon offers superlative wilderness fishing for grayling, lake trout, Arctic char and cutthroat trout. The services of a guide, or a stay at a fishing lodge, are highly advisable ways to learn how to pursue Yukon angling. Licenses are required for all fishing; numerous regulations protect this resource for the future.

British Columbia's towering mountain ranges peel snow from incoming Pacific storms like upside-down ice scrapers. Some areas receive more than 400 inches of snow a year, beneath which, at higher elevations, glaciers form. Naturally, this creates world-class skiing. The province's more northerly location means its ski areas, especially in the interior, are not as subject to the occasional rain and warm temperatures that afflict Cascades resorts in Washington and Oregon. The season generally runs from mid-November through April; Blackcomb Mountain at Whistler operates through August.

SKIING

Whistler benefits from this climatic largesse, but that's not the only reason it's the top-rated ski resort in North America. Its careful design development as a pedestrian village makes it exceptionally appealing for extended stays, and its huge vertical drop (one mile, on Blackcomb Mountain) means skiers spend much more time skiing than riding lifts. Whistler offers dozens of other attractions and activities; it has a chapter all to itself because it truly is one of Canada's top visitor destinations.

Although none of B.C.'s other ski areas are as well-known, vertically vast and developed as Whistler, they have heeded its success and are also pursuing attractive mountain village development approaches. Mount Washington, in Strathcona Park on Vancouver Island; Sun Peaks, north of Kamloops; Silver Star, east of Vernon; and Big White, east of Kelowna, are the best-known and most-developed second-tier resorts. See the regional chapters for more information. There are also a couple dozen other smaller areas, mostly geared to day use, throughout B.C.

Another fast-growing, high-profile (and pricey) alternative is heli-skiing, whereby skiers are lifted in the morning to wilderness peaks and spend the day plunging through untracked powder. Several major operators in the Cariboo, Chilcotin and Rocky Mountains offer this option; see the respective chapters for more information.

Cross-country skiing is popular in B.C.'s interior; many B.C. provincial parks maintain trail networks, as do most of the major ski resorts. Local Visitor Info Centres can supply maps and trail guides; in winter, only the major regional centers—Kamloops, Kelowna, Penticton, Williams Lake, Prince George and so on—are open. For information on BC Parks, including cross-country skiing, visit the B.C. Parks website at wlapwww. gov.bc.ca/bcparks.

For general information on winter sports in the province, including a comprehensive guide to all the ski areas, call the Tourism B.C. helpline at 800-663-6000 and ask for the B.C. *Ski/Winter Adventure Guide*, which also covers cross-country skiing, snow-mobiling and even snowshoeing.

SkiBC is a booking agency for lodging at most major B.C. resorts, from Whistler to the Rockies. ~ 888-676-9977; www.ski bc.com.

Although there is no alpine skiing in the Yukon, dedicated cross-country areas are found near Whitehorse and Dawson City, and the entire province is open to wilderness ski-trekking from November through April.

BOATING   With uncounted thousands of lakes; tens of thousands of miles of undammed rivers, including one of the longest in the world, the Fraser; and 16,780 miles (27,000 km) of saltwater shoreline, British Columbia offers boaters limitless territory. Freshwater kayaking and canoeing have many fervent practitioners in B.C.

Rentals are available in almost every resort area, and numerous outfitters specialize in supplying wilderness canoe and kayak trips. The best-known are around the Gulf Islands, Barkley Sound and Clayoquot Sound along Vancouver Island; and Desolation Sound north of the Sunshine Coast; but many other trips are possible. Canoe enthusiasts are drawn to Bowron Lakes, Tweedsmuir Park, Powell River and Murtle Lake in Wells Gray Park.

B.C.'s many rivers offer thrills galore, but whitewater kayak enthusiasts can find something here available almost nowhere else on earth—surfing the standing waves of tidal rapids, such as the one at Skookumchuck Narrows on the Sunshine Coast. The **Sea Kayak Association of BC** is the source for expert information about saltwater kayaking. ~ 604-290-9653; skabc.org. The **Recreational Canoeing Association of British Columbia** serves a similar function for freshwater canoeing. ~ 604-437-1140; www.bc canoe.com. **The Whitewater Kayaking Association of BC** is a good source of information about the province's many world-class rivers; 604-515-6376; www.whitewater.org.

Boating and sailing are also highly popular in B.C.; there are dozens of major marinas and hundreds of smaller ones. Some offer boat rentals to visitors; however, the Pacific Coast is a tricky, temperamental marine environment and boating is not a wise choice for non-experts.

The same hazards apply to kayaking and canoeing: on most major lakes and coastal inlets, for instance, surrounding mountains make afternoon thermal winds a significant problem in the summer. Waterborne adventures are only to be undertaken by experienced individuals who have acquired local information beforehand. With that caveat, this area is exceptional for boating.

TWO

Vancouver

Vancouver enjoys every advantage a city could have. With an unsurpassed natural setting, an ideal geographic location and a bustling economy, its population is vibrant and diverse, its parks are fabulous and its cultural life vigorous. Its hotels and restaurants are among the finest in the world; it is politically and socially progressive; its climate is mild but not dull. It's surrounded by rich farmland, clean blue waters and gorgeous snow-capped mountains.

All these attributes are ideal for visitors, so it's no surprise that Vancouver is one of the most popular travel destinations in North America. The city's abundance fills the plate for every type of visitor. These virtues are exactly what so appealed to the International Olympic Committee when it chose the city (in conjunction with Whistler) to host the 2010 Winter Olympics. Vancouver's diversity was especially attractive—for example, organizers were able to find volunteers currently living in the metro area who speak each of the three-score languages native to the visiting Olympic participants and spectators.

Nature has long provided for human needs here. B.C.'s First Nations thrived in the mild climate of the region for centuries, fishing salmon-filled waters, picking wild berries and harvesting shellfish for food and relying on cedar for clothing and shelter. Europeans first made an appearance in the 1770s, when Captain James Cook sailed through searching for the Northwest Passage and stopped to trade with the native inhabitants. Britain didn't lay claim to the area until Captain George Vancouver's visit in 1792.

Stories of the incredible bounty of wildlife brought trappers and traders; when the fur trade began to wane, the Fraser Gold Rush of 1858 was just gaining speed, and the lower Fraser Valley proved ideally situated as a jumping-off point for what became a flood of treasure-seekers when the Cariboo gold fields opened in 1860. Logging provided another boost to the frontier economy. Gastown, the first settlement in what is now Vancouver, grew around an early sawmill. Vancouver itself was just a hastily built shantytown of 400 residents when a catastrophic fire in 1886 forced it to rebuild; the city's future was ensured with the announcement that the transcontinental Canadian Pacific Railroad would terminate there. With the railroad and a natural harbor, Vancouver's importance as a shipping center soon became paramount. Incorporation quickly followed the railroad announcement, and that same year a shipment of tea from China was Vancouver's first inbound cargo. Wood went back the other way; some of the long, knot-free beams in Beijing's Imperial Palace were logged along Burrard Inlet. When the Panama Canal opened in 1914, Vancouver assumed even greater importance as a gateway for outbound grain from the prairies.

Although the economy in British Columbia is shifting from its traditional base on what the land provides—logging, fishing and mining—Vancouver remains a processing and shipping center. One of every four jobs in B.C. is connected to trade, and Vancouver's port is Canada's largest. Visitors to Stanley Park can see evidence of this by the dozens of freighters moored just offshore awaiting dock time. Since the World's Fair in 1986 focused worldwide attention on all the region has to offer, tourism has grown to assume an ever-greater importance in the province, and it was a reflection of the times in 1998 when technology surpassed timber as an employer. Not surprisingly, Vancouver-area residents are on average the best-educated in Canada. Add to this mix Swiss-style banking regulations that attract investment from around the world, and you have a truly dynamic urban economy.

Canada's Pacific gateway in fact as well as image, Vancouver is now one of the economic and political centers of the Pacific Rim—huge amounts of Alberta and Saskatchewan wheat headed for Asia pass through Vancouver, for instance, and international summits have drawn political leaders such as former U.S. President Bill Clinton to the city. (His favorite Vancouver activity is the same as mine—running along the Stanley Park Seawall.)

Vancouver is also a bustling cruise-ship departure port; the vast majority of passengers bound north on Alaska cruises depart from the Canada Place cruise-ship dock. Not surprisingly, tourism is the city's top industry. More than 9 million visitors a year reach Vancouver—four times the metro area's population.

The city has long attracted immigrants from Asia, most recently from Hong Kong, although that tide has slowed now that control of the colony has reverted to China—in fact, some of the early '90s arrivals who took advantage of their British passports to leave Hong Kong for Vancouver have headed back now that life seems stable in Britain's former Asian colony. Even so, Vancouver's Chinatown remains one of the three largest in North America, behind New York and San Francisco, and other Asian communities continue to grow. There are now more Singhs in the Vancouver phone book than there are Simpsons. The city also has strong Italian, Greek, French, Indian, Pakistani, Japanese and Russian communities, and is a popular destination for European travelers. The West End (adjoining Stanley Park) is the most densely populated urban district in North America, much resembling a European city neighborhood with its residential towers, street side shops and cafés. The Vancouver visitor can hear more than a dozen languages in a day's journey through the city, a reflection of its vital, cosmopolitan nature.

The combination of exceptional scenery, heady cultural life, mild climate, economical production costs and attractive exchange rates has made Vancouver a film-industry center that ranks with San Francisco and sometimes exceeds Toronto (much to the latter's chagrin). "The X-Files" was taped here, along with a half-dozen other American TV shows and literally dozens of films a year. Aside from the cachet this brings the city, it's an economic boon—more than C$1 billion (US$790 million) and 70 productions a year. With several major recording studios, Vancouver is also a center for the Canadian music industry; pop mavens Sarah McLachlan and Bryan Adams make their home here.

Climate is one of the major attractions for the film industry; the relatively mild winters make production possible year-round. Yes, it does rain—35 to 60 inches a year, depending on exactly where you are in the metro area. And winters can be chilly; afternoon highs in January are likely to barely creep above freezing. But nighttime lows rarely drop below 25°F (-8°C), and major snowfalls are equally rare. The moderating influence of the saltwater has prompted city parks managers to plant palm trees in the south-facing gardens next to the English Bay Beach bathhouse, where they thrive.

Summertime highs, also moderated by the water, rarely exceed 80°F (26°C). The dry season is July, August and September. That's also peak visitor season; Vancouver hotel occupancy rates approach 100 percent from early July to early

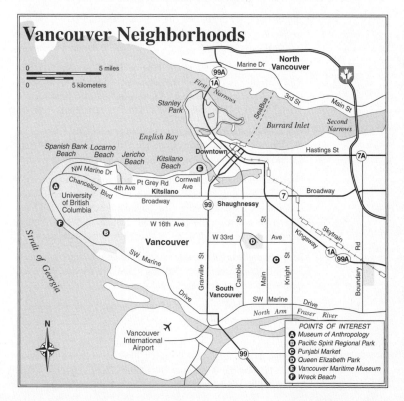

Vancouver Neighborhoods

POINTS OF INTEREST
Ⓐ Museum of Anthropology
Ⓑ Pacific Spirit Regional Park
Ⓒ Punjabi Market
Ⓓ Queen Elizabeth Park
Ⓔ Vancouver Maritime Museum
Ⓕ Wreck Beach

Text continued on page 50.

Three-day Weekend

Vancouver

Like New York and San Francisco, Vancouver is ideally suited to the traveler willing to put on good walking shoes and see the city from street level. The following three-day trip involves a lot of walking, but you'll gain a real appreciation for the city's cultural and geographic diversity. The key: Go in early May or October. The weather is almost always nice, crowds are minimal, and all the city's hotels offer excellent bargain packages.

Day 1
- Check in early to the cozy **Wedgewood** (page 55) (ask for a room on the third floor or higher) or art-infused **Listel Vancouver** (page 77) (get a room on the back side of the hotel, away from Robson). Other choices: the classic **Fairmont Hotel Vancouver** (page 55) or ultra-sharp **Metropolitan Hotel** (page 56).

- Hit the street for the ten-minute walk to **Canada Place** (page 51) to see the famed "sails" and the view of Burrard Inlet and the North Shore mountains.

- Backtrack a few minutes to the **Marine Building** (page 51), taking 15 minutes to check out the amazing art deco friezes and decorations. Then lunch at **Imperial Chinese Seafood Restaurant** (page 59), one of the best Mandarin/dim sum restaurants in town.

- Pick up the waterfront walkway and head around Coal Harbour to the **Vancouver Aquarium** (page 75). Visit the lower-level Arctic Canada exhibit, admiring the underwater grace of the beluga whales.

- Head back on the wonderful **Stanley Park seawall promenade** (page 76), walking counter-clockwise to pass the totem poles, under the Lions Gate Bridge, by **Samish Rock**. Stop at **Third Beach** for a rest on the golden sand, then on to Second Beach, along **Lost Lagoon** and into the **West End** residential district.

- Return along **Robson Street** (page 61) to people-watch, and duck into the **Vancouver Art Gallery** (page 52) to visit the floor devoted to Emily Carr's work.

- Dine at **Bacchus** (page 57), the Wedgewood's intimate French-Mediterranean restaurant.

Day 2
- Another day on foot. After breakfast, head down Burrard to False Creek, catching the Aquabus or False Creek Ferry across the water to **Granville Island** (page 84).

- Stroll through **Granville Public Market** (page 84) on the island, checking out spots you'll want to return for lunch. Then head down Duranleau Street to the **Sport Fishing Hall of Fame & Museum** (page 85), an intriguing facility that also holds model trains and ships.

- Return to the **market** for an early lunch at the food stalls.

- Head off the island and up to 4th Avenue to catch a bus to the **Museum of Anthropology** (page 83), paying special attention to the Hall of Totems and Bill Reid's marvelous "Raven and the First Men." Don't forget to wander outside to check out the traditional **Haida village** built on a bluff overlooking English Bay.

- Back on the bus to Granville Island. Need some gifts? The **Kids Only Market** and the **BC Wood Co-op** (page 91) are worth a stop, as are any of a dozen galleries offering Northwest art and crafts.

- One of the ferries will take you back across False Creek for dinner at **C** (page 58), Vancouver's most amazing seafood restaurant.

Day 3
- Today you need a rental car, available at several locations near your hotel. After breakfast, head down Georgia Street to the **Stanley Park Causeway** and across towering **Lions Gate Bridge** (page 76) to the North Shore.

- First stop is in **West Vancouver** on Marine Drive for muffins and coffee at **Bean Around the World** (page 111) or at the legendary **Savary Island Pie Shoppe** (page 111). Be sure to pick up something for lunch later.

- Five miles west on Marine Drive, watch carefully for the small wooden sign indicating **Lighthouse Park** (page 113). A half-hour hike down one of the many paths in this beautiful preserve will bring you to one of numerous rocky headlands, where you can perch in the sun, admire the view of the city, and eat the lunch you brought along.

- Back at the car, head back east on Marine, then up Capilano Canyon to the end of the road and the lift base for **Grouse Mountain** (page 104). The ride up in the Skyride gondola takes 15 minutes and opens up the very best view of the Vancouver metropolitan area.

- Head back downtown to your hotel to get dressed for dinner at **Diva** (page 59), the glitzy capital of West Coast cuisine.

- Catch a concert by the **Vancouver Symphony Orchestra** (page 62) at the Orpheum, or a show by one of the city's many resident theatre companies.

September, so advance booking is essential, even with more than 16,000 hotel rooms in the metro area. Those wishing to avoid crowds are best advised to visit before June—the weather is often fine in April and May—or after Labor Day, when Indian summer can last until mid-October.

Winter visitors will encounter rain and, occasionally, blustery Pacific storms. However, November through April is when Vancouver's cosmopolitan nature blooms, with literally thousands of concerts, plays and other performances. The city promotes this as Vancouver's "Entertainment Season," and most hotels participate in package offerings that are excellent bargains.

Despite all its development, Vancouver remains a friendly, low-key community. It values its past; heritage designation is found on many buildings around town, and the ethic that supports this is evident in the modern Cathedral Place office tower, which was deliberately designed to reflect the architecture of its two venerable neighbors, Christ Church Cathedral next door and the Fairmont Hotel Vancouver across the street. The much-discussed Canadian penchant for courtesy is in full force here—you won't hear many car horns honking, even at rush hour, and the panhandlers who inhabit lower downtown and Gastown are extraordinarily civil compared to those in other urban areas. Except for corporate workers, dress is stylish but informal; few restaurants require coat and tie, and an opera or symphony performance brings as many Vancouverites dressed in jeans as in suits. Fashionable jeans, mind you.

Many of the city's social conventions are more European than North American. One local store advises would-be shoplifters that their karma will suffer. A Vancouver woman writer, assigned by a local magazine to pursue her daily life topless for a week, was intrigued to find that pretty much nobody cared. "No one questioned my right to be shirtless or was anything other than friendly," she wrote. "Later, when I took off my shirt during a visit to Seattle, cars screeched to a halt and people gaped and shouted."

The city also holds fast to an anti-freeway ethic. As in San Francisco, no four-lane controlled-access road traverses Vancouver; visitors heading north–south through the city must use city streets. Heading north through Stanley Park, travelers cross the object of what passes for a true controversy in Vancouver: what to do with the Lions Gate Bridge. The community resoundingly rejected proposals in 1998 to replace the bridge entirely, opting instead for a modest upgrade that has done little to speed traffic flow. Even so, in Vancouver it's still possible to accomplish the fabled recreational triple header: the energetic visitor in late spring can ski, sail and play a round of golf all in one day. Now that's leisure. Perhaps this fact should lead to a new Olympic triathlon event—few other cities on earth could entertain the notion.

The fate of the bridge—and of traffic flow in general—returned to the public agenda when Vancouver, along with Whistler, won the bid to host the Olympics in 2010. Most of the snow-based events will take place in Whistler; the city lies between the airport and the ski area. How to get people there? The provincial and federal governments have embarked on an upgrade of the Sea to Sky Highway that leads north to Whistler, and Vancouver's light rail system will be extended to the airport. (A fact visitors in any year, never mind 2010, will appreciate.)

So even though 2 million people now call the Vancouver metro area home, the city is in no hurry to . . . well, to be in a rush. More than a century ago the first meeting of the Vancouver City Council was delayed because no one remembered to bring pen and paper to record the minutes. That low-key approach to things still pervades the city: the Corporate Resources Group of Geneva declared Vancouver the most livable city in the world in 1997, and serene residents seem to agree. Visitors are well advised to adopt the same approach. In fact, the very best way to see Vancouver is on foot. Most of downtown is within a 15-minute walk of the major centrally located hotels, and walking is what suits the city best, summer or winter.

Central Downtown

If your picture of downtown is an office world that rolls up the sidewalk at 6 p.m., Vancouver will dispel that. It is a vibrant financial and corporate center, to be sure, but a beautiful harbor setting with snow capped mountains behind, historic districts, galleries and gardens set downtown Vancouver apart. Even in the heart of the financial district, intriguing shopping centers, glitzy restaurants, small cafés and numerous plazas and courtyards flavor the metal-and-glass architecture that typifies the modern Vancouver look. Among other things, the city's finest hotels, most of its public buildings, and the theater district, are all within a ten-block area—as is the famed Robson Street shopping district.

SIGHTS

Vancouver Tourist Info Centre offers detailed and comprehensive information to visitors, covering not just Vancouver but all of British Columbia. Closed Sunday from October to mid-May. ~ Plaza Level, Waterfront Centre, 200 Burrard Street; 604-683-2000; www.tourismvancouver.com.

There's a great view of the harbor from **Canada Place**, Vancouver's trade-convention center and cruise-ship terminal. From the bow of this landlocked behemoth you can scan the waterfront, taking in the broad sweep of North Vancouver and the

AUTHOR FAVORITE

sights The **Marine Building** was once (when it opened in 1930) the tallest building in the British Commonwealth. Today its 21 stories put it in the shadow of nearby office towers but I still consider it an art deco masterpiece. A wraparound frieze with terra-cotta figure work depicts the history of exploration and seafaring along the Pacific Coast; the richly colored tile lobby, with recessed lighting, is intended to evoke a Mayan temple. ~ 355 Burrard Street.

spectacular mountains behind it. Bridges arch to port and starboard, ships lie at anchor in the harbor and an occasional ferry plies the narrow waterway. Cynics suspect that the notorious peaked-fabric roof of the new Denver International Airport was stolen from the Canada Place profile, which is supposed to suggest ship sails. A hotel and IMAX theater round out the complex. ~ At the foot of Howe Street.

Nearby, a glass elevator zips you up to the aptly named **Lookout!** circular viewing deck high atop Harbour Centre. With a 360-degree view of Vancouver and environs, plaques pointing out all the major sights, guides present to answer all questions and a brief multimedia presentation on the highlights of the city, this is one of the best places to get your bearings. It's overpriced, though, and if you want the best view, try Grouse Mountain or Queen Elizabeth Park. Admission. ~ 555 West Hastings Street; 604-689-0421; www.vancouverlookout.com.

Housed in what was once the central courthouse, part of it designed by the legendary F. X. Rattenbury, the **Vancouver Art Gallery** has four floors of galleries showcasing the works of international and Canadian contemporary artists. The Emily Carr Gallery, featuring many of her drawings and paintings of the coastal rainforests and First Nations inhabitants, is the best place to familiarize yourself with B.C.'s best-known classical painter. The building's back (south) steps are a popular gen-X hangout, and the front (north) of the art gallery is ground zero for social and political protests in Vancouver. Closed Monday in winter. Admission. ~ 750 Hornby Street; 604-662-4700; www.vanart gallery.bc.ca.

Adjacent **Robson Square**, below the current government offices and courts, is the site of concerts and lectures and has a skating rink. The various steps and plazas beside the multi-level fountain are popular with downtown workers for alfresco picnic lunches. ~ 800 Robson Street; 604-660-2830.

Christ Church Cathedral is the oldest surviving church in Vancouver, dating to 1895. Originally a parish church, this sandstone structure with buttresses and steep gabled roof was designed to mimic English parish churches; it was designated a cathedral in 1929. Plans by the diocese in the '60s to tear it down evoked a community outcry. It's frequently a site for free concerts. ~ 690 Burrard Street; 604-682-3848; www.cathedral.vancouver.bc.ca.

Just east along Georgia, the lobby of the **Hong Kong Bank of Canada** offers passersby rotating art exhibits—usually with an international flavor—such as photos of Pacific Basin indigenous peoples. And the Alan Storey sculpture that swings through the lobby, a massive 90-foot, 3500-pound aluminum pendulum, is both fascinating and slightly intimidating: stand directly beneath

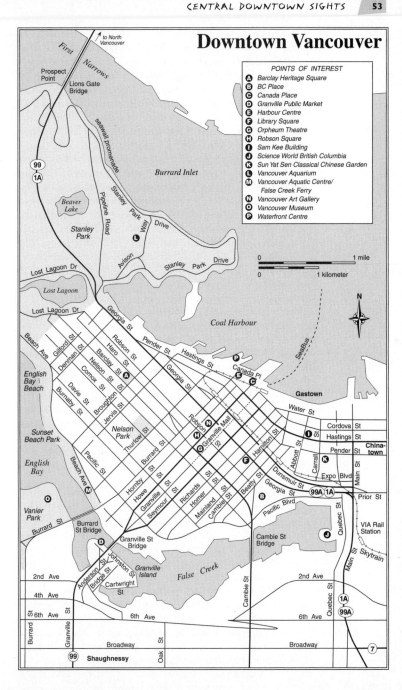

Downtown Vancouver

to North Vancouver

First Narrows

Prospect Point

Lions Gate Bridge

seawall promenade

99
1A

Beaver Lake

Stanley Park

Pipeline Road

Stanley Park Way

Avison

Drive

Ⓛ

Stanley Park Drive

Burrard Inlet

POINTS OF INTEREST

Ⓐ Barclay Heritage Square
Ⓑ BC Place
Ⓒ Canada Place
Ⓓ Granville Public Market
Ⓔ Harbour Centre
Ⓕ Library Square
Ⓖ Orpheum Theatre
Ⓗ Robson Square
Ⓘ Sam Kee Building
Ⓙ Science World British Columbia
Ⓚ Sun Yat Sen Classical Chinese Garden
Ⓛ Vancouver Aquarium
Ⓜ Vancouver Aquatic Centre/
    False Creek Ferry
Ⓝ Vancouver Art Gallery
Ⓞ Vancouver Museum
Ⓟ Waterfront Centre

Lost Lagoon Dr

Lost Lagoon

Lost Lagoon Dr

Coal Harbour

0   1 mile

0   1 kilometer

N

SeaBus

Georgia St

Robson St

Pender St

Hastings St

Ⓟ

Canada Pl

Ⓒ

Gastown

Water St

Cordova St

Ⓘ

Hastings St

China-town

Pender St

Beach Ave

Gilford St

Denman St

Barclay St

Haro St

Nelson St

Comox St

Ⓐ

English Bay Beach

Davie St

Burnaby St

Broughton St

Jervis St

Georgia St

Robson

Ⓝ

Granville Mall

Abbott St

Carrall St

Ⓚ

Expo Blvd

Sunset Beach Park

Nelson St

Thurlow

Nelson Park

Ⓗ
Ⓞ

Ⓕ

Hamilton St

Dunsmuir St

99A 1A

English Bay

Pacific St

Burrard St

Hornby St

Howe St

Granville St

Seymour St

Richards St

Homer St

Mainland St

Cambie St

Beatty St

Georgia St

Ⓑ

Pacific Blvd

Prior St

Ⓞ

Vanier Park

Ⓜ

Beach Ave

Burrard St

Burrard St Bridge

Granville St Bridge

Ⓓ

Anderson St

Johnston St

Granville Island

Cartwright St

Cambie St

Cambie St Bridge

False Creek

Quebec St

VIA Rail Station

Ⓙ

Skytrain

2nd Ave

4th Ave

6th Ave

Burrard St

Granville St

6th Ave

Cambie St

2nd Ave

6th Ave

Quebec St

Main St

1A

99A

99

Shaughnessy

Oak St

Broadway

Broadway

7

it for a minute and see if your heart rate doesn't elevate a tad. Open during business hours. ~ 885 West Georgia Street.

Built in 1927, the **Orpheum Theatre** was once the largest in Canada and the Pacific Northwest. The ornate interior is neo-Spanish Baroque with many arches, columns and interlaced moldings. Community support for its heritage forestalled a plan to divide the Orpheum into several smaller cinemas. The city bought it in the early '70s and it became the home of the Vancouver Symphony. ~ 884 Granville Street; 604-665-3050.

Library Square is an architectural highlight of Vancouver's decade-long building boom—much loved by the citizens who paid for it, although disdained by architects. Vancouver Public Library's Central Branch is the centerpiece: a stunning, monumental oval building cast in reddish concrete, designed by Canadian architect Moshe Safdie to hint at the Roman Coliseum. Its many windows and unusual angles capture and reflect light like a prism. With six floors of books and reference materials—1.2 million items— the library is one of the largest in North America. Coffee shops and small cafés under the atrium along the retail parkade offer nourishment to browsers and serious researchers alike. ~ 350 West Georgia Street; 604-331-3600; www.vpl.vancouver.bc.ca.

The shining geodesic dome so prominent on the Vancouver skyline as you approach the city from the south was Expo Centre during the 1986 Exposition and is now home to **Science World British Columbia**. Fascinating hands-on exhibits let you blow square bubbles, light up a plasma ball, dance on a giant synthesizer keyboard and more. Kids throng here, but the accompanying adults seem to have just as good a time. The OMNIMAX **Theatre** upstairs features a variety of exciting films shown on one of the largest screens in the world. There are separate admission charges for the museum and theater. ~ 1455 Quebec Street; 604-443-7440, fax 604-443-7430; www.scienceworld.bc.ca.

LODGING   It can be expensive to stay in the city, especially in the downtown core, and especially in high season (June through August). Fall and winter promotions drop prices dramatically at many hotels, and a recent boom in new lodging construction somewhat oversaturated the market. As a result, some hotels are actively soliciting extra business—such as renting rooms for four-hour afternoon liaisons. If you bring your car, expect to pay an additional C$10–$15 per day to park at most downtown hotels. You will also pay the Goods and Services Tax (17 percent) on all hotel accommodations; if 7 percent of this tax amounts to over C$7, you can claim a rebate for this percentage by filling out a form (available from your hotel) and mailing it to Revenue Canada.

Located in the heart of the business and entertainment district, the **Sutton Place Hotel** offers luxury accommodations at prices comparable to (and in some cases lower than) other top hotels in town. Rooms are elegant, with classical decor punctuated by a blend of antique reproductions and botanical prints; the suites have enormous marbled bathrooms with deep European-style tubs and separate showers. Personal service is the signature here. Sutton Place is one of the few downtown hotels that welcomes pets in its longer-term-rental suites and apartments. ~ 845 Burrard Street; 604-682-5511, 800-961-7555, fax 604-682-5513; www.suttonplace.com. ULTRA-DELUXE.

Even more compact—its entrance is barely visible on Hornby— is the **Le Soleil**, an all-suite hotel that aspires to neo-Italian elegance, with rich brocades, maroon and burgundy decor, and an opulent lobby. Rooms are cozy but sumptuous, and the lobby holds two massive and richly exotic canvases that evoke tropical languor. ~ 567 Hornby Street; 604-632-3000, 877-632-3030, fax 604-632-3001; www.lesoleilhotel.com. DELUXE.

Home away from home for the British royal family since it opened in 1939, the **Fairmont Hotel Vancouver**, peaked by a chateau-style oxidized copper roof, is a landmark. The calling card of this posh property is Old World elegance. Rooms are spacious and well appointed with polished antiques, plump chairs, large writing desks and tall windows that open to the surrounding scenery. Bathrooms are a bit small (typical of the period in which they were built) but elegant nonetheless. The lobby lounge and 900 West restaurant are popular gathering places. ~ 900 West Georgia Street; 604-684-3131, 800-257-7544, fax 604-662-1924; www.fairmont.com. ULTRA-DELUXE.

The **Crowne Plaza Hotel Georgia** is a welcome addition to the lodging scene in central downtown—an addition with a history, as it's a heritage property (1927 vintage) that was once the city's

AUTHOR FAVORITE

With just 83 guest rooms, the **Wedgewood** exemplifies the fine boutique hotel concept. Rooms are spacious and elegantly decorated; hotel owner Eleni Skalbania personally selected most of the furnishings, which exhibit a personal touch not found in many places. Pastel colors as well as satin and other rich fabrics warm the ambience. Special soundproofed windows keep the urban street bustle admirably at bay. The service is friendly and low-key, and the location could hardly be better—Robson Street is a half-block away, and most other downtown attractions are within minutes. The adjoining restaurant lounge is a popular evening gathering spot. ~ 845 Hornby Street; 604-689-7777, 800-663-0666, fax 604-608-5348; www.wedgewoodhotel.com. ULTRA-DELUXE.

snazziest. Now it's a lovingly refurbished, comfortable hotel with a sumptuous wood, marble and brass lobby, and high-ceilinged rooms that have plenty of character. Ask for an upper-floor room if traffic noise bothers you. ~ 801 West Georgia Street; 604-682-5566, 800-663-1111, fax 604-642-5579; www.hotelgeorgia. bc.ca, e-mail general@hotelgeorgia.bc.ca. MODERATE TO DELUXE.

Super, Natural British Columbia operates a free reservation hotline to help visitors arrange accommodations in all price categories. ~ 800-663-6000; www. snbc-res.com.

There's a reason the **Four Seasons Vancouver** consistently shows up in top-ten rankings for North America. The service here is incomparable, devoted to dozens of tiny details that escape the average hotel. Head out the door to go jogging, for instance, and the doorman will greet your return with a dry towel. The extensive fourth-floor fitness center opens onto a waterfall garden and courtyard, perfect for inner-city contemplation. ~ 791 West Georgia Street; 604-689-9333, 800-819-5053, fax 604-684-4555; www.fourseasons. com/vancouver. ULTRA-DELUXE.

The **Metropolitan Hotel** was built in 1984 as a Mandarin Oriental property, and little expense was spared—in fact, its per-room construction cost was the highest in North America at the time. The 197 rooms are sleek and modern, with oak cabinetry, wool carpets and marble baths. The health club, including squash and racquetball courts, is excellent for a hotel of its size. The Met's restaurant, Diva, is one of Vancouver's best-known practitioners of West Coast cuisine. ~ 645 Howe Street; 604-687-1122, 800-667-2300, fax 604-643-7267; www.metropolitan.com, e-mail reservations@van.metropolitan.com. DELUXE.

The view from the **Fairmont Waterfront** captures the essence of Vancouver: in the foreground is the commercial hubbub of Canada Place; beyond that is Burrard Inlet, with sailboats and container ships; beyond that, the Lions Gate Bridge and Grouse Mountain. More than half the 489 rooms are positioned to look out on this vista—be sure to ask for one. There's also an extensive herb garden on the patio adjoining the swimming pool. ~ 900 Canada Place Way; 604-691-1991, 800-257-7544, fax 604-691-1999; www.fairmont.com/waterfront. DELUXE TO ULTRA-DELUXE.

The **Delta Pinnacle** is a modern high-rise just above the Coal Harbour area (and thus close to Stanley Park and Canada Place). Lots of light wood, brushed metal and glass mark the sleek decor; and all the staff sport individual headsets to respond instantly to queries and requests. ~ 1128 West Hastings Street; 604-689-8188, 877-814-7706, fax 604-605-8881; www.delta hotels.com. DELUXE.

The **Pan Pacific** has an enviable location—atop Canada Place and its convention and cruise-ship facilities. Each of the 506 rooms has a view of Vancouver and the harbor. The Pan Pacific concentrates on expert, knowledgeable service. The fairly compact rooms feature elegant modern decor with subtle Asian touches. The multilevel lobby is an architectural delight. ~ 999 Canada Place; 604-662-8111, 800-937-1515, fax 604-685-8690; www.panpacific-hotel.com, e-mail reservations@panpacific-hotel.com. ULTRA-DELUXE.

The rooms at the **St. Regis** are spacious and comfy, even if the decor is a bit circumspect. Nothing fancy here—and that includes the prices, which are about as economical as you can get in a centrally located downtown hotel. Most of the 72 rooms are suites; winter rates are exceptionally low. The theater district is just three blocks away. ~ 602 Dunsmuir Street; 604-681-1135, 800-770-7929, fax 604-683-1126; www.stregishotel.com, e-mail reserve@stregishotel.com. MODERATE.

DINING

Its entrance is right on Robson, but **Cin Cin** would be easy to miss if you weren't looking. The restaurant itself is upstairs, a surprisingly large and spacious dining room whose Mediterranean decor and cuisine have long been among the city's most popular. The fresh-baked bread, rich soups and grilled meats and seafoods here are all highly flavored and imaginatively conceived. No lunch on Saturday and Sunday. ~ 1154 Robson Street; 604-688-7338, fax 604-688-7339; www.cincin.net, e-mail info@cincin.net. MODERATE TO DELUXE.

Bacchus is the dining room at the Wedgewood hotel, an intimate restaurant whose food might be described as elegant French Mediterranean. It's always hearty, always highly flavored, and always perfectly prepared; the lamb dishes are standouts. After dinner, the cigar room beckons. ~ 845 Hornby Street; 604-608-5319; www.wedgewoodhotel.com. DELUXE.

When your wallet is plump and it's time to indulge your taste buds, head for longtime favorite **The William Tell**, poshly appointed with fine European art and a few antique crossbows in keeping with its name. Your gastronomic experience might start with smoked B.C. salmon, followed by grilled veal with morel mushrooms or Fraser Valley duck breast in a yam and maple syrup demiglaze. Items on the seasonal menu supplement are always good choices, as are the extraordinary set meals presented in conjunction with shows at the Queen Elizabeth Theatre. Reservations recommended. No dinner on Monday. ~ Georgia Court Hotel, 765 Beatty Street; 604-688-3504, fax 604-683-8810; ww.thewmtell.com. ULTRA-DELUXE.

If you're in the mood for Italian food, you can't go wrong by heading to one of the region's five restaurants in the Umberto dynasty. The service and decor are impeccable and the food always tasty: Caprese salad, antipasti and pasta are reliable choices. For alfresco dining on sunny days, step out to the villa-style, terra-cotta courtyard of **Il Giardino**. Check their website or the phone book for addresses and phone numbers of other Umberto locations. No lunch on Saturday. Closed Sunday. ~ 1382 Hornby Street; 604-669-2422; www.umberto.com, e-mail inquire@umberto.com. DELUXE TO ULTRA-DELUXE.

Le Crocodile serves hearty and rich French provincial dishes such as cassoulet; the nightly specials are inviting and the crowded buzz of the place creates an energizing, cosmopolitan air, though the service can be a bit snotty and the portions don't match the prices. Even so, for many travelers, this remains the favorite Vancouver restaurant. No lunch on Saturday. Closed Sunday. ~ 909 Burrard Street; 604-669-4298; www.lecrocodilerestaurant.com. ULTRA-DELUXE.

Spicy northern Chinese cuisine is showcased brilliantly at **Kirin Mandarin**, a large, stylish restaurant with creamy gold walls adorned with prints. An emphasis on fresh local seafood is evidenced by well-stocked fish tanks at the rear of the dining area. Shellfish dishes are especially noteworthy, including lobster and crab prepared with a ginger sauce or chili-spiked sea scallops. Stop by for daily dim sum. ~ 1166 Alberni Street; 604-682-8833, fax 604-688-2818; www.kirinrestaurant.com. MODERATE.

HIDDEN ▶ **Presto Panini** is inconspicuous, but not hard to find—right in the heart of downtown—no doubt the reason it's hard to get a table here at lunch. The menu is simple—Italian soups, salads, pastas and panini sandwiches. The list of sandwiches is extensive—with two dozen concoctions scooped onto toasted focaccia—and excellent. Service is efficient, portions filling. Closed Sunday. ~ 859 Hornby Street; 604-684-4445. BUDGET TO MODERATE.

Some of the food at **900 West** is so rich and delectable that you'll want to ask the chef exactly what went into it. No problem—the line cooks are hard at work behind the bar. The airy,

AUTHOR FAVORITE

The decor at **C**, the seafood restaurant overlooking False Creek, is flashy—lots of wood, metal and glass, exposed pipes and modern furniture, along with kitschy touches such as fishing lures on the restroom doors. The food is equally innovative, including entrées such as octopus bacon–wrapped scallops and foie gras with persimmon jam. Fish dishes are cooked to perfection, with only the freshest seafood used; and you can round off dinner with one of C's 15 types of tea. Seasonal lunch. ~ On the False Creek Pier, 1600 Howe Street; 604-681-1164; www.crestaurant.com, e-mail info@crestaurant.com. DELUXE.

high-ceilinged room has two dozen tables, which seem surprisingly intimate in the big open space. The seasonal menu features lamb, poultry and ahi tuna dishes. Desserts are as sumptuous as the main courses. Closed Sunday. ~ Fairmont Hotel Vancouver, 900 West Georgia Street; 604-669-9378; www.fairmont.com. DELUXE.

Diva is one of the capitals of Vancouver cuisine. This stylish, glitzy restaurant serves superlative dishes based on Northwest ingredients with an Asian flair. Smoked black cod might be served with lightly sautéed oriental vegetables—or it might arrive with hearty mashed potatoes. A frequent dining spot for theater-goers, the atmosphere is upscale; this isn't the place for jeans and a T-shirt. Try to save room through dinner to sample the cheese course afterward; you'll have to select among two dozen exceptional European and North American cheeses. ~ Metropolitan Hotel, 645 Howe Street; 604-602-7788; www.metropolitan.com/diva. DELUXE.

Vancouver food experts often rate **Imperial Chinese Seafood Restaurant** the best in town for dim sum; it's also a wonderful purveyor of traditional Mandarin cuisine. Furthermore, it's in the beautiful historic Marine Building, an art deco masterpiece, and the views are fabulous. ~ 355 Burrard Street; 604-688-8191. MODERATE.

At **Herons**, the Fairmont Waterfront's signature restaurant, chef Daryle Ryo Nagata has indulged his passion for herbs by turning the hotel's second-floor poolside courtyard into an herb garden—and incorporating the results into almost every dish, such as barbecued salmon with sorrel. Theme dinners take on intriguing flavors, such as the notorious aphrodisiac dinner offered around Valentine's Day. The decor matches the hotel's, lots of glass and metal, with an excellent view of the harbor. Breakfast, lunch and dinner served. ~ 900 Canada Place Way; 604-691-1991. DELUXE.

Villa del Lupo chef Julio Gonzalez-Perini practices food as art. Each dish is not only exquisitely flavorful, it's visually striking—swirls of sauce, artfully layered dashes and splashes of ingredients. The pastas, all handmade, are especially fine. The basement wine cellar (which guests can sometimes use for very intimate private parties) is extensive. ~ 869 Hamilton Street; 604-688-7436, fax 604-688-3058; www.villadellupo.com, e-mail info@villadel lupo.com. DELUXE.

Vancouver's explosion of coffee shops has become, if anything, greater than Seattle's. Although Starbucks dominates, there are many fine local purveyors; the best downtown is **Trees**, a   ◄ HIDDEN
small enclave in the financial district just a couple of blocks from Canada Place. They roast their own all-organic coffees; even better, the best cheesecake muffins downtown are baked in the kitchen out back. ~ 450 Granville Street; 604-684-5060, fax 604-684-5026. BUDGET TO MODERATE.

Generous breakfasts and lunches attract a mixed clientele to the **Elbow Room Café**, which is decorated with autographed photos of movie stars. Start your day with the lumberjack or English breakfast, eggs Benedict, pancakes or an omelette. For lunch try a Monte Cristo, clubhouse or shrimp sandwich. Hamburgers are big and popular. The staff is supposed to treat customers insouciantly, if not outright insultingly; the owners say you have to have personality to fit in. Weekend breakfasts are popular. ~ 560 Davie Street; 604-685-3628, fax 604-685-4338; www.theelbow roomcafe.com. BUDGET.

HIDDEN ►   **El Caravan** is definitely not fancy, but it offers two advantages: its location is in the heart of the theater district (just behind the Orpheum, in fact) and its food is tasty and economical. The best choice is the buffet, which allows diners to choose among a dozen soups, salads and main dishes. ~ 809 Seymour Street; 604-682-7000. BUDGET.

SHOPPING   **Sinclair Centre**, housed in a fortress-like heritage granite complex near Canada Place, is composed of four handsome heritage buildings refurbished and joined, including Vancouver's old post office. It has a dozen high-end retail shops and a lower-level food court. **Leone** (604-683-1133) is a high-fashion boutique with a generous selection of designer apparel ranging from Armani to Versace. ~ 757 West Hastings Street; 604-659-1010.

Holt Renfrew isn't a boutique, but within the store the various departments are so elegant, and offer such fine merchandise and personable service, that it's like shopping at a boutique. ~ 633 Granville Street; 604-681-3121; www.holtrenfrew.com.

At the **Marion Scott Gallery**, the First Nations theme extends to works in bone and ivory, as well as other traditional materials. High quality and matching prices. ~ 481 Howe Street; 604-685-1934.

* * *

CALLING ALL CHOCOHOLICS AND HUNGRY DINERS

Fleuri Restaurant, well-known for outstanding Continental cuisine, also hosts an incredible Chocoholic Bar from 6 to 10 p.m. each Thursday, Friday and Saturday night, attracting hordes of sweet-toothed locals. There are 12 to 16 different chocolate items on the buffet (crêpes, fondues, cakes, covered fruits) that change daily. The café also features what may be the city's best Sunday brunch (be sure to try the croissant bread pudding); a seafood buffet on Friday and Saturday; and high tea daily. Reservations highly recommended. ~ Sutton Place Hotel, 845 Burrard Street; 604-642-2900; www.suttonplace.com, e-mail fleuri@suttonplace.com. MODERATE TO DELUXE.

Few would dispute the fact that the **Eaton's** building down-town, ironically opposite the Vancouver Art Gallery, is, well, un-attractive; locals call it the White Whale. Now that Sears has taken over the chain and rebranded it, disdain for the building is diminished a bit by the fact it almost stood empty, a fate that would have made it also a white elephant. ~ 701 Granville Street; 604-685-7112.

You'll find only high-style urban chic clothing at **A-Wear**, a trendy boutique in the heart of the financial district. ~ 350 Howe Street; 604-685-9327.

Just a block away is the north entrance to the **Pacific Centre Mall**, notable mainly for the fact that it's built entirely beneath street-level office complexes, and shoppers need never brave Van-couver's elements. Most of the stores within are fairly routine, but **La Jolie Madame** (604-669-1831) is an excellent European lux-ury lingerie outlet. ~ 700 West Georgia Street; 604-688-7236.

Another popular downtown shopping area is **Robson Street**. It's nicknamed Vancouver's Rodeo Drive because of the sheer number of see-and-be-seen sidewalk cafés and upscale boutiques. A recent epidemic of international chain stores has robbed it of its once-unique character, but enough distinctive shops remain to warrant a stroll along the street. And the people-watching is fab-ulous—so many people crowd Robson so much of the time that at one intersection (Robson and Thurlow), there are thriving cof-fee shops (two of them Starbucks) on three of the four corners.

If you feel compelled to acquire a Vancouver souvenir, by far the best place to do so is **Oh Yes Vancouver**, which offers a rea-sonably intelligent assortment of T-shirts, sweatshirts, postcards and, yes, paperweights. ~ 1167 Robson Street; 604-687-3187. A block on down, **Chachkas** lives up to its name, with a notably upscale selection of knick-knacks, gew-gaws and other oddments. ~ 1075 Robson Street; 604-688-6417.

Escents is a B.C.–born maker and purveyor of fine aroma-therapy products, ranging from oils to lavish soaps and emollients. Just walking in the store is an aromatic delight. ~ 1172 Robson Street; 604-682-0041.

Any self-respecting European shopping district would have a good lingerie store, and so does Robson: **La Vie en Rose**. The qual-ity and selection here are good, the prices affordable. Also a good selection of swimwear. ~ 1001 Robson Street; 604-684-5600.

Nearby, at **La Casa del Habano**, visitors can try out the fine (and expensive) Cuban cigars prohibited in the States. The selec-tion (exclusively Cuban) and expertise are superb here. ~ 980 Robson Street; 604-609-0511.

Tea experts consider **Murchie's** (a branch of the famed Victoria store) one of the world's great tea stores. With dozens of types ranging from pekoes to exotics, prices get as high as US$63 (C$99) an ounce. Want to test some out? Grab a seat at the tea and coffee bar. ~ 970 Robson Street; 604-669-0783.

NIGHTLIFE Vancouver's arts and entertainment scene is one of the most dynamic in North America; during the peak entertainment season in the winter, literally dozens of performances take place every night. The **Vancouver Alliance for Arts & Culture** arts-event clearinghouse offers comprehensive information on musical, theatrical, cultural and artistic happenings in the city. Tickets are available for some events. ~ 938 Howe Street; or call the **Arts Hotline** at 604-681-3535; www.allianceforarts.com.

The **Vancouver Opera Association** (604-682-2871) stages productions several times a year at the Queen Elizabeth Theatre and Playhouse, also home to **Ballet British Columbia** (604-732-5003) as well as major theater productions and visiting musicals. The opera is especially known for its periodic avant-garde productions that challenge the conventions of classic opera. ~ Theatre and Playhouse, Hamilton Street between Georgia and Dunsmuir streets; 604-665-3050.

The **Vancouver Symphony Orchestra** (604-876-3434; www.vancouversymphony.ca) provides first-rate entertainment at The Orpheum, a glittering multilevel vaudeville theater built in the mid-1920s that's worth a visit in itself. The symphony's repertoire encompasses Baroque to modern music, and Canadian performers and composers are given special attention. ~ Orpheum, 884 Granville Street.

Pacific Cinematheque is a nonprofit venue devoted to film, focusing on rarely seen foreign and classic films and festivals devoted to film genres. Two films are screened every night. ~ 1131 Howe Street; 604-688-3456.

Vancouver Playhouse Theatre is the city's major traditional company, offering a full program of mainstream productions in fall, winter and spring. ~ Hamilton at Dunsmuir; 604-877-3311. **Metro Theatre** concentrates on modern drama. ~ 1370 Southwest Marine Drive; 604-266-7191. The **Vancouver Professional Theatre Alliance** represents all the professional dramatic companies in the greater metro area. ~ 604-608-6799.

There are hundreds of clubs, discos, cabarets, lounges, pubs and taverns in Vancouver; we touch on only a few popular selections here. A complete listing of all the acts at all the clubs, taverns and bars appears every Thursday in the *Georgia Straight*.

Richard's on Richards, with its refined wood, brass and stained-glass decor, adult-oriented rock and live Top-40 bands on weekends, attracts a mixed crowd, predominantly upscale businesspeople. Wednesday is salsa night. Hip-hop comedy is a popular feature here. ~ 1036 Richards Street; 604-688-1099.

In the Crease

It's true, Canadians are just as crazy about sports as their neighbors to the south, and they show it by filling up stadiums to root for their teams. In general, you won't see the fans here devolve to the level of rudeness typical in some other locales, but that doesn't mean they never get worked up—a major victory or defeat can send fans into the streets.

Whether the home team is playing well makes a difference, of course—but either way, sitting in the stands here is likely to get you a taste of an international pastime with its own regional flavor. It's a great way to see a section of the culture you might not find at the opera (though in these parts, don't be too surprised if you see that mirthful guy in row E again tomorrow night—at *La Traviata*).

The place to go for pro games in Vancouver is at the east end of downtown. Two side-by-side covered arenas here, **General Motors Place** and **BC Place**, house Vancouver's professional sports teams. The **Vancouver Canucks**, the city's NHL franchise, play at GM Place; the city was at fever pitch when the Canucks appeared in the Stanley Cup finals in 2004. (They lost.) Ticket information for the Canucks is at 604-899-4610. The **BC Lions**, members of the wild and woolly Canadian Football League, play at BC Place, the world's largest stadium under an air-supported roof when it opened in 1983. The Lions won the Grey Cup, Canada's professional championship, in 2000; for ticket information, call TicketMaster, 604-280-4400. GM Place is at Dunsmuir Street and Expo Boulevard; BC Place is between Expo Boulevard, Smithe Street and Pacific Boulevard South. The **BC Sports Hall of Fame & Museum** is at BC Place, with interesting exhibits devoted to notable provincial athletes and sporting events. (The world's first professional hockey championship was won in 1914 by a B.C. team from Victoria.) Admission. ~ 777 Pacific Boulevard South; 604-687-5520.

On a slightly different note, the **Terry Fox Memorial** (on the plaza at the foot of Robson Street leading to BC Place) honors one of the Vancouver area's most famous native sons. Fox, a cancer patient who lost a leg at the age of 18, captured the Canadian (and global) imagination in 1980 with his attempt to run solo across Canada. He made it from Newfoundland to Thunder Bay, Ontario, before a recurrence of his cancer brought his quest to an end. Fox died less than a year later. ~ At the intersection of Robson and Beatty streets.

Liquor flows and singles connect, both at high speed, at **The Roxy**, an after-work watering spot swarming with Vancouver's young professionals. ~ 932 Granville Street; 604-331-7999.

If you don't like hockey, don't venture into the **Shark Club**, where dozens of TV monitors are tuned to Canada's national madness. During hockey interregnums, other sports manifest themselves. As sports bars go, this one is a bit more refined than most. ~ 180 West Georgia Street; 604-687-4275.

For an unhurried drink and quiet conversation, a good bet is the **Gérard Lounge**, a genteel gentlemen's-style club; since it's in the Hollywood-favorite Sutton Place Hotel, this is one place to spot visiting celebrities as well. ~ 845 Burrard Street; 604-682-5511.

Other nearby hotels offer comfortable lounges. At **Bacchus** in the Wedgewood, jazz piano and excellent drinks pack the small lounge area every night; there's a cigar room that is also an excellent place to spot celebrities. ~ 845 Hornby Street; 604-608-5319. The Fairmont Hotel Vancouver's lobby opens onto **900 West**, whose lounge attracts a bustling crowd weeknights. The wine tasting bar, with 55 wines available by the glass, is an excellent innovation. Jazzy piano here, too. ~ 900 West Georgia Street; 604-669-9378.

O'Doul's is a smoky, bustling, intimate chophouse/lounge that presents excellent jazz vocals nightly. It's in the Listel Vancouver along Robson's ever-busy scene. ~ 1300 Robson Street; 604-684-8461.

HIDDEN ▶   It's hard to get into the **Railway Club**. All those people are lined up outside to hear hot B.C. and Canadian bands upstairs. It's one of the trendiest places in town; if you're in a major hotel, see if the concierge can help get you in. ~ 579 Dunsmuir Street; 604-681-1625.

At **BaBalu**, the ambience is smoke and tapas, with live bands offering music to match. ~ 654 Nelson Street; 604-605-4343.

The **Gate** is a ballroom devoted to big-beat sounds—swing, jump, big band. ~ 1176 Granville Street; 604-688-8701.

IN THE KNOW

The most authoritative guide to Vancouver dining, theater, music and other events is the venerable *Georgia Straight*, a free weekly (one of the last of the original Sixties counterculture papers left on the West Coast) with comprehensive coverage of the city's cultural life. It's available at most coffee shops, bookstores, hotels, restaurants and newsstands. Keep an eye out as well for *CityFood*, a monthly tabloid devoted to the dining scene, and *Taxi*, a hip club guide.

At **Yale Hotel,** blues is the predominant theme, with live local and national acts. ~ 1300 Granville Street; 604-681-9253.

Not surprisingly, Celtic music is big in Vancouver. The **Rogue Folk Club** presents about 60 concerts a year at local venues, featuring traditional and Celtic music and dance. ~ 604-736-3022. The **Irish Heather** offers live traditional Irish music Wednesday through Sunday nights, with a traditional Irish open jam Sunday afternoon. ~ 217 Carroll Street; 604-688-9779.

▼▼▼▼▼▼▼▼▼▼▼▼▼▼▼▼

Gastown/Chinatown/East End

The east side of Vancouver is a sharp contrast to downtown—funkier, older, in a few places still slightly run-down. Hundreds of heritage buildings, many wonderfully restored, dot the Gastown, Chinatown, Yaletown and East Side neighborhoods, vastly outnumbering skyscrapers; Yaletown consists of more than 40 converted warehouses, some a century old. Instead of glitzy, upscale restaurants, low-key, hidden ethnic and local eateries await the adventurous traveler. The Commercial Drive area east of Chinatown is one of Vancouver's hippest scenes; it's known as a lesbian hangout. Farther east and southeast, residential neighborhoods offer Vancouver's most affordable housing, with many early-20th-century homes now being snapped up and refurbished by young professionals.

One thing remains the same as elsewhere in the city: walking, especially in Gastown and Chinatown, is by far the best way to enjoy this lively area. (Please note that one street—East Hastings from the central downtown and on through Chinatown and the east end—has become one of Canada's most active drug-dealing districts, with some attendant violence. Visitors are best advised to avoid this street near and after dark and to avoid the corner of Hastings and Main entirely.)

SIGHTS

There are numerous photo-worthy spots in **Chinatown,** which stretches along Pender Street between Carrall and Gore streets. North America's third-largest Chinese community, this crowded neighborhood is particularly festive during holiday periods. Holiday or not, it's a wonderful area to tour on foot, poking into the many food stalls and cafés to sample redolent, spicy delights ranging from honey-roasted quail to exotic tropical fruits. The culturally adventurous traveler can hardly have more fun in Canada than to spend four hours in Vancouver's Chinatown, deliberately trying out unfamiliar things.

Among the most intriguing sights is the extremely narrow **Sam Kee Building** (Pender and Carrall streets), listed in *Ripley's Believe It or Not!* as the skinniest building in the world at just six feet wide. Along the way you'll also see brightly colored,

Chinatown in a Half-day

There's no way to truly experience the flavor of Vancouver's Chinatown but on foot. It can be done in half a day, starting at 10 a.m. or so, leaving plenty of time to return to your hotel and relax before dinner. Make sure you bring a camera, a handful of Canadian currency, and a spirit of adventure.

SAM KEE BUILDING   Start at the corner of Pender and Carrall, where the Sam Kee Building (page 65)—the world's narrowest—demonstrates not only how valuable a slice of land can be, but how a single exotic distinction can bring something world fame.

DR. SUN YAT SEN CLASSICAL CHINESE GARDEN   A half block west on Pender, a huge decorative gate leads into a courtyard that holds the entrance to the Dr. Sun Yat Sen Classical Chinese Garden (see below). Handcrafted by Chinese artisans, using materials imported from mainland China, this marvelous walled garden, with its finely shaped wood and stone, and its carefully grown shrubs and trees, is an exceptional oasis of calm in the midst of the city.

CHINESE BENEVOLENT ASSOCIATION BUILDING   Return to Pender and head east. Across the street, at 108 Pender Street, is the Chinese Benevolent Association Building, the finest remaining example of the early-20th-century Tong architecture. Its lavish paint and recessed balconies are typical of the style; Tongs, although they have a colorful reputation, were mostly just clan associations devoted to maintaining community vitality.

elaborately carved facades of buildings housing herbalists, bakeries, dim sum parlors, silk or souvenir shops and open-front produce stands.

Also be sure to stop by the jewel of Chinatown, the **Dr. Sun Yat Sen Classical Chinese Garden**, a unique garden that seems to have been magically transported to Vancouver from China. In fact, much of it was: Many of the elements, including the architectural and artistic components, rocks and pebbles (but not the plants) were shipped in from China. This Ming Dynasty–style garden is the first such classical garden to be built outside China. Admission. ~ 578 Carrall Street; 604-662-3207.

A bit farther on Pender Street is the 1912 **Sun Tower Building**, which, at 272 feet, was once briefly the tallest building in the British Empire and site of a daring escape stunt pulled off

GOOD EATS   The next block of Pender, east of Main, is the busiest district of **food stalls** and produce and seafood shops. Here's where adventurous appetites can find fruits you've never seen—my favorite is the tangy, purple dragon fruit—and savor barbecued meats and sausages. I particularly favor the honey-glazed roast quail at **Kam Tong**, 276 East Pender Street. A swing south on Gore Street for a block takes you past the best seafood shops, with live fish and crustaceans of every description; when you return to Pender and head back down the north side of the street, you'll encounter herb and Chinese medicine stores where you can find salves for every ill known to man—if you speak Mandarin.

AFTERNOON TEA   When you arrive back at Main, it's time to cleanse your palate with a stop at **Ten Lee Hong Tea & Ginseng** (page 71) for tea service; jasmine tea is a wonderful early afternoon choice. Be sure to pick up some ginseng candy for snacks.

HOME SHOPPING   Heading back west on Pender, you cross Main and encounter the best furniture and houseware stores in Chinatown. Rosewood and porcelain abound; it's not all good, but quite a bit is sufficient to induce a little acquisitive ardor. You bet they take credit cards.

CHINESE CULTURAL CENTRE   When you reach Columbia, turn left (south) and go a half-block to the Chinese Cultural Centre (555 Columbia Street), a facility that holds rotating craft and art exhibits and has a memorable permanent collection of carved jade statuary and jewelry. It's not for sale, but if you need to seek quiet to cast off Western mercenary impulses, the **public meditation garden** adjacent to the Sun Yat Sen garden is behind the cultural center. Fifteen minutes on a bench here will admirably clear your mind for the cosmopolitan evening ahead.

by Harry Houdini during the height of his career. Builder Louis Taylor, a newspaper publisher, deliberately intended the half-clad caryatids (maidens) atop the tower to offend Edwardian sensibilities. ~ 100 West Pender Street; 604-683-2305.

Colorful **Gastown**, named after saloonkeeper "Gassy" Jack Deighton whose statue stands in Maple Tree Square (Alexander and Carrall streets), is where the original townsite was in 1867. This touristy heritage area of cobbled streets, Victorian street lamps and storefronts, charming courtyards and mews is chock-full of antique and souvenir shops and international eateries.

On the corner of Cambie and Water streets, the world's first **steam clock** wheezes out musical chimes on the quarter hour. Although it looks old, the two-ton clock dates back to 1977—a promotional creation by the leaders who restored Gastown. A picture taken in front of the steam clock seems to be essential for visitors to Vancouver. ~ 604-669-3525.

Yaletown is a former warehouse district, south of Chinatown and Gastown, turned trendy by conversion of its buildings into galleries, restaurants and stores. Many of the district's lofts have been transformed into condominiums, and modern high-rises are beginning to dot the district. Even so, it retains a funky, slightly industrial air found nowhere else in central Vancouver. It's what Granville Island was like before the latter was completely gentrified. The main streets of the restaurant district are Hamilton and Mainland streets, well worth a stroll up one and down the other.

HIDDEN ►   The **Roundhouse Community Centre**, built for one of Yaletown's snazzy new residential developments, Concord Pacific, preserves its namesake old railyard facility, plus an antique Canadian Pacific engine. The gallery inside the center often features shows by Yaletown artists and craftmakers. ~ 181 Roundhouse Mews; 604-713-1800.

LODGING   There are few accommodations in the east end of downtown; that's why the **YWCA Hotel/Residence** is such a pleasant surprise. It is clean, modern and safe; its 155 units range from four-to-a-room family lodgings to singles much like any mainstream hotel. There are kitchens on some floors; TVs and private baths are available; and, of course, the YWCA exercise facilities are extensive. It's quite close to GM Place, BC Place, the theater district and Chinatown. ~ 733 Beatty Street; 604-895-5830, 800-613-1424, fax 604-681-2550; www.ywcahotel.com. BUDGET TO MODERATE.

Jodie Foster won her first Academy Award in 1988 with *The Accused*, set in New England though filmed in Vancouver.

Situated directly across the street from BC Place and just down from GM Place, the **Georgian Court Hotel** is the best deluxe property close to these sports and concert venues. It's also just a five-minute stroll from Chinatown. The hotel's mauve and indigo rooms include many nice touches, such as three-way light bulbs, soundproof windows and roomy bathtubs. ~ 773 Beatty Street; 604-682-5555, 800-663-1155, fax 604-682-8830; www.georgiancourt.com, e-mail info@georgiancourt.com. DELUXE.

You know it's different the instant you walk in the **Opus Hotel** lobby: An "altar" sparkles with the light from a couple dozen votive candles, and sitting stools front the reception desk. It's hip, chic and distinctive—just what Yaletown needs. Rooms feature vibrant walls, faux-wood ebony fixtures, ambient lighting and platform beds. Bathrooms include a window-wall facing outside, with a long granite slab and brushed-stainless bowl sink. Ask for a room on the side, not facing Davie, if you like quiet. There are both a tapas bar and French bistro on-site. ~ 322 Davie Street;

604-642-6787, 866-642-6787, fax 604-642-6780; www.opus
hotel.com, e-mail info@opushotel.com. DELUXE.

Dining in Chinatown means entering a kaleidoscopic world of **DINING**
colors, sounds, smells and tastes, with exotic ingredients and flavors behind every door. The adventurous traveler can simply walk
the streets having a look, choosing on the basis of sight or smell;
there are literally dozens of small lunch counters and backroom
cafés. Here are a few more established options:

The **Pink Pearl Restaurant** is a dim sum emporium, a cavernous dining room where black-clad waiters and waitresses roll
out dozens of steam-tray delectables on trundle carts. Dine on this
finger food while enjoying the Chinese artwork adorning the walls.
Hugely popular with Vancouverites. Best to take a taxi to this
east end location—don't walk. ~ 1132 East Hastings Street; 604-
253-4316, fax 604-253-8525; www.pinkpearl.com. MODERATE.

Garden Villa Seafood Restaurant is hard to find—you go   ◀ HIDDEN
through a courtyard and up a flight of stairs to enter a cozy,
crowded room where the dim sum emphasizes seafood—shrimp,
crab, fish, shellfish. There are dozens of kinds to choose from; go
with friends or family so you can sample everything without
overeating. ~ 127 East Pender Street; 604-688-3877. MODERATE.

The fare at Chinatown's **Buddhist Vegetarian Restaurant** is   ◀ HIDDEN
typified by simplicity and abundance. Most dishes consist of a
tureen of soup, noodles, curry or some combination of the three,
enough for a full meal at a most reasonable price. Try the Eight
Treasures won ton soup. The ambience is modest, the food rich
and filling. ~ 137 East Pender Street; 604-683-8816. MODERATE.

Asia is vast and diverse, and Chinatown's name does not limit
its scope. **Phnom Penh** is a highly regarded Cambodian restaurant
where the flavors are sharper and spicier than you'll find in most
Chinese restaurants. The soups and barbecued chicken are standouts here. ~ 244 East Georgia Street; 604-682-5777. BUDGET TO
MODERATE.

Vietnamese food is, compared to other Asian cuisines, fairly
simple. The classic dish, *pho*, is a big bowl of noodles, meat, broth
and garnishes such as cilantro, lime and chiles. That's the main
attraction at **Pho Hoang**, Chinatown's best Vietnamese eatery.   ◀ HIDDEN
Finish your meal with Vietnamese coffee, slowly dripped into
condensed milk while you eat. ~ 238 East Georgia Street; 604-
682-5666. BUDGET.

When wandering around Gastown, it's hard to miss the ro-
tund, dancing monks touting their pastas, steak and lobster painted
on the side of **Brother's Restaurant**. Waiters in Franciscan habits
fit right in with the dark, monastic decor of this fun, family-style
eatery. As promised, the food is good (especially the seafood and
prime rib). ~ 1 Water Street; 604-683-9124, fax 604-689-2767;
e-mail brothersrestaurant@telus.net. MODERATE TO DELUXE.

Sandwiches, fresh shucked oysters and wood-roasted pizzas are the specialties at **SteamWorks Brewing**—not to mention a tasty selection of craft beers, and a lunch and dinner ambience that's all happy bustle. ~ 375 Water Street; 604-689-2739. MODERATE.

Yaletown is a popular former warehouse district converted to restaurants, dancehalls, stores and cafés. The **Hamilton Street Bar & Grill** offers gourmet pub food in an attractive rehabbed warehouse setting; the pizzas, sandwiches, salads and pastas are well above average. Try the calamari—it's fabulous. Great beer selection. ~ 1009 Hamilton Street; 604-331-1511. MODERATE.

It seems like the staff outnumbers the customers at **Cioppino's**, one of the snazziest and most popular of the restaurants in Yaletown. The food is superb—Northern Italian freshened with a Northwest flair, such as the namesake cioppino, a rich seafood stew—but the service is what stands out. Raise your eyebrow and someone will be there instantly to see what you want. The decor is what you might call renovated-warehouse glitz, with huge beams and low amber light. ~ 1133 Hamilton Street; 604-688-7466; www.cioppinosyaletown.com. DELUXE.

Yaletown Brewing, a frequent local poll winner in its category, serves up craft beers, dependable pub food—sandwiches, salads, pastas—and an innovation for Vancouver: an extensive selection of hot sauces, some of which frequently seem to disappear into pockets and purses. ~ 1111 Mainland Street; 604-681-2739; www.yaletownbrewing.com. MODERATE.

If only breads were the fare at **Ecco il Pane** it would be worth a visit—the hearty, European-style loaves are thick and flavorful. But what they do with those breads at lunch is even more enticing: consider a cornmeal-crusted fried oyster sandwich, or a simple bowl of country stew served with thick slices of rye bread. ~ 238 West 5th Street; 604-873-6888. BUDGET TO MODERATE.

The crowd is chic, the buzz is high-energy, the food is hot and highly flavored at **Havana**, located in the burgeoning Commercial

AUTHOR FAVORITE

I find that seafood is rarely executed as expertly as at **Blue Water**, the sensational centerpoint of Yaletown dining. The signature appetizer tower features a dozen delights, ranging from crabcakes to sushi; the entrées take peerless ingredients such as salmon and cod, fancy them up a bit (pumpkin-seed crust) and leave the flavor intact. Desserts include handmade sorbets and a sensational lemon tart. Lots of glitz and glamour here, with black-clad young professionals hugging the sushi bar. The wood-decor and open ceiling are a delight, and the service is matchless. ~ 1095 Hamilton Street; 604-688-8078. DELUXE.

Drive see-and-be-seen district. The fare is nominally Caribbean here, with the typical Northwest slant—crab is Dungeness, for instance. It's hardly possible to not have fun at Havana. ~ 1212 Commercial Drive; 604-253-9119. MODERATE.

The bagels at **Solly's** are made on site each morning. The cream cheese, pastrami, lox and smoked salmon are the highest quality. And the cinnamon buns are frequently voted the best in town in local dining polls. In other words, this is a classic neighborhood deli, just a half-block off the vibrant East Main shopping district. ~ 189 East 28th Avenue; 604-872-1821. BUDGET.

There's nothing fussy about Hungarian food, so what you get at the **Budapest Restaurant** are full plates of chicken, schnitzels, potatoes and bowls of goulash, all quite genuine and excellently made. Don't leave without carefully inspecting the pastry display; Budapest's heavy banana bread loaves are thick and rich, and they last a week. ~ 3250 Main Street; 604-877-1949. BUDGET TO MODERATE.

◄ HIDDEN

The biggest challenge at **Mario's Gelati** is choosing among the dozens of flavors of gelati, sorbets and frozen yogurts. Here is every fruit, berry and chocolate possibility you could imagine—and some no one could imagine, except the chefs at this Vancouver institution. ~ 88 East 1st Avenue; 604-879-9411. BUDGET.

In Chinatown, the **Beijing Trading Company** carries an intriguing selection of herbs, teas and food products. ~ 89 East   Pender Street; 604-684-3563. Like most furniture/artifacts stores in Chinatown, **Yen Hua** has some junk. But there is also a healthy selection of good-quality tables, chairs, vases and such. ~ 173 East Pender Street; 604-662-3832.

SHOPPING

Ten Lee Hong Tea & Ginseng has a wide variety of ginseng preparations to restore youth and vigor; and dozens of varieties of tea, ranging from classic oolong to jasmine. Stop in for a quick tea ceremony to clear your palate of all its food-stall adventures. ~ 500 Main Street; 604-689-7598.

Ming Wo has just one stock in trade—cookery. But this shop at the edge of Chinatown is peerless in its selection: If you need a 21-inch stainless-steel wok, here's where you'll find it. The inventory is not limited to Asian cooking gear; pots, pans, plates and utensils of every description crowd the shelves and bins. ~ 23 East Pender Street; 604-683-7268.

Biz Books has titles devoted to a popular Vancouver industry—show business (film, theater, television). Also software, tapes, scripts and more. ~ 136 East Cordova Street; 604-669-6431. The **Magpie Magazine Gallery** carries more than 2000 (yes, two thousand) titles; that'll keep browsers busy for a while. ~ 1319 Commercial Drive; 604-253-6666.

Nearby, Gastown teems with souvenir shops full of T-shirts, totems, maple sugar (not local—it's from Eastern Canada), smoked salmon and other regional items.

The **Inuit Gallery** offers extremely high quality and high-dollar Northwest Coast First Nation and Inuit art. It's worth a visit just to look, even if you can't really think about buying. ~ 345 Water Street; 604-688-7323. **Spirit Wrestler Gallery** focuses on masks and carved stone from Inuit and Northwest Native artists. ~ 8 Water Street; 604-669-8813.

Hill's Indian Crafts is one of the older purveyors of First Nations work in Vancouver, focusing on Cowichan, West Coast and Inuit arts. The store also has outlets in Victoria and Nanaimo. ~ 165 Water Street; 604-685-4249. Next door, **Frances Hill's** offers a vast selection of Canadian crafts and products, ranging from oilskin dusters to pottery and sweaters. ~ 151 Water Street; 604-685-1828.

The theme at **LightHeart** matches its name—kitchenware with a whimsical touch. All is high quality; some is handcrafted. ~ 100-535 Howe Street; 604-684-4711.

HIDDEN ▶   **McLeod's** looks exactly like a used bookstore should—shelves stuffed with books, and more books piled on floors, windowsills, tables in heedless profusion. In fact, any stationary, flat surface is covered with books. Specialties include Canadiana, art and history, and an extensive mystery section. And where else would you find a whole shelf devoted to Sacco and Vanzetti? ~ 455 West Pender Street; 604-681-7654.

It seems like there are a zillion antique and curio shops in the Gastown area; one of the best is **Salmagundi West**, an engaging collection of clothes, jewelry, household goods and such. The owner has a fetish for horns, so if you need an antique trumpet or other heraldic instrument, this is the place. ~ 321 West Cordova Street; 604-681-4648.

HIDDEN ▶   Located on the edge of Gastown, **Sikora's** is a modern oddity, a store with just one type of merchandise—classical music. But what a selection! With thousands of CDs, classical music lovers will find artists and recordings they'll never see in mainstream

❖❖❖

SUMMER STROLLS

In summer only, costumed local historians offer **guided walking tours** of Gastown. ~ 604-683-5650. The **Architectural Institute of BC** offers six different summer walking tours that explore the history of the city's buildings in a variety of neighborhoods, from Gastown to the West End. ~ 604-683-8588, fax 604-683-8568; www.aibc.bc.ca, e-mail communications@aibc.bc.ca.

American music stores, no matter how large. The staff is admirably knowledgeable and opinionated; ask which recording of Mahler's Second Symphony is best, and they'll tell you. ~ 432 West Hastings Street; 604-685-0625.

The question is whether **Button Button** is more amazing because it's a store devoted entirely to, yes, buttons—or because a store devoted entirely to buttons does a thriving business. At any rate, whatever button you need, this is the place. ~ 422 West Cordova Street; 604-687-0067.

The biggest and most notable store in Yaletown is **Chintz & Company**, a fabulous, cavernous collection of what the store calls treasures and curiosities. The selection ranges from seriously overstuffed armchairs to eclectic lamps—and they do mean eclectic. ~ 950 Homer Street; 604-689-2022.

Any observation of the modern publishing scene will lead to the suspicion that there are a lot of books devoted to cooking and food. A visit to **Barbara-Jo's Books to Cooks** reveals just how many: this marvelous Yaletown store carries about 3000 separate titles, ranging from the latest cookbooks to rare and out-of-print classic texts. Evening events feature presentations by leading B.C. chefs. ~ 1128 Mainland Street; 604-688-6755.

◀ HIDDEN

At **Vancouver Cigar Company**'s walk-in humidor room, fanciers will find cigars from almost every corner of the world, including unusual Brazilian smokes. The selection covers a large number of Cuban makes, as well as Dominican, Nicaraguan and Honduran. Prices are competitive with most other Vancouver outlets, and it's open late in the evening to serve the Yaletown after-dinner crowd. ~ 1093 Hamilton Street; 604-685-0445.

A profusion of antique and curio shops make the Main Street district, southeast of downtown, an excellent spot for a leisurely stroll. At **Curios–City Arts & Antiques**, country furniture dominates. Some of the large pine pieces are fairly reasonably priced. ~ 3851 Main Street; 604-876-0900.

In the heart of the antique district, **The Blue Heron** serves as a sort of informational gateway—it specializes in titles relating to antiques, curios and collectibles, as well as history and Canadiana. ~ 3516-A Main Street; 604-874-8401.

Kestrel Books offers an excellent general stock of used natural history, arts, literature and reference books. ~ 3408 Cambie Street; 604-872-2939.

The **Purple Onion Cabaret** is a popular Gastown club offering food, music, dancing and cigars. Closed Monday through Wednesday. ~ 15 Water Street; 604-602-9442.

NIGHTLIFE

Touchstone Theater offers a progressive program of drama and performance art at Firehall Arts Centre east of Gastown. ~ 280 East Cordova Street; 604-689-0926.

▼▼▼▼▼▼▼▼▼▼▼▼▼▼▼▼▼

West End/Stanley Park

Vancouver's West End is a wonderful, cosmopolitan neighborhood that reflects all the best features of urban life—high density but comfortable and quiet (and expensive) apartment and condo complexes contribute to an almost nonstop bustle. Denman Street is the major thoroughfare; at lunchtime and in the early evening it's almost as crowded as Robson, although it's more of a low-key, neighborhood street. The crown jewel of the West End is Stanley Park, widely considered one of the outstanding city parks in the world—and rightly so. This 1000-acre park offers more recreational and entertainment options than you can imagine.

SIGHTS

In the West End, the **Community Arts Council Gallery** offers an eclectic and frequently changed sampling of works by local and regional artists; it's also a visual-arts resource and information center. ~ 837 Davie Street; 604-683-4358.

At **Barclay Heritage Square,** the exquisite semiformal Victorian garden is a special delight in late spring when the many rhododendrons bloom. The square also contains several historic homes, the best of which is the **Roedde House Museum**, a restored early West End mansion open for tours and tea each afternoon. ~ Located four blocks north of Davie Street, at Barclay Street and Broughton Street; 604-684-7040.

HIDDEN ►

Nearby, at **St. Paul's Anglican Church,** parishioners have painted a **medieval labyrinth** on the church hall floor. The geometric circular path is supposed to evoke harmony and peace; the church itself is a heritage 1905 wood structure. ~ 1130 Jervis Street; 604-685-6832.

STANLEY PARK   Stanley Park is almost as big as the rest of downtown Vancouver, but only the outer 20 percent of this green grove that pokes out into Burrard Inlet at the head of the downtown peninsula is developed for recreational use. Six hundred acres of the park's land is undeveloped forest; as a result wildlife abounds, including herons, owls, eagles, beavers, coyotes, flying squirrels, gray squirrels and the ubiquitous raccoons. (Please do not feed any of the animals, especially raccoons, which look cute but can be quite dangerous.) ~ 604-257-8400.

Dedicated in 1888, the park is the subject of several engaging legends. Although it looks like virgin old-growth forest, most of it was in fact logged by 1870; sufficient time has elapsed since then to allow the trees to grow back to mature size, and tracts of ancient forest left by the loggers are indeed scattered throughout the park. And while Vancouver city founders deserve some credit for the foresight involved in petitioning Ottawa to deed over as a park what had been a military reserve, it was also a scheme promoted by railroad barons and land developers to boost the value of property in the West End (it worked). Stanley Park still serves as a focus for social and political currents—its famed zoo was closed in 1992 by the city's voters, who objected to confining wild animals.

A similar movement is targeting the popular **Vancouver Aquarium**, so far unsuccessfully. At the Aquarium, about a quarter-mile inside the park, you'll find resident dolphins and beluga whales, as well as nearly 700 other species of marine life in the museum's numerous exhibits. The dolphin shows are well presented and popular with children. Even more intriguing are the aquarium's new "beluga encounters," where patrons go behind the scenes to meet the whales, feed them and learn their many endearing traits. Afterward, you can stroll through the tropical rainforest room and listen to the birds chitter as you peer at crocs or piranhas. A Pacific Canada exhibit includes the aquarium's own manmade stream, with its own race of salmon returning to spawn each year. An outdoor viewing deck on the west side of the compound allows free looks at the seal and beluga whale pools. Admission. ~ 604-659-3474; www.vanaqua.org.

You can enter the nearby **Children's Farm Yard** to frolic with the llamas, goats and other little critters. You can also ride the miniature railway, a scaled-down version of the first train to cross Canada. Call for winter hours. Admission. ~ 604-257-8530.

Rose aficionados will want to stroll through the lovely **Rose Garden**, crowning glory of the city's parks. The fragrant collection in this mid-size formal garden is sure to contain one or two specimens you'd like to have in your own yard. Late summer is the best time to visit for the full effect. ~ Located near the park's entrance just off Georgia Street; 604-257-8400.

The best approach to touring the rest of the park is to first stop at the **Lost Lagoon Nature House** at the west end of Alberni Street   ◄ HIDDEN
just above the south shore of Lost Lagoon, and pick up a park map plus pamphlets explaining the various sights.

READ ALL ABOUT IT

Of the city's two daily papers, the *Province* most resembles a British tabloid, with lots of stories about animals and human foibles, while the *Sun* takes a more sober, business-minded view of the world. The *Vancouver Review* is a very fine, progressive literary quarterly available free at local bookstores and coffee shops. *BC Bookworld*, another free quarterly found at bookstores and newsstands, not only offers extensive insight into the vigorous provincial publishing scene, it's the best roundup of the many bookstores and literary happenings in both Vancouver and Victoria.

Making your way around the seawall promenade, you'll pass a statue of Lord Stanley, the rose gardens, the Royal Vancouver Yacht Club, Deadman's Island, the Nine O'Clock Gun, an array of Kwakiutl and Haida totem poles and the "girl in a wetsuit" statue next to the historic figurehead from the S.S. *Empress of Japan*.

Continue along the promenade to **Prospect Point Lookout**, at the far northern tip of the park, which boasts a great view of the **Lions Gate Bridge**. Once one of the longest suspension bridges in the world, it stretches over Burrard Inlet's First Narrows (it's also called the First Narrows Bridge) to the slopes of West Vancouver. The bridge was built in 1938 by the Guinness family so residents could travel to their housing subdivisions on the north shore. The government bought the bridge in 1963.

Siwash Rock, the hollow tree, and Second, Third and English beaches, favorites of sunbathers and water enthusiasts, finish out the seawall route. Second Beach has a heated outdoor pool. Not far off the seawall between Second and Third Beach is a Western red cedar (now dead) that the National Geographic Society believes was the largest in the world. The promenade continues on around False Creek past English Bay Beach, past Science World and around to the University of British Columbia; the truly energetic can trek the entire 37 kilometers (22.5 miles) in a day on bike or inline skates.

To get to know the wild interior of the park, hikers will enjoy the miles of trails through thick coniferous forest; **nature walks** depart the Lost Lagoon Nature House on Sundays in the summer. The walks are free, but preregistration is required; call 604-257-8544. Birdwatchers will probably prefer to perch quietly at the edge of **Beaver Lake** or **Lost Lagoon** to peer at Canada geese, rare trumpeter swans and other waterfowl. For children, there's the **Variety Kid's Water Park** (a wonderful, watery play area complete with slides, water cannons and a pint-size, full-body blow drier), and a fire-engine playground.

AUTHOR FAVORITE

The best way to take in all of Stanley Park's sights is to bike or hike along the divided six-mile **seawall promenade**. Beware of the crowds that head for the seawall on sunny weekends; weekday midmornings are the best times for visitors to take in the sights. If I'm pressed for time or not up for the several-hour jaunt around the perimeter path, I just hop in the car and follow the one-way scenic drive signs from the park's main entrance off Georgia Street to hit most of the highlights.

The **Coast Plaza Hotel & Suites at Stanley Park** is by far the best   **LODGING**
lodging near Stanley Park. With 269 airy, large rooms and suites
just off Denman looking out over the park, its location is unsurpassed for West End visitors. ~ 1763 Comox Street; 604-688-
7711, 800-663-1144, fax 604-688-5934; www.coasthotels.com.
MODERATE TO DELUXE.

Prime downtown location and lots of room space were long
the drawing cards at **Pacific Palisades**—but this '60s-era property
was sorely in need of renovation. That's what happened in 2000
when the San Francisco–based Kimpton Group bought the property and gave its designer free rein. Now bright colors abound—
orange, green (including chartreuse gingham-check carpet!) and
persimmon in the rooms, a rainbow of glass and tile in the lobby.
It won't appeal to everyone, but it is visually memorable. The
other virtues of the place—including a lavish health club—remain the same, and the Kimpton service is unsurpassed. ~ 1277
Robson Street; 604-688-0461, 800-663-1815, fax 604-688-4374;
www.pacificpalisadeshotel.com, e-mail reservations@pacificpali
sadeshotel.com. DELUXE.

At **Listel Vancouver**, hotel managers hit on a charming and
clever idea a while back: Why not collaborate with local galleries
for the art used to decorate guest rooms and hallways? The result,
two "gallery floors" of high-art rooms, is engaging. Local galleries
show off the best by (usually) local artists; and guests get to enjoy
a level of decor unmatched at mid-range hotels. The suites are as
fine as any in town. Gay-friendly. ~ 1300 Robson Street; 604-684-
8461, 800-663-5491, fax 604-684-7092. DELUXE.

Planning to be in Vancouver a while? **The Residences on
Georgia** are sparkling, offer fabulous views, provide an excellent
location—and are surprisingly economical for those staying a
week or more. You get a spacious suite, with a big kitchen and
plenty of living space, for less than you'd pay nightly at one of the
major first-class hotels. Most suites are booked far in advance,
so it's a good idea to call well ahead. ~ 1288 West Georgia Street;
604-891-6100, fax 604-891-6168; www.vancouverextended
stay.com. DELUXE.

The West End Guest House, a pink Victorian a block off bustling Robson Street, offers a personable alternative to the area's
hotels and motels. Each of the eight guest rooms (two of which
are suites), filled with a mixture of antiques, has a personality of
its own. All have private baths and plush feather mattresses, duvets and luxurious linens. The multicourse morning repast and
the afternoon sherry with nuts and summertime iced tea on the
sun deck are a gourmand's delight. Free bikes for guests' use.
Gay-friendly. ~ 1362 Haro Street; 604-681-2889, 888-546-3327,
fax 604-688-8812; www.westendguesthouse.com, e-mail info@
westendguesthouse.com. DELUXE TO ULTRA-DELUXE.

It's not hard to tell from its layout that the three-story **Barclay Hotel** was at one time an apartment building, though renovations have really spruced up the public areas. Rooms are a bit tight, with mix-and-match furniture, minuscule bathrooms and air conditioning. The suites provide an affordable (though not cheap) alternative for families. Facing on Robson near all the restaurants and boutiques, the location is its best attribute. ~ 1348 Robson Street; 604-688-8850, fax 604-688-2534; www.barclayhotel.com, e-mail infos@barclayhotel.com. MODERATE TO DELUXE.

The **Burrard Motor Inn** has standard, motel-style accommodations in a good central location. A crotchety old elevator takes guests to upper-level, medium-size rooms arranged in a quadrangle around the carport hidden under a rooftop garden. Furnishings are run of the mill, but parking is free, virtually unheard of in downtown Vancouver. There are a few kitchenette units available. ~ 1100 Burrard Street; 604-681-2331, 800-633-0366, fax 604-681-9753. MODERATE.

The **Kingston Hotel Bed and Breakfast** is an unusual find in downtown Vancouver. This 1910 woodframe with the large green awning and red neon sign was recently renovated inside and out to look more like a European B&B. The tiny rooms are clean and offer the bare necessities—vanity sink, dresser, bed, small closet. There's a shared bath down the hall; eight rooms with private bath and TV are larger. There's a sauna, and a continental breakfast is served in the lobby. ~ 757 Richards Street; 604-684-9024, 888-713-3304, fax 604-684-9917; www.kingstonhotelvancouver.com. BUDGET TO DELUXE.

Hostelling International—Vancouver Downtown is perfectly situated—just a 10 to 15 minutes' walk from Stanley Park, Granville Island, Gastown and the business district. With space for more than 200 hostelers, its rooms are clean and functional. Laundry, recreation, cooking, meeting and studying facilities are available. Dozens of organized activities are offered every day, but wanderers will find almost limitless opportunities within easy reach. ~ 1114

AUTHOR FAVORITE

There's nothing too fancy about the rooms at the ivy-covered **Sylvia Hotel**. But I find the accommodations are spacious and practical, with comfortable furnishings. Many of the suites have kitchenettes and dining areas. The price is right, too, economical even in summer's high season. The location is divine—right on English Bay, the only hotel so close to the beach. ~ 1154 Gilford Street; 604-681-9321, fax 604-682-3551; www.sylviahotel. com. BUDGET TO MODERATE.

Burnaby Street; 604-684-4565, 888-203-4302, fax 604-684-4540; www.hihostels.ca, e-mail info@hihostels.ca. BUDGET.

Located several blocks east on bustling Granville Street is **Hostelling International—Vancouver Central**, which offers private rooms with private baths in addition to four-bed dorm rooms. There's also a lively bar on-site. ~ 1025 Granville Street; 604-685-5335, 888-203-8333, fax 604-685-5351. BUDGET.

Local office workers line up on the sidewalk at lunchtime to get a table at **Stepho's**, a fairly traditional Greek taverna that serves up heaping platters of excellent roast lamb or fish. One platter is a bountiful meal at a most reasonable price—about US$7. ~ 1124 Davie Street; 604-683-2555. BUDGET TO MODERATE.

DINING

At **Wrap Zone** the fare is focused: giant tortillas filled with lots of stuff. "Stuff" ranges from curries to salmon to beans to meat and veggies. Service is quick and the price is definitely right—lunch for two is about C$9 (US$6). ~ 1711 Davie Street; 604-608-6711. BUDGET.

Don't miss **Liliget Feast House**, a "First American" (Canadian for American Indian) "longhouse" serving the native cuisine of the Pacific Northwest. You'll feast your eyes on Vancouver's most unique menu, then fill your belly with venison soup, barbecued duck breast, clam fritters and alder-barbecued salmon. On the side are steamed fern shoots and wild rice. For dessert, how about cold raspberry soup or whipped *soapallalie* (Indian ice cream), washed down with a cup of juniper tea? Call for winter hours. ~ 1724 Davie Street; 604-681-7044; www.liliget.com, e-mail info@liliget.com. MODERATE TO DELUXE.

◀ HIDDEN

With its bordello decor and prime Northwest haute cuisine, funky **Delilah's** in the West End is one the locals usually prefer not to share. As you arrive, you'll be handed a seasonal menu—perhaps grilled venison, pan-roasted duck and seared Arctic char. Next, sidle up to the bar for one of their famous martinis to keep you happy during the longish wait to be seated and served. Dinner only. ~ 1789 Comox Street; 604-687-3424; www.delilahs.ca, e-mail info@delilahs.ca. DELUXE TO ULTRA-DELUXE.

At **Mum's Gelati**, the ice creams and sorbets are handmade and delicious, and the servings are generous. Noteworthy are the berry concoctions, which do not smother the fruit taste with sugar. Italian-style espresso is also available. ~ 849 Denman Street; 604-681-1500. BUDGET.

◀ HIDDEN

Of the dozens of cafés and small eateries along Denman, near Stanley Park, **Bojangles** is a bit snazzier than most but still offers an economical lunch for visitors who've spent the morning in the park. The deluxe sandwiches are exceptionally good. A small outdoor seating area faces south, into the sun, along a side street.

~ 785 Denman Street; 604-687-3622, fax 604-687-3613; www. bojanglescafe.com. BUDGET TO MODERATE.

Tropika offers a fine introduction to Malaysian cuisine. If you really don't know what you're getting into, order satay (marinated meat skewered and grilled); if you've had some exposure, you'll appreciate the spicier starred selections. They specialize in curries. ~ 1128 Robson Street; 604-737-6002. MODERATE.

Most Vancouverites label **Fogg 'n' Sudds** the place for the widest selection of beer, ale and other brewed beverages (literally dozens of choices) from around the world. The menu also offers well-made typical pub fare such as fish-and-chips and burgers. ~ 1323 Robson Street; 604-683-2337, fax 604-669-9297. BUDGET TO MODERATE.

HIDDEN ► Unlike most tapas cafés, the menu at **Tapastree** is not so long you need a lengthy perusal to satisfy your curiosity. The two dozen plates here vary from Asian to comfort food—curried vegetables, pan-fried oysters, scalloped potatoes. It's just two blocks from Stanley Park, perfect after a trek around the seawall. ~ 1829 Robson Street; 604-606-4680; www.tapastree.ca. MODERATE.

The **Robson Public Market**'s food court is a fine place to stop for an inexpensive lunch after wandering Stanley Park or Denman Street. Among the cafés and food counters is **Robson Teriyaki** (604-683-9105), with good teriyaki as well as yakisoba. ~ 1610 Robson Street. BUDGET.

Capers is a large natural-foods market that serves top-notch soups, sandwiches, salads, pastas and baked goods, all well priced and healthy. The original Capers (there are three) is in West Vancouver. ~ 1675 Robson Street; 604-687-5288. BUDGET.

HIDDEN ► It's just a small, side-street café, but **Crepe La Bretonne** makes crêpes in the genuine French Brittany style, using whole wheat flour, starting from scratch. The fillings make breakfast or lunch equally savory. ~ 795 Jervis Street; 604-608-1266. BUDGET.

HIDDEN ► Tucked into the landscape along the new Coal Harbour Promenade, **The Mill Marine Bistro** honors the area's maritime past with both its name and its menu, which offers dozens of sa-

---

PICKLED FIRE

Kim chee, the fiery Korean pickle of cabbage, garlic and hot peppers, is an acquired taste. Once you acquire it, the problem becomes acquiring decent kim chee. **Ma-Dang-Coul**, a tiny Korean lunch counter on Denman, has superb kim chee, as well as other typically Korean dishes—mostly big bowls of stew, soup or noodles. Though the decor is nothing special, the food here more than compensates. ~ 847 Denman Street; 604-688-3585. BUDGET.

vory, economical seafood plates, many tapas-style, such as garlic prawns and mushroom caps stuffed with shrimp. On Saturdays, soup is free with a sandwich; and sundaes are only $1.99 on, of course, Sundays. ~ 1199 West Cordova Street; 604-687-6455; www.millbistro.ca. MODERATE.

A splendid view of the harbor, reliable moderately priced seafood, and a convivial atmosphere draw loyal diners back again and again to **Cardero's**, which perches on piers by the Coal Harbour Marina. Snag a window table on a winter night for a romantic view of the bay outside; the grilled fish are best. ~ 1583 Coal Harbour Quay (end of Cardero and Nicola streets); 604-669-7666; www.carderos.com. MODERATE TO DELUXE.

The **Robson Public Market**, which has over two dozen retail stores, is a fine place to duck in on a rainy day and browse through the food stands and small shops. ~ 1610 Robson Street; 604-682-2733.

SHOPPING

Lush is exactly what its name implies—a redolent profusion of lotions, soaps, oils and other cosmetics and body-care products. It's an outpost of a popular European chain; all the products are natural and organic. ~ 100–1025 Robson Street; 604-687-5874.

A high-style boutique on the west side of town, **Boboli** features imported European clothing for men and women. ~ 2776 Granville Street; 604-736-3458.

Reliance on and support for Northwest artists is what distinguishes **Buschlen Mowatt Fine Arts**, a sleek gallery near Stanley Park. Among other well-known names, Carmelo Sortino and Z. Z. Wei, whose vivid expressionist paintings are gaining international renown, exhibit here. ~ 1445 West Georgia Street; 604-682-1234, 800-663-8071.

It wouldn't make much sense to shop for furniture while traveling, but fabric is another story. At **K.A. International** the upholstery and drape fabrics in stock are the finest European materials—available almost nowhere else in North America. It's a great place to daydream, if you don't want to spend C$20 a yard for sofa covering. ~ 1237 Burrard Street; 604-408-1533.

ENGLISH BAY BEACHES (NORTHERN SHORE)

BEACHES & PARKS

Connected by Stanley Park's seawall promenade, silky English Bay Beach and broad Sunset Beach Park are prime candidates for a long sunset stroll. Within walking distance of the city center, they are a favorite of businesspeople out for a lunch break or there to catch the last rays after work during the week. There are restrooms, changing rooms and intermittent food stalls. During good weather, artists and craftmakers often set up booths along the promenade. Although the bay's waters are by no means tropical, July, August and September bring enough warming to occasion a dip for all but the most delicate swimmers. The best time is during an afternoon incoming tide, the waters of which are warmed by the sun-heated sand. The nearby palm gardens make the scene seem quite tropical. Kayaks and sailboards are available for rent during summer months at the English Bay Beach bathhouse. ~ Off Beach Avenue on the southwest side of town; 604-257-8400, fax 604-257-8427.

Stanley Park's first eight pairs of gray squirrels were a gift from New York to Vancouver in 1909.

STANLEY PARK 🏃 🚲 🏊 Beautiful Stanley Park is a green oasis in downtown Vancouver. Highlights include the aquarium, children's farmyard, seawall promenade, children's water park, a miniature railway, scenic lighthouses, totem poles and statues, pitch-and-putt golf, tennis courts, an evening gun salute (each day at 9 p.m.), open-air theater, a swan-filled lagoon, nature house and miles of trails through thick coniferous forest, some of it undisturbed old growth. Second and Third bathing beaches are extremely popular among sun lovers and water enthusiasts. Second Beach boasts a heated outdoor pool; Third Beach is a long, broad, sandy stretch facing southwest and thus sun-warmed in the afternoon. Park facilities include restaurants and concession stands, restrooms, showers and picnic facilities. Please do not feed the indigenous raccoons; although they seem cute, they are actually a major urban menace. ~ Follow Georgia Street heading west through downtown to the park entrance; 604-257-8400, fax 604-257-8427.

Kitsilano & Granville Island

False Creek, the saltwater inlet that divides downtown Vancouver from the rest of the city, forms a geographically and culturally distinct border between the glittering highrise city center northward and the more compact, smaller-scale urban neighborhood southward. The area is marked by hundreds of small shops and cafés along Broadway and 4th streets; surrounding them are ultra-popular small apartments, duplexes and older homes.

Farther south, in Shaughnessy, turn-of-the-20th-century mansions recall the timber industry's heyday; and south of there, the proliferation of "monster homes," huge pseudo-French chalet houses on small lots, signifies the influx of Hong Kong money in the early '90s.

Westward, toward the University of British Columbia, the Kitsilano district has gently matured from a counterculture capital in the '60s to a progressive, quiet residential area today. The neighborhood closest to English Bay is the locale of choice for professional families; it contains some of the finest Craftsman-style homes to be seen on the West Coast, especially in the vicinity of Vanier Park, where the Maritime Museum and Vancouver Museum are found.

Several of the city's leading museums are along the south shore of English Bay. One of the finest is the University of British Columbia's famed **Museum of Anthropology**, with sunlit galleries of Northwest Coastal First Nation totems, chests, canoes, jewelry, ceremonial masks, clothing and contemporary native artwork. Although the museum is best-known for its collection of towering totems, housed in a beautiful hall looking out over the water, other facets are equally compelling. A whole room is devoted to legendary First Nations artist Bill Reid's carving, "Raven Discovering the First Men." The museum's entire collection of indigenous Pacific Rim artifacts, artworks and crafts is housed on glass-enclosed shelves so visitors can see it all. There's no charge to visit the true-to-life Haida longhouse and totems behind the museum; you may even find a carver at work on a totem there. Closed Monday from September through May. Admission (free Tuesday evenings). There's a parking fee, too; have change ready. ~ 6393 Northwest Marine Drive; 604-822-3025; www.moa.ubc.ca.

SIGHTS

In a city with a plethora of parks and gardens, what distinguishes the UBC **Botanical Garden** is the way the plantings have been worked into the indigenous forest. Paths wind among large old second-growth hemlocks and firs, with 400 types of rhododendrons (non-native) and azaleas thriving in the shade of the open forest. The park is big (70 acres), so allow time for an unhurried stroll. Admission. ~ 6804 Southwest Marine Drive (a mile past the Museum of Anthropology); 604-822-9666; www.ubcbotanical garden.com.

The nearby **Nitobe Memorial Garden** is considered one of the finest Japanese gardens in North America. This strolling garden with teahouse has narrow paths that wind through two-and-a-half acres of serene traditional Japanese plantings and across gracefully arched bridges over the still pond. Folks come here for the cherry blossoms in April, irises in June and flaming red Japanese maples in October. Closed weekends in winter. Admission. ~ UBC campus, 1903 Lower Mall; 604-822-6038; www.nitobe.org.

◄ *HIDDEN*

The garden theme continues just above Shaughnessy at **VanDusen Botanical Garden**, a 55-acre expanse of lavishly landscaped gardens that offer blooms in every season. With everything from palms to alpine flowers, the garden ably demonstrates the horticultural diversity possible in Vancouver. Admission. ~ 5251 Oak Street; 604-878-9274; www.vandusengarden.org.

Samples of First Nations artifacts along with intriguing collections of European costumes, tools, furniture and relics portraying the rapid colonization of the area are also found at the **Vancouver Museum**, located on a small green peninsula in English

Bay known as Vanier Park. Next door, the **H. R. MacMillan Space Centre** (604-738-7827, fax 604-736-5665; www.hrmacmillan spacecentre.com) augments regular astronomy programs and musical laser-light shows with multimedia theater, a motion simulator and occasional performances of live, avant-garde music. Closed Monday in winter. Separate admission to museum and space centre. ~ 1100 Chestnut Street; 604-736-4431, fax 604-736-5417; www.vanmuseum.bc.ca.

Nearby is the **Vancouver Maritime Museum**, documenting the maritime history of British Columbia, including the glory of international steamship travel. The museum has an extensive collection of model ships. Housed in the connected A-frame is the Royal Canadian Mounted Police supply ship, the St. Roch, now a National Historic Site; it was the first ship to pass successfully through the Northwest Passage in both directions. Touring the ship gives a good impression of the cramped life seafarers used to live. In summer, other historic boats, such as the S.S. Master, the Northwest's last operating steam tug, moor in the museum's harbor. Closed Monday from September to mid-May. Admission. ~ 1905 Ogden Avenue; 604-257-8300, fax 604-737-2621; www. vmm.bc.ca, e-mail genvmm@vmm.bc.ca.

Across a short bridge from downtown Vancouver lies **Granville Island**. Refurbished by the federal government, Granville contains everything from parkland to craft studios to a cement factory. Once an industrial area, today it is a classic example of urban funk gone chic. Corrugated-metal warehouses have been transformed into sleek shops, while rusting cranes and dilapidated steam turbines have become decorative pieces. There are several **working studios** to view.

The **Granville Public Market** (see below for more information) is the centerpiece of the island. Of course, getting to the market is half the adventure: you can walk, drive or catch the **False Creek Ferry**, a charming tub-like boat that chugs back and forth, from behind the Vancouver Aquatic Centre (south end of Thurlow

AUTHOR FAVORITE

sights   The focal point of Granville Island is the **Granville Public Market**, and no wonder. This 50,000-square-foot collection of stalls selling fresh fish, fruits, vegetables and other goodies is a great place to observe Vancouver's international flavor. Many of the stalls are operated by recent immigrants offering their native foodstuffs, ranging from Ukrainian pirogies to Thai curries. Just to remind everyone of the area's industrial past, a cement plant still operates east of the market. ~ 604-666-6477.

Street). ~ 604-684-7781. The **Aquabus**, a competing enterprise, also offers passage across and along False Creek in small jitneys from various docks. ~ 604-689-5858; www.aquabus.bc.ca

A quick stop at the **Info Centre** to see the orientation film and pick up a map helps you focus on what you want to explore. ~ 1398 Cartwright Street; 604-666-5784; www.granvilleisland.com.

A few blocks away at the **Sport Fishing Hall of Fame &**   ◄ HIDDEN
Museum, the angling aficionado will find an extensive collection of rare and antique rods and reels, along with a fine collection of fly-fishing photographs. There's also a model-ship exhibit, and upstairs is one of the world's largest collections of model train pieces. ~ 1502 Duranleau Street; 604-683-1939.

Leave time for an informal 30-minute tour of the **Granville Island Brewing Company**, the first microbrewery in Canada and home of Island Lager. Tastings are offered at the end of the tour. The brewery's main production facilities have moved to larger quarters in the suburbs; here they brew special and experimental batches, so visitors may help determine the fate of new products. The brewery store also offers an extensive selection of B.C. wines. Admission. ~ 1441 Cartwright Street; 604-687-2739.

Not only is the **Granville Island Hotel** in a dandy location, right   **LODGING**
in one of Vancouver's most popular attractions, it's a handsome boutique hotel with much to offer. Each guest room is different, decorated in warm woods and brocade fabrics; the views over False Creek are smashing; and there's even a small atrium with hot tub and exercise equipment. Gay-friendly. ~ 1253 Johnston Street; 604-683-7373, 800-663-1840, fax 604-683-3061; www. granvilleislandhotel.com, e-mail reservations@granvilleislandhotel. com. DELUXE.

Shaughnessy Village is unique—the world's largest bed and   ◄ HIDDEN
breakfast, it advertises itself, and who could argue? This 13-story complex near the Broadway shopping district features 240 rooms at bargain prices, with security, parking, an internet café, spa, sun tanning, a billiards room and more. Rooms range from cruise ship–style bunk units to two-room suites. Breakfast is served in the restaurant, so you get your choice among a variety of hot, fresh-cooked meals. ~ 1125 West 12th Avenue; 604-736-5512, fax 604-737-1321; www.shaughnessyvillage.com, e-mail info@ shaughnessyvillage.com. BUDGET TO MODERATE.

Throughout the year there are affordable rooms available at the **Conferences and Accommodation at** UBC, a budget alternative to Vancouver's pricey downtown hotels. Single and twin rooms in the dorm buildings are generally full of students during the school term but are available in the summer. "Triple suites" (one-bedroom apartments with kitchenette and private bath) are always available. Guests can get an inexpensive meal in the Student Union Building cafeteria. ~ 5961 Student Union Boulevard; 604-822-1000, fax 604-822-1001; www.bcconferences.com, e-mail reservations@housing.ubc.ca. BUDGET TO DELUXE.

Hostelling International—Vancouver Jericho Beach enjoys a prime setting on English Bay at lovely Jericho Beach. Housed in what was once military barracks, there is space here for more than 275 hostelers in the many dorm-style rooms with shared baths; the few couple/family rooms go quickly. With fully equipped communal kitchens, laundry facilities, cafeteria and lounge with big-screen television, this is easily one of the fanciest hostels you could hope to visit. The hostel is only open May through September. ~ 1515 Discovery Street; 604-224-3208, 888-203-4303, fax 604-224-4852; www.hihostels.ca. BUDGET.

Guests at **Penny Farthing Inn** are served afternoon sherry in this heritage home's beautiful private garden. Not far from UBC, the 1912 Edwardian is in the famed Kitsilano neighborhood, near beaches and parks, cafés and restaurants. Of the four rooms, two are suites; all have private baths and cable TV. Smoke-free. Gay-friendly. ~ 2855 West 6th Avenue; 604-739-9002, fax 604-739-9004; www.pennyfarthinginn.com, e-mail info@pennyfarthing inn.com. MODERATE.

Of the five suites in **Columbia Cottage**, all have private baths and color television. This 1920s art deco–style home is in a heritage neighborhood not far from the Broadway/4th Avenue shopping districts, and within a ten-minute drive of downtown. Guests enjoy a full breakfast, laundry facilities and free parking. Children are welcome. Gay-friendly. ~ 205 West 14th Avenue; 604-874-7787; www.columbiacottage.com, e-mail info@columbiacottage. com. MODERATE TO DELUXE.

HIDDEN ▶

Although it's on a back street in a quiet neighborhood, nearby public transportation makes **Beautiful Bed & Breakfast** accessible to Vancouver's main attractions, including downtown and the UBC, both of which are just minutes away by bus. Housed in a spacious, attractive colonial-style home, the inn's four rooms include a honeymoon suite with marble fireplace and a balcony. Breakfast is served in a formal dining room with silver service. No children under 14 allowed. ~ 428 West 40th Avenue; 604-327-1102, fax 604-327-2299; www.beautifulbandb.bc.ca. MODERATE TO DELUXE.

DINING

The Kitsilano and Broadway neighborhoods were the center of Vancouver's counterculture in the '60s and '70s, and remain distinctive in their personality—including a wide selection of small cafés and restaurants, many of them little-known outside their immediate neighborhood.

Students at the **Pacific Institute of Culinary Arts** learn their   ◄ *HIDDEN*
craft by preparing full-gain gourmet meals, which then have to
be enjoyed by someone. Might as well be you: the menus are
broad and entertaining, and the price can't be beat, about C$35
(US$28) for the institute's "wine & dine" evenings, which fea-
ture multicourse meals accompanied by appropriate wines. Still
not economical enough? Mondays are often two-for-one nights.
These are the gourmet chefs of the future, so the preparations
can be fairly inventive. ~ 1505 West 2nd Avenue; 604-734-4488;
www.piachef.com. MODERATE.

Shijo Japanese Restaurant, atmospherically appointed with
tatami, bronze lamps and black wood accents, is popular with
the downtown crowd. Sushi, vegetarian dishes and traditional
Japanese fare are prepared with an innovative twist. Barbecued
shiitake mushrooms is one of the standout dishes. ~ 1926 West
4th Avenue; 604-732-4676, fax 604-731-4589. MODERATE.

The last time we stopped by **Sophie's Cosmic Café** on a weekend, diners were lined up outside the door. Inside, people were
piling into Naugahyde booths and gazing at the pennants, pictures and antique toys that line this quirky café. There are
omelettes and high-fiber Belgian waffles for breakfast, and falafel
and veggie burgers later in the day. Dinner gets downright sophisticated as Sophie cooks up quesadillas, oysters and chicken
Rouchambeau. There's a heated outdoor patio. A scene. ~ 2095
West 4th Avenue; 604-732-6810, fax 604-732-9417. BUDGET TO
MODERATE.

John Bishop is widely credited with starting Vancouver's modern fine-dining scene. Many newer restaurants have since seized
the spotlight, but the food, service and atmosphere at **Bishop's**
remain among the best in the city, and Bishop himself still greets
his guests, making sure they receive the best hospitality possible.
The cuisine is expertly made West Coast food, featuring B.C. ingredients wherever possible. ~ 2183 West 4th Avenue; 604-738-
2025. DELUXE.

AUTHOR FAVORITE

The cuisine at **Lumiere** is sensational, often chosen the best in
Vancouver by critics and diners. Each evening's fixed-menu dinner presents
a selection of highly inventive, French-inflected West Coast dishes—very
contemporary, but lacking the fussiness of some such places. You'll be
both amazed and well sated, just as I am when I have the good fortune to dine here. ~ 2551 West Broadway; 604-739-8185. DELUXE.

A natural-foods market with a lunch/deli counter and café in the interior courtyard, **Capers** offers Northwestern cuisine made with organic, whole-grain, free-range ingredients. Vegetarians will have a field day here. ~ 2285 West 4th Avenue; 604-739-6676. BUDGET.

Can man live by bread alone? Vancouverites are tempted to try by the offerings at **Terra Breads**, a superb bakery focusing on rich, hearty, whole-grain loaves. A smattering of accompaniments (spreads and sandwich fillings) rounds out the fare here, but bread is the focus. ~ 2380 West 4th Avenue; 604-736-1838. Also in the Granville Public Market; 604-685-3102. BUDGET.

It was while living in Kitsilano that author William Gibson first coined the term "cyberspace."

Naam is a deservedly well-known natural foods restaurant. The ambience is woody and funky, the fare whole wheat, veggies and tofu. The soups are excellent. Keep your eyes open for New Age celebrities. ~ 2724 West 4th Avenue; 604-738-7151. BUDGET.

The fare is surprisingly genuine, considering its northerly locale, at **Fatzo's Barbeque Smokehouse**—slow-roasted chicken, pork and beef with the usual accompaniments such as potato salad and cole slaw. Portions are large and the meat is lean. The decor and ambience are neo-diner, but it's all brand-new. ~ 2884 West Broadway; 604-733-3002. MODERATE.

HIDDEN ►

Indian and Pakistani elements color the contemporary Northwest cuisine at **Star Anise**, an elegant small restaurant well-known among Vancouver food devotees. Seafoods such as smoked ahi and vindaloo sea bass mesh intriguingly with roast lamb and grilled emu with portobello paté and scalloped potatoes—prototypical examples of the fusion cuisine the city is renowned for. ~ 1485 West 12th Avenue; 604-737-1485; www.staranise.ca, e-mail info@staranise.ca. DELUXE.

Gourmands literally come from around North America to line up at **Vij's**, the namesake high-style Indian bistro of Vikram Vij's path-breaking cuisine. The culinary inventions are simply astounding—just imagine buttermilk curry or lamb popsicles! The line heads out the door as Vij's does not take reservations, so get there early. ~ 480 West 11th Avenue; 604-736-6664; www.vijs.com. MODERATE TO DELUXE.

Set near the conservatory at the peak of Queen Elizabeth Park, the elegant **Seasons in the Park Restaurant** enjoys sweeping views of the Vancouver skyline and the mountains towering above the North Shore. The seafood and Continental dishes are seasonal, and specials from the daily menu are always on a par with the outstanding vista. Bill Clinton and Boris Yeltsin dined here during a 1993 summit. Weekend brunch. ~ Cambie Street at

33rd Avenue; 604-874-8008, fax 604-874-7101; www.seasons hilltopbistro.com/home.html, e-mail info@vancouverdine.com. DELUXE TO ULTRA-DELUXE.

Inevitably you are going to end up on Granville Island. Should hunger strike while you're touring the shops and artist studios, check out the food stalls at the **Granville Public Market**. Here you'll find a fish-and-chips shop, a souvlaki stand, a juice and salad bar, a deli, Russian and Southeast Asian food stands, and even a fresh soup outlet. Among others, be sure to pass by **The Stock Market** (604-687-2433), where cooks fire up the stove for several large tureens of thick soup every morning, and the lunch counter is packed by noon. At **Zara's Pasta Nest** (604-683-2935), the pasta salads are unexcelled because the noodles have been hand-made, probably that morning. And **Kaisareck Delicatessen** (604-685-8810) offers no-nonsense, meat-and-cheese filled sandwiches, Austrian style. ~ Johnston Street. BUDGET.

Another spot for a fine view of the city lights, this time from water level on the Granville Island Wharf, is **Bridges**. The restaurant is one of the hot spots of the dining elite, who may choose from the elegant dining room, the relaxed bistro or the convivial pub. The fare here ranges from standard and nouvelle preparations of seafood and meats to basic pasta and finger foods. Reservations are recommended for the dining room. Be forewarned: Some readers claim it too touristy. ~ 1696 Duranleau Street; 604-687-4400; www.bridgesrestaurant.com, e-mail info@bridgesres taurant.com. MODERATE TO DELUXE.

SHOPPING

A strip of intriguing shops lies along **4th Avenue** and **Broadway** between Burrard and Alma streets. Situated between Granville Island and the University of British Columbia campus, this is the Kitsilano neighborhood. Since the '60s and '70s, time and gentrification have transformed the area from Vancouver's countercultural center into a spiffy district of smart shops and comfortable homes.

Farther east along Broadway, another vigorous and intriguing shopping district has sprung up devoted to sporting goods and outdoor recreation. The major impetus is the huge **Mountain Equipment Co-op** store. Here, active Vancouverites can acquire anything from thermal socks to climbing pitons to Everest-expedition tents. Parkas, sleeping bags, boots, skis, kayaks and canoes, biking gear—if it happens outdoors, Mountain Equipment has the relevant supplies. Members get a small discount, but anyone can shop here, and the prices are competitive. It's also an unsurpassed information clearinghouse, with books, maps, pamphlets and knowledgeable staff to answer questions about outdoor recreation throughout B.C. ~ 130 West Broadway; 604-872-7858; www.mec.ca.

Across the street, **Altus Mountain Gear** focuses on expedition-quality mountaineering equipment. ~ 137 West Broadway; 604-876-5255. And a few doors down, **A. J. Brooks Outfitters** has excellent prices for boots and shoes, among other things. ~ 147 West Broadway; 604-874-1117.

HIDDEN ▶ The entrance to ITMB has, on the wall, the largest world map ever published—and its orientation betrays its origin. Vancouver-based publisher Jack Joyce put the Western Hemisphere in the center because he was tired of Eurocentric map drawing. The International Travel Maps and Books store has dozens of self-published maps for exotic locales, ranging from B.C.'s Cariboo to Mongolia. But there are also maps, globes and guides from all sources (it's a major Michelin distributor). In other words, no matter where you're thinking of going, they have the map. ~ 530 West Broadway; 604-879-3621.

Among the dozens of fine bookstores in Vancouver, **Book Warehouse** is the most comprehensive discount house. Most titles are 20 to 70 percent off the publisher's list price. ~ 632 West Broadway; 604-872-5711.

Just off 4th is **T**, one of the district's more intriguing shops, which also doubles as a tea room. Devoted entirely to teas, T has more than 250 black-tea varieties, ranging from common types such as Earl Grey to rarities such as a robust Tanzanian leaf. Fruit and herbal teas and pastries round out the offerings. Those interested in a quiet respite during a shopping haul can stop for fresh-brewed tea and biscuits. ~ 1568 West Broadway; 604-730-8390; www.tealeaves.com.

The **Travel Bug** is devoted to books about travel and guides for the same, along with maps, atlases and such. ~ 2667 West Broadway; 604-737-1122.

Banyen Books and Sound is a Kitsilano favorite with a New Age perspective—lots of titles about self-improvement, meditation, spiritual exploration and healing arts. There's quite a collection of CDs and videos in the same vein, as well. ~ 2671 West Broadway; 604-732-7912.

AUTHOR FAVORITE

If it's edible and delectable, **Meinhardt Fine Foods** no doubt has it. While this South Granville institution stocks fresh produce and meats, it's most noted for an amazing selection of imported ingredients ranging from cinnamon to escargot. I'm certainly impressed. ~ 3002 Granville Street; 604-714-3131.

Yoka's offers a rich inventory of coffee, chocolate, honey and tea—quite an appropriate combination, actually. The coffees are roasted on the premises, and the honeys are B.C.-grown products. Exotic teas and Belgian chocolate round out the selection. ~ 3171 West Broadway; 604-738-0905.

Wanderlust is a store devoted to aiding its namesake urge. Here the traveler will find guidebooks, maps, language books, accessories and some luggage—along with considerable expertise on travel, especially in British Columbia and Western Canada. It's not a travel agency, it's a travel aid. ~ 1929 West 4th Avenue; 604-739-2182.

Chocolate is an indigenous Western Hemisphere treat, and at Chocolate Arts, Haida artist Robert Davidson has combined fine dark chocolate with First Nations designs to create comestibles that are aesthetically pleasing before and after you eat them. These are the nighttime pillow treats guests receive at a number of luxury downtown hotels. ~ 2037 West 4th Avenue; 604-739-0475.

Vancouver is a chocoholic's paradise, with an unusual number of fine chocolate shops scattered throughout the city. A favorite is Daniel Le Chocolat Belge, which uses top-quality Belgian chocolate to create truffles and other confections. ~ 4447 10th Avenue West; 604-224-3361.

The main draw on Granville Island is the Public Market, with rows of vendors selling fresh produce, flowers, pastas, wines, baked goods, seafood and meats, along with the section of fast-food outlets proffering an international array of delectables (see Dining, above). But virtually the whole island has seen its warehouses and small factories converted to galleries and shops. The BC Wood Co-op is a display gallery for carvers and craftspeople throughout the province who use native materials and traditional techniques to make wondrous furniture and housewares. ~ 1592 Johnston Street; 604-408-2553. Malaspina Printmakers Gallery features work by Canadian artists. ~ 1555 Duranleau Street; 604-688-1827. Eagle Spirit Gallery concentrates on work   ◄ HIDDEN by Northwest Coast Native artists, including masks, totems and jewelry. ~ 1814 Maritime Mews; 604-801-5205.

Okanagan Wine Shop focuses on the growing array of B.C. wines and dessert liqueurs, including the highly sought-after ice wines that have earned so much notice lately. ~ In the Public Market; 604-684-3364.

The Kids Only Market at the island entrance of Granville Island's Public Market is a mall full of toy stores, children's clothing shops and a tykes' beauty salon. ~ 1496 Cartwright Street; 604-689-8447.

Feet are the focus at Run Inn, a store devoted exclusively to walking and running and gear for both. There's much more than shoes, although footwear is the foundation of the store. ~ 2236 West 41st Avenue; 604-267-7866.

Punjab Cloth House is the largest fabric store on Main Street in the Punjabi Market, with hundreds of bolts of brocade, silk, satin and other exotic fabrics, in equally exotic colors. ~ 6660 Main Street; 604-325-8383.

The dark and passionate swirls of First Nations art have been incorporated by designer **Dorothy Grant** into a line of truly distinctive apparel. Also available at her boutique is a collection of Northwest artwork. ~ 1656 West 75th Avenue; 604-681-0201; www.dorothygrant.com.

NIGHTLIFE There is plenty of innovative theater to choose from on Granville Island. The **Carousel Theatre** offers family-oriented classical and contemporary productions. ~ 1411 Cartwright Street; 604-685-6217. There's a wide variety of shows with a multicultural flair at the nearby **Waterfront Theatre**. ~ 1410 Cartwright Street; 604-685-1731. The **Playwrights Theatre Center** hosts the Annual Vancouver New Play Festival, showcasing the works of Canadian playwrights. ~ 1405 Anderson Street; 604-685-6228; www.playwrightstheatre.com. One of the largest nonprofit theaters in Canada (and a training ground for stars such as Michael J. Fox) is the **Arts Club Theatre**. ~ 1585 Johnston Street; 604-687-1644. This is the home of the **Vancouver TheatreSports League**, one of the top improvisational groups in the world, which produces 260 shows a year, as well as private, corporate and special events. ~ 604-738-7013.

The **Hot Jazz Society** presents swing and modern jazz. ~ 2120 Main Street; 604-873-4131.

The **Coastal Jazz and Blues Society Hotline** lists what's going on in the numerous jazz clubs around town. ~ 604-872-5200. The **Cotton Club** on Granville Island is a New York–style restaurant and lounge with live jazz. ~ 200-1833 Anderson Street; 604-738-7465.

◆◆

LITTLE INDIA

The **Punjabi Market** is a small district of shops, cafés and service businesses just southeast of Queen Elizabeth Park. Here you'll find dozens of jewelers, cloth merchants, clothiers, spice importers and the like, all serving Vancouver's large and dynamic East Indian community (for whom a wedding can cost up to C$40,000, thus the many bridal shops). If you'll ever have any use for gold-fringed lavender brocade, this is the place. ~ Main Street between East 49th and 51st avenues.

Bridges, a subdued but trendy bistro on Granville Island, is fairly quiet and a good place to savor a glass of wine and the lights of the city dancing on the water of False Creek. ~ 1696 Duranleau Street; 604-687-4400.

Naam is a natural foods café with music to match—folk, New   ◀ *HIDDEN*
Age—in the evenings. ~ 2724 West 4th Avenue; 604-738-7151.

Vancouver's dynamic Arts Club Theatre Company took over the **Stanley Theatre** a few years ago, and the result is a sensational renovation of an art deco classic. Built as a moviehouse, it's now used for stage productions that range from Cole Porter musical revues to premieres of locally written plays. ~ 2750 Granville Street; 604-687-1644.

Casino gambling is legal here, with half the profits going to local charities; for a little roulette, sic bo or blackjack action, try the **Great Canadian Casino.** ~ 709 West Broadway; 604-872-5543.

QUEEN ELIZABETH PARK 🏃 Taking the place of two stone   **BEACHES**
quarries that once supplied building materials for the city, this 130-   **& PARKS**
acre park now features various ornamental gardens showcasing the indigenous plants of the coast, along with two rock gardens that reflect the land's past. At 501 feet above sea level, the park affords the best views of downtown Vancouver, crowned by the mountains of the North Shore and the famous lions—two mountain peaks for which Lions Gate is named. You'll find a restaurant, restrooms, picnic facilities, 18 tennis courts, lawn bowling lanes, frisbee golf and a pitch-and-putt golf course. ~ Located at Cambie Street and 33rd Avenue; 604-872-5513.

PACIFIC SPIRIT REGIONAL PARK 🏃 This wonderful park was created from UBC endowment lands, partly in response to city plans to build a road in the area. Students protested (literally sitting down in front of the bulldozers), and the ultimate result is 20 miles of forest trails along the bluff overlooking English Bay. Dozens of hikes through mature woods are possible; maps are available at the park center, and most trailheads along 16th Street have maps posted. Aside from trails, there's no development. ~ North of 16th Street between Kitsilano and UBC; the park center is at 4915 West 16th Street.

Wreck Beach 🏖 Of the many beaches in and around Van-   ◀ *HIDDEN*
couver, this undeveloped (and unspoiled) sandy stretch across from the University of British Columbia on the tip of Point Grey Peninsula is the major *au naturel* spot in town. Students make up the majority of the sun worshipers here. There are outhouses, seasonal concession services and a phone at the top of the trail. ~ Located south of Nitobe Garden and the Museum of Modern Art off Northwest Marine Drive; a steep, twisting trail opposite the university residences leads from the road to the beach; 604-224-5739.

ENGLISH BAY BEACHES (SOUTHERN SHORE) 🏊 🚣 Stretched around the north face of Point Grey Peninsula on the opposite side of the bay, Kitsilano, Jericho, Locarno and Spanish Bank beaches attract hordes of windsurfers, sunbathers, picnickers and swimmers, but are spacious enough not to feel overcrowded. There's a heated outdoor saltwater pool (open during the summer; fee) at Kitsilano Beach in case the sea is too nippy. You'll find restrooms, lifeguards (in summer), changing rooms and intermittent food stalls. Kitsilano is the beach volleyball center of Vancouver. Jericho and Spanish Bank are popular for skimboarding and sailboarding. ~ Kitsilano Beach is at Cornwall Avenue and Arbutus Street; Jericho, Locarno and Spanish Bank beaches are accessible off of Northwest Marine Drive; 604-257-8400.

Vancouver Gay Scene

Although the West End is nominally considered the gay neighborhood, in reality Vancouver's gay and lesbian community is well assimilated into Vancouver proper and no area dominates. The highlight of recent history for the gay community came when Vancouver hosted the Gay Games in 1990—a turning point for acceptance of gay lifestyles. Since then openly gay politicians have been elected to the B.C. legislature, and the annual gay pride parade is a popular community event.

Information, support and referrals can be found at the **Gay and Lesbian Centre** in the West End. ~ 1170 Bute Street; 604-684-5307, Helpline: 604-684-6869.

The Vancouver **Gay and Lesbian Business Association** serves the community with an on-line directory. ~ 101-1001 West Broadway; 604-878-4898; www.glba.org.

LODGING

Offering five guest rooms, **Nelson House** is a three-story Edwardian located near Barclay Heritage Square. Each of the four rooms (one has a shared bath) is individually decorated. Lounge by the cozy fireplace in the living room. The top-floor suite has a fireplace, deck and hot tub. Enjoy the full breakfast. Nonsmoking; children are allowed by prior arrangement only. ~ 977 Broughton Street; 604-684-9793, 866-684-9793; www.downtownbandb.com. MODERATE TO ULTRA-DELUXE.

The **Lotus Hotel** offers 110 rooms in an older brick building shaded by green awnings. Thoroughly renovated, the rooms feature refrigerators, carpeting and contemporary furniture. It's the home of several of the city's more popular gay nightclubs. ~ 455 Abbott Street; 604-685-7777, fax 604-685-7067. MODERATE.

Housed in an exquisitely renovated 1897 Victorian home, **O Canada House**'s six elegant, comfortable rooms all feature private baths and are furnished with period antiques. Guests are served a gourmet three-course breakfast. It's just a ten-minute walk to Granville Island, and 15 minutes to Stanley Park. ~ 1114 Barclay Street; 604-688-0555, 877-688-1114, fax 604-488-0556; www.ocanadahouse.com, e-mail info@ocanadahouse.com. MODERATE TO DELUXE.

Hawks Avenue Bed & Breakfast serves women only in a heritage townhouse located in a calm neighborhood just ten minutes from downtown. The six rooms are comfortable and quiet. Guests enjoy a full breakfast and easy street parking. ~ 734 Hawks Avenue; 604-253-0989. BUDGET TO MODERATE.

Little Sisters is an adult bookstore serving the gay and lesbian community. Magazines and videos are also available here. ~ 1238 Davie Street; 604-669-1753.

SHOPPING

The **Lotus Sound Lounge** offers music played by a deejay. A mixed gay and lesbian crowd frequents the dancefloor at this contemporary lounge. ~ The Lotus Hotel, 455 Abbott Street; 604-685-7777.

NIGHTLIFE

Jupiter Billiards is a classic pool hall with a cozy lounge; Wednesday is cabaret night. ~ 1216 Bute Street; 604-609-6665. The **Edge Coffee Bar** is a low-key gathering place, open late. ~ 1148 Davie Street; 604-688-3395.

F212 is a sleeker and more modern version of the traditional gay steam bath, as much a spa for men as a steam bath. ~ 1048 Davie Street; 604-877-4765.

The **Odyssey** presents gay shows aimed at men. ~ 1251 Howe Street; 604-689-5256. **Penthouse Night Club** periodically features "Diva's Den" for women. ~ 1019 Seymour Street; 604-683-2111.

> Pick up a copy of Vancouver's free gay bi-weekly, *Xtra West*, at coffee shops, cafés and gay haunts.

The **Hotel Dufferin** has shows ranging from drag to karaoke; drinks and rooms are also available. ~ 900 Seymour Street; 604-683-4251. **The Royal Hotel** is another casual after-work gathering spot for drinks; nightly shows range from drag to live music. ~ 1025 Granville Street; 604-685-5335.

English Bay is downtown's most popular beach. That's why Peter Rainier set up his **Ocean West** kayak operation here, but it also happens to be the best set-off point for a wonderful half-day trip around Stanley Park, or around the bay to the UBC campus and Wreck Beach. Rainier leads guided trips, including a picnic lunch. The company also has extended trips into the islands along the Sunshine Coast. ~ At the English Bay Beach Bath House, corner

Outdoor Adventures

KAYAKING

of Denman and Davie streets; 604-688-5770, 800-660-0051. The **Vancouver Rowing Club** is ideally situated at the neck of Stanley Park on Burrard Inlet; it's a membership club, but accommodations for visitors can be made through hotel concierges.

SURFING & WIND-SURFING

English Bay is ideal for many of the waterborne board sports—sailboarding, skimboarding at Spanish Beach, wakeboarding, etc. Supplies, rentals and local information are available at **Pacific Boarder,** a shop catering to every board sport known. ~ 1793 West 4th Avenue; 604-734-7245; www.pacificboarder.com.

Skimboards are the focus at **PD's Hot Shop,** which also offers free tidal charts so boarders can figure out when to ride the incoming tide on local flats. ~ 2868 West 4th Avenue; 604-739-7796.

BOATING

With 5000 miles of sheltered water in easy reach, Vancouver and southwestern British Columbia afford many opportunities to float. You can rent a powerboat or a sailboat and head north to the Sunshine Coast, where Desolation Sound has the warmest waters north of Mexico; you can hop into an inflatable raft and paddle the Chilliwack River whitewater; or you can simply rent a kayak for a morning paddle around Stanley Park.

Although Canada does not require a license to operate either a powerboat or a sailboat, **Blue Pacific** requires that you prove your expertise before you rent one of its vessels. Otherwise, Blue Pacific will set you up for a three- to five-day skippered cruise; you can learn sailing basics or laze around on the deck. ~ 1519 Foreshore Walk; 604-682-2161.

Fishing charters, mostly for salmon, leave right from downtown. Two established operators are **Bites-on Salmon Charters,** 877-688-2483, www.bites-on.com; and **Coho Sports,** 604-435-7333, www.cohosports.com.

A VIEW TO REMEMBER

Located in the center of Vancouver, **Queen Elizabeth Park**, the site of two stone quarries that once supplied building materials for the city, is a 130-acre park that features ornamental gardens with indigenous plants, along with two rock gardens that reflect the land's past. It's also one of the best places to get a view of downtown. **Bloedel Conservatory** rests at the park's highest point, just above Seasons in the Park restaurant. Compact but packed chock-full with tropical plants and birds, it's a comforting place to visit during Vancouver's dark and rainy winters. Admission. ~ Cambie Street and 33rd Avenue; 604-257-8584.

There are dozens of golf courses and practice facilities in and around Vancouver. **Last Minute Golf** is a service specializing in finding tee times at local courses. ~ 604-878-1833.

GOLF

Pitch-and-putt facilities are located in **Stanley Park** (604-681-8847) and in **Queen Elizabeth Park** (604-874-8336).

Near the Fraser River, **Fraserview Golf Course** is an 18-hole public course. ~ 7800 Vivian Street; 604-280-1818. **University Golf Club** is a championship course near UBC, ideal for a game after visiting the Museum of Anthropology. ~ 5185 University Boulevard; 604-224-1818. **McCleery Golf Course** is also along a Fraser River channel, and is open year-round, weather permitting. ~ 7170 McDonald Street; 604-280-1818. **Langara** is an 18-hole course open seasonally (not winter), probably the quickest to reach from downtown. ~ 290 West 49th Avenue; 604-280-1818.

There are more than 80 locations in the Vancouver area with tennis courts: most are free and first-come, first-served; all are open for play year-round, weather permitting. Call the Park Board (604-257-8400) for a list of locations other than those listed here. Some of the area's outlying resorts provide tennis facilities for guests as well.

TENNIS

WEST END/STANLEY PARK   Of the 21 tennis courts in **Stanley Park**, six charge minimal fees for reserved playing times; the rest are free.

KITSILANO & GRANVILLE ISLAND   **Kitsilano Beach Park** has ten public courts charging minimal fees (only during warm-weather months). ~ Cornwall Avenue and Arbutus Street. Other parks with courts include **Queen Elizabeth Park**, just off Cambie Street, and **Jericho Beach Park**, off Northwest Marine Drive.

Vancouver city streets are no place for recreational bicycle riders, even if the city's drivers are courteous: there's just too much traffic. But who could complain—with a lengthy trail that winds along the waterfront from Canada Place, around Stanley Park, down along False Creek and out English Bay to UBC, you can literally ride all day. Vancouver's waterfront path links up with interior paths in Stanley Park and Pacific Spirit Park, where bikers will find hills and solitude.

BIKING

WEST END/STANLEY PARK   Cyclists should stick to the protected 5.5-mile seawall path around the perimeter of **Stanley Park**. Please observe the separation line demarcating foot and wheeled traffic, especially on crowded sunny days.

KITSILANO & GRANVILLE ISLAND   To avoid busy streets, try the shoreside paths at Jericho Beach and English Bay and the pathways that parallel Chancellor and University boulevards and

15th Avenue on the scenic campus of the University of British Columbia. It's possible, sticking to these paths, to bike all the way to Stanley Park and around the seawall, a trek totaling 37 kilometers.

Bike Rentals & Tours   Just a few blocks from the main entrance to Stanley Park, **Spokes** is the best location to rent bikes for West End cycling. After your ride, trade in your bike for a double cappuccino; they serve that, too. ~ 1798 West Georgia Street; 604-688-5141.

Guided biking tours in the Vancouver metro area are offered by **VeloCity Cycle Tours**. ~ 604-924-0288.

HIKING   With two vast parks easy to reach from downtown, low-key hiking is an everyday possibility in Vancouver. Stanley Park's numerous interior paths wind through quiet, fairly uncrowded forest, as do the steeper trails that lead up from the waterfront in Pacific Spirit Park on the west end of Kitsilano. It's not wilderness, but here a dedicated walker can enjoy quiet woods for many miles. All distances listed for hiking trails are one way unless otherwise noted.

WEST END/STANLEY PARK   The Stanley Park seawall **path** (5.5 miles/9 km), carefully divided to accommodate cyclists, skaters and pedestrians, is easily the most popular hike in town. There are also numerous paths that plunge into the thickly forested acres of the park. Among the many interior paths, one of the best is the trail to **Beaver Lake** (1 mile/2 km) from the vicinity of the Aquarium.

HIDDEN ▶   **KITSILANO & GRANVILLE ISLAND**   Pacific Spirit Regional Park (30 miles/50 km) crisscrosses 1000 acres of parkland on Point Grey Peninsula, offering easy to moderate hikes through this largely unmarked ecological reserve. Here you're more likely to run into a blacktail deer or bald eagle than another hiker. A map is available from the Greater Vancouver Regional Parks office (604-432-6350), or at the park center (4915 West 16th Street).

SKATE THE DAY AWAY

Inline skating is perhaps the most serene way to enjoy the lengthy seawall promenade path that circles Stanley Park, False Creek and English Bay. You can literally skate all day if you want. (But please stick to the separate lane supplied for wheeled traffic.) Lessons and rentals are available at **Outaline**, the skaters' supply store near the old Expo grounds. ~ 1251 Pacific Boulevard; 604-899-2257.

Driving in Vancouver is a bit more like the European experience—all traffic funnels through the city on broad boulevards where a courteous but frenetic air dominates. One peculiarity American drivers need to note: Left-turn signals are rare, and turn lanes rarer still. Thus it's best not to occupy the left lane, lest you get stuck behind a driver waiting to turn left across oncoming traffic.

Transportation

CAR

From the West Coast of the United States, **Interstate 5** turns into **Route 99** after crossing the Canadian border at Blaine and proceeds northwest through Vancouver's suburbs, skirting the airport, and into the city core where the name changes once again, this time to **Granville Street**. The **Trans-Canada Highway (Route 1)** connects Vancouver with points east in Canada. Both highways become four-lane expressways outside central Vancouver, but the freeways do not penetrate the downtown core.

Vancouver International Airport offers domestic charters and flights by Harbour Air and Whistler Air Services. International airlines include Air Canada, Air China, Air New Zealand, Alaska Airlines, American Airlines, British Airways, Cathay Pacific Airways, Continental Airlines, Delta Air Lines, Horizon Air, Japan Airlines, KLM, Korean Air, Lufthansa, Northwest Airlines, Qantas, Singapore Airlines and United Airlines. ~ www.yvr.ca.

AIR

Airport express buses operated by **The Airporter** depart every 20 to 30 minutes from the arrival level of the Main Terminal building and stop at the bus station and most major hotels in downtown Vancouver. ~ 604-946-8866, 800-668-3141. **Translink** buses also serve the airport; catch #424 from the airport and then transfer to #98 at Airport Station, which will take you right into downtown Vancouver. ~ 604-953-3333; www.translink.bc.ca.

A taxi or limousine ride from the airport to downtown should run C$25–$30 (US$16–$19) and take about 20 to 25 minutes. **Vancouver Limousine** is an established airport-to-downtown carrier. ~ 604-421-5585.

Between May and October, cruise ships call regularly at the terminal at **Canada Place**, an architectural stunner under Teflon-coated white "sails." ~ 999 Canada Place; 604-666-6068.

FERRY

BC Ferries provides service between Vancouver Island and Tsawwassen (an hour south of downtown Vancouver), Horseshoe Bay (half an hour northwest of downtown) and Langdale on the southern Sunshine Coast and Earls Cove and Saltery Bay on the northern Sunshine Coast. ~ 888-273-3779; www.bcferries.bc.ca.

Greyhound Bus Lines offers service to and from the United States. ~ 1150 Station Street, Vancouver; 800-231-2222 from the

BUS

U.S., 800-661-8747 from Canada; www.greyhound.com. **Maverick Coach Lines** provides service to various points within B.C. ~ 604-940-2332, 877-330-8773; www.maverickcoachlines.bc.ca

TRAIN

VIA Rail Canada (800-561-8630 within Canada; www.viarail.ca) at 1150 Station Street in Vancouver provides rail service throughout Canada and connects with **Amtrak** (800-872-7245; www.amtrak.com) to points within the United States.

CAR RENTALS

Rental agencies at Vancouver International Airport include **Alamo Rent A Car** (800-462-5266), **Avis Rent A Car** (800-879-2847), **Budget Rent A Car** (800-299-3199), **Hertz Rent A Car** (800-263-0600), **Thrifty Car Rental** (800-847-4389) and **National Car Rental** (800-227-7368).

Discount Car Rentals (604-273-5565) has an office in the neighboring suburb of Richmond and offer free airport pickup.

PUBLIC TRANSIT

Translink governs Vancouver's expansive transit system, with buses, the SkyTrain and the SeaBus covering all the main arteries within the city and fanning out into the suburbs. Running on a 16-mile, mostly elevated track between Canada Place downtown and the suburb of Surrey, the SkyTrain is a good way to see some of the major sights of the city. You can also get a great view of the skyline from the water aboard the SeaBuses that cross Burrard Inlet between downtown and the North Shore. The handy *Transportation Services Guide for Greater Vancouver* tour guide, day passes and timetables are available from Travel Info Centres. A book of ten tickets that covers all three zones in the metro area costs C$36. ~ 604-953-3333; www.translink.bc.ca.

TAXIS

Cab companies serving the airport include **Bel-Air Taxi** (604-433-6666), **Black Top and Checker Cabs** (604-731-1111), **Vancouver Taxi** (604-255-5111) and **Yellow Cab** (604-681-1111).

TOURS

Manfred Scholermann of **Rockwood Adventures** leads urban and urban-wilderness hikes and walking tours. Areas include Chinatown, Gastown, Stanley Park and out-of-city attractions such as Lighthouse Park and Lynn Canyon. Scholermann, a former gourmet chef, also prepares picnic lunches guaranteed to be as memorable as the hikes. ~ 604-926-7749, 888-236-6606; www.rockwoodadventures.com.

Even though "The X-Files" departed Vancouver for Los Angeles before finally going off the air, fans can avail themselves of a tour that visits many places used to depict some of the best-known locales in the show, such as the local building that was the location for Dana Scully's apartment (Pendrell Suites, whose owners have established these tours). Tours can be customized by tour guide **Emilia Palombi** and can include shooting locations for other popular productions filmed in Vancouver. ~ 604-609-2770.

THREE

Lower Mainland & the Sunshine Coast

One of Vancouver's finest features is its proximity to nature; the image of the city is inextricably linked to the North Shore mountains, which provide a stunning backdrop to the urban skyline. Just a few minutes from the heart of the city, this lush, green slope holds scenic beaches, ecology centers and campgrounds. Easily reached by transit, this area also offers a great bird's-eye view of the metropolitan district for those who climb its slopes even a little way.

As you head up the Fraser Valley from Vancouver, the communities change from metropolitan suburbs to mountain towns; vistas that had been horizontal become more vertical; rainfall increases and temperatures become more extreme. The gentle river delta narrows until you reach the Coast Range mountains near Hope. Here the Fraser River surges powerfully through a narrow canyon.

This is the Lower Mainland, a fringe of lowland that fronts the shoulders of the mountains. Although near the coast, the Fraser Delta is quite warm in the summer; thus this swath of temperate terrain has long been agricultural, with cattle ranches, berry, vegetable and truck farms and, more recently, vast clumps of greenhouses.

It is also the Vancouver metropolitan area. Masses of people inhabit delta towns (one of which is in fact called Delta) and commute to urban employment centers—chiefly Burnaby, Richmond and Surrey, as well as Vancouver itself. Traffic on Route 1 in and out of Vancouver experiences the same rush-hour tangles as suburban expressways elsewhere in North America, as does Route 99 south of the city—somewhat obscuring the fact that a number of noteworthy destinations are in the Lower Mainland not far from Vancouver.

The valley was long inhabited by First Nations people who thrived on the dependable salmon runs and mild climate; the tall cedar, cottonwood and fir forests supplied most of their other needs. Although Spanish explorers made forays into the Fraser Delta as early as 1791, the initial European settlement, at Fort Langley, was begun by the Hudson's Bay Company in 1827. Hudson's Bay focused on furs for its inland commerce, but diversified by shipping salted salmon from Fort Langley in 1831, and soon added shingles and timber bound for Hawaii.

The discovery of gold in the B.C. interior in 1856 made the Fraser Valley a geographic conduit. Queensborough—soon renamed New Westminster—became the provincial capital in 1859, and small towns sprang up along the lower valley as settlers sought to profit from the gold rush. The settlers needed cattle, timber, grain and other supplies for the arduous journey through the Coast Range, and the Lower Mainland's commercial and agricultural character was established. The arrival of the transcontinental railroad in 1886 cemented the region's reliance on trade; the next year saw the first shipment of tea and silk from Asia through Vancouver and on to Britain by rail and transatlantic steamer. Though the provincial capital has since returned to Victoria, the valley's economy still relies on timber, trade, farming, regional commerce and government offices. The Lower Mainland holds more than 5000 farms encompassing 260,000 acres of crop- and pastureland. There are 140,000 cattle, 1.5 million square feet of greenhouse space, and fields producing 80 percent of B.C.'s vegetables and berries.

All that is changing as urban growth spreads farther out from Vancouver. About 2 million people live in the lower Fraser Valley—half the population of British Columbia. Even so, the area's history, agriculture and natural wealth are clearly evident, even to drivers barreling through on the Trans-Canada, because farms and pastures surround the highway corridor, dense forests blanket the foothills nearby and steep peaks vault up—sometimes almost vertically—above the valley floor. Even in the middle of the vast Vancouver suburbs, it's remarkably scenic. And with all the farms and preserved wetlands, the Fraser Valley and Delta are excellent areas for birdwatching.

Head the other direction from Vancouver, west and north up the inland coast, and just 30 miles from Vancouver growth is barely an issue. The reason: restricted access. Ferries are the only way to get to the Sunshine Coast, which, with approximately 2400 hours of sunshine each year, lives up to its name. This region is made up of small, quiet fishing and logging communities strung along 90 miles of shoreline between Langdale, a short ferry ride from Horseshoe Bay in West Vancouver, and Lund, the gateway to Desolation Sound Marine Park. Another short ferry ride between Earls Cove and Saltery Bay connects the northern and southern sections of the coast. The ferry trips give visitors the sense that they're touring islands, even though the Sunshine Coast is firmly attached to the mainland.

The region is a gem for anyone who loves the outdoors, with mild weather and enough hiking, camping and water activities to please one and all. The locals, mainly loggers, anglers and artists, are friendly and upbeat, willing to share recommendations for what to see and do in their neck of the woods. Except for warm summer weekends, the Sunshine Coast is not yet inundated by tourists and retains a rustic, low-key air.

The separation provided by Burrard Inlet creates more than just a spatial difference between North and West

North and West Vancouver

Vancouver and the main city. For one thing, the climate is different: the mountains above catch and hold weather, and rain and snow often pour down on the North Shore when Vancouver itself is dry. Thus the three ski areas in the slopes above the North Shore; all three often receive prodigious amounts of (admittedly wet) snow, and in fact one area was open for skiing on Canada Day, July 1, in the exceptional weather year of 1999.

The North Shore is Vancouver's portal to the B.C. wilderness. Head into the mountains here and you'd wind up in Garibaldi Provincial Park—if you could make it, as it's largely untracked and virtually impassable. The two cities themselves are swank bedroom communities for Vancouver proper; West Vancouver, in particular, with its expansive views of the water, holds Canada's costliest real estate and most elite homes.

SIGHTS

Vancouver's North Shore is home to the **Capilano Suspension Bridge and Park,** a swaying footbridge built in 1889, 230 feet above the chasm cut by the Capilano River. This is the highest and longest footbridge in the world, and one of those tourist attractions notable partly because it is, well, a major tourist attraction. You pass through a park complete with totem poles and a souvenir-filled trading post to reach the bridge. The Treetops attraction takes visitors through the rainforest canopy on rope bridges. Admission. ~ 3735 Capilano Road, North Vancouver; 604-985-7474; www.capbridge.com.

Up the road a bit is the **Capilano Salmon Hatchery,** where the public can take a self-guided tour and learn about the life cycle of this important fish. ~ 4500 Capilano Park Road, North Vancouver; 604-666-1790, fax 604-666-1949.

HIDDEN ►

The surrounding **Capilano River Regional Park** offers excellent nature hikes, a good view of the Lions (the two distinctive skyline peaks north of Vancouver) and a cost-free alternative to the suspension bridge for seeing the river's gorge. (See Beaches & Parks, below.) ~ One mile above Route 1 along Capilano Road; 604-224-5739.

Continue up Capilano Road, which turns into Nancy Greene Way, and you'll arrive at **Grouse Mountain**, where visitors catch the Skyride gondola to the mountain peak complex to ski, hike, see the incredible high-tech mythology and history presentation about Vancouver in "The Theatre in the Sky" or settle in for a meal at one of the restaurants. The view of Vancouver and out to the Gulf Islands is stupendous, and the 100-passenger gondola ride, up a *very* steep slope to 3700 feet, is bracing. The gondola leaves every 15 minutes. Admission. ~ 6400 Nancy Greene Way, North Vancouver; 604-984-0661; www.grousemountain.com.

HIDDEN ►

Atop Grouse Mountain is **Hiwus Feasthouse**, a cedar longhouse in which guests enjoy a traditional native dinner—salmon, fiddleheads, shellfish, oyster mushrooms, berry tart—while watching a very entertaining presentation of First Nations legends, chants

Text continued on page 108.

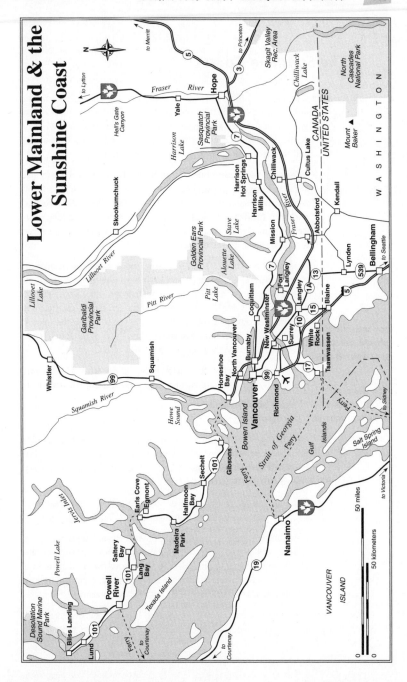

Lower Mainland & the Sunshine Coast

The Sunshine Coast

Day 1 • Catch an early ferry at Horseshoe Bay for Langdale. Be sure to get in line well ahead of time (or try out the BC Ferries reservation system) in summer and on weekends. While you're crossing Howe Sound, keep your eyes peeled for orcas, harbor seals, bald eagles and the occasional osprey looking for breakfast.

• After you reach **Langdale**, get on Route 101 and head north just as far as **Gibsons** (page 127). Stop at this small enclave for a stroll around the numerous art galleries and craft shops. Be sure you duck into **Molly's Reach** (page 127), a restaurant whose long service as a Canadian TV locale gives it the same cultural significance that the Cheers bar in Boston has for Americans.

• Head back up Route 101 to **Sechelt**. Check into **Beachcomber Marine Spa & Cottage** (page 130), have a bite of lunch and then grab a kayak for a late afternoon paddle in beautiful Sechelt Inlet. Ask host Chris McNaughton for precise directions to the First Nations **pictographs** (page 128) on the rocks across the inlet. If you have time, stop in at **Porpoise Bay Provincial Park** (page 135), one of the prettiest in the lower half of B.C.

• Head down to Sechelt for dinner, either at the **Blue Heron Inn** (page 132) or, for more down-home cuisine, the **Lighthouse Pub** (page 132).

Day 2 • Another early start. (You'll sleep in the third day.) Head on up 101, a scenic hour drive that takes you past **Halfmoon Bay**, **Pender Harbour** and **Ruby Lake** to Earls Cove and the half-hour ferry ride to the upper Sunshine Coast.

• Continue on 101 to Powell River, stopping at Willingdon Beach for a guided walk along the **Willingdon Beach Trail** (page 143).

• Head on up a mile to the historic **Powell River Townsite** (page 128) (north of the newer town), slowing down to gawk at the attractive Craftsman homes on the bluff above the road. Take note of the "hulks," the scuttled barges and boats that form the harbor for **Norsk Canada**'s (page 128) pulp-mill log booms.

• Another half-hour north brings you to **Lund**. This little cove is the end of the road, theoretically where the ribbon of asphalt that started all the way down in California ends. Have a late lunch at the **Lund Hotel café** (page 132) or **Nancy's** (page 134), following that with a stroll through the marina to look at the yachts that pull in here on their way north along the Inside Passage to Alaska.

- Backtrack a bit, then head east to check in at **Desolation Resort** (page 131). Let's hope you asked them to make reservations for you at the nearby **Laughing Oyster** (page 133)—it's the best dinner spot between here and Sechelt, and the view is splendid.

Day 3
- After a leisurely breakfast, head down to the resort dock to grab a couple of kayaks for a relaxing paddle up **Okeover Arm** to **Desolation Sound** (page 138). Be sure to bring your swimsuit because the water warms up here in late summer and you'll want to find a quiet cove for a saltwater swim. Take your time cruising the many small bays and islands in this marine park, watching for wildlife on shore and marine mammals in the park. If the tide's low enough, check out the amazing sea life in **tidepools** along rocky shores.

- Back at the lodge, you might as well see if there's room for you at the Laughing Oyster for dinner again. Before dinner, a short stroll along the beach takes you past **Okeover Arm Provincial Park** (page 136), a pretty spot with a sandy tideflat.

Day 4
- Time to start heading back to the city. Best to leave Desolation Resort by 10:30 a.m.; on your way back, south of Powell River, detour off the highway for a half-hour to **Palm Beach Regional Park** (page 136), the perfect place for an early picnic lunch and a stroll along this beautiful beach.

- From here to Sechelt, including the Earl's Cove ferry, will take about three hours. You could stop in downtown Sechelt—which looks ever so much like a California coastal village—for an early dinner at the **Old Boot** or **Sunfish Café** (page 132), then catch an evening ferry back to Horseshoe Bay.

- On the ferry ride back across Howe Sound to Horseshoe Bay, enjoy the summer evening sunset over the Strait of Georgia and the many islands westward.

and songs. The hand-carved beams and masks in the longhouse are stunning, the food is good and the presentation is sufficiently engaging that, by the end of the evening, the mostly Anglo guests are themselves up and dancing around. Closed in winter. Admission includes the gondola fare. ~ 6400 Nancy Greene Way, North Vancouver; 604-980-9311.

With a five-acre children's park where kids can get to know cows, goats, chickens, sheep and other farm animals, **Maplewood Farm** is a great stopover for families. Seasonal demonstrations explain the age-old rhythms of farm life. Closed Monday. Admission. ~ 405 Seymour River Place, North Vancouver; 604-929-5610; www.maplewoodfarm.bc.ca.

HIDDEN ►   **Park & Tilford Gardens** was a 1968 gift to the North Shore by a local brewing company. Now well-established, the different theme gardens (roses, herbs, perennials, native plants, oriental garden, conservatory) offer constantly changing displays almost year-round. At Christmas more than 50,000 lights convert the grounds to a twinkling wonderland. ~ 333 Brooksbank Avenue, North Vancouver; 604-984-8200.

At the **North Vancouver Museum & Archives** displays on pioneer logging, shipbuilding and farming detail how the area evolved from a resource-based economy to a suburban center. Coast Salish artifacts depict the lifestyles of the original inhabitants. Closed Monday (archives closed Sunday). ~ 209 West 4th Street, North Vancouver; 604-987-5618; www.district.north-van.bc.ca/nvma.

LODGING   The **Bed and Breakfast at Laburnum** is a breath of fresh air in North Vancouver, offering welcome respite for weary travelers. There are four posh deluxe-priced guest rooms (each with private bath) within the elegant, antique- and art-filled main house. Of the two ultra-deluxe housekeeping cottages on the grounds, the larger has an extra sleeping loft, making it suitable for families. The smaller, nestled in the prim English garden, is designed for romance. The food here is also memorable. ~ 1388 Terrace Avenue, North Vancouver; 604-681-2889, fax 604-904-8812; www.laburnumcottage.ca. DELUXE TO ULTRA-DELUXE.

For a roadside chain motel, the **Holiday Inn Express** in North Vancouver has many virtues. It's remarkably clean and quiet, there is a nice palm-shaded swimming pool, the service is superior, and both local telephone calls and the morning continental breakfast are free. Capilano Canyon and Grouse Mountain are just minutes away. ~ 1800 Capilano Road, North Vancouver; 604-987-4461, 800-663-4055, fax 604-984-4244; www.hiexpressnv.com. MODERATE.

The **Grouse Inn** near the north end of the Lions Gate Bridge has 80 tidy but plain, motel-style rooms decorated in earth tones.

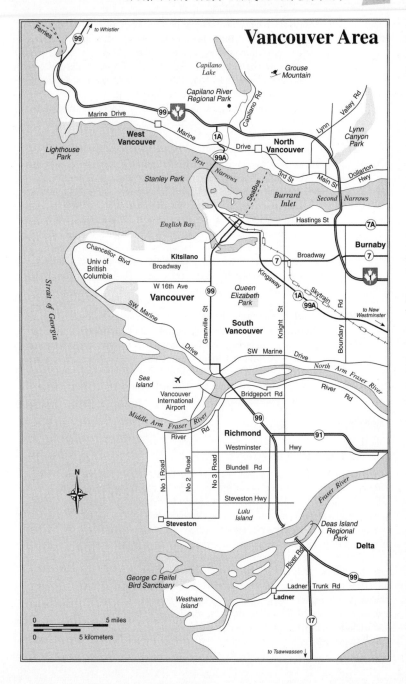

Standard rooms have the basics—full bath, queen bed, cable TV, small table and chairs—though a few are set up as family suites and others have kitchenettes. There's a playground and heated pool. Continental breakfast included. ~ 1633 Capilano Road, North Vancouver; 604-988-7101, 800-779-7888, fax 604-988-7102; www.grouseinn.com. MODERATE TO DELUXE.

HIDDEN ►   If you're looking for quiet, **BayView B&B at Green Gables West**'s perch in an exclusive residential neighborhood above West Vancouver is the place. A spacious, neat home at the end of a little-traveled cul-de-sac, BayView has a four-room suite on the main floor and two three-room suites upstairs. Canadian and European antiques adorn the rooms. All offer panoramic views of English Bay, Stanley Park, the city skyline and the Lions Gate Bridge. Its grounds are equally stunning, with beautifully landscaped gardens and a quaint gazebo. Guests are greeted with a plate of steaming fresh cookies; a full breakfast is served. Despite its bucolic locale, it's just 15 minutes from downtown Vancouver. ~ 1270 Netley Place, West Vancouver; 604-926-3218, 800-208-2204, fax 604-926-3216; www.bayview-bb.com, e-mail bayview@bayview-bb.com. MODERATE TO ULTRA-DELUXE.

DINING   Despite the name, **Kilby's** is not an Irish pub. If anything, the decor and cuisine here suggest Tuscany or California, with deeply **HIDDEN ►**   flavored meats—try the lamb that's spent two days in a spiced honey–red wine marinade—and richly sauced pastas. The salads are excellent. The bright, cheery interior is vaguely Mediterranean. ~ 3108 Edgemont Boulevard, North Vancouver; 604-990-4334. MODERATE.

AUTHOR FAVORITE

I love the remarkable serenity that reigns within **Thistledown House**, an elegant mansion-turned-small-inn at the west edge of North Vancouver. This 1920 Craftsman-style masterpiece was built by a North Shore timber tycoon; his legacy includes two massive firs in the front yard that were spared the chainsaw. The interior boasts custom woodwork everywhere, maple and mahogany floors, arched doorways and a huge fireplace/sitting room. The four rooms in the main house have numerous nooks and crannies, private baths and eclectic, arty furnishings. The Apple Tree suite in back is crafted like the main house, with its own fireplace, sitting area, soaking tub and garden view. Breakfasts are gourmet repasts featuring excellent coffee. ~ 3910 Capilano Road, North Vancouver; 604-986-7173, 888-633-7173, fax 604-980-2939; www.thistle-down.com. MODERATE TO DELUXE.

Neighborhood pubs are a much-loved part of life in Canada, and the **Black Bear** is the most popular in North Vancouver. Housed in a handsome Craftsman building, the restaurant offers a good selection of ale and beer, and an outstanding menu of not-your-usual pub fare: peppercorn steak with Irish whiskey sauce, pulled pork sandwiches, Indonesian curry pastas. There's also tasty burgers, but you can opt for chicken, ostrich and salmon instead of ho-hum beef. ~ 1177 Lynn Valley Road, North Vancouver; 604-990-8880, fax 604-990-8860. BUDGET TO MODERATE.

For a million-dollar view of the city and seafood to match, **The Salmon House on the Hill**, perched in the heights of the North Shore fits the bill. The specialty here is fresh British Columbia salmon grilled over alderwood, but the prawns and scallop brochettes and rack of lamb are also worth trying. Lunch, dinner and Sunday brunch. Reservations recommended. ~ 2229 Folkestone Way, West Vancouver; 604-926-3212, fax 604-926-8539; www.salmon house.com. MODERATE TO DELUXE.

Beach Side Café prepares outstanding, original dishes; it's often voted the top restaurant on the North Shore in local dining polls. The menu boasts an imaginative mix of such entrées as grilled beef tenderloin medallion with leeks, and halibut wrapped in pancetta. The decor is a simple combination of white tablecloths and straight-back chairs; if the weather's nice, be sure to ask for a table on the deck, with an outstanding view of the water. ~ 1362 Marine Drive, West Vancouver; 604-925-1945. MODERATE TO DELUXE.

◄ HIDDEN

Village Fish is a traditional seafood store much favored by locals. There's fresh crab, prawns and salmon among the many selections. Ask for some Indian candy (honey-cured salmon) to take with you as you leave. ~ 1482 Marine Drive, West Vancouver; 604-922-4332. BUDGET.

The coffee at **Savary Island Pie Shoppe** is poor, but it's a secondary attraction after the sumptuous array of baked goods that make a perfect breakfast. The pecan/cranberry muffins are the best anywhere. Heading to Whistler today? Grab a loaf of bread and take lunch with you. ~ 1533 Marine Drive, West Vancouver; 604-926-4021. BUDGET.

Right across the street from Savary Island Pie Shoppe, **Bean Around the World** offers much better coffee—roasted on-site—and friendlier service. The adjacent bakery turns out a rich selection of muffins, breads and pastries every morning; it's hard to find a seat here around 8 a.m. but worth a few minutes' wait. Breakfast and lunch only. ~ 1522 Marine Drive, West Vancouver; 604-925-9600. BUDGET.

Tucked into the back of a health food store, **Capers Café** specializes in wholesome dishes such as quiche, salads, seafood and vegetarian plates. The outdoor patio provides views of Burrard

Inlet. ~ 2496 Marine Drive, West Vancouver; 604-925-3316.
MODERATE.

SHOPPING   Across Burrard Inlet in North Vancouver, **Lonsdale Quay Market** is a tri-level atrium mall on the waterfront. In addition to post-card views of the Vancouver skyline, this bustling shopping center combines trendy stores with a farmer's market. It's not quite as funky and diverse as Granville Island, but it is a great place to spend money, people-watch and survey the shoreline. From downtown Vancouver, the SeaBus takes 15 minutes to cross Burrard Inlet, docking right next to the quay. ~ End of Lonsdale Avenue, North Vancouver; 604-985-6261.

BEACHES & PARKS   **CAPILANO RIVER REGIONAL PARK** 🚶‍♂️ 🛶 Just up the road from the higher-profile, privately operated Capilano Suspension Bridge, this 177-acre park encompasses Cleveland Dam and the canyon below it, wrapping around the commercial suspension bridge. An extensive trail network winds along the canyon, through second-growth forest with a few massive old-growth "leave" trees; among other things, it's a good place to see how relatively un-varied a dark, dense second-growth forest can be. The trails cross the gorge at several points, offering a good sense of the canyon's narrow defile. It's possible to begin or end a hike here that stretches all the way to the waterfront below. At the upper end of the park, the dam's spillway gives one of the best views of the Lions, the two peaks crowning the North Shore mountains for which the Lions Gate Bridge was named. Several entrances to the park along Capilano Road offer access to the trail network. ~ One mile above Route 1 along Capilano Road; 604-224-5739.

LYNN CANYON PARK 🚶‍♂️ 🛶 It's much shorter (though slightly higher) than the Capilano Suspension Bridge, but there's no charge to venture out onto Lynn Canyon Suspension Bridge, stretched 240 feet above the rapids of Lynn Canyon. This pretty, 617-acre park also has a fine ecology center. Facilities include restrooms,

sights

AUTHOR FAVORITE

With towering old-growth Douglas firs and cedars, numerous well-laid hiking trails winding through the woods, and a half-dozen splendid little coves and bays to stop for lunch, **Lighthouse Park** is the finest such preserve in the Vancouver area. Often used as a stand-in for other locales during movie and TV productions, the park is nonetheless rarely crowded. It's my first choice for a relaxing picnic and walk whenever I'm in the area. See page 113 for more information.

picnic facilities, nature trails and a concession stand as well as the ecology center. Please heed the signs warning of the dangers on nearby cliffs. ~ 3663 Park Road, North Vancouver; 604-981-3103.

LYNN HEADWATERS REGIONAL PARK 🏃 ⌙ Upstream from Lynn Canyon is a chunk of wilderness within easy reach of the city. Backcountry trails lead to waterfalls and secluded spots along the river. ~ Lynn Valley Road, three miles (5 km) north of Route 1.

CAPILANO RV PARK 🏃 Located under the north end of Lions Gate Bridge, this private venture is the closest camping option you will find. While it's primarily set up for recreational vehicles, there are a few grassy tent sites. Reservations can be made for hookups only, and are essential during the busy summer months. There are restrooms, showers, picnic tables, a playground, a lounge, laundry, a pool and a whirlpool. ~ 295 Tomahawk Avenue, North Vancouver; 604-987-4722, fax 604-987-2015; www.capilanorv park.com, e-mail info@capilanorvpark.com.

▲ There are eight tent sites and 125 sites with hookups; C$22 to C$32 per night. Pet charge, C$2 per day.

LIGHTHOUSE PARK 🏃 This exceptional regional park is on the last point of land along the North Shore; thus the vistas from its many rocky outlooks range from Vancouver, and Mount Baker beyond, to the Strait of Georgia. The park also contains the finest remaining old-growth forest in the immediate Vancouver area, including some massive red cedar and Douglas fir trees. An eight-mile (14 km) trail system offers ample hiking; many of the best viewpoints are on rocky outcrops along the trails. ~ Follow Marine Drive from downtown West Vancouver six miles (10 km) west and watch for the entrance sign on the south side of road; 604-432-6350.

▼ ▼ ▼ ▼ ▼ ▼ ▼ ▼ ▼ ▼

Fraser Delta

The Fraser Delta south and east of Vancouver is one of the most productive agricultural regions in North America. Once the province of cattle growers and vegetable truck farms, in the past half-century it has become the center of the B.C. greenhouse industry. Here, with long summer days and mild winters, growers produce warm-climate crops such as tomatoes, peppers, squash and melons practically year-round. The many greenhouses and specialty farms offer eminently worthwhile visitor stops—although millions of tourists buzzing by on Route 99 seem not to realize it.

The delta is also one of the most important spots on the West Coast for birds migrating along the Pacific Flyway. Despite the pressures of urban growth, tens of thousands of acres of marsh, intertidal wetland and delta bog have been preserved, offering unparalleled opportunities to see snowy owls, puffins and many other rarely viewed avians.

The three major cities that comprise this area—Richmond, Surrey and Delta—are suburban and ex-urban boroughs whose rapid development has brought enormous change to the region. Steveston, for instance, a small enclave on the Fraser River within Richmond, has been a commercial fishing harbor for a century; now, as it transforms into a historic village, it is rapidly being surrounded by urban development such as vast condominium and apartment complexes.

And the greenhouse operators who turned pasture land into more intense agriculture are in turn facing urban conversion of their land. Richmond has become an important center for Asian immigrants, boasting a Buddhist temple and a Chinatown second only to that east of downtown Vancouver. Shopping centers, small industrial parks and suburban subdivisions round out development in the area.

Perhaps because it's so close to the border that they whiz right on by, U.S. travelers tend to overlook White Rock, a peaceful seaside town about 40 minutes from downtown Vancouver that claims Canada's best climate (as do several other B.C. towns)—and has a couple of palm trees growing right along the main drag for proof. Canadians and European visitors flock to White Rock's small inns, motels and B&Bs; on summer weekend afternoons the town is astir with people using the beachside promenade or strolling the avenue of small shops, cafés and restaurants behind it.

SIGHTS   Between the two arms of the Fraser River, across the Oak Street Bridge from Vancouver, the transforming industrial suburb of Richmond conceals a few treasures. The Richmond **Buddhist Temple** advertises itself as the best example in North America of Chinese palatial architecture—and it's instantly apparent exactly what that means. This sprawling, gilded, ornate complex is a rainbow of gold leaf, figured carvings and exquisite statuary. A bonsai garden embraces the entrance; courtyards seem to go on forever; tile-roof buildings loom above. A thousand candles signify meditative moments; be sure to add your own. ~ 9160 Steveston Highway, Richmond; 604-274-2822.

On the northern tip of Westham Island, at the foot of the Fraser Delta, blue turns to white in November when 25,000 snow geese arrive at the **George C. Reifel Bird Sanctuary**. This area is one of the most important waterfowl habitats in North America, serving as a rest stop for hundreds of thousands of migratory birds on their way to or from nesting grounds farther north. More than 230 species of birds have been seen here, including the rare black-crowned night heron. ~ Located at the end of Westham Island Road, six miles west of Ladner, off of Fraser River Road; 604-946-6980.

Deas Island, a spur of land in the Fraser River between Richmond and Delta (it's actually attached to Delta), is almost entirely occupied by **Deas Island Regional Park**. Here you'll find walking trails that pass through nesting grounds of local and migratory fowl, as well as a village site with restored heritage buildings from the beginning of the 20th century. ~ Follow Route 99 south through the George Massey tunnel, take the 62B Street/River Road exit, go north about a mile and a half and turn left onto the Deas Island Road.

Burns Bog is the largest peat bog on the West Coast—once 12 times the size of Stanley Park. Today it has been whittled down by development and conversion to farmland, and just a scant portion remains undisturbed. But that part, contained within the **Delta Nature Reserve**, offers 148 acres of meadow, bog, cedar woods and unparalleled wildlife-viewing opportunities from its three loop trails. ~ Route 91 and Nordel Way, Delta; 604-572-0373; www.burnsbog.org.

◄ HIDDEN

Continuing south along Route 99 for 30 miles (50 km), you'll approach the U.S. border. Before you do, you'll come upon **White Rock**. There isn't anything notably glamorous about the place. In fact, it seems ever so much like the small British beach towns it drew its inspiration from. That's what makes it charming—no big resorts, no famous sights, no fancy shops. Facing south into the sun, with a Mediterranean cast to the houses climbing the slope that fends off northerly storms, it does offer a balmier clime than most of the rest of B.C. Innumerable places serve fish-and-chips, and lots of happy couples stroll hand in hand along the promenade. For a tourist destination, it's charmingly low-key.

Built in 1986 with assistance from the national and provincial governments, the **White Rock Promenade** spans 1.25 miles of the town's gray-sand beach. Paved in brick, with numerous benches, it's a great place for a walk or a run; the sun keeps it warm, but the harbor breeze prevents extreme heat. When the tide's out a truly vast expanse of gray-sand beach lies exposed, attracting many

AIRPORT ART

Vancouver International Airport in Richmond is frequently voted by air travelers as one of the best in North America. The spacious, airy and uncrowded design contributes much to its user-friendly nature—and the airport has one of the premier pieces of art in Canada. Bill Reid's "Jade Canoe" is a stunning bronze sculpture that represents the races of man arriving on earth; it's in the outer lobby of the International Terminal. ~ Airport information, 604-207-7077; www.yvr.ca.

sandcastle builders young and old. A .25-mile pier leads out into deeper water; you can toss crab pots in the water here if you're interested in hand-caught seafood. Not far south of the pier, the White Rock that lent the city its name sits on the slope above the beach. At 486 tons, it's staying put. If it was not truly white historically, liberal coats of paint ensure that it is now. ~ Along Marine Drive in downtown White Rock. Please note that White Rock's parking meters are in force until midnight along the promenade.

Built into the restored 1912 railroad depot, the **White Rock Museum and Archives** offers revolving exhibits focused on regional cultural and natural history. There's an on-site gift shop and a visitor information booth just south of the depot. ~ 14970 Marine Drive, White Rock; 604-541-2222, fax 604-541-2223.

HIDDEN ▶

Set in a bucolic meadow just above the tideflats, **Historic Stewart Farm** is a serene place for a picnic, and offers a good look at late-19th-century life in the Fraser Delta. The restored farmhouse, outbuildings, barns and antique apple orchard all hint at simpler times. During summer and fall, costumed interpreters explain just how "simple" life really was more than a century ago. Admission. ~ 13723 Crescent Road (just north of White Rock), Surrey; 604-502-6456.

Peace Arch Provincial Park is actually in both the United States and Canada, as the two countries have declared it "international territory." Aside from the famed arch, which honors the neighborly relations between the two countries, there are extensive gardens, walking paths and picnic areas. Stroll along the paths away from the highway; this is a remarkably peaceful spot, with great views out over Semiahmoo Bay. ~ Along Route 99/5, at the U.S./Canada border; 604-924-2200.

LODGING

Seasoned travelers ordinarily avoid airport hotels, but the **Fairmont Vancouver Airport** is a remarkable property that's worth a stop if you're heading out of Vancouver on a morning flight. Built right in the terminal's east end, the hotel is a high-tech marvel with computerized gadgets galore—lights flick on automatically when you enter a room. The room decor is discreetly luxurious, with plum fabrics and maple-burl desks, and vast baths that include tiled showers and a soaking tub. Substantial insulation keeps jet noise to a minimum (not zero, though), and the reception area has an intriguing space-age look (hotel staffers stand at solo terminals). Prices are deluxe, but off-season the hotel offers some remarkable bargain packages. ~ Vancouver International Airport; 604-207-5200, 800-441-1414, fax 604-248-3219; www. fairmont.com. DELUXE TO ULTRA-DELUXE.

HIDDEN ▶

Perched halfway up the hill above Boundary Bay from the White Rock Promenade, **Villa Marisol** has one of the finest vantages you could expect from a B&B, with distant islands and peaks jutting into the sunset. It also provides luxurious modern accommodations in a California-style house; the two guest suites have superlative views, expansive bedrooms and baths, cushy beds and balconies. One has its own fireplace and solarium, the other is right by an outdoor hot tub. For those in mauve moods, pastel color schemes dominate. An elegant breakfast is part of the tab. ~ 1389 Archibald Road, White Rock; 604-535-9735. DELUXE.

DINING

As a quasi–beach resort, White Rock has at least a dozen ice cream stands along its waterfront drive. The best of them all is undoubtedly **White Mountain Ice Cream**, where they advertise homemade goods and deliver the best you can imagine. The acid test is vanilla—it's practically perfect at White Mountain. The ice cream here is enough reason to visit the town. ~ 14909 Marine Drive, White Rock; 604-538-0030. BUDGET.

If it's a full-scale breakfast you're after, you want "The Big One" at **Holly's Poultry in Motion**. The plate comes piled high with eggs, hash browns, toast and ham or bacon. Lunch entrées, sandwiches and burgers are similarly generous. ~ 15491 Marine Drive, White Rock; 604-538-8084. BUDGET.

NIGHTLIFE

Over in Surrey, a half hour south of Vancouver, is the only drive-in movie theater left in British Columbia; the rest have become flea markets or weedlots. **The Hillcrest** is still popular during warm-weather months—all 500 spaces are usually occupied on weekend nights. It's not all nostalgic; high technology has replaced the speaker stands, and the soundtrack is now beamed to each car by radio. Thursday nights are one-price-per-carload; bring a station wagon (remember those?) and a bunch of friends and go back to simpler times. ~ 18694 Fraser Highway, Surrey; 604-576-2324.

BEACHES & PARKS

DEAS ISLAND REGIONAL PARK 🚶 🚲 🐎 ⚓ Encompassing most of a small island in one of the Fraser River's main channels,

AUTHOR FAVORITE

Tapas are the fare at **Cielo**, one of the Mediterranean-style eateries on Marine Drive, White Rock's main drag. But the restaurant's chefs have expanded the usual range of these Spanish appetizer plates. I come for such nontraditional items as breaded eggplant, calamari and grilled chorizo, and the preparations are excellent. Three plates make an ample amount for two, and the atmosphere is a bit more elegant than the typical pub eatery found on Marine. ~ 15069 Marine Drive, White Rock; 604-538-8152, fax 604-538-1237. MODERATE TO DELUXE.

Text continued on page 120.

Old Salt Village

Tucked in the southwest corner of Richmond is the old fishing village of Steveston. The cannery here was once the largest in B.C.; at the turn of the 20th century, 10,000 seasonal workers labored at plants up and down the Fraser River to pack the salmon then so abundant. As recently as 1979, fish canning, commercial fishing and shipbuilding were still major industries.

Today Steveston is a charming spot where visitors can get a taste of the watery ways of old as the place reinvents itself. Alongside historic attractions, small shops, art and craft galleries and cafés are being developed as the area shifts from an industrial derelict to a heritage village. There's an active wharf where visitors can buy fresh fish and shellfish right off the boats. For general information, visit www.steveston.bc.ca.

The **Gulf of Georgia Cannery** has been converted to a museum with a model canning line, historic artifacts and photographs and exhibits explaining the fishing industry. Kids especially love the ultra-realistic fish-cleaning line. Closed in winter. Admission. ~ 12138 4th Avenue; 604-664-9009.

The **Britannia Heritage Shipyard** was converted from a cannery to a shipyard in 1918; it survived until 1980. Now it's an eight-acre waterfront park the City of Richmond is slowly restoring to a heritage attraction, with role players demonstrating skills such as rope-making and steam-bending. Closed Monday. ~ 604-718-8050.

A slightly different dimension of the local history is depicted at the **Steveston Museum**. Here you can find plenty about the area's early fishery days, but also some background on the major contributions made by Japanese settlers between 1900 and World War II, and on the lamentable episode in which nearly all the Japanese Canadians here (and elsewhere in B.C.) were brought to internment camps during the war. ~ 3811 Moncton Street; 604-271-6868.

If you have a chance to spend the night in Steveston, there are a couple of good options for lodging. Right in the heart of things, the **Steveston Hotel** has been providing visitors a place to stay since long before the village became an attraction for anyone but fishermen. Compact—its 25 rooms include suites and some with shared baths—and distinctive, the hotel offers full services such as a restaurant, steam bath and sauna and cable TV. ~ 12111 3rd Avenue; 604-277-9511, fax 604-277-3188; www.

stevestonhotel.com, e-mail info@stevestonhotel.com. BUDGET TO MODERATE.

Visitors at **The Villager B&B** are within walking distance of all the attractions, yet in a quiet neighborhood. Two units have queen or twin beds and private baths; breakfast is served in a conservatory overlooking the rhododendron gardens. ~ 11111 6th Avenue; 604-275-0550, fax 604-275-0563; www.villagerbb.com, e-mail villager@attcanada.ca. BUDGET.

As for eateries in the village, **Dave's Seafood** restaurant holds a prominent spot on the Steveston Landing boardwalk, but its beginnings were humble enough—a modest nearby café on Moncton Street (still serving plentiful orders of fish-and-chips). The newer, bigger Dave's has the same reliable food, plus a splendid view of the harbor and a sun-filled patio during good weather. ~ 3800 Bayview Street #108; 604-275-4347. BUDGET TO MODERATE.

The fare is simplicity itself at **Pajo's**, and the location is marvelously inconspicuous, right on the wharf by the entrance to the dock. The reason this tiny outlet has enjoyed unparalleled success for years is the food: it's the best fish-and-chips around, and the hamburgers and chowder keep pace. Closed in winter. ~ Government Wharf, at the foot of 3rd Street; no phone. BUDGET.

As you'd expect, shopping in Steveston is best done by strolling through the small historic village's center. Once given over to fishing and marine supply stores, the village now offers an ever-growing array of gift shops, bookstores and art galleries.

Gerry's Books has a wide selection of used books—and we do mean wide. With 40,000 volumes on the shelves, this is a book-lover's paradise. ~ 3651 Moncton Street; 604-272-6601.

Irish Fancy specializes in fine wool clothing—sweaters, capes, coats and jackets, hats and caps—from Ireland and Great Britain. ~ 3866 Bayview Street #110; 604-272-1101.

Nikaido Gifts offers Japanese and Asian dolls, pottery, kimonos and other decorative items. ~ 3580 Moncton Street #150; 604-275-0262.

For more information on Steveston, call Parks Canada at 604-664-9009, or the Steveston Community Society at 604-241-5555.

this park provides extensive riparian habitat to stroll through and watch for birds and small mammals; also canoeing or kayaking along the river's slough. There are three restored heritage buildings as well, including a 1905 Queen Anne–style residence and a one-room schoolhouse. ~ Located two miles from Route 99; go north from the Route 17 interchange near Ladner, then left onto the Deas Island Road; 604-432-6350.

BOUNDARY BAY REGIONAL PARK 🚶 🚲 🐎 🛶 ⛵ 🏊 It's hard to say whether this spectacular shoreline park is more popular with people or birds. It includes a ten-mile trail, sand dunes, wide tideflats, salt marshes, lagoons and extensive wildlife populations. Hikers, cyclists, horseback riders and birdwatchers frequent the park, which, because of its south-facing exposure, is often balmier than its surroundings. This is a great place to go on a nice spring or autumn day. ~ Located one mile south of Route 17, along the road to the ferry terminal, Tsawwassen.

HIDDEN ► **CAMPBELL RIVER VALLEY REGIONAL PARK** 🚶 🚲 🐎 This wonderful park, east of White Rock, is a rarity in Vancouver—1000 acres of largely deciduous forest, the result of century-old farming and logging operations. With extensive trails wandering through forest and field it's an excellent place to while away a long afternoon, especially on a clear autumn day. ~ Five miles east of Route 99 on 16th Avenue, White Rock; 604-432-6350.

▼▼▼▼▼▼▼▼▼▼▼▼
East Fraser Valley

Except for those who detour to Harrison Hot Springs, most visitors speed through the east Fraser Valley on the Trans-Canada Highway, headed for more alluring locales east, west and north. What they're missing is a string of exceptional heritage sites along the valley, where European settlers first set up shop in the Lower Mainland. There are also several popular provincial parks in the mountainous foothills that ring the valley.

SIGHTS

Just off Route 1, east of downtown Vancouver, is **Burnaby Heritage Village**, one of the largest and finest historical attractions in British Columbia, with 30 restored buildings and role players, garbed in period costumes, depicting life in the region around the turn of the century. Be sure to stop for a cone in the ice cream parlor, and see if there's a silent movie running in the cinema. There's also a fabulous operating vintage carousel. Closed late January to early May and from September to October. Admission. ~ 6501 Deer Lake Avenue (Deer Lake Park), Burnaby; 604-293-6501.

Deer Lake Park itself, surrounding the heritage village, is a nice place for a picnic. The gardens up the hill from the heritage village are especially fine, and on clear days the views of the lake and Vancouver skyline are excellent. ~ At Canada Way and Gilpin Street, just off Route 1.

South of Burnaby is New Westminster, where you'll find the **Irving House**. Built in 1865, when New Westminster was the ◄ *HIDDEN* chief city along the Fraser River and Vancouver did not even exist, this is one of the finest heritage houses in B.C.—owned for most of its history by spinster sisters, it has many original furnishings and fixtures, such as brocaded early-Victorian wall-paper. The **New Westminster Museum** next door maintains extensive exhibits devoted to the Royal Engineers who built the Cariboo Road upriver. Call for winter hours. Admission. ~ 302 Royal Avenue, New Westminster; 604-527-4640.

Continuing along Route 1 another 15 miles (9 km) brings you to **Fort Langley**. First founded in 1827, the fort shut down in 1886, and had been used as a farm until it was declared a national historic site in 1923 and a national park in 1955. Since then, restoration of the palisades and many of the buildings has created a feeling similar to that at Fort St. James, another former Hudson's Bay outpost far to the north. Costumed guides and role players explain and demonstrate activities such as blacksmithing, fur tanning and barrel making. The **Langley Centennial Museum** has an extensive collection of First Nations art and artifacts. Nearby, the **BC Farm Machinery Museum** holds antique steam tractors, stump pullers and other mechanical marvels—including a Tiger Moth airplane used for crop dusting. The surrounding village features shops, cafés and antique stores. Admission. ~ One mile northeast of Route 1 at Langley; 604-513-4777.

> British Columbia's birthplace is Fort Langley—the "big house" in this erstwhile Hudson's Bay Company post is where the territory was declared a crown colony in 1858.

Back on the north bank of the Fraser River just outside Mission, Benedictine monks welcome visitors in the afternoon to **Westminster Abbey**, a working monastic retreat on the slope ◄ *HIDDEN* overlooking the river. Towering stained-glass windows mark the abbey's church. Visitors may attend liturgies, or stay at the abbey for a contemplative retreat of their own. The abbey's meditation bench, at the end of a short trail, offers an excellent vista of the Fraser Valley. It's hard to find—call for directions or stop at the Mission Visitor Info Centre for a map. ~ North of Route 7, just outside Mission; 604-826-8975.

Xa:ytem Interpretive Centre is the site of a 9000-year-old village inhabited by the Lower Mainland's Sto:lo people, thus the oldest known dwelling spot in B.C. Smallpox depopulated it in the mid-1800s. Visitors today can tour a longhouse, learn about First Nations heritage and ponder a massive stone held sacred by aboriginal peoples. Open in summer and fall only. Admission. ~ 35087 Lougheed Highway, two miles east of Mission; 604-820-9725.

Few facilities were more vital to settlement of B.C. than the trading posts along routes to the interior. The **Kilby Store** living history site is a reconstructed early-20th-century general store that served the Harrison Mills community; today, visitors can inspect shelves stocked with sundries and piece goods, and sample 1920 cuisine in the café. There's also an exhibit depicting the history of the nearby Sto:lo villages. Children can weigh out beans and flour for themselves and crank an old telephone. Closed October through April. Admission. ~ One mile off Route 7 on the east side of the Harrison River, Harrison Mills; 604-796-9576.

B.C.'s hot springs offer frequent reminders that this area is along the Ring of Fire; of the many spots to seek the sort of bone-deep relaxation only hot mineral water can provide, **Harrison Hot Springs** is a long-established area whose proximity to Vancouver has meant development of typical visitor amenities such as resort hotels, restaurants and golf courses. There's a public pool filled from the springs, which spew forth potash/sulphur water at well over 120°F (about 60°C). The nearby lake is where the hot water was first discovered: a gold prospector capsized his canoe and, instead of freezing as he expected, he stayed warm enough to survive and report his good fortune. ~ Along Route 9, about 50 miles (85 km) east of Vancouver; visitor info at 604-796-3425; www.harrison.ca.

Brian Minter, a well-known B.C. garden expert and radio commentator, has put his expertise to work creating **Minter Gardens**, a major horticultural enterprise exemplifying the green-thumb possibilities of the East Fraser lowlands. There's a maze, an aviary, topiary animals, a fragrance garden and numerous other delights for those who appreciate the horticultural life. Closed in winter. Admission. ~ One mile north of Route 1 at the Route 9 interchange (exit 135) east of Chilliwack; 604-794-7191, 888-646-8377.

LODGING   Fields of lavender and echinacea surround **Tuscan Farm Gardens B&B**, a lavish, tile-roofed, stucco estate where guests stay in accommodations situated in a separate farmhouse. Each of the three suites features hardwood floors, private bath and country furniture such as four-poster beds. Breakfasts are served in the garden in good weather. ~ 24453 60th Avenue, Langley (call for directions first!); 604-530-1997, fax 604-532-0350; www.tuscanfarmgardens.com, e-mail heather@tuscanfarmgardens.com. DELUXE.

First built in 1887, the **Traveler's Hotel** believes itself to be B.C.'s oldest. A marvelous restored clapboard house set just back from a historic intersection known as Five Corners, the hotel has four upstairs rooms furnished in period Victorian style, and offers sumptuous breakfasts based on Fraser Valley produce, such as eggs and salmon. ~ 21628 48th Avenue, Langley; 604-533-5569; www.langleybedandbreakfast.com. MODERATE TO DELUXE.

Salmon River Guest House is a charming, quiet, garden-sheltered home in Fort Langley, within minutes of the historic park and the village's cafés and shops. The two guest rooms share a bath with a clawfoot tub; there's a sitting room, and one of the guest suites can accommodate three. ~ 8812 Glover Road, Fort Langley; 604-888-7937; www.fortlangley.com. MODERATE TO DELUXE.

Set in pastoral farmland on the north side of the Fraser Valley, **Harrison Mills Country House** occupies a supremely quiet spot   ◀ HIDDEN

in the middle of a Christmas tree farm. Its four rooms are all decorated in country fashion, but in this case that means comfortable elegance—rich quilts and afghans—rather than rustic utility. There's also an upstairs reading room/library and an indoor hot tub. ~ 828 Kennedy Road, Harrison Mills; 604-796-0385, 800-551-2511, fax 604-796-2214; www.bbcanada.com/countryhse. MODERATE TO DELUXE.

Harrison Hot Springs Resort, the major visitor facility at its eponymous hot springs, is a sizable resort in and of itself. With 306 units (including a dozen cottages and a luxurious tower), two restaurants, its own golf course and beach, extensive hot pools, baths and saunas, plus recreation ranging from windsurfing to tennis, it's a fully stocked destination. Recent visitors have complained, however, that the resort is in dire need of refurbishing. As with any B.C. resort, off-season packages can be good bargains. ~ 101 Esplanade, Harrison Hot Springs; 604-796-2244, 800-663-2266, fax 604-796-3682; www.harrisonresort.com. MODERATE TO DELUXE.

AUTHOR FAVORITE

Rowena's Inn occupies a 160-acre estate on the Fraser River, and its heritage is deep: The land was part of a grant by Queen Victoria, and the current owners' antecedents—Charles Pretty, Sr., and Charles Nelson Pretty—were key figures in the B.C. timber industry. The inn has been fashioned from the Pretty mansion and still holds many family heirlooms. Guests can also enjoy the pool, hot tub, or fishing on the river. Five rooms in the main house all have private baths; there are also two self-contained guest cottages. Closed in January. ~ 14282 Morris Valley Road, Harrison Mills; 604-796-0234, 800-661-5108, fax 604-796-0280; www.rowenasinn.com. DELUXE TO ULTRA-DELUXE.

Little House on the Lake is the low-key alternative to the big hotel in Harrison Hot Springs. This log-home B&B is, as its name suggests, right on the lake; its four suites offer spacious accommodations with skylights, private bath, balconies and other amenities including fireplaces and CD players. The Captain's Cottage offers a more private retreat for two, with the same amenities as the in-house suites. There's a library, hot tub, beach and dock on the lake. ~ 6305 Rockwell Drive, Harrison Hot Springs; 604-796-2186, fax 604-796-3251, 800-939-1116; www.littlehouseonthelake.com. DELUXE TO ULTRA-DELUXE.

HIDDEN ►

The view of Cultus Lake and the Cascade Foothills from **Retreat on the Ridge** is spectacular—it's tucked atop a ridge south of Chilliwack—but the serenity and quiet are the most appealing attractions here. With five cozy housekeeping cabins overlooking the valley, and a fantastic hot tub nestled between fir trunks at the edge of the slope, it's a great place for utter relaxation. ~ 46782 Thornton Road, Chilliwack; 604-819-8599, fax 604-858-3878; www.retreatontheridge.com. DELUXE.

DINING

Wendel's Books, despite its name, contains a delightful small café in downtown Fort Langley. Yes, there are books for sale (just in case you need a hefty volume on Canadiana) but there is also a full menu of hearty breakfast plates, dandy sandwiches (the chickpea and rice on naan bread is great) and fresh-baked pastries and desserts. ~ 103-9233 Glover Road, Fort Langley; 604-513-2238. BUDGET.

SHOPPING

Travelers who like fresh agricultural produce will find more than 50 Fraser Valley farmsteads that offer their produce directly from the farm. Choices range from fresh dairy treats—even old-fashioned milk in a glass bottle with the cream on top—to free-range emu, pheasant and chicken. There are numerous berry farms, many vegetable producers, greenhouses and several orchards that grow antique and rare apples and other fruits. The Fraser Valley Farm Fresh Products guide includes a map and a description of the member producers. It's widely available at Visitor Info Centres, produce stands and area stores. Further information can be found at their website, www.bcfarmfresh.com.

Chilliwack in particular, long famed for its August and September sweet corn, is positioning itself as an agritourism destination, with a number of local farms drawing visitors to see

HIDDEN ►

what goes on as well as buy their products. **Greenhill Acres**, perched atop a hill above the Fraser Valley, offers guests the chance to see rare stock animals such as Highland cattle, watch the farm's notorious pumpkin cannon do its thing in the fall and buy farmstead products such as goat cheese. ~ 47090 Greenhill Road, Chilliwack; 604-858-9917. At **Willow Lane Herb Farm**, guests learn about the many savory and aromatic plants they can add to their own gardens; handmade lavender soap exemplifies what can be done with herbs. ~ 42090 South Sumas Road; 604-823-6492.

GOLDEN EARS PROVINCIAL PARK   **BEACHES & PARKS**
Coast Range ridges and peaks tower above this scenic valley and its Alouette Lake. It looks like a wilderness postcard, but it's only an hour from Vancouver. The valley was once the center of a large-scale railroad logging operation; the abandoned railbeds form a vast network of foot, mountain-bike and horse trails that lace the hills above the lake. Despite the popularity of the park, development is confined to the Alouette Lake shore, and most of the park remains deep wilderness, verging to the north into Garibaldi Provincial Park outside Whistler. ~ Located six miles northeast of Pitt Meadows; follow Alouette Lake Road north from downtown Maple Ridge; 604-924-2200; wlapwww.gov.bc.ca/bcparks.

▲ There are 403 vehicle/tent sites in three campgrounds, both right above the lakeshore at the far end of the park's access road; C$22 per night. There is also one developed wilderness camping area; C$8 per night.

CULTUS LAKE PROVINCIAL PARK
Nestled in the foothills of the Cascades, with a warm lake, long sandy beaches, four campgrounds and virtually limitless recreation opportunities—and all within an hour of Vancouver—this is arguably British Columbia's most popular park. That also makes it one of the most crowded: get here early or forget it, if you're camping. In the peak summer months, campsite reservations are crucial. That said, if you can pull in on a Tuesday in late July, spend a couple days and move on before the weekend rush, it's a heck of a nice place to rest from the road. Commercial recreation facilities ranging from go-carts to golf adjoin the park. ~ Located

WILDLIFE CARVED IN HOPE

Hope, where early pioneers and gold rushers began their trek into the B.C. interior, hopes to gain new renown as the "chainsaw carving capital of Canada." It's largely the doing of one local artist, Pete Ryan, who was inspired to turn a local cedar tree dying of trunk rot into a massive statue of a bald eagle. Since then he has transformed two dozen similarly afflicted trees into carvings depicting B.C. wildlife. Although scattered around town, many of the carvings are in Hope Memorial Park; the Hope Visitor Info Centre has maps delineating where the other carved trees are. ~ Visitor Info Centre, 919 Water Avenue, Hope; 604-869-2021.

on Cultus Lake Road, ten miles (17 km) south of Chilliwack, off Route 1; 604-824-2300; wlapwww.gov.bc.ca/bcparks.

▲ Four separate campgrounds, all near the lake, have 298 vehicle/tent sites. The only one right on the lake is Delta Grove. No hookups; C$22 per night.

HIDDEN ▶ **CHILLIWACK LAKE PROVINCIAL PARK** 🏃 🚲 ⛵ 🎣 🛶 🚤 🛥️ 🚣 This smallish park is also in the Cascade foothills, like Cultus Lake, but is somewhat more remote and less developed, and therefore less crowded as well. It's also tucked farther back into the mountains, which loom precipitously above the lake. Many wonderful hiking trails lead from the park into the hills. The Chilliwack River, which begins at the lake, is a popular spring and early summer rafting locale. ~ Located 30 miles (52K) southeast of Chilliwack along the Chilliwack River Road; 604-858-7161; wlapwww.gov.bc.ca/bcparks.

▲ There are 146 vehicle/tent sites fairly close to the lake; C$12 per night.

SASQUATCH PROVINCIAL PARK 🏃 🚲 🛶 🎣 🏕️ 🛶 🚤 🛥️ Nestled in a foothill valley along Harrison Lake—once an important route north into the gold fields of the Cariboo—this small park has three interior lakes as well as its frontage on Harrison. Its second-growth forest, largely deciduous, is famed for fall color. Today, the broad sand beach of Harrison Lake is the site, each September, of the World Championship Sand Sculpture Competition. The winning sculptures remain on display for a month. ~ Located three miles (5 km) north of Harrison Hot Springs on East Harrison Lake Road; 604-824-2300; wlap www.gov.bc.ca/bcparks.

▲ There are 176 vehicle/tent sites in three campgrounds near the two highest lakes; C$14 per night.

HIDDEN ▶ **SKAGIT VALLEY RECREATION AREA** 🏃 🚲 🏇 🎣 🛶 🚣 At the end of a long, winding gravel road, this is probably the most remote and least crowded major park in the Lower Mainland region. Tucked in the Skagit Valley below Manning Provincial Park, it features a rain-shadowed climate holding the most westerly stand of ponderosa pines in Canada, as well as wetter ravines with old-growth rainforest. Native rhododendrons are scattered through the woods. Park development is confined to the valley floor, which offers access to many miles of wilderness trail. The U.S. border forms the southern end of the park; Ross Lake extends a mile or so into Canada here. ~ Located 20 miles (36 km) southeast of Hope, at the end of Skagit Valley Road; 604-824-2300; wlapwww.gov.bc.ca/bcparks.

▲ There are 142 vehicle/tent sites at three campgrounds, one on Ross Lake; C$14 per night.

With a 100-mile shoreline that stretches along the northeast side of the Strait of Georgia, the Sunshine Coast is bordered by sandy beaches, secluded bays and rugged headlands. It reaches from Howe Sound in the south to Desolation Sound in the north. This area is rustic, even a bit worn around the edges, but don't let that stop you. There are many pleasant sites, plus a good number of artists in residence whose work is worth checking out. Activities taking advantage of the coast's marvelous landscape—kayaking, hiking, golf, diving—also abound.

Sunshine Coast

Despite its many charms, the Sunshine Coast is often mysteriously uncrowded. Travelers seem to shy away from the ferry passage—even though thousands endure much longer rides to reach Vancouver Island and fight their way through the crowded beachfront resorts that lie directly across the water from Powell River. I've always found the Howe Sound crossing, with islands and Coast Range foothills looming up in the mist, exceptionally beautiful.

A quick ferry trip up the North Coast from Vancouver will land you on **Bowen Island,** a once bucolic but still serene and very scenic isle in Howe Sound with its own ferry service from Horseshoe Bay. A half century ago this was Vancouver's answer to Coney Island, a day-trip getaway for city residents. It has since become a bedroom community for Vancouverites who need not go into the city every day, or are willing to face a daunting commute. It is also resuming its role as a getaway spot, with numerous small inns, cafés and shops in and around the town of Snug Cove. The ferry ride takes about 20 minutes. ~ Island information, Bowen Island Chamber of Commerce, 604-312-1102; www.bowenisland.org.

SIGHTS

Go up to the Mill View-point above Powell River for a look at the "Hulks," a half-moon breakwater of ten cement ships protecting the floating logs waiting to be processed.

From Horseshoe Bay the ferries for the southern Sunshine Coast bring you to Langdale; as you wind your way up Route 101 from there, one of the first areas of interest is the port town of **Gibsons.** Be sure to stop at **Molly's Reach** on Route 101, for years the setting for a popular Canadian television series, "The Beachcombers," and still a restaurant. ~ 604-886-9710.

The **Elphinstone Pioneer Museum** maps the history of European pioneers in the area. Artifacts from the daily life of these settlers are on display. The museum also houses a massive collection of sea shells. Open by appointment only in winter. Closed Sunday and Monday. ~ 716 Winn Road, Gibsons; 604-886-8232.

Next stop on the lower coast is the **House of Héwhîwus,** or House of Chiefs, the center of government, education and entertainment for the self-governing Sechelt Indian band. Photographs and artifacts relating the history of the tribe are on display in the **Tems Swîya Museum** (604-885-2273). Ask for directions to the totems and grouping of carved figures behind the complex. Closed some Sundays (call ahead). ~ 5555 Route 101, Sechelt; 604-885-2273, fax 604-885-3490; e-mail slb@secheltnation.net.

HIDDEN ▶

If you have an interest in archaeology, rent a boat and head north up the inlet from Porpoise Bay to view ancient Indian **pictographs** on the faces of the cliff walls looming above the water. The pictographs are very difficult to see; local guidance is essential.

From the trailhead near the town of **Egmont**, it takes approximately an hour to stroll the well-posted trail in order to see **Skookumchuck Narrows**, a natural phenomenon of rapids, whirlpools and roiling eddies created by massive tidal changes pushed through the narrow inlet. If you arrive at low tide you can view the marine life in tidal pools near Roland Point.

HIDDEN ▶

Taking the next ferry hop, from Earls Cove to Saltery Bay, brings you to the **Lang Creek Salmon Spawning Channel** about midway to Powell River. During the peak spawning season (September to November) you can get a close look at pink or chum salmon making the arduous journey upstream. ~ Route 101.

Nearby at **Mountain Ash Farm** the kids can play with little pot-bellied pigs, chickens, goats, sheep, emus and llamas while you visit the country store for a look at specialty foods, kitchenware and the farm's own fresh produce. Closed Monday and Tuesday. Admission. ~ 10084 Nassichuk Road, Kelly Creek; 604-487-9340.

The **Powell River Historical Museum**, an octagonal building just across from Willingdon Beach, houses a fine collection of regional memorabilia including furniture, utensils and hand tools of pioneers and indigenous people along with a photo and print archive that has material dating back to 1910. Closed weekends. Admission. ~ 4800 Marine Avenue, Powell River; 604-485-2222, fax 604-485-2327; www.armourtech.com/~museum, e-mail museum@aisl.bc.ca.

For a further lesson in the history of the area, take the heritage walk through the **Powell River Townsite** to view the early-1900s homes, churches and municipal buildings of this old company town. Some of the finest homes, exceptional examples of Arts & Crafts and Craftsman styling, are visible on the bluff just above the highway as you come into the old townsite. Maps are available from the **Visitor Info Centre**. Closed weekends in winter. ~ Info Centre, 4690 Marine Avenue, Powell River; 604-485-4701; www.discoverpowellriver.com, e-mail info@discoverpowell river.com.

During the months of June, July and August you can take a free two-hour tour of the Norsk Canada pulp and **paper mill**, the lifeblood of Powell River. The tour gives you an inside view on the process of turning logs into lumber and paper products, from water blasting the bark off through forming pulp sheets to rolling the finished newsprint, and Pacifica is justifiably proud of the efforts it has made to reduce pollution from the mill. No children under 12 permitted. Closed weekends in winter. ~ For information and reservations, contact the Powell River Info Centre, 604-485-4701.

LODGING

There are virtually no big resorts or major chain hotels in this area. Motels, inns and lodges are sometimes a shade worn but generally are friendly and inexpensive—part of the coast's unique charm.

The building that houses the **Lodge at the Old Dorm** was once just that—a dormitory for crews that piloted steamships to the island more than a half-century ago. Completely refurbished and decorated to reflect its steamship heritage, each of the five rooms is named after one of the boats that used to serve the island before BC Ferries took over the route. Breakfast goodies include fresh-baked muffins, waffles and pancakes. ~ 460 Melmore Road, Bowen Island; 604-947-0947, fax 604-947-0547; www.lodgeattheolddorm.com, e-mail old-dorm@infoserve.net. BUDGET TO MODERATE.

Sea Garden Retreat is a deluxe getaway B&B in Gibsons with two bedrooms in one unit served by a private entrance. The adjacent tropical atrium features a hot tub and sauna. Breakfasts are lavish affairs with fresh fruit and juice and baked goods. Gay-friendly. ~ 1247 Gower Point Road, Gibsons; 604-886-4643, 866-886-4643, fax 604-886-4619; www.seagardenretreat.com, e-mail info@seagardenretreat.com. MODERATE.

The **Royal Reach Motel and Marina** offers clean, basic accommodations in 32 simple rooms that are pretty much the same. Nondescript furnishings include one or two double beds, a long desk/television stand, plain bedside table and lamps, a mini-fridge,

BONNIE BEDS

A bed and breakfast since 1922, **Bonniebrook Lodge** is a charming yellow clapboard house overlooking the Strait of Georgia. Four guest rooms, each with a different color motif, feature flocked wallpaper and Victorian-style furnishings such as marble-topped tables and hand-carved beds. Two of the rooms have water views. Forty campsites for tents and RVs (half of the sites have hookups) are also available on the grounds behind the house. ~ 1532 Ocean Beach Esplanade, Gibsons; 604-886-2887, 877-290-9916, fax 604-886-8853; www.bonniebrook.com, e-mail info@bonniebrook.com. BUDGET TO MODERATE.

electric kettle and a small bathroom. Ask for one of the water-front rooms that looks out over the marina and Sechelt Inlet. You can also book a bay cruise, on a sailboat or powerboat, with the proprietor. Rowboats and paddleboats also for rent. ~ 5758 Wharf Road, Sechelt; 604-885-7844, fax 604-885-5969. MODERATE.

Beachcomber Marine Spa & Cottage is on a splendid site overlooking Sechelt Inlet. Guests choose among three lower-level rooms, with a TV room and outdoor hot tub nearby. The property reaches down to the waterfront, for those who care to set off into the inlet for a paddle. ~ 6398 Gale Avenue North, Sechelt; 604-885-0900, 877-399-2929; www.beachcomberbb. com, e-mail beachcomberbb@dccnet.com. DELUXE.

Although **Lord Jim's Resort** is a Coast Hotels property, this resort north of Sechelt is much more like a fine small inn than a chain hotel. With just 25 units, it offers both lodge rooms and cabins, plus a sauna, pool, game room and fine-dining restaurant. Bed-and-breakfast rates are available, as are fishing charters and other activities including hiking. The site, located just above a small, private cove, is exceptional. The restaurant is well-known locally as a good place to get a fine dinner. ~ Ole's Cove Road, Halfmoon Bay; 604-885-7038, 888-757-3474, fax 604-885-7036; www.lordjims.com, e-mail lordjims_resort@dcc net.com. MODERATE TO DELUXE.

HIDDEN ► **Burchill's Bed & Breakfast By The Sea** is actually a stand-alone cabin that can hold six to eight people, with single and double beds, private baths, a fireplace, kitchen, saltwater pool, and breakfast supplies provided. It's on the waterfront, with a panoramic view of Malaspina Strait; guests can use the B&B's rowboat. ~ 5402 Donley Drive, Halfmoon Bay; 604-883-2400; www.bb canada.com/478.html. MODERATE.

Lowes Resort, a Pender Harbour institution since 1952, offers a range of accommodation options including 11 housekeeping cottages and 13 tent/RV spaces among the permanent mobile-home units on the grounds. White paint, blue trim and flower baskets adorn the rustic little housekeeping cottages, each furnished with a vinyl couch and chairs, a laminated table, blond-wood furniture and a separate bedroom. The bathrooms are tiny. This is a suitable spot for families on a budget. The marina makes it a good choice for fishing and diving fans as well. ~ 12841 Lagoon Road off Route 101, Madeira Park; 604-883-2456, 877-883-2456, fax 604-883-2474; www.lowesresort.bc.ca, e-mail visit@lowesre sort.bc.ca. BUDGET TO ULTRA-DELUXE.

Turning **Ruby Lake Resort** into a popular destination has been a labor of love for—believe it or not—an entire family from Milan, Italy. The Cogrossi clan has taken a once-shabby road-side resort, upgraded the restaurant and accommodations, and has fashioned a bird habitat on the surrounding 90 acres. The lagoon at the center of the resort is a popular stop for colorful wood ducks on the annual migrations to and from the North. The ten cottages and two suites offer comfortable housing for guests who hike and canoe nearby; they're equipped with mini-refrigerators and TVs. The rustic lakeside tents sit on raised cedar platforms and boast four-poster beds and personal docks with private canoes. The restaurant features sensational Northern Italian cuisine. ~ RR#1, Madeira Park (Route 101); 604-883-2269, fax 604-883-3602; www.rubylakeresort.com, e-mail info@rubylakeresort.com. MODERATE.

> Over 80 species of birds, including blue herons, turkey vultures and ospreys, visit the lagoon at Ruby Lake Resort.

With furniture that appears to be stuck in at odd angles to make it all fit, the motel-style guest rooms at the **Beach Gardens Resort and Marina** are nothing special, equipped with the basics. There are also cabins and kitchenette units available. Extra amenities include the private marina, dining room and weight room. ~ 7074 Westminster Avenue, Powell River; 604-485-6267, 800-663-7070, fax 604-485-2343; www.beach gardens.com, e-mail bgarden@beachgardens.com. BUDGET TO DELUXE.

Within moments of arriving at the charming **Beacon B&B and Spa** and getting settled into one of the two inviting bedrooms or the roomy downstairs suite, you'll begin to unwind and feel right at home. It's hard to tell whether to attribute this to the genuine hospitality or the cozy, down-home decor. Whatever the case, the congenial hosts, large hot tub, great ocean view, proximity to the beach and thoughtful touches like plush robes and scrumptious breakfasts make this one of the most delightful lodging options in the region. ~ 3750 Marine Avenue, Powell River; 604-485-5563, 877-485-5563, fax 604-485-9450; www.beaconbb.com, e-mail stay@beaconbb.com. DELUXE.

Powell River's **Old Courthouse Inn** is in the middle of the historic townsite, not far from the lower end of Powell Lake and its popular canoe route. The heritage building, handsomely refurbished, holds very comfy dorm-style and private rooms, with an on-site café, cable TV and ready access to outdoor activities. The inn is non-smoking. ~ 6243 Walnut Street, Powell River; 604-483-4000, 877-483-4777; www.pacificspirit.org/oldcourthouse, e-mail oldcourt@telus.net. BUDGET TO MODERATE.

Set amid mature fir trees overlooking Okeover Arm, **Desolation Resort's** ten deluxe cedar chalets are all different, all private, all with expansive views of the water. With a private dock and 900 feet of waterfront, it's a perfect gateway to the famed Desolation Sound Marine Park, which can be reached in easy day trips from the resort. All the guest chalets are fully furnished

◄ HIDDEN

for self-sufficient stays and can accommodate up to ten people. Some have hot tubs on the decks overlooking the water. Closed mid-November to early December. ~ 2694 Dawson Road (off Malaspina Road), Powell River; 604-483-3592, fax 604-483-7942; www.desolationresort.com, e-mail info@desolationresort.com. DELUXE.

Acquired by the Sliamon Native Band, the **Lund Hotel** has been spruced up and modernized—each of the 27 rooms in the motel adjoining this heritage property has a scenic mural painted by a local artist. Stay here and you can truly say you've been to the end of the road; Route 101 stops at the hotel parking lot. The hotel café is a dependable place for sandwiches, fish and chips and the like. ~ End of Route 101; 604-414-0474, 877-569-3999, fax 604-414-0476; www.lundhotel.com, e-mail info@lundhotel.com. MODERATE.

DINING

HIDDEN ▶

Gibsons Fish Market, a smallish outlet on the main drag above the landing, does a booming business with tasty takeout fish-and-chips. It may not look like much, but there's usually a crowd lined up on the front sidewalk. ~ 294 Gower Point Road, Gibsons; 604-886-8363. BUDGET.

Another good bet is **Robbie's**, where the breakfasts are unstinting combinations of pancakes, sausage, eggs and toast; lunches are soups and hearty sandwiches; and there's a separate menu for kids. ~ Cedars Inn complex, 895 Sunshine Coast Highway, Gibsons; 604-886-9090. BUDGET TO MODERATE.

The **Blue Heron Inn**, a delightful waterfront home-turned-restaurant on picturesque Porpoise Bay, is home to masterful creations. The daily menu uses fresh regional produce and seafood in the dishes. Reservations suggested. Closed Monday and Tuesday. ~ Sechelt Inlet Road and Delta Street, Sechelt; 604-885-3847, 800-818-8977; www.bigpacific.com. DELUXE.

The salads and soups are superior at the **Sunfish Café**, and the sandwiches benefit immensely from the fact the café is part of the Wild Flour Bakery. Desserts feature dandy pastries and cakes, naturally. ~ 5530 Wharf Street, Sechelt; 604-885-0237. BUDGET TO MODERATE.

Throngs of people crowd into the **Old Boot** in downtown Sechelt for handmade pizza, pastas and other Italian specialties. Plan to wait on warm summer nights, but it's worth it. ~ 5530 Wharf Street, Sechelt; 604-885-2727. BUDGET TO MODERATE.

HIDDEN ▶

They make hamburgers by hand, on order, never frozen, at **Lighthouse Pub** in the back end of Sechelt, overlooking Sechelt Inlet. The rest of the pub food menu is equally down-home and well done, including their tasty soups and salads. The fish-and-chips are among the best in B.C. ~ 5764 Wharf Road, Sechelt; 604-885-9494. BUDGET.

Coffees are hand-selected, organically grown and fairly traded at **Strait Coffee Traders** just outside Sechelt. Furthermore, they're good. You can also munch on muffins, pastries and light lunches. This is the most popular coffee house in the lower Sunshine Coast. ~ Field Road and Route 101; 604-885-9757. BUDGET.

The menu focuses on traditional Continental dining at **Lord Jim's Resort**; it's the setting and execution that distinguish this fine restaurant at Halfmoon Bay. ~ Ole's Cove Road, Secret Cove (Halfmoon Bay); 604-885-7038; www.lordjims.com. MODERATE TO DELUXE.

Folks over 19 can stop by the **Royal Canadian Legion Hall Branch 112** for a super-cheap supper of chicken and chips, Salisbury steak or juicy burgers. This is actually one of the nicest (and only) places in Madeira Park to get a meal, but the bar inside means that only those of legal drinking age can enter. The salt-of-the-earth folks here might even let you in on a hand of cribbage or a fevered dart game. ~ 12829 Lillie's Lake Road, Madeira Park; 604-883-0055, fax 604-883-2005; e-mail rc@uni serve.com. BUDGET.

Loyal customers sometimes drive the full length of the Sunshine Coast just to stop at the **Hamburger Stand**. The reasons are basic: No frozen meat patties here; no pre-cut frozen french fries; milkshakes and malts whipped up the old-fashioned way. Try the fish-and-chips, too. ~ 12905 Madeira Park Road, Madeira Park; 604-883-9655. BUDGET.

The **Shingle Mill Bistro and Pub**, situated at the tip of Powell Lake, has large windows on three sides so the views of this beautiful, evergreen-trimmed lake are enjoyed. It's no surprise that

AUTHOR FAVORITE

The view from the **Laughing Oyster** is sensational, looking out over Okeover Arm and north toward Desolation Sound. The seafood dinners at this country restaurant are equally memorable, including the seafood platter for two that includes just about every sea creature the chefs can find on the market that morning—salmon, rockfish, shrimp, oysters, crab, scallops and more. Even though it's remote, reservations are essential on summer weekend nights. I vote it one of the best seafood restaurants in B.C. ~ Malaspina Road at Okeover Arm; 604-483-9775. MODERATE.

they serve grilled B.C. salmon in this waterfront eatery, but the steak *au poivre*, chicken in puff pastry, and fusilli primavera are unexpectedly good. Items from the dinner menu are available in the relaxed bistro. ~ 6233 Powell Place, Powell River; 604-483-2001, fax 604-483-9413. MODERATE TO DELUXE.

Nancy's is a small café/bakery in Lund, just above the harbor, with a nice outdoor seating area and a generous selection of fresh-baked breads, muffins and pastries. Naturally, the breads form the basis for filling lunchtime sandwiches. Lunch only. ~ Lund, across from the marina; 604-483-4180. BUDGET.

SHOPPING

An admirable devotion to local artists distinguishes **Gift of the Eagle Gallery** in Gibsons. There are many talented artists on the Sunshine Coast, and the paintings, sculpture, pottery and fiber art here would pass muster in any gallery in B.C. ~ 689 Gibsons Way, Gibsons; 604-886-4899.

HIDDEN ►

They're pricey—C$1600 and up—but the custom-made cowboy boots Norman Bashor fashions at **Trident Boots** are exquisite. Inlaid designs, perfect fit and matchless finish mark Bashor's craft, which he sells to customers across North America. ~ Molly's Lane, Gibsons Landing, Gibsons; 604-886-4622; www.trident boots.ca.

For First Nations arts and crafts, including masks, drums, totems and baskets, visit the Sechelt Indian Band's **Tsain Ko Gift Shop**. Closed Sunday in winter. ~ 5555 Route 101, Sechelt; 604-885-4592.

You'll find fine representations of local art (serigraphs, pottery, woodwork, watercolors, jewelry, sculpture) at Gibsons' **Westwind Gallery**. Closed Sunday. ~ 292 Gower Point Road #14, 604-886-9213; Halfmoon Bay's **Anchor Rock Gallery** ~ 5646 Mintie Road, 604-885-7472; and Powell River's **Gallery Tantalus** ~ 4555-C Marine Avenue, 604-485-4662.

HIDDEN ►

Cranberry Pottery, a working studio, offers functional and affordable handmade stoneware in varying designs and glazes. Closed Sunday. ~ 6729 Cranberry Street, Powell River; 604-483-4622; www.cranberrypottery.bc.ca.

◆◆◆

SUNSHINE STUDIOS

There's an abundance of artists living in small communities along the Sunshine Coast, and many of them are happy to open their studios to visitors. Contact the Sunshine Coast Arts Council for tour information. Closed Monday. ~ Corner of Trail and Medusa streets, Sechelt; 604-885-5412.

Along the Sunshine Coast you'll find fairly slim after-hours pick- **NIGHTLIFE**
ings, limited primarily to friendly, no-airs local taverns and pubs
that occasionally have dance space, live music or karaoke and
great water views.

A popular neighborhood hangout, **The Blackfish Pub** has
very occasional live music and karaoke. ~ 920 Route 101 at
Show Road, just outside Sechelt; 604-886-6682.

Thursday to Saturday night you can shake your thang to live
rock and R&B at **Wakefield Inn**. ~ 6529 Sunshine Coast Highway,
Sechelt; 604-885-7666.

Powell River has an amiable establishment in which to spend
a comfortable evening after canoeing the lakes. Kick back with a
brew and a view overlooking Powell Lake at the **Shingle Mill Bistro
and Pub**. ~ Route 101, Powell Lake (north end of Powell River);
604-483-3545.

PORPOISE BAY PROVINCIAL PARK 🏃 🛶 🎣 🚣 One of the   **BEACHES**
prettiest parks along the coast, Porpoise Bay has a broad, sandy   **& PARKS**
beach anchored by grass fields and fragrant cedar groves. This is
a favorite base for canoeists who come to explore the waterways
of the Sechelt Inlets Marine Recreation Area. You'll also find excellent sportfishing. The park has restrooms, showers, picnic tables, an adventure playground, an amphitheater, nature trails,
visitor programs and a fall chum salmon run. Parking fee, $3. ~
Located northeast of Sechelt off Porpoise Bay Road; 604-898-
3678, 800-689-9025; wlapwww.gov.bc.ca/bcparks.

▲ There are 86 tent/RV sites (no hookups); C$20 per night.
They also have cyclist sites with showers; C$10 per night.

SALTERY BAY PROVINCIAL PARK 🛶 🚣 🚤 🛥 🚣 This
lovely oceanside park with twin sandy beaches enjoys grand
views of Jervis Inlet, where sharp-eyed visitors often catch
glimpses of porpoises, whales, sea lions and seals. Scuba divers
flock to the park to visit the nine-foot bronze mermaid resting
beneath 60 feet of water not far offshore from the evergreen-
shrouded campground. Swimming and offshore salmon fishing
are excellent. There are restrooms, picnic sites, fire pits and disabled diving facilities. ~ Located off Sunshine Coast Highway, 17
miles south of Powell River; 604-898-3678, fax 604-898-4171;
wlapwww.gov.bc.ca/bcparks.

▲ There are 42 tent/RV sites (no hookups); C$14 per night.

FRANCIS POINT PROVINCIAL PARK 🏃 🚤 This is the Sunshine   ◄ *HIDDEN*
Coast's newest park, an exquisite shoreline expanse of 160 acres
that was saved from development by a large donation from a famed
U.S. software magnate. The park's rare, "very dry maritime"
ecosystem features Douglas fir and madrona forest; hiking trails
lead three kilometers or so into the park, along several peaceful

sandy coves. ~ Follow Francis Peninsula Road to Merrill Road, parking is at the end; 604-885-9019.

HIDDEN ▶   **PALM BEACH REGIONAL PARK** 🚻 🏖 There are no palms at this small, exceptionally obscure little park about three miles (5 km) south of Powell River. Instead, there's a delightful picnic area and access to a gorgeous half-mile stretch of white-sand beach looking out toward Vancouver Island. It's quite hard to find— look for inconspicuous signs on the southwest side of the road. ~ Palm Beach Road, off Route 101; turn at Lang Bay Road.

POWELL FOREST CANOE ROUTE 🚶 🏖 🛶 With eight fjord-like lakes interconnected by rivers, streams and miles of hiking trails, it is possible to make three-day or week-long portage canoe trips in this beautiful northern Sunshine Coast recreational area. There are more than 200 miles of hiking trails around Powell River. Best time to make the trip is between March and November; lakes at upper elevations tend to freeze, and roads are inaccessible during winter months. Facilities include outhouses, picnic tables, hiking trails (the inland lake trail is wheelchair accessible), and a camping supply store. ~ Jumpoff point for the canoe route is Lois Lake, accessed by the canoe mainline; 604-485-4701, 877-817-8669, fax 604-485-2822; www.discoverpowellriver.com, e-mail info@discoverpowell river.com.

▲ Permitted at any of the 30 recreation sites. Prices vary from C$7 per night at some of the forestry campsites to C$20 per night at municipal and provincial campsites around the area.

WILLINGDON BEACH MUNICIPAL CAMPSITE 🚶 🏖 The sandy, log-strewn, crescent beach bordered by acres of woods draws a big summertime crowd to this comfortable campground. Some of the campsites are right up on the beach, while others in a grove of cedar are more secluded. The site has great, though unsupervised, swimming. You'll find restrooms, showers, a laundry, a barbecue area, playgrounds, a nature trail and a seasonal food stall. ~ Located immediately off Marine Avenue in the Westview section of Powell River; 604-485-2242.

▲ There are 81 sites, half with full hookups; C$15 to $36 per night. Monthly winter rates are available.

OKEOVER ARM PROVINCIAL PARK 🎣 ⛴ 🚻 🏖 🚤 🛥 🛶 This small park is literally at the end of the road, the terminus of Route 101's long run from South America. This is a popular one-night stopover for kayakers and boaters heading into Desolation Sound, although it's a fine place to wind up a Sunshine Coast trip. The park is on the waterfront, and swimming, hiking and biking

Saltery Bay Provincial Park was named for the Japanese fish-saltery settlement located in the area during the early 1900s.

along back roads are possible activities. ~ One mile east of Lund, off Route 101; 604-898-3678; wlapwww.gov.bc.ca/bcparks.

▲ There are five vehicle/tent sites, four walk-in sites; C$12 per night.

DESOLATION SOUND MARINE PARK ⚓ 🛶 🚤 🎣 This park is made up of 37 miles of shoreline and several islands. The waters here are very warm and teem with diverse marine life, making the area ideal for fishing (excellent for cod or salmon), swimming, boating and scuba diving. The park is wild and undeveloped, with magnificent scenery at every turn. There are a few onshore outhouses and numerous safe anchorages. Because of the balmy summer climate, and the fact that cold sea water doesn't enter protected inlets and bays, the water here often reaches tropical warmth in later summer. ~ Boat access only from the coastal towns. Easiest access is from Powell River; 604-898-3678, fax 604-898-4171; wlapwww.gov.bc.ca/bcparks.

▲ There are several walk-in wilderness campsites; no charge. Two developed boat-access campgrounds have pit toilets and information shelters.

Outdoor Adventures

FISHING

The tremendous variety of fish in southwestern British Columbia waterways provides an array of exciting challenges for the angler. In the mountain country, you can flyfish or spin-cast in high alpine lakes and streams for rainbow trout, Dolly Varden, steelhead or kokanee salmon. On the coast, you'll find chinook, coho, chum, pink and sockeye salmon and bottom-dwelling halibut, sole and rockfish. Licenses for both fresh- and saltwater fishing are required (charter operators can usually provide them); regulations change frequently.

Lowes Resort operates eight-hour fishing charters in Pender Harbour for salmon, rock cod and Pacific snapper. Gear and licenses are available. ~ Lagoon Road, Madeira Park; 604-883-2456. **Lord Jim's Resort** offers similar services from its location at Halfmoon Bay north of Langdale. ~ RR2, Ole's Cove, Halfmoon Bay; 604-885-7038, 888-757-3474.

RIVER RUNNING

Scenic floats and whitewater rafting are immensely popular around Vancouver, especially on the Chilliwack River, 65 miles east of the city.

Hyak Wilderness Adventures runs guided whitewater-rafting trips on the Chilliwack River in the spring, when snow still caps surrounding mountains. By summer, the focus shifts to the Thompson River, with its desert scenery. Rapids along these rivers range from Class II to Class V. You can actively participate by paddling or go the lazy route and let the guides do the work. ~ 3823 Henning Drive, Burnaby; 604-734-8622, 800-663-7238; www.hyak.com.

CANOEING & KAYAKING With spectacular fjords, sounds and bays, the Lower Mainland and Sunshine Coast offer some of the best kayaking and canoeing in North America. The most popular locales are Indian Arm (northeast of Vancouver), Howe Sound, Sechelt Inlet, Powell Lake and Desolation Sound on the Sunshine Coast. All feature undeveloped shores, towering mountains, pristine waters and the chance to see many wild animals—and all demand expert guidance before you set out since winds and currents are daily challenges.

NORTH AND WEST VANCOUVER Ocean West Expeditions runs a summer-only kayak rental operation in Vancouver near Stanley Park, but the company also offers extended guided trips into Desolation Sound and the islands along the Sunshine Coast. ~ At the English Bay Beach Bath House, corner of Denman and Davie streets, Vancouver; 604-688-5770, 800-660-0051; www.oceanwest.com. Canadian Outback Adventures also offers five-day guided kayak trips into Desolation Sound. ~ 657 Marine Drive #100, West Vancouver; 604-921-7250, 800-565-8735.

> The 32-mile-long Powell River is the second-shortest river in the world. (Oregon's D River is the shortest at 120 feet.)

Indian Arm is a true glacial fjord, a narrow, 15-mile inlet off Burrard Inlet that cuts a swath northward into the North Shore Mountains just outside Vancouver. With the peaks of Mount Seymour Provincial Park towering above to the West, and miles of undeveloped shoreline along the inlet, it's a genuine wilderness experience just minutes from the city. **Lotus Land Tours** offers guided day trips by kayak into Indian Arm, and will pick up visitors in town at their hotels, providing transportation and outfitting along with a picnic lunch. ~ 1251 Cardero Street, Suite 2005, Vancouver; 604-684-4922, 800-528-3531.

SUNSHINE COAST On the road to Whistler, **Sewell's Marina** offers boat rentals to visitors who want to tour the calm waters of Howe Sound—perhaps taking a day trip to Bowen Island, setting off on a fishing jaunt, or simply finding their own secluded beach for a picnic. Charters and sightseeing tours are also available. ~ 6695 Nelson Avenue, Horseshoe Bay; 604-921-3474.

Desolation Sound Marine Park and the 40-mile **Powell Forest Canoe Route**, which includes eight breathtaking lakes and lush, interconnecting forests, are ideal spots for canoes. "Powell Forest Canoe Route is as beautiful as the more popular Bowron Lake route in northern British Columbia, but it's less populated by people in canoes," explains a local outfitter. Maps for the canoe route are available from the Powell River Forest Service. The entire route takes up to a week, but unlike Bowron Lakes, it's possible to drop in at a couple spots along the way and do an abbreviated version of the route. All told, there are six miles (11 km) of portages on the route; some have canoe racks. As with almost all coastal lakes and inlets, afternoon winds can be quite high. ~ 7077 Duncan Street, Powell River; 604-485-0700; www.roughlife.com.

To rent a canoe for one or eight days, contact **Wolfson Creek Ventures** in Powell River. You can tackle it alone with a rental or take a guide as you explore the Powell Forest Canoe Route. ~ 9537 Nassichuk Road, Powell River; 604-487-1699; www. canoeingbc.com. Experienced kayakers can rent craft for the day from **Sunshine Kayaking Ltd.** in Gibsons, on Howe Sound. Longer tours and kayaking classes are also offered. ~ RR4 S12 C18, Gibsons, BC V0N 1V0; 604-886-9760.

Even though Sechelt Inlet is reasonably protected, a guide service will make a kayak trip safer and more productive—especially when it comes to finding the famed water-side pictographs, and understanding the inlet's ecology. The guides at **Porpoise Bay Kayaks** will teach beginning paddling techniques, lead the way across the inlet, and haul out a dandy snack or lunch just at the right moment. ~ 604-885-5950.

DIVING

A thick soup of microscopic plant and animal life attracts and feeds an abundance of marine life that in turn attracts divers in growing numbers. Although quite cold, these waters are also home to colorful anemones, sea cucumbers, and the world's largest octopus. Add to this the array of wrecks and underwater sights (such as a nine-foot bronze mermaid in Saltery Bay as well as the largest artificial reef in North America—a 366-foot destroyer that sank and is now a diver's paradise), and it's easy to understand the popularity of scuba diving around Vancouver and the Sunshine Coast.

Dive charters to local waters, the Gulf Islands and Howe Sound are arranged by **Great Pacific Diving**. Rentals and lessons are also available. ~ 1236 Marine Drive, North Vancouver; 604-986-0302; www.greatpacific.net. **Aqua Sapiens** charters excursions in British Columbia and Washington. Gear and lessons (from resort to technical instructor certification) are available. ~ 1386 Main Street, North Vancouver; 604-985-3483.

BOATING

With 5000 miles of sheltered water in easy reach, Vancouver and southwestern British Columbia afford many opportunities to get out on the water. You can rent a powerboat or a sailboat and head up to the Sunshine Coast, where Desolation Sound has the warmest waters north of Mexico (in the summer), or you can hop onto an inflatable raft and paddle the Chilliwack River's whitewater.

NORTH AND WEST VANCOUVER   At **Sewell's Marina** they'll give you a short instruction course on running their safe, low-key powerboats and then, if the weather's calm, send you off into Howe Sound to cruise over to Bowen Island or to one of the sound's more remote isles. ~ 6695 Nelson Avenue, West Vancouver (Horseshoe Bay); 604-921-3474.

GLIDING

With dependable daily thermals rising up the nearby canyon walls, Hope is the gliding capital of the Lower Mainland. The **Vancouver Soaring Association** is based at Hope Airport and has three planes and nine gliders to provide training for beginners or experts. Saturday and Sunday are the best days for beginners; arrive early and put your name on the flight list. It's about US$40 for a 20-minute flight as a passenger. ~ Located at the Hope Airport, take the Flood–Hope exit off Route 1; 604-869-7211; www.vsa.ca.

GOLF

Golf in the Lower Mainland and along the Sunshine Coast is bound to involve water in some way. Even if there isn't much of it on the course, the location or the view will likely encompass a body of water—English Bay, the Strait of Georgia, one of the rivers.

EAST FRASER VALLEY   The **Sandpiper Golf Club** avails itself of the Fraser River Valley's beautiful landscape to make this 18-hole course an aesthetic experience. Golfers may share the course with eagles, hawks, herons and other migratory birds. Four sets of tees offer golfers of any level the chance to have fun. Golfers can combine a game with dinner and an overnight stay at nearby Rowena's Inn (see Lodging), a restored riverside estate. ~ 14282 Morris Valley Road, Harrison Mills; 604-796-1000, 877-786-1001.

SUNSHINE COAST   Open year-round, the 18-hole **Myrtle Point Golf Club** has splendid views of Texada and Vancouver islands. ~ C-5 McCausland Road, RR #1, Myrtle Point; 604-487-4653. An occasional elk can be seen emerging from the surrounding lush vegetation to wander across one of the fairways at the nine-hole **Pender Harbour Golf Club**. ~ Sunshine Coast Highway, Pender Harbour; 604-883-9541. The **Sunshine Coast Golf and Country Club** is an 18-hole semiprivate course. With challenging greens, the tree-lined par-71 course isn't too long and is good for the average golfer. ~ 3206 Sunshine Coast Highway, Roberts Creek; 604-885-9212, 800-667-5022.

SKIING

The majestic range crowning Vancouver's North Shore offers three fine ski areas within minutes of the city center.

The glittering string of lights visible each night on the North Shore across the inlet from downtown Vancouver marks the arc-lit runs of **Grouse Mountain**, where residents head after work to get in some slope time. The resort offers 25 runs, a variety of lifts, a snowboard park and a snowshoeing park. There's also outdoor skating on a pond. ~ 6400 Nancy Greene Way, North Vancouver; 604-984-0661; www.grousemtn.com.

On a clear, fogless day, Burnaby and Richmond are visible from the 20 ski runs at **Mount Seymour**. Good novice runs make this a best bet for beginners or those who want to avoid hot doggers. Downhill runs are serviced by a network of chairlifts and tows and are open for night skiing. Though the skiing here is mainly beginning and intermediate (80 percent of the runs), Mount Seymour attracts international professional snowboarders who come for the natural terrain in its three parks. Third Peak, the most northerly, offers good views of Garibaldi Provincial Park to the north. Hilly cross-country trails run through the adjacent Mount Seymour Provincial Park. ~ 1700 Mount Seymour Road, North Vancouver; 604-986-2261; www.mountseymour.com.

Cypress Bowl, with 35 runs on two lift-served mountains, boasts the longest vertical run of the local resorts. Snowboarders share the runs with downhill skiers. A third area features 10 miles of groomed cross-country trails tracked for both classic and skate skis. Night skiing and backcountry skiing trails are available in the provincial park. ~ Cypress Provincial Park, West Vancouver; 604-926-5612; www.cypressmountain.com.

BIKING

Although mountain biking on logging roads is gaining in popularity, over-the-road cycling presents some challenges. There is no protected bike path along Route 101, the main artery of the Sunshine Coast, and the rocky shoulder drops off entirely at times, forcing bikers onto the highway. However, the moderately challenging trip from Langsdale to Earls Cove (50 miles/81 km) is popular nonetheless. The backcountry of the entire coast is laced with marked and unmarked logging trails leading off Route 101 just waiting to be explored by intrepid mountain bikers; a detailed map of the trails between Jervis Inlet and Lund is available from the Powell River Travel Info Centre. ~ Info Centre, 4690 Marine Avenue, Powell River; 604-485-4701.

FLOATING OVER FRASER ISLAND

There's hardly any better way to experience the pastoral beauty of the Fraser Valley than in a hot-air balloon, which can drift quietly over farms and delta wetlands. **Balloons Above the Valley** offers flights daily during the summer from Langley Airport. ~ Call for reservations and directions; 604-533-2378.

Bike Rentals   On the Sunshine Coast, you can rent bikes at **Taws Cycle and Sports.** ~ 4597 Marine Avenue, Powell River; 604-485-2555.

HIKING   Because it is backed along its entire length by the steep Coast Mountains, hiking in the Lower Mainland and Sunshine Coast region usually involves heading uphill . . . sometimes quite steeply uphill. The rewards are spectacular scenery and the chance to disappear into undeveloped wilderness quite close to the city. All distances listed for hiking trails are one way unless otherwise noted.

NORTH AND WEST VANCOUVER   Capilano Pacific Trail (4.5 miles/7 km), which starts in North Vancouver's Capilano River Regional Park, passes from massive Cleveland Dam to Ambleside Park through sections of coastal rainforest and offers great views of the Lions, the twin mountain peaks soaring majestically above the dam.

There are many short, lovely trails within Capilano River Regional Park, offering smashing perspectives of the canyon and cool strolls through the maturing second-growth forest. The best trail is **Giant Fir**, which takes you by a particularly massive tree (one of the few big firs left by the loggers a century ago), then back down across the canyon on a footbridge.

Norvan Falls (9.5 miles/15 km) offers a more rugged backcountry trek for the experienced hiker through the wilderness areas of Lynn Headwaters Regional Park. The shorter **Lynn Loop Trail** (3 miles/5 km) affords views of Lynn Valley and passes an abandoned cabin. Call 604-985-1690 for trail conditions.

Every afternoon dozens (sometimes hundreds) of Vancouver office workers traipse across the Lions Gate Bridge, wend their way to the Grouse Mountain parking lot, tie on hiking boots and stretch their hamstrings *really* well. They're about to climb the **Grouse Grind** (1.5 miles/2.5 km), the trail that covers the same ascent the airtram does. Yes, it is quite steep. It's a lot of altitude—1400 feet—but the average reasonably fit person can do it in a couple hours. (The record is about 32 minutes!) When you get to the top, you stretch some more, have a beer at the Rusty Rail bar, and pay a few bucks to ride back down on the airtram. This is fitness with a view. *Please heed the signs when the Grind is closed for avalanche danger; several hikers perished in a snowslide a couple years back.* ~ The Grouse Mountain parking lot is 15 minutes north of the Lions Gate Bridge on Capilano Drive—you can't miss the signs.

EAST FRASER VALLEY   The trail circling **Buntzen Lake** (8 miles/13 km) in the recreation area of the same name northwest of Port Moody is both scenic and invigorating. On the north side, bluffs invite the adventurous to dive in the lake for a refreshing, cool dip. The full loop takes about four hours, but it's mostly level. ~ On Sunnyside Road, near Belcarra Park; follow Ioco Road out of downtown Port Moody.

The trail circling the **Pitt–Addington Marsh** wildlife management area (2–4 miles/5–8 km) offers viewing towers as well as dikes to allow visitors a good look at the wetland wildlife common here, which includes eagles, osprey, swans, beavers and numerous kinds of waterfowl. ~ Five miles (9 km) north of Pitt Meadows off Harris Road; access is from Grant Narrows Regional Park.

SUNSHINE COAST The **Soames Hill Mountain Trail** (1.5 miles/2.5 km) is a brisk stair climb to an elevation of 800 feet followed by expansive views of Howe Sound and the surrounding mountains and villages. ~ From North Road (upper highway) turn left on Chamberlain, then left on Bridgeman.

Soames Hill is otherwise known as "the knob" because of its appearance to passengers on ferries approaching Langdale.

The **Smuggler's Cove Marine Park Trail** (.5 mile/1 km) is an easy walk leading to the cove once used to smuggle in contraband and Chinese immigrants and now home to an array of seabirds. ~ Trailhead is located off Brooks Road approximately six miles north of Sechelt.

Mount Valentine Trail (approximately 1 mile/1.5 km) is a short walk on a gravel path followed by a steep climb up a stone staircase leading to panoramic views of Malaspina and Georgia straits, Vancouver Island, Powell Lake and the surrounding hamlet of Powell River. ~ At the end of Crown Street in Powell River.

The **Willingdon Beach Trail** in Sechelt begins at the Willingdon Beach campsite, following shore north a couple miles along an old log skid road. Along the way, old-growth forest and leftover logging artifacts convey a sense of the Sunshine Coast's early history.

Inland Lake Trail (8 miles/13 km) offers a longer hike over a well-maintained circuit of boardwalks and bridges through scenic swamp areas and skirting lovely Inland Lake. The entire trail is wheelchair accessible, and several handicapped-accessible shelters and fishing wharfs are along the way. ~ Just off Route 101, a half-mile north of Powell River.

The **Sunshine Coast Trail** is a work in progress, but when all 111 miles (180 km) are finished its backers hope it will develop an allure similar to better-known trekking routes on Vancouver Island. The trail begins at a remote site in Desolation Sound; access is by water taxi from Lund. It follows the coast range through old-growth and second-growth forest, crossing high ridges and dipping down to the water at several points along the way, finishing at Saltery Bay near the BC Ferries terminal. Numerous access points along the route allow shorter hikes; the entire length takes more than a week. Several small inns and lodges lie along the route for those who want a break from the wilderness camps along the trail. ~ For more information and a detailed map contact the Powell River Visitor Info Centre; 604-485-4701.

Transportation

CAR

From the West Coast of the United States, Route 5 turns into **Route 99** after crossing the Canadian border at Blaine and proceeds northwest through Vancouver's suburbs and into the city core where the name changes once again, this time to Granville Street. The **Trans-Canada Highway** (**Route 1**) connects Vancouver with points east in Canada.

Route 99, referred to as the **Sea to Sky Highway** from Horseshoe Bay northward, picks up again in North Vancouver, hugs the rugged coastline and continues north into the mountains to Whistler.

Route 101, the only major thoroughfare through the Sunshine Coast, connects Langdale to Earls Cove and Saltery Bay to Lund, the northernmost point of this long, transcontinental highway with its southern terminus in Chile. Yes, this is the same road that follows Washington State's Olympic Peninsula and the California coastal valleys—theoretically, anyway.

AIR

Vancouver International Airport offers domestic charters and flights by Harbour Air and Whistler Air Services. International airlines include Air Canada, Air China, Air New Zealand, Alaska Airlines, American Airlines, British Airways, Cathay Pacific Airways, Continental Airlines, Delta Air Lines, Horizon Air, Japan Airlines, KLM, Korean Air, Lufthansa, Northwest Airlines, Qantas, Singapore Airlines and United Airlines. ~ www.yvr.ca.

Pacific Coastal Airlines offers scheduled service between Vancouver and Powell River; 604-273-8666, 800-663-2872.

FERRY

BC Ferries provides service between Vancouver Island and Tsawwassen (an hour south of downtown Vancouver); between Horseshoe Bay (half an hour northwest of downtown) and Bowen Island; and between Horseshoe Bay and Langdale on the southern Sunshine Coast and Earls Cove and Saltery Bay on the northern Sunshine Coast. When traveling Route 101 up the Sunshine Coast from Langdale to Earls Bay, allow at least two hours transit time. BC Ferries offers discount fares to travelers making a circle up the Sunshine Coast, across to Vancouver Island and back down. ~ 888-223-3779; www.bcferries.bc.ca.

CAR RENTALS

Rental agencies at Vancouver International Airport include **Alamo Rent A Car** (800-462-5266), **Avis Rent A Car** (800-879-2847), **Budget Rent A Car** (800-299-3199), **Hertz Rent A Car** (800-263-0600), **Thrifty Car Rental** (800-847-4389) and **National Car Rental** (800-227-7368).

Discount Car Rentals (604-273-5565) has an office in the neighboring suburb of Richmond and offer free airport pickup.

PUBLIC TRANSIT

Translink governs Vancouver's expansive transit system, with buses, the SkyTrain and the SeaBus, covering all the main arteries within the city and fanning out into the suburbs. Running on a 19-mile, mostly elevated track between Canada Place downtown and the suburb of Surrey, with 20 stations along the way, the SkyTrain is a good way to see some of the major sights around Vancouver. Trains leave every three to five minutes. You can also get a great view of the skyline from the water aboard the Sea Buses that cross Burrard Inlet between downtown and the North Shore, docking at Lonsdale Quay. The handy *Discover Vancouver on Transit* tour guide, day passes and timetables are available from Travel Info Centres. ~ 604-953-3333.

TOURS

Pressed by the growth of another Lower Mainland crop—houses —the Fraser Delta's farms have adopted survival tactics ranging from organic agriculture to specialty crops. Specialty Agricultural Tours offers day-long trips designed to acquaint visitors with both the old and the new in Fraser farming. Clients travel quiet back roads to visit working family farms, chat with farm family members, and enjoy some of the fresh produce raised here. ~ 7064 48th Avenue, Delta; 604-946-3929.

A half-century ago Vancouverites piled onto steam ferries for a day at Bowen Island. Today, Harbour Air Seaplanes does a quicker version: you can board a floatplane at Vancouver Harbour, fly to Bowen for dinner at a Snug Cove restaurant, take the ferry back to Horseshoe Bay and a limousine back to downtown Vancouver. ~ 604-688-1277; www.harbour-air.com.

FOUR

Whistler

In its short history—the first lift opened in 1966, and the resort village itself dates to 1978—this ski destination has gained a peerless international reputation and is now among the top attractions in North America. Now that it is sharing the 2010 Winter Olympics with Vancouver, Whistler will gain even more international prominence. It's already consistently rated number one in North America by *Ski* magazine—ahead of such better-known destinations as Aspen, Vail and Sun Valley.

Just 75 miles north of Vancouver (about a two-hour drive) Whistler is close enough for a day trip from the city. But there's far too much to see and do in only one day—skiing is just the start—and first-time Whistler visitors who haven't allowed themselves at least a night in the resort will regret it once they get there.

With island-dotted Howe Sound to the west and the verdant Coastal Range to the east, there are enough sights along the Sea to Sky Highway to make driving the narrow, winding road slow but enjoyable. Parks and scenic pullouts along the way are perfect for a picnic or a stretch, and the terrain is stunning. Along the way, several attractions in the Squamish area deserve at least a glance, but that's only a prelude.

Once you arrive in Whistler, which is in a small valley surrounded by towering mountains, you'll see memorable sights in every direction. Whistler advocates happily point out that, among other things, virtually every guest room in the city has an alpine view—a fact made possible by the mountainous surroundings on every side.

Although the area's economy originally depended on logging, mining and trapping, the first settlers to arrive in the early 1900s realized right away the potential of the area's beauty, so it's no surprise that some of the first structures were built as vacation retreats, most geared toward fishing and hunting (both of which remain popular activities). Skiing began in earnest in 1966 with the opening of the Garibaldi Lift Company in Whistler. A stylized European village resort was constructed 12 years later at the convergence of Blackcomb and Whistler mountains.

Those who have never been here are often mystified by the resort's huge popularity. After all, Whistler is by ski-industry standards somewhat remote from major population centers. It's nowhere near as large, as venerable or as publicized as Aspen, Vail or Sun Valley. And then there's the oft-heard concern about the damp, heavy snow found along Pacific Northwest coastal mountains.

First things first: the snow is usually excellent, an average fall of 30 feet, because Whistler is behind the Coast Range front and not exposed directly to damp Pacific air; its base is relatively high, 2200 feet; and its two mountains offer skiing up to 7500 feet. In fact, on Blackcomb Mountain, glacier skiing continues into August; this is a popular spot for racers to train, although not a very sensible choice for recreational skiers because the tickets are pricey and the hours short—the glacier is given over to training in the morning. In winter, the varied terrain (more than 7000 acres, 200 trails, three glaciers, 12 bowls and that huge 5280-foot vertical) offers something for every skier: vast untracked bowls and steep, expert pitches as well as long, luxurious intermediate runs, the lengthiest of which stretch seven miles. There's a marked difference between the two mountains, by the way, in atmosphere and clientele. Whistler is the family mountain, Blackcomb the mountain favored by younger, more extreme skiers and snowboarders.

Crucial to Whistler's popularity is the design of the two villages: the slapdash development that followed the valley's early growth was halted in 1975 and today Whistler and its residents take development standards very seriously. The result is a place particularly suited to pedestrians. Vehicular and foot traffic are kept separate, which contributes to the high-mountain village atmosphere. The vast majority of Whistler's visitors spend their days on foot or on skis and leave their cars parked. An extensive network of trails serves cross-country skiers in the winter and joggers, skaters, bicyclists and walkers in the summer.

These qualities are among the attributes that appealed to the International Olympic Committee. The resort is accustomed to major international competitions, having hosted several World Cups. It already has virtually all the necessary facilities—the only major additions will be a Nordic complex northwest of the main village, and some new audience seating for awards ceremonies. Not much new lodging will be built, so tickets and rooms will be at a premium.

Although summer used to be the slow season at Whistler, an explosion of golf and other recreational development is attracting a growing crowd of warm-weather visitors. Hiking, tennis, sailing, fishing, canoeing, rafting, biking and horseback riding are among the activities that draw people up here; lodging and dining rates are considerably lower than in winter and the cobbled walkways of Whistler Village are alive with street entertainers—jugglers, clowns, dancers, musicians.

Whistler and Blackcomb villages are separate, but they meet at the foot of the two mountains—as do the main lifts serving them. Whistler is the bigger village, a stone- and brick-paved warren of cafés and shops at ground level with hotels above. The Upper Village (i.e., Blackcomb) is newer, and thus has a bit less character. However, it is also the home of several of the snazziest hotels and restaurants at the resort. Because the two villages are directly at the foot of the two ski mountains, visitors must crane their necks to check out the alpine magnificence above.

The whole area is remarkably compact; a slow walk between the two villages might consume ten minutes.

Even during ski season (November through April) you'll find no shortage of parking—a big problem at many resorts—because the main village is built atop a massive underground garage and a huge parking lot is carefully hidden amid the trees between Whistler and Blackcomb villages.

The rest of the valley is devoted to top-drawer residential areas well-hidden in the forest, a few more economical accommodations along the main highway, golf courses stretched amid a string of pretty lakes and a utilitarian area stashed away at the foot of the valley, whimsically named "Function Junction."

Squamish and Pemberton, the two bookend communities that each lie about a half-hour from Whistler, are developing their own visitor amenities while they also serve as bedroom communities for resort workers. Squamish (fondly known as "Squish" to fans of its climbing and water sports) is increasingly well-known as a recreation center. From here you can go rafting on the Squamish River, climbing in the cliffs and mountains surrounding Squamish, diving and kayaking in Howe Sound and sailboarding in the upper end of Howe Sound. The area where the river's current meets the sound's water regularly produces "nuclear" winds akin to those of the Columbia Gorge farther south.

Upriver from Squamish, in the Brackendale area, great numbers of bald eagles settle in for the winter. One winter, the count was 3769 eagles, the highest concentration of these birds on earth. Not surprisingly, eagle-watching floats are a chilly but popular winter activity.

Pemberton, for its part, is a farming community (the valley is known for seed potatoes) now adding golf and country-inn vacationing to its attractions.

Because of its near-coastal location, Whistler's climate is mild—rarely bitter cold in winter, warm but not hot in summer. The average midwinter high temperature is a mild 23°F, the low 11°F. The average midsummer high is in the 70s, nighttime lows in the low 50s. In the summer, brief afternoon thundershowers roll off the peaks over the valley, quickly washing the village and moving on to leave behind rainbows painted across the mountain ridges.

Popular annual events in Whistler include a roots music weekend in July, a classical music weekend in August, Oktoberfest in early October and Cornucopia, a wine and food festival, in mid-November. New Year's Eve brings a torchlight parade down the mountainside, followed by a family-oriented First Night celebration. There are typically a half dozen major ski-race events at Whistler each year, including alpine, snowboard and freestyle World Cup meets.

The road to Whistler, the remarkable and scenic Sea to Sky Highway (see below), is a narrow thread of asphalt glued to the granite cliffs along Howe Sound—not a place for haste. The proliferation of hot-shot drivers who suffer Grand Prix delusions has led the province to boost traffic enforcement considerably and set up a hotline for callers to report aggressive drivers. Just relax: You'll get there in a bit over two hours at a moderate pace. Let the Porsches and Ferraris roar by; they'll get what's coming to them.

SIGHTS   The way to Whistler, the **Sea to Sky Highway** (Route 99), is a spectacular ribbon of road hugging the sometimes precipitous mountain wall that borders Howe Sound. Dozens of waterfalls cascade down the slope on the inland side of the road; glimpses of islands, the sound and the far shores offer vistas on the water side. In the distance, snowy peaks appear and disappear regularly. Because it's a winding two-lane road much of the way, use the numerous pullouts to gawk at the scenery, especially during winter, when the road may be icy and the driver behind you, on the way to Whistler for the umpteenth time, isn't interested in the view. The frequent signs advising of rockfall hazard aren't there for decoration: be watchful, especially during rainstorms. Also, the signs urging citizens to report reckless drivers have been occasioned by the Route 99 cowboys who think they're James Bond.

Though the highway is being upgraded in some stretches for the 2010 Olympics, it will remain a two-lane artery along a fair portion of its length—a fact most Whistler residents embrace. (They don't want their town to be at the end of a freeway.) The

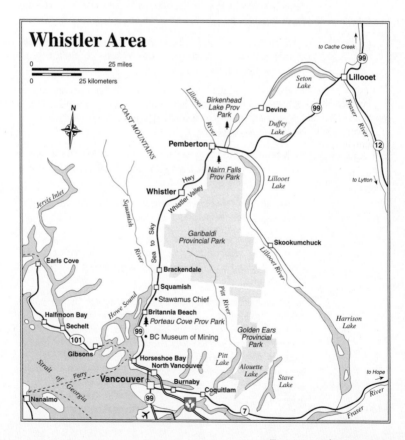

Whistler Area

Text continued on page 152.

Whistler Whistle-stop

A resort village designed to keep cars out of sight demands a day spent on foot to experience its real character. That's one of the best reasons to head for Whistler in the off-season (May through September). Crowds are down, the weather's great, and prices are dandy. This itinerary can be adapted for winter, too, by simply substituting snow-based morning activities.

- Arrive in the late evening and check into the **Summit Lodge** (page 157), one of Whistler's best compromises between luxury and value.

- Next morning, start your day with coffee and muffins at **Auntie Em's Kitchen** (page 160) across the street.

- If you're here in winter, hit the slopes or the cross-country trails. In summer, head up to the **Whistler Village gondola** base to rent a bike for the morning.

- Cycle studs can catch a lift up the mountain for a rousing career back down; a more sedate but equally appealing option is to head out on the **Valley Trail** (page 172), a 15-mile path that winds out to Green Lake and back.

- Arriving back at the base just after noon, head downhill along the Village stroll, stopping at **Ingrid's Village Café** (page 160) for a cup of soup and a thick-headed sandwich.

- Check out **The Grocery Store** (page 163) after that to see what a boutique grocer in a world-class resort stocks.

- Be sure to observe the diverse social milieu—Whistler is that rarity, an upscale resort that draws young and old, hip and conservative, wealthy and not. Then wander along the brick plazas for a couple hours.

- Ignore all the name-brand stores you pass; they don't have anything different from what you'd find at branches in dozens of other resorts. Do make sure to see the astounding bear collection at **Bear Pause** (page 163) and soothe your aromatic psyche at **Escents Aromatherapy of Whistler** (page 163), a Whistler-born shop now growing into Vancouver and Victoria. In case you ever wanted to own a Tony Curtis painting, **The Plaza Galleries** (page 163) is the place.

- Once you hit Lorimer, pass the post office, head right toward the creek and rejoin the Valley Trail system. Nearby you'll encounter **Rebagliati Park**, a small island in the creek bed named for Whistler's Olympic gold medal–winning freestyle skier, who's at least as well known for declaring his fondness for recreational cannabis use. It's also the best place for a vantage of Blackcomb Mountain, whose 5280-foot lift-served vertical drop is the greatest in North America.

- Head uphill a bit to reach the Upper Village at the base of Blackcomb—just in time for dinner at **La Rua** (page 161), Whistler's best restaurant. A meal here will be so rich and filling that the after-dinner stroll necessary to take you back to your room is just that—necessary.

- Still going? There's an excellent cigar room at the **Bearfoot Bistro** (page 161). If your feet are not worn out, try Whistler's most popular music venues, the **Longhorn Saloon** (page 164) or **Boot Pub** (page 164).

majority of the Olympics visitors are expected to travel to and from Vancouver by bus.

As you're cruising up the Sea to Sky Highway, you'll pass a couple of sights worth a detour just before you reach the town of Squamish. First will be **Shannon Falls**, a high, shimmering ribbon of tumbling water immediately off the highway. Hundreds of visitors stop here, but it's worth a few moments despite the crowds—especially in the spring, when torrents of water roar down from snowmelt above. Be careful on the rocks beneath the falls; they're quite slippery; and take note of the steam donkey, an archaic logging machine once used to drag logs, on display along the trail.

Next you'll come to the **Stawamus Chief**, often called, incorrectly, the second-largest monolith in the world after the Rock of Gibraltar; at 1900 feet (622 meters) it's actually the second-largest in the British Commonwealth. On a fine day there will be climbers dangling all about the face of this mountaineer's dream—its 180 different routes draw 160,000 international climbers and hikers a year. It became a provincial park in 1995 under an ambitious B.C. natural conservation program.

HIDDEN ▶

At the **Brackendale Eagle Reserve**, a thin strip of land along each side of the Squamish River preserves the all-important riparian cottonwood forest that is home each winter to more than 2000 wintering bald eagles. This park is open to visitors during eagle-watching season (November–March), but it's no place for rowdy behavior, as eagles will stop feeding when disturbed. Respect the natural inhabitants, and keep a thoughtful distance from feeding or roosting eagles. Most of the eagles are on the west bank of the river, opposite the reserve's public access; binoculars are a good idea. ~ In Brackendale, three miles (5 km) north of Squamish, take Depot Street off Route 99, then follow Government Road southwest to the riverside dike, which is the access to the viewpoint.

The nearby **West Coast Railway Heritage Park** offers the largest collection of antique railroad rolling stock, locomotives and other railroad artifacts in Western Canada. Admission. ~ 39645 Government Road, Brackendale; 604-898-9336, 800-722-1233.

The **Squamish Chamber of Commerce** offers information for Squamish and the entire region, including Brackendale. ~ 37950 Cleveland Avenue, Squamish; 604-892-9244; www.squamish chamber.bc.ca.

Once you're in Whistler, the staff at **Central Guest Services** (604-932-3434) will try to answer almost any question you can conjure up or will direct you to someone who can. Heading for a Whistler store, café or restaurant? Don't hesitate to call for directions—many places are really rather tucked away—and be sure to pick up one of the resort association's excellent maps of the villages and the valley.

The **Whistler Activity and Information Centre** is the local clearinghouse for events, recreation and public services such as parks and trails. ~ 4040 Whistler Way, Whistler; 604-932-2394; www.whistler-resort.com.

One of the more interesting heritage attractions in Whistler is **Rainbow Park,** the site of the area's first vacation retreat and now a day-use park. This is also the best spot for a view of the valley and the Blackcomb and Whistler mountains. ~ Alta Lake Road, Whistler.

For an in-depth look at the history of the area, visit the **Whistler Museum and Archives Society**, a quaint museum next to the public library in Whistler Village that houses relics, artifacts, documentary videos and a worthwhile slide presentation (which must be booked for viewing). Call ahead for hours. Admission. ~ 4329 Main Street, Whistler; 604-932-2019, fax 604-932-2077; www.whistlermuseum.org, e-mail info@whistlermuseum.org.

Skookumchuck Hot Springs, a distant but popular destination in the Lillooet River Valley south of Mount Currie, is located along the Lillooet River, on the original Cariboo wagon road that took gold rushers into B.C.'s interior in the 1870s. This long drive from Whistler—allow three hours—is a substantial day trip. Even so, weekends can be quite crowded, as bathers flock to the unique setup where taps regulate water flow from the cold and hot springs. The facilities and grounds, which are on private property, are maintained voluntarily by users. The nearby First Nations town of Skookumchuck has a picturesque, oft-pho-

◄ HIDDEN

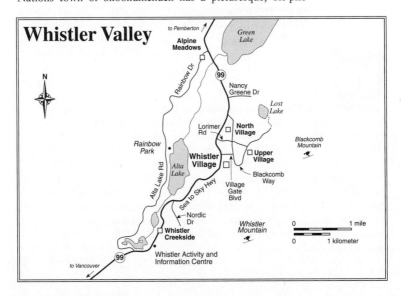

tographed pioneer church. ~ Located 50 miles (77 km) south of
Pemberton; follow Route 99 to the turnoff to Lillooet Lake Road,
which becomes the Lillooet River Road.

LODGING   Before you get to Whistler, you'll pass through Squamish on the
Sea to Sky Highway, and there's at least one good reason to stop
here. The clientele the **Howe Sound Inn & Brewing Company** seeks
is betrayed by the inn's exterior granite climbing wall, sauna,
storage lockers for recreational equipment, and microbrewery.
The 20 "character rooms" are comfortable if undistinguished, with
rustic inn decor; the restaurant concentrates on local fish and game.
To ensure that guests find their way out and back, there's a map
room. ~ 37801 Cleveland Avenue, Squamish; 604-892-2603, 800-
919-2537, fax 604-892-2631; www.howesound.com. MODERATE.

With a spanking-new (2003) facility and a great location, the
Squamish Hostel draws travelers to this recreation center between Vancouver and Whistler. Aside from a selection of both
dorm and private rooms, the hostel has a staff with considerable
expertise on the area's activities, from climbing to riding. Many
options are within walking distance. Free high-speed internet is
a big plus. ~ 38490 Buckley Avenue, Squamish; 604-892-9240,
800-449-8614; www.squamishhostel.com. BUDGET.

Once you make it up the valley, there's a wide range of options for lodging. The central accommodations number for
Whistler is 604-664-5625, 800-944-7853; www.tourismwhistler.
com. A consortium of smaller Whistler inns also maintains a website at www.whistlerinns.com. A continuing village controversy
over the creation of B&Bs in residential neighborhoods may
someday shut down some of the resort's smaller, family-owned
guest houses, but the issue has been tied up in court for years.

sights

AUTHOR FAVORITE

The Whistler area has enough upscale, high-octane attractions
that it's a bit like eating too much foie gras. That's why I like the **B.C.
Museum of Mining**, whose down-to-earth tour takes you deep into
what was once the highest-yielding copper mine in the British Empire
(and is now a major source of toxic pollution into Howe Sound). Mining
isn't just old news in B.C., by the way; it's still among the province's top
five industries. Tours include a stop inside the mountain to watch workers wield mining equipment. The kids will enjoy panning for gold in the
small pool set up for just that purpose. Closed most of December and
January. Admission. ~ Route 99, Britannia Beach; 604-896-2233;
www.bcmuseumofmining.org.

Several of the larger lodging operators in town have central booking numbers. The **Whistler Lodging Company** manages 1200 units, all luxury suites, in a dozen different spots; package rates can be remarkably good. ~ 604-684-9378, 800-777-0185, fax 604-633-2948; www.whistlerlodgingco.com. **WhiskiJack Resorts** manages more than a dozen properties, some of which are condos. ~ 604-932-6500, 800-944-7545, fax 604-932-3268; www.whiskijack.com. **Whistler Chalets** offers condos and specializes in resort homes and executive chalets from one to four bedrooms. ~ 604-932-6699, 800-663-7711, fax 604-932-6622; www.whistlerchalets.com.

Whistler also has a number of clearinghouses that arrange rentals of private homes in the resort, including **Whistler Home Holidays**. ~ 604-938-9256, 888-644-7444, fax 604-938-9259.

Hostelling International—Whistler is located on Lake Alta, ten minutes from Whistler Village. Accommodations are basic here, with men's and women's dorms and a private room upstairs, and a kitchen, dining room and game room downstairs overlooking the lake. There's also a sauna. ~ 5678 Alta Lake Road, Whistler; 604-932-5492, fax 604-932-4687; www.hihostels.ca. BUDGET.

◄ HIDDEN

Similarly basic is the **Shoestring Lodge**, where most of the rooms are of the dorm variety—a bed or two or four, a TV, a rudimentary closet. Most rooms share baths. The decor is minimal. Ah, but you came to ski, right? And the price: in winter, a bed can be had for around US$20. The lodge operates its own free shuttle to the lifts, about five minutes away. And one of the most popular youth hangouts in town, the Boot Pub, is in the same building. ~ 7124 Nancy Greene Drive, just off Route 99, Whistler; 604-932-3338, fax 604-932-8347; www.shoestring lodge.com. BUDGET.

Just a five-minute stroll from the Creekside Gondola base, the **Southside Lodge** is also an excellent bargain for those who come to Whistler to ski, not spend money. Economical and functional, the lodge is close to Route 99 and offers both dorm and private rooms in typical hostel style—with some upscale touches such as cable TV and VCR in all rooms. ~ 2102 Lake Placid Road, Whistler; 604-932-3644. BUDGET.

A nicer alternative is the UBC **Whistler Lodge.** You still need to provide your own food and bedding and will share cubicles with other hostelers, but this rustic lodge set above a quiet residential section offers lots of pleasant extras like a sauna and jacuzzi, a barbecue and fire pit off the large deck, ski-equipment/bike storage locker, kitchen, laundry, game lounge, separate television/ movie room and internet access. Book well in advance—at least two months—for the ski season. ~ 2124 Nordic Drive, Whistler;

604-932-6604, fax 604-822-4711; www.ubcwhistlerlodge.com.
BUDGET.

Even if the outward appearance of **Chalet Luise** is a bit stereo-typical, the eight rooms within are spruce and cozy, simply fur-nished with pine fixtures and furniture. All rooms have private baths and down comforters; the honeymoon suites, which have fire places, are especially appealing, but much less costly than sim-ilar accommodations at the major hotels. Hearty German-style breakfasts come with a stay here. ~ 7461 Ambassador Crescent, Whistler; 604-932-4187, 800-665-1998, fax 604-938-1531; www.chaletluise.com. MODERATE.

HIDDEN ▶   Its location in a quiet residential area means **Lorimer Ridge Pension** is pleasantly apart from Whistler's bustle; but the main village and lifts are just a few minutes' walk. Rooms are spacious and handsomely appointed, with duvets and private baths; some have balconies and fireplaces. There's a billiards room, too. ~ 6231 Piccolo Drive, Whistler; 604-290-3641, 888-988-9002, fax 604-938-9155; www.lorimerridge.com, e-mail info@lorimerridge.com. MODERATE.

If you seek an all-out alpine experience, you'll do well to choose **Edelweiss**, a charming European-style pension complete with window boxes and rosemaling on the chaletlike exterior. There are eight simply furnished guest rooms with private bath-rooms and down comforters. A small guest lounge shares space with the sunny breakfast room where guests are treated to a hearty meal. The French and German proprietors are avid skiers who post a ski bulletin daily for guests. There's even a whirlpool and sauna for post-slope relaxation. ~ 7162 Nancy Greene Drive, Whistler; 604-932-3641, 800-665-2003, fax 604-938-1746; www.pensionedelweiss.com. DELUXE.

The Coast Whistler Hotel is farther from the lifts but has re-sort amenities such as a dining room, pub, fitness room, sauna, hot tub, shiatsu massage clinic and heated pool. Guest rooms are boxy, with basic, light-wood furniture, mini-fridges and cramped bathrooms; some have built-in window seats to take advantage of the views. Request a corner unit or one with vaulted ceilings—they seem to be roomier and are the same price. ~ 4005 Whistler Way, Whistler; 604-932-2522, 800-663-5644, fax 604-932-6711; www.coastwhistlerhotel.com. DELUXE.

The townhomes at **Glacier's Reach** are akin to those you'd find in any luxurious resort development—compact but fully fur-nished, comfortable and practical. All have separate entrances, kitchens and dining nooks; most have hot tubs; decor is attractive, low-key and conventional. In other words, this is a mainstream Whistler accommodation—and like most such places, a relatively good value, especially for families. The lower Whistler village is just minutes away, as is the valley trail system that serves joggers and cross-country skiers. ~ 4388 Northlands Boulevard, Whistler; 604-905-4746, 800-580-6645, fax 604-905-4724; www. whistlerstays.com. MODERATE TO DELUXE.

Lifestyles of the Rich and Famous dubbed the **Fairmont Château Whistler**, located at the base of Blackcomb Mountain, "Whistler's premier address" with good reason. The property is strikingly elegant and brimming with Old World charm. Guests enjoy alpine views from more than 500 rooms, all smartly furnished with country-style wood furniture, queen or king beds, mini-bars and large bathrooms. The Blackcomb lift base is just seconds from the hotel's back door. Château Whistler also operates an 18-hole golf course (designed by Robert Trent Jones, Jr.), and the hotel's restaurant, The Wildflower, is one of Whistler's best-known venues for new-wave West Coast cuisine. ~ 4599 Château Boulevard, Whistler; 604-938-8000, 800-441-1414, fax 604-938-2055; www.fairmont.com, e-mail chateauwhistlerresort@fairmont.com. ULTRA-DELUXE.

> The Whistler village site was once a garbage dump!

Le Chamois shares the same prime ski-in, ski-out location at the base of the Blackcomb runs. However, its smaller proportions (only 50 rooms) allow for a high degree of personal attention. The guest rooms are spacious, with large bathrooms, kitchenettes and designer touches evident throughout the decor; some of the studio rooms are especially wonderful, with two-person jacuzzi tubs in the living room area set before bay windows overlooking the slopes and lifts. These units are actually condos (some owned by royalty); each room's decor is different. ~ 4557 Blackcomb Way, Whistler; 604-932-8700, 800-777-0185, fax 604-905-2576; www. whistlerstays.com. ULTRA-DELUXE.

The **Marriott Residence Inn** typifies the mainstream accommodations available in Whistler. It's on Blackcomb Mountain, about 100 yards up from the lift base; so, as with many of Whistler's hotels, you ski out in the morning and ski right back to the hotel back door in the afternoon. The architecture features massive fir log beams, slate floors and wood siding. The rooms are attractive suites, done in wood and warm fabrics, with a small kitchen and dining area. There's a free continental breakfast in the lobby every morning, and a pool, a sauna, hot tubs and basic exercise facilities. Most rooms look out on the mountain or out over the valley. ~ 4899 Painted Cliff Road, Whistler; 604-905-3400, 888-905-3400; www.marriott.com. DELUXE.

The **Summit Lodge** is a low-key, midscale property whose location right at the end of the Whistler Village stroll puts guests in the heart of the Whistler experience. Part of San Francisco's popular Kimpton Group lodging chain, the Summit features comfy rooms with rudimentary kitchenettes, balconies and tasteful decor—tile rather than marble in the baths. Not only is a decent continental breakfast included in the room rate, they'll bring it to your room with a newspaper at the time you specify. ~ 4359 Main Street, Whistler; 604-932-2778, 888-913-8811, fax 250-932-2716; www.summitlodge.com. MODERATE TO DELUXE.

HIDDEN ►   The **Lost Lake Lodge** is an example of a more remote Whistler accommodation—"remote" meaning it's all of five minutes from a lift. The inn is constructed from massive wood beams and rock facings, with an interior decor scheme you might call upscale rustic—lots of wood, homey fabrics, functional furnishings. Kitchens and dining nooks are standard, as are ample closets; many rooms have bunk beds for kids. The very private pool area looks out on the trees lining the Fairmont Château Whistler Golf Course. ~ 4660 Blackcomb Way, Whistler; 604-905-7631, 866-580-6647, fax 604-905-0365; www.whistler-lostlakelodge. com. MODERATE TO DELUXE.

The **Pan Pacific Lodge** is designed to look more like a château; within, much like a château, all the 121 units are suites—no mere hotel rooms here. The decor is subdued and upscale, lest it detract from the amenities: every room has a fireplace, full kitchen, soaker tub, balcony, and floor-to-ceiling windows. The pool and hot tubs outside have unobstructed views of Whistler Mountain. The service is expert, quiet and discreet. ~ 4320 Sundial Crescent, Whistler; 604-905-2999, 888-905-9995, fax 604-905-2995; www. panpac.com. ULTRA-DELUXE.

HIDDEN ►   Rarely does one find a place as pretty and tranquil as **Brew Creek Lodge** near a major international resort like Whistler. Located off Route 99 about 15 minutes down the valley from Whistler proper, the site is well-hidden back in the forest about a mile from the main road. Its six-room log lodge, two guest houses and one cabin are all furnished in rustic yet upscale fashion, with fir paneling and trim; the grounds, with the namesake creek running by, are peaceful and attractive. Hot tub and sauna are also available. It's a B&B; while the kitchen does not offer lunch or dinner, full catering can be provided for groups. ~ 1 Brew Creek

AUTHOR FAVORITE

The view across Green Lake at **Edgewater Lodge** is so sublime that I sometimes find it hard to tear myself away to actually go skiing—even though the ski area base is just ten minutes away. Access to the valley's extensive network of cross-country trails is just steps from the lodge's porch. In summer, of course, those wanting activities can just hop in a canoe, or fling a fly on the lake from shore. See page 159 for more information.

Road, Whistler; 604-932-7210, fax 604-932-7223; www.brew
creeklodge.com. MODERATE TO DELUXE.

At the upper end of Whistler Valley, the **Edgewater Lodge** sits
on the edge of Green Lake. Not surprisingly, the lodge's 12 rooms
have stunning views of the lake, as does the dining room, which
serves exceptional Northwest cuisine. The accommodations
themselves are large and comfy, simply furnished; six boast a living room. Breakfast (homemade cereal, pastries, jam) is included
for guests; there's a hot tub at water's edge. What more could anyone need? ~ 8841 Route 99, Whistler; 604-932-0688, 888-870-
9065, fax 604-932-0686; www.edgewater-lodge.com. DELUXE.

Tucked away in a subalpine valley northwest of Whistler
Village, **Callaghan Backcountry Lodge** can be reached only by   ◀ HIDDEN
snowcat. Nestled amid a grove of cedars, the chaletlike lodge itself has eight private rooms, a fireplace-warmed sitting area,
games and lounging facilities; it can handle groups up to 22.
Meals are catered for guests, and since the rate includes all meals,
it's not as steep as a night at some of Whistler's high-end properties. And the skiing! Simply strap on your skis and head out
the door into the valley, which will be the site of the Nordic
events during the 2010 Olympics (and the lodge will no longer
be so remote). ~ Callaghan Valley; 604-938-0616, fax 604-932-
5251; www.callaghancountry.com. DELUXE.

The **Farmhouse B&B** is on ten pastoral acres outside Pem-   ◀ HIDDEN
berton, overlooking meadows in the foreground and the steep,
snowy pitches of Mount Currie in the near distance. The house
itself contains an extensive library and collection of regional art.
The three guest rooms have country furnishings and share baths.
The full farm breakfast includes oodles of fresh fruit and potatoes. ~ 7611 Meadows Road, Pemberton; 604-894-6205; www.
bbcanada.com/farmhouse, e-mail farmhouse@uniserve.com.
MODERATE.

Pemberton Valley Vineyard & Inn is a deluxe log lodge set in
the middle of pinot gris, chardonnay and other cool-climate grapes
in the Pemberton Valley countryside. More like an inn than a B&B,
each of the three rooms has a private entrance, bath, fireplace
and deck. Although the vines on the property are still young, the
inn's owners make wine with grapes from the Okanagan; be sure
to sample some. ~ 1427 Collins Road, Pemberton; 604-894-5857,
877-444-5857; www.whistlerwine.com, e-mail bradner@whistler
wine.com. BUDGET TO MODERATE.

Any town populated by climbers, boarders, rafters and other out-   **DINING**
door types needs a good burger bar. In Squamish, **Mountain
Burger House** is a hugely popular hangout. Its hamburgers, sandwiches, breakfasts (served 24 hours) and other staples are sizeable and economical, and the tableside conversation ranges from

windy (sailboarders) to stony (climbers). ~ 38198 Cleveland Avenue, Squamish; 604-892-5544. BUDGET.

The abundance of fresh seafood at the **Crab Shack** is complemented by nautical decor and an oyster bar. In addition, you can order pasta, steak or chicken while cracking jokes with the entertaining wait staff. There's occasional live music in the bar. ~ 4005 Whistler Way, Whistler; 604-932-4451, fax 604-938-0118; www.whistlercrabshack.com, e-mail crabshack@telus.net. DELUXE TO ULTRA-DELUXE.

Araxi, a bright and airy restaurant with congenial staff, has been a dependable favorite in town since its beginning. The menu features creative Italian cuisine. Breads, sausages and pasta are all house-made. The dining room is often overflowing with customers, while the bar is best for a rousing drink with your friends. The huge selection of craft beers and single malt scotches is a popular draw for after-ski revelers. ~ 4222 Whistler Village Square, Whistler; 604-932-4540, fax 604-932-3348; www.araxi.com, e-mail araxi@direct.ca. MODERATE TO DELUXE.

Auntie Em's Kitchen is one of Whistler's better soup-and-sandwich cafés. Nothing fancy, but you get a good, quick meal for your money. The morning muffin selection is exceptional. Breakfast, lunch and dinner. ~ 4340 Lorimer Road, Whistler; 604-932-1163. BUDGET.

HIDDEN ▶ At **Ingrid's Village Café** the tradition of savory home cooking continues in this family-owned tiny bistro on the village plaza a few minutes from the central lift base. Soups and bulging sandwiches are fresh-made daily; breakfasts are heaping platters of eggs, potatoes, toast and sausage. It's hard to find a better value in Whistler. ~ 4305 Skiers Approach, Whistler; 604-932-7000. BUDGET.

Of the several Japanese restaurants in Whistler Village, **Sushi Village** is the one locals visit most often. This place is busy, so service can be slow to a fault, but the atmosphere is serene, the decor clean-cut and the food quite good, especially the tasty tempura and à la carte sushi items. ~ 4272 Mountain Square, Whistler; 604-932-3330; e-mail sushivil@whooshnet.com. MODERATE TO DELUXE.

Another romantic spot slightly removed from the bustle of the central village is **The Wildflower**, an elegant restaurant decorated to echo the Old World charm of its setting in the Fairmont Château Whistler. The award-winning chef focuses on fresh Pacific Northwest cuisine featuring organically grown regional herbs, veggies, fruits, eggs and meat. Seafood is also a specialty of the house, with a Tuesday-night buffet. The Sunday brunch is a bargain considering the quality, as is the breakfast buffet. ~ 4599 Château Boulevard, Whistler; 604-938-2033, 800-866-5377, fax 604-938-2020; www.fairmont.com. MODERATE TO ULTRA-DELUXE.

Caramba! sounds Mexican, but it's really not. It's comfort food—black-bean soup, roast chicken, grilled salmon, pizzas from an alder wood–fired oven. Yes, there's even macaroni and cheese. ~ 4314 Main Street #12, Whistler; 604-938-1879. BUDGET TO MODERATE.

With high-octane coffee, high-energy baristas, high-carb pastries (this is not Atkins land) and great soups and sandwiches for midday munching, **Moguls Bakery and Cafe** is a one-stop beverage and culinary fuel station for visitors headed out for a day of activity. ~ 4202 Village Square, Whistler; 604-932-4845. BUDGET.

Il Caminetto di Umberto is one of the pioneers of fine Whistler cuisine, and has been awash in a sea of publicity as a result. Magazine readers frequently vote it tops among the resort's restaurants, and there's no question that its Northern Italian–tinged fare, favoring B.C. ingredients, is excellent. The decor is dark and romantic, but the atmosphere crowded and cheery. The service is polished. If you like restaurants with flash and dash that also deliver the goods—good food—this is a great choice. It does get crowded: reservations are highly advised. ~ 4242 Village Stroll, Whistler; 604-932-4442. DELUXE.

Citta's Bistro is popular chiefly for its outdoor tables, which in good weather are filled to overflowing with customers doing as much people-watching as anything else—the vantage over the main plaza in Whistler Village is perfect. For food you'll find mainstream bistro sandwiches, pizzas, nachos and such. This is a place to see and be seen. ~ 4232 Village Stroll, Whistler; 604-932-4177. MODERATE.

There's no mistaking the underlying chophouse philosophy at **Bearfoot Bistro**—fine meats and wines, a cigar room appended to the dining area. No tofu or alfalfa sprouts here: beef, lamb and hearty fish dishes are the menu mainstays, and the cigar selection

AUTHOR FAVORITE

The food at **La Rua** is quite simply fantastic. This inconspicuous Blackcomb restaurant concentrates on West Coast cuisine, which it executes flawlessly. Local ingredients such as Pemberton sheep cheese, salmon, lamb and potatoes are stirred in succulent and inventive concoctions—a plate of brie pan-fried with blue cornmeal, sun-dried tomatoes and pine nuts, for instance. The soups are thick and rich, the pastas wildly flavored, the service superb. I never miss a chance to try the house-made ice creams and sorbets. Dinner only. ~ Le Chamois, 4557 Blackcomb Way, Whistler; 604-932-5011. DELUXE.

leans to equally hearty Cubans. The decor is wood, rattan, tile and stone. Reservations are advised on weekends. Dinner only. ~ 4121 Village Green, Whistler; 604-932-3433. DELUXE.

HIDDEN ► **Gone Bakery & Soup Company** has two notable virtues: its breads, soups, sandwiches and salads are all made fresh every morning, and they're bargains—by any standard, let alone the rarified price structure that prevails at Whistler. You can have lunch here for less than US$5 (C$8). It's a bit hard to find, hidden in a corner of Village Square. Ask around—locals will surely be able to direct you. If you want the full selection, show up before 1:30—the best items sell out early. ~ 4205 Village Square, Whistler; 604-905-4663. BUDGET.

Pony Espresso is quintessential Pemberton—down-home, funky, dependable, economical. The decor is remarkable: recycled wood paneling, mismatched chairs, an entertaining bulletin board—looking for a local anti-logging protest? Good coffee drinks, fine muffins and scones, and panini for lunch. At dinner, it turns into an eclectic bistro with pasta, fish and sandwiches. ~ 1426 Portage Road, Pemberton; 604-894-5700. BUDGET.

Locals love **Pamela's Cook Shack** for its hearty, down-to-earth and economical platters of home cooking—breakfast plates piled high with eggs, hash browns, toast, sausage and pancakes; heaping sandwiches and rich soups. Its roadside ambience doesn't look like much, but the food sticks with you. ~ 1961 Sea to Sky Highway, Pemberton; 604-894-3677. BUDGET TO MODERATE.

SHOPPING As a village, however recent its development, Whistler has attempted mightily to create the sort of folksy, small-town atmosphere that is marked worldwide by small specialty shops lining winding streets. It succeeds to a remarkable extent: what detracts from this ambience the most is the invasion of international upscale brand stores that are identical to those you'll find in other glitzy resorts.

Most of the best shopping in Whistler is done in the village, where you can wander the paved walkways to discover specialty shops like **Mountain Craft Gallery**, with its wide range of items in glass, bronze, ceramic, wood, textile and new media. ~ 4295 Blackcomb Way #101, Whistler; 604-932-5001.

Outdoor lovers will appreciate the assortment of climbing and hiking gear and backcountry equipment available at **The Mountain Shop**. ~ Delta Mountain Plaza, Whistler; 604-932-2203. **Escape Route North** also carries the latest in adventure gear. ~ 4350 Lorimer Road #113, Whistler; 604-938-3228. **Fanatyk Co.** offers all the latest equipment, boots and clothing for the serious snow shredder. ~ 4433 Sundial Place #6 (in St. Andrews House), Whistler; 604-938-9455.

Chocoholics will be in seventh heaven at the **Rocky Mountain Chocolate Factory**, one of a chain of similar stores. ~ 4190 Springs Lane, Whistler; 604-932-4100.

Several shops in Town Plaza offer more distinctive fare than the usual. The man-size stuffed bear outside **Bear Pause** isn't for sale, but if he were, the price would run past $4000. Inside is a fine selection of more sensible bears, ranging from C$15 to $150, including some in collectors' series. Why would teddy bears be collectibles? Stop in and ask. ~ 4314 Main Street #19, Whistler; 604-905-0121. A few doors away, **Escents Aromatherapy of Whistler** starts with essential oils—rosemary, lavender and such— and adds a dizzying array of lotions, oils, soaps, scents, potions and emollients. ~ Town Plaza, 4314 Main Street #20, Whistler; 604-905-2955.

The cigar craze continues to thrive in Whistler, and connoisseurs certainly have their choice—there are four purveyors in town. **Whistler Cigar Co. Limited** is the best, with a fine selection and reasonable prices. They'll happily deliver to local hotels. ~ 4557 Blackcomb Way, Whistler; 604-905-2423. Like its parent store in Vancouver, **Vancouver Cigar Company's** Whistler branch is large and plentifully stocked, with a large walk-in humidor, but definitely pricey. Of course, when you want a truly fine cigar, price should be of little object. ~ 4314 Town Plaza #31, Whistler; 604-932-6099, 800-766-5318.

The Plaza Galleries have a unique distinction: among their artists are celebrities such as Tony Curtis and Anthony Quinn. Keep your eyes open for the occasional Rembrandt or Picasso, too. It's all very ritzy. ~ 4314 Main Street #22, Whistler; 604-938-6233.

The Grocery Store is what it's called, and that's exactly what it is. This main village institution is notable for two things: it's a community center of sorts, with a vast bulletin board and steps out front perfect for meeting folks. It's also remarkably well-stocked for such a tiny space; if you're in a kitchen unit at

FLIP OUT!

Here's an astoundingly clever attraction set up each summer at the foot of Blackcomb Mountain, circus trapeze instruction from **Blackcomb Aerial**. Kids (and especially nervy adults) are taught basic skills by professional acrobats, and then make their own first flight, all safely belayed. It's impossible to bring a youngster near this without provoking wide-eyed amazement. Fee. ~ Located just south of Fairmont Château Whistler; 604-932-3434.

Whistler, you can get almost anything you'd need here, at surprisingly reasonable prices. ~ 4211 Village Square, Whistler; 604-932-6222.

Armchair Books is small, but it stocks an intriguing collection of tomes for every kind of reader, going far beyond the usual bestseller mentality at the major chain stores. Social commentary and philosophy are strong points. ~ 4201 Village Square, Whistler; 604-932-5557.

Tired of all the upscale foofaraw? Head over to Pemberton, where the biggest shopping experience is the general store, and just outside town, at **North Arm Farm**, the inventory ranges from asparagus to zucchini. Some of the crops, such as raspberries and strawberries, are available for picking by visitors; at any rate, with a wide variety of fruit and vegetables, any visitor is bound to find something to like. Closed November through April. ~ 1888 Sea to Sky Highway (3 miles/5 km east of Pemberton); 604-894-5379, fax 604-894-6650.

Pique, a free weekly, is an interesting and dynamic guide to Whistler community events, entertainment and dining, available not only in Whistler but at numerous cafés in Vancouver as well.

NIGHTLIFE You'll find a good selection of lounges, taverns and discos in Whistler Village. The après-ski scene is big everywhere—one of the most popular spots is the **Longhorn Saloon**, with a deejay nightly and one of Whistler's largest dancefloors. Live bands play periodically, too. ~ Carleton Lodge, Whistler; 604-932-5999. At **Buffalo Bill's Bar & Grill**, nightly entertainment ranges from comedy on Tuesdays to party music on weekends. ~ 4122 Village Green, Whistler; 604-932-6613.

Rustic and rowdy **Garfinkel's** offers a variety of music, including reggae and jazz. Cover for live shows. ~ 14308 Main Street, Whistler; 604-932-2323. The glitzier **Savage Beagle Bar** has an eclectic mix of sounds: hip-hop, house, classic rock and salsa. ~ 4222 Village Stroll, Whistler; 604-938-3337. **Maxx Fish** caters to a teen and early-20s crowd with hip-hop and house grooves. Fans of the weird shouldn't miss the nightclub's occasional "foam party." Yes, that's exactly what it sounds like. ~ 4228 Village Stroll, Whistler; 604-932-1904.

The **Boot Pub** is one of Whistler's most popular hangouts. Located in the Shoestring Lodge, a bargain hotel along Route 99, this tavern fills nightly with a twenty- and thirty-something crowd there to listen to an eclectic lineup of Celtic, rock, groove and folk-rock. Free pool on Sunday. ~ 7124 Nancy Greene Drive, Whistler; 604-932-3338.

Tommy Africa's is the place for dance and groove music. ~ 4216 Gateway Drive #101, Whistler; 604-932-6090.

The slate at **Moe Joe's** ranges from movies on Monday and disco on Tuesday to live bands (mostly rock) on weekends. ~ 4115 Golfers Approach, Whistler; 604-935-1152.

The refined **Mallard Bar**, with a large fireplace, soft piano music and expansive views of the Blackcomb Mountain base, is infinitely suitable for a quiet drink with friends. ~ Fairmont Château Whistler, 4599 Château Boulevard, Whistler; 604-938-8000.

The **Bearfoot Bistro** offers a neighboring wine bar and champagne lounge for late-night relaxation and live jazz acts. ~ 4121 Village Green, Whistler; 604-932-3433.

PORTEAU COVE PROVINCIAL PARK   **BEACHES & PARKS**
Porteau Cove is a favorite among scuba enthusiasts because of its sunken ships and concrete reefs full of marine life located not far off the rocky beach. This long, narrow park stretches along the BC Rail tracks on the east shore of picturesque Howe Sound. Swimmers and kayakers are also welcome. Restrooms, showers, picnic facilities, an amphitheater and a divers' changing room are available. Parking fee, $5. ~ Located off the Sea to Sky Highway, 15 miles north of Horseshoe Bay; 604-898-3678.

▲ There are 59 developed sites for tents and RVs (no hookups); C$22 per night. You'll also find 15 walk-in campsites; C$10 per night. Very popular, reservations recommended.

STAWAMUS CHIEF PROVINCIAL PARK Aside from the famed monolith, which draws climbers from around the world, this park has some short woodsy hikes and a steep trail to the top of the Chief. ~ On Route 99, just past Shannon Falls and just before coming into Squamish.

▲ There are 63 developed vehicle sites at a former unofficial climbers' campground, turned into a public park in 1995; C$8 per night.

ALICE LAKE PROVINCIAL PARK This 900-acre park is tucked up against towering Coast Range mountains, with deep forests surrounding the small lake. Picnicking, canoeing, swimming and general loafing are all pleasant options here. ~ Located nine miles (13 km) north of Squamish along Route 99; 604-898-3678; wlapwww.gov.bc.ca/bcparks.

▲ The 88 developed sites around the lake fill up very early on weekends; C$18.50 per night.

GARIBALDI PROVINCIAL PARK Named for Mount Garibaldi, its crowning point, this awe-inspiring park is made up of 480,000 acres of intriguing lavaland, glaciers, high alpine fields, lakes and dense forests of fir, cedar, hemlock, birch and pine. Much of the terrain is wilderness; it's often considered the true backcountry experience closest to Vancouver, and Garibaldi's

196 established wilderness walk-in campsites represent the highest number in any B.C. provincial park. Thirty-six miles of developed trails lead into the five most popular spots—Black Tusk/ Garibaldi Lake, Diamond Head, Singing Pass, Cheakamus and Wedgemont Lake. All the trails depart from points along Route 99, including one within Whistler Village. You'll find restrooms; picnic tables; shelters; and nature, bike and cross-country ski trails (biking is restricted to the Cheakamus area).

Exploring beyond these spots, Garibaldi Park also consists of forest canyons, high-alpine tundra, and permanent snowfields and glaciers, all of which are rarely reached by visitors. In the brief summer (July through September) those who do venture deeper into the park experience an awesome landscape of volcanic peaks and mesas, flower-strewn meadows, deep forests and towering peaks.

You can try for rainbow and Dolly Varden trout in most of the park's lakes—especially Mamquam (Diamond Head area), Garibaldi, Cheakamus, Russet and Barrier—but swimming is *very* cold. Garibaldi attracts climbers and mountain bikers, but most park visitors are simply there to hike and take in the magnificent scenery. Parking fee, $3. ~ Located 40 miles north of Vancouver off the Sea to Sky Highway (Route 99), north of Squamish; 604-898-3678; wlapwww.gov.bc.ca/bcparks.

▲ There is a 34-bunk hike-in shelter with propane stoves (seven-mile hike) at Diamond Head; you must bring your own gear; C$10 per night. There are two hike-in campgrounds at Garibaldi Lake (six-mile hike); with propane stoves; C$5 per night. Camping is also permitted at several other designated sites throughout the park; some have huts, all are walk-in; open fires are prohibited everywhere.

BRANDYWINE FALLS PROVINCIAL PARK 🏃 🛶 The high light of this small park is its 230-foot waterfall; winding nature trails are also close at hand. The sparsely wooded campsites perched

I SPY A BALD EAGLE

In winter, when more than 3000 bald eagles arrive to roost in the Squamish River's cottonwoods and feast on spawning salmon, the **Brackendale Art Gallery** offers maps and information as well as daily guided walking tours of the eagle reserve in December and January. Call ahead to book tours. ~ On Government Road, Brackendale; 604-898-3333. Farther downriver, trumpeter swans alight in the Squamish River delta in the late fall. Call the Squamish Chamber of Commerce for more information. ~ 604-892-9244.

alongside the highway can be a bit noisy at high-traffic times (weekends). There are restrooms, picnic facilities, fire pits, and nature and hiking trails. Parking fee, $3. ~ Located approximately 60 miles north of Vancouver on the Sea to Sky Highway (Route 99); 604-898-3678; wlapwww.gov.bc.ca/bcparks.

▲ There are 15 developed sites; C$14 per night.

NAIRN FALLS PROVINCIAL PARK 🏃 ⏝ A thundering waterfall is the centerpiece of this small park on the road between Whistler and Pemberton. The waters of the Green River pour through a deep cleft in the granite, creating a roar that not only testifies to nature's power but mutes the sound of the nearby highway. A short (1 mile/1.5 km) trail leads to the vantage point overlooking the falls. ~ About three miles (5 km) south of Pemberton, 15 miles north of Whistler, along Route 99; 604-898-3678.

▲ The 88 sites fill up early on weekends; C$12 per night.

BIRKENHEAD LAKE PROVINCIAL PARK 🏃 🚲 🏕 ⚓ ⏝ 🏊 ⛵ ⏝ This somewhat remote park, at the end of an 11-mile (18 km) gravel road, offers a spectacular Coast Range setting, with a pretty lake, deep forests, abundant wildlife and good fishing. Moose, bears and mountain goats are among the indigenous animals; fish include kokanee salmon, rainbow trout, Dolly Varden and whitefish. ~ Located 11 miles northwest of Devine; follow the signs from Route 342; 604-898-3678.

◄ *HIDDEN*

▲ There are 85 vehicle campsites and 6 walk-in sites; C$12 per night.

It's no surprise, with soaring mountains, rumbling rivers and streams, gem-colored lakes and every kind of weather imaginable, that the Whistler area is famed for its recreation—not just skiing, but hiking, fishing, river sports, sailboarding and climbing. Squamish is the mecca for serious boarders, climbers and such; Whistler offers more sedate activities, ranging from golf to horseback riding. Outfitters and guides for virtually every endeavor are available in all three towns: Squamish, Whistler and Pemberton. The **Whistler Valley Adventure Center** is a central clearinghouse for all of the resort's various guided and unguided adventure enterprises. ~ 4283 Mountain Square, Whistler; 604-932-6392.

▼▼▼▼▼▼▼▼▼▼▼▼▼▼
Outdoor Adventures

In the coastal waters of Howe Sound, chinook, coho, chum, pink and sockeye salmon and halibut, sole and rockfish abound in season. In the mountain streams, you can fish for rainbow trout, Dolly Varden, steelhead or kokanee salmon. Be sure to check on regulations and procure the necessary licenses (see Fishing in Chapter One for details on these matters).

FISHING

Whistler Fishing Guides is an assortment of local experts on area angling techniques and locales. ~ 604-932-4267.

Steve's Fishin' supplies everything you'll need for a guided fishing trip on the Squamish or Mamquam River. ~ Box 12, Squamish, BC V0N 3G0; 604-892-5529.

RIVER RUNNING

There are mountains, glaciers and waterfalls visible from guided rafting trips on several local rivers, including the Green and Squamish.

Sunwolf Outdoor Centre takes float trips down the Squamish and other area rivers. ~ 70002 Squamish Valley Road, Brackendale; 604-898-1537. One of B.C.'s most arresting sights is that of winter-bare cottonwoods festooned with thousands of bald eagles along the Squamish River. Dress warm—very warm—for eagle-watching float trips pioneered by **Canadian Outback Adventures**, a Vancouver company. They'll pick you up at your Vancouver or Whistler lodging. ~ 657 Marine Drive Suite 100, West Vancouver; 604-921-7250, 800-565-8735; www.canadian outback.com.

CANOEING & KAYAKING

Whistler's five beautiful lakes are ideal locations for canoeing and kayaking. Rentals and tours are available through **Whistler Outdoor Experience Co.** from mid-May to mid-October. You'll see waterfalls and bird life on a self-guided tour of the serene River of Golden Dreams. ~ Fairmont Château Whistler or Edgewater Lodge; 604-932-3389. **Sea to Sky Kayaking** offers instruction and rentals. ~ 2557 Mamquam Road #101, Squamish; 604-983-6663. In Pemberton, **Canadian Voyageur Canoe Co.** leads leisurely excursions on the Lillooet and Ryan rivers. ~ Pemberton; 604-894-5900.

The **Squamish Spit**, a narrow neck of land at the juncture of the Squamish River and Howe Sound, has wind conditions perfect for windsurfing. It's becoming almost as famous as the Columbia

BEST OF BOTH WORLDS

In summer, the ski resort and local golf operators collaborate to offer **Ski & Golf Esprit**, or "ski & tee," which provides two mornings of ski instruction on Blackcomb Glacier followed by two afternoon rounds of golf, including a clinic and a caddy, at two of the best valley courses. The service runs from the end of June to the end of July. It's a bit pricey (about US$350/ C$550) but how many people can say they've skied and golfed in the same day? Includes lunch and lift tickets; you provide your own stamina. ~ 604-932-3434.

Gorge farther south. **North Shore Ski & Sailboard** in North Vancouver provides rentals as well as area information. ~ 1625 Lonsdale Avenue, North Vancouver; 604-987-7245.

Although the Stawamus Chief is the most prominent and most-utilized climbing attraction in the area, Garibaldi Provincial Park holds a number of wilderness climbs, including the Black Tusk. Reaching the Garibaldi destinations involves major expeditions since it is a daunting backcountry park.

Squamish area cliffs and walls are not for novices, but several local shops offer equipment, instruction and general advice to interested visitors. **Slipstream Rock & Ice** provides rock climbing instruction and guides. ~ Box 219, Brackendale, BC V0N 1H0; 604-898-4891, 800-616-1325. **Squamish Rock Guides** offers climbing tours and lessons for all levels. ~ Box 1786, Squamish, BC V0N 3G0; 604-815-1750; www.squamishrock guides.com. **Vertical Reality Sports Store** rents and sells rock-climbing equipment; they also have tour packages available. ~ 38154 2nd Avenue, Squamish; 604-892-8248.

The **Whistler Alpine Guides Bureau** maintains a roster of certified guides who can lead climbing expeditions into the rugged mountains of Garibaldi Park. ~ 604-938-9242; www.whistler guides.com. Whistler guests can hone their outdoor rock skills indoors at the **Great Wall Underground**. ~ 4340 Sundial Crest, Whistler; 604-905-7625.

The Whistler area has achieved considerable renown as a golf destination. Two courses along Route 99 would make good golf stops on the way to Whistler. **Furry Creek Golf & Country Club**, south of Squamish, offers great views of the Squamish Valley and Howe Sound. ~ Route 99, 11 miles (16 km) south of Squamish; 604-896-2224. **Squamish Valley Golf & Country Club** is between Squamish and Whistler. ~ 2458 Mamquam Road, Squamish; 604-898-9521.

Top-caliber courses wind along the valley and the scenery is hard to beat. The **Whistler Golf Club** is an 18-hole public course designed by Arnold Palmer with five lakes and two creeks. ~ 4001 Whistler Way, Whistler; 604-932-3280.

The narrow, mountainous **Château Whistler Golf Club** course is surrounded by trees and has scenic views of Blackcomb and Whistler mountains. Designed by Robert Trent Jones, Jr., the elevation gain is more than 400 feet—and you'll know exactly how much it changes every step of the way, because the club's golf carts have onboard GPS computers that figure yardage, elevation and other factors. (Club selection is still up to you.) ~ 4612 Blackcomb Way, Whistler; 604-938-2092.

Nicklaus North Golf Club, the second course in Canada designed by Jack Nicklaus, winds along Green Lake five minutes from the main village. ~ 8080 Nicklaus North Boulevard, Whistler; 604-938-9898.

Designed by Robert Cupp and set at the foot of breathtakingly precipitous Mount Currie in Garibaldi Park, **Big Sky Golf and Country Club** is in the upper end of the Pemberton Valley 25 minutes from Whistler. The 7001-yard course offers mountain views in every direction. Child care is available at the club. ~ 1690 Airport Road, Pemberton; 604-894-6106.

Pemberton Valley Golf & Country Club is a championship course with fabulous mountain views from its lowland setting. ~ 1730 Airport Road, Pemberton; 604-894-6197.

RIDING STABLES

What do you do with ski-mountain access roads in the summer? Turn them over to horses, among other things; riding aficionados can depart from the lift base for scenic half-day or full-day treks. The other popular riding area is the beautiful Pemberton Valley, a pastoral lowland surrounded by shimmering high peaks.

In Squamish, **Sea to Sky Stables** offers trail rides, wagon rides and, in the winter, sleigh rides. October-to-March eagle tours on horse back follows the Cheakamus River—you'll spy osprey, bald eagles and golden eagles. ~ Off Route 99, on Squamish Valley Road, about eight miles north of Squamish; 604-898-3934; www.seatoskystables.com.

Whistler Outdoor Experience Co. leads guided rides during the summer through the Pemberton Meadows and along Ryan Creek and the Lillooet River. Winter sleigh rides provide views of glacier-fed Green Lake and a ring of mountains. ~ 8841 Route 99; 604-932-3389, 877-386-1888. The **Blackcomb/Whistler** resorts collaborate to offer horseback rides from the base of the two mountains in the summer. ~ By the Whistler/Blackcomb ticket lodge at the base of the Blackcomb gondola; 604-932-3434.

In Pemberton, **Pemberton Stables** takes guided rides and overnight pack trips through the valley's unmatched scenery. ~ P.O. Box 7, Pemberton, BC V0N 2L0; 604-894-6615. The setting for **Punch Creek Trail Rides** in the valley north of Pemberton is simply spectacular. With towering peaks overhead, and lovely woods and meadows below, one- and two-hour rides are leisurely and serene. Small groups mean little waiting, ample individual attention. ~ Pemberton Meadows Road, ten miles (18 km) north of Pemberton; 604-894-6086.

BIKING

Mountain biking on rough alpine trails or paved paths around Lost Lake and along the Valley Trail, which connects the village with nearby residential areas, parks and lakes, is the rage on summer days. Daredevils go for the mountain descents, often taking a helicopter or gondola to the peaks so they don't expend the energy needed for zooming down the dry ski runs.

The Slippery
Slopes

No other area in North America offers the expanse of Whistler's vertical drop and alpine village atmosphere. From top to bottom it's exactly one mile, 5280 feet; there are 7071 acres of skiable terrain, including vast areas of glacier and snowfield; dozens of lifts can haul more than 52,000 skiers an hour. No surprise that more than two million skiers a year come to Whistler—one of the few resorts on earth that can claim that many customers.

For all that, side-by-side Whistler and Blackcomb mountains are known for their informal, family-friendly atmosphere. Locals worried that the character might change when the corporation that owns Blackcomb, Intrawest, took over Whistler in 1998; but the atmosphere so far seems unchanged.

For those interested in such distinctions, Blackcomb is the haunt of the experts and snowboarders, Whistler the family mountain. A leisurely descent down Whistler's meandering green trails affords the beginner a couple hours of bucolic gliding. On the other hand, the Blackcomb Glacier offers hot dogs unparalleled steeps and drops.

You could spend a week here and not ski any slope twice. In addition to all of Whistler's perks, the prices benefit from that U.S./Canada exchange rate—an adult ticket is far less (US$55/C$75 or so) than at any major resort in the United States. Furthermore, the snow's great. It averages 30 feet a year, and is set just far enough back from the marine influence to be reasonably dry. Ski zealots throughout North America consider Whistler, quite simply, the best. Blackcomb and Whistler mountains each offer boarders a snowboard park outfitted with half-pipes.

Between the two mountains, skiers will find 34 lifts (including more than a dozen high-speed gondolas and quad lifts) taking them to more than 200 marked runs. Ski and snowboard lessons are available for those just starting out. The official season runs from late November through May, then starts again for glacier skiing in mid-June. ~ Resort information, 4165 Springs Lane, Whistler; 604-932-3434, 800-766-0449; www. whistler-blackcomb.com.

Bike Rentals & Tours   In business since 1985, **Whistler Backroads Mountain Bike Adventures** is Whistler's original mountain-bike tour company. Tours range from easy sightseeing rides through the valley to customized excursions over challenging terrain. Combination trips incorporating biking, kayaking, hiking and rock climbing are also popular. If bikes aren't your thing, you can also embark on canoeing excursions or naturalist-led walks. Closed in winter. ~ 604-932-3111, fax 604-932-1204; www.backroadswhistler.com.

Bike rentals at the foot of the Whistler gondola are supplied by **Glacier Shop**, along with expert advice on the most appropriate way to get back down from the top. ~ Whistler Village Gondola base; 604-905-2252.

Corsa Cycles is the bike rental place in Squamish. They also offer bike tours. ~ 38128 Cleveland Avenue, Squamish; 604-892-3331; www.corsacycles.com.

Whistler Outdoor Experience Co. offers a guided descent of Blackcomb Mountain as well as slower-paced bike tours of parks and lakes. ~ 8841 Route 99; 604-932-3389, 877-386-1888.

HIKING   Garibaldi Provincial Park, one of the premier wilderness enclaves in southern British Columbia, backs Whistler to the south and is thus the most popular hiking destination from the resort valley (and Squamish). Several moderate trails lead to pretty alpine meadows; more serious treks head back toward the virtually impassable Garibaldi highlands. There is also good hiking in the mountains around Pemberton, with numerous developed trails.

All distances listed for hiking trails are one way unless otherwise noted.

WHISTLER   There are trails in the Whistler area for all levels. **Valley Trail** (15 miles/24 km roundtrip) is a bustling paved walkway/bike path/cross-country ski trail that winds through town, connecting Alpha, Nita, Alta, Lost and Green lakes, the village

For a neck-craning view of the Stawamus Chief, the famous monolith that brings climbers here from around the world, follow the very steep gravel **Stawamus Chief Trail** (2 miles/4 km) from the south end of the parking lot, around the concrete barricade onto the pavement remnants of the old highway. After 300 feet (100 meters), follow the heavily used climbers' path into the woods on the right, which brings you to the base of the granite wall in about ten minutes. *Please note:* Climbing on the monolith itself is for trained, equipped and experienced experts only.

and the various residential areas. ~ Access at dozens of places in town—the main parking area is a central starting point.

Lost Lake Trails (12 miles/22 km total) serve as cross-country ski trails during the winter and make for fairly level summer hiking paths (with some paved areas) through the forested area between Lost and Green lakes. In the winter, access to the tracked paths and log warming hut is under a fee ticket system (children and seniors free). ~ 604-932-6436.

Singing Pass–Russet Lake (6.75 miles/11 km), an alpine hiking trail up the Fitzsimmons Creek Valley just behind Whistler Village, and the graded **Garibaldi Lake Trail** (5.5 miles/9 km), located off Route 99 south of town, are both prime options for experienced hikers interested in heading to the steep fringes of Garibaldi Provincial Park. The trail to Garibaldi Lake leads into the heart of the park, past a phenomenal geologic formation known as the Barrier—a mountainslide that forms the dam creating the upper valley's lakes. Two overnight shelters are found on the far shore of Garibaldi Lake, and beyond that are hundreds of square miles of untracked wilderness and rugged alpine terrain. ~ The Garibaldi Lake trailhead is just south of Daisy Lake along Route 99.

The **Rainbow Lake Trail** (4 miles/7 km) offers a less-crowded trek into alpine country, passing first through established second-growth fir/hemlock/cedar forest, then topping out at the lake amid alpine meadows at about 4300 feet/1455 meters. ~ Trailhead is on Alta Lake Road just south of Alpine Meadows.

The **Whistler Interpretive Forest** southwest of the main village holds trails of diverse length, character and difficulty. The **Riparian Interpretive Trail** (1 km) leads through young forest with numerous signs identifying the various trees and shrubs, including most of the major coastal species. The **Riverside Trail** (3 miles/4.5 km) leads along the Cheakamus River, offering access along the way to more demanding mountain trails and several lakes in the interior. ~ Route 99 at "Function Junction," three miles (5 km) west of Whistler Village.

PEMBERTON AREA The short walk into the **Joffre Lakes Provincial Recreation Area** (1 mile/2 km) is scenic and not particularly taxing, and makes a good rest break along the last leg of the Sea to Sky Highway for those driving to Lillooet. ~ Located seven miles (11 km) east of Mount Currie along Route 99.

The western trailhead for one of B.C.'s most famous and daunting wilderness hikes, the **Stein Valley** traverse, is at Lizzie Falls, ten miles (16 km) south of Mount Currie (see the Hiking section in Chapter Seven).

Blackcomb Helicopters offers visitors the chance to experience the growing Canadian phenomenon of airborne drop-in hiking. Four-hour excursions—from beginner to advanced—are offered June through September. ~ 8621 Fissile Lane, Whistler; 604-938-1700; www.blackcombhelicopters.com.

Transportation

CAR

Route 99 is the highway to and through Whistler from Vancouver; theoretically, this is the same Route 99 that begins far south in California and wends its way up the West Coast. The stretch from Horseshoe Bay (the Vancouver Island ferry terminal a half-hour west of the Lions Gate Bridge) northward is the famed **Sea to Sky Highway**, a winding ribbon of pavement that sometimes literally clings to a narrow shelf above the waters of Howe Sound, beneath the towering Coast Mountains. Although you will see hot-shots whizzing by, this road is not for speed demons; aside from the danger and dis-courtesy, it is heavily patrolled by the RCMP, and the province now has a hotline for drivers to report highway cowboys. Be pre-pared for winter conditions past Squamish any time from November to April; signs advise of road conditions ahead.

AIR

Whistler Air Services Ltd. offers twice-daily summer floatplane service between downtown Vancouver and the resort. Whistler-bound flights depart at 9:30 a.m. and 5 p.m. from Coal Harbour. Flights to downtown Vancouver leave Green Lake, located a mile-and-a-half (3 km) north of Whistler Village, at 8:30 a.m. and 4 p.m. ~ 604-932-6615, 888-806-2299.

BUS

Greyhound Bus Lines provides six-times-a-day bus service from Vancouver to Whistler. ~ 1150 Station Street, Vancouver; 604-482-8747 in Vancouver, 604-932-5031 in Whistler; www.grey hound.com.

Whistler Express offers bus service directly from Vancouver International Airport to the resort, six times daily. ~ 604-266-5386 in Vancouver, 604-905-0041 in Whistler.

CAR RENTALS

Rental agencies in Whistler include **Avis Rent A Car** (604-932-1236), **Budget Rent A Car** (604-932-1236, 800-268-8900) and **Thrifty Car Rental** (604-938-0302, 800-367-2277).

PUBLIC TRANSIT

Whistler Transit, the local operator for BC Transit, runs buses connecting Whistler Creek and Whistler Village every 15 min-utes. ~ 604-932-4020.

TAXIS

Cab companies serving Whistler include **Whistler Taxi** (604-932-3333), **Sea to Sky Taxi** (604-932-3333) and **Limojet Gold Limou-sines** (604-273-1331, 800-278-8742), all of which offer flat-rate service between the resort and Vancouver International Airport.

Numerous companies offer airborne sightseeing and charter services in the Whistler area. **Whistler Air Services** (604-932-6615, 888-806-2299), **Blackcomb Helicopters** (604-938-1700), and **Pemberton Helicopters** (604-932-3512) are in the immediate Whistler area. **Glacier Air** (604-898-9016) runs floatplane services in the Squamish area.

AIR TOURS

FIVE

Victoria

Those of us who appreciate Victoria for its many virtues are bemused by the city's "old England" persona. Although not a complete fabrication, it's really no more intrinsic to Victoria than veneer is to an armoire. Yes, there are a number of heritage buildings whose design, heft and character hint at Victorian London. Yes, the B.C. legislature is housed in the "Parliament Building." High tea is a daily tradition—for tourists, at least—and one of the world's finest tea shops is right downtown. There's a wax museum, as British an institution as you can get; and the newspaper features almost daily novelty stories about animals, just like the British tabloids. Victoria's most splendid mansion was built before the turn of the 20th century by a tycoon, Robert Dunsmuir, who built his fortune, like so many British barons, on coal. One of North America's best-known formal gardens, Butchart Gardens, draws thousands of visitors daily at its summer peak, and handsome rose gardens abound throughout the city. Trim, well-kept homes with neat lawns line tidy streets.

This heritage is absolutely genuine: founded in 1843 as a Hudson's Bay Company post and made a colonial capital in 1862, Victoria was indeed one of the outposts of the British Empire. Ships that pulled into the Inner Harbour in the 1880s might well have departed Hong Kong or Sydney six weeks before.

So far, sounds quite British indeed. But there is much more to Victoria—starting with the incredible diversity brought by its Asian cultural heritage. After all, the second largest Chinatown in North America was once Victoria's, home to thousands of workers brought over to build railroads. And, like the rest of British Columbia, more recent waves of immigration from across the Pacific have indelibly flavored the city.

Thus the visitor will find an engaging mix of old and new, British and Asian, colonial and New World, all swirled into a sort of postmodern cultural curry that brings Victoria international popularity. Curry, in fact, constitutes one facet of this appeal at the Fairmont Empress, the quintessential Victoria institution: the best meal to be had at the Empress' informal dining room, the Bengal Lounge, is at the lounge's curry buffet bar. In the mornings at the Empress, the breakfast room (Kipling's) serves three types of breakfast: Asian, European and North American. It's the most culturally wide-ranging breakfast buffet you're likely to find anywhere. High tea, however, is still the afternoon standby upstairs in the lobby lounge. And of course you can get beef Wellington at the Empress Room, the hotel's dark-wood-paneled formal dining room.

Even though vestiges of colonial character remain, this is definitely not stiff-upper-lip territory. Dress codes have relaxed, for instance; jeans are welcome at high tea. And the territory beyond the central city offers a dizzying array of landscapes, similar to climbing a steep mountain. Not far outside Victoria you'll find, in succeeding order, expansive suburbs like those in any growing city, pastoral farmland that might seem North European were it not for the distinctive Northwest vegetation, wild storm-tossed ocean coasts, primeval old-growth forests and rugged mountains.

Much of Vancouver Island, in fact, is an untamed land. Stretching 280 miles along the Pacific coastline of Canada and the United States, it encompasses some 12,400 square miles—the size of Holland. Divided by high, steep mountains, most of this mass shields the lower mainland of British Columbia from the torrential rains and gale-force winds brought by the ocean. Because the island does cross the 49th parallel, the general boundary between the United States and Canada, its southern one-fifth, including Victoria, is on the same latitude as parts of Washington State.

Geography and the elements have conspired to make the southern part of the island a haven where farming, tourism and commerce thrive. A number of picturesque villages and towns are perched on the coast outside Victoria—Sooke, with its famed small inns, is especially notable. The Malahat Drive offers fabulous views of Washington's Olympic Mountains, the Gulf Islands and the Saanich Peninsula, which is dotted with small farms, orchards and gardens.

For the most part, the Victoria area's climate is gentle, thanks to the moderating influence of the North Pacific and the rain-shadow effect of the Olympic Mountains to the south. The summers can be blissful with long, sunny, warm (but not hot) days. The climate of Victoria and the southeastern part of the island is akin to that of the Mediterranean—dry, cool summers and mild, rainy, foggy winters. The average July high temperature is 67°F (20°C); the average January high is 43°F (6°C). Eight months of the year are frost-free, and rain is rare in June, July, August and September. It is no accident that many Canadians choose to retire here. In fact, more Canadians retire to Greater Victoria than anywhere else in the country.

Victorians are so fond of their climate that, in an inspired bit of promotional gimmickry, once a year the city undertakes the annual "Blossom Count" during the last week in February. Residents go out in their yards and count how many flowers are blooming—crocuses, daffodils, azaleas, rhododendrons, camellias and so on. They call the number into local radio stations, which add up the total and then publicize it throughout Canada, most of which at that point is snowbound. The annual blossom count number has been as high as four billion (yes, billion with a "b").

Of course, with just a couple minor exceptions residents are not counting native flowers, and the Victoria area's development has not come without some cost. The

Saanich Peninsula once held large tracts of an ecosystem known as oak savannah, very similar to terrain a thousand miles south in California. Today the savannah is almost gone, the rarest ecosystem in Canada, replaced by housing and farms. (You can see hints of what it looked like on Rockland Hill east of downtown Victoria, where a number of beautiful old oaks remain, and in Beacon Hill Park.)

All these facets—climate, geography, cultural history—have combined to create a bucolic lifestyle that somewhat resembles—surprise—parts of southern England. Much of the population is retired working people; small farms and cottage gardens dot the countryside; the *Victoria Times Colonist* even employs a columnist who writes on equestrian matters.

Prior to settlement by white explorers, the island's Native people lived close to the land. The Nootka or Nuu-chah-nulth lived on the west, the Coast Salish to the south and east and the Southern Kwakiutl to the north. These people thrived on the natural bounty of the region, principally the salmon, cedar and wild berries. Spanish explorers first came to the island in 1592, followed by Captain James Cook in 1778. Vancouver Island is the namesake of George Vancouver, the British naval captain who negotiated the island away from Spain in 1795.

In 1843, Hudson's Bay Company representative James Douglas established a fort, named after Britain's Queen Victoria, where Bastion Square sits on Wharf Street today, just above the Inner Harbour, an admirably protected anchorage. Coal mining, fishing, logging and fur trading brought settlers to other parts of the island, and Victoria became the island's commercial, government and cultural center. It filled a similar role for all of British Columbia until the Cariboo gold rush a decade later brought fortune seekers to the mainland.

Fortunately, the island's wealth of wildlife has adapted to human use of the land. Home to all six species of Pacific salmon, the waters surrounding the island make for excellent fishing (although certain stocks are declining) and offer a supply of natural food for orca whales, sea lions and seals. These waters also contain huge numbers of seabirds. The mountains and highlands harbor Roosevelt elk, black bears, blacktail deer, marmots, wolves and cougars—in fact, Vancouver Island is the mountain lion capital of the world, with a greater density of these animals than anywhere else.

Victoria has been the seat of the provincial government since 1868 and is B.C.'s second largest city, but there remains a cozy and quaint look to the place. It overflows with flowers, the yards are graced with tulips, rhododendrons and roses, the window boxes and hanging planters filled with geraniums and lobelia. Victoria's economy rests on the shoulders of government and tourism—just as it has, for the most part, for a century and a half. Almost 20 percent of the city's residents have government jobs, and another 40 percent perform service jobs, reflecting the visitor industry's reliance on three million tourists a year.

The adventurous Vancouver Island visitor can begin a trip with a cosmopolitan day or two in Victoria, staying in an elegant historic hotel, having high tea, shopping and dining in style. Follow that with a wilderness jaunt in deep forests or along storm-tossed shores, trekking the home ground of wolves, bears and eagles. Then return to Victoria for a bit of decompression back in civilized climes.

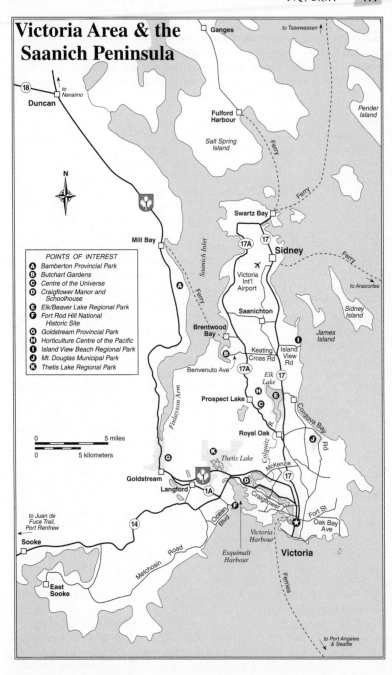

Victoria Area & the Saanich Peninsula

POINTS OF INTEREST

Ⓐ Bamberton Provincial Park
Ⓑ Butchart Gardens
Ⓒ Centre of the Universe
Ⓓ Craigflower Manor and
   Schoolhouse
Ⓔ Elk/Beaver Lake Regional Park
Ⓕ Fort Rod Hill National
   Historic Site
Ⓖ Goldstream Provincial Park
Ⓗ Horticulture Centre of the Pacific
Ⓘ Island View Beach Regional Park
Ⓙ Mt. Douglas Municipal Park
Ⓚ Thetis Lake Regional Park

0   5 miles
0   5 kilometers

Ganges
to Tsawwassen
to Nanaimo
Duncan
18
Pender Island
Fulford Harbour
Salt Spring Island
Swartz Bay
Sidney
17A   17
Mill Bay
Saanich Inlet
Victoria Int'l Airport
to Anacortes
Sidney Island
Saanichton
James Island
Brentwood Bay
Keating Cross Rd
Island View Rd
Benvenuto Ave
17A
Elk Lake
Prospect Lake
Royal Oak
Cordova Bay Rd
Mt. Douglas
McKenzie
17
Thetis Lake
Goldstream
Langford
1A
Craigflower
Fort St
Oak Bay Ave
to Juan de Fuca Trail, Port Renfrew
14
Ocean Blvd
Victoria Harbour
Sooke
Metchosin Road
Esquimalt Harbour
Victoria
East Sooke
Ferries
to Port Angeles & Seattle
Finlayson Arm
Colquitz R
Ferry

▼ ▼ ▼ ▼ ▼ ▼ ▼ ▼ ▼ ▼ ▼ ▼ ▼
Downtown Victoria

The City of Gardens lends itself admirably to walking—with a few exceptions, 90 percent of what's worth seeing can be reached on foot. And that's by far the best way to experience the historic city's amazing variety of shops, cafés and small vendors, concentrated on the north side of downtown.

SIGHTS

The place to get information, and a good place to start a stroll through the city, is the **Travel Info Centre**, on the Inner Harbour. ~ 812 Wharf Street; 250-953-2033, 800-663-3883; www.tourism victoria.com, e-mail info@tourismvictoria.com.

Visitors get a good overview of the city by taking a horse-drawn tour with **Tally-Ho Sightseeing**, whose steeds have been clip-clopping their way through the streets since 1903. ~ Inner Harbour; 866-383-5067, fax 250-920-0181; www.tallyhotours. com.

Another company offering horse-drawn outings is **Victoria Carriage Tours**. ~ Tours leave from the corner of Belleville and Menzies streets; 250-383-2207; www.victoriacarriage.com.

The granite-faced **Inner Harbour promenade** features dozens of plaques honoring the many ships that have played a role in Victoria's history—an apt reminder that the harbor is the reason the city is here, and that in the past it truly was a colonial capital from the days Britain's ships ruled the seas. The harbor docks usually have a number of opulent yachts and sailboats to gawk at, and buskers such as singers and jugglers ply the promenade daily.

The **Fairmont Empress** is Victoria's unofficial central landmark facing the Inner Harbour. Opened in 1908, it reflects the gentility of an earlier time. The Palm Court, with its stained-glass dome, is renowned for afternoon teas and tropical plants. Designed by Francis Rattenbury, the same architect who designed the Parliament, the building is such an icon that the air around it seems filled with fireflies—actually the glimmer of flash bulbs as tourists take snapshots. ~ 721 Government Street; 250-384-8111, fax 250-389-2747; www.fairmont.com.

On the ground floor of the Empress you'll find **Miniature World**, a quintessentially British attraction, with more than 80 diminutive illustrations of history and fantasy. Miniature World includes the world's smallest operational sawmill, two of the world's largest dollhouses and one of the world's largest model railways. Admission. ~ 649 Humboldt Street; 250-385-9731, fax 250-385-2835; www.miniatureworld.com, e-mail info@miniature world.com.

Just east of the Empress is **Crystal Garden**, once an enclosed swimming pool built in 1925 (the largest saltwater pool in the British Empire) and now a glass-roofed tropical aviary with hundreds of colorful blossoms and more than 75 varieties of birds

Two-day Getaway

The West Coast Shore Getaway

Day 1
- Start by heading west out of Victoria on Route 14, Sooke Road, to **Point-No-Point Resort** (page 213), the popular collection of comfortable, semirustic cabins beyond Sooke about 15 minutes. Make sure you've reserved a cabin with a private hot tub on the oceanside deck. After you check in, stroll out on the resort's headland to watch waves crash and see if any whales are passing by.

- Drive back through Sooke and up the Sooke River Road to **Sooke Potholes Provincial Park** (page 214), where a quiet walk in the woods can be followed by a plunge in the river's cool pools.

- Or head for **East Sooke Park** (page 214) for a more demanding hike through native forest of fir and madrona down to rocky headlands along the shore.

- Return to Sooke in time for dinner at **Sooke Harbour House** (page 213). (You made the reservation a month ago, of course.)

- The only sensible thing to do after dinner is to head back to your cabin and sink into the hot tub.

Day 2
- After morning coffee, ask the resort kitchen to pack you a picnic lunch; a day of beachcombing beckons. Head west to **China Beach Provincial Park** (page 215), hiking ten minutes down to this beautiful strand of sand for a leisurely walk.

- **Sombrio Beach** (14 miles/20 km from China Beach on Route 14) is a great place to take your picnic lunch, another ten-minute stroll down to a gravel beach.

- After lunch, the focus shifts from beaches to tidepools at **Botanical Beach Provincial Park** (page 215). At low tide, hundreds of pools are exposed for visitors to look at the colorful marine inhabitants. Leave them there, please. If the day's low tide is in the morning, reverse the day's itinerary to start at Botanical Beach and finish at China Beach.

- Have dinner back at Point-No-Point Resort, whose food is not quite as exotic as Sooke Harbour House's—but the view of the Pacific is unsurpassed and the seafood preparation is expert.

- Back in that hot tub. Hopefully the moon will bronze the Pacific below your room and the memory will fasten indelibly in your mind.

including penguins and flamingos, plus the world's tiniest butterflies in the summer. Kids especially enjoy the remarkably sociable flamingos. Admission. ~ 713 Douglas Street; 250-381-1213, fax 250-383-1218.

Across Belleville Street, just south of the Fairmont Empress, lies a complex anchored by the **Royal British Columbia Museum**, the one attraction all Victoria visitors should make ample time for. Canada's most visited museum focuses on the history of British Columbia—its land and people from prehistoric times to the present—in a personal and evocative way. Visitors sit among totem poles, walk inside a longhouse and learn stories of native people and the changes they encountered. Detailed dioramas depict the island's natural ecosystems, from rainforest to wind-tossed sea stack. Museum guests can also stroll down the streets of Old Town, plunge into the bowels of a coal mine and walk through the *Discovery*, a replica of the ship used by Captain Vancouver. This museum is often the only venue in the country for major international exhibits. Within the museum, the National Geographic IMAX theatre schedules big-screen films about natural, historic and cultural wonders. Admission. ~ 675 Belleville Street; 250-356-7226, 888-447-7977, fax 250-387-5674; www.royalbcmuseum.bc.ca.

Part of the museum complex is **Thunderbird Park**, a postage stamp–sized park covering only a quarter of the block. The park is the site of ten or so magnificent totem poles and a longhouse in which natives demonstrate the crafts of carving and beading during the summer. ~ Belleville and Douglas streets.

Just behind the park, adjacent to the museum is **Helmcken House**, built in 1852 for pioneer doctor J. S. Helmcken. This is British Columbia's oldest residence on its original site. Rooms decorated in the style of the period are furnished with pieces brought around Cape Horn from England by Victoria's founding families. The library includes Dr. Helmcken's medicine chest and medical instruments. Recorded audio presentations narrated by various family members relate tales about the house and family. Call for winter hours. Admission. ~ 10 Elliott Street beside the Royal British Columbia Museum; 250-361-0021, fax 250-356-7796; www.heritage.gov.bc.ca/helm/helm.htm.

HIDDEN ► From here you can take a detour (just a couple blocks south) to a Victorian Italianate cottage known as **Emily Carr House**, where British Columbia landscape painter Emily Carr, a Canadian national heroine, was born in 1871 and lived her girlhood years. Historians have restored the home with period wall coverings and furnishings to make it look as it did when she lived there. Carr was also an author, and her gardens have been re-created from her books, excerpts of which stand on plaques among the vegetation. Closed mid-October to mid-May except the month of December. Admission. ~ 207 Government Street; 250-383-5843; www.emilycarr.com.

A walk in the **James Bay neighborhood**, one of the city's more fashionable areas, takes you past several restored Victorian and Edwardian homes. Continue south on Government Street to Holland Point, turn right and walk along the waterfront. After a couple of blocks, take another right turn and head north on Menzies Street back toward the Inner Harbour.

Another side detour leads to a lesser-known heritage attraction in Victoria. **St. Ann's Academy** was first built in 1871, with additions in 1886 and 1910, and was slated for conversion to a major tourist center until community disdain for the idea forced the pro-

◄ HIDDEN

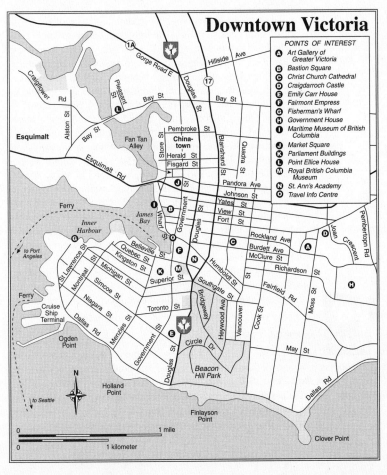

Downtown Victoria

POINTS OF INTEREST

- **A** Art Gallery of Greater Victoria
- **B** Bastion Square
- **C** Christ Church Cathedral
- **D** Craigdarroch Castle
- **E** Emily Carr House
- **F** Fairmont Empress
- **G** Fisherman's Wharf
- **H** Government House
- **I** Maritime Museum of British Columbia
- **J** Market Square
- **K** Parliament Buildings
- **L** Point Ellice House
- **M** Royal British Columbia Museum
- **N** St. Ann's Academy
- **O** Travel Info Centre

vincial government to change plans. The chapel is open to the public and the main building has been converted into an interpretive center. The gardens and grounds are century-old horticultural masterpieces, including a quarter-mile of walks lined by cedar, poplar, plane, beech and cypress trees. A 300-year-old Garry oak south of the formal garden is one of the last left in downtown Victoria. ~ North of Beacon Hill Park, 835 Humboldt Street; 250-953-8828.

Over on the corner of Quadra and Rockland streets is the century-old **Christ Church Cathedral**, one of the largest churches in Canada. It's the seat of the Anglican bishopric of B.C.; there's a bookstore and church archives, and a pioneer cemetery adjacent to the cathedral. ~ Quadra Street, between Rockland and Burdett avenues; 250-383-2714, fax 250-383-2744; www.christchurch cathedral.bc.ca.

The **Parliament Buildings** are in the block west of the Royal British Columbia Museum. The legislative buildings are Francis Rattenbury's architectural salad of Victorian, Romanesque and Italian Renaissance styles with 33 copper-covered domes, deliberately designed to mimic their more famous counterparts in London. At night they are outlined with more than 3000 twinkling lights (one of B.C.'s most frequently snapped photographs). A statue of Queen Victoria stands in front of the buildings, and one of Captain George Vancouver tops the main copper dome. Guided tours explain historic features and the workings of the provincial government. Closed weekends from Labor Day to mid-May. ~ 501 Belleville Street; 250-387-3046, fax 250-356-5876.

Located across the street is the **Royal London Wax Museum**, also designed by Rattenbury as the Victoria terminal for the Canadian Pacific Steamships. The Acropolis-style building contains wax sculptures of Princess Diana, President George W. Bush and some 300 other Josephine Tussaud figures; additions depend on the affairs of public life. The likenesses of the American figures are poor, but the royal family is very lifelike. You will want to keep young children out of the Horror Chamber with its gruesome depictions of decapitations and other methods of torture,

sights

AUTHOR FAVORITE

Dozens of spectacular First Nations ceremonial masks are mounted in large dark cabinets—each one spotlit and thus brought to life—at the **Royal British Columbia Museum**. You can easily imagine how they seemed in the coastal lodges a century ago during firelit ceremonies; I was transfixed until a guard hustled me out at closing time. Other collections capture my imagination as well. See page 182 for more information.

but adolescents love it. Admission. ~ 470 Belleville Street; 250-388-4461, fax 250-388-4493; www.waxworld.com.

On the water side of the Wax Museum are the **Pacific Undersea Gardens,** a salute to British Columbia life below water, which, even though these are northern climes, can be quite colorful. At regularly scheduled intervals, divers swim behind windows in the enclosed aquarium tanks to show and tell visitors about the sea creatures of the region. Admission. ~ 490 Belleville Street; 250-382-5717, fax 250-382-5210; www.pacificunderseagardens.com, e-mail pug@obmg.com.

You can continue out Belleville Street by car, cab, bus or bicycle to picturesque **Fisherman's Wharf,** a working fishing pier. Moorage allows for up to 400 boats, but the little bay often is jammed with many more, tied up to one another. If the fishing fleet is in, visitors can buy fresh fish from the docks. ~ Corner of Dallas Road and Erie Street.   ◄ *HIDDEN*

Continue back around the Inner Harbour past the Empress and head north on Wharf Street to **Bastion Square.** This is where James Douglas established Fort Victoria in 1843–44, but the buildings here now—including warehouses, offices, saloons and waterfront hotels—were constructed in the late 1800s, the city's boom period. The buildings, many of them red brick, have been restored and now house restaurants, shops and art galleries. The square itself is home to a couple dozen craft and gift booths during good weather. ~ Off Wharf Street between Fort and Yates streets.

The **Maritime Museum of British Columbia** is housed in a large, turreted building that was originally the Provincial Court House. The museum depicts British Columbia's maritime history from its early days to the present. It includes nautical charts, an extensive model-ship collection, brassware from old ships, Navy uniforms and an incredible vessel—*Tilikum*, a 38-foot dugout canoe that sailed from Victoria to England at the turn of the 20th century. The museum's lighthouse includes both old and new apparatus, along with the history of the characters who ran the equipment. Admission. ~ 28 Bastion Square; 250-385-4222, fax 250-382-2869; www.mmbc.bc.ca, e-mail info@mmbc.bc.ca.

The **Victoria Bug Zoo** is a combination store/natural attraction that Victoria kids adore: This miniature insect zoo offers the chance to see and even touch creepy-crawlies such as tarantulas, scorpions, millipedes and mantises. Periodic overnight sleepovers allow children to, er, see what comes out at night. The gift store stocks exotic honey, among other things. Admission. ~ 631 Courtney Street; 250-384-2847, fax 250-389-2847; www.bugzoo.bc.ca, e-mail bugs@bugzoo.bc.ca.

Walking over to Government Street and north to Johnson Street brings you to **Market Square,** which incorporates the original Occidental Hotel—the choice of many Klondike gold miners in 1898, it's now a favorite area for shopping and dining. ~ Government and Johnson streets.

Although Victoria is a cosmopolitan city, it's not far from some of the deepest wilderness in Canada. You can learn about that, and about the never-ending threats to B.C.'s environment, at the **Western Canada Wilderness Committee** chapter storefront. Maps, pamphlets and protest announcements paint a vivid picture of the ongoing battle to save the province's ancient forests. ~ 651 Johnson Street; 250-388-9292; www.wilderness committee.org.

The Parliament Buildings opened in 1897 to coincide with Queen Victoria's diamond jubilee.

Following Fan Tan Alley north another block leads to **Chinatown** at Government and Herald streets. In the late 19th century, Victoria's Chinatown was second largest on the continent, trailing only that of San Francisco. (It lost the distinction to Vancouver.) The Chinese immigrants headed to British Columbia to work on the railroad and to mine for coal and gold. Approaching Chinatown from Government Street, you see the ceramic-tiled **Gate of Harmonious Interest** with two hand-carved stone lions, gifts from Suzhou, Victoria's sister city in China, standing guard. **Fan Tan Alley**, dubbed Canada's narrowest street, is a block-long warren of boutiques and artists' studios.

HIDDEN ►

The **scenic marine drive** along the coast is the best route for views of the water, the coast, the Olympic Mountains and some of Victoria's most elegant homes. Starting at Mile 0 (at the intersection of Dallas Road and Douglas Street), the end of the Trans-Canada Highway, follow the signs as the drive winds along the coast. You pass through Oak Bay, around part of Cadboro Bay, to Mount Douglas Park and the Saanich Peninsula. At Elk Lake, you can turn left onto Route 17 to head back to Victoria.

Esquimalt Harbour, three miles (4.5 km) west of the Inner Harbour, is the home of Canada's Pacific naval fleet. The CFB **Esquimalt Naval and Military Museum** depicts the history of the base all the way back to its founding in 1865. Tours of a historic naval boat and dockyard are also available. Closed Sunday. ~ 250-363-4312.

LODGING

Lodging in Victoria presents the same challenge as elsewhere in popular cities—it can be expensive, especially during high season. Numerous luxurious hotels line the Inner Harbour, and several others charge luxurious prices for mediocre to shoddy rooms. Budget and moderate accommodations can be found, but these are often farther from downtown. With more than 7000 rooms, however, Victoria offers every traveler plenty of options.

Victoria's high season is June to October; the rest of the year the city's hotels offer superlative off-season packages that often bring room rates down near 50 percent of the summer tariff. The weather isn't as dependable, but it often isn't bad (and sometimes great), and the streets aren't thronged with crowds of bus-borne tourists. For more information, call **Tourism Victoria**, whose accommodation line provides travelers with current rates and availability at a full range of places. ~ 800-663-3883, fax 250-382-6539; www.tourismvictoria.com, e-mail info@tourismvictoria.com.

There are dozens of fine bed-and-breakfast inns throughout Victoria, many in heritage houses and mansions; contact **Blue Dolphin Travel** (250-479-1986, 866-247-2421; www.bluedolphin-travel.com, e-mail reservations@bluedolphin-travel.com). A dozen of the city's luxury B&Bs can be found at their common website, www.victoriafinest.bc.ca/bb.

The dominant sight in Victoria's Inner Harbour is the stately, neo-Gothic **Fairmont Empress**. Canadian Pacific Railways commissioned architect Francis Rattenbury, the designer of the Parliament Buildings around the corner, to design this magnificent property. Although its 475 guest rooms can be quite expensive, the service is unfailingly courteous, accommodations are tasteful and the off-season bargains can make it actually reasonable. The Empress itself is far from hidden, but it does have hidden rooms— eight rooms on the sixth floor of the north tower, the so-called **Romantic Attic** under the gables, which are quiet and spacious   ◄ HIDDEN and offer great views. If you don't mind walking up one flight of stairs (the elevators don't reach this floor) ask for one of these when you book. Amenities include a swimming pool, sauna, spa, health club, lobby, shopping arcade and lovely grounds. ~ 721 Government Street; 250-384-8111, 800-441-1414, fax 250-389-2747; www.fairmont.com. ULTRA-DELUXE.

Almost directly across the street from the Parliament complex, **Birdcage Walk Guesthouse** is in a 1907 heritage home and features five suites with private baths, some with kitchens, all furnished with period antiques, and reasonable rates for such a prime location. ~ 505 Government Street; 250-389-0804, 877-389-0804, fax 250-389-0348; e-mail birdcagebnb@hotmail.com. BUDGET TO MODERATE.

Admiral Inn, on the Inner Harbour, is a basic motel with 32 straightforward, clean rooms, all with refrigerators, 25 with kitchenettes. Continental breakfast is included. ~ 257 Belleville Street; 250-388-6267, 888-823-6472; www.admiral.bc.ca, e-mail admiral@admiral.bc.ca. BUDGET TO MODERATE.

For luxury accommodations along the Inner Harbour near the Parliament Buildings, the **Hotel Grand Pacific** is one of the city's finest. The lobby and other public areas are airy and lavish affairs. The rooms and suites offer views of the harbor or downtown; the new west wing offers one of the city's best views of the Inner Harbour. Facilities include an indoor swimming pool, sauna, whirlpool, health and fitness equipment, restaurant and lounge.

~ 450 Quebec Street; 250-386-0450, 800-663-7550, fax 250-380-4475; www.hotelgrandpacific.com. DELUXE.

Magnolia Hotel & Spa has an estimable location just a block from the Inner Harbour and the Government Street shopping district. The 63 handsome rooms and suites are decorated in cream and blue and luxuriously furnished, including soaking tubs and separate shower stalls. If noise bothers you, be sure to ask for an upper-floor room away from the popular brewpub bar. Room rates include a continental breakfast. ~ 623 Courtney Street; 250-381-0999, 877-624-6654, fax 250-381-0988; www.magnoliahotel.com, e-mail sales@magnoliahotel.com. ULTRA-DELUXE.

A brisk walk or shuttle or ferry ride from the downtown attractions, the **Coast Harbourside Hotel & Marina** faces a 42-slip marina. Marine colors of teal blue, dark mahogany, original art and watery motifs are found throughout the hotel. The 132 guest rooms and suites, each with private balcony, bar and computer hookup. Pick your view: the harbor or the Olympic Mountains. The hotel features an indoor/outdoor pool and deck, with whirlpool, sauna and exercise room. They also offer free parking and a courtesy van to downtown. ~ 146 Kingston Street; 250-360-1211, 800-663-1144, fax 250-360-1418; www.coasthotels.com. DELUXE TO ULTRA-DELUXE.

Haterleigh Heritage Inn is an opulent 1901 Victorian home just a block from the harbor. This six-room bed and breakfast has a downstairs whose vast stained-glass windows draw in cascades of prismatic light; the hand-wrought dark woodwork lends a cozy element. All rooms have private baths, most also have whirlpool tubs. Rates include a full gourmet breakfast and afternoon refreshments. ~ 243 Kingston Street; 250-384-9995, 866-234-2244, fax 250-384-1935; www.haterleigh.com. ULTRA-DELUXE.

HIDDEN ►   The **Rosewood Victoria**'s sunny yellow stucco exteriors, airy conservatory and lush landscaping keep the place in tune with Victoria's Mediterranean climate. The rooms continue this theme, with bright floral wallpapers and quilts, and English country decor touches such as canopied beds. Each of the 17 rooms has a balcony or patio and a private bath; some have fireplaces. The inn is located two blocks from the Parliament complex. ~ 595 Michigan Street; 250-384-6644, 800-335-3466, fax 250-384-6117; www.rosewoodvictoria.com. MODERATE TO DELUXE.

The **Laurel Point Inn** is a modern resort hotel with a location any such facility would envy; its own tongue of land at the entrance to the Inner Harbour. The 200 rooms include 65 suites; all are decorated in light, natural colors that help bring the outside in. All have water views; the basic rooms are fairly compact yet airy. Pool, sauna, health club and restaurants are part of the complex. Downtown is just a five-minute walk. ~ 680 Montreal

Street; 250-386-8721, 800-663-7667, fax 250-386-9547; www.laurelpoint.com. DELUXE.

Even after renovating its 45 rooms, the **James Bay Inn** still fills the bill for price-minded travelers. It is located in a residential area among heritage homes and small cafés (near the Carr House; in fact the inn is where Carr died) but is quite convenient to downtown. The hotel, which opened in 1911, features light-oak paneling and period furnishings in the lobby. Guest rooms are small but comfortable. Rent for a week and you get two nights for free. A pub and restaurant are on the premises. A few travelers have found the service here a bit gruff. ~ 270 Government Street; 250-384-7151, 800-836-2649, fax 250-385-2311; www.jamesbayinn.com. MODERATE.

Battery Street Guesthouse is an option for budget-minded travelers to Victoria. Its four comfortable, compact rooms include breakfast, and the quiet location near Beacon Hill Park is just a ten-minute walk from the Inner Harbour. ~ 670 Battery Street; 250-385-4632; www.batterystreetguesthouse.com. BUDGET TO MODERATE.

Dashwood Manor Bed and Breakfast, a gracious Tudor mansion built in 1912, sits next to Beacon Hill Park and offers unobstructed views of the Strait of Juan de Fuca and the Olympic Mountains. Breakfast is a make-it-yourself affair, with ingredients provided in the kitchenettes in each of the rooms. Three of the 14 guest rooms have fireplaces. The grounds are impeccable and the rooms are clean. In the evening, there's wine and cheese. ~ 1 Cook Street; 250-385-5517, 800-667-5517, fax 250-383-1760; www.dashwoodmanor.com, e-mail frontdesk@dashwoodmanor.com. MODERATE TO DELUXE.

A truly hidden discovery for couples seeking a romantic getaway is **Humboldt House Bed & Breakfast,** which looks like a   ◄ HIDDEN
private residence. A Victorian home built in 1895 and tastefully renovated in 1988, it includes six suites. The library has walls full of books and a fireplace. The rooms are individually decorated with stained glass and have whirlpools and fireplaces. Guests are

AUTHOR FAVORITE

How can you come to Victoria and not stay at the **Fairmont Empress** at least once? This grande-dame hotel is a real holdover from the British Empire and is known throughout the world for its British-style elegance and wonderful afternoon teas. Local author Julie Lawson wrote a children's book, *In Like a Lion,* about a legendary 1992 incident in which a cougar became trapped in the hotel's parking garage! (The lion was peacefully removed.) See page 187 for more information.

served champagne and truffles on arrival and breakfast is delivered to their room via a two-way compartment. ~ 867 Humboldt Street; 250-383-0152, 888-383-0327, fax 250-383-6402; www.humboldthouse.com, e-mail rooms@humboldthouse.com. ULTRA-DELUXE.

A large 1905 Edwardian-style home, the **Beaconsfield Inn** has a turn-of-the-20th-century ambience with antique pieces, stained glass, an oak fireplace, a 14-foot beamed ceiling and the original dark paneling. The nine guest rooms vary in charm, but all include down comforters and antiques. Many feature canopy beds, whirlpools and fireplaces. Guests can also partake of afternoon tea, sherry hour in the library and a full gourmet breakfast in the original dining room or sun room, all included in the rate. ~ 998 Humboldt Street; 250-384-4044, 888-884-4044, fax 250-384-4052; www.beaconsfieldinn.com, e-mail info@beaconsfieldinn.com. DELUXE TO ULTRA-DELUXE.

Millionaire R. P. Rithet built the Beaconsfield Inn in 1905 as a wedding present for his daughter, Gertrude.

Abigail's is just four blocks east of downtown. This Tudor inn has a European ambience with colorful, well-kept gardens and a bright interior. The foyer features marble floors and an open oak staircase that leads to the guest rooms. The sitting room is luxurious with hardwood floors, a leather sofa, a fireplace and fresh flowers. Each of the 23 rooms and suites has down comforters and antiques, and some boast whirlpool baths, fireplaces and vaulted ceilings. Included in the rate is an evening social hour with appetizers in the library and a gourmet breakfast served in the dining room. Free parking. ~ 906 McClure Street; 250-388-5363, 800-561-6565, fax 250-388-7787; www.abigailshotel.com, e-mail innkeeper@abigailshotel.com. DELUXE TO ULTRA-DELUXE.

For low-cost accommodations close to downtown, try the **Cherry Bank Hotel**, a hotel/rooming house. The full breakfast included with your room is the best part of the deal. The dining room is cozy, clean and attractive, which is more than can be said for the rooms, which, at their best, feature an eclectic mix of cast-off furniture, draperies and bedspreads. ~ 825 Burdett Street; 250-385-5380, 800-998-6688, fax 250-383-0949; e-mail cherrybank@pacificcoast.net. MODERATE.

What has been *the* place for basic accommodations is the **Victoria Hostel**, sandwiched between historic buildings and offices in the downtown area. The hostel has two kitchens, a game room, a lounge, an eating area, a library, a bicycle-storage area, laundry facilities and hot showers. There are 108 beds, dormitory-style, and five small family rooms. Private double-occupancy rooms are available with reservation. ~ 516 Yates Street; 250-385-4511, 888-883-0099, fax 250-385-3232; www.hihostels.ca, e-mail info@hihostels.ca. BUDGET.

Swans Suite Hotel, in a restored brick heritage building along the harbor in downtown Victoria, has a colorful pub and restaurant as well as 29 hotel rooms. Each contemporary unit features designer decor and includes a full kitchen, dining area and original art on the walls. ~ 506 Pandora Avenue; 250-361-3310, 800-668-7926, fax 250-361-3491; www.swanshotel.com. MODERATE TO DELUXE.

Ocean Island Backpackers Inn is a funky but very economical property in the west end of downtown Victoria, near Chinatown. Facilities include a music/games room, a licensed pub, kitchen, internet access, storage and parking. The 115 beds include some private rooms, and there is no curfew. Rates start as low as C$18.95 (US$12). ~ 791 Pandora Avenue; 250-385-1788, 888-888-4180, fax 250-385-1780; www.oceanisland.com, e-mail get-it@oceanisland.com. BUDGET.   ◄ HIDDEN

Things are always jumping at the Strathcona Hotel, a venerable downtown institution that includes several popular restaurants, pubs and nightclubs. The 82 rooms are decorated in period furnishings but offer data-ready phones and cable TV. Since the rooms are in the main tower (a solid heritage structure), they're reasonably quiet despite all the goings-on; to be sure, ask for one at the back of the building. ~ 919 Douglas Street; 250-383-7137, 800-663-7476, fax 250-383-6893; www.strathconahotel.com. MODERATE.   ◄ HIDDEN

The Bedford Regency Hotel, across from Victoria Bay Centre, has 40 individually decorated guest rooms feature marble fireplaces, beds with down comforters and pillows, and window boxes overflowing with colorful flowers. A complimentary full breakfast is served in the hotel's Belingo 1140 Lounge and fresh coffee or tea is placed outside each room in the morning. ~ 1140 Government Street; 250-384-6835, 800-665-6500, fax 250-386-8930; www.bedfordregency.com. ULTRA-DELUXE.

The Brass Bell B&B is not only hidden, it's afloat. This 1931 wooden cruiser is moored in the West Bay; guests stay aboard and are provided breakfast at a restaurant of their choice, plus transportation out and about aboard Harbour Ferries. The quarters are compact and cozy, resembling a tidy room in an English country inn. It would be hard to find a better place to watch the sun set on the harbor scene. ~ 4530 Markham Street; 250-748-1033; www.islandnet.com/~brass, e-mail brass@islandnet.com. DELUXE.   ◄ HIDDEN

Spinnakers Guesthouse started out as Canada's first licensed brewpub, and that's still the core of its identity. But over the years owner Paul Hadfield has added a most engaging inn to his menu by acquiring heritage homes in the pub's neighborhood and creating a quiet, inconspicuous accommodation complex right around   ◄ HIDDEN the pub. Three homes ranging from a late-19th-century Victorian to a mid-20th-century Asian-inflected two-story comprise the inn; all the suites are spacious and beautifully furnished and private. Spinnakers is just across the Blue Bridge from downtown, and thus away from the downtown frenzy. ~ 308 Catherine Street; 250-384-2739, 877-838-2739, fax 250-384-3246; www.spinnakers.com, e-mail spinnakers@spinnakers.com. MODERATE TO DELUXE.

HIDDEN ▶ The **Selkirk Guest House–Hostel** is a historic waterfront home along the Gorge (an arm of Victoria Harbour) that offers economical accommodation, an excellent location, and amenities such as a hot tub, kitchen facilities, and even canoes for guests to use for poking around the channel. The three rooms have private baths; there are also two dorm rooms. ~ 934 Selkirk Avenue; 250-389-1213, 800-974-6638, fax 250-389-1313; www.selkirk guesthouse.com, e-mail info@selkirkguesthouse.com. BUDGET TO MODERATE.

DINING   **Sam's Deli** is the best and most convenient spot along Government Street to start a day of shop-browsing with a good cup of coffee and a muffin or pastry. Nothing fancy, but it's good. Breakfast and lunch only. ~ 805 Government Street; 250-382-8424; sams deli.com. BUDGET.

How can anything at the Fairmont Empress be hidden? Easy: so much attention focuses on the hotel's lobby, tea service and
HIDDEN ▶ upscale shops that visitors overlook the **Bengal Lounge**, a dining room with enough character to deserve its own storybook. Formerly the hotel's library, the lounge is decorated with curios reflecting the colonial era—a tiger-skin wall hanging (donated by the Maharajah of India in 1960), Indian ceiling fans. The curry is served buffet-style at lunch and dinner (there's also an all-day à la carte menu). ~ Fairmont Empress, 721 Government Street; 250-384-8111, fax 250-389-2747; e-mail theempress@fairmont. com. DELUXE.

The other "hidden" restaurant at the Empress is **Kipling's**, the downstairs breakfast room, which offers, in essence, three different morning buffets: North American breakfast (pancakes, scrambled eggs), European breakfast (breads, muffins, mueslix, herring), and Asian breakfast (pickled fruits, rice, miso soup). It's not overly expensive—children cost just C$1 for each year of their age—and where else could you find such varied options? ~ Fairmont Empress, 721 Government Street; 250-389-2727. MODERATE.

James Bay Tea Room and Restaurant is a homey place with photographs of English royalty overlooking tables set close together with hand-crocheted tea cozies insulating every teapot. This place, which serves afternoon tea daily, is popular with the older crowd. Lunch and tea service served all day. ~ 332 Menzies

Street; 250-382-8282, fax 250-389-1716; www.jamesbaytea room.com, e-mail jamesbaytearoom@shaw.ca. MODERATE.

The charming and graceful Japanese restaurant **Yokohama** features a large sushi bar, the best place in town for such fare. You can get authentic Japanese entrées here as well as sushi and familiar favorites such as tempura, sukiyaki and ginger pork in the main dining area or in private tatami rooms. ~ 980 Blanshard Street; 250-384-5433, fax 250-384-5438; www.yokohama restaurant.ca, e-mail info@yokohamarestaurant.ca. MODERATE TO DELUXE.

The Keg Steakhouse and Bar is an informal restaurant, one of the most popular, reasonably priced places in downtown. Its dining room offers great views of the Inner Harbour. Entrées include prime rib and grilled shrimp. Try the Classic Meal, a sirloin or New York steak served with seasonal vegetables and Caesar salad or salad bar. Dinner only. ~ 500 Fort Street; 250-386-7789, fax 250-386-5201. MODERATE TO DELUXE.

Siam Thai serves up some of the tastiest Thai food in Victoria. The atmosphere is dark and quiet, with soft lighting lending a bit of mystery to this ethnic eatery. Only fresh ingredients are used in the entrées, which include *larp gai* (diced chicken with spicy lime juice, onions and vegetables) and scallop *prik paow* (sautéed scallops with and red peppers, onions, mushrooms and chile paste). ~ 512 Fort Street; 250-383-9911, fax 250-380-8990. MODERATE.

The atmosphere and decor at **Cafe Brio** could hardly be finer. Housed in a renovated stucco home along Antique Row, the interior is lined with fir plank floors and 18-foot ceilings. Walls are blush peach with fine art prints, including a conspicuous Modigliani nude. The food is Pacific Northwest/Northern Italian, and most dishes feature artful stacks of ingredients—for example, potatoes piled under arugula and bok choy, all topped with halibut. The cooking is expert and the service is friendly. The much-sought-after booths are often reserved weeks ahead, even in the

AUTHOR FAVORITE

Widely considered Victoria's best Indian restaurant, **Da Tandoor** offers a mainstream but expertly prepared selection of items from the subcontinent that once was, after all, just another post in the Empire. As the restaurant's name suggests, tandoori kabobs are the specialty, along with the vindaloo stews, poultry and lamb preparations that typify Indian foods. You can also get Indian and Pakistani prepared foods here, in case you need a good jar of hot lime pickle for the road. ~ 101 Fort Street; 250-384-6333. MODERATE.

off-season. ~ 944 Fort Street; 250-383-0009, 866-270-5461; www. cafe-brio.com, e-mail cafebrio@pacificcoast.net. MODERATE TO DELUXE.

HIDDEN ►   Crowds line up outside the **Blue Fox** on weekend mornings to get in this small Fort Street café. They've come for heaping platters of breakfast—huge omelettes, piles of hash browns and toast, or redolent huevos rancheros—and equally filling lunch, including that endangered rarity: handmade hamburgers. Breakfast is available all day, of course. ~ 919 Fort Street; 250-380-1683. BUDGET.

Victoria residents have long favored **Villa Rosa** for traditional Italian food, with hearty marinara sauces, savory soups and rich lasagna. The location is perfect for dinner after an afternoon prowling the Fort Street antiques district. ~ 1015 Fort Street; 250-384-5337. MODERATE.

Personal restraint is necessary when you walk into **Captain Cook's Bakery**—unless you are truly in need of a half-dozen pies, sweet breads and other pastries. There's usually a daily pie special, and the croissants are first-rate. ~ 1019 Fort Street; 250-386-4333. BUDGET.

Historic Bastion Square contains one of Victoria's best dining spots. **Camille's Restaurant** is romantic and elegant with brick walls, balloon curtains and linen tablecloths. This intimate restaurant prepares delicious West Coast and Pacific Rim cuisine, such as local Muscovy duck with an orange-and-lavender demiglace and spice-crusted venison on beet and barley risotto. The breads and desserts are heavenly. Camille's also has an extensive wine cellar. Dinner only. ~ 45 Bastion Square; 250-381-3433, fax 250-381-3403; www.camillesrestaurant.com, e-mail info@camillesrestaurant.com. DELUXE.

Delicious Greek food, including moussaka, souvlaki and spanakopita, along with standard steaks and seafood are served at **Periklis**, a convivial, *taverna*-style restaurant with dining areas on three levels and Greek posters on the walls. Greek and belly dancing draw big crowds on the weekends in winter and seven nights a week during the summer. No lunch on weekends. ~ 531 Yates Street; 250-386-3313, fax 250-386-5531. MODERATE.

BUN ON THE RUN

On down Fort Street, **Sally Bun** is an admirably simple establishment: Each day the cooks bake up dozens of buns filled with curries, vegetables, meats and other unusual stuffings. One bun is a more than adequate lunch; two are ample for dinner; and in either case the tariff is less than C\$5 per bun. ~ 1030 Fort Street; 250-384-1899. BUDGET.

Locals recommend the **Blue Crab** for seafood. It's fresh, filling and dependable, if not wildly inventive. The harborside setting is appropriate to the cuisine. As always, salmon, halibut and local crab are the best choices. The Sunday brunch is one of the best seafood repasts in Victoria. ~ 146 Kingston Street; 250-480-1999. MODERATE.

Bean Around the World is a cozy, friendly and top-quality coffee shop in Chinatown. The coffee is custom roasted, and the muffins and pastries are fresh and filling. It also serves light lunches. ~ 533 Fisgard Street; 250-386-7115. BUDGET.

For a traditional Chinese restaurant in the heart of Chinatown, try **Don Mee**. Go through the door under the neon sign and walk up a long, burgundy-carpeted staircase to the large dining area. The food here is good, portions are ample and the presentation is upscale. People come for the Cantonese-style seafood dishes like lobster in ginger sauce or crab with black beans. Favorites include Szechuan chicken and fresh vegetable dishes. The dim sum, served for lunch daily, is especially good. ~ 538 Fisgard Street; 250-383-1032, fax 250-383-8387; www.donmee.com. MODERATE.

The other Chinese cuisine mainstay in Victoria is **Ming's**, a spruce modern building where the cooking is classic Mandarin—no heavy use of chiles here except in the curries—and the service is practically obsequious. In other words, it's just like Chinese restaurants were a half-century ago. One of the best items on the menu is *lo han jai*, a savory Buddhist vegetarian concoction. ~ 1321 Quadra Street; 250-385-4405. MODERATE.

Outdoor dining made warm and cozy by fireplaces and overhead heaters is the draw at **Il Terrazzo**. Here they serve sophisticated Northern Italian cuisine on an intimate, plant-filled brick terrace off Waddington Alley. Daily specials yield such possibilities as grilled lamb chops seasoned with garlic and fresh mint or baked halibut with fresh raspberry sauce. No lunch on weekends in winter. ~ 555 Johnson Street; 250-361-0028, fax 250-360-2594. MODERATE TO DELUXE.

John's Place advertises "real food, real prices," and delivers—breakfast plates and lunch and dinner platters are filling, fairly priced and well made. There's nothing exciting here (omelettes, pancakes, burgers, burritos and such) but the atmosphere is congenial, the service friendly and the food, well, real. ~ 723 Pandora Avenue; 250-389-0711, fax 250-389-0799. BUDGET.

Victoria's downtown is chock full of fascinating shops. Best buys are locally made candies, sweaters made by Cowichan Indians, Haida carvings and silver, British Columbia jade, weavings and pottery, books on Canada and goods imported from Britain. Shopping starts with tiny stores in the Empress Hotel and extends

SHOPPING

north on Government Street. Be sure to wander the several side alleys that contain some small but interesting shops.

HIDDEN ▶ If you happen to be in town on a Saturday, be sure to swing by the corner of Superior and Menzies streets, southeast of the Parliament Buildings, to browse the **James Bay Community Market**. Open early May to early October, the market brings in dozens of craft-makers, local growers and small food booths. You can find everything from peppermint soap to apple butter, all locally made. ~ www.jamesbaymarket.com.

Roger's Chocolates is *the* place for connoisseurs of fine chocolates. Housed in a 1903 building with a tiled floor, dark-oak paneling and oak-and-glass display cases, the shop is full of Dickensian charm. The chocolate is the classic, well-sweetened British variety. Roger's started offering chocolates to Victorians in 1885, and ever since fans have been returning for the hugely popular "Victoria Creams." ~ 913 Government Street; 250-727-6851, 800-663-2220, fax 250-727-6854; www.rogerschocolates.com.

A few doors down, the **Edinburgh Tartan Shop** offers genuine Scottish tartans, plus an extremely fine (and, during sales, surprisingly economical) selection of woolen garb ranging from pinstripe suits to, yes, kilts. ~ 921 Government Street; 250-953-7790. A second location is in the Empress Hotel's arcade. ~ 721 Government Street.

Hill's Native Art avows that everything in this somewhat cluttered store is authentic—and there are some worthwhile pieces of Native art in the general pile of tourist-oriented stuff. ~ 1008 Government Street; 250-385-3911.

Just next door, **Avoca** offers another famed Irish product, woolen clothing—coats, scarves, hats and trousers, all exceptionally made and handsome. ~ 1009 Government Street; 250-383-0433.

For Irish linen, tablecloths, doilies, fine handkerchiefs and embroideries, visit the **Irish Linen Store**. ~ 1019 Government Street; 250-383-6812; www.irishlinenvictoria.com.

Northern Passage Gallery offers art, crafts and gift books that focus on Canadian materials. The store stocks a number of decent prints of Emily Carr paintings. ~ 1020 Government Street; 250-381-3380.

For a look at a beautifully restored old building, stop by **The Spirit of Christmas**. It's located in an 1886 bank building with high ceilings, large, arched windows and dark-oak and glass display cases containing a multitude of whimsical ornaments, music boxes, nutcrackers, Disney characters and collectibles. ~ 1022 Government Street; 250-385-2501, fax 250-385-7272.

Even if you brought all your reading with you, stop at **Munro's Books** to see this neoclassical heritage building with high ceilings and carved details, formerly the head office of the Royal Bank.

The bookshop, one of the finest in western Canada, holds more than 50,000 titles of Canadian, British and American works. ~ 1108 Government Street; 250-382-2464, 888-243-2464; www.munrobooks.com, e-mail service@munrobooks.com.

Right next door to Munro's—this is surely no mere coincidence—is the best place in Victoria to have a pot of tea and peruse recent literary acquisitions, if you happened to pick some up next door. **Murchie's** is *the* purveyor of fine teas and coffees; you can also sample some delectable pastries. Here you can buy teas that go for as much as C$99 an ounce—not quite the price of gold, but closer than tea neophytes would suspect. Afternoon tea is served in their tea salon. ~ 1110 Government Street; 250-383-3112, fax 250-383-3255; www.murchies.com.

One vestige of Victoria's colonial British heritage is evident at **Old Morris Tobacconist**—the humidor is devoted to pipe tobaccos, not cigars. The cigars are found in the main counter, and the sales personnel have a most intriguing offer to make U.S. citizens who fancy Cuban cigars. Stop in and inquire while you check out the selection. ~ 1116 Government Street; 250-382-4811; www.oldmorris.com.

Just down the street, **Cowichan Trading Co.** offers a generous selection of Cowichan sweaters, the famed water-resistant wool garments made up the road in the Cowichan Valley. ~ 1328 Government Street; 250-383-0321.

Bay Centre, a multilevel shopping mall located in the heart of Victoria, has more than 90 shops and opens to an interior courtyard with a fountain under skylights and arches. Bay Centre, Canada's answer to JC Penney (now owned by Sears), offers goods from all over the Commonwealth, especially china and woolen products. ~ Government and View streets; 250-389-2228, fax 250-381-5285.

Located within the Bay Centre is the **Hudson's Bay Company**, the Canadian company that pioneered settlement of the West. Now more widely known simply as The Bay, it still carries

AUTHOR FAVORITE

Simply walking into **Silk Road** is a delight for the senses. This aromatic shop offers fine teas, essential oils and bath products, and the staff is constantly offering samples to browsers. The broad selection of teas includes nontraditional blends that incorporate herbs and other embellishments, such as green tea and sour cherry. The bath salts are also quite inventive, incorporating exotic ingredients like fir needles and geranium. ~ 1624 Government Street; 250-388-6815.

Shop 'til You Drop

I hate to shop. But Victoria's astounding plethora of stores and cafés makes it irresistible, especially in the off-season when crowds are light and holidays loom. Surrender to the urge and allow a whole day—with a few sidetrips for more socially redeeming sights.

FORT STREET Start bright and early—say, 7:45—at the **Blue Fox** (919 Fort Street) (page 194), the popular breakfast joint where huge platters of comfort food will fuel your trek. Linger long enough to allow the street's many antique stores to open—most at 9 a.m., some not 'til 10. Up one side and down the other, there is an almost dizzying number of stores devoted to chintz and china, art and schlock, treasures and trivia. I'd make a point of checking out **Lunds Auctioneers and Appraisers** (926 Fort Street), which has wonderful furniture you can't possibly get home, much less afford; **Wells Books** (824 Fort Street), a relic of the day that books were valued as objects; and **Romanoff & Company** (837 Fort Street), where the china and housewares glitter and shine. But I spent most of my time in a humbler place, **Roger's Jukebox** (1071 Fort Street), where the used CDs are not only stacked floor to ceiling, but Roger himself can comment on almost every title in the place.

CHINATOWN This one-block district (Fisgard Street between Government and Store streets) is experiencing incursion from non-Asian shops, but you can still find dragon fruit, barbecued quail and herbal concoctions that have no name in English. Strangely enough, **Fan Tan Alley**

the famous Hudson's Bay point blankets and top brands of English china and woolens. It also houses a gallery featuring bay history art. ~ 1150 Douglas Street; 250-385-1311, fax 250-385-9247; www.hbc.com.

If you want to try a more modern approach to chocolate—dark and tangy rather than sweet and milky—stop by **Chocolaterie Bernard Callebaut**. This descendant of the famed European chocolate family set up operations in Calgary a couple decades ago, and is now known for making some of the finest chocolate in Canada. ~ 623 Broughton Street; 250-380-1515.

The focus is strictly contemporary at **Fran Willis Gallery**, a welcome change of pace for shoppers who have strolled Victoria's seemingly endless array of quaint little shops devoted to traditional goods and arts. Here, on the second floor of a heritage building, has been taken over almost entirely by occidental merchants, including another dandy record store, **The Turntable** (107 Fan Tan Alley). Don't you need a copy of the Jefferson Airplane's first album?

STORE STREET   Two remarkable institutions of commerce inhabit this old warehouse district just above the Upper Harbour. **Capital Iron** (1900 Store Street) is an indescribable purveyor of indelibly useful items (pliers and socks, say) and incredibly useless artifacts like harbor buoys. Two blocks down, **Chintz & Company** (1720 Store Street) offers modern versions of all those antiques up on Fort Street. How many lamps does the human race need, anyway?

HERALD STREET   Heading back up Herald toward Government, you'll pass **Kiss & Tell** (531 Herald Street). Yes, it is what it looks like: a very upscale, low-key adult store.

GOVERNMENT STREET   This is the real thing, a tourist-centered shopping street where schlock shops alternate with the best in town. The Native arts-and-crafts shops range from dubious to cluttered, but **Murchie's** (1110 Government Street) and **Munro's Books** (1108 Government Street) are indisputably worthy stops—it's time for afternoon tea, anyway. Across the street, three garment stores offer all the finery anyone could need in a northern climate: **Avoca** (1009 Government Street) Irish woolens, **Irish Linen Store** (1019 Government Street) and **Edinburgh Tartan Shop** (921 Government Street). Yes, they do have kilts at the latter. No, you won't find me buying any.

Now it's an easy stroll back to any downtown hotel, and since you didn't actually buy anything but a CD or two, it takes little effort. Wait a minute—you didn't tumble for that bungee harness at Kiss & Tell, did you? Don't blame it on me.

modern Canadian artists exhibit works reflecting the vivid, experimental side of the country's artistic community. Solo shows change monthly. ~ 1619 Store Street #200; 250-381-3422.

Fort Street between Blanshard and Cook streets is known as Antique Row with antique maps, stamps, coins, estate jewelry, rare books, crystal, china, furniture and paintings. Three or four antique malls have been carved out of historic buildings along Fort. The entire three-block stretch from Blanshard to Cook is the best antique row in Western Canada—credit all the retirees who have moved to Victoria and discovered a need to divest themselves of stuff.

Romanoff & Company has a fine European-flavored collection of china and dinnerware, plus other housewares. ~ 837 Fort Street; 250-480-1543. **Lunds Auctioneers and Appraisers** has a large stock of very fine furniture and furnishings, plus Tuesday auctions. ~ 926 Fort Street; 250-386-3308. **Pacific Editions** provides framing for prints and paintings, and has an extensive selection of contemporary Northwest Coast art. ~ 942 Fort Street; phone/fax 250-388-5233, 877-388-5234.

HIDDEN ▶
Alcheringa Gallery offers a visually and intellectually tantalizing look at Pacific aboriginal art, mostly masks and small totems. The pieces on display are colorful and exquisite, but what's most interesting is the similarity from one end of the Pacific Rim to the other. The characteristics of design and ornamentation found in New Zealand and New Guinea bear striking resemblances to those of the north B.C. coast. ~ 665 Fort Street; 250-383-8224; www.alcheringa-gallery.com.

Bookstores are among Fort Street's wonders for the vintage-minded browser. **Wells Books** is a simply enormous storehouse of antique, rare and secondhand books, specializing in nautical and scholarly texts, plus old postcards and photographs. ~ 824 Fort Street; 250-360-2929. **Russell Books** is Vancouver Island's largest collection of used books; adding in its stock of discount new books reaches half a million. ~ 734 Fort Street; 250-361-4447. At

HIDDEN ▶
the **Antiquarian Print Room** maps and prints range as far back as the 16th century. ~ 840 Fort Street, second floor; 250-380-1343.

HIDDEN ▶
There are more than 11,000 CD titles in **Roger's Jukebox**, a dandy little store on Fort Street, but that's only the beginning. Roger Pinfield also publishes a catalog of rare records (his real passion), and he promises any buyer that a defective CD can be mailed or brought back for a refund or exchange. ~ 1071 Fort Street; 250-381-2526.

An impressive selection of recycled kitchenware awaits at **Revive**, including utensils, dishes, pots and pans that, while used, are still better than most modern versions. ~ 1088 Fort Street; 250-385-8500.

The Turntable is a cubbyhole with used records, CDs and tapes stacked ceiling-high. The selection of '60s and '70s rock is especially intriguing. ~ 3 Fan Tan Alley #107; 250-382-5543.

Back toward the waterfront, **Dark Horse Books** concentrates on used theater, science fiction, mystery, New Age, alternative press, fantasy and philosophy titles. ~ 623 Johnson Street; 250-386-8736.

HIDDEN ▶
Common wisdom says you shouldn't heed the instruction in the name of **Kiss & Tell**, an adult store near Chinatown. That being the case, I won't tell exactly what the bungee harness is for, but they'll be happy to explain. ~ 531 Herald Street; 250-380-6995.

Walk into **Ethos** and you step back 30 years to the early '70s—incense, beads, candles and other oddments that look best in black light accompanied by the Grateful Dead. There's even macramé! ~ 574 Johnson Street; phone/fax 250-382-2131.

There's nothing antique about most of the inventory at **Chintz & Company**, but it is one of the finest stocks of contemporary china, dinnerware, tableware and other housewares in B.C. In fact, there's nothing chintzy about it. ~ 1720 Store Street; 250-381-2404.

> The Victoria booksellers publish a pamphlet listing used and antiquarian book buyers and merchants. Look for the guide in bookstores, coffee shops and cafés.

Capital Iron advertises that there's no store like it, and they're not kidding. This hardware/marine supplies/outdoor gear emporium occupies an old warehouse building at the lower end of downtown, and all manner of items you didn't know you need can be found here. The basement is the most entertaining—need a hand-cranked printing press? Out in the yard, old boats and buoys are on hand for those who need such. You don't have to buy (or need) a thing to have fun here. ~ 1900 Store Street; 250-385-9703.

NIGHTLIFE

Victoria's free-distribution news and entertainment weekly is *Monday Magazine,* widely available in coffeehouses, bookstores and cafés. It offers the most comprehensive overview of the arts and entertainment in the city. The *Victoria Times Colonist* publishes a weekly entertainment calendar in its Thursday edition.

Hush, a gay-friendly danceclub, features house music. Deejays provide music Wednesday through Sunday 'til 2 a.m. Every Sunday night there's a drag show. Cover. ~ 1325 Government Street; 250-385-0566.

For a more cultured evening, Victoria offers several options. The well-respected **Pacific Opera Victoria** performs at the **Royal Theatre** (250-385-0222, 250-386-6121; www.pov.bc.ca) at 805 Broughton Street.

The **Victoria Symphony** presents concerts featuring international conductors and artists from September through May. On the first weekend in August the symphony holds the celebrated "Symphony Splash," a free, open-air concert where the orchestra plays from a barge in the harbor. They also do a summer pop series. ~ 846 Broughton Street; tickets, 250-385-6515; information, 250-385-9771; www.victoriasymphony.bc.ca.

In the Fairmont Empress, the **Bengal Lounge,** with its high ceilings, potted plants and rattan furnishings, is fit for the raj. The Utopian murals above the bar were donated by the King and Queen of Siam on their visit in 1936. It is a comfortable, old-money place for a drink. ~ 721 Government Street; 250-384-8111.

Deep Nightclub offers Top-40 music for dancing. Cover. ~ Market Square; 250-383-7844.

Victoria has a variety of pubs, comfortable and affordable spots that either feature beers made on the premises or stock a wide variety of local and imported beers and ales. Whether in historic buildings or cottage breweries, you are apt to find a game of darts and a number of skilled competitors. One of the liveliest pub crowds is found at the **Swans Suite Hotel**, where you can hear great local jazz combos several nights a week and see a changing and colorful collection of local and international art. ~ 506 Pandora Avenue; 250-361-3310, 800-668-7926; www.swans hotel.com.

The Strathcona Hotel is a hoppin' place almost every night of the week, with an array of nightclubs that only Victoria could offer. The biggest is the **Sticky Wicket**, a pub with a cricket theme and five levels of dining and entertainment rooms. **Big Bad John's** calls itself a hillbilly bar, but its real persona is a sports bar, with big-screen TVs covering sports around the world. **Legends** is an eclectic dance club, with music ranging from live artists to deejay-led beach parties and frat bashes. Occasionally big-name artists take the stage for live shows. ~ 919 Douglas Street; 250-383-7137.

> The tallest totem pole in the world, carved from a single log in 1958, stands in Beacon Hill Park.

Centennial Square arts center includes the original City Hall (dating back to 1878) and the **McPherson Playhouse**. The playhouse is a restored baroque and Edwardian-style Pantages Theatre seating 800. It hosts stage plays, classical and pops concerts, dance performances, films and touring lectures. ~ Government and Pandora streets; 250-386-6121.

A favorite spot for karaoke (yes, this is quite popular in B.C.) singalongs is the **Karaoke Club**. ~ 1961 Douglas Street; 250-382-5853.

Jazz, swing and world music is the focus at **Millennium Jazz Club**. Live acts on weekends. ~ 1650 Store Street; 250-360-9098.

Bar Victoria caters to dancers of all stripes with Top-40 and '80s hits. Closed Sunday and Monday. Cover. ~ 1417 Government Street; 250-386-1717.

The **Jet Lounge** offers live swing dancing, with lessons, on Wednesday, and an assortment of music ranging from R&B to Top-40 the rest of the week. ~ 751 View Street; 250-920-7797.

The **Tudor House Sports Pub** has dancing Friday and Saturday, and trivia free-for-alls on Sunday and Thursday nights. ~ 533 Admirals Road; 250-382-5625.

PARKS

BEACON HILL PARK This sedate park near downtown, founded in 1882, contains forest, open grassy areas, ponds and Goodacre Lake, a wildfowl sanctuary. Among gardens that bloom nearly year-round you will also find lawn bowling, a century-old cricket pitch, the Mile 0 marker of the Trans-Canada Highway and a children's petting zoo in the summer, all at the southwestern corner where Dallas Road and Douglas Street meet. The massive rhododendrons are a century old; peak blooming season is April through

June. Facilities include restrooms, picnic areas, tennis courts, a playground, lawn bowling, baseball and soccer fields, a children's wading pool and a water play area. ~ Along Douglas Street, a ten-minute walk southeast of the Empress Hotel; 250-361-0600, fax 250-361-0615; e-mail margaretm@city.victoria.bc.ca.

Beyond the heart of Victoria, some of the city's most important landmarks include a castle fit for a queen and the house

Victoria Neighborhoods

where Her Majesty actually stays on her visits. The itinerary also features Victoria's major art gallery and a leading museum of Victoriana. If you have half a day at your disposal, it's definitely a chance to savor the city's heritage.

The **Art Gallery of Greater Victoria** is one of Canada's finest art museums. This gallery features Canadian art, European pieces from the 15th through 20th centuries and the only Shinto shrine outside Japan, plus a large Asian art collection. A portion of the gallery is housed in Spencer Mansion, built in 1890, which features a dramatic staircase, a Jacobean ceiling and a dollhouse with many intricate details. Admission (Monday is free). ~ 1040 Moss Street; 250-384-4101; www.aggv.bc.ca, e-mail aggv@aggv.bc.ca.

SIGHTS

A couple of blocks southwest is **Government House**, where the Queen of England and her family stay when they visit Victoria. It is the official residence of the Lieutenant Governor, the Queen's representative in British Columbia. When royalty is not visiting, the public can stroll through the formal lawns and gardens, which boast a lily pond, waterfall and extensive collection of roses. It's a pleasant, uncrowded (and free) contrast to the frenzy of Butchart Gardens. ~ 1401 Rockland Avenue; 250-387-2080; www.ltgov.bc.ca. The surrounding **Rockland** neighborhood boasts dozens of splendid heritage homes, ranging from late Victorian to Craftsman style.

◀ HIDDEN

If you enjoy Victorian furnishings, you will want to see **Point Ellice House**, which contains British Columbia's most comprehensive collection of Victorian furnishings and art in its original setting. The house was built around 1862. Visitors also can stroll through a wonderful 19th-century garden where afternoon tea is served daily (reservations required) throughout the summer. Many Victoria residents consider this a better afternoon tea than the Empress's; it's certainly more economical. The house can be reached by a ten-minute ferry ride from Victoria's Inner Harbour (ferry information, 250-480-0971). Limited winter hours; call ahead. Admission. ~ 2616 Pleasant Street off Bay Street; 250-380-6506; collections.ic.gc.ca/peh.

Prince and Princess Abkhazi began shaping a piece of land in the Fairfield neighborhood into a garden in the late '40s, paying special attention to the natural attributes to the site—magnificent old Garry oaks, glacier-carved slabs of granite, the gentle slope of the land. The result, a garden that literally flows across the landscape, was turned over to the Conservancy of B.C. in 2000 and **Abkhazi Garden** is now one of the many garden attractions in the city. Admission. ~ 1964 Fairfield Road; 250-598-8096; www.conservancy.bc.ca.

HIDDEN ▶

LODGING

HIDDEN ▶

Fairholme Manor is just down the street from Craigdarroch Castle and next door to Government House, and it fits admirably in such lofty surroundings. The 1885 estate occupies most of an acre on Rockland Hill, with spacious lawns and gardens surrounding it. The high-ceilinged Italianate manor house saw brief life as apartments, and the five guest suites are thus extra-spacious and well-furnished. Hostess Sylvia Main, Austrian by birth, serves European-style breads and pastries at breakfast. ~ 638 Rockland Place (call for directions—it's hidden well off the main street); 250-598-3240, 877-511-3322, fax 250-598-3299; www.fairholmemanor.com, e-mail info@fairholmemanor.com. DELUXE.

Many of the furnishings in **Amethyst Inn** were shipped around Cape Horn in barrels of protective molasses—they and this exquisite 1885 Victorian mansion remain in pristine condition today. The decorative frieze girdling the high walls of the public rooms is incredibly intricate, and the European tilework on the fireplaces is priceless. Every room has a soaker tub, spa or antique clawfoot tub. ~ 1501 Fort Street; 250-595-2053, 888-265-6499, fax 250-595-2054; www.amethyst-inn.com, e-mail innkeeper@amethyst-inn.com. DELUXE.

Claddagh House Bed and Breakfast has four guest rooms, a patio and garden open to guests and serves a hearty breakfast. Although tucked away in a quiet residential area, it is convenient

AUTHOR FAVORITE

You'll need your own or public transportation to head out east on Fort Street to **Craigdarroch Castle**. Robert Dunsmuir had the house built for his family after new coal deposits were found in 1869, making him, the overseer of the Hudson's Bay Company, British Columbia's first millionaire. Alas, Dunsmuir died before the house was finished. Today, visitors can tour Craigdarroch, furnished in turn-of-the-20th-century style featuring 39 rooms on five floors with stained-glass windows, intricate hand-set woodwork, period furniture and turrets. It's likely the most opulent house in all of B.C. Admission. ~ 1050 Joan Crescent; 250-592-5323, fax 250-592-1099; www.craigdarrochcastle.com, e-mail info@craigdarrochcastle.com.

to tourist attractions, shopping and the ocean. Gay-friendly. ~ 1761 Lee Avenue; 250-370-2816, 877-377-2816, fax 250-592-0228. ULTRA-DELUXE.

Oak Bay Guest House is a 1912 bed and breakfast furnished with period antiques. The 11 rooms provide garden views and private baths, some with clawfoot tubs. Relax by the living-room fireplace or enjoy a book in the sun room. Gay-friendly. ~ 1052 Newport Avenue; 250-598-3812, 800-575-3812, fax 250-598-0369; www.oakbayguesthouse.com, e-mail stay@oakbayguesthouse.com. MODERATE TO DELUXE.

The **Oak Bay Beach Hotel** is a large Tudor-style inn right above the water in Oak Bay. The cozy rooms are furnished with antiques, and the lobby, dining room and pub all offer that dark wood–trimmed, slightly cramped feeling of a genuine English beachside hotel. Although it's right on the Marine Scenic Drive, the surrounding neighborhood is pleasant and peaceful. ~ 1175 Beach Drive; 250-598-4556, 800-668-7758, fax 250-598-6180; www.oakbaybeachhotel.com. DELUXE.

If you don't mind student housing without frills, the **University of Victoria Housing Services**, 20 minutes north of downtown, offers more than 800 rooms, including breakfast in the residence dining room, from May 1 to August 30. ~ P.O. Box 1700, Finnerty Road, Victoria, BC V8W 2Y2; 250-721-8395, fax 250-721-8930; housing.uvic.ca. BUDGET TO MODERATE.

About a quarter of the way from Victoria to Sidney in a quiet residential area on the edge of its namesake park is the **Quality Resort at Mount Douglas Park**. The hillside lodge features large relief carvings of birds and marine life. The 44 rooms are contemporary and comfortable. Suites have balconies with ocean or park views, and some have fireplaces, jacuzzis and kitchenettes. Breakfast is included in the tab. ~ 4550 Cordova Bay Road; 250-658-2171, 888-303-2133, fax 250-658-4596; www.qualityresortmd.com. MODERATE TO DELUXE.

The Gorge Waterway extends northwest from the Inner Harbour. Here you will find a large number of less expensive motels. The **Travelodge** is one that offers the most quality and service for your money. The motel appeals to families because of its indoor pool, twin saunas, restaurant and lounge. Just a few minutes drive from downtown, the motel has 73 clean guest rooms that are decorated in cool colors and feature oak trim. Some rooms and 12 one-bedroom suites have kitchenettes. ~ 229 Gorge Road East; 250-388-6611, 800-565-3771, fax 250-388-4153; www.travelodgevictoria.com, e-mail info@travelodgevictoria.com. MODERATE.

The **Aerie** resort is one of Canada's most conspicuous inns, an over-the-top Mediterranean-style complex resting astride Malahat Mountain. With a dizzying array of levels, angles and perspectives, it sprawls along the hill like a Greek resort; but inside the decor and ambience aim for Roman Empire opulence, with columns and canopy-draped beds, whispering baths and neoclassic statuary. The air of sensuous decadence is bolstered by the restaurant's legendary multicourse dinners (see "Dining" below). ~ 600 Ebedora Lane, Malahat; 250-743-7115, 800-518-1933, fax 250-743-4766; www.aerie.bc.ca, e-mail resort@aerie.bc.ca. ULTRA-DELUXE.

DINING

HIDDEN ▶

The menu at **Blighty's Bistro** is a savory combination of down-home pub food with gourmet inflections, leading to such unusual offerings as a curry mulligatawny stew; paté, bacon and mushrooms; and salmon stuffed with curried cream cheese. The ambience is neighborhood bistro, and the service could hardly be friendlier. ~ 2006 Oak Bay Avenue; 250-592-5111. MODERATE.

For a truly English dinner or afternoon tea, meander out to the **Blethering Place**. There you will find the silver-haired set gossiping over hours-long tea, and families stopping by for supper. The fare includes crumpets, tarts, scones, Welsh rarebit, steak-and-kidney pie and decadent desserts. ~ 2250 Oak Bay Avenue; 250-598-1413, fax 250-592-9052; www.thebletheringplace.com, e-mail tearoom@thebletheringplace.com. BUDGET TO MODERATE.

The **Marina Restaurant** not only has a smashing view of Oak Bay and the Lower Mainland in the distance, it offers excellent seafood and pastas, along with house-made breads. There's also a very fine sushi bar putting local fish and shellfish to good use. This place is extremely popular with residents. ~ 1327 Beach Street; 250-598-8555, fax 250-598-3014; www.marinarestaurant.com. MODERATE TO DELUXE.

An 1855 carriage house six miles from downtown is the site of the **Six Mile Pub**—the spitting image of an old English pub with hanging lamps, oak moldings, dart boards and stained-glass windows. At lunch expect traditional pub fare such as Cornish pasties or steak-and-kidney pie. Changing specials at dinner may include charbroiled salmon or vegetable stir-fry. ~ 494 Island Highway; 250-478-3121, fax 250-478-8765; www.sixmilepub.com, e-mail info@sixmilepub.com. BUDGET TO MODERATE.

AUTHOR FAVORITE

Almost all the ingredients at **Paprika** are island-grown, from sage and rosemary to free-range chicken and lamb—which is why I try to dine here whenever I'm in the area. The culinary thrust is French provincial—there's a lobster or shellfish bisque every night—and entrées are typically roasted or braised meats and fish. Although the food is sensational, the atmosphere is low-key; this is a neighborhood restaurant. ~ 2522 Estevan Avenue; 250-592-7424. DELUXE TO ULTRA-DELUXE.

The **Beacon Drive-in** is a Victoria institution, offering all the usual drive-in items—burgers, fries, shakes, ice cream and hearty breakfasts—made the old-fashioned way. Be sure to try an island favorite, the oyster burger. ~ 126 Douglas Street; 250-385-7521 or 250-385-3653. BUDGET.

The Aerie resort includes one of Victoria's most sensational restaurants, sitting atop the Malahat summit. Located outside greater Victoria on the way to Duncan, the dining room boasts a 23-carat gold-leaf ceiling and panoramic views stretching from the Gulf Islands to the Olympic Mountains. The menu changes, depending on availability of the freshest local ingredients, ranging from wild mushrooms to barnacles grown in island tidepools. Entrées such as sage-and-pancetta-crusted pheasant breast or roasted venison loin with a matsutake mushroom sauce attract enough high-flying guests that a helicopter pad was added to the restaurant and 29-room guesthouse. ~ 600 Ebedora Lane, Malahat; 250-743-7115, 800-518-1933, fax 250-743-4766; www.aerie.bc.ca. ULTRA-DELUXE.

SHOPPING

The Oak Bay area offers an array of boutiques and specialty stores on Oak Bay Avenue featuring designer clothing, English toffees, New Age toys and games, crafts and jewelry. **Avenue China & Chintz** typifies the district, with a pleasing and eclectic array of elegant housewares and decor items. ~ 2225 Oak Bay Avenue; 250-595-1880.

The Cook Street neighborhood also has a small shopping district, the most notable venue of which is **Cook Street Village Wines**, a store specializing exclusively in B.C. estate wines. Floor-to-ceiling shelves hold dozens of rare vintages (some otherwise available only to high-end restaurants and hotels), including an impressive array of ice wines. Naturally, the store personnel maintain great expertise on the province's vintages. ~ 242 Cook Street; 250-995-2665.

◄ HIDDEN

Mayfair Shopping Centre is one of the largest and most upscale shopping centers on the island. It contains more than 130 shops specializing in men's and women's fashions. ~ A mile from downtown near Douglas Street and Finlayson Avenue; 250-383-0541.

NIGHTLIFE

In Oak Bay, east of downtown Victoria, **The Snug Pub** at the Oak Bay Beach Hotel attracts locals and visitors alike. It has a warm, British atmosphere with plaster walls, dark-wood beams, a large bar and fireplace. The balcony, open in summer, overlooks the ocean. ~ 1175 Beach Street; 250-598-4556, fax 250-598-6180.

BEACHES & PARKS

THETIS LAKE REGIONAL PARK 🏃 🏊 ⬛ Just five miles from the city center, this park affords opportunities for walking, hiking and solitude through more than 1900 acres of rolling hills, fir and cedar forest and lake frontage. You can swim in the lake during the summer. There are picnic areas and restrooms. ~ Off Route 1, about five miles northwest of downtown Victoria; 250-478-3344, fax 250-478-5416.

MOUNT DOUGLAS MUNICIPAL PARK 🏃 🔭 On the east side of the Saanich Peninsula, this 500-acre park has forests of arbutus (madrona), fir and cedar, a beach and Mount Douglas peak. Visitors can drive a one-and-a-half-mile paved route to a parking area and then hike a short distance to the peak where the view stretches in all directions. You can swim here in summer. You'll find picnic areas and restrooms. ~ Located about five miles northeast of downtown Victoria off Route 17 and Royal Oak/Cordova Bay Road; 250-475-1775.

Saanich Peninsula

One of Vancouver Island's leading tourist attractions, Butchart Gardens, is the Saanich Peninsula's primary draw. This area also offers a host of other garden retreats featuring exotic flora from all over the world.

SIGHTS

Traveling north on Route 17 from Victoria toward Sidney, signs direct you to **Butchart Gardens**, a haven for anyone who appreciates the spectacle of lush, estate garden design. Dating back to 1904, the industrious wife of the manufacturer of Portland Cement turned a quarry pit created by her husband into a fabulous sunken garden. Today, Jennie Butchart's project (still run by the Butchart family) is a world-famous, 55-acre display garden, which includes the Rose Garden, the Italian Garden, the Japanese Garden, the Star Pond and the Ross Fountains. The gardens, joined by a series of walkways, display glorious color and rare and exotic plants, although critics find the overall impression a bit too artificial. Fireworks displays are offered every Saturday night in July and August. In summer the bus-borne crowds can be a bit much (some of the paths are rather narrow) so it's a good idea to come early in the day. Christmastime features an extensive lighting display. Admission. ~ 800 Benvenuto Avenue; 250-652-5256, 250-652-4422 (winter), 866-652-4422, fax 250-652-3883; www.butchartgardens.com, e-mail email@butchartgardens.com.

Returning south on Route 17, on a hilltop overlooking Elk Lake, stands a white dome. Here the **Centre of the Universe** houses what in 1918 was the largest telescope in the world, a 65-inch optical masterpiece that still offers a stunning view of the heavens—tour visitors get to turn the massive instrument. On Saturday night visitors can hear nontechnical talks about astronomy. The nearby interpretive center offers exhibits on Canadian contributions to space exploration, and lots of interactive displays for kids. Closed Sunday and Monday from November through March. ~ Little Saanich Mountain, 5071 West Saanich Road, Victoria; 250-363-8262; www.hia-iha.nrc-cnrc.gc.ca/cu.

Off Route 17, you can stop at the **Horticulture Centre of the Pacific**, where perennial displays are all labeled. You walk on forest paths to see a fabulous display of Asian lilies, a rose garden with more than 100 kinds of miniature roses, a creek flanked with ferns and hostas, and the rhododendron vale. There's a winter garden of fruit trees and a fuchsia arbor, providing the center with flowers year-round. Admission. ~ 505 Quayle Road, Saanich; 250-479-6162, fax 250-479-6047; www.hcp.bc.ca, e-mail hcp.info@hcp.bc.ca.

When Route 17 intersects with Route 1, head west on Route 1 and follow the signs to **Craigflower Manor and Schoolhouse**. Craigflower grew out of the requirement that in order to have a lease on Vancouver Island, the Hudson's Bay Company had to colonize it—the precursor to homesteading. Craigflower is one of four farms planned by the company. Some 25 families arrived from Scotland in 1853 to live on and work the farm. Visitors can tour the Georgian-style farmhouse built for bailiff Kenneth McKenzie in 1856, which contains furnishings and articles brought from Scotland. There is also a heritage garden with heirloom plants. Closed mid-September to mid-May. Admission. ~ 110 Island Highway, corner of Craigflower and Admirals roads, View Royal; 250-383-4627, fax 250-744-2251; www.heritage.gov.bc.ca.

◀ **HIDDEN**

Craigflower Schoolhouse is the oldest school building in western Canada.

The **Marine Ecology Station** in Sidney Harbor is a small floating research center that has an aquarium and a marine interpretive exhibit open to the public. Admission. ~ 9835 Seaport Place, Sidney; 250-655-1555.

Near Butchart Gardens, ferries and the airport, the **Best Western Emerald Isle Motor Inn** is convenient and the rooms have kitchenettes. No designer interiors here, but the decor is functional. The 63 rooms (including 12 two-room suites), some of which are nonsmoking, are clean. Amenities include laundry facilities, a restaurant, whirlpool baths, a sauna and a health spa. ~ 2306 Beacon Avenue, Sidney; 250-656-4441, 800-315-3377, fax 250-655-1351; www.bwemeraldisle.com, e-mailfrontdesk@bwemeraldisle.com. MODERATE TO DELUXE.

LODGING

"Miraloma" is what B.C. Lieutenant Governor Walter Nichol called his Saanich Peninsula summer home in the 1920s. Designed by B.C. architect Samuel Maclure, the house featured fir-slab exteriors, tree-trunk posts and balconies and spruce, cottonwood and fir paneling inside. This home is now **Shoal Harbour Inn**, a five-suite guest house and country restaurant. The guest rooms, all upstairs, feature pine and country furnishings and private bathrooms; two have fireplaces. Continental breakfast is included. ~ 2328 Harbour Road, Sidney; 250-656-6622, 877-956-6622; www.shoalharbourinn.com. MODERATE TO DELUXE.

Iris Garden Country Manor is a bed and breakfast housed in a modern estate built by a contractor who had ample time, material and expertise—thus the huge indoor pool that's part of the complex. The four units, decorated in bright colors, have private baths and feather beds. The common areas are equally spacious. Butchart Gardens is a quick ten-minute drive. ~ 5360 West Saanich Road; 250-744-2253, 877-744-2253, fax 250-744-5690; www.irisgardenvictoria.com, e-mail stay@irisgardenvictoria.com. MODERATE TO DELUXE.

HIDDEN ►

The four cabins at the **Compass Rose Cabins & Marina** are not only waterfront, they are over the water on pilings, facing west on Brentwood Bay just north of Butchart Gardens. Each cabin is a clean, light and airy space with a loft bedroom and sitting, dining and cooking areas downstairs. Full meal service is available at an adjoining restaurant. Guests can rent canoes and kayaks on-site, either for a leisurely cruise on the bay or a crowd-free quick trip to the back entrance at Butchart Gardens. ~ 799 Verdier Avenue, Brentwood Bay; 250-544-1441, fax 250-544-1015; www.compassrosecabins.com, e-mail compassrosecabins@shaw.ca. MODERATE TO DELUXE.

Perched on pilings above the water, the handsome new **Brentwood Bay Lodge** is both an ultraluxurious destination resort (and spa) and a dive center, the only PADI-certified center in Canada. The attraction for divers is the depths of adjacent Saanich Inlet, one of the best dive spots in B.C.; but the lodge itself, a handsome cedar contemporary structure overlooking the water, offers guests every amenity, from the simple (plush terrycloth bathrobes) to the more exotic—multijetted massage showers. The lodge is about 10 minutes from Butchart Gardens. ~ 849 Verdier Avenue; 250-544-2079, 888-544-2079, fax 250-544-2069; www.brentwoodbaylodge.com. ULTRA-DELUXE.

DINING

Seahorses Café is right on the water next to the Brentwood Bay ferry dock—a suitably marine environment for this lovely little seafood bistro. Shellfish, prawns and fish dishes dominate, with the fresh sheet menu the best choice—you might find fresh oysters in phyllo with garlic, for instance. The outdoor deck is a great choice in nice weather. ~ 799 Verdier Avenue, Brentwood Bay; 250-544-1565. MODERATE.

BEACHES & PARKS

ISLAND VIEW BEACH REGIONAL PARK 🏃 ⚓ 🚤 🛥 On the eastern shore of the Saanich Peninsula, the weather has molded this relatively flat park with rolling sand dunes at the north end and a long beach at the water's edge. The beach, full of fine, white sand, is strewn with sculpture-like driftwood. The water is cold, although some do swim in it. The park offers views of Mount Baker, De Haro Strait and the San Juan and Gulf islands. Facilities include picnic areas and restrooms. ~ Located northeast of Victoria on the Saanich Peninsula off Route 17 and Island View Road; 250-478-3344, fax 250-478-5416.

ELK/BEAVER LAKE REGIONAL PARK Lush wetlands, tranquil forests and hilltop vistas surrounding Elk and Beaver lakes (good trout and bass fishing) provide more than 1000 acres of habitat for many birds, including owls, woodpeckers and ducks. There are picnic areas and restrooms. ~ Located north of Victoria off Route 17 and Beaver Lake Road; 250-478-3344, fax 250-478-5416.

GOLDSTREAM PROVINCIAL PARK This park provides two distinct vegetation zones—dry ridges with dogwood, lodgepole pine and arbutus (madrona), and wetter areas with 600-year-old Douglas fir, western red cedar, western hemlock, Pacific yew, black cottonwood and big-leaf maple, as well as many wildflowers. A salt marsh, where the Goldstream River flows into Finlayson Arm, contains mosses, lichens and liverworts. Each October, the river draws thousands of salmon returning to spawn. The river got its name after gold was discovered there, but the find was a small one. You'll find picnic areas and restrooms. ~ Off Route 1, ten miles northwest of Victoria; 250-391-2300, fax 250-478-9211; wlapwww.gov.bc.ca/bcparks.

▲ There are 159 tent/RV campsites (no hookups); C$22 per night.

Esquimalt Area

West of Victoria, the Esquimalt area, surrounding Esquimalt Harbour, is home to Fort Rodd Hill, one of the region's most important landmarks. As you head west a bit more you reach Sooke, a great place to get a taste of the rugged West Coast.

SIGHTS

Fort Rodd Hill National Historic Site, a 44-acre park of rolling hills, an open, parade-grounds area, woods and beach is in this region. The fort was built in 1895 to protect the entrance to the Royal Navy Yards in Esquimalt Harbour. It became a park in 1962. Visitors can see restored batteries and the restored Fisgard Lighthouse, which features exhibits on navigation and shipwrecks—of which there have been hundreds along Vancouver Island's West Coast. There is a film at the entrance of both sites. Admission. ~ Ocean Boulevard off the Old Island Highway, Esquimalt; 250-478-5849; www.parkscanada.gc.ca/fortroddhill.

The Fisgard Lighthouse at Fort Rodd Hill National Historic Park is the oldest lighthouse on the Pacific Coast.

Continuing west on Route 14 brings you to **Sooke**, a former logging and fishing town on Sooke Inlet, now becoming a travel destination and bedroom community for Victoria. This is a good spot to start or end a trip to the wild regions farther west, or simply hide away in quiet lodgings near the water. The Sooke visitor information center is just after you cross the Sooke River bridge on the main highway, at the museum. ~ 2070 Phillips Road, Sooke; 250-642-6351, fax 250-642-7089; www.sooke.museum. bc.ca, e-mail info@sooke.museum.bc.ca.

LODGING   A bed and breakfast that started as a 1940s log cabin and grew to include a cedar addition with five guest rooms, **Ocean Wilderness** offers travelers a secluded seaside retreat. Set on five oceanfront acres just outside Sooke, the original log cabin is now the inn's breakfast area, and accommodations in the addition are adorned with romantic canopy beds and eclectic antiques; some rooms have two-person soaker tubs. Decks overlook the water or garden. Gayfriendly. ~ 109 West Coast Road, Sooke; 250-646-2116, 800-323-2116, fax 250-646-2317; www.oceanwildernessinn.com. MODERATE TO DELUXE.

Sooke Harbour House, famous for its restaurant, is also an exquisite small inn, with 28 elegant, sumptuous rooms, fascinating grounds—much of the restaurant's provender is grown here—and wonderful walking territory on the beach nearby. The guest rooms are light, wood-trimmed and exceedingly comfortable; many have hot tubs and fireplaces, and all are different. ~ 1528 Whiffen Spit Road, Sooke; 250-642-3421, 800-889-9688, fax 250-642-6988; www.sookeharbourhouse.com, e-mail info@sookehar bourhouse.com. DELUXE TO ULTRA-DELUXE.

HIDDEN ►   **Winter Creek House** is not only hidden, it's exquisitely isolated. Perched on a landing in the forest north of Sooke, this beautiful small cabin was handbuilt by owners Ken and Patti from local wood, much of it milled on site. The warm and cozy interior includes a small kitchenette, gas fireplace and luxurious bath; outside, in the shade of mature second-growth firs, is the extravagantly soothing Japanese soaking tub. This is an ideal place to while away a rainy winter weekend; Patti's handmade meals (breakfast is included) are sumptuous. ~ Phillips Road, north of Sooke (call for directions); 250-642-4768, 866-642-4768; www.wintercreek house.com. MODERATE.

HIDDEN ►   **Point-No-Point Resort** is the sort of place that draws intensely loyal repeat visitors to its spectacular beachfront location west of Sooke. All of its wood cabins have fireplaces, baths and kitchens; many of the rooms and suites have private hot tubs. All told there are 25 units, all different. The beautiful 40-acre property has hiking trails, secluded beach coves and rocky headlands with bracing Pacific views. Even in winter reservations are necessary well in advance for weekends. ~ 1505 West Coast Road, Sooke; 250-646-2020, fax 250-646-2294; www.pointnopoint resort.com. BUDGET TO DELUXE.

The finest lodging in Port Renfrew is **Arbutus Beach Lodge**, a comfy small inn facing the beachfront and harbor. The five up-stairs rooms are compact, but all feature private bath. The first-floor common area offers lots of sitting space to watch the area's often tempestuous weather. Kitchen access is included. ~ 5 Queesto Drive, Port Renfrew; 250-647-5458, fax 250-647-5552; www.arbutusbeachlodge.com. MODERATE.

Some of the finest dining in Canada is offered by **Sooke Harbour House**, a white clapboard inn surrounded by colorful gardens on a bluff above Sooke Harbour's Whiffen Spit. In a setting of refin-ished pine and maple furnishings with whimsical folk art accents, the dining room offers a changing menu. There's an emphasis on fresh seasonal ingredients and local seafood that might include sea urchin roe or fresh skate served with cranberry vinegar. Suckling kid, duck and rabbit are among the possible meat choices. The vast majority of herbs and vegetables served in the restaurant are grown in the inn's gardens, with an emphasis on unusual flavors and in-gredients, such as fuchsia berries and begonia blossoms. The in-ventive cuisine led to the restaurant's designation as the best din-ing room in Canada by *Gourmet* magazine. Winter closures; call ahead. ~ 1528 Whiffen Spit Road, Sooke; 250-642-3421. ULTRA-DELUXE.

DINING

The obvious contrast is **Mom's Cafe**, where West Coast hikers often repair after their treks to indulge in—what else?—huge plat-ter breakfasts and hamburgers. It's not fancy fare, but it seems like it after a week on the trail. ~ 2036 Shields Road, Sooke; 250-642-3314. BUDGET.

The restaurant at **Point-No-Point Resort** serves West Coast cuisine prepared with local produce and seafood. Afternoon tea service is always popular, too. ~ 1505 West Coast Road, Sooke; 250-646-2020. MODERATE.

◄ *HIDDEN*

AUTHOR FAVORITE

Of all the restaurants in Canada, **Sooke Harbour House** is unsurpassed—and best-known—because owners Sinclair and Frederique Philip invented what all their imitators since have been doing: unique, flavorful, surprising cuisine based on local ingredients. It's the first (and last) place I tasted sea cucumber, which was harvested in the bay just below the inn. See above for more information.

BEACHES & PARKS

A note about using parks and beaches in the Sooke area: Do not leave valuables in your car, as the region has been plagued by gangs of thieves that prowl the trailhead and picnic area parking lots. It's best to leave valuable items in your hotel room, but if you can do nothing else, make sure they're locked in the trunk.

EAST SOOKE PARK 🚶 ⛵ 🛶 🌊 This huge regional park is where the West Coast begins. The 3500-acre park encompasses beautiful arbutus trees clinging to the windswept coast. You'll find small pocket beaches, rocky bays and islets for beachcombing and tidepooling. It features six miles of rugged coast trails and 30 miles of trails through forest, marsh and field with opportunities to view orca whales, sea lions, harbor seals, Columbian black-tailed deer and cougar. The park has views of the Strait of Juan de Fuca and the Olympic Mountains. You'll find picnic areas and restrooms. ~ Located about 25 miles southwest of Victoria off East Sooke Road on Becher Bay Road; 250-478-3344, fax 250-748-5416.

In September, check out the large number of bald eagles, hawks and other raptors that stop at East Sooke Park during their migration.

BAMBERTON PROVINCIAL PARK 🚶 ⛵ 🛶 🚣 🚤 🌊 The warm waters of the Saanich Inlet make this park, with a 750-foot sandy beach, attractive to swimmers. The park contains many arbutus trees in a second-growth forest. The Saanich Peninsula, Mount Baker and the Gulf Islands form the backdrop to water and mountain views from this park. Picnic areas and restrooms are the only facilities. ~ Located northwest of Victoria off Route 1 at the northern foot of Malahat Drive; 250-391-2300, fax 250-478-9211; wlapwww.gov.bc.ca/bcparks.

▲ There are 50 tent/RV sites (no hookups); C$14 per night. For camping reservations, call 800-689-9025.

SOOKE POTHOLES PROVINCIAL PARK 🚶 🚴 ⛵ The potholes are pockets in the riverbed that form dandy swimming holes in summer; with its high-mountain watershed source, the Sooke River runs clear and cool all summer. In the fall, salmon runs use the river, and a nearby gully (Todd Creek) in winter holds a spectacular waterfall. ~ Located four miles (7 km) north of Sooke at the end of the Sooke River Road; 250-391-2300; www.sooke potholes.com.

JORDAN RIVER RECREATION AREA 🏄 🚣 🚤 This small spit fronts the Pacific next to the Jordan River. Property of a local timber company, it's a popular hangout for island surfers who take advantage of the good break along the beach. ~ In Jordan River, just east of the bridge, on the main highway.

▲ There are approximately two dozen informal vehicle and tent campsites; there's no privacy, and the weekend partying can get intense, but they're free.

CHINA BEACH PROVINCIAL PARK 🏃 🎣 ⚓ The parking lot for this roadside park is in a dense and dark second-growth forest—offering no hint to the marvelous oceanside old-growth spruce forest and long sandy beach found at the end of a 15-minute walk. Once on the beach, hours of leisurely beachcombing are possible, and ambitious hikers can trek all the way back to Jordan River. All hikers should consult a tide table before undertaking any major beach walks, and stay alert for rogue waves. This is also the start of the Juan de Fuca Trail (see page 224). ~ Located 20 miles (37 km) west of Sooke on West Coast Road; 250-391-2300.

BOTANICAL BEACH PROVINCIAL PARK 🏃 🎣 ⚓ This western terminus of the Juan de Fuca Trail (see page 224) is the best place to poke among tidepools in the Victoria/Sooke area. Make sure you check the tide tables for a good low tide (at least below four feet) and plan to spend hours just watching the anemones, chitons, mussels, crabs and other inhabitants of the rocky pools. It's especially popular with kids. ~ Located two miles (3 km) southwest of Port Renfrew; 250-391-2300.

FRENCH BEACH PROVINCIAL PARK 🏃 🚣 ⛵ 🎣 🐟 ⚓ 🛥 ⛴ Visitors have the opportunity to see whales in the spring from this mile-long, sand-and-gravel beach on the Strait of Juan de Fuca. The park also contains second-growth forest. There are picnic areas, modest nature trails and extensive playground facilities. ~ Located west of Sooke off Route 14 near Jordan River; 250-391-2300; www.wlapwww.gov.bc.ca/bcparks.

▲ There are 69 tent/RV sites (no hookups), with exceptional privacy; C$14 per night. Part of the campground remains open in winter. Reservations, 800-689-9025.

Gulf Islands

Ready for some island-hopping? Whether you're into beaches, arts and crafts, birdwatching, dining or just plain looking around, there is something here for everyone. The Gulf Islands provide plenty of activities—swimming, windsurfing, scuba diving, beachcombing, boating, bicycling, hiking and horseback riding—to suit families and outdoor enthusiasts of all abilities.

These islands are isolated places where residents enjoy a bucolic lifestyle. At sunset, basking like a group of sea turtles in the water, the islands are like shadows, amorphous shapes in muted shades of blue, mauve and gray stacked up behind one another. Sisters of the San Juan Islands in Washington State, they include mountain peaks, sandy beaches, and pastoral farms. And much like the San Juan Islands, they lie in a rain shadow that brings them drier, sunnier weather than most of the rest of the coastal region. Much favored by artists, musicians and writers—especially Salt Spring—the islands are excellent places to seek spiritual renewal.

Geographically they are granite blocks, with many rocky faces and outcroppings along the shorelines. The landscape is a beautiful mix of broad meadows and fir-and-madrona (arbutus) woodland that's much more open than the rainforests common throughout most of B.C.

Except for a few small towns, the Gulf Islands are rural, pastoral and undeveloped, with residents scattered among farms and serene homesteads. In fact, one of the great pleasures of visiting (or living on) the islands is patronizing the numerous honor-system farmstands along the backroads. These range from established small farms to a box of tomatoes put out by a rural resident. The climate is Mediterranean-like—mild and dry. BC Ferries provides passage to all the major islands from Tsawwassen and Swartz Bay; call 888-BC-FERRY. Harbour Air (250-537-5525, 800-665-0212) also provides scheduled floatplane service to several of the islands from Vancouver. For information about all the islands, visit www.gulfislands.net.

SIGHTS

Salt Spring Island is the largest, most populated and most frequently visited of the islands. It's renowned for its artists and craft-makers; several of Canada's best-known painters live here, and there are 15 galleries and more than 40 studios. Mid-June to mid-September a dozen of the galleries in Ganges proper stay open late Friday evenings for visitors to browse. For Salt Spring information, call the island Chamber of Commerce at 250-537-4223; www.saltspringisland.com.

The largest village on Salt Spring Island is **Ganges**, a pedestrian-oriented, seaside hamlet about 20 minutes up-island from the ferry terminal, where visitors flock to a summer-long arts-and-crafts fair, art galleries and the Saturday morning market. The **Visitor Info Centre** for the islands is here. ~ 121 Lower Ganges Road; 250-537-5252, fax 250-537-4276.

Salt Spring Island was first settled in the 1850s by freed American slaves; European settlers and expatriate Hawaiians followed. The island today is famed for its beautiful landscape, featuring

AUTHOR FAVORITE

Not only is **Ruckle Provincial Park** the Gulf Islands' largest—a 1200-acre expanse of meadow and forest with broad, rocky beaches and superb views—it is a piece of Salt Spring history. The Ruckle family homestead dates to 1876, and the park still includes a working sheep farm operated by members of the family. Closed November through March. Admission. ~ At the east end of Beaver Point Road, three miles (5 km) east of Fulford Harbour, Salt Spring Island; 250-391-2300.

wide meadows, calm beaches, expansive views and arbutus and Garry oak woodlands. Numerous B&Bs, small inns and low-key cafés serve the summertime visitor explosion.

Pender Island, population 1500, is really two islands connected by a narrow wooden bridge that affords splendid views of Browning Harbour. Medicine Beach in Bedwell Harbour and Hamilton Beach in Browning Harbour are popular picnic spots. The Driftwood Centre and Port Washington are locations of several galleries. ~ Pender Island Chamber of Commerce, 888-420-3737; www.penderislandchamber.com.

If you are a diver, the Gulf Islands provide a number of good locations. Divers often see octopi, wolf eels, sea cucumbers, sea stars, sea urchins and sea pens. Shore dives include Vesuvius Bay on Salt Spring Island for sighting octopus and ling cod; Fulford Harbour, opposite the ferry terminal, with a shallow area perfect for seeing crabs and starfish; and Tilley Point on North Pender Island for interesting kelp beds. Near Thetis Island, the *Miami*, a steel- and coal-carrying freighter that sank in 1900, is covered with interesting vegetation and marine life. The *Del Norte*, a 190-foot side-wheel passenger steamship that sank in 1868, is between Valdez and Galiano islands and appropriate only for more advanced divers.

LODGING

There are very few hotels, major resorts or classic motels on the islands—an integral part of their charm. The **Gulf Island B&B Registry** books for several dozen lodges and small inns. ~ 250-539-5390, 888-539-5390.

Hastings House is perhaps the highest-profile lodging on Salt Spring. This luxurious estate inn is renowned for its fine cuisine, elegant grounds and sumptuous accommodations. There are ten guest suites in the 16th-century Sussex-style manor house, all decorated with fireplaces and antique, country English furnishings. The atmosphere is definitely high-end; this is one of the few places in all western Canada where men are asked to wear jackets to dinner. ~ 160 Upper Ganges Road, Salt Spring Island; 250-537-2362, 800-661-9255, fax 250-537-5333; www.hastingshouse.com.DELUXE TO ULTRA-DELUXE.

At **Eagles Nest B&B** on the hills outside Ganges, the views across the water to Vancouver and Mount Baker are fabulous, sufficient to distract guests from the gargantuan breakfasts they receive. Muffins, fruit, waffles, eggs, sausage—all local provender—provide fuel for a day of wandering the shops and cafés in Ganges or biking the country roads toward Mount Maxwell. The one unit, a cedar chalet, offers a private outdoor shower and hot tub. Pet-friendly. ~ 115 Sollitt Road, Salt Spring Island; 250-537-2129, fax 250-537-2178; www.ssieaglesnestbandb.com. BUDGET TO MODERATE.

HIDDEN ►   There are four cottages at **Maple Ridge** resort on St. Mary Lake; each is a cozy cedar structure with sundeck, kitchens, private baths and an outdoor firepit and picnic table. The resort has its own beach and docks on the lake and access to hiking trails up the mountain behind. Canoes, rowboats, kayaks, sailboards and a small sailboat are available for guest use; the lake is famed for bass and trout fishing. ~ 301 Tripp Road, Salt Spring Island; phone/fax 250-537-5977; www.mapleridgecottages.com. BUDGET TO MODERATE.

The **Salt Spring Island Hostel** is, like so many island lodging, in the countryside on forested grounds (the hostel has ten acres), with ocean beach and a quiet lake nearby. Accommodations run the gamut from traditional hostel dorm rooms to a teepee, a gypsy caravan and two treehouses. Kitchen and other facilities are on site. Closed mid-October to mid-March. ~ 640 Cusheon Lake Road, Salt Spring Island; 250-537-4149; www.beacom. com/ssihostel, e-mail hostel@saltspring.com. BUDGET.

The three luxurious suites at **Salt Spring Lodge** perch atop a hill overlooking Ganges Harbour, and thus enjoy a sensational view. Each suite has a soaking tub, lots of wood trim, and a king-size bed with down comforters. ~ 641 Fulford-Ganges Road, Salt Spring Island; 250-537-9522, fax 250-537-9522; www.saltspring lodge.com, e-mail info@saltspringlodge.com. DELUXE.

Summerhill Guest House is right on the water, so the activities at this B&B quite naturally focus on the water—swimming, canoeing, kayaking, fishing, sailing are all available. The house itself is an understated private home; the three rooms all have private baths, and two have private decks. Gay-friendly. ~ 209 Chu-An Drive, Salt Spring Island; 250-537-2727, fax 250-537-4301; e-mail summerhill@saltspring.com. BUDGET TO MODERATE.

Green Rose Farm is a restored 1916 Edwardian farmhouse in the middle of a 17-acre farmstead with orchards, meadows and forest. The house features extensive wood trim, with a breakfast room and reading room; one of the three upstairs rooms has a fireplace, and all have private baths. Hiking and kayaking areas are nearby. Gay-friendly. ~ 346 Robinson Road, Salt Spring Island; 250-537-9927. MODERATE.

Situated on four acres, **Cusheon Lake Resort** has fully equipped log and A-frame cabins, all with kitchens and lake views, some with fireplaces. There's an outdoor hot tub. Fishing, swimming and boating are available. ~ 171 Natalie Lane, Salt Spring Island; phone/fax 250-537-9629, 866-899-0017; www.cusheonlake.com, e-mail resort@cusheonlake.com. BUDGET TO MODERATE.

The cozy cedar kitchenette cottages at **Salt Springs Spa Resort** are lined up facing the water, but it's not the view that brings most guests here. The adjacent spa draws on the salt spring for which the island is named; baths and other spa treatments soothe guests not already relaxed by the peaceful location. ~ 1460 North Beach Road, Salt Spring Island; 250-537-4111, fax 250-537-2939; www.saltspringspa.com. MODERATE TO DELUXE.

Perched on a bluff above Stonecutters Bay, **Anne's Oceanfront Hideaway** is deliciously secluded at the end of a private road on the island's north end. The four upstairs rooms are decorated in shades of blue or green and burgundy, with private baths, soaking tubs, plush mattresses and balconies. The extensive book and video library offers entertainment. ~ 168 Simson Road, Salt Spring Island; 250-537-0851, 888-474-2663, fax 250-537-0861; www.annesoceanfront.com, e-mail annes@saltspring.com. MODERATE TO DELUXE.

◄ HIDDEN

Saturna Island is one of the least crowded of the Gulf Islands, largely rural and undeveloped—perfect for a small vineyard and inn. That's what **Saturna Lodge** has created, an all-in-one getaway that retains its low-key atmosphere while offering guests luxurious accommodations, gourmet meals, and lots of relaxing activities on the property or at nearby beaches. The wine shop and tasting room offer a glimpse at a burgeoning new industry in the islands. Closed November through March. ~ Saturna Island Road, Saturna Island; 250-539-2254, 888-539-8800, fax 250-539-3091; www.saturna.ca. DELUXE.

The Inn on Pender Island, with 12 rooms and a hot tub, sits on seven acres of wooded tranquility near Prior Centennial Provincial Park, where hiking, bicycling and beachcombing are in abundance. Three cabins have private hot tubs and fireplaces. Breakfast is included in the room price. ~ 4709 Canal Road, Pender Island; 250-629-3353, 800-550-0172, fax 250-629-3167; www.innonpender.com. MODERATE TO DELUXE.

The newest resort in the islands is **Poet's Cove**, a snazzy new retreat set in its namesake cove (once just a popular marina) in the inner inlet (Bedwell Harbour) on Pender Island. The cedar main lodge is just above the beach; above that are deluxe cottages of stone and wood, with full kitchens, hot tubs and every other imaginable luxury, decorated in elegant green tones. The

PRIVACY PLUS

Spindrift has its own secluded, forested six-acre peninsula overlooking the ocean at Welbury Point. The six self-contained, somewhat rustic cottages are decorated with local pottery and crafts; each has a kitchen, shower and private decks. The grounds include headland forests and a private white-sand beach. ~ 255 Welbury Point, Salt Spring Island; 250-537-5311; www.spindriftsaltspringisland.com. BUDGET TO DELUXE.

entire complex includes a pool, dock, tennis courts and virtually limitless activities such as biking, hiking, kayaking and wildlife watching. ~ 9801 Spalding Road, South Pender; 250-751-1223, 888-512-7638; www.poetscove.com. DELUXE.

HIDDEN ▶   Though it's just a small, quiet facility, **Sun Raven Wellness Retreat** offers many of the same services you'd find at a full-scale spa—massage, reiki, aromatherapy, scrubs, sauna and outdoor pool, even a traditional First Nations sweat lodge. The rooms are spare but offer queen-sized beds and utterly nutritious breakfasts. Both the ferry dock and island restaurants are within walking distance. ~ 1356 MacKinnon Road; 250-629-6216; www.sunraven.com. MODERATE.

DINING   Dinner at **Hastings House** is a highly rated upscale affair (jackets required for men). The cuisine features the famed Salt Spring Island lamb and cheese, plus local seafood and produce, much of it from the estate itself. One seating nightly. ~ 160 Upper Ganges Road, Salt Spring Island; 250-537-2362. ULTRA-DELUXE.

Barb's Buns Bakery is the sort of community institution almost every island has—and needs. Here locals gather for morning coffee, muffins and pastries, and to traffick in local gossip. Everything is made from scratch, and the results fit almost every budget for breakfast. ~ 121 McPhillips Avenue, Salt Spring Island; 250-537-4491. BUDGET.

HIDDEN ▶   Situated in a cozy, small heritage home overlooking Ganges, **Restaurant House Piccolo** is widely considered the finest gourmet bistro on Salt Spring. The menu embraces island lamb, salmon and venison, served with French provincial flair. There are only eight tables, so reservations are highly advised. ~ 108 Hereford Avenue, Salt Spring Island; 250-537-1844. MODERATE.

Seafood is the theme at **Oystercatcher**, an informal eatery right on the harbor in Ganges. Be sure to start with a plate chosen from the day's fresh oyster varieties—usually a half-dozen types are available—and if you want to veer from the seafood theme, the lamb burger, made from island-grown meat, is dandy. ~ 104 Manson Road, Salt Spring Island; 250-537-5041. MODERATE.

HIDDEN ▶   Grab a sandwich, burrito or a savory pizza—or just a plate-filling salad—at the harborfront **Tree-House Cafe**, and get a good seat for the weekend-evening music concerts. The singers set up under the huge, spreading tree for which the café is named, and the music soars as the stars come out. ~ 106 Purvis Lane, Salt Spring Island; 250-537-5379. BUDGET.

Vesuvius Inn labels itself, simply, a neighborhood pub—a distinction that seasoned B.C. travelers know often means darn good food, along with the usual complement of beer and ale. The food, naturally, focuses on simply prepared fish and shellfish, with fish and chips an obvious and excellent choice. The views from the

deck across to Vancouver Island are exceptional. ~ 805 Vesuvius
Bay Road, Salt Spring Island; 250-537-2312. BUDGET.

Though it's tucked into a small shopping center, the **Pistou Grill**   ◄ HIDDEN
is definitely the best independent restaurant on Pender Island. The
menu offers bistro-style food with an Asian flair, such as braised
lamb, caesar salad with pappadam bread, and shrimp and salmon
entrées. The space is cozy and friendly—and small, so make reservations. ~ Driftwood Centre; 250-629-3131. MODERATE.

CUSHEON LAKE 🏊 Cusheon is an interior freshwater lake   **BEACHES**
with a large swimming area—and the water is quite warm. The   **& PARKS**
small regional park here offers a beach, picnic tables and playground facilities. ~ Located on Cusheon Lake Road, six miles (10
km) south of Ganges, Salt Spring Island.

VESUVIUS AND BADER BEACHES 🏊 Vesuvius and Bader are
popular ocean beaches on the island's west side, where the water
is warmest. Because it sits at the edge of the forest, Bader provides
much more privacy, but the sandy beach is small. ~ Vesuvius Bay
Road, four miles (6 km) north of Ganges, Salt Spring Island.

RUCKLE PROVINCIAL PARK 🏃 Ruckle is the largest park in the
islands. It's the site of a pioneer homestead (the family still occupies part of the land). There's a working sheep farm, a broad
meadow and a steep headland with great views out over Swanson
Channel. Closed November through March. ~ Located on Bridgeman Road, ten minutes east of the ferry terminal; 250-391-2300;
wlapwww.gov.bc.ca/bcparks.

▲ There are 70 walk-in shoreline sites—get there early on
summer weekends—and 6 RV sites right by the road; C$14 per
night.

MOUNT MAXWELL PROVINCIAL PARK 🏃 The views at the top
of Mount Maxwell are simply awesome, embracing all the Gulf
Islands, the sound and Georgia Strait beyond, and mainland mountains. Hiking trails ring the mountain, the highest point in the
Gulf Islands. The road up may not be suitable for RVs and low-
slung cars. ~ Located on Mount Maxwell Road, 15 minutes
southwest of Ganges.

FLOCKING TO THE GULF ISLANDS

Birdwatching is a prime activity on the Gulf Islands. Cormorants, harlequin
ducks, gulls, oystercatchers, turkey vultures, ravens, ospreys and bald eagles
are commonly seen. Other birds include tanagers, juncos, bluebirds, fly-
catchers, blackbirds and sparrows. Many of these birds can be seen in
the island's parks.

MOUAT REGIONAL PARK   Mouat is a pleasant, wooded glade offering camping and picnicking facilities. It's in the middle of Ganges, at the foot of Ganges Hill; the name honors early island settlers from Scotland. ~ Seaview Avenue, Ganges.

▲ There are 15 sites, often spoken for quite early in the day; C$15 per night.

The archipelago includes almost 200 islands, but only five have a population of more than 250—Salt Spring, Pender, Galiano, Mayne and Saturna.

PRIOR CENTENNIAL PROVINCIAL PARK   Prior Centennial Park is a pleasantly wooded spot near Bedwell Harbour on Pender Island. Although the park is just inland, two nice beaches are within easy walking distance, as are fishing and boating sites. Closed mid-September to mid-May. ~ Bedwell Harbour Road, five miles (8 km) south of Otter Bay; 250-391-2300; wlapwww.gov.bc.ca/bcparks.

▲ The 17 sites here are often reserved weeks ahead of time; C$14 per night.

MOUNT NORMAN REGIONAL PARK   The hike to the top of the highest point on Pender is a pleasant 1.5-mile climb to a windswept ridge top that affords fantastic views of Bedwell Harbour, almost directly below. ~ Ainslie Point Road, South Pender Island.

Outdoor Adventures

FISHING

Victoria is positioned for incredible sportfishing, primarily for salmon but also for bottomfish such as rock cod, ling cod, red snapper and the occasional halibut. Besides the great angling possibilities, there's the unsurpassed natural backdrop of scenery and wildlife: snowcapped mountains, old lighthouses, sea lions, whales, bald eagles, herons and other water birds.

It's crucial to check local regulations before fishing. Some streams and lakes are closed to fishing at certain times; threats to the viability of salmon runs have caused complete closures on saltwater fishing for some species. In 1999, for instance, coho salmon fishing was closed in much of the water around Vancouver Island. Of course, charter guides and license agencies will have the latest information on season openings. (See the Fishing section in Chapter One for further details.)

It's just a few minutes' drive from downtown Victoria to the marinas where charter outfits operate saltwater fishing trips. **Adam's Fishing Charters** has a standard charter package for a minimum of four hours for up to four people, as well as more customized trips. ~ Inner Harbour; 250-370-2326; www.adamsfishing charters.com. **Kingfisher Charters** provides the usual bait, tackle and license for a minimum four-hour charter for up to four people. ~ 950 Wharf Street; 250-479-8600, 888-479-8600; www.king fisher1.com.

Oak Bay Charters provides bait and tackle for up to five people on charter trips into the protected waters around Victoria. Charter sightseeing excursions are also available. ~ Oak Bay Marina, 2141 Newton Street; 250-598-1061; www.oakbaycharters.com.

Kayaking is an up-close way to explore the coastal inlets of Vancouver Island, where plenty of sea mammals, birds and other wildlife will keep you company.

KAYAKING

Ocean River Sports rents single or double kayaks to individuals, but only to those with kayaking experience. During the summer the store offers a three-hour "get your feet wet" introductory class for people who want to find out more about kayaking. Experienced kayakers can join one of the scheduled two- to three-day trips to the southern Gulf Islands or inquire about customized trips to other locales. ~ 1824 Store Street; 250-381-4233, 800-909-4233; www.oceanriver.com.

There are several popular and worthwhile dive spots around Victoria and Sidney; the waters of northern Puget Sound offer many marine wonders, including the world's largest octopus. Easily accessible from downtown Victoria, **Ogden Point Breakwater** on Dallas Road is a marine park where diving depths range from 20 to 100 feet. Not the best dive spot, but one that's great for snorkeling and exploring tidepools is **East Sooke Park**, between Victoria and Sooke. For advanced deep-sea diving, try **Race Rocks**, also a marine park, where high-current activity stirs up much marine life.

DIVING

Between Victoria and Sidney, on the Saanich Peninsula, there's suitable shore access at **10-Mile Point**, the ecological reserve, although it has strong currents and is not for beginners. **Saanich Inlet** is several hundred feet deep with a sharp 200-foot drop and little tidal exchange, so there's no current.

DOWNTOWN VICTORIA Frank White's Dive Store rents equipment and can provide information and directions for you and your diving buddy or buddies. The shop sponsors group shore dives every Saturday at 10 a.m. and monthly night dives on every second Thursday. You can also arrange a private dive trip with a dive master. ~ 1855 Blanshard Street, Victoria; 250-385-4713, 800-606-3977. **Great Ocean Adventures** rents gear and operates a dive charter vessel for full-day trips to the lower Gulf Islands, Race Rocks and wreck dives along the artificial reefs off Sidney. ~ 1636 Cedar Hill Crossroad, Victoria; 250-475-2202, 800-414-2202.

SAANICH PENINSULA For rentals and instruction, visit **Frank White's Dive Store**. On Sunday, the shop sponsors a drop-in dive. ~ 2200 Keating Cross Road, Saanichton; 250-652-3375.

BOATING

Boating and sailing are popular all around Victoria, the southeastern side of Vancouver Island and in the waters surrounding the Gulf Islands. Victoria is the terminus of the famed Whitbread Classic in the spring. The waters off the west coast are often too rough for relaxed boating, but some pleasure charters are available.

For bareboating (that is, without a guide) rentals of sailboats or powerboats, contact **Bosun's Charters Ltd.** Closed weekends in the winter. ~ Bosun's Landing, Sidney; 250-656-6644; www.bosuns.bc.ca. Besides bareboat rentals, **Seahorse Sailing Inc.**'s sailing school and yacht service runs three- to six-day charters up to the wilderness area of Desolation Bay and over to the Gulf Islands. ~ 2240 Harbour Road, Sidney; 250-656-6644, 800-226-3694; www.seahorsesailing.com.

HANG GLIDING & PARAGLIDING

With steep nearby mountain flanks facing south into the sun, the Victoria area is a dependable venue for hang gliding. Malahat, north of the city, is the most popular launch point; from here the views of the Saanich Peninsula and Strait of Georgia are breathtaking.

By calling the **British Columbia Hang Gliding/Paragliding Association** you can get more information about the sport in the province. ~ 250-767-6717.

GOLF

The oak savannah landscape of the Saanich Peninsula is a natural for golf, with broad meadows flanked by mature trees. Canadians are golf-crazy, and the phenomenon is especially acute in the Victoria area, which has a large population of retirees.

DOWNTOWN VICTORIA There's a mean 16th hole at **Cedar Hill Municipal Golf Course.** It's a par-four downhill, with a two-tiered elevated green. ~ 1400 Derby Road; 250-595-3103. The nine-hole par-three **Henderson Park Golf Course** is fun for beginners.

AUTHOR FAVORITE

Little more than an hour from Victoria, the **Juan de Fuca Trail** is a kinder, gentler southerly cousin to the West Coast Trail. Stretching from Port Renfrew southeast to Jordan River, this 30-mile (50 km) shoreline path takes about four easy days, with several access points along the way (so two-day jaunts are possible), and primitive free camping at various points. Wide beaches, steep headlands, tidepools, dense forests and lots of wildlife are the draws. Trailheads are at China Beach, near Jordan River; and Botanical Beach, near Port Renfrew. *Do not leave valuables in your car while using the trail.* ~ Along Route 14 from China Beach, 21 miles (35 km) north of Sooke, to Botanical Beach, just outside Port Renfrew; 250-391-2300.

You'll only need three clubs to play this course, and you can rent them there. Closed in winter. ~ 2291 Cedar Hill Road; 250-370-7200. Just as the name suggests, **Olympic View Golf Club** offers views of the Olympic Peninsula from its 18 holes. It's cut out of the wilderness, about 25 minutes from Victoria. ~ 643 Latoria Road; 250-474-3671. The nine-hole **Prospect Lake Golf Club** is a challenging course set on the shore of Prospect Lake. ~ 4633 Prospect Lake Road; 250-479-2688. The executive nine-hole **Royal Oak Golf Course** is just minutes from the ferry. ~ 540 Marsett Place; 250-658-1433.

SAANICH PENINSULA Glen Meadows Golf and Country Club is a semiprivate 18-hole championship course that has hosted the World Lefthanders golf tournament and the British Columbia Open. Also available are three tennis courts and a curling rink. ~ 1050 Mctavish Road, Sidney; 250-656-3921.

Golf Central is a Victoria-based service that offers shuttle transportation, tee times, caddy booking and other golf assistance throughout southern Vancouver Island. Working arrangements with nine local courses facilitate the objective—getting out on the links. ~ 250-380-4653.

Although Victoria's terrain is perfect for cycling, the city's streets **BIKING** and walkways are often very crowded; and many walking paths prohibit bicycles. One of the best bets for great views of the water and the Olympic Mountains is **Victoria's Beach Drive**, a six-mile route that passes through lovely Victorian neighborhoods near the ocean. It's an easy ride, with only a few low hills. But use caution on Beach Drive; it's winding and there is often considerable motor traffic. The **Galloping Goose Trail** is a multiuse section of the Trans-Canada Trail, an erstwhile railbed turned into recreation path. You can pick it up in downtown Victoria and head west toward Sooke and beyond into the mountains. ~ Capital District Regional Parks; 250-478-3344.

For a map of bike routes in the area, contact the **Greater Victoria Cycling Coalition**. ~ 1275 Oscar Street, Victoria; 250-381-2453.

Bike Rentals **Sports Rent** provides bikes and inline skates, as well as equipment for camping and water sports. ~ 1950 Government Street #3, Victoria; 250-385-7368. **Cycle BC Rentals** has several locations that rent bikes and scooters. Closed in winter; call for hours. ~ 747 Douglas Street, 250-885-2453, 866-380-2453; 950 Wharf Street, 250-385-2453; www.cyclebc.ca.

Although the Victoria area is quite urbanized, an extensive net- **HIKING** work of hiking trails leads through the city and its many parks, into the suburbs and on into the mountains beyond. The Sooke area is especially fine for summer hiking. All distances listed for hiking trails are one way unless otherwise noted.

DOWNTOWN VICTORIA   The **Harbour Walkway** (6 miles/10 km) is a network of boardwalks, pathways and broad sidewalks that takes the resourceful wanderer from Ross Bay, around the Inner Harbour, and out to West Bay in Esquimalt. Victoria Harbour Ferries can take visitors to the start, or several points along the way; ask at the Visitor Info Centre across from the Empress. Another resource is the Capital Regional District (250-478-3344), which manages thousands of acres of parks in the Victoria area with 180 miles (300 km) of paths and trails. For information on trails outside the greater Victoria area, call BC Parks at 250-391-2300.

For an easy stroll around the Inner Harbour take the **West-song Way Walk** (just over 2 miles/3 km). From there you can watch all kinds of water vessels, including float planes, passenger cata-marans, fishing boats and yachts.

VICTORIA NEIGHBORHOODS   There's a maze of trails in **Thetis Lake Park**. Trails loop around Upper Thetis and Lower Thetis Lakes and along Craigflower Creek.

The **Norn Trail** (less than 1 mile) at Mount Douglas Munici-pal Park (250-425-5523) is an easy walk on a well-marked route with plenty of trees. It joins the **Irvine Trail** to reach the summit of Mount Douglas. Hikers can access the Norn Trail from the park-ing lot at the intersection of Cordova Bay Road and Ash Road.

SAANICH PENINSULA   On the **Island View Beach Regional Park loop** (1.5 mile/2 km roundtrip), visitors can take an easy hike from the parking lot at Island View Park; the trail meanders through fragile sand dunes and has views of the beach and Haro Strait.

The **Lakeside Route** (6.3 miles/10 km) at Elk/Beaver Lake Regional Park is a shaded and well-groomed trail of wood chips and wooden bridges through the beaches surrounding Elk and Beaver lakes.

The trail system within **John Dean Provincial Park** (total of 6 miles/9.5 km of trails) provides views of Saanich Inlet, fertile farm-land and orchards. Take East Saanich Road (Route 17A) north from Saanich eight miles (15 km) to Dean Park Road; the park is 1 mile east.

Goldstream Provincial Park's **Goldmine Trail** (1 mile/1.6 km) is a dirt pathway that travels past a miner's spring and out to Squally Reach Lookout.

The **Galloping Goose Regional Trail** (37 miles/60 km) is a popular multi-use path. Favored by hikers, bicyclists and horses, it begins in downtown Victoria, winds through farmland of Met-chosin then into the semiwilderness of the Sooke River Valley and up the hills, providing ocean views. As a former railroad

Whale Watching

Whale-watching excursions are relatively new to Victoria, beginning in the late 1980s. It's big business on the island now, but it's also big trouble for the whales, who have been forced to endure as many as 100 boats pounding the waters above them on busy summer days. Whale numbers have begun to decline, and some activists are calling for a halt to whale watching. The constant harassment seems to drive the orcas off their usual feeding grounds, and inhibits mating.

The inland waters around Vancouver Island are known for orca (or killer) whales, porpoises, harbor seals, sea lions, bald eagles and many species of marine birds. Visitors also may see the occasional minke whale, gray whale or elephant seal. Whale-watching season extends from March through October; late March and April are best for gray whales. You can also look for little black-and-white Dall's porpoises that play off the bow or follow behind in the wake when you're out on one of these cruises. By July and August, cruise operators are very busy, so it's best to call as much as a week ahead for reservations.

Official regulations and widely accepted ethics attempt to govern whale watching, and commercial operators usually observe the guidelines. Unfortunately, some private boat operators ignore all decent standards of behavior, sometimes even chasing whales outright. Keep in mind that orcas and other whales don't care for boaters buzzing them any more than we would like helicopters hovering over our houses.

Dozens of tour operators, most based in Victoria, run whale-watching trips. The two listed here are among the most responsible and cautious among the operators, trying to minimize their impact on the whales. **Seacoast Expeditions** can accommodate 12 people per boat on its three-hour whale-watching cruises, which begin in April. ~ Ocean Pointe Resort Hotel, 45 Songhees Road; 250-383-2254, 800-386-1525; www.orcaspirit.com. **Five-star Whale Watching** offers three-hour cruises with trained naturalists, departing from the Inner Harbour. ~ 706 Douglas Street; 250-388-7223, 800-634-9617; www.5starwhales.com.

I'd like to urge travelers to consider whether it's essential to go on a whale-watching "hunt" at all. If you must, some operators lead kayak trips, which are much less invasive. If you do take a commercial motor-boat tour, please make sure beforehand that the tour operator intends to respect the whales' need for peace and quiet. Pressure from visitors is likely to have the greatest impact on the industry. And if your charter guide seems to be getting too close, please object.

bed, most of it's perfect for long bike roads but a bit monotonous for walking.

A network of trails, good for hikers, bikers and horseback riders, winds around and up **Cobble Hill**, providing superb views of the Cowichan Valley, Salt Spring Island and the Saanich Peninsula. The hill summit is about 1000 feet above sea level; trails range from a quarter mile to two miles (3 km) in length. ~ Five miles west of Route 1, just north of Shawnigan Lake.

▼▼▼▼▼▼▼▼▼▼
Transportation

CAR

Vancouver Island lies across the Strait of Juan de Fuca from the state of Washington and across the Strait of Georgia from mainland British Columbia. Victoria and the southeastern communities are accessible from either. **Route 14** runs from Victoria through Sooke to Port Renfrew on the west coast. The **Trans-Canada Highway (Route 1)** goes from Victoria to Nanaimo; at 7699 kilometers, connecting St. John's, Newfoundland, to Victoria, BC, it's the world's longest national highway. **Route 17** is a four-lane freeway from the ferry terminals at Swartz Bay and Sidney, past the airport and down the Saanich Peninsula to the Victoria outskirts. Count on a half-hour to 45 minutes to traverse the entire distance.

AIR

The **Victoria International Airport** is located 20 minutes from Victoria in Sidney. Carriers here include Air Canada, Horizon Air, Pacific Coastal Airlines and WestJet. Direct service is available to Vancouver and Seattle. ~ www.cyyj.ca.

Airport bus service between downtown Victoria and the Victoria International Airport is provided by the AKAL **Airport Shuttle Bus**. ~ 250-386-2525.

Helijet Airways offers jet helicopter service into downtown Victoria from downtown Vancouver, and then on to Seattle, and from Victoria Harbour to Vancouver Airport—a quick and very scenic way to get around. ~ 250-382-6222, 800-665-4354; www.helijet.com.

FERRY

Ferries provide daily, year-round sailings to Victoria and Nanaimo. The number of sailings daily usually increases in the summer, but it is advisable to call for up-to-date schedules and rates. High travel times, especially holiday weekends, produce long line-ups at ferry terminals; plan to arrive early.

Travelers wishing to depart from the United States can take Black Ball Transport, Washington State Ferries or Victoria Clipper to Victoria. **Black Ball Transport** takes vehicles and foot passengers from Port Angeles to Victoria's Inner Harbour. ~ 109 East Railroad Avenue, Port Angeles, WA, 360-457-4491; 430 Belleville Street, Victoria, BC, 250-386-2202; www.ferrytovictoria.com.

Washington State Ferries takes vehicles and foot passengers on a scenic route through Washington's San Juan Islands between Anacortes, WA, and Sidney, BC, and buses take foot passengers to downtown Victoria from Sidney. ~ Seattle, WA; 206-464-6400, 800-843-3779.

The **Victoria Clipper** ships are 300-passenger, high-speed jet catamarans that run year-round between Seattle's Pier 69 and Victoria's Inner Harbour with separate trips to the San Juan Islands from May through September. ~ U.S., 800-888-2535; Seattle, WA, 206-448-5000; Victoria, BC, 250-382-8100; www. victoriaclipper.com.

BC Ferries travels year-round from Tsawwassen, just south of Vancouver, to Swartz Bay, a scenic half-hour drive by car or bus from Victoria. Long, long lines in the summer suggest trying out B.C.'s ferry reservations system; call the main ferries number. ~ Victoria, BC, 250-386-3431; within B.C., 888-223-3779; www. bcferries.com. Crossing time is about an hour and a half.

Victoria's Harbour Ferries offer tours of the Inner Harbour and the Gorge waterway, the narrow harbor arm that divides the city to the northwest. The ferries are also the waterborne bus system for Victoria; look for the distinctive red "Ferry Stop" signs along the waterfront. ~ 250-708-0201.

TRAIN

VIA Rail provides Vancouver Island rail service between Victoria and Courtenay, with stops at Nanaimo. ~ 888-842-7245; www. viarail.ca.

CAR RENTALS

Agencies in downtown Victoria and at the Victoria airport include **Avis Rent A Car** (800-331-1084, 250-386-7726), **Budget Rent A Car** (800-668-9833, 250-953-5300), **Hertz Rent A Car** (within the U.S., 800-654-3001; within Canada, 800-263-0600), **Island Rent A Car** (250-384-4881) and **National Car Rental** (800-387-4747, 250-386-1213).

Island Coach Lines (250-385-4411) has bus service between Victoria and other points on Vancouver Island. **B.C. Transit** (250-

◆◆

FLOATING OVER VICTORIA

Floatplanes offer a unique experience as they take off on the water and land directly in Victoria's Inner Harbour. **Kenmore Air** has a daily schedule to Victoria from the Seattle area and also goes to Nanaimo in the summer. ~ 206-486-1257, 800-543-9595; www.kenmoreair.com. **Harbour Air**, the B.C. coast's major operator, flies from Victoria to the Gulf Islands, Vancouver and other coastal destinations. ~ 604-682-2964, 800-665-0212; www.harbour-air.com.

382-6161) provides local bus service throughout the greater Victoria area. B.C. Transit and Victoria Regional Transit Commission offer public transit service to the disabled called **Handy** DART (250-727-7811).

TAXIS

In the Victoria area, you will find **Bluebird Cabs** (250-382-4235, 800-665-7055), **Empress Taxi** (250-381-2222, 800-808-6881) and **Victoria Taxi** (250-383-7111, 888-842-7111).

TOURS

Like many nonprofit institutions devoted to the natural world, the **Royal British Columbia Museum** has launched an eco-tour program devoted to the subject areas the museum features in its galleries. Tours include the Carmanah old-growth forest; local bat colonies; sea lion migration routes; forest mushroom hunts; south island history; and Pacific coast storms. All tours are one-day trips, conducted by experts in their field, ranging in price from C$42 to C$90 (US$27 to US$58). ~ 250-387-5745.

In Victoria, the local architectural society offers free **architectural walking tours** of the city during summer months; call 800-667-0753. **Victorian Garden Tours Ltd.** conducts guided tours year-round of the city's heritage gardens; the fee includes transportation and umbrellas. ~ 250-380-2797; www.victoriagardentours.com. **Victoria's Harbour Ferries** offer tours of the Inner Harbour and the Gorge, the narrow harbor arm that divides the city to the northwest. ~ 250-708-0201.

Midnight Sun Adventures offers rainforest and West Coast trips from one to three days, and encompassing old-growth forests, Pacific beaches, and Vancouver Island's caves. ~ 250-480-9409, 800-255-5057.

SIX

North Vancouver Island

Cold blue seas, towering mountains, icy glaciers, deep forests, sunny sand beaches: the geographic contrasts of Vancouver Island are so vast they make the island as fascinating as it is scenic, and the northern section of the island exemplifies this fact. With vast sounds and inlets cutting into the rugged coastline, steep peaks forming the spine of the island, ancient temperate rainforests (many clear-cut in the past half century) and broad gentle beaches, there's a variety of climatic and topographic conditions for visitors to enjoy. Some of the island's most popular resort areas are like balmy, semiarid ocean communities much farther south. Others are wilderness lodges where thousands of square kilometers of trackless terrain begin outside the door. Many of the island's First Nations inhabitants still occupy remote coastal villages reached only by boat.

At one spot (Tofino) palm trees grow in the cool but mild coastal climate. Not far away, at Strathcona Park, glaciers cling to the mountainsides as a result of yearly winter dumps of 10 to 20 feet of snow. In between, at the heads of the vast fjords that crease the west coast, towering forests thrive under the influence of 10 to 20 *feet* of rain. Over the mountains and down the other side, from Parksville/ Qualicum to Campbell River, the peaks' rain shadow produces a dry and sunny climate similar to the Sunshine Coast across the Strait of Georgia. Families flock here in summer to play in the sun on long sandy beaches. With snow-capped wilderness peaks visible on both sides, the contrast epitomizes how B.C.'s precipitous topography has determined its character.

Ironically, although it is right on the coast, Vancouver Island was one of the last North American locales discovered by European explorers. Inhabited for thousands of years by Coast Salish and Nootka natives who depended on cedar, salal, shellfish and salmon for their livelihoods, the island was visited by Chinese Buddhist monks who sailed there in 499 and called it Fusang when they returned to Asia. A millennium later a Greek navigator working for the Spanish discovered a wide strait, marked by a pillar of rock at its entrance. The straight is still called Juan de Fuca, after the Spanish name the Greek navigator had taken.

Famed explorer James Cook anchored in Nootka Sound in March 1778 on his way home from the voyage in which he discovered Hawaii. A short time later a dispute between the British and the Spanish over the island was resolved in England's favor, and a young British physician, James MacKay, was the first white resident of the island. Furs, coal, timber and fish spurred settlement and development of Vancouver Island—especially a valuable coal field in the area of Nanaimo, which made a tycoon of a Scottish immigrant named James Dunsmuir. Dunsmuir's mines were shipping a million tons of coal a year by 1890, but were notoriously unsafe. An 1887 explosion at Number One Mine in Nanaimo killed 150 miners. Every May 3 the Nanaimo bastion commemorates this disaster by flying the flag half-mast.

Northwest lumber was in demand in California as the Gold Rush fueled a boom in San Francisco. The first major mill began operation in Port Alberni in 1856. Loggers after that hopscotched around the island, stripping hillsides near good anchorages and then moving on. In the 20th century the addition of roads and railroads extended timber operations into the interior; most of the island's roads have been built for the sake of lumber, and only later converted to general use. In the past quarter-century the ever-growing tourism industry has begun to outstrip timber in economic importance. It's a telling oddity to see signs promoting concrete fencing in a region famed for its cedar lumber.

Visitors can avail themselves of excellent boating, beachcombing, wildlife viewing, fishing, hiking, golf, skiing and just plain relaxing. Two of the most intriguing spots are hidden away along distant inlets, reachable only by boat or float plane. The island's West Coast is a world-famous destination for boaters whose craft range from kayaks to sleek, modern yachts; tricky winds, currents and shoals mean it is not for beginners, however.

Pacific Rim National Park is a breathtaking stretch of coastline that draws one million visitors a year in the brief summer season. Similar crowds pour into the Parksville area's string of campgrounds, motels and time-share resorts. In late summer, Campbell River draws anglers from around the world for its salmon fishing. Such numbers don't mean you can't escape people on the island, however; it's easy to do in the off-season, and still possible in the summer. Hikers who head to Cape Scott, for instance, where the weather can be tempestuous most of the year, are virtually certain not to bump into other people.

The fact that relaxed vacationers can play golf or laze on sunny beaches just 60 miles southeast of Cape Scott, one of the wildest spots on the continent, typifies north Vancouver Island. It's both wild and civilized. It's remote but easily reachable—the Parskville resorts are just four hours from Vancouver by car, and a plane flight from Seattle or Vancouver to Tofino takes about an hour.

The island's north half even offers cultural and political interest. It's almost all Crown (public) land, but until recently Canada's major timber companies had virtually undisputed access to clear-cut the old-growth forests that blanketed the island a century ago. Heated protest by environmentalists over this practice culminated in 1993 near Clayoquot Sound when activists from around the world blockaded a bridge over the Kennedy River on the only highway leading in. Hundreds were arrested, and the global spotlight shone on the area. Today, although the timber industry has not shut down, little logging takes place near Clayoquot

Text continued on page 236.

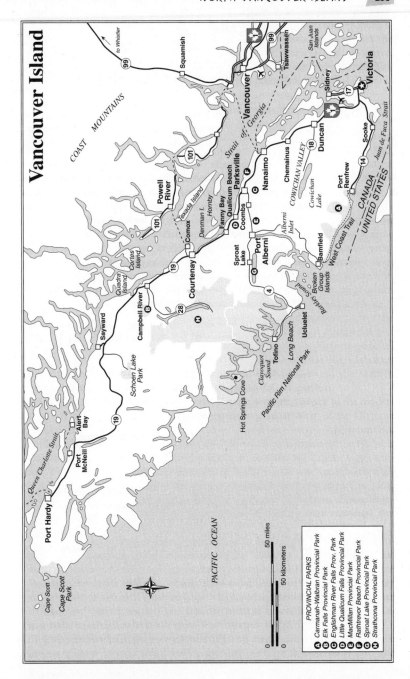

Vancouver Island

COAST MOUNTAINS

to Whistler

Squamish

99

Vancouver

Tsawwassen

San Juan Islands

Sidney

Victoria

17

Duncan

Sooke

Juan de Fuca Strait

14

Port Renfrew

CANADA
UNITED STATES

West Coast Trail

Cowichan Lake

COWICHAN VALLEY

Chemainus

Nanaimo

Strait of Georgia

101

Powell River

101

Texada Island

Hornby

Fanny Bay

Denman I.

Comox

Cortes Island

Quadra Island

Sayward

19

Campbell River

28

Courtenay

Schoen Lake Park

19

Alert Bay

Port McNeill

Port Hardy

Queen Charlotte Strait

Cape Scott

Cape Scott Park

PACIFIC OCEAN

Qualicum Beach

Parksville

Coombs

Sproat Lake

Port Alberni

Alberni Inlet

Bamfield

Barkley Sound

Broken Group Islands

4

Ucluelet

Tofino

Long Beach

Pacific Rim National Park

Clayoquot Sound

Hot Springs Cove

N

50 miles

50 kilometers

PROVINCIAL PARKS
A Carmanah-Walbran Provincial Park
B Elk Falls Provincial Park
C Englishman River Falls Prov. Park
D Little Qualicum Falls Provincial Park
E MacMillan Provincial Park
F Rathtrevor Beach Provincial Park
G Sproat Lake Provincial Park
H Strathcona Provincial Park

In and Around Tofino and Ucluelet

Day 1 • After catching an early ferry to **Nanaimo**, head west on Route 4 toward Tofino, stopping for 15 minutes at **MacMillan Provincial Park** (page 252), by Cameron Lake, to wander through Cathedral Grove's old-growth fir forest.

• Head through Port Alberni, along beautiful **Sproat Lake** (page 253), admiring the sheer peaks of the island ranges just south of the lake. When you come down to the West Coast, stop in at Pacific Rim National Park's **Wickaninnish Centre** (page 255), just north of the Y junction where the road splits to either Tofino or Ucluelet. Map in hand, head up the road for a quick look at **Long Beach** (page 261), almost always packed with surfers; then continue on to the **Schooner Trail** (page 272) parking lot. This relaxing 20-minute hike takes you through old-growth spruce forest to a pristine, uncrowded little beach.

• Check in at the **Wickaninnish Inn** (page 258), Tofino's premier lodge; or **Chesterman Beach Bed and Breakfast** (page 257) just down the road.

• Before dinner, a stroll along beautiful Chesterman Beach is a great way to clear your head of work-week travails. Be sure to stop and visit the master carver employed by the Wickaninnish; both his skill and his perspective are sharp.

• Have dinner at the intimate and inventive **Raincoast Café** (page 259).

Day 2 • After breakfast at the Wick, or your B&B, head into Tofino proper to visit the **Common Loaf Bake Shop** (page 260)—Grand Central Station for the West Coast's alternative culture—and the **Raincoast Interpretive Centre** (page 255), whose compact exhibits on the Clayoquot Sound ecosystem make clear why it's so valuable.

• Time to check out the real thing. Hop on a charter cruise, first stop—**Meares Island** (page 255). The short trail through this majestic old-growth forest leads to the "Hanging Garden Tree," a millennium-old cedar overgrown with other plants and trees. It was the poster "mascot" for the 1993 campaign to save Clayoquot Sound from logging.

- Back in the boat for the 45-minute cruise up **Clayoquot Sound** to **Hot Springs Cove** (page 254), the highlight of the trip. On your journey, watch for whales, dolphins, seals and eagles. When you reach the hot springs dock, don't dawdle on the trail to the changing room—the best pools fill up fast.

- Dine tonight at **The Pointe** (page 259), where chefs blend local seafood, produce and herbs into sensational dinners. If you're lucky, the surf will be up enough to lash the headland just below the restaurant's huge picture windows.

Day 3
- Can you say "Ucluelet"? Your host at **Ocean's Edge B&B** (page 258), Bill McIntyre, will be happy to teach you once you've checked in to this small inn overlooking the Pacific at the southwest edge of town.

- After a cup of coffee, enlist McIntyre, a retired national park naturalist, to lead you to a local cove for a stroll through the fascinating **tidepools** of the Ucluelet Peninsula.

- This afternoon, rent a kayak for a short paddle into the backwaters of **Barkley Sound** (page 269).

- You've had enough upscale food now, so for dinner I recommend a visit to a local pub for fish-and-chips or an oyster burger, a popular and very worthy West Coast favorite.

- Afterwards, you may opt to tuck in early, especially if you made reservations for the 6:30 a.m. Nanaimo ferry out of Ucluelet (you'll be back in Vancouver by 9:30 a.m.).

and Barkley Sounds, and the regional economy depends on tourists—many of whom come to see the marvelous forests that remain.

The best times of year to visit North Vancouver Island are June and September, when the weather is moderate—daytime highs of 65–75°F (20–25°C) with little rain—and the peak season's crowds are gone. April and October can both offer sunny, calm days as well, along with virtually no other visitors. July and August are warmer on the east side; highs can reach 85–95°F (30–35°C). On the west coast, fog often rolls in overnight and doesn't dissipate until early afternoon. On both sides, these are the months when every lodging and campground is booked, and advance reservations are essential.

In the winter, the east side is rainy and chilly. The coast is wracked by downpours and massive storms; the largest wave ever recorded, 140 feet, was registered by a Canadian Coast Guard buoy off Cape Scott. Snow is rare in the lowlands, but copious in the mountains.

▼▼▼▼▼▼▼▼▼▼▼▼▼▼▼▼▼

Strait of Georgia Coast

The territory north of Victoria on the road to Nanaimo is the heartland of the timber industry—at least, it used to be. Here are old sawmills, log dumps, museums, pulp mills, and miles and miles of trees. Most of the latter are second- or even third-growth forest, as the original trees were felled long ago in colonial days. Duncan itself is the center of the Cowichan Valley, a pastoral region of farmsteads and, lately, a small but growing wine industry. Here, the Cowichan First Nation people are noted for their wool garments, and the city has adopted a totem theme. Nanaimo, about 70 miles (114 km) north of Victoria, is an old industrial town now evolving into a commercial center because of its status as a major ferry terminal.

As you go farther north, you reach the Parkville–Qualicum Beach area—these days mostly notable as an enclave of family beach resorts—and the farming and fishery areas of Comox and Campbell River, which are also departure points for some of the more remote islands in the region.

SIGHTS

The towns on Vancouver Island's protected eastern shore tend to be more low key than the more proper British Victoria.

The logging community of **Duncan**, 35 miles (55 km) north of Victoria, is the site of the **British Columbia Forest Discovery Centre**, where you ride the rails behind a steam locomotive through a typical Northwest forest, across a trestle over Somenos Lake to the train station. Once there you can walk around the 100-acre park to see early logging equipment, the Log Museum exhibiting logging artifacts, the Jones Building with historic photos and displays explaining the history of logging. There's also a picnic area and playground. Closed mid-October through March. Admission. ~ 2892 Drinkwater Road, RR4, Duncan; 250-715-1113, fax 250-715-1170; www.bcforestmuseum.com.

Duncan is also home to a collection of some 60 **totem poles**, ten of which are along the highway and the others scattered about town.

Visitors have an opportunity to experience authentic traditions of the Cowichan people at the **Quw'utsun' Cultural and Conference Centre** in Duncan. Today, the Cowichan Band, with about 4000 members, is the largest group of native peoples in British Columbia. During the summer, you can see carvers at work and watch women spin and knit authentic Cowichan sweaters. Call to make a reservation for the midday salmon barbecue with two shows of interpretive dancing. An audiovisual presentation gives a sense of the Cowichan spiritual traditions, which are closely tied with the earth and nature. The center also includes a fine-art gallery and a smaller gift shop. Admission. ~ 200 Cowichan Way, Duncan; 250-746-8119, 877-746-8119, fax 250-746-4143; www.quwutsun.ca.

Tourism information for the island as a whole is available at 250-754-3500; ask for the annual illustrated guide to travel in and around Vancouver Island.

Nearby, the **Cowichan Bay Maritime Centre** is a small museum devoted to local boating and boat-making history. Be sure to check out Salish carver Herbert Rice's fine canoes and other wood arts. Closed November through March. ~ 1781 Cowichan Bay Road, Cowichan Bay; 250-746-4955; www.classicboats.org.

West of Duncan, **Cowichan Valley** is a small but distinctive vineyard and orchard region where some very fine cool-climate wines, as well as fruit ciders, are produced. "Cowichan" is the transliteration of a Native word that means "warm land," and the valley does enjoy a sunnier, balmier climate than other parts of Vancouver Island. To reach the valley, head west from Duncan on Route 18.

Cowichan Valley wineries all use estate-grown grapes, ranging from classic cool-climate types such as pinot gris to unusual varieties such as Ortega. A half-mile west of Route 1, three miles (5 km) south of Duncan, **Blue Grouse Vineyard** is a traditional family-run farm winery with a tasting room and wine shop. Closed Monday and Tuesday, and Sunday in winter. ~ 4365 Blue Grouse Road; 250-743-3834, fax 250-743-9305; www.bluegrousevineyards.com.

Four miles (7 km) south of Duncan and set on 34 acres, **Cherry Point Vineyards'** wine-tasting room is open daily. ~ 840 Cherry Point Road; 250-743-1272, 866-395-5252, fax 250-743-1059; www.cherrypointvineyards.com.

Located one mile west of Duncan, **Vigneti Zanatta** has been a family-owned vineyard winery for over four decades. With regular tastings, a "library vineyard" that displays unusual grape varieties, and gardens surrounding the early-1900s house, this is a sweet place on a sunny afternoon. There's a gift shop here and a restaurant that serves traditional Italian food. Closed Monday and Tuesday and from January to early March. ~ 5039 Marshall Road, Duncan; 250-748-2338.

Chemainus is a small water-side town that hit on an inventive scheme to revive community spirit about two decades back—adorn the town's buildings with local history murals. Now there are dozens, and Chemainus is famous for its outdoor art gallery. ~ Visitor information, 250-246-3944; www.chemainus.com.

HIDDEN ▶

Heading back to the coast and up Route 1 about 30 miles (50 km) from Duncan brings you to **Nanaimo**, a hidden destination right under the noses of visitors who pass through it on their way from the mainland-to-island ferry terminus. The city's name grew out of its native title, "Snenymo," meaning "great and mighty people." White pioneers came to the area after large deposits of coal were discovered in 1851. The city was incorporated in 1874 and today its economy rests on fishing, forestry, port business and tourism.

Its name is also preserved forever in the famous Nanaimo Bar chocolate dessert, although no one has been able to ascertain for certain where or when the recipe originated—or whether it was anywhere near Nanaimo.

The **Nanaimo District Museum** gives visitors an experience of the city's past by taking them through a coal-mining tunnel, blacksmith's shop, general store and barbershop in a turn-of-the-20th-century town; also here are a restored miner's cottage, dioramas depicting the history and culture of the Nanaimo First Nations people and an area focusing on Chinatown. Closed Sunday and Monday in winter. Admission. ~ 100 Cameron Road, Nanaimo; 250-753-1821; www.nanaimo.museum.bc.ca.

There's a self-guided historical walking tour of Nanaimo detailed in a map available at the **Tourism Nanaimo Beban House.** Closed Sunday in winter. ~ 2290 Bowen Road, Nanaimo; 250-756-0106, 800-663-7337, fax 250-756-0075; www.tourism.nanaimo.bc.ca, e-mail info@tourism.nanaimo.bc.ca.

AUTHOR FAVORITE

With hundreds of traditional European cider-apple trees, **Merridale Estate Cidery** is the largest such enterprise in western Canada. Merridale hard ciders are available at many locations in B.C., but only a visit to the farm allows an understanding of the unique process by which hard cider is made. Merridale's annual harvest festival takes place over several weekends in September and October; aside from watching the pressing, visitors can buy local crafts and foods—and, of course, cider from last year's press. ~ 1230 Merridale Road, Cobble Hill; 250-743-4293, 800-998-9908, fax 250-743-9310; www.merridalecider.com.

The **Hudson's Bay Bastion,** a 30-foot-tall building, was built on the waterfront in 1852, ostensibly to protect white settlers from the natives. But because the Indians proved to be peaceful, the fort really didn't protect anything. Since 1910 it has been a museum depicting Nanaimo's heritage. ~ Located just south of the Seaplane Terminal along the harbor, Nanaimo.

Route 19 from Nanaimo follows the coast north and before long (20 miles/35 km) brings you to the crowded (in summer, at least) sea-and-sand stretch between Parksville and Qualicum Beach.

In the Parksville–Qualicum Beach area, you can stop by **St. Anne's Anglican Church,** one of the oldest churches on the island. A group of 45 farmers in the area used oxen to haul the logs for building it. The log church features stained-glass windows. Closed weekends. ~ 407 Wembley Street at Church Road, Parksville; 250-248-3114, fax 250-248-3295; e-mail stedmund@island.net.

The **Craig Heritage Park and Museum** displays artifacts from the local area, including an old schoolhouse, fire engine and period cottages. Very limited winter hours; call ahead. ~ 1245 East Island Highway, Parksville; 250-248-6966.

If you visit the **Big Qualicum Fish Hatchery** during the fall spawning season, you can watch the salmon thrashing their way upstream to lay their eggs. After the staff "milk" the salmon eggs, the eggs are placed under controlled conditions for hatching. There are hiking trails and a picnic area on the grounds. ~ Located off the East Island Highway, ten miles (16 km) north of Qualicum Bay; 250-757-8412, fax 250-757-8741.

In the foothills near Qualicum Beach is **Horne Lake Caves Provincial Park,** one of the finest cave systems in B.C. One-hour family tours are available on weekends in June and September and daily during July and August. Helmets and lights for longer treks can be rented on site during business hours; bring warm clothing and sturdy shoes. Admission. ~ Horne Lake Caves Road, ten miles (16 km) west of Qualicum Beach; 250-757-8687 to book tours in advance; www.hornelake.com.

From Parksville, a few miles west on Route 4 is the little town of **Coombs** with its (thoroughly modern) Old West look of boardwalks and hitching posts amid a collection of novelty shops. In the summer, goats graze on the thatched roofs of some of the shops. Once a Salvation Army settlement project, Coombs has metamorphosed into a small tourist town with putt-putt golf, ice cream parlors and a plethora of antique malls.

West of Coombs is **Butterfly World,** where visitors can see all stages of butterfly life, including egg laying and caterpillar rearing. The most colorful area is the tropical indoor garden where butterflies sip nectar, court and flit among colorful blossoms. Also check out the aviary, koi pond and gift shops. Closed November to mid-

March. Admission. ~ Located one mile west of Coombs on Route 4; 250-248-7026, fax 250-752-1091.

The B.C. Ministry of Forests has created a self-guided **forest tour** along the road from Parksville to Tofino, with signs and interpretive waysides interspersed every 20 miles (30 km) or so. Guide pamphlets are available at tourist info centres. ~ Contact the Nanaimo Forest office, 250-751-7001; or the Timber West Info Centre, 250-749-3244.

The Parksville–Qualicum Beach area is a hugely popular (and hugely crowded, in summer) family vacation stretch of coast, with literally dozens of motels, resorts, campgrounds and combinations of all the above. In midsummer, low tides often draw the water out a half-mile, leaving acres of sun-warmed sand to play on and pockets of equally warm shallow water to play in. (And sometimes it seems like all those acres are needed to handle all the people.) ~ Visitor information, 250-248-3613.

Farther north, just past Fanny Bay, a renowned oyster-farming inlet, is the ferry departure point to **Denman and Hornby Islands**, two side-by-side enclaves in the Strait of Georgia with broad, oyster-and-clam-filled beaches. Both are typified by many B&Bs and small inns, with craft shops and art galleries on Hornby more common than on largely rural Denman. Ferries run roughly hourly during the summer.

On **Hornby**, which advertises itself as the "undiscovered Hawaii of British Columbia," several south-facing bay beaches offer water warm enough for pleasant swimming, notably at **Tribune Bay Provincial Park**. Nearby, at **Helliwell Provincial Park**, a three-mile (5 km) trail leads up to spectacular bluffs from which the setting sun outlines the main island's peaks in an amber glow.

Back on Vancouver Island the highway north to Campbell River passes through the **Comox Valley**, a pastoral agricultural area whose many fruit and produce stands reflect the area's rain-sheltered, balmy summer climate. U-pick farms and farm stands offer berries, fruits and vegetables ranging from lettuce to corn.

From Comox it's about an hour's drive up Route 19 to **Campbell River**, which claims to be the "Salmon Capital of the World" (so does Port Alberni, by the way). The area's many fishing lodges range from ultra-deluxe to plain and economical; floatplane service, scheduled and charter, from Seattle and Vancouver brings high-end anglers to the area in less than two hours. ~ Visitor information, 250-287-4636.

Several islands reached by ferry from the north half of Vancouver Island offer even more in the way of bucolic remoteness. **Quadra Island** is fairly well-developed and settled, with numerous visitor amenities. The ferry departs from Campbell River.

Cortes Island is reached by ferry from Quadra; this more sparsely settled island is excellent for beachcombing, forest walks, and general serenity. It's at the foot of Desolation Sound, the summer cruising and kayak area where inlet waters sometimes reach tropical temperatures.

The peaceful ambience of another century surrounds the 1890s estate at **Fairburn Farm Country Manor** outside Duncan. This 120-acre working sheep farm offers six rooms and a quiet cottage, all with private baths. Guests can enjoy sitting in the library or strolling through the forest; the breakfasts feature homegrown natural foods, including breads, eggs and jams. Closed in winter. ~ 3310 Jackson Road, Duncan; 250-746-4637; www.fairburnfarm.bc.ca, e-mail info@fairburnfarm.bc.ca. MODERATE.

LODGING

◀ HIDDEN

Sunflower Inn B&B is also in the countryside just south of Duncan. This peaceful retreat on a seven-acre farm has three units with views, balconies and a shared bath. There's a lounge, as well as orchards and meadows for guests to wander through. ~ 3415 Glenora Road, Duncan; 250-748-7910, 800-953-6572, fax 250-748-7920; www.sunflowerinn.ca, e-mail rrensing@cowi chan.com. BUDGET.

Newly restored and wonderfully cozy, the cottages at **Greendale Lodge** are tucked under huge firs and cedars along the banks of the Cowichan River. Rustic but completely comfortable, each cottage is different, and all have kitchen facilities. There's a barbecue on the premises, and guests can fish, boat or swim in the river from the property. ~ 8012 Greendale Road, Lake Cowichan; 250-749-6570, fax 749-6590; www.cowichan.com/green dale, e-mail agreen@cowichan.com. MODERATE.

◀ HIDDEN

Deer Lodge was built back in the days (1947) when a "motel" was a quiet small inn by the highway. Luckily for this Mill Bay

AUTHOR FAVORITE

Cortes Island is definitely remote—and thus ideal for **Hollyhock**, a New Age healing and retreat center patterned after Findhorn in Scotland. With a woodsy lodge and cabins scattered about the extensive grounds and fabulous gardens, this is a place for an extended stay. That's exactly what most Hollyhock visitors are there for; the center offers a diverse catalog of retreats and learning workshops, ranging from therapeutic massage to herbal remedies to healthy cooking. Visitors can just plain relax, too. ~ Highland Road, south of Cortes Bay; 800-933-6339; www.hollyhock. bc.ca. ULTRA-DELUXE.

facility, the highway moved a couple hundred yards west, leaving the motel on a peaceful hillside overlooking the bay. Each of the 24 suites is clean, cozy and different; many have kitchens and fireplaces, and all look out on the splendid view. ~ 2529 Route 1, Mill Bay; 250-743-2423, 800-668-5011. BUDGET TO MODERATE.

HIDDEN ▶   **Rosebank Cottages** look ever so much like they were transplanted from a British seaside town; each is a distinctive clapboard building with kitchen, sitting room, bedrooms and a porch. The grounds slope gently down to the beach, and Mount Baker glistens in the distance. ~ 2631 Mill Bay Road, Mill Bay; 250-743-5541. BUDGET TO MODERATE.

Although **Dream Weaver B&B** looks Victorian, the house is actually quite new, with cedar-shake siding. Its broad porch overlooks Cowichan Bay; the four sizable suites all have private baths. Three have whirlpool tubs, and all have CD players, VCR and TV. ~ 1682 Botwood Lane, Cowichan Bay; 250-748-7688, 888-748-7689; www.vancvouverisland-bc.com/dreamweaver, e-mail dream wvr@islandnet.com. MODERATE TO DELUXE.

The Victorian **Pacific Shores Inn** has three suites (each sleeping two to four people) with kitchens and private entrances. Two of the suites feature washers and dryers, making them ideal choices for families. For a romantic getaway, rent the Fairy Tale Cottage with its unique stonework and wood detailing, fireplace and private deck and yard. ~ 9847 Willow Street, Chemainus; 250-246-4987, fax 250-246-1051; e-mail inkeeper@island.net. MODERATE TO DELUXE.

The **Coast Bastion Inn** has rooms that feature wood furniture, designer color schemes and views of the water. The inn has a sauna, whirlpool and exercise room, restaurant, café and pub. ~ 11 Bastion Street, Nanaimo; 250-753-6601, 800-663-1144, fax 250-753-4155; www.coasthotels.com, e-mail infobastion@coasthotels.com. MODERATE TO DELUXE.

INN A PRIVATE PLACE

The **Ships Point Inn** sits on a private point of land overlooking Fanny Bay and Denman Island. The beach is littered with oysters; you can pick a few and have lunch if you like. The inn is surrounded by gardens with dozens of varieties of roses. There are four rooms, all with views; there's also a private cottage. A communal hot tub overlooks the bay. The gourmet breakfast includes mouth-watering coffee, homemade breads and pastries, and herb-infused omelettes. Dinners are available with advance notice. ~ 7588 Ships Point Road, Fanny Bay; 250-335-1004, 877-742-1004, fax 250-335-1014; www.shipspoint.com, e-mail info@shipspointinn.com. MODERATE TO DELUXE.

The **Best Western Dorchester Hotel** offers oceanfront views from most of its 70 Victorian-themed units. Built on the former site of the old Windsor Hotel and Opera House near the Bastion, the hotel also has a restaurant, rooftop garden and a library. ~ 70 Church Street, Nanaimo; 250-754-6835, 800-661-2449, fax 250-754-2638; www.dorchesternanaimo.com, e-mail info@dorchester nanaimo.com. MODERATE TO DELUXE.

With white stucco walls and amazing fuchsia/indigo awnings, the **Buccaneer Inn** has a Mediterranean flair. But it's in a quiet, back-street location and is actually the closest accommodation to the BC Ferries Departure Bay terminal. The spacious studios and suites (one is a fireplace suite) all have a separate private bath; suites all have a kitchen. ~ 1577 Stewart Avenue, Nanaimo; 250-753-1246, 877-282-6337; www.thebuccaneerinn.com. DELUXE.

◄ *HIDDEN*

Just minutes away from the **Nanaimo Hostel** is the BC Ferries dock; the departure dock for Newcastle Island park; and numerous cafés and pubs in central Nanaimo. The 40 beds are dorm style, and there's a communal kitchen, TV room, laundry and camping area. ~ 65B Nicol Street, Nanaimo; 250-753-1188. BUDGET.

Surrounded by woods on three sides, **Beach Acres Resort Hotel** opens onto a large, secluded beach. The 55 beachfront and forest cottages and oceanview condos with kitchens and fireplaces are clean and comfortably furnished. Amenities include a pool, whirlpool, sauna, tennis courts, laundry and restaurant. ~ 1051 Resort Drive, Parksville; 250-248-3424, 800-663-7309, fax 250-248-6145; www.beachacresresort.com, e-mail reservations@ beachacresresort.com. ULTRA-DELUXE.

In the middle of Beach Acres Resort, but not associated with it, is the **Maclure House Inn**, a Tudor-style mansion that houses a good restaurant on the ground floor and sumptuous B&B rooms above. Three large rooms and one suite are furnished with Edwardian antiques; two rooms overlook the ocean, and the suite has a sitting room with a fireplace. Breakfasts are excellent, three-course samplings of the restaurant's fare. ~ 1015 East Island Highway, Parksville; 250-248-3470; www.maclurehouse.com, e-mail stay@maclurehouse.com. MODERATE.

◄ *HIDDEN*

The **Island Hall Beach Resort** is in downtown Parksville on nearly 1000 feet of sandy beach. This resort opened its doors in 1917 with 24 rooms. Now it has grown to 44 units. Rooms are light and bright with a mixture of older and contemporary furnishings. The resort also features a seasonal pool, whirlpool, restaurant, pub and lounge. ~ 181 West Island Highway, Parksville; 250-248-3225, 800-663-7370, fax 250-248-3125; e-mail ishall@ island.net. MODERATE TO ULTRA-DELUXE.

Wood paneling, plush carpets and water views mark the 43 rooms at the **Parksville Beach Resort**, right on the beach in this sunny resort town north of Nanaimo. Rooms have either two queen or two double beds, and some include kitchenettes. The resort itself has two beach volleyball courts, a whirlpool and sauna, an indoor pool, horseshoe pits and tennis courts. A playground and water park are next door. ~ 161 West Island Highway, Parksville; 250-248-6789, 888-248-6789, fax 250-248-4789; www.parksvillebeachresort.com, e-mail info@parksville beachresort.com. MODERATE TO ULTRA-DELUXE.

Down beds, private entrances and antique furnishings mark the two units at **Madrona Point Waterfront B&B** on Nanoose Bay. Guests can make use of canoes, kayaks, sailboards and bicycles available for rent. The hot tub overlooks the beach. ~ 1344 Madrona Drive, Parksville; 250-468-5972. BUDGET.

Once a private boys' school, the Tudor-style **Qualicum Heritage Inn** sits on three acres on a bluff overlooking Georgia Strait. Half the inn's 70 rooms have water views and some include fireplaces. A lounge, dining room, neighborhood pub and beach access round out the scene; six golf courses are nearby. ~ 427 College Road, Qualicum Beach; 250-752-9262, 800-663-7306, fax 250-752-5144; www.qualicumheritageinn.com, e-mail info@ qualicumheritageinn.com. MODERATE.

Outer Island R&R is in the middle of 13 acres of fields and orchards near Tribune Bay on Hornby Island. With five luxurious rooms, a private cottage, a tennis court and a heated pool, it would be easy to stay put—but the beach at Tribune Bay is just minutes away. ~ 4785 DePape Road, Hornby Island; 250-335-2379, 800-364-1331, fax 250-335-0606; www.outerisland.bc.ca, e-mail retreat@outerisland.bc.ca. MODERATE TO DELUXE.

HIDDEN ► Set on ten acres in the countryside west of Courtenay, the **Comox Lake Hostel** is near Strathcona Park and offers guests hiking and biking along the Comox River, sailboarding on Comox Lake, and easy access to skiing in the mountains nearby. There are outdoor barbecues, a kitchen and laundry and camping facilities. The hostel will pick travelers up at the train or bus station in Courtenay. ~ 4787 Lake Trail Road, Courtenay; 250-338-1914. BUDGET.

Painter's Lodge is Campbell River's best-known fishing resort. Like other area resorts, fishing charters leave from the lodge's dock daily, and the best fishing grounds are often minutes away. The resort often offers off-season, budget packages that include direct floatplane service from Seattle or Vancouver. Modern rooms, gourmet dining facilities, a fitness center and tennis courts are available. ~ 4100 Discovery Drive, Campbell River; 800-663-7090; www.painterslodge.com. DELUXE.

Next door to Painter's is **The Dolphins Resort**, a much more low-key lodge also devoted to fishing. Its 18 rustic-style cabins are self-contained units with fireplaces and kitchens, furnished with lodge-style antiques. Lodge staff will prepare meals if desired; guests have access to complete guided fishing services. ~ 4125

Discovery Drive, Campbell River; 250-287-3066, fax 250-286-6610; www.dolphinsresort.com, e-mail fish@dolphinsresort.com. ULTRA-DELUXE.

Although it's remote and secluded, **April Point Lodge** leaves little luxury undone. With elegant suites and guesthouses (37 units in all), fireplaces, hot tubs, meeting facilities—even a sushi bar—it's little wonder April Point draws quite a few business customers who fly in from Vancouver or Seattle. On Quadra Island, the lodge can be reached by road; it also has a marina. All guest facilities face the water; fishing is obviously a major attraction. The dining room focuses on gourmet seafood preparations. ~ April Point Road, Quadra Island; 250-285-2222, 800-663-7090, fax 250-598-3366; www.aprilpoint.com. DELUXE.

> The original Duncan post office, built in 1913, is now the town's city hall.

Just as in a traditional "big house," massive cedar beams form the superstructure of **Tsa-Kwa-Luten Lodge,** one of just two Native-owned guest inns in B.C. Large, comfortable rooms with fireplaces warm guests, but a myriad of outdoor adventures beckon: fishing, kayaking, looking for pictographs or just plain beachcombing. All rooms face the water. ~ Cape Mudge, Quadra Island; 250-285-2042, 800-665-7745, fax 250-285-2532; www.capemudgeresort.bc.ca, e-mail tkllodge@connected.bc.ca. DELUXE.

Strathcona B&B is a comfy wood chalet at the entrance to its namesake park, with both dorm-style and private family rooms. Breakfasts are hearty affairs designed to fuel skiers for long days at Mount Washington. The same operators run the even more economical Mount Washington Hostel. ~ 1375 Henry Road, Mount Washington; 250-898-8141; www.strathconabandb.com. BUDGET TO MODERATE.

The **Strathcona Park Lodge** offers good access to its namesake park. You can stay in a simple budget-priced room or a fully equipped cabin with a private bath (moderate to deluxe). An ultra-deluxe-priced chalet has eight bedrooms and three decks. ~ Route 28, an hour west of Campbell River; 250-286-3122, fax 250-286-6010; www.strathcona.bc.ca. BUDGET TO ULTRA-DELUXE.

DINING

You can discern the **Coffee Mill**'s philosophy about its brew from its web address: seriouscoffee.com. It's a legitimate description, too, with good strong coffee drinks and excellent muffins and pastries. If you're around at lunch there are soups and sandwiches; the fireside sitting area is dandy. No dinner. ~ Frayne Road and Route 1; 250-743-3371. BUDGET.

The ice cream is handmade and all natural at the **Udder Guys** store on Cowichan Bay—using only fresh milk from nearby dairies. The pies are pretty darn good, too. ~ 1750 Cowichan Bay Road, Cowichan Bay; 250-746-8981. BUDGET.

Glow World Cuisine is the newest entrant in fine dining in Nanaimo. With a Hollywood-style decor—high-backed plush red booths—and parchment-paper menus, the ambience matches the inventive cooking. Try the salmon and rhubarb compote, or tapas plates usch as green curry crab and apple slices. ~ 7 Victoria Road, Nanaimo; 250-741-8858. MODERATE TO DELUXE.

The **Lighthouse Bistro** is designed to look like a lighthouse built into a white, Cape Cod–style building with light blue trim. The restaurant has a great view of the harbor, especially from the tables on their large deck, and a menu that changes with the local fish in season, such as blue marlin or trout. The pub upstairs serves the same menu, including the smoked salmon corn chowder. ~ 50 Anchor Way at the Seaplane Terminal, Nanaimo; 250-754-3212. MODERATE TO DELUXE.

In Parksville, visit **Kalvas**, a large log-beam building, for fine French and German fare. You can feast on East Coast lobster, fresh local crab and oysters. ~ 180 Moilliet Street, Parksville; 250-248-6933. DELUXE TO ULTRA-DELUXE.

HIDDEN ▶ The **Maclure House Inn**, in the middle of Beach Acres Resort, is a Tudor-style mansion that represents gourmet dining on this stretch of the island coast. Lunches feature hearty soups and fish dishes; dinners offer excellent Continental entrées, utilizing fresh island ingredients such as local oysters, cheese and lamb. Breakfast, lunch and dinner served. ~ 1051 Resort Drive, Parksville; 250-248-3470. MODERATE.

For English-style fish and chips, try Parksville's **Spinnaker Seafood House**. The comfortable restaurant has a nautical theme, and the eclectic menu includes fresh seafood, pizza, hamburgers and salads for eating in or taking out. ~ 625 East Island Highway, Parksville; 250-248-5532. BUDGET TO MODERATE.

As in so many other small towns across British Columbia, the best place to find dinner in Campbell River is a neighborhood pub. Join the locals at the **Royal Coachman**, where the pub chefs offer up excellent soups and salads, as well as sandwiches, fish-and-

COWICHAN CRAFTS

In Duncan, the **Quamichan House** at the Quw'utsun' Cultural and Conference Center offers one of the largest selections of authentic native arts and crafts on the island, including original paintings, jewelry, carvings, masks, rattles, drums, Cowichan knitted items and books on the culture and art of native Northwest coastal peoples. ~ 200 Cowichan Way, Duncan; 250-746-8119, fax 250-746-4143; www.quwutsun.ca, e-mail askme@quwutsun.ca.

chips and dinner specials. The pub is located in a timber-framed Tudor-style building. ~ 84 Dogwood Street at 2nd Avenue, Campbell River; 250-286-0231. BUDGET TO MODERATE.

With the Strait of Georgia at its feet, the fare at **Sushi by the Sea** is quite appropriate—sushi rolls using fresh ingredients such as salmon and shrimp. You'll also find teriyaki and noodle dishes. Located in the Anchor Inn, the restaurant affords superb views across the water. ~ 261 Island Highway, Campbell River; 250-286-1131. MODERATE.

Take your sweet tooth to **Steiner Bakery and Coffee Shop**: the pastries, muffins and other goodies here are German-style. Be sure to pick up a loaf of bread for lunch, too. ~ 231 Dogwood Street, Campbell River; 250-287-7323. BUDGET.

With an extensive buffet and salad bar, the vegetarian cuisine at **Bar None Café** is certain to leave no one hungry. There are also hot entrées, nightly specials, a juice and cappuccino bar, and delectable desserts. Closed Sunday. ~ 244 4th Street, Courtenay; 250-334-3112. BUDGET.

◄ *HIDDEN*

SHOPPING

Judy Hill operates a very large gallery in Duncan that represents two dozen local and First Nations artists and craftmakers, including Reg Davidson and Roy Vickers. ~ 22 Station Road, Duncan; 250-746-6663.

Hill's Native Art features handmade Cowichan sweaters, small replicas of totem poles, carvings, jewelry and prints. ~ 76 Bastion Street, Nanaimo; phone/fax 250-755-7873; www.hills nativeart.com.

The **Crow's Nest Marine Chandlery** offers a full line of nautical supplies, but you don't have to be a waterborne traveler to find something here you'll need. Binoculars, outerwear, camping and fishing gear are on hand—and check out the selection of clocks and electronic gear. ~ 1797 Comox Avenue #204, Comox; 250-339-3676.

For all its pseudo-Tudor flavor, Vancouver Island has a strong Western heritage. That's what visitors will find on display at **Ridgerider**, where the top-of-the-line custom Western wear includes fancy boots, handmade leather jackets, hats and other adornments such as moccasins and belts. There's a selection of Coast Native artwork and handcrafts, too. ~ 920 Island Highway, Campbell River; 250-286-3554.

NIGHTLIFE

Nightlife isn't plentiful outside Victoria, but that doesn't mean you can't have an enjoyable time in some of the island's southeastern communities. Try Nanaimo's **Dinghy Dock Pub**, reached by a ten-minute ferry ride (ferry information 250-753-8244). The pub offers locally brewed beers and other spirits and spectacular views of Nanaimo, its harbor and Newcastle Island. Closed mid-October to spring. ~ 8 Pirate's Lane, Protection Island; 250-753-2373, fax 250-741-8244.

Nanaimo has a handful of **theater companies**, including the Nanaimo Theatre Group, Yellow Point Drama Group and Malispina College Drama Group. For information on all groups, call 250-756-0106.

BEACHES & PARKS

NEWCASTLE ISLAND PROVINCIAL MARINE PARK 🏃 🚴 🛶 🛥 🚤 ⛴ ⛵ Over 750 acres of woods and sandy beaches on an island in Nanaimo Harbor afford views of Vancouver Island and the mainland's Coast Mountains. The park features sandstone ledges and sandy, gravel beaches. Cast a rod for salmon. There are picnic areas, a playground, restrooms, over 130 feet of docks, a visitors center and a snack bar in the summer. ~ In summer, scheduled foot-passenger ferry service departs from behind the Nanaimo Civic Arena off Route 1, north of downtown. Cars are not allowed; 250-754-7893.

The area near Newcastle Island Provincial Marine Park was a site for coal mining and sandstone mining in the mid-to-late 1800s.

▲ There are 18 tent sites available on a first-come, first-served basis; C$14 per night.

RATHTREVOR BEACH PROVINCIAL PARK 🏃 🚴 🛶 🎣 ⛵ 🚤 ⛴ Located between Nanaimo and Parksville, this park's popularity lies within its sandy beach. There are also a wooded upland area, excellent birdwatching during the spring herring spawn and views of Georgia Strait. There are picnic areas, restrooms and showers. Parking fee, C$5. ~ Located about two miles south of Parksville off Route 19; 250-954-4600.

▲ There are 174 tent/RV sites (no hookups); C$22 per night. There are also 24 walk-in sites; C$14 per night.

ENGLISHMAN RIVER FALLS PROVINCIAL PARK 🏃 🚴 🛶 🎣 ⛵ Forests of cedar trees surround a crashing waterfall in this lush park that encompasses 240 acres. Large groves of hemlock and fir also can be found in the park. A good time to visit is in the autumn, when the maple trees offer a colorful contrast to the evergreens. You'll find picnic areas and restrooms. Parking fee, C$3. ~ Located west of Parksville off Route 4; 250-954-4600.

▲ There are 105 tent/RV sites (no hookups); C$17 per night.

LITTLE QUALICUM FALLS PROVINCIAL PARK 🏃 🛶 ⛵ Although a neighbor of Englishman River Falls Park, this area is much drier. Consequently, visitors see more pine, Douglas fir and arbutus (madroña) trees in this park that straddles the Little Qualicum River. Don't miss the impressive waterfalls splashing down a rocky gorge. Fish for salmon and take a dip in Cameron Lake. Picnic areas and restrooms are the only facilities. Parking fee, C$3.

~ Located 11 miles west of Parksville off Route 4; 250-954-4600, fax 250-248-8584.

▲ There are 91 tent/RV sites (no hookups); C$17 per night. Reservations: 604-689-9025, 800-689-9025; www.discover camping.ca.

FILLONGLEY PROVINCIAL PARK 🏃 🚴 ⛵ ⛴ 🚣 ⤵ This pretty, small park offers a creek for children to splash in, a long gravel and shell beach and grassy meadows to stroll through. Extended beach walks are possible at low tide. ~ Located four miles east of the ferry landing, on Lambert Channel Road, Denman Island; 250-954-4600.

▲ There are 10 vehicle/tent sites nicely situated up from the beach; C$17 per night.

STRATHCONA PROVINCIAL PARK 🏃 ⛵ ⤵ This is B.C.'s old-   ◄ *HIDDEN*
est provincial park, a half-million-acre enclave in the middle of Vancouver Island four hours north of Victoria. It offers popular day hikes from Paradise Meadows on the Forbidden Plateau, which can also serve as the starting point for extensive back-country pack trips. Intrepid hikers might want to try for 1443-foot Della Falls, one of the ten highest waterfalls in the world, accessible only by boat and foot on the Gold River side of the park. Less determined visitors can simply relax in the Buttle Lake campground. ~ Located an hour west of Campbell River on Provincial Route 28; 250-954-4600.

▲ Campsites at Buttle Lake (86 sites) or Ralph River (60 sites) are on a first-come, first-served basis; C$14 from Memorial Day through September, $C9 the rest of the year.

MIRACLE BEACH PROVINCIAL PARK 🏃 🚴 ⛵ ⛴ 🚣 ⤵ Although this major park is close to the Island Highway and just south of Campbell River, the fact that it's a bit distant from the Parksville area holds crowds down a little, compared to Englishman River and Rathtrevor. The beach is just as nice, and the campground, while huge, is well laid out. ~ Located 15 miles (24 km) north of Courtenay along Route 19; 250-954-4600.

▲ There are 193 vehicle sites; C$22 per night.

ELK FALLS PROVINCIAL PARK ⛵ ⤵ Just outside Campbell River, this park abuts a river famed for its winter steelhead runs; in summer, nearby lakes and streams offer excellent trout fishing. The day-use area provides good swimming on hot summer days. ~ Located one mile (2 km) west of Campbell River; 250-954-4600.

▲ Some of the 121 sites have limited facilities; C$14 per night.

SMELT BAY PROVINCIAL PARK 🏃 🚴 ⛵ 🎣 ⛴ 🚣 ⤵ The   ◄ *HIDDEN*
bay fills with millions of spawning smelt in the spring, but that's not what draws most visitors to this small shoreline park. This

remote corner of Cortes Island is peaceful and beautiful, and the waters warm to practically balmy levels in the summer. ~ The island is two ferry rides from Campbell River. Located in the southwest corner of Cortes Island, about ten miles (16 km) south of the ferry landing on Smelt Bay Road; 250-954-4600.

▲ There are 22 vehicle sites; C$14 per night.

Alberni Inlet

Route 4 heads west across the island from Parksville toward Pacific Rim National Park. On the way is Port Alberni, at the end of a long inlet that opens out to Barkley Sound. Perched on a small corner of land here is Bamfield, south of which is the West Coast Trail section of Pacific Rim.

SIGHTS

Port Alberni is mostly of interest to travelers as a jumpoff point for Sproat Lake and Barkley Sound. This small industrial city at the end of an inlet that almost divides the island has an extensive logging history; the first mills here predate 1900, although none of those are still operating. A small selection of highway motels awaits travelers who are unlucky enough to lack reservations on the *Lady Rose* or at a lodge out on the coast.

Board the **MV Lady Rose** for a unique experience traveling the Alberni Inlet aboard a freighter, the likes of which have served the hidden, remote communities on the island's west coast for over 50 years. Passengers on the day-long trips can see deliveries of fish food to commercial fish farms, asphalt shingles to individuals reroofing their homes and mail to residents of communities such as Kildonan. Kayakers can be dropped off at the Broken Group Islands. Tourists should realize that the boat is primarily a freighter, so don't expect a naturalist or an interpretive guide with fascinating commentary. ~ Argyle Pier; 250-723-8313, 800-663-7192 (April to September), fax 250-723-8314; www.lady rosemarine.com.

HIDDEN ►

Just outside Alberni is the **R. B. McLean Heritage Lumber Mill**, a steam-powered sawmill that was in commercial use from

---

BOMBS AWAY

Just outside Port Alberni at Sproat Lake, take the time to view a hidden attraction, the **Flying Tankers, Inc.**; a private fire protection service. Although not regularly scheduled, and certainly not developed for tourists, the sight of the largest firefighting aircraft in the world dropping 6000 gallons of water on the lake in a test run is almost too impressive for words. ~ 9350 Bomber Base Road, off Lakeshore Road, Port Alberni; 250-723-6225; www.martinmars.com.

1925 to 1965. Now restored and open to visitors, it offers a genuine taste of what sawmills used to be like before computers, lasers and the other technologies took over. ~ On Smith Road 4 miles (6 km) northwest of Port Alberni; 250-723-2181.

Not long ago the road from Port Alberni to Bamfield was open mostly to logging traffic. Today, with the timber market slumping and the road much improved, it's a fairly easy two-hour drive in a passenger car. Along the way you'll see hundreds of square miles of forest and the aftermath of logging, pass by several inviting lakes, and arrive at the end of the road in one of the most remote communities the average visitor can get to in North America. In British Columbia, only Telegraph Creek, the Nass Valley and Atlin compare. (See Chapter Eleven.)

Bamfield is built along two sides of a beautiful narrow inlet   ◄ HIDDEN
on Barkley Sound. When the road finally reached the town, it stopped on the east side, and the west half of town remains accessible only by boat. Thus the town has a truly split personality, the west being much quieter and slower-paced than the east. (Bamfield split in earnest in the mid-'80s when a road to the west side was proposed; many west side residents opposed it, and the community was bitterly divided. Eventually the plan, which would have been extremely costly, was dropped.) Water taxis connect the two; on the west side, a boardwalk is the town's main street, a charming 15-minute stroll past a few small inns, a coffee/curio stand, the grocery store and post office. An overnight visit to west Bamfield is like a massage for the psyche, soothing and serene.

Best Western Barclay with 86 rooms is the largest hotel in town.   **LODGING**
It features an attractive lobby, a coffee shop, dining room, sports bar and lounge. Accommodations are clean, fairly standard rooms and suites. Amenities include a heated outdoor pool, whirlpool, fitness center, and sauna. ~ 4277 Stamp Avenue, Port Alberni; 250-724-7171, 800-563-6590, fax 250-724-9691; www.best westernbarclay.com, e-mail reservations@bestwesternbarclay. com. DELUXE.

Coast Hospitality Inn may be the best place to stay in town if you don't mind the absence of a pool. The lobby features comfortable seating in front of a fireplace. The inn has 49 rooms in soft colors with firm beds and standard motel furniture. Exercise room on-site. ~ 3835 Redford Street, Port Alberni; 250-723-8111, 800-663-1144, fax 250-723-0088; www.coasthotels.com, e-mail info@coasthospitalityinn.com. DELUXE.

You could hardly ask for a more perfect setting than that occupied by **Eagle Nook Ocean Wilderness Resort**. Built on a nar-   ◄ HIDDEN
row neck of land dividing a back bay in the most remote corner of Barkley Sound, Eagle Nook is surrounded by forest and quiet

inlets. The bay is perfect for kayaking among the tidepools; a huge oyster bed is nearby; salmon and halibut fishing are not far. A system of trails leads into the mountains behind. The 23 rooms are spacious and comfortable and the dining room offers cuisine superior to that at most outback lodges. Access by boat and floatplane only; the lodge owners also operate China Creek Marina outside Port Alberni, so that's where the lodge's water taxi departs from. Closed October through April. ~ Jane Bay, Barkley Sound (Box 575), Port Alberni; 250-723-1000, 800-760-2777, fax 250-723-2736; www.eaglenook.com. DELUXE.

HIDDEN ► **Imperial Eagle Lodge** sounds more imposing than it is; it's actually a very nice B&B at the south end of west Bamfield. Four rooms with comfortable beds and furnishings surround a beautifully landscaped yard; there's also a nice two-bedroom cottage with cooking facilities. Breakfast is served in a smartly appointed dining room overlooking Bamfield Harbor; gourmet dinners are also available on request, after which guests can repair to the hot tub on the deck. The Bamfield boardwalk is just five minutes away. Lodge owner Jim Levis, who also operates fishing charters, picks up guests on the east side once you arrive in Bamfield. ~ Box 59, Bamfield; 250-728-3430; www.imperialeaglelodge.com. MODERATE.

DINING It would be hard to leave hungry after a meal at **Little Bavaria**, which seduces local appetites with overflowing plates of traditional German favorites such as schnitzel, as well as salmon, crab and other local seafood. The Bavarian Platter offers meat, sausage, potatoes, noodles, rolls and vegetables for two at about C$35. No lunch on weekends. ~ 3035 4th Avenue, Port Alberni; phone/fax 250-724-4242; www.littlebavariarestaurant.com. MODERATE.

Dining options on the water side of Bamfield boil down to the **Bamfield Inn**, which offers an array of seafood-based lunches and dinners ranging from chowder to grilled salmon. Burgers, fish-and-chips and pub-type fare round out the menu. ~ Located on Government Dock, at the north end of the boardwalk, Bamfield; 250-728-3354. BUDGET TO MODERATE.

BEACHES & PARKS **MACMILLAN PROVINCIAL PARK** 🏃 On the shores of Cameron Lake, this 336-acre park, available for day-use only, provides access to Cathedral Grove, a large stand of old-growth Douglas fir. Some of the trees are 800 years old, and the largest are 250 feet tall and nearly ten feet in diameter. Walking through this ancient forest can be a spiritual experience, but the area is so popular it is being "loved to death" by tourists. A huge blowdown a few years ago inspired park managers to build a scaffold-walk that lifts visitors above the devastation, offering a unique perspective on this fairly common ancient forest phenomenon. Parking fee, C$3. ~ Located west of Parksville, about 11 miles east of Port Alberni off Route 4; 250-954-4600.

SPROAT LAKE PROVINCIAL PARK

On the north shore of Sproat Lake just west of Port Alberni, this park is a water enthusiast's paradise. The lake is warm and sunny, perfect for summer swimming. Fishing is excellent for steelhead, trout and salmon. Visitors can walk a short distance through the woods to see prehistoric petroglyphs. Facilities are limited to picnic areas and pit toilets. Parking fee, C$3. ~ Located eight miles northwest of Port Alberni off Route 4; 250-954-4600.

The Douglas firs at MacMillan Provincial Park are believed to have survived a fire some 300 years ago because of their fire-resistant bark, nearly a foot thick on some of the trees now.

There are 59 tent/RV sites (no hookups); C$17 to $20 per night.

STAMP RIVER PROVINCIAL PARK

This park offers pleasant walks among the stands of cedar and fir, and an area for contemplation near the waterfall. Visitors can view salmon jumping up the fish ladders in summer and fall. Steelhead and cutthroat trout also invite anglers. Picnic areas and primitive campsites are the only facilities. ~ Located about eight-and-one-half miles north of Port Alberni off Route 4 on Beaver Creek Road; 250-954-4600.

There are 23 tent/RV sites (no hookups); C$14 per night.

CHINA CREEK MARINA & CAMPGROUND

This private facility, just outside Port Alberni, is one of the best spots to gain access to Barkley Sound, with boat rentals and water-taxi service available. The marina also operates a charter service, and this is the departure point for guests going to Eagle Nook Ocean Wilderness Resort. The best tent campsites are numbers 49, 50 and 55 along the beach. ~ On the Bamfield Road, 10 miles (16 km) west of Port Alberni; 250-723-9812.

There are 318 sites, most with hookups; C$15 to C$25 per night.

POETT NOOK CAMPGROUND & MARINA

Along a secluded, pristine cove just off the Alberni–Bamfield Road, this private campground has a store, boat launch, fuel service, and fishing charter service. Appropriately enough, the owners' names are Salmon: the cove is on Barkley Sound, site of a famous late-summer/early-fall salmon run. ~ Along the Bamfield Road, 45 miles (72 km) from Port Alberni; 250-758-4440; www.geocities.com/poettnook.

Most of the 150 sites have hookups; C$12 to C$20 per night.

West Coast

The Long Beach Peninsula is a spur of land that protrudes into the Pacific, dividing Barkley and Clayoquot Sounds. Tofino, at one end, is simultaneously a major visitor center and the entry point for Clayoquot Sound; Ucluelet, at the other, is a major entry point for Barkley Sound, one of the premier kayaking destinations in the world. In between the two towns lies the northern part of Pacific Rim National Park, a long expanse of scenic, broad sandy beach broken by rocky headlands. The park and the two towns draw one million visitors a year, mostly in June, July and August, so it can get quite crowded in the summer, when reservations are essential not only at local lodgings but at the national park campgrounds. April/May and September/October are quieter times to visit—sometimes with surprisingly good weather. August days frequently begin with fog on the coast, followed by afternoon sun. In winter the whole area is periodically thrashed by North Pacific storms, and visitors (many of whom come just to experience the storms) have the place pretty much to themselves.

SIGHTS

Except for still-recovering, leftover clearcuts along the road coming in, the whole region could hardly be more scenic.

Tofino itself is socially and economically unique: thousands of visitors mingle with hundreds of counterculture transients (established residents call the latter "shrubs") and the timber/fishing lifestyle remains alive, although diminished, around the edges of the tourism economy. Clayoquot and Barkley sounds, meanwhile, are where many of the '60s-era U.S. draft dodgers wound up; some still inhabit remote island outposts accessible only by water. All these elements mix on the streets of Tofino in the summer high season. The town itself has about 2000 residents year-round. ~ Visitor information, 250-725-3414.

sights

AUTHOR FAVORITE

Hot Springs Cove, 40 minutes north of Tofino by boat, is on a headland facing the Pacific where very hot (120°F/50°C) water issues from a fissure about 100 feet above the water line and pours down a rock passage to the ocean shore. Bathers can stand under a blistering waterfall shower, or select a spot to lounge in a half-dozen small pools below the waterfall. In the lowest pools (my favorite), as the tide comes in, waves wash in cooling water every 30 seconds or so, offering an instant contrast that, combined with the view, is available at no other U.S. or Canadian hot spring.

With a perspective admirably close to neutral, the **Raincoast Interpretive Centre** in Tofino is a good place to learn the secrets of the deep forests that surround Clayoquot Sound—and the uses people make of the forest ecosystem. A handsome mural that covers one wall of the center is a marvelous depiction of the many plants and animals that inhabit these forests; a small selection of posters and books is available to visitors. ~ 316 Main Street, Tofino; 250-725-2560.

Meares Island, in Clayoquot Sound just outside Tofino, was saved from logging by protests in 1993. A nature trail winds through this incredible old-growth forest of cedars and hemlocks; visitors can access the island by hiring a water taxi in Tofino.

Pacific Rim National Park offers visitors a wide range of scenery and activities. The park has three separate units. The southernmost portion, on the south side of Barkley Sound, holds the West Coast Trail, which is for experienced wilderness hikers only. The middle portion is in Barkley Sound, where the Broken Islands are home to more than 100 beachheads ranging from large rocks to mile-long islands. Kayaking the Broken Group is one of the world's premier ocean kayak trips, a two- to seven-day journey that provides unparalleled scenery and solitude.

The Long Beach unit, between Tofino and Ucluelet, is a lengthy expanse of broad beach that seems unspoiled once you walk out on the sand. Here, between Ucluelet and Tofino, you will find the **Wickaninnish Centre**, an interpretive center offering exhibits on Pacific Ocean history. Visitors can see powerful waves rolling up on the beach, watch nature presentations, participate in day hikes and view whales, seals and sea lions. There's also a restaurant with views of the surf and spectacular sunsets. The center is closed October to mid-March. ~ Along Route 4, between Ucluelet and Tofino; the visitors center is on the east side of the highway just north of the turnoff to Ucluelet; 250-726-7721, fax 250-726-4720; www.parkscanada.gc.ca/pacificrim, e-mail pacrim.info@pc.gc.ca.

The two sounds, Clayoquot and Barkley, are sparkling expanses of sapphire water with hundreds of islands whose coves harbor inviting sandy beaches. In the distance, the towering peaks of the island's spine reveal glaciers when the clouds lift long enough to see them. The Pacific is a constant presence; the sound of its surf and tang of its salt air are everywhere. Boating is a hugely popular activity but should not be undertaken by inexperienced visitors.

Ucluelet, (pronounced you-CLUE-let), at the south end of Pacific Rim National Park, has been a fishing village for centuries—originally of the Nu-chalnulth band. More recently, the town has served as an outpost for the fur and timber trades—and now for the tourist trade—as well as fishing. ~ Visitor information, 250-726-4641.

LODGING

HIDDEN ►

The turnoff to **Red Crow Guest House** is a discreet sign marking a driveway along the road into Tofino—just what you'd expect for a B&B as quiet and secluded as this is. The two guest rooms on the lower floor of this large timber structure all face a peaceful back bay where birds flock and guests can use the inn's canoe to wander. Wood floors, spacious rooms and rustic furnishings mark the rooms; one room has a fireplace, and both have private entrances onto a verandah that receives full morning sun. The Garden Cottage, up above the house, has room for a family of six, including kitchen. A path leads around the property through the old-growth cedars and hemlocks. ~ 1084 Pacific Rim Highway, Tofino; phone/fax 250-725-2275; www.tofinoredcrow. com, e-mail relax@tofinoredcrow.com. MODERATE.

HIDDEN ►

Cable Cove Inn is the nicest small inn right in Tofino, with six rooms facing northwest toward Clayoquot Sound and the Pacific. Decorated in forest green, blue and beige, the rooms reflect the prevailing colors of the island. All six rooms have private baths, but no phones or TVs; guest awake to find a tray of juice, coffee and tea outside their door. Breakfast in the common area consists of fresh baked goods. One suite has a fireplace, four-poster bed and French doors that open onto a deck with a private hot tub. ~ 201 Main Street, Tofino; 250-725-4236, 800-663-6449, fax 250-725-2857; www.cablecoveinn.com. MODERATE.

The best thing about **Duffin Cove Resort** is that it offers views of the ocean from a bluff a block away from downtown. Eleven suites and kitchen units with garage-sale furniture and two cottages with fireplaces on the beach are a winter storm-watcher's delight. ~ 215 Campbell Street, Tofino; 250-725-3448, 888-629-2903, fax 250-725-2390; www.duffin-cove-resort.com, e-mail duffin@island.net. DELUXE.

Ocean Village Beach Resort is a nest of 51 comfortably rustic duplex and single cedar chalets on McKenzie Beach, a quarter-mile of protected sandy beach facing the Pacific Ocean. The units feature an eating area with table and benches, a sitting area and a sleeping area or separate bedroom and bath. The resort also includes an indoor swimming pool, hot tub and laundromat. ~ 555 Hellesen Drive, Tofino; 250-725-3755, fax 250-725-4494; www. oceanvillageresort.com, e-mail info@oceanvillageresort.com. MODERATE.

Pacific Sands Beach Resort, located on Cox Bay, which borders Pacific Rim National Park, offers 54 housekeeping suites with contemporary furnishings, fireplaces and views of the beach and the ocean. Three of the suites have hot tubs. ~ 1421 Pacific Rim Highway, Tofino; 250-725-3322, 800-565-2322, fax 250-725-3155; www.pacificsands.com, e-mail info@pacificsands.com. DELUXE TO ULTRA-DELUXE.

If you want a more intimate experience, try **Chesterman Beach Bed and Breakfast,** which offers three private units with fireplaces, including a charming cottage, a spacious suite and a cozy honeymooner's room, on the beach by the same name. After a visit to the island's west coast, owner Joan Dublanko fell in love with the place. Her hospitality and tasty breakfasts match her enthusiasm. ~ P.O. Box 72, Tofino, BC V0R 2Z0; 250-725-3726, fax 250-725-3706; www.chestermanbeach.net, e-mail surf sand@island.net. DELUXE.

Set just back from Cox Bay, in a fringe of old-growth cedar and Sitka spruce, **Long Beach Lodge** is a handsome wood structure with sensational views of the coast, a homey atmosphere and a fantastic great room with huge fir beams and a granite fireplace. Half the rooms face directly on the beach; they are furnished with thick beige carpet and hand-crafted wooden furniture covered in plaid, and have two-person soaking tubs. ~ 1441 Pacific Rim Highway, Tofino; 250-725-2442, fax 250-725-2402; www.longbeachlodgeresort.com. DELUXE.

In the early 19th century, during the era of sailing ships, the West Coast of Vancouver Island was dubbed "Graveyard of the Pacific" for the number of shipwrecks that occurred there.

BriMar is a small B&B inn on beautiful Chesterman Beach, set back in the forest fringe. One of the three guest bedrooms is a cozy loft with a woodstove and clawfoot tub. Dozens of local activities beckon, but simply strolling the beach is as good as any. Gay-friendly. ~ 1375 Thornberg Crescent, Tofino; 250-725-3410, 800-714-9373; www.brimarbb.com. MODERATE TO DELUXE.

West Wind Guest House is set on an acre of lushly landscaped garden in Tofino. The self-sufficient cottage sleeps six; the in-house private suite has its own sundeck. There's a glass-covered hot tub in the garden. Gay-friendly. ~ 1321 Pacific Rim Highway, Tofino; 250-725-2224, fax 250-725-2212; www.tofinoaccommo dation.com, e-mail stay@tofinoaccommodation.com. MODERATE.

Since the actual hot spring is on its own little peninsula, and a provincial park to boot, **Hot Springs Lodge** isn't right at Hot Springs Cove. But it is the next best thing—right across the bay, five minutes away at the Hesquiaht First Nation village. All six units include kitchenettes with private baths, and guests enjoy exclusive access to a nearby wilderness beach. Transport over to the hot spring is provided by the lodge hostess. Access is by float-plane or water taxi from Tofino. ~ Clayoquot Sound; 250-670-1106. MODERATE.

◀ HIDDEN

The owners of **Clayoquot Wilderness Resort** have big plans for their floating inn, which was moved in 1997 from Barkley Sound to its present mooring about 20 minutes out of Tofino by boat. Now ensconced on a quiet back bay at the toe of the foot-hills leading into Strathcona Park, the lodge will be supplemented by cabins on the property behind it. There are also two lakes for fishing and swimming, and a small hydro dam that replaces the usual noisy generator. The setting is outstanding, the lodge comfortable, the cooking great—let's hope they don't develop it so much that the term "wilderness" no longer applies. Fishing on nearby lakes and rivers is often excellent, even when salmon aren't running in the Sound. Canoeing, hiking and horseback riding await non-anglers. Closed end of October through April. ~ Quait Bay, Clayoquot Sound (boat or floatplane access only); 250-726-8235, 888-333-5405, fax 250-726-8558; www.wildretreat.com, e-mail info@wildretreat.com. DELUXE.

Snug Harbour Inn is situated on a rocky cliff overlooking a small cove that does indeed seem snug—but it's the inn itself that most deserves the adjective. Four suites, all with private baths and fireplaces, and a large hot tub on the deck provide an air of romantic luxury. ~ 460 Marine Drive, Ucluelet; 250-726-2686, 888-936-5222, fax 250-726-2685; www.awesomeview.com, e-mail asnughbr@island.net. DELUXE.

HIDDEN ► Not only is **Ocean's Edge B&B** in a spectacular setting—perched on a headland overlooking the entrance to Ucluelet's harbor—the host, Bill McIntyre, is a retired Pacific Rim National Park naturalist. Thus you get a beautiful modern room with queen bed and down quilt, great breakfasts, superlative views, and a walking encyclopedia of the area's natural wonders, ranging from tiny shore creatures to the gray whales that can be seen offshore in spring and fall. The three rooms here have private baths. No children. ~ 855 Barkley Place, Ucluelet; 250-726-7099; www.oceansedge.bc.ca. MODERATE.

AUTHOR FAVORITE

Perched on a rocky point thrusting out into the Pacific not far from Pacific Rim National Park and Clayoquot Sound, the **Wickaninnish Inn** has a spectacular setting under any circumstances. During the West Coast's sometimes phenomenal winter storms, it's an unparalleled natural experience. Each of the 76 spacious rooms faces the ocean and includes a soaking tub, a large-screen television, a refrigerator, a fireplace and furniture made from recycled old-growth fir, cedar and driftwood. A full-fledged spa rounds out the luxury lodge experience. Critics rave about dinner at The Pointe, the inn's restaurant, but what I liked just as well was a sumptuous breakfast that made several uses of local huckleberries and marionberries. ~ Osprey Lane at Chesterman Beach, Tofino; 250-725-3100, 800-333-4604, fax 250-725-3110; www.wickinn.com, e-mail info@wickinn.com. DELUXE.

Tauca Lea is a waterfront adventure resort on a wooded peninsula in Ucluelet. Each of the 24 one- and two-bedroom suites has a water view, private deck, fully equipped kitchen, gas fireplace, six-foot soaker tub and private garage. Kayaking, canoeing, diving and other water adventures are available right from the resort's dock. ~ 1971 Harbor Drive, Ucluelet; 250-726-4625, 800-979-9303; www.taucalearesort.com. DELUXE.

The **Canadian Princess Resort** is unique in that 30 of its 76 rooms are aboard the ship of the same name (which served from 1932 to 1975 as a hydrographic survey vessel). Consequently, these moderately priced staterooms are small, and many share a bath. Three buildings contain 46 spacious, contemporary rooms and loft suites with fireplaces, decks and views of the ship and the harbor. The resort also includes ten fishing boats and a nautical-themed restaurant and lounge for guests. ~ Ucluelet Harbor, Ucluelet; 250-726-7771, 800-663-7090, fax 250-726-7121; www. canadianprincess.com, e-mail info@obmg.com. MODERATE TO ULTRA-DELUXE.

A block from the Ucluelet marina is the **Thornton Motel**, which has 19 rooms and suites with standard furnishings, some with kitchenettes. It is popular with the fishing crowd. ~ 1861 Peninsula Road, Ucluelet; 250-726-7725, fax 250-726-2099; www. thorntonmotel.com, e-mail thorntonmotel@yahoo.com. MODERATE TO DELUXE.

At the **West Coast Motel**, views of the harbor from some of the 21 rooms make up for the rather standard motel decor. Nonsmoking rooms are available. Added advantages are an indoor swimming pool, gym, sauna and tanning salon. The dining room (open summer only) overlooks the harbor. ~ 247 Hemlock Street, Ucluelet; 250-726-7732, fax 250-726-4662; www.westcoastmotel.com, e-mail wcmotel@island.net. MODERATE TO DELUXE.

DINING

The surrounding environment sets the tone at **The Pointe**, the restaurant at the Wickaninnish Inn just outside Tofino. With hand-carved cedar beams framing picture windows that overlook the surf, the theme is seafood and West Coast produce ranging from oyster mushrooms to blackberries to B.C. wines. The cuisine is superb, the service friendly, the setting incomparable. Yes, it is a bit pricey by Tofino standards (entrées range up to $30) but worth it. Reservations are advisable during high travel periods. ~ Osprey Lane at Chesterman Beach (two miles south of Tofino along Route 4); 250-725-3100. DELUXE TO ULTRA-DELUXE.

The **Raincoast Café** features West Coast seafood, pastas and main dishes with a Northern Italian tinge served in a quiet, refined atmosphere in the heart of Tofino—a definite improvement on the standard tourist fare available at so many restaurants in town. Reservations are a good idea on weekends and during the summer. ~ 4th and Campbell streets, Tofino; 250-725-2215. MODERATE TO DELUXE.

There's a lot to be said for good pub food, and that's exactly what you'll find at the **Blue Heron Marine Pub** at the Weigh West Resort. Fish-and-chips, burgers and fries, surprisingly good salads and a hockey game on the TV—it's the order of the day here. The more upscale restaurant next door isn't as good as the pub. ~ 634 Campbell Street, Tofino; 250-725-4266. BUDGET TO MODERATE.

Everybody needs a cup of coffee and a muffin in the morning. The best place to get them in Tofino is the **Common Loaf Bake Shop**, where the espresso makers are capable and the baked goods are filling. You'll also find calzones, pizzas and curries. The bulletin board is also the news center for the counterculture community in Clayoquot Sound, if you want to find out who's protesting what this month. ~ 180 1st Street, Tofino; 250-725-3915. BUDGET.

Perched on a knoll above the harbor, the **Schooner Restaurant** is a cozy place with a loyal local following and a slate of excellent food. Cedar plank walls and a nautical decor are the backdrop to entrées such as poached salmon in a yogurt-dill caviar sauce, pepper steak, ribs, salads and seafood, all prepared and presented with care. Breakfast is served in summer. Closed over Christmas. ~ 331 Campbell Street, Tofino; 250-725-3444, fax 250-725-2100; www.schoonerrestaurant.com, e-mail vicsdine@island.net. MODERATE.

The Harbor View Restaurant, located on the second story of the West Coast Motel, features log-beamed ceilings and panoramic views of the Ucluelet harbor and the mountains beyond. The menu emphasizes seafood, steaks and salads. Closed in winter. ~ 247 Hemlock Street, Ucluelet; 250-726-3441. MODERATE.

SHOPPING   Even the owners can't quite explain the odd assortment of items available at **Beaches Market & Garden**—plants and foodstuffs.

AW, SHUCKS

At **Oyster Jim's** the name says it all. There is a real Jim, an immigrant to B.C. from Colorado, who grows his superb oysters in the back bays of Clayoquot Sound. At his shop on the main road into Ucluelet, you get not only oysters, as fresh as they can be, but savvy advice on what to do with them. My favorite: buy a dozen, carry them out to a log on Long Beach at Pacific Rim National Park, and shuck them on the spot for lunch or dinner. ~ Located one mile north of Ucluelet along Route 4; 250-726-7350.

Visitors might not buy too many potted bushes, but a warm day demands a stop for one of the market's "colossal cones"—ice cream piled as high as you want for just C$1.50. You might also appreciate the fresh oysters and produce. ~ 1184 Pacific Rim Highway, Tofino; 250-725-3259.

Wildside Booksellers is fairly small, but as the name implies it has an excellent selection of natural history and outdoor recreation books geared toward the West Coast. Summer reading selections and social activism books round out the book fare. ~ 320 Main Street, Tofino; 250-725-4222.

The **Eagle Aerie Gallery** is as much a cultural experience as it is an art gallery. The building was designed by native artist Roy Henry Vickers and constructed by his brothers. The gallery is built in the longhouse style with adzed cedar paneling and massive totem cornerposts. Effective lighting, evocative subject material and a background of taped native chanting and drumming inspire a spirit of reverence unlike almost any other place. The gallery represents Vickers' art only. ~ 350 Campbell Street, Tofino; 250-725-3235, 800-663-0669.

Nearby, the **House of Himwitsa** gallery offers a good selection of native art including limited-edition prints, silver jewelry, weavings, carvings, beaded items and pottery. ~ 300 Main Street, Tofino; 250-725-2017.

You won't find nightclubs on the rugged West Coast. Some bars and lounges offer sunset views. The bar at **The Loft Restaurant** is not on the water, but it has a casual, nautical theme and lots of fishing tales told 'round its bar, attracting locals and visitors alike. ~ 346 Campbell Street, Tofino; 250-725-4241.

NIGHTLIFE

MAQUINNA PROVINCIAL PARK (HOT SPRINGS COVE) 🖐 🛶 Reached only by boat, this park holds the justly famed hot springs that occupy a small ravine above the seashore. Provincial officials have built a dock about a half-mile from the hot springs; a boardwalk leads through a serene coastal spruce forest to the springs, where there's a changing house. ~ Located 45 minutes north of Tofino by boat, at the north end of Clayoquot Sound; 250-954-4600.

BEACHES & PARKS

◄ HIDDEN

▲ Six free, primitive tent sites are located east of the dock, along the shore.

PACIFIC RIM NATIONAL PARK Cliffs, islands, bog and beach are just some of the topography visitors discover at this vast, 158,400-acre park. The reserve is divided into three units: Long Beach, the Broken Group Islands and the West Coast Trail.

Long Beach 🖐 🚵 🐎 🛶 🎣 🚣 ⛴ 🛥 ⚓ The most accessible section of the reserve, Long Beach is a six-mile stretch of sand and surf between rocky outcroppings. Most of the park includes a rocky shoreline that supports tidepools full of barnacles, mussels, starfish, hermit crabs and anemones. Sitka spruce thrive just behind the pockets of sandy beaches and the rocky outcroppings. Farther inland are cedar, hemlock, fir and areas of bog and muskeg with pine and laurel. The forest floor is redolent with moss, ferns, huckleberry and salmonberry. The park is also an ideal spot for seeing harbor seals, sea lions, river otters, mink and a vast array of resident and migrating birds, including hundreds of rufous hummingbirds that arrive in spring to enjoy the salmonberry blooms and raise their young in the forest fastness. Beach hiking is excellent. Nine marked trails traverse old-growth rainforest. Facilities include picnic areas, restrooms and a restaurant. Parking fee, C$10. ~ Route 4 (Pacific Rim Highway) between Ucluelet and Tofino, 62 miles west of Port Alberni; 250-726-7721.

▲ Green Point Campground has 55 primitive walk-in sites situated above the beach and 94 inland tent/RV sites with beach access; C$18 to C$21 per night. To reserve a drive-in site, call 800-689-9025.

Broken Group Islands 🏃 🛶 🚣 🚤 🚢 ⛵ With more than a hundred islands and islets in Barkley Sound, this is kayak and sailboat territory. Accessible only by boat, these remote islands are an excellent place to see wildlife ranging from eagles to sea lions; diving is excellent. Composting toilets are available in the camping areas. ~ The MV *Lady Rose*, a mail boat that also takes passengers and kayaks, makes trips to Bamfield, Sechart Lodge at Sechart Bay and Ucluelet; 250-723-8313, 800-663-7192.

▲ There are primitive campsites on eight of the islands; C$8 per adult.

West Coast Trail 🏃 This demanding 47-mile stretch between Bamfield and Port Renfrew follows a turn-of-the-20th-century trail constructed to aid shipwrecked mariners. Hikers need to be prepared for five to eight days traversing an irregular, slippery trail, often knee-deep in mud, with some headlands requiring tricky climbs up rope ladders. The weather is also notoriously cranky, exposed as the coast is to incoming Pacific storms. All told, it is one of the most difficult hikes in North America—and that's a big part of the attraction. The scenery is unsurpassed—tidepools, cliffs, fjordlike inlets and small bays, stunning stretches of sandy beach, sea stacks and the chance to see gray whales, sea lions, seals, orcas and thousands of shorebirds and seabirds.

Experienced hikers recommend timing your journey to the tides so you can walk at least partway along rock shelves ex-

Valley of the Spruces

It's a long drive on gravel roads—basically upgraded logging roads—to **Carmanah–Walbran Provincial Park**, a remote corner of Vancouver Island's West Coast. The reward is access to a world-class rainforest valley, one of the last major untouched Sitka spruce forests in B.C. The rainforest ecosystem here is a remnant of the ancient forests that once covered the entire coast and ranged hundreds of miles inland. All of the organisms—from microscopic fungi to skyscraping spruces and all the insects, birds, mammals, fish, ferns, flowers, lichens and vines in between—are linked in a chain of interdependence that defies measure in terms of its complexity and subtlety. Biologists consider intact eco-islands such as Carmanah–Walbran doorways into the world as it once appeared, holding crucial secrets to the future health of the planet.

The valley's giant spruces, some almost 300 feet tall and a millennium old, are among the largest in the world—but the area is so remote that they weren't publicly known until 1988. Conservationists worked tirelessly to save the trees from logging, and the area was declared a park in 1990. An adjoining valley, so remote that provincial officials strongly discourage entry, was added to the park later.

In the main valley, visitors can hike and keep a watchful eye out for resident deer, bears, cougars and other forest creatures. Most of all, you can admire some of nature's finest and most impressive handiwork. Although the tallest tree in Canada, the 300-foot (95 meter) Carmanah Giant, is nearby, trails to it are closed to limit impact as much as possible; but the park's accessible valley contains more than 230 spruces taller than 225 feet (75 meters), and the hills above hold many giant cedars as well.

If you want to sleep among the giants, you can camp at one of the 12 developed tent sites (near the parking lot) or hike in to one of the wilderness sites located upstream along Carmanah Creek. Free, short-term vehicle camping is also permitted in the parking lot.

The park is located about 80 miles (130 km) from Duncan; from here follow Route 18 west, then follow the signs to Nitinat Lake, then to Carmanah–Walbran. It's a long drive—two to three hours from Nanaimo or Cowichan, two hours from Port Alberni—and the last half hour takes you by some dishearteningly large clearcuts, which run right to the edge of the park. The contrast within the park is gratifying, and very educational. ~ 250-954-4600; wlapwww.gov.bc.ca/bcparks.

posed at low tide—but one must be vigilant not to get caught along a headland on an incoming tide. Access to the southern trailhead is west of Port Renfrew. The northern trailhead access is near Bamfield. Park officials restrict trail use to about 8000 hikers a year; reservations in advance are essential during June, July and August, and hikers pay a per-person fee of C$80 (about US$50) for permits. Closed October through April. ~ Access to the Bamfield and Port Renfrew trailheads is by improved gravel roads, but they are still active logging roads as well. The MV *Lady Rose* (250-723-8313, 800-663-7192) drops hikers at Bamfield. For reservations and permits, call 800-663-6000.

Approximately 290 native archaeological sites (including remnants of fish traps and camps) have been identified within Pacific Rim National Park.

North Coast

North of Campbell River, the highway leads through dense forest, narrow valleys and towering peaks. Much of the forest has been cut, and there are few visitor services and attractions until you reach Port Hardy, the debarkation point for BC Ferries Discovery Coast and Queen Charlotte Islands cruises.

SIGHTS

Alert Bay is a tiny First Nations community on equally small Cormorant Island, reached by ferry from Port McNeill. Once a thriving salmon canning center, this community is the home of the 'Namgis First Nations people. At the **U'mista Cultural Centre** visitors can see the remarkable masks and potlatch regalia confiscated by the Canadian government in the 1920s, when the federal government was attempting to squelch Native culture. Closed weekends in winter. Admission. ~ On Front Street, Alert Bay, near the ferry dock; 250-974-5503; www.umista.org. Nearby, what was once the tallest **totem pole** on earth rises to more than 150 feet (52 meters). (A pole raised in Victoria in 1994 surpassed it.)

From Port McNeill, it's only 20 miles (36 km) to the last town on the north coast. Aside from its traditional character as a commercial and industrial center, **Port Hardy** serves two distinctly different types of travelers—adventurers bound for the storm-tossed wilderness at Cape Scott, and more sedate journeyers catching a ferry to Bella Coola or Prince Rupert. In either case the town has plenty of facilities—motels, RV parks, cafés and stores—to serve visitors. As in Prince Rupert and Bella Coola, it's imperative that ferry passengers have reservations for a place to stay the night before boarding a ferry. During the peak summer travel season the town of 5000 can quite literally fill up.

Port Hardy has a pretty **seawall promenade** along the town harbor, a Fishermen's Wharf, several nice small parks and a museum depicting traditional First Nations life and the Danish settlements that were the first European habitations in the area. Several well-known fishing lodges are nearby.

Stop by the Port Hardy **Visitor Info Centre**, located in the center of town, for lodging reservations and local orientation. ~ Market Street; 250-949-7622.

The road west from Port Hardy, a well-maintained gravel road, leads past the legendary Shoe Tree, which may or may not be the first of its kind. it's about 8 kilometers (5 miles) west of the junction with Highway 19; nearby is supposedly a more modern cousin, the Bra Tree.

Cape Scott Park, an hour past Port Hardy, is one of the most remote, forbidding and storm-tossed wilderness destinations in B.C. (See Beaches & Parks, below.) Deep forests, rocky headlands and long, unmarked beaches await the intrepid explorers who don't mind walking through terrain that can fling freezing rain in their faces without a hint of warning.

LODGING

Alert Bay, reached only by ferry, is surely one of the most remote sites in the world for a hostel. Nonetheless, a former chapel converted into **Pacific Hostel—Alert Bay** does a thriving business in the summer, when travelers come through to experience the small island's First Nations culture and marine attractions. Like the island itself, the hostel is small, with a capacity of just 12 in clean, functional rooms. ~ 549 Fir Street, Alert Bay; 250-974-2026. BUDGET.

Travelers to Port Hardy in July and August must make reservations beforehand since the inns are usually fully booked by visitors planning to leave on a northbound ferry the next morning. Call the **Port Hardy Chamber of Commerce** at 250-949-7622.

The quiet, park-like setting around **Pioneer Inn** makes this family-friendly lodging perfect for relaxing after a long ferry ride or a long drive up the island. The laundry, playground, kitchen units and complimentary coffee make life easier for families traveling with kids. ~ 4965 Byng Road, Port Hardy; 250-949-7271, 800-663-8744, fax 250-949-7334; e-mail pioneer@island.net. MODERATE.

With phones, banquet facilities, a lounge and a restaurant, the 50-unit **Thunderbird Inn** is a business-class hotel in the center of Port Hardy, close to town services and the ferry terminal. The pub offers entertainment on weekends. ~ 7050 Rupert Street, Port Hardy; 250-949-7767, 877-682-0222, fax 250-949-7740; www.thunderbirdinn.com. MODERATE.

Located in a quiet residential area of Port Hardy, **Kay's B&B** offers a lot to guests—ocean views, cable TV in every room, gourmet continental breakfast, free ferry shuttle. Two units are self-contained suites; two share baths. No credit cards. ~ 7605 Carnarvon Road, Port Hardy; 250-949-6776. BUDGET.

Quarterdeck Inn is a spiffy modern structure set right at the edge of Port Hardy harbor, the most upscale lodging in Port Hardy. The spacious rooms are modern, furnished in cheery colors; the marina, restaurant and hot tub are all handy amenities for those departing or awaiting ferry passage. ~ 6555 Hardy Bay Road, Port Hardy; 250-902-0455, 877-902-0459, fax 250-902-0454; www.quarterdeckresort.net. MODERATE.

HIDDEN ► **Great Bear Lodge** is actually located on the Central Coast, across from north Vancouver Island, but access is from Port Hardy. The floating lodge, moored in a quiet inlet, affords access to unparalleled adventure—bear watching, wilderness hiking and fishing, rainforest experiences. The solar-powered lodge makes a low impact on the delicate environment, and the lodge maxes out at ten guests in its five rooms. ~ Port Hardy; 888-221-8212; www.greatbeartours.com. DELUXE.

HIDDEN ► Like several other island accommodations, **Duval Point Lodge** is a floating inn, north of Port Hardy, reached only by boat. Catering to anglers, it's also a good choice for anyone who wants to spend quiet days canoeing or kayaking or just serenely enjoying the protected shore. The attractive, wood-sided lodge can accommodate up to 16 in various comfortable room configurations; housekeeping facilities are available. ~ Box 818, Port Hardy; 250-898-8431, 877-282-3474; www.duvalpointlodge.com, e-mail duval@island.net. MODERATE.

DINING   **Snuggles**, in the Pioneer Inn, has Port Hardy's best dining fare. The menu encompasses mainstream dishes such as salmon, crab, steaks and chicken dishes, with pastas, soups and salads to diversify dinner. ~ 4965 Byng Road, Port Hardy; 250-949-7494. MODERATE.

The cuisine is mainstream Cantonese and Mandarin at **Kan's Kitchen**—chow mein, fried rice, hot pots and stir fries—but it's filling, flavorful and economical. Takeout is available for folks headed to the ferry dock to wait in line. ~ 7053 Market Street, Port Hardy; 250-949-8998. BUDGET TO MODERATE.

HIDDEN ► **I.V.'s Quarterdeck Pub** sports a marine atmosphere and the pub food—fish and chips, burgers, soups and salads—is quite good. It's one of the few places in town where residents will likely outnumber visitors. ~ 6555 Hardy Bay Road, Port Hardy; 250-949-6922. BUDGET.

BEACHES & PARKS   **SCHOEN LAKE PARK** 🏃 🐎 ⛵ 🎣 This spectacular park is situated in the high country along the spine of the island, with jagged snowy peaks ringing the lake. It is remote and not very crowded, except on holiday weekends. Swimming and fishing in the lake are excellent, and the backcountry is truly wilderness, with few established trails. ~ The park is located two hours southeast of Port McNeill, 15 miles (25 km) south of Route 19.

HIDDEN ►

▲ Nine campsites, fairly primitive by provincial park standards, are at the foot of Schoen Lake; $14; 250-954-4600.

QUATSE RIVER CAMPGROUND Set in the groves along the riverside, this park offers quiet sites for vehicle and tent campers. Flush toilets, full hookups, laundry, hot showers, firepits and more make this full-service commercial campground a good choice in an area lacking provincial parks. Reservations are a good idea for summer travel. ~ 8400 Byng Road, Port Hardy; 250-949-2395.

▲ There are 62 tent/RV sites with full hookups; C$14 to C$20 per night.

CAPE SCOTT PARK 🖐 This remote thumb of land, the island's northwest corner, is a notoriously distant and forbidding area. The road stops at the park's border; from there you're on foot, and the terrain is ideal for adventurers. Trails are almost always muddy and hard to follow. Storm-wracked, deeply forested, with huge headlands along untracked beaches, Cape Scott is for those who like their wilderness truly untouched—definitely not for the inexperienced. ~ Located 40 miles (63 km) west of Port Hardy; 250-954-4600.

◄ HIDDEN

▲ The seven designated, no-fee campgrounds are all walk-in.

Although B.C.'s coho (silver) salmon runs have been in danger, Vancouver Island still offers incredible sportfishing for king (chinook) and sockeye salmon, and also for bottomfish such as rock cod, rockfish and the occasional halibut. Besides the great angling possibilities, there's the unsurpassable natural backdrop of scenery and wildlife: snowcapped mountains, old lighthouses, sea lions, whales, bald eagles, herons and other water birds.

Outdoor Adventures

FISHING

Make sure to check on local fishing regulations and equip yourself with the appropriate licenses. For more information, see Fishing in Chapter One.

STRAIT OF GEORGIA COAST To arrange a fishing charter in the Campbell River area, try **Painter's Lodge**—trips to the prime waters leave their docks daily. ~ 4100 Discovery Drive, Campbell River; 800-663-7090; www. obmg.com. Another excellent resource here is **The Dolphin Resort** next door. ~ 4125 Discovery Drive, Campbell River; 250-287-3066; www.dolphinsresort.com. On Quadra Island, **April Point Lodge** will take you to your limit. ~ April Point Road, Quadra Island; 250-598-3366, 800-663-7090; www.obmg.com.

As you angle along the west coast of Vancouver Island, you might even see an occasional bear walking along the coast.

ALBERNI INLET **Bamfield Inn** runs charters in the sound and the ocean, and provides the usual bait, tackle and license for groups of two or three. ~ 75 Boardwalk, Bamfield; 250-728-

3354. **Imperial Eagle Lodge,** just down the boardwalk, also has charters of Barkley Sound; expect salmon, halibut and rockfish on the May-to-September trips. ~ Box 59, Bamfield BC, V0R 1B0; 250-728-3430; www.imperialeaglelodge.com.

WEST COAST Located right next to Pacific Rim National Park, **Weigh West Marine Resort** offers charters for salmon and halibut. If you've brought your flyfishing gear, Weigh West has saltwater flyfishing packages. ~ 634 Campbell Street, Tofino; 250-725-3277, 800-665-8922; www.weighwest.com. **Chinook Charters** specializes in offshore jaunts. ~ Tofino; 250-725-3431, 800-665-3646.

WHALE WATCHING Vancouver Island is known for orca (or killer) whales, porpoises, harbor seals, sea lions, bald eagles and many species of marine birds. Watch also for the occasional minke whale, gray whale or elephant seal. Whale-watching season extends from April through September. June is the best time to see the orcas; March and April are best for gray whales, which pass near the island on their migration to Alaska from Mexico. A few whales stop in Clayoquot Sound for the summer; local cruise operators usually know where they are. In July and August, cruise operators are very busy, so try to call at least a day or two ahead for reservations.

STRAIT OF GEORGIA COAST Robson Bight, located north of Campbell River, is famed for the orca pod that inhabits the fish-rich waters in the summer months. **Robson Bight Charters** operates out of Sayward, a small logging community an hour from Campbell River, and offers a high success rate to guests on its whale-watching cruises. ~ P.O. Box 99, Sayward; 250-282-3833, 800-658-0022 in B.C.

WEST COAST In Ucluelet, **Subtidal Adventures** operates both Zodiacs and a cabin cruiser, offering fishing and whale-watching trips. ~ 877-444-1134. In Tofino, the **Whale Centre** is a major

OF MUSHROOMS AND MINKE WHALES

Two excellent Pacific Rim naturalists offer visitors their services, leading nature walks and adventures in the area for reasonable hourly or daily rates. **Adrienne Mason** of Raincoast Communications is based in Tofino, and can explain natural phenomena as diverse as salamander egg sacs and old-growth cedar root balls. Guided forest and beach hikes concentrate on Pacific Rim National Park and the islands of Clayoquot Sound. ~ 250-725-2878. **Bill McIntyre** is based in Ucluelet and offers impeccable credentials: he's a retired Pacific Rim National Park naturalist. Understandably, his expertise in marine and tidepool habitats is extensive; every little rock along the beach has a creature attached, and McIntyre can tell its tale. ~ 250-726-7099.

tour operator for whale-watching and Clayoquot Sound cruises. ~ 411 Campbell Street; 250-725-2132, 888-474-2288.

NORTH COAST Stubbs Island Whale Watching has been in business since 1980, long before orca-watching cruises became popular; their base, Telegraph Cove, is just a half-hour from the prime orca grounds. ~ P.O. Box 7, Telegraph Cove (near Port McNeill in the north of the island); 250-928-3185, 800-665-3066; www. stubbs-island.com.

Kayaking is an up-close way to explore the coastal inlets of Vancouver Island—especially Clayoquot and Barkley Sounds, both known for their wilderness kayaking opportunities. Quiet coves, unspoiled beaches and plenty of sea mammals, birds and other wildlife typify kayak trips on the island's waters.

KAYAKING

ALBERNI INLET Access to Barkley Sound's Broken Islands is provided from Port Alberni by the **MV Lady Rose**, which can also arrange kayak and equipment rentals. The boat will drop kayakers in the islands to begin their trip, and pick them up at a prearranged later date. ~ 5425 Argyle Street, Port Alberni; 250-723-8313.

WEST COAST No experience is necessary to join one of **Tofino Sea Kayaking Co.**'s guided day trips or overnight excursions into Clayoquot Sound along Vancouver Island's west coast. Longer excursions, lasting six days, head farther into Clayoquot Sound. Rentals are available too. Closed mid-October to mid-March. ~ 320 Main Street, Tofino; 250-725-4222, 800-863-4460.

Remote Passages Sea Kayaking in Tofino also offers guided trips into Clayoquot and Barkley sounds. ~ P.O. Box 624, Tofino, BC V0R 2Z0; 250-725-3330, 800-666-9833; www.re motepassages.com.

NORTH COAST Kayaks offer an exquisitely thrilling way to experience whale watching. **Northern Lights Expeditions** has been running sea-kayaking expeditions out of Port McNeill for nearly 20 years. Trips are based from campsites in Blackfish Sound and Johnstone Strait. A lodge-based trip is also available. Kayaking near foraging and frolicking orca is a big attraction for both novice and experienced kayakers. Northern Lights provides all equipment, including rain gear. ~ P.O. Box 4289, Bellingham, WA 98227; 360-734-6334, 800-754-7402.

There are many popular and worthwhile dive spots around Vancouver Island. Clayoquot and Barkley sounds both offer rich subtidal terrain, although it's important to go with locally knowledgeable guides because currents can be hazardous.

DIVING

Besides equipment rental and training, **Octopus Adventures Dive Center** offers certification classes and can arrange boat dives. ~ 4924 Argyle Street, Port Alberni; 250-723-3057.

SURFING

Surf's up along Pacific Rim National Park's Long Beach section. A dry suit is essential; the waters never warm past 60°F.

Surfboards, sailboards and similar equipment are available in Tofino at **To Live To Surf**, where you can also get expert advice on the winds and waves along the coast. ~ 1180 Tofino Highway; 250-725-4464.

BOATING

Boating and sailing bring thousands of people to the waters around Vancouver Island; in fact, the circumnavigation of the island, which takes a month, is one of the world's best-known gunkholing cruises. It is not for beginners, however, and should not be undertaken even by experienced boaters without gaining expert advice from local marine operators. Tides and winds, fog and rain make the route challenging as well as spectacular. The waters off the west coast are often too rough for relaxed boating, but some pleasure charters are available.

At **China Creek Marina**, visitors can rent day-cruisers for a spin through Barkley Sound. ~ Located on the Bamfield Road, ten miles (16 km) west of Port Alberni; 250-723-9812.

GOLF

With a fairly dry, sunny summer climate, the island's numerous golf courses offer duffers long days, spectacular scenery and verdant surroundings. The large retired community in the Vancouver area means there's a healthy local golf-fan base to support quite a few courses all the way north to Campbell River.

For some beautiful views of central Vancouver Island, try the 18-hole **Eaglecrest Golf Club**. ~ 2035 Island Highway West, Qualicum Beach; 250-752-6311, 800-567-1320. **Morningstar International Golf Course** hosts one of the events on Canada's professional golf tour. The holes have four sets of tees, so this course can provide a challenge to most golfers. ~ 525 Lowry's Road, Parksville; 250-248-8161, 800-567-1320.

The **Long Beach Golf Course**, just before you get to Tofino, boasts year-round access because of the area's mild climate and the course's good drainage. This nine-hole course also has a driving range, pro shop, coffee shop and campground. ~ Airport Road, 2 miles (3 km) south of Tofino; 250-725-3332.

Stay two nights at the **Crown Isle Resort**, a snazzy north island golf community, and the day's golf round is free. The resort's course has been rated the top public layout on Vancouver Island. ~ Courtenay; 888-338-8439.

BIKING

Most island highways are not ideal for bicyclists since there is little provision for safety. But the situation gets better on the West Coast, where the traffic is a bit less frantic and the roads less tortuous.

The **Long Beach Highway** from Tofino to Ucluelet is a perfect bike ride; parts of the road near the two towns have a paved pathway alongside the highway. Although there's more traffic, the highway (Route 4) along the north side of **Sproat Lake** offers spectacular views of the lake and the snow-capped coastal peaks in back.

Bike Rentals   **Fiber Options** offers rentals in the Tofino area. ~ 120 4th Street, Tofino; 250-725-2192.

HIKING

One of the most famous (and arduous) treks in North America, the West Coast Trail draws seasoned wilderness travelers to Vancouver Island. But many other less demanding trails—especially in Pacific Rim National Park—serve day-hikers and casual strollers. All offer the chance to experience the wonderful forests and sandy beaches of the island. All distances listed for hiking trails are one way unless otherwise noted.

STRAIT OF GEORGIA COAST   The **Cowichan River Footpath** (11 miles/19 km) follows one of the most popular recreational corridors on south Vancouver Island. The river is famed for its steelhead trout fishing, but the path is enjoyed by many non-anglers. It stretches northwestward from Duncan, transecting Cowichan River Provincial Park. ~ The trailhead is five miles west of Route 1; maps are available at the Duncan Visitor Info Centre.

WEST COAST   Gold Mine Trail (approximately 1 mile/1.6 km) begins just west of the Pacific Rim National Park information center on Route 4 for a nonstrenuous hike through a forest of amambilis fir, red cedar, hemlock, Douglas fir and red alder. The remains of mining machinery, including part of a dredge, can still be found on the beach. ~ Located just west of the Pacific Rim National Park Information Centre on Route 4.

   South Beach Trail (approximately .5 mile/1 km) starts behind the Wickaninnish Centre and winds through a stand of Sitka spruce. Side trails lead to rocky or sandy coves surrounded by headlands. At the far end of Lismer Beach, a boardwalk climbs over a bluff to South Beach. At the top of this bluff, the **Wickaninnish Trail** (1.5 miles/2.5 km) leads to the left, but continuing to the right takes hikers past groves of moss-enshrouded Sitka

◆◆

JOURNEY DOWN THE COAST

The most arduous trek on Vancouver Island is the **West Coast Trail** (47 miles), stretching along the west coast. Hikers need to be prepared for the five- to eight-day journey on an irregular slippery trail. There are tidepools, fjordlike cliffs, opportunities to see Pacific gray whales, sea lions, harbor seals, shorebirds and sea birds. ~ Access to the southern trailhead is at Port Renfrew. The northern trailhead access is at Bamfield.

spruce and western hemlock. ~ Access is from the Wickaninnish Centre, off Route 4 about ten miles north of Ucluelet.

The **Wickaninnish Trail** (1.5 miles/3 km) links Long Beach to Florencia Bay. Hikers can access this trail via the South Beach Trail or from the Florencia Bay parking lot.

The Wickaninnish Trail is a part of the early Tofino–Ucluelet land route that used beaches, forest trails and sheltered inlets to link the two towns before a road was built farther inland.

The **Schooner Trail** (1.2 miles/2 km) is a good route to observe the near-shore transition from cedar-hemlock forest to spruce, which is able to withstand the wind-driven salt spray common in winter. The trail crosses a small salmon-spawning stream and ends at a lovely beach.

NORTH COAST The First Nations village of Ahousat invites visitors to experience the wilds of **Flores Island**, one of the outermost islands in Clayoquot Sound. Here exquisite sandy beaches face the power and ceaseless drive of the Pacific, while on the quiet eastern side ancient forests bear undisturbed testament to the lush power of the winter rains. Village residents guide visitors on their walks. The trip begins with a scenic boat ride from Tofino through Clayoquot Sound. Fee. ~ 250-670-9696.

Transportation

CAR

Vancouver Island lies across the Strait of Juan de Fuca from the state of Washington and west across the Strait of Georgia from mainland British Columbia. The north part of Vancouver Island is accessible from either direction. The **Trans-Canada Highway** (**Route 1**) goes from Victoria to Nanaimo; from there, the **Inter-Island Highway** (**Route 19**) heads north to Port Hardy. **Route 4** goes from the Parksville–Qualicum Beach area west to Port Alberni, leading to the west coast communities of Ucluelet and Tofino. Driving time from Nanaimo to Port Hardy is five to eight hours; from Nanaimo to Tofino, three to four hours.

AIR

The **Victoria International Airport** is 20 minutes from Victoria in Sidney. Carriers include Air BC, Horizon Air, Pacific Coastal Airlines and WestJet; nonstop service is available from Vancouver, Seattle and Calgary. ~ www.cyyj.ca.

Nanaimo Airport is served by Air Canada and Canadian Western Airlines. ~ www.nanaimo-airport.com.

Harbour Air is the major floatplane operator on the B.C. coast, offering charter and scheduled service throughout the islands from Vancouver and Victoria. ~ 800-665-0212; www.harbour-air.com.

Floatplanes offer a unique experience as they take off on the water and land directly in island harbors. **Kenmore Air** has a daily schedule to Victoria from the Seattle area and also goes to Nanaimo in the summer. ~ 206-486-1257, 800-543-9595; www.kenmoreair.com.

NW Seaplanes offers direct floatplane service from Seattle to numerous spots on Vancouver Island, including Bamfield, Barkley Sound, Tofino, Port Hardy, Port McNeil and Campbell River. ~ 425-277-1590, 800-690-0086; www.nwseaplanes.com.

The **BC Ferries** run from Horseshoe Bay (north of Vancouver) to Nanaimo is the main access to north Vancouver Island. Ferries leave roughly every other hour; although the boats are huge, extensive lineups occur on weekends and holidays—and especially on holiday weekends. ~ 604-444-2890 outside B.C., 888-223-3779 within B.C.; www.bcferries.com. **FERRY**

Travelers wishing to depart from the United States can take Black Ball Transport, Washington State Ferries or Victoria Clipper to Victoria. **Black Ball Transport** takes vehicles and foot passengers from Port Angeles to Victoria's Inner Harbour. ~ 109 East Railroad Avenue, Port Angeles, WA, 360-457-4491; 430 Belleville Street, Victoria, BC, 250-386-2202; www.ferrytovictoria.com.

Washington State Ferries takes vehicles and foot passengers on a scenic route through Washington's San Juan Islands between Anacortes, WA, and Sidney, BC. ~ Seattle, WA, 206-464-6400.

The **Victoria Clipper** ships are 300-passenger, high-speed jet catamarans that run year-round between Seattle's Pier 69 and Victoria's Inner Harbour, with separate trips to the San Juan Islands from May through September. ~ Seattle, WA, 206-448-5000, 800-888-2535; Victoria, BC, 250-382-8100.

VIA Rail provides Vancouver Island rail service between Victoria and Courtenay, with stops at Nanaimo. ~ 800-842-7245 (within the U.S.), 888-842-7245 (within Canada); www.viarail.ca. **TRAIN**

Agencies in downtown Victoria and at the Victoria airport include **Avis Rent A Car** (800-879-2847), **Budget Rent A Car** (800-268-8900), **Hertz Rent A Car** (800-263-0600), **Island Rent A Car** (250-384-4881), and **National Car Rental** (800-227-7368). National also has local offices in Nanaimo (250-386-1213), Courtenay (250-334-0202), Campbell River (250-923-7278) and Port Hardy (250-949-7121). Budget has an office in Nanaimo (250-754-7368). **CAR RENTALS**

Island Coach Lines (250-385-4411) operates bus service between Victoria and other points on Vancouver Island. **BUS**

In Tofino, **Jamie's Whaling Station** is the oldest tour operator; they run both boats and Zodiacs, and offer trips to Hot Spring Cove as well as whale-watching and fishing trips. ~ 606 Campbell Street, Tofino; 250-725-3919, 800-667-9913. **Sea Trek** offers sightseeing tours and whale-watching cruises from Tofino. ~ 250-725-4412, 800-811-9155; www.seatrektours.bc.ca. **TOURS**

SEVEN

Okanagan

The Salish Indian phrase *pen tic ton* is said to mean "a place to live forever," and it's easy to see why the original inhabitants felt that way about this region. In south-central British Columbia—ringed by mountains, watered by high-country streams, marked by deep, clear lakes, with valleys turned south into the sun—the setting is incomparable. The climate is Canada's hottest, with more than 2000 hours of sunshine a year; winter is relatively mild by north-of-the-border standards. The valley floors and side slopes are a paradise of orchards, vineyards, farms and hay meadows. The beaches along lakes Okanagan, Osoyoos, Skaha and Shuswap offer delightful stretches of golden sand. Dry, warm midsummer days are long and languorous, with light clinging to the northwest sky above the valley well past 10 p.m. No wonder early settlers chose to adopt the Salish description of the valley when they named Penticton, the capital of the south Okanagan.

In the high country between the Okanagan and the Fraser, vast rolling grasslands cradle lakes that abound with Kamloops rainbow trout. Below are the Thompson and Fraser rivers, powerful, roiling waterways that once blocked pioneer and prospector passage into the B.C. interior. Some of North America's largest salmon runs follow the two rivers to their spawning grounds. Even though Canada's major transcontinental highway, Route 1, passes by on the south shore, Shuswap Lake boaters can reach undeveloped roadless shores in just a couple of hours.

Once upon a time, Americans thought this region was bound to join the United States. Long inhabited by native Okanagan peoples, the area at first drew only trappers and prospectors seeking gold in the surrounding mountains. When gold was indeed found—farther north, in the Cariboo—this provoked the sort of annexation interest that brought California into the U.S. fold, under similar circumstances; but after much wrangling the boundary was finally fixed at the 49th parallel, in 1846.

The line passes through Osoyoos Lake, the southernmost of the Okanagan chain and Canada's warmest body of water. The first settlers in the valley were prospectors and suppliers who used it as a route to the gold fields, then decided to stay and establish ranches amid the region's abundant natural hay meadows.

The Okanagan Valley's first apple trees were planted by Father Charles Pandosy, an Oblate friar who established a mission near Okanagan Lake in 1860. (You can still see his restored compound in a park in Kelowna.) The valley didn't really become a fruit-growing capital until the late 19th century, after the Canadian Pacific transcontinental railroad made transportation in and out of Okanagan easy. As rail lines and modern irrigation practices spread through the valley, the region was transformed into the lush quilt of orchards, vineyards and vegetable fields visitors find today.

The Okanagan and Fraser river valleys, once given over mostly to hay meadows, evince the rapid growth of one of B.C.'s newest industries: ginseng production. Thousands of acres of hayfields have been plowed under, raised beds installed, and shade canopies draped overhead. Kamloops is a major ginseng processing center; one consequence, however, has been a steep rise in the cost of hay to B.C. ranchers.

The region honors its heritage at a number of pioneer ranches, interpretive recreations of Native villages, missions and early mills. These sights show the sorts of challenges this gentle land presented and how early residents responded. Where the Trans-Canada Highway clings to impossible canyon walls above the river, gold rushers once scrambled through with mules—first in the canyon above Hope in 1858, then farther north in the Cariboo in 1860.

Although gold is still extracted here (visitors can pan for it themselves) the area's treasures now come from what the land grows. The region's bounty—fruit and vegetables—is available at countless stands and small stores along valley roads. Prices for peaches, apricots, pears, plums, cherries, strawberries, raspberries, grapes, tomatoes, apples and dozens of other delights all seem roughly comparable no matter where you stop. Many stands offer organic produce; organic or not, it's best to pick a stand that's associated with an orchard.

Visitor information for the entire region is available from **Thompson-Okanagan Tourism** at 800-567-2275 or www.thompsonokanagan.com.

▼▼▼▼▼▼▼▼▼▼▼▼▼

Hope to Kamloops

The main road from Vancouver east—the Trans-Canada Highway, Route 1, the country's major continental thoroughfare—passes through some amazing geographic contrasts. At Hope, the eastern end of the lower Fraser Valley, towering mountains close in on the flat river bottomland, and the thick rainforest vegetation reflects the wet, cool maritime climate.

Just 100 miles up the road, after traversing a deep canyon, you will reach dry, desertlike rangeland. At Cache Creek, midsummer temperatures of 100°F (44°C) are common, and rainfall is less than ten inches a year. The topography is still mountainous, but the lower slopes are sere grassland and sagebrush, even cactus. Welcome to B.C.'s southern interior, where rugged topography and contrasting climates are the norm all the way east to the Rockies.

SIGHTS

While the scenery along the road from Hope to Cache Creek is spectacular—narrow canyon walls, rowdy rivers, distant snow-capped peaks—**Route 1** is an attraction all by itself. This stunning example of engineering is the original Cariboo Road, famed as the route into the gold fields that put British Columbia on the map in the 1860s; this was still a single-lane road just a half century ago, and the sharp curves and many tunnels (seven between Hope and Lytton) testify to the difficulties the highway engineers faced.

Yale, 15 miles (25 km) up the canyon from Hope, is where panners first found gold in the Fraser. It's also where a huge rock blocks the Fraser to most navigation; thus Yale was the starting point of the Cariboo Road, and at one time a booming gold rush center. The **Historic Yale Museum** recalls those days with a slide show, exhibits and artifacts, plus a gold-panning sluice. (The "gold" is salted, of course.) Closed Tuesday and in winter. Admission. ~ 31179 Douglas Street, Yale; 604-863-2324.

At **Hell's Gate**, 20 miles (32 km) north of Yale, the Fraser roars through a narrow gap in the rock that terrified early explorers and settlers. This is where a 1913 construction landslide blocked the river to migrating salmon, virtually wiping out the Fraser's bountiful runs. In 1946, the United States and Canada cooperated on construction of fish passageways to restore the runs, and by 1990 the Fraser once again was home to more than 20 million salmon a year. The **Hell's Gate Airtram** is a pricey but exciting way to have a look at the river and the fishways; the tram descends about 500 feet, swinging across the river at the last minute. At the bottom is a somewhat tacky tourist village—shops, cafés, exhibits—perched on a bench directly above the surging river. If you really need a hand-painted rock depicting a salmon, this is where to get it. Those who want to substitute shoe leather for money can hike down a half-mile to the bottom; it's a steep but well-maintained gravel road. The trailhead is 100 yards south of the Airtram parking lot. Closed November through March. Admission. ~ 43111 Trans-Canada Highway, 20 miles north of Yale; 604-867-9277; www.hellsgateairtram.com.

HIDDEN ►

If you backtrack a couple of miles downstream from Hell's Gate itself, you'll find the historic **Alexandra Bridge**. Now closed to vehicles, it remains from earlier highways. A ten-minute forested walk brings you to the bridge, which is a sturdy steel truss span open to foot traffic. It passes over a narrow gap (not as narrow as Hell's Gate, though) in the canyon through which the Fraser surges and it's free. An interpretive display recounts the history of road-building in the canyon. ~ Located 19 miles (30 km) north of Yale, 2 miles south of Hell's Gate, on Route 1. Leave your car in the parking area on the west side of the road and walk down to the bridge.

Drive another hour north on Route 1 along the Fraser River and you'll come to Lytton, where the Thompson River joins the Fraser in a confluence that betrays the different characters of the two rivers—the cleaner, greenish water of the Thompson is distinct as much as a half mile downstream. The **Lytton Ferry**, one mile north of town off Route 12, has operated since 1894, providing a free cable-drawn five-minute passage to the west bank of the Fraser. The ferry, one of the last of its kind, uses baffles to turn the river's own current into motive force.

Stein Valley Nlaka'pamux Heritage Park near Lytton is one ◀ *HIDDEN* of B.C.'s environmental triumphs, a vast, unlogged, untracked

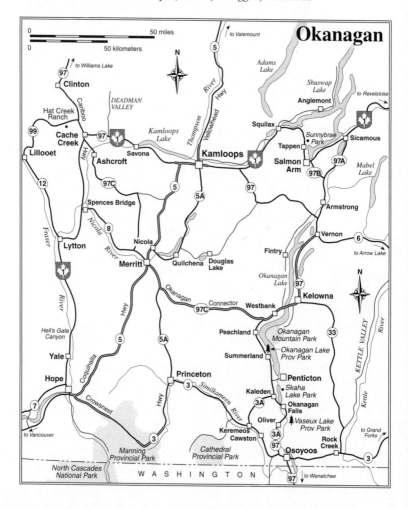

Okanagan

valley through which one of the Northwest's best wilderness treks passes. A public campaign conducted by conservationists and the Lytton First Nations band saved the valley from clear-cutting in the mid-1980s. The uncrowded eight- to ten-day hike through the park traverses rugged terrain. You can also take day hikes here. ~ The park entrance is four miles north of Lytton, off Route 12.

North from Lytton, Route 1 follows the Thompson River; at Cache Creek the road joins Route 97, the Cariboo Highway. If you take this road north for six miles, you can check out **Hat Creek Ranch**. Hat Creek found prosperity in the 19th century both as a true ranch and as a way station along the Cariboo Road. Now it is one of B.C.'s most popular heritage sites, with restored original buildings, amiable costumed role players and a Shuswap First Nations interpretive village just upstream. Visitors can enjoy wagon jaunts along the original Cariboo Road, which runs through the middle of the ranch. There's a café and gift shop, too. The cowboy rodeo, featuring working cowboys from nearby ranches, is a late-August treat. Closed mid-October to mid-May. Admission. ~ Half a mile west of Route 97, 6 miles (11 km) north of Cache Creek; 250-457-9722, 800-782-0922.

A short detour on the other side of Route 1 (a few miles south of Cache Creek; take the Route 97C east from Ashcroft) is a much different sort of spectacle. High above the Thompson, mining continues today—especially at the **Highland Valley Copper Mine**, the largest open pit mine in North America, producing 265,000 metric tons a day. (A little less than half of that is actual ore.) Although the mine discontinued public tours in 1998, the pit is quite visible from Route 97C, which connects Ashcroft and Logan Lake. ~ Route 97C, 25 miles (40 km) east of Ashcroft.

At the **Logan Lake Visitor Info Centre**, visitors can see at close range a gargantuan shovel, bucket and ore-haulage truck used at

sights

AUTHOR FAVORITE

Before loggers, ranchers or farmers ever saw the Thompson Valley, the First Nations Secwepemc (Shuswap) people called it home, spending summers in reed shelters and winters in dugout houses. I got a thorough impression of this traditional life at **Secwepemc Heritage Park and Museum**, where a faithful reproduction of a winter pit-house village depicts five different periods of Shuswap life from 5000 years ago to the 19th century. The museum's exhibits and interpretive displays offer a glimpse at a lifestyle utterly linked to the salmon that came up the Thompson each year and to the berries that grew along its banks. Admission. ~ 355 Yellowhead Highway (Route 5), on the north bank of the South Thompson River, north of Kamloops; 250-828-9801.

the mine. Closed mid-October to early May. ~ Box 1060, Logan Lake; 250-523-6322; www.loganlake.ca.

Back on Route 1, traveling east will bring into view **Kamloops Lake,** a ten-mile-long stretch of the Thompson where the river widens, famed as the home of the Kamloops rainbow trout, which is known for achieving great girth and size. Anglers especially prize the great fighting power of this fish, which is found naturally throughout the region's many lakes and streams and has been stocked even farther afield in B.C. The contrast between the lake and the arid desert around it is striking. ~ Located 19 miles (31 km) east of Cache Creek along Route 1.

The day-trip excursion up **Deadman Valley** is an opportunity   ◄ HIDDEN
to see, in one fairly short drive, all the attractions of this area. The road starts at the west end of Kamloops Lake, down in the Thompson River valley amid desertlike terrain; it traverses low-elevation scrub rangeland, which turns into mid-elevation hay meadows, passes into the transition pine/fir zone and winds up in montane territory along several pretty lakes. Along the way, you'll pass odd geological formations known as the **Deadman Hoodoos**— tall columns of eroded breccia, about halfway up the east slope of the valley on private land about 10 miles (17 km) north of Kamloops Lake. Deadman Road becomes troublesome for passenger cars after about 30 miles (49 km) at Vidette Lake, a high-country lake with good fishing early and late in the summer. ~ The Deadman turnoff on Route 1 is about 20 miles (32 km) east of Cache Creek, 3 miles (5 km) west of the Route 1 bridge at the west end of Kamloops Lake.

Kamloops, at the east end of Kamloops Lake, is Central B.C.'s unofficial capital, a thriving town whose dependence on three lagging industries—timber, mining and agriculture—hasn't slowed its growth to almost 80,000 residents. This is still hot, dry desertlike rangeland, but the mountains above hold some of B.C.'s best hiking, fishing and hunting. Kamloops itself is a government and commercial center, more of an overnight stop than a travel destination. With more than 1000 ranches in the region, it's also a cattle-country capital. Stop by the **Visitor Info Centre** for brochures, maps and general information on the area. ~ 1290 West Trans-Canada Highway, Exit 368, Kamloops; 250-374-3377, 800-662-1994; www.city.kamloops.bc.ca.

Kamloops is also the center of B.C.'s growing ginseng industry. **Sunmore Ginseng,** one of the largest processors, offers visitors a brief tour and exhibits on the supposedly magical root in all its many product applications, which these days range from tea to chewing gum. ~ 925 McGill Place, Kamloops; 250-374-3017; www.sunmore.com.

The **Wanda-Sue paddlewheeler** only seems like a historic at-   ◄ HIDDEN
traction. Although it harks back to a long heritage of sternwheel

boating on B.C.'s inland lakes and rivers, this 85-foot tour boat was actually built by a Kamloops resident in the late 1970s. Two-hour cruises in spring, summer and fall offer a relaxing way to see the river and its valley up close. The galley serves snacks and beverages. Admission. ~ Old Kamloops Yacht Club, Riverside Park, 1140 River Street, Kamloops; 250-374-7447.

The **Kamloops Museum & Archive** contains exhibits on local pioneers, and includes a brief depiction of the exploits of Billy Miner, the American outlaw who robbed a Canadian Pacific train nearby in 1906, and was tried and convicted in Kamloops. ~ 207 Seymour Street, Kamloops; 250-828-3576.

HIDDEN ▶

Across the street, **St. Andrews on the Square** is a spectacular restoration of an 1887 Gothic-style Presbyterian church, now a community hall. ~ 159 Seymour Street, Kamloops; 250-377-4232.

The hills around Kamloops hold some of the world's finest grasslands, rolling terrain that harbors untold miles of bunch-grass prairie, old-growth ponderosa pine and dryland Douglas fir.

HIDDEN ▶

The **Lac du Bois Grasslands** northwest of Kamloops preserve a substantial tract of this terrain. Motorized access and camping are limited, but the park offers many opportunities for hiking, wild-life watching, ecological exploration or just simply appreciating the beauty of the high prairie. ~ Access is five miles north of Kam-loops off Route 5; wlapwww.gov.bc.ca/bcparks.

Set a few miles east of Kamloops in a pretty, arid ravine with sagebrush and ponderosa pine providing natural landscaping, the **Kamloops Wildlife Park** is an impressive operation. Basically a well-run open-air zoo, its focus is on wildlife indigenous to British Columbia, especially endangered or threatened animals; a pleasant series of paths takes visitors through the extensive grounds, and there's a short miniature train ride for kids. The holiday lighting display in November and December is particularly impressive. Admission. ~ Located off Route 1 (south side), 8 miles (13 km) east of Kamloops; 250-573-3242; www.kamloops wildlife.com.

An alternative to Route 1 is the **Coquihalla Highway** (Route 5), which connects Hope to Kamloops through the town of Merritt. It's a modern engineering marvel that crosses the high terrain above the Fraser Canyon, shortening the route between Vancou-ver and Kamloops by almost two hours. The four-lane highway has only one real exit—Merritt—and one toll booth, between Hope and Merritt, where the toll is C$10. The **Okanagan Connector** (Route 97C), another four-lane mountain highway, connects Merritt to Kelowna, and features a 60-mile (97-km) chain link fence (the longest in North America) to keep wildlife off the road. Both of these impressively scenic roads cross considerable high-elevation terrain and are subject to snow and ice in late fall, win-ter and early spring.

The **Douglas Lake Ranch**, which occupies much of the highlands between Merritt and Kelowna, encompasses almost a half-million acres of land, and is the largest working cattle ranch in North America. Visitors to the ranch headquarters at Douglas Lake can check out branded shirts at the ranch store, learn about ranch operations from the ranch newsletter and stock up on grass-fed Douglas Lake beef from the freezer. While it's still largely a working cattle ranch, with 16,000 head of cattle, the ranch's future is clouded because of the legal and financial troubles of owner Bernie Ebbers, the former Worldcom magnate. There are several visitor accommodations, and a few spots are available for day-fishers on the ranch's lake. (See Lodging, below.) ~ From Kamloops, take Route 5A south about 50 miles (80 km) to the Douglas Lake Road turnoff; ranch headquarters are 16 miles (26 km) east; www.douglaslake.com.

Early-20th-century American bandit Billy Miner is believed to be the originator of the command "Hands up!"

LODGING

Although there is only one four-star hotel (the Grand Okanagan in Kelowna) the region has a myriad of small hotels, motels, inns and B&Bs. Toll-free assistance with lodging, tours and other visitor attractions is available from **Okanagan Central Reservations**. ~ 800-663-1900. Visitor accommodations are less common in the Thompson and Fraser canyons; since the Trans-Canada Highway (Route 1) passes through, roadside motels typify the lodging options there, with a few notable exceptions.

Perched on a bluff overlooking the Thompson River, the **Garuda Inn** is one of B.C.'s oldest accommodations, parts of the building dating to 1862. Recently taken over by new owners, the pink stucco-sided inn has shed its somewhat rowdy character and is now a serene retreat where classical music fills the café and sunlight splashes through the windows. Rooms feature eclectic pastel decor and wide windows. ~ 3642 Merritt-Spences Bridge Highway, Spences Bridge; 250-458-2311, 877-354-1997, fax 250-459-2318; www.garudainn.com, e-mail garudainn@hotmail.com. MODERATE.

◀ HIDDEN

It's amazing that things seem so tranquil at the **Lakeside Country Inn** in Savona. Canada's transcontinental highway and busiest railroad pass within a half-mile of here. But it's well off the highway and all the rooms face away from the hubbub, toward the lake, so serenity reigns. The six rooms are quiet, decorated in blue and white with rattan furniture and custom-made armoires that conceal the TV setups. Each room has a balcony or patio adjacent to it, looking out on the landscaped grounds and garden; four units have kitchen facilities. You can swim at the private beach, or borrow a boat for a quiet Kamloops Lake paddle. Breakfast is served in the glass-enclosed garden patio. This is a perfect stop on the way to or from a week in the interior, and much nicer than most of the lodging in Kamloops a half-hour away. Closed in winter. ~ 101 Savona Access Road, Savona; 250-373-2528, 800-909-7434, fax 250-373-2432; www.lakesideinn.bc.ca, e-mail info@lakesideinn.bc.ca. BUDGET TO MODERATE.

The **South Thompson Inn** has an enviable setting on the high, grassy banks of the South Thompson River, creating the sense of an oasis in this desert valley. With 48 airy, high-ceilinged rooms (inexplicably given names in a British theme), pine plank floors, coordinated country-pattern wallpaper and bed linen, the ambience is upscale rustic. There's a pool, a large hot tub, adjacent golf course and extensive horseback riding facilities. Though it's only six miles outside Kamloops, it feels a bit like a guest ranch. ~ East of Kamloops on the north side of the South Thompson River Road; 250-573-3777, 800-797-7713, fax 250-573-2853; www.stigr.com, e-mail theinn@stigr.com. MODERATE TO DELUXE.

If you must spend the night in Kamloops, the **Riverland Motel** is a clean, standard place with one major advantage over most others: it's well off the highway and, more important, well removed from the railroad line. The riverside site is pleasant and the 58 rooms are functional if sparsely furnished. ~ 1530 River Street, Kamloops; 250-374-1530, 800-663-1530, fax 250-374-1534; www.riverlandmotel.kamloops.com, e-mail riverlandmotel@kamloops.com. BUDGET TO MODERATE.

Hostelling International–Kamloops is in a restored courthouse at the west end of downtown, with many of the building's original features and decorations intact. There are 68 beds (some shared rooms and some private) and shared baths; plus laundry, a TV lounge and a fully equipped kitchen. ~ 7 West Seymour

AUTHOR FAVORITE

The **Quilchena Hotel** opened in 1908 along the stagecoach route between Kamloops and Vancouver, and the ranch family that built it hoped a railroad would soon follow. None did, and the opening of the Coquihalla Highway meant road traffic bypassed the hotel, too. Nonetheless, the place, 12 miles (20 km) northeast of Merritt, thrives. The restored three-story Edwardian structure offers 17 spacious rooms furnished in period style—some with the original furniture from the day the hotel opened. Still operated by the same family, the hotel is a wonderful weekend getaway from Vancouver. Spend your time at Nicola Lake, at the adjacent golf course, horseback riding on the ranch, or just plain lazing on the veranda or in the saloon (also original), which features a bar complete with bullet holes. ~ Route 5, Quilchena; 250-378-2611, fax 250-378-6091; www.quilchena.com, e-mail info@quilchena.com. MODERATE.

Street, Kamloops; 250-828-7991, fax 250-828-2442; www.hi hostels.ca. BUDGET.

Of the many high-country fishing lodges in the Kamloops area, **Roche Lake Resort** is one of the best—good fishing, excellent accommodations, a beautiful setting on a high-country lake outside Kamloops. The 14 two-bedroom cedar chalets offer complete self-sufficiency, if guests wish; there's also a restaurant and lounge, a pool, a hot tub and some camping facilities. Packages include use of boats and meals. ~ Off Route 5A, 20 miles (33 km) southeast of Kamloops; phone/fax 250-828-2007; www.roche lake.com, e-mail info@rochelake.com. MODERATE TO DELUXE.

Salmon Lake Resort is one of the facilities at Douglas Lake Ranch. This is a full-fledged family resort, with campsites, RV sites and a dozen small cabins, all overlooking the lake at the headwaters of the Salmon River. It's a gorgeous setting, with fish jumping in June and September, and there's plenty for non-anglers to do, with a playground, convenience store and horseback riding facilities. The 11 modern, trim cabins are one- or two-bedroom, all with kitchens, private baths and wood-burning stoves. ~ At Salmon Lake, about 22 miles (38 km) northeast of Quilchena; 250-350-3344, 800-663-4838, fax 250-350-3336; www.douglas lake.com, e-mail info@douglaslake.com. MODERATE.

A native wood, batten-and-board structure on the shore of a lake in a pine woods setting, the **Stoney Lake Lodge** is really there for just one reason: fishing. Stoney and nearby Minnie Lake offer superb angling for enormous rainbow trout amid the grasslands that made this area famous as cattle country. This Douglas Lake Ranch lodge also features an outdoor hot tub, horseback riding and an on-site fly-master who will tie the best patterns for you on the spot. Boats are supplied for guests. The eight rooms are large and functional. The ranch also operates several remote, high-country fishing cabins. ~ At Stoney Lake, about 10 miles (16 km) east of Quilchena; guests must obtain the combination for the locked ranch gate; 250-350-3344, 800-663-4838, fax 250-350-3336; www.douglaslake.com, e-mail info@douglaslake. com. MODERATE TO DELUXE.

◀ HIDDEN

Sundance Guest Ranch is among the biggest and best-known guest ranches in B.C. Located just outside Ashcroft, it's easily reached from Vancouver and can occasionally be a bit crowded. On the high benchland above the Thompson River, it's in one of B.C.'s sunniest and warmest areas. Among other things, that means the riding season, from mid-March to late October, is longer than at other B.C. guest ranches. It also makes the outdoor pool more enjoyable for visitors. All 28 guest rooms are air-conditioned and furnished in a style that verges on ranch kitsch—maroon-and-white-checked bedspreads, shingled interior walls.

Rides head out twice daily. ~ Route 97C, 5 miles (8 km) south-east of Ashcroft; 250-453-2422, fax 250-453-2554; www.sun dance-ranch.com, e-mail sundance@wkpowerlink.com. DELUXE.

Right in the town of Nicola, five miles north of Merritt, the historic **Nicola Ranch** makes several of its heritage buildings available to travelers. The Banker's House is a tidy one-bedroom clapboard structure with a living room and kitchen; the Court-house across the street is a massive five-bedroom, two-bath man-sion with a full kitchen and dining room that all told rents for about the same as an executive suite in a downtown Vancouver hotel. ~ Route 5A, Nicola; 250-378-6499, 888-708-7388, fax 250-378-2727; www.nicolaranch.com, e-mail info@nicolaranch. com. MODERATE TO DELUXE.

DINING

HIDDEN ►

Every morning Donna Horsting and her helpers load several dozen loaves of bread into the ovens at **Horsting Farm Market** outside Cache Creek. The bread is mostly cooled but still moist by the time lunch rolls around, when Mrs. Horsting slices it in order to make the tastiest sandwiches in B.C.'s interior. She loads on meat, tomatoes, onions, lettuce—all sliced at that minute—pours out a dollop of soup and hands it to you. You can fill up on fresh fruits and vegetables, too, most grown right on the prop-erty. If you're around in September, be sure to try the Jonah red apples—they're as good as apples get. ~ Route 97, 1 mile (2 km) north of Cache Creek; 250-457-6546. BUDGET.

HIDDEN ►

The **Savona General Store** doesn't look like much—a classic roadside storefront with racks of convenience items inside. But the pizzas here are made from scratch using hand-rolled dough and top-notch ingredients, and they taste like it. ~ Savona Access Road, Savona; 250-373-0022. BUDGET.

Coffee is roasted daily on the premises at **The Grind** in Kam-loops, and the baristas are expert. That makes it easily the best java in central B.C. Great muffins and pastries, too. Like most true hardcore coffeehouses, if you ask for drip coffee, they'll make an Americano instead. ~ 476 Victoria Street, Kamloops; 250-828-6155. BUDGET.

This Old Steak & Fish House is the closest thing to a fine din-ing restaurant in Kamloops. Housed in a historic mansion over-looking downtown, its ambiance is Edwardian, its cuisine West Coast meats and fish, including excellent Canadian beef and sal-mon. Reservations are a good idea on weekends. ~ 172 Battle Street, Kamloops; 250-374-3227. MODERATE TO DELUXE.

The **Quilchena Hotel** is a long way from almost anywhere—45 minutes from Kamloops, a half-hour from Merritt, three-and-a-half hours from Vancouver. But its dining room draws patrons from all those locales— as much for the atmosphere as for the food. The building is a 1908 Edwardian masterpiece, with 18-

foot ceilings and original turn-of-the-20th-century furnishings, including the much-discussed bullet holes in the bar. The food concentrates on seafood and, not surprising for a place owned and operated by a cattle ranch, excellent beef. ~ Route 5, Quilchena; 250-378-2611. MODERATE TO DELUXE.

At **Cariboo Jade & Gifts**, the focus is on B.C. jade, a mineral that, while not the equal of fine Asian jade, can be made into handsome carved and polished artifacts that range from napkin rings to animal carvings, candleholders and the like. Visitors can watch artisans work the jade. ~ 1093 Todd Road, Cache Creek; 250-457-9566.

SHOPPING

Like so many locally owned B.C. bookstores, **Merlin Books** in Kamloops does a commendable job of finding and stocking local-interest and Canadian titles, including an ample array of tales about the surrounding Cariboo country. There's also a generous selection of fiction and general-interest books. ~ 448 Victoria Street, Kamloops; 250-374-9553.

Although all the best fishing spots are in the mountain lakes around Kamloops, the town itself is a supply and outfitting center. **Kamloops Fly Shop** has angling equipment, including a vast selection of flies specific to the region's lakes, plus other fishing-related gear—as well as the most important commodity of all: knowledge about the area. ~ 1366 Hugh Allen Drive, Unit 104, Kamloops; 250-377-8461.

Valhalla Pure is a Western Canada chain of outdoor outfitters, with gear ranging from long johns to longboats. The Kamloops outlet is also a good source for maps, outdoor guides, rumors and advice. ~ 261 6th Avenue, Kamloops; 250-377-0157.

Andy Knight is the owner of **Knight's Saddlery** and a master craftsman who turns leather into functional works of art. The store carries a full line of Western wear and gear, but it's Knight's saddles and tack that are exceptional. Even if you don't need a new saddle, it's worth a stop to look at what careful hand tooling can accomplish. ~ 2776 Voght Street, Merritt; 250-378-5733.

HAND TO MOUTH

Stop at a U-pick orchard and fill your own sack with ripe cherries, apricots, peaches or apples. Universal U-pick practice is that you pay for what you take; what you eat on-site is free. So a fruit-picking stop is not only the best way to select the best fruit, it's an excellent lunch or afternoon snack. It's also the quintessential way to absorb the best of the area— summer sun, pastoral beauty, clean orchard air and the unsurpassed taste of hand-picked, tree-ripened fruit.

BEACHES & PARKS

MANNING PROVINCIAL PARK 🚶 🚴 🏇 🎿 🏕 ⚓ This is one of British Columbia's most popular and most accessible parks. With towering peaks and towering old-growth forests, it offers a chance to see in a relatively short drive the major mountain ecological zones of southern B.C. Hiking, camping and wildlife watching occupy visitors in the summer, skiing and snowshoeing in the winter. ~ Located along Route 3, 20 miles (32 km) east of Hope; 250-840-8836.

▲ Four campgrounds have 355 vehicle/tent sites; C$14 to C$22 per night.

STEIN VALLEY NLAKA'PAMUX HERITAGE PARK 🚶 🚴 🏇 ⚓ This magnificent park north of Lytton is one of the environmental triumphs of the 1980s in British Columbia. The Stein River watershed is the largest major unlogged valley near Vancouver; now a remote wilderness park, it offers hardy visitors the chance to hike through unspoiled lowland forest, passing beautiful Stein Lake, and then crossing alpine high country to wind up near Lillooet Lake. Bears, moose and other wilderness wildlife species are numerous. This six- to ten-day, 50-mile (80-km) trek is considered by many the equal of the far more famous (and more crowded) West Coast Trail on Vancouver Island. Although not quite as arduous, it is long. There are three cable car river crossings. Easier family day hikes are possible in the lower valley. ~ Off Route 12, 4 miles (6 km) north of Lytton on the west bank of the Fraser River; 250-455-2304.

▲ Wilderness camping only; C$10 per night.

JUNIPER BEACH PROVINCIAL PARK 🚴 ⛵ 🎣 ⚓ This hot desert spot is in the Thompson River canyon just below Kamloops Lake. The beach itself offers nice access to the river; the campground is just above the beach, and there's not much else to

CITY SLICKERS

Cowboys do not ever say yee-haw—unless they're jesting, that is. You can learn this and other details of the rangeland life on the **Kamloops Cattle Drive**, an annual event city slickers can join. This five-day July ride traverses the high country around Kamloops, and there really is a herd of cattle involved. Okay, it's a small herd, and the 300 to 500 riders that participate are a few more than necessary. Participants get feed for their horse, three meals a day and transportation to the start site; horse rentals are available. Although expert equestrian skills aren't necessary, this is not an event for beginners. Saddle conditioning beforehand is recommended. ~ 250-372-7075, 800-288-5850, fax 250-372-0262; www.cattledrive.bc.ca.

the park. It's just a warm place to laze away a weekend. ~ Route 1, 11 miles (18 km) east of Cache Creek; 250-315-2771.

▲ There are 30 vehicle/tent sites with little visual separation; C$17 per night.

The drive along Route 1 from Kamloops to Shuswap Lake reveals just how quickly the climate and environment can change in B.C.'s interior. From sheer desert to

▼▼▼▼▼▼▼▼▼▼
Shuswap Lake

verdant inland forest takes less than an hour, and the Shuswap Lake area is a mellow, summer-warm, lush green region. Salmon Arm, at the south end of the lake, is the main town around here, and Shuswap Lake itself, a deep, uniquely H-shaped body of water with more than 600 miles of shoreline, offers watery fun for visitors each summer. ~ Salmon Arm Visitor Information, 877-725-6667.

About 40 miles east of Kamloops is Shuswap Lake. Once every four years an immense run of sockeye salmon returns to the **Adams River**, just north of Shuswap Lake; at several points this has been the world's largest single sockeye run, topping out at 4 million fish. It's a heartening example of how the Fraser River system's salmon have revived over the past half century. During the dominant year runs (the next is 2006) a festival takes place at **Roderick Haig-Brown Provincial Park**, the conservation preserve that encompasses the length of the river. Thousands of people come from all over the world to watch the salmon spawn and to learn about fisheries conservation and management. It's a remarkable sight. The runs the other three years are smaller, but still noteworthy. The park at other times is a peaceful, beautiful stretch of riparian terrain, with cottonwood, birch and pine trees shading the clean waters of the river. ~ On the Squilax–Anglemont Road, 3 miles (5 km) from Route 1, across the Squilax Bridge; 250-955-0861.

SIGHTS

The cars occupying the lot outside the **White Post Auto Museum** are a mixed bunch—rusted-out Edsels, cherried Plymouths, a T-bird or two. The cars inside are much finer, including a couple of glistening Cadillacs with towering fins and price tags to match. There's a wall of hubcaps, a long bench of engine blocks. If you really love something here, you can probably buy it, as most everything is on consignment. Tourist attractions like this are an endangered species in the Planet Hollywood era. Admission. ~ Route 1, Tappen, 10 miles (16 km) west of Salmon Arm; 250-835-2224.

Salmon Arm is a friendly town at the south end of Shuswap Lake, the commercial center of the Shuswap district. The town pier stretches into the lake quite a distance; free summer-evening concerts are presented here in the "Wednesdays on the Wharf" series. The bay and shore in Salmon Arm comprise the **Nature Bay Bird Sanctuary**, covering one of the largest undeveloped inland river deltas in B.C.; a public park stretches eastward along the bay from the pier. Each year in May and June, hundreds of grebes return here to court and mate, a ritual that involves dances on the water—which fans say is every bit the equal of the more famous courtship dance of Canada's loons. For information, contact the Salmon Arm Chamber of Commerce, 250-832-6247.

HIDDEN ▶   **Gort's Gouda Cheese Farm** is at the foot of the Salmon River valley, just outside Salmon Arm, and the cheese you buy is the product of the pastures and grain fields around the farm. Tours are available to learn how the cheeses are made; your appetite whetted by that, don't leave without some of their exquisite gouda and hearty Swiss. The smoked and aged gouda wheels are the best. ~ 1470 50th Street Southwest (Salmon River Road), Salmon Arm; 250-832-4274.

Haney Heritage Village is a restored pioneer settlement in the woods just outside Salmon Arm. The refurbished heritage home, church, schoolhouse, gas station, firehouse and farm buildings give a good impression of life here at the turn of the 20th century. Summer only. Admission. ~ Route 97B, a half mile off Route 1, southeast of Salmon Arm; 250-832-5243.

Sicamous, at the south end of Shuswap Lake, is the capital of the area's booming vacation houseboat industry (see Outdoor Adventures at the end of the chapter). There's a nice beachfront park at the inlet from Mara Lake, the smaller upstream lake that feeds Shuswap Lake.

LODGING   **Quaaout Lodge** is one of just two Native-owned lodges in B.C.; like its counterpart on Quadra Island, Quaaout is in a forest overlooking the water. Here the water is Little Shuswap Lake, a clean, warm lake along which First Nations people—in this case the Little Shuswap Indian band—have lived and prospered for thousands of years. The lodge fronts a long, fine beach on Little Shuswap and has expansive grounds (including a summertime tepee group). The lodge doors, hand-carved out of old-growth fir, depict two standing bears. The lodge's 72 rooms are spacious and modern, and most have lake views; six mini-suites have whirlpool tubs and fireplaces. There's a pool and fitness center, canoes and bikes are available for rent and the lodge restaurant is known for its excellent inland cuisine. The tepees rent for C$10 (US$6.50) a night. This is the closest accommodation to the Adams River and its famous sockeye run. Guests occasionally have the chance to participate in a sweat lodge with the band's chief. ~ Located on the north shore of Little Shuswap Lake, across the Squilax Bridge; 250-679-3090, 800-663-4303, fax 250-679-3039; www. quaaout.com, e-mail quaaout@quaaout.com. BUDGET TO DELUXE.

HIDDEN ▶

Part of Hostelling International, the **Squilax Store Hostel** is a most unusual place. For one thing, its historic (1934) refurbished building is home to a large summertime colony of yuma bats, which help keep the lakeside mosquito numbers low. For another, the hostel accommodations (the capacity is 24) are in retired CN Railroad cabooses set below the store along Shuswap Lake's outlet. Two private rooms are available in the main building, along with an organic grocery store. ~ Route 1, Squilax; 250-675-2977; www.hihostels.ca, e-mail shuswap@hihostels.ca. BUDGET.

Furnished with authentic period antiques, the four second-floor bedrooms (three with private bath) of the **Trickle Inn** share an enclosed-porch sitting room looking out over Shuswap Lake. But the best accommodation is up on the third floor, in a spacious loft (private bath) with a small balcony overlooking the backyard orchard. Guests enjoy gourmet three-course breakfasts and, if they wish, can reserve a chance to taste Harper's superb and inventive dinner cuisine, ordinarily available only to members of her dining club. (The club's popularity reflects the fact that, for gourmet cooking in the Salmon Arm area, Trickle Inn is just about it.) ~ Route 1, 7 miles (11 km) west of Salmon Arm; 250-835-8835; www.trickleinn.com, e-mail trickle@trickleinn. com. MODERATE.

You have to make an effort to find the **Salmon River Lodge**. ◄ HIDDEN
It's in the hills above the Salmon River valley, along a country lane; the B&B itself sits back on a quarter-mile gravel drive. Here a small guest house and main house offer traditional European-style B&B bedroom and shared bath facilities, plus there's a larger suite in modern but nondescript housing. A pool and extensive gardens round out the grounds, and llamas, ducks, geese and other animals will keep you company. Breakfasts are German-style—muesli, fresh bread, eggs and sausage. Closed November through March. ~ 5011 Salmon River Road, between Armstrong and Salmon Arm; 250-546-6929. BUDGET.

Totem Pole Resort has an enviable location at the end of the paved road on the north side of Shuswap Lake's southern arm.

AUTHOR FAVORITE

The **Trickle Inn** is far from inconspicuous—it's a huge, white Victorian mansion along Route 1 west of Salmon Arm. But in a way its visibility obscures the hospitable nature of Carol Harper's inn. In addition, the 1904 house's solid construction (it was owned by a lumber baron) keeps the rooms quiet despite its proximity to the highway. See above for more information.

All its wood-sided, semirustic cabins, chalets and duplex units face the lake, and the facilities are designed for longer stays, with full kitchens, laundry and a convenience store. While you're here you can canoe the lake, swim, hike the hills behind, sunbathe, birdwatch, play tennis, relax in the spa or sauna—even though it's fairly small (14 units), the resort has ample amenities. Yes, there is a totem pole, an 85-footer with an osprey nest on top. ~ Canoe Point Road, Sunnybrae; 250-835-4567; www.totempole resort.com, e-mail inquiries@totempoleresort.com. MODERATE TO DELUXE.

DINING

The **Chocolate Bean** was the first gourmet coffee shop in Salmon Arm, and it's still the most reliable. The muffins and scones are made fresh each morning and, naturally, the selection of chocolates is extensive. ~ 250 Alexander Street, Salmon Arm; 250-832-6681. BUDGET.

Moose Mulligan's is housed in an airy building overlooking the channel between Mara and Shuswap lakes in Sicamous. Although the menu is mainstream—chicken, steak, pizzas—it's the best food available in the houseboat capital. Try Mulligan's beef stew sandwich, served on a sourdough bun. ~ 1122 Riverside Street, Sicamous; 250-836-3603. MODERATE.

BEACHES & PARKS

ADAMS LAKE PROVINCIAL PARK 🚲 🏊 🎣 🛶 🚤 Just at the toe of Adams Lake, this small, low-key park has a nice setting, ample recreation opportunities, and less tendency to attract crowds than other Shuswap region parks. It'd be a good base to use while taking in the Adams River salmon runs downstream from the park. ~ Located 10 miles (16 km) north of Route 1, along the Squilax-Anglemont Road; 250-955-0861.

▲ There are 28 primitive sites set in the forest away from the lake, about 20 yards from shore; C$9 per night.

SHUSWAP LAKE PROVINCIAL PARK 🏃 🚲 🏇 🏊 ⛷ 🎣 🚤 🚣 This huge—and hugely popular—campground, beach and picnic spot is on the warm north shore of Shuswap Lake's main arm. Set on the delta of Scotch Creek, the park holds

---

A REAL MEAT MARKET

Most towns in inland B.C. have something that's a rarity below the border—a local butcher. Salmon Arm has three. The one I like best is **Petty's Meats**—Bernard Petty buys his own meat on the hoof, slaughters it in back, cuts and smokes it himself. Try the kielbasa or garlic sausage; with a loaf of bread, it makes a scrumptious picnic lunch. ~ Route 1, just west of Salmon Arm; 250-832-3756. BUDGET.

a thick, mixed forest of pine, birch, cottonwood and fir. The long beach faces south into the sun. Copper Island, a mile offshore, is a well-known boat destination that's also part of the park. There's an amphitheater, a children's playground, showers, interpretive displays and nature programs. Crowds are permanent in the July/August peak travel season. ~ On the Squilax–Anglemont Road, 11 miles (18 km) east of Squilax; 250-955-0861.

▲ Set in the park's thick forest, the 270 vehicle/tent sites offer fairly good visual and sound separation; C$22 per night.

SUNNYBRAE PARK 🏊‍♂️ 🛶 This quiet, overlooked spot is about   ◄ HIDDEN
ten minutes from Route 1, a great place to have a picnic and a cooling dip in Shuswap Lake. There's no camping, so there's little crowding. ~ Sunnybrae Road, 2 miles (3 km) east of Route 1.

HERALD PARK 🚶 🚲 🛶 🚣 🏊‍♂️ ⛵ About a half-hour off Route 1, this park has a campground, a sandy beach, a picnic area and other visitor facilities. But what distinguishes it is the trail leading to **Margaret Falls**, a spectacular cataract about 1 mile (2 km) from the main park. The trail leads along a lush stream canyon, past old-growth cedars, to the toe of the falls. ~ Sunnybrae Road, 7 miles (12 km) east of Tappen; 250-955-0861.

▲ There are 51 vehicle/tent sites with good visual separation; C$22 per night. Reservations recommended: 800-689-9025.

From Salmon Arm and Shuswap ▼▼▼▼▼▼▼▼▼▼▼▼▼▼▼▼▼▼▼
Lake, it's hardly a half-hour drive **Kelowna and North Okanagan**
south along Route 97 into the
Okanagan proper. The Okanagan Valley is a lush, warm land full of orchards and vineyards. The most significant geographical feature is Okanagan Lake, stretching south from the town of Vernon to Penticton; other lakes in the chain reach nearly to the U.S. border. Kalamalka Lake, a small jewel parallel to Okanagan Lake, is on the way south, and about halfway down the valley is Kelowna, the busy, cosmopolitan town that's the largest of the Central Okanagan.

Drive south from Salmon Arm and before long you'll reach the   **SIGHTS**
area's preeminent sight, **Okanagan Lake**, which can accurately be called a must-see because, well, it's impossible not to see it. At 76 miles (123 km) long, one to three miles wide, and 1000 feet deep, it's a truly impressive body of water. The main lake never freezes; its level doesn't vary much, either, although the only thing resembling a dam is a small weir at Penticton that's barely eight feet high. This large body of water is fed mostly by springs; despite the fact that only a few small streams enter it, the lake water is fully replaced three times a year.

HIDDEN ▶

The North Okanagan has long been a lush grassland. With little of the undisturbed prairie left, the **Allan Brooks Nature Centre** was created by the Vernon community to offer access to this unique habitat and its wildlife. Located on a knoll southeast of Vernon, the center's observation facility offers panoramic views, as well as exhibits depicting the surrounding ecosystem. Allan Brooks was a local wildlife artist. Closed in winter. ~ 250 Allan Brooks Way (off Commonage Road southwest of Vernon); 250-260-4227.

Several of B.C.'s historic ranches have been converted to heritage sites; of them all, the **O'Keefe Ranch**, near the northern tip of Okanagan Lake, is the most extensive and entertaining. It's also the most crowded; the parking lot out front is full of tourist cars, vans and charter buses. It's best to go in the morning, as the chance to stroll quietly through the grounds is important to the atmosphere. The general store, stocked with period goods, is fascinating. The **O'Keefe Mansion** is an elegant Victorian with hand-crafted touches that hint at the beginning of the Craftsman style. There are numerous ranch outbuildings, ranging from root cellar to cowboy bunkhouse. The tiny chapel is a popular spot for weddings. All these elements are original, lovingly restored. You can hitch a ride in the stagecoach that wends its way through the grounds. There's also a restaurant and gift shop. Closed in winter. Admission. ~ Route 97, 5 miles (8 km) northwest of Vernon; 250-542-7868; www.okeeferanch.bc.ca.

Heading south, Route 97 passes along **Kalamalka Lake**, a sparkling emerald-sapphire gem (the color depends on the light) separated from Okanagan Lake by a range of hills and a highway. Hemmed by ridges and cliffs, the setting seems particularly Mediterranean. **Kalamalka Lake Provincial Park** is a day-use site, abuzz in summer, with two nice beaches and several nature trails through wetland bird habitat. ~ The park is on the east side of Kalamalka Lake, 2 miles (3 km) from Route 97, just south of Vernon; 250-494-6500.

Kelowna (Kuh-loan-ah) lies in a wide fertile vale halfway down 76-mile-long Okanagan Lake; locals still remember crossing the lake by ferry before the highway bridge was built in the 1950s. The economic and cultural center of the Okanagan region and one of British Columbia's biggest interior cities, it has a busy airport, a vibrant downtown, many beautiful residential sections and a lively cultural scene. Hotels and inns are clustered around the downtown and outlying beaches.

Visitor information on Kelowna and the surrounding region is available at the **Kelowna Visitors and Convention Bureau**. ~ 544 Harvey Avenue, Kelowna; 250-861-1515, 800-663-4345; www.kelownachamber.org.

It is also the gateway most travelers from the east use into the Okanagan. Built between the mountains ringing Okanagan Lake, Kelowna's setting is as spectacular as the rest of the valley's towns. What sets it apart is a bit of urban bustle and cosmopolitan verve, including symphony concerts, a municipal arena (with a minor-league hockey team) and a top-notch restaurant or two.

Kelowna takes its visitor industry seriously—witness the four young people, the **Biz Patrol**, downtown merchants hire every summer to stroll the urban center, answering tourist questions and, when not otherwise occupied, serenading passersby with Western folk songs.

At the **Wine & Orchard Museums**, two separate institutions sharing space in a historic packinghouse in downtown Kelowna, exhibits explain the development of the valley's two major agricultural enterprises. The Orchard Museum (250-763-0433) includes a marvelous display of antique fruit box label art. The Wine Museum (250-868-0441) briefly depicts the fairly recent development of the area's fine wineries, and offers sample wines for sale from most vintners. ~ 1304 Ellis Street, Kelowna.

Appropriately enough for a city attracting large numbers of Asian tourists, Kelowna has a superb Japanese garden. With a trickling stream, a koi pond, soothing landscaping and little wooden bridges, **Kasugai Garden** is a calm oasis in the midst of the downtown bustle, right behind City Hall. ~ Queensway Avenue opposite Pandosy Street. ◄ HIDDEN

Nearby, the **Kelowna Art Gallery** is expanding its collection of B.C. art and has a small gift shop. Admission. ~ 1315 Water Street, Kelowna; 250-762-2226.

Busloads of Japanese tourists regularly disembark in downtown Kelowna to take pictures of a statue—not just a statue depicting some venerable human hero, mind you. This one's undulating form represents **Ogopogo**, the aquatic monster supposedly inhabiting Okanagan Lake, an object of much fascination across the Pacific. The human phenomenon surrounding the statue is at

AUTHOR FAVORITE

sights It's easy to see why the pioneer founders of the **O'Keefe Ranch** snapped up this bucolic site at the north end of Okanagan Lake. The rich grassland fed a prosperous cattle-raising operation that grew into a major way station as well. Kids love cruising around the property in the old stagecoach and checking out the farm animals, while I can never pass up the antique woodstove collection. See page 292 for more information.

least as interesting as the art itself. ~ In Kelowna City Park, at the corner of Abbott Street and Bernard Avenue.

It's not hard to see why Father Charles Pandosy chose the spot he did for his mission in 1859. With tall cottonwoods lining nearby Mission Creek, rich grass carpeting the meadows and the ridges and mountains lending perspective to the view, it's a **HIDDEN ►** lush place. Today the restored buildings at **Pandosy Mission Provincial Heritage Site** offer modern visitors a chance to see just how simple—and peaceful—the valley's first white pioneers found it. Father Pandosy's own bedroom above the chapel is preserved more or less as it was when he used it over a century ago.

The thick beams and hand-carved logs forming the buildings are as solid as ever. ~ At Benvoulin and Casorso roads in east Kelowna.

Kalamalka Lake has been dubbed "lake of a thousand colors" because of the water's shifting hues.

Guisachan Heritage Park is one of Kelowna's original ranches, now a popular spot for picnics, weddings and social gatherings. The beautiful gardens, with Edwardian perennials, antique roses and rhododendrons, are in bloom five months of the year; the original 1891 mansion, the summer residence of Lord Aberdeen, is now a restaurant serving West Coast cuisine. ~ 1060 Cameron Avenue; 250-862-9368 (restaurant).

The nearby **Benvoulin Heritage Church**, built in 1892 as a Presbyterian church, is a wood-sided pioneer structure open for tours on summer afternoons. ~ 2279 Benvoulin Road, Kelowna; 250-762-6911.

LODGING

The luxurious interior makes the **Lakeside Illahee Inn's** superb location icing on the cake for visitors seeking an elegant lakeside **HIDDEN ►** experience. With a provincial park in back and Kalamalka Lake in front, guests enjoy vast opportunities for walking, swimming, boating and wildlife watching. The five rooms feature private baths and entrances, and all have access to the lakeshore hot tub and private sandy beach. ~ 15010 Tamarack Drive, Vernon; 250-260-7896, 888-260-7896, fax 250-260-7826; www.illahee.com, e-mail info@illahee.com. MODERATE TO DELUXE.

Vernon's Lodged Inn Backpackers Hostel is one of the many such independent guesthouses in B.C. There are 30 beds, two kitchens, laundry facilities, a TV/VCR lounge, extremely economical rates, and you'll get expert advice about the North Okanagan's many recreational opportunities. ~ 3201 Pleasant Valley Road, Vernon; 250-549-3742, 888-737-9427, fax 250-549-3748; e-mail lodgedinn@telus.net. BUDGET.

The **Royal Anne Hotel** is right downtown in Kelowna, within walking distance of parks, beaches, restaurants and stores—not to mention the Ogopogo statue—and the Kelowna hockey arena. The 60 guest rooms are medium-size, pleasantly comfortable and feature in-room coffee. ~ 348 Bernard Avenue, Kelowna; 250-763-2277, 888-811-3400, fax 250-763-2636; www.royalanne hotel.com, e-mail guestservices@royalannehotel.com. BUDGET TO MODERATE.

Located in downtown Kelowna is the **Kelowna SameSun International Hostel**. This facility has private and shared accommodations. Amenities include pool tables, internet access, kitchen and laundry facilities, and lounge areas. ~ 245 Harvey Avenue, Kelowna; 250-763-9814, 877-562-2783; www.samesun.com/kelowna.htm, e-mail samesun@home.com. BUDGET.

Housed in a heritage home downtown, close to Kelowna City Park and lakefront attractions, **Mad Cadder Guesthouse** has a main-floor bedroom with private bath, and a separate suite with a kitchen that sleeps four people. Gay-friendly. ~ 911 Borden Avenue, Kelowna; 250-763-3558, 877-763-3525. MODERATE.

The red tile–roofed **Grand Okanagan** is the most visible hotel in Kelowna, situated as it is on the lakeshore at the edge of downtown. It's also usually considered the best hotel in the valley; the 205 rooms range from standard business fare to expansive multiroom suites with wet bars, sitting rooms and the like. The decor is a bit boring—country-club modern—but the service and furnishings are professional and sparkling. For an extra treat, book a package with the hotel's spa and enjoy massages, facials and a jacuzzi suite. ~ 1310 Water Street, Kelowna; 250-763-4500, 800-465-4651, fax 250-763-4565; www.grandokanagan.com, e-mail reserve@grandokanagan.com. ULTRA-DELUXE.

The **Hotel Eldorado** came to its current site by barge when it was moved from its original location farther south; then, after it burned, it was rebuilt exactly as it had been—which is to say, a charming late Edwardian, dark wood–paneled small historic inn. Perched on the lake just south of Kelowna, its restaurant and outdoor lounge are popular gathering spots. The 20 rooms are all simply but elegantly furnished, and reasonably priced. Boat-bound travelers can moor at the dock out front. It's best to ask for a third-floor room to escape the noise from the bar below. ~ 500 Cook Road, Kelowna; 250-763-7500, fax 250-861-4779; www.eldoradokelowna.com. MODERATE TO DELUXE.

◄ HIDDEN

The view from **Ravenhills B&B**, on a slope overlooking golf courses, orchards, vineyards, Kelowna and the lake, is unsurpassed. And the house was designed to take advantage of it, with huge expanses of west-facing glass. The large bedrooms each have a private bath and adjoining sitting room; there's a pool, hot tub and private entrance. ~ 396 Viewcrest Court, Kelowna; 250-764-0141, fax 250-764-0182. MODERATE.

Ted Turton was born in the big stone manor house he and his wife now operate as a splendid B&B in the orchard slopes above Kelowna. The **Manor House** is big, comfy and exquisitely built;

◄ HIDDEN

dating to 1905, the wainscoting, clear-fir floors and heritage furnishings make it a truly memorable heritage inn. There are two guest rooms on the second floor, with views out over the surrounding orchards and valley. Guests can enjoy sampling the many heritage apple varieties on the property. ~ 2796 K.L.O. Road, Kelowna; 250-861-3932, fax 250-861-4446; www.manor houseokanagan.com, e-mail info@manorhouseokanagan.com. MODERATE TO DELUXE.

HIDDEN ▶ Set in a quiet area of fields in the hills north of Kelowna, the **Grapevine B&B** is a peaceful oasis in the bustle the city has become. Housed in a handsome two-story white clapboard rambler, the three upstairs rooms (one with private bath) have dormers, thick duvets, ample room and privacy; the color scheme is soothing blues and greens. The delectable three-course breakfasts include fresh-baked goods, fruits and a hearty egg dish, as well as excellent Kelowna-roasted coffee. There's a pleasant backyard patio at the foot of a hill garden to which birds flock. ~ 2621 Longhill Road, Kelowna; 250-860-5580, 800-956-5580, fax 250-860-5586; www.grapevineokanagan.com, e-mail info@ grapevineokanagan.com. MODERATE.

The **Lake Okanagan Resort** is big, but that doesn't mean it's impersonal. Far from it—this family-friendly resort complex takes special care to make vacations enjoyable for parents and kids. In fact, guests during the peak season can avail themselves of child-care "adventure camps" that are quite inventive—a once-a-week parade through the complex, for instance, featuring floats, costumes, animals, songs and whatever else the kids and their counselors have dreamed up. Adult activities include golf, tennis, hiking, horseback riding, boating, swimming, exercising and general lounging about. The 140 units (most are time-shares) range from pleasantly utilitarian, in need of a little upkeep, to smashingly new and luxurious. All have kitchen facilities of some sort, although the resort's dining room wins accolades for its gourmet

REST AND RECREATION

The **Manteo Resort** is a dandy place for families, with numerous recreational amenities ranging from splash pools to sandy beaches to an on-site movie screening room. There are also a heated indoor pool, hot tubs, saunas, water slides, a tennis court, a putting green and a marina—if your kids can't find something to do here, there's no hope. The 72 rooms are comfortable but not glitzy, with blue and maroon decor. Fourteen lakefront villas offer more spacious accommodation for longer stays. ~ 3766 Lakeshore Road, Kelowna; 250-860-1031, 800-445-5255, fax 250-860-1041; www.manteo.com, e-mail refresh@manteo.com. DELUXE.

Okanagan cuisine (especially the seafood buffet). ~ 2751 West-
side Road, 19 miles (30 km) north of the Route 97 lake crossing
on the west shore of Okanagan Lake; 250-769-3511, 800-663-
3273, fax 250-769-6665; www.lakeokanagan.com, e-mail
info@okanaganresort.com. DELUXE.

Bird-lovers flock to **Wicklow By the Lake Bed & Breakfast,**   ◄ HIDDEN
a modern house in a lakeside neighborhood across Okanagan
Lake from Kelowna, because of its estimable setting next to a
four-acre shoreline bird sanctuary and below an estate winery.
You can simply sit on the back porch—where breakfast is served
in good weather—and enjoy the avian show and the serene vista.
Yellow-winged blackbirds, ducks, geese, grosbeaks, songbirds
and many other migratory types are profuse in the summer;
Lloyd and Johanne O'Toole have counted dozens of different
species. Or see if Lloyd will take you for a spin in his boat, past
the marsh, around the lily-pad duck nests and out onto the main
lake for an exhilarating cruise through Ogopogo territory. Three
rooms in the main house offer cozy quarters, with shared bath;
a detached guest house is much larger. Breakfasts are excellent,
and feature a delicious egg concoction called, naturally, the
Wicklow egg nest. ~ 1454 Green Bay Road, Westbank; 250-768-
1330, 877-708-5805, fax 250-768-1335; www.bbexpo.com/bc/
wicklow.htm. BUDGET TO MODERATE.

The main drag in downtown Kelowna is Bernard Avenue; not   **DINING**
surprisingly, many of the city's most interesting eating establishments are on this street.

Doc Willoughby's, a favorite downtown lunch stop, offers
pasta, sandwich and entrée plates, along with good soups and
salads. The Western/rustic interior decor is attractive and the service is amiable. The brewpub operation adds a craft beer element
to lunch and dinner, with entertainment on weekend nights. ~
353 Bernard Avenue, Kelowna; 250-868-8288. MODERATE.

The fare at the **Bohemian Bagel Cafe** far exceeds those simple boiled breakfast biscuits in vogue today. Full breakfasts are
made from ingredients such as homemade Canadian bacon,
brown eggs and local sausage, and you won't leave hungry. The
coffee is dependable, too. ~ 363 Bernard Avenue, Kelowna; 250-
862-3517. BUDGET.

De Montreuil is arguably the finest restaurant in Kelowna,
specializing in what it calls Cascadian cuisine—Continental and
Mediterranean dishes infused with Okanagan ingredients. Diners
choose a fixed-price meal ranging from two to five courses, and
select among dozens of dishes such as Alberta lamb chops, lin-
guine with squid, vegetables and hot sauce and fresh apricot
crème brulée. A fine collection of local art decorates the walls.
The tab illustrates the general tenor of pricing in Okanagan; a

five-course dinner is just C$35 (about US$23). ~ 368 Bernard Avenue, Kelowna; 250-860-5508. MODERATE TO DELUXE.

At **The Grateful Fed Deli** you get solid fare with no frills—hearty sandwiches, salads and soups at reasonable prices. Pasta salads are also good. Lunch only. ~ 509 Bernard Avenue, Kelowna; 250-862-8621. BUDGET.

Yes, the lounge downstairs below **Coyote's Waterfront Restaurant** looks a lot like a singles bar: it is (Rose's Waterfront Pub; see Nightlife, below). It's also the center of an annual biker convocation that confounds downtown Kelowna. But the restaurant upstairs does an exceptional job with its Southwest/neo-Italian cooking, especially pastas and fajitas. They even have genuinely hot sauces, a revelation in the B.C. interior. ~ 1352 Water Street, Kelowna; 250-860-1266. BUDGET TO MODERATE.

HIDDEN ► The **Pioneer Country Market and Museum** not only serves up made-to-order sandwiches and such staples as potato salad, it offers a vast array of pickles, condiments, jams and other products made from locally grown materials—most, in fact, grown in the market's own fields out back. Closed Sunday in winter. ~ 1405 Laurence Road, Kelowna; 250-762-2544, fax 250-762-2544; www.pioneercountrymarket.com, e-mail info@pioneercountrymarket.com. BUDGET TO MODERATE.

HIDDEN ► The **Harvest Dining Room** is in a remarkable setting, a golf course molded around an old apple orchard. The view past the clubhouse fountain/garden to Okanagan Lake and the west-side mountains is superlative, especially in the late evening when the sun sets. The food is expertly prepared Okanagan/West Coast cuisine, including dishes such as grilled eggplant and roast salmon. The dining room is no secret to members, but it's open to the general public as well. ~ 2725 K.L.O. Road, Kelowna; 250-862-3177. MODERATE TO DELUXE.

The **Bunkhouse Restaurant** is at Orchard Greens Golf Club, but it's not really a traditional clubhouse restaurant. In fact, it's the best place in Kelowna to get fish and chips and other pub foods, in healthy servings at reasonable prices. ~ 2775 K.L.O. Road, Kelowna; 250-868-3844. BUDGET TO MODERATE.

Every night **Mama Rosa**, a traditional Italian restaurant, serves up pasta, breads and sauces made fresh that day. The pizzas are equally tasty. ~ 561 Lawrence Avenue, Kelowna; 250-763-4114. BUDGET TO MODERATE.

SHOPPING   Among the many minerals extracted from B.C.'s mountainous terrain, Okanagan opals are one of the most recent discoveries. No, they're not the quality of Australian opals; however, they are quite pretty semiprecious stones. You can see them at **Okanagan Opal, Inc.**, in Vernon, where you can also book a visit to the dig site to look for your own. ~ At the junctions of Routes 97 and 97A, 5 miles (8 km) north of Vernon; 250-542-1103.

In a grassland valley with a long-established dairy industry, cheese making has long been a local art. At **Village Cheese Company**, visitors can watch master cheese maker Ivan Matte as he crafts dozens of traditional and flavored cheeses, sample the results and load up with wheels to take home. There's also ice cream and other local food products such as jams and syrups. ~ 3475 Smith Drive, Armstrong; 250-546-8651.

Geert Maas is an incredibly industrious Dutch transplant to Canada who decided to locate his studio in an airy pasture north of Kelowna. Lo and behold, his sculpture output surpassed his interior space, and the bigger pieces began to take root in the pasture; the result, **Geert Maas Sculpture Gardens & Studio**, is ◀ HIDDEN an intriguing stop near the Kelowna Airport. The bigger pieces are pricey, but smaller ones suitable for gifts can be had at fairly sensible prices, and the quality and style range from modest to striking—worth a look around, in any case. Call ahead for hours. ~ 250 Reynolds Road (1 mile/2 km) west of Route 97, Kelowna; 250-860-7012.

Locally owned **Mosaic Books** thrives (in spite of competition from chain mega-bookstores) because it does an especially good job of stocking titles of regional interest, as well as maps and adventure guides. The coffee shop invites leisurely introspection. ~ 411 Bernard Avenue, Kelowna; 250-763-4418, 800-663-1225.

Rose's Waterfront Pub is where the action is after work in down- **NIGHTLIFE** town Kelowna—especially once a summer when a modest gathering of bikers takes place at the pub. The rest of the time young singles meet to check each other out over drinks. ~ 1352 Water Street, Kelowna; 250-860-1141.

The bar at the **Hotel Eldorado** is where white-collar professionals head after work; in warm weather every table on the deck

---

OKANAGAN APPLE WAGON

In the Okanagan, orcharding has been a part of life for a century, but it remains a mystery to the average North American. If you want to know why some apples are grown in paper bags and then sold for $15 apiece, take a horse-drawn wagon tour (both fun and educational) of **Kelowna Land & Orchard**'s extensive (140 acres) holdings. KLO now includes a spiffy restaurant, the Teahouse, with a spectacular view of the Okanagan Valley, and gourmet food that relies heavily on local fruits and vegetables. ~ 2930 Dunster Road, Kelowna; 250-763-1091.

overlooking the lake is filled from 5:30 p.m. to dusk. The bar's nachos and appetizers are better than average. Reggae, blues and Caribbean bands provide music on weekends. ~ 500 Cook Street, Kelowna; 250-763-7500.

Not surprisingly, there's a country music club in Kelowna, the **OK Corral**. Line dancing, a mechanical bull, a games room and a horizontal bungee (go see for yourself) keep folks on their toes six nights a week. ~ 1978 Kirschner Road, Kelowna; 250-763-5554.

BEACHES & PARKS

KELOWNA CITY PARK Although this is right at the foot of downtown, all the urban activity nearby doesn't detract from the beach, playground, picnic areas, extensive gardens and other amenities. There are several concession stands and a children's water playground. ~ On Abbot Street at the west end of downtown Kelowna.

GYRO PARK Because this beach faces west, the afternoon winds tend to pick up as they come downlake and off the opposite shore. Thus, this is one of the top windsurfing spots around Kelowna. There's also a kids' playground and a concession stand. ~ At the end of Pandosy Street, south of downtown Kelowna.

HIDDEN ►   **ROTARY PARK** This is one of the nicest, quietest beaches in Kelowna, not far from the Hotel Eldorado in the south end of town. The sandy beach faces south, into the sun and pretty much out of the prevailing winds; it's inhabited by families, but there's plenty of room for all. There's also a nice picnic area. ~ On Lakeshore Drive a mile south of downtown Kelowna.

HIDDEN ►   **BERTRAM CREEK PARK** This 41-acre regional district park is one of the area's hidden gems, a pretty expanse of quiet beach south of Kelowna near Okanagan Mountain Park, used mostly by local residents. There's a nice playground, volleyball courts and nature trails—and virtually no tour buses or noisy motors. ~ Located at the end of Lakeshore Drive, 3 miles (5 km) south of Kelowna.

OKANAGAN MOUNTAIN PARK This marvelous, wild landscape climbs the steep cliffs and ridges above a big turn on Okanagan Lake south of Kelowna—the supposed haunt of Ogopogo, who issues from beneath the cliffs that plunge into the deep waters of the lake. No roads penetrate the park—with 20 miles (33 km) of undeveloped shoreline, most of the park is accessible only by trail or by boat. Hikers and bikers must bring their own water. Much of the park's upper area was burned in the big 2003 fire that seared the countryside. ~ Lakeshore Drive, 5 miles (8 km) south of Kelowna; 250-766-1835.

▲ The six marine wilderness campgrounds are reachable only by boat; 48 sites, C$5.

OKANAGAN LAKE PROVINCIAL PARK

Driving past this popular park on Route 97, you'd have a hard time envisioning its extent. The slope the highway hugs is so steep it cuts off the view of what's directly below—one of B.C.'s most-visited (and one of its most unusual) campgrounds. Instead of relying on native vegetation, as park developers would do today, the originators of this place planted 10,000 trees of exotic species ranging from Russian olive to Norway maple. The result is an established arboretum that cools the park. Bring lots of film—across the lake is the underwater cave beneath Okanagan Mountain Park that Ogopogo supposedly inhabits. Snap an actual picture and your vacation would become very, very profitable. ~ On Route 97, 8 miles (13 km) north of Summerland, about 25 miles (40 km) south of Kelowna; 250-494-7643.

> Built in 1958, the Okanagan Lake Bridge is North America's longest floating bridge.

▲ There are 168 vehicle/tent sites in two campgrounds on the slope above the lake; moderate visual separation between sites; C$22 per night. The north campground closes in winter.

BEAR CREEK PROVINCIAL PARK

Located on the west side of Okanagan Lake opposite Kelowna, Bear Creek Provincial Park is another highly popular camping/picnicking spot; the No Vacancy sign often goes up by 5 p.m. on Fridays. Besides a beach, playgrounds and nature center, across the road there's a charming hike up a narrow canyon to Bear Creek Falls. In the fall, Lake Okanagan kokanee (landlocked sockeye salmon) spawn in the creek. Closed November to April. ~ Westside Highway, 5 miles (8 km) north of the Route 97 lake crossing; 250-769-6825.

▲ The 122 vehicle/tent sites are fairly closely spaced; C$22 per night.

FINTRY PROVINCIAL PARK

One of B.C.'s newer parks, this striking spot, on a large thumb of land in Okanagan Lake, was once an estate; the stone summer house remains. More interesting today are the soaring old-growth ponderosa pines, among the largest in Canada, that dot the easterly grounds of the park. These are truly giants among trees, even by B.C. standards. The north-facing beach is somewhat subject to wind on hot summer afternoons. Too often plagued by bears in September, when the estate's antique apple orchard dropped its fruit, the park recently underwent a drastic remedy when managers bulldozed the orchard into oblivion. ~ Westside Highway, 20 miles (33 km) north of Route 97; 250-260-3590.

◀ HIDDEN

▲ There are 100 vehicle/tent sites in a pine woods near the old estate buildings and close to the beach; not much visual separation between sites; C$22 per night.

▼▼▼▼▼▼▼▼▼▼▼▼
South Okanagan

At the south end of Okanagan Lake is Penticton, the visitor, cultural and business center for the southern Okanagan Valley, situated on a tongue of land between Skaha and Okanagan lakes. Many of the area's fine wineries are in the countryside, a verdant quilt of orchards, vineyards and farms.

Below Penticton, on the shores of the smaller Skaha Lake, are the towns of Kaleden and Okanagan Falls, and as you go farther down Route 97, you reach Osoyoos, the Okanagan's southernmost town. Nearby is the Pocket Desert, where cactus blooms and desert scrub make the area look for all the world as if it were 1000 miles farther south.

The Similkameen, the next valley west of Okanagan (along Route 3), is a stunning narrow vale resting between steep ridges that lead to snow-capped peaks. With the river lined by tall cottonwoods and green pastures, and orchards and vegetable fields spreading up the lower slopes, it looks as much like Shangri-la as you are ever likely to see in North America. Keremeos, the main town on this stretch of Route 3, calls itself the "fruit stand capital of Canada," a slight embellishment of reality. But there's no denying the sheer fertility of the land, as you're faced with choosing among peaches, peppers, apples, pears, grapes and dozens of other fresh treasures.

SIGHTS

Most people use Penticton as the starting point for exploring the South Okanagan region. With a bounty of restaurants, hotels and stores serving the visitor trade, Penticton is a bustling, sometimes slightly rowdy town. Once known somewhat scornfully for

DEVIL OF THE LAKE

Just because the Loch Ness Monster gets most of the publicity doesn't mean it's the only creature lurking in a deep lake. Okanagan can claim the second-most famous, **Ogopogo**—the subject of several documentaries made by Japanese TV crews. Named N'ha-a-itk by the original Salish inhabitants, the "Devil of the Lake" is supposed to have a long, serpentine body with dark green skin and a large head. Most sightings take place in Peachland, south of Kelowna, where the lake plunges under steep cliffs at Okanagan Mountain Park. The best-known sighting was at Bear Creek Provincial Park, where a local salesman shot video footage of the creature. Scientific analysis demonstrated he'd actually seen a very large beaver, but Ogopogo believers remain steadfast. The Penticton Chamber is offering C$2 million to anyone who provides irrefutable proof that the monster exists. They mean a photo, not a carcass.

"peaches and beaches," the town today offers those in ample measure, as well as some slightly more sophisticated attractions.

Penticton's Wine Country Visitor Centre borrows a page from a similar facility in Napa, California, 1000 miles south, offering visitor information, maps and pamphlets that describe hundreds of area attractions, and racks of wine from all the area's major vintners. This is the place to begin a south Okanagan winery tour. ~ 888 Westminster Avenue West, Penticton; 250-492-4103, 800-663-5052.

A six-mile jog up the west shore of Okanagan Lake will take you to Summerland, where the Agricultural Research Station's **Ornamental Gardens** are a tranquil oasis on a high bench above Okanagan Lake. With formal beds, strolling paths, many rare plants and a xeriscape garden, this 15-acre parcel is idyllic indeed. ~ 4200 Route 97, Summerland; 250-494-6385.

Back at lake level, moored at the north end of Penticton at the edge of Riverside Park, the **SS Sicamous** is a restored example of the paddlewheelers that once plied Okanagan Lake before reliable roads encircled it. The nearby **rose garden** is brilliant with blooms all summer. ~ Lakeshore and Riverside drives, Penticton.

Excellent municipal beaches line the shores at both ends of town—that is, on Skaha and Okanagan lakes. Rental concessionaires offer boats, sailboards, canoes and other watercraft at both lakes as well.

Hundreds of orchards and fruit and vegetable stands line the road between Penticton and Osoyoos, sometimes right along the valley floor, sometimes above the lakes on high benches of land.

About a half-hour south of Penticton, you can see dozens of types of waterfowl flock to **Vaseux Lake Provincial Park**, a bird sanctuary between Okanagan Falls and Oliver. Naturally, there are Canada geese, as well as numerous ducks, gulls, swans and widgeons. It's also a good spot to spy partridge, thrashers, hummingbirds, hawks, eagles and the rare white-headed woodpecker. Trails lead through the thick brush along the lake to viewing blinds. Bighorn sheep inhabit the cliffs around the lake on the east side of the highway; there's a small provincial campsite nearby. ~ Located at the south end of Vaseux Lake along Route 97; BC Parks information, 250-497-6810.

As you continue south through Oliver along Route 97, stop at the **Desert Interpretive Centre**. Here Canadians marvel at what really is unique north of the border—a true desert landscape, with prickly pear cactus, yucca, sagebrush and other desert plants. The dry, sandy terrain receives just ten inches of rain a year, and desert wildlife includes rattlesnakes, owls and canyon wrens. You can't exactly call the sand hills dunes, but the area is definitely out of the ordinary. Guided tours only, along the center's

The South Okanagan

Few places in Canada offer the chance to experience as much scenic diversity as the South Okanagan. From desert to montane surroundings takes just a few minutes of driving; along the way history, good food and the chance to see rare wildlife flavor the experience. It's beautiful any time of year, but the best time by far is late September or October, when the cottonwoods and fruit orchards are in full, glowing fall color, and the fruit stands and restaurants are all offering the valley's harvest.

SIMILKAMEEN RIVER VALLEY   Head west out of Osoyoos on Route 3, climbing rapidly up the foothills from antelope-brush desert into ponderosa pine highlands. When you top the first pass and descend into the Similkameen River Valley, the pastoral field-and-orchard setting backed by steep-sided mountains demands a roadside stop just to take it all in. On your way up the valley, be sure to pull into **Harker's Fruit Ranch** (page 310), one of Canada's oldest organic farms, specializing in delectable peaches. ~ Route 3, Cawston.

KEREMEOS   Continue west on Route 3 until you come to Keremeos (30 miles/46 km), site of the **Grist Mill** (page 305), which dates back to 1877 and is now devoted to restoring Victorian food production methods. Water drives the stone grinding wheel; antique grains are grown on the slope above the pretty little creek; picnic tables rest in the shade of tall cottonwoods. Be sure to try out their full-flavored heirloom apples in fall, and pick up a sack of the best whole wheat flour you can get. ~ Upper Bench Road, Keremeos; 250-499-2888. Nearby, **Orchard Blossom Honey** relies on surrounding vineyards and orchards for its production. ~ Upper Bench Road, Keremeos; 250-499-2821. **Crowsnest Vineyard** has a gorgeous site on a bench overlooking the valley. ~ Surprise Drive, Cawston; 250-499-5129. Head northeast out of town on Route 3A, and it's 20 miles (32 km) through montane highlands back to the Okanagan Valley; see if you can glimpse the **Keremeos Columns**

boardwalk. Closed in winter. ~ Two miles (3 km) north of Osoyoos, off Route 97 on 146th Avenue; 250-495-2470.

With a lake that has waters reaching 70°F (25°C) or warmer in the summer (Osoyoos Lake) and a semi-arid landscape, the town of **Osoyoos** has adopted an Iberian theme. Although it's clearly contrived, it is more successful than similar theme schemes adopted by other North American towns. Red-tile roofs and pastel stucco buildings give the village a somewhat Mediterranean air.

(page 306), a basalt formation, in the mountain slopes above. You'll skirt Skaha Lake and pass through Okanagan.

VINEYARD LANDS   South from Okanagan Falls, have a lunchtime sampling of what most consider Canada's best wine. Dozens of wineries along Route 97 welcome visitors on a regular basis: Try Blue Mountain Vineyards (you'll need an appointment–good luck!) or Tinhorn Creek, among the most notable. Connoisseurs often rate **Blue Mountain Vineyard**'s deeply flavored vintages the best in Canada; in fact, you can't find the wines for sale at retail outlets since virtually all the production is snapped up by gourmet restaurants and luxury hotels. You can call to see if the winery is open for visitors, however; when it is, limited wine purchases are available. Tours by appointment only. ~ Allendale Road, two miles (3 km) east of Okanagan Falls; 250-497-8244. At **Tinhorn Creek Vineyards**, newly developed varieties of hardy vinifera grapevines went into full production in 1995. Red wines predominate. ~ Road 7 off Route 97, just north of Oliver; 250-498-3743, fax 250-498-3228.

VASEUX LAKE   At Vaseux Lake, five miles (8 km) south of Okanagan Falls, keep your eyes peeled on the east side of the road for the bighorn sheep that inhabit the hillsides. The small lake park is a good place for a stroll into wetlands teeming with birds, including the rare white-headed woodpecker. (Not so rare here; I saw one in the first two minutes.)

DESERT INTERPRETIVE CENTRE   From here south through **Oliver** (it's 30 miles/45 km back to Osoyoos) is the densest concentration of fruit and vegetable stands in Canada, literally dozens on each side of the road. Once you're almost back to Osoyoos, just a mile north of town is the Desert Interpretive Centre (page 303). Guided tours along the boardwalk expose visitors to the rare ecosystem now almost gone from the valley. ~ 146th Avenue, Osoyoos; 250-495-2470.

ANARCHIST VIEW   Once back to Osoyoos, head east four miles (7 km) up Route 3 on **Anarchist Mountain** to the viewpoint near the top, where the valley vista is unsurpassed and the sunsets paint the sky over the westward mountains.

If you want an interesting detour, follow Route 3A northwest from Osoyoos and after 19 miles (30 km) you'll arrive at **Keremeos**, which boasts thousands of acres of orchards and farms that supply perhaps hundreds of roadside fruit stands.

The main attraction here is the **Grist Mill**, built in 1877. The building and its original equipment, lovingly restored as a provincial heritage project, are now producing flour once again—using the waterwheel power that ran the mill during its first incarna-

◀ HIDDEN

tion. You can buy the stone-ground wheat flour, tour the homestead's heritage gardens and historic interpretive wheat displays and savor the best cup of coffee to be had between Penticton and the Vancouver metroplex. ~ Upper Bench Road, Keremeos; 250-499-2888.

HIDDEN ▶

Much of the Northwest's interior is volcanic in origin; this is, after all, along the Ring of Fire. The **Keremeos Columns** just outside their namesake town are towering, 100-foot (30-meter) basalt pillars that form a wall on the face of Orofino Mountain east of town. The best viewpoint is along Route 3A, 3 miles (5 km) northeast of Keremeos. The columns themselves can only be reached by passing through private property.

From Keremeos, you can take the gravel Cathedral Park Road southwest to **Cathedral Provincial Park**, a craggy land of lakes and strange rock formations that covers more than 80,000 acres between here and the U.S. border. ~ Cathedral Park Road, 20 miles southwest of Keremeos; 604-795-6169.

LODGING

HIDDEN ▶

At **God's Mountain Crest Chalet**, guests not only get a fabulous view of Skaha Lake and the lower Okanagan Valley, they get plentiful doses of self-made lodging entrepreneur Ulric Lejeune's philosophy. Lejeune believes you must "sing your own song"; his fanciful B&B certainly exemplifies that. The seven rooms are airy and comfortable, the setting unsurpassed, the common areas uniquely decorated and the breakfasts bountiful. If you're lucky, Ulric's wife Ghitta, who is often susceptible to culinary inspiration, will offer one of her multicourse dinners while you're there. Regardless, be sure to ask Ulric about his priceless collection of classical music LPs. This is a truly hidden place; Ulric deliberately has no sign at his driveway. Look for the white gazebo along East Lake Shore Road on the east side of Skaha Lake. ~ RR2, South 15, Comp. 41, Penticton; 250-490-4800; www.godsmountain. com. DELUXE.

Hostelling International—Penticton is in a downtown turn-of-the-20th-century home just blocks from the southern tip of Okanagan Lake and convenient to shops, cafés and restaurants. The hostel's capacity is 50 in an assortment of shared and private rooms; there's a kitchen, parking and a patio with barbecue. ~ 464 Ellis Street, Penticton; 250-492-3992, 866-782-9736, fax 250-492-8755. BUDGET.

It's hard to imagine a better resort setting than that enjoyed by **Ponderosa Point**. Its log cabins occupy a quiet sandy spit jutting out into Skaha Lake at the foot of Kaleden, an orchard-and-residence enclave that climbs the steep west hillside overlooking the lake. The two dozen one-, two- and three-bedroom cottages include full kitchen facilities and ample living space; three larger

A-frames accommodate up to six people. The beach is literally just seconds away. Tennis, sailboarding, rowboating, sailing and canoeing are on-site possibilities; the resort sponsors children's activities during high season. Because jet skis are prohibited, it's a bit quieter than other nearby spots. Popular with repeat visitors; it's a good idea to reserve many months ahead. ~ Box 106, Kaleden, BC V0H 1K0; 250-497-5354. DELUXE.

Sandy Beach Lodge & Resort has one of the best sites in the ◀ *HIDDEN* Okanagan, at the end of the road on Okanagan Lake's quiet side, in Naramata. Its long sweep of golden-white sand fronts a set of comfortably appointed modern log cabins; there are also six rooms in the main lodge. Cottages include kitchens, fireplaces and a deck with a barbecue. Tennis, canoeing, swimming, sailing and just plain relaxing occupy the time. Reservations in peak summer months are necessary as much as a year ahead. ~ Sandy Beach Road, Naramata; phone/fax 250-496-5765; www.sandy beachresort.com. DELUXE.

It's a good thing the lakeside road system around **Lake Osoyoos Guest House** is perfect for a lengthy jog. Best put in a 5K the night you stay here, because in the morning you will face hostess Italia Sofia Grasso's fresh-made Italian-style croissants. She uses olive oil, not butter; inexplicably, that makes them exponentially better than traditional croissants, and mortals cannot resist any number of these. The three guest rooms are spacious and quiet, with private baths, facing the lake; two have access to a small kitchen, assuming anyone would need a meal on the same day you've had Italia's breakfast. Ask her to make her good, strong Italian coffee, too. No credit cards, please. ~ 5809 Oleander Drive, Osoyoos; 250-495-3297, 800-671-8711, fax 250-495-

AUTHOR FAVORITE

Despite the explosion of adventure accommodations in Western Canada, **Cathedral Lakes Lodge** remains one of a kind, a classic European-style mountain hiking lodge—with the distinction of being located in a wilderness. I can't think of a better way to hike than in Cathedral Provincial Park's magnificent alpine scenery, followed by a gourmet lodge dinner and a soak in the hot tub. The food here, vaguely German to complement the Bavarian-style decor, is way above average for backcountry lodges, and lodge operator Richard Padmos' area expertise is unmatched. Just don't ask him where I caught my limit of trout four days in a row—I swore him to secrecy. See page 308 for more information.

5310; www.lakeosoyoosguesthouse.com, e-mail bbgrasso@vip. net. BUDGET TO MODERATE.

Brookvale Holiday Resort has the nicest setting on Lake Osoyoos, with a long, south-facing golden sand beach, tree-shaded campsites, sleeping cabanas, a boat ramp, playground and plenty of RV hookups. ~ 1219 45th Street, Osoyoos; 250-495-7514, 888-495-7514, fax 250-495-2730; www.brookvalecampground. com, e-mail info@brookvalecampground.com. BUDGET.

Villa Blanca is in one of the most spectacular locations you can imagine for a small B&B, high up on the side of Anarchist Mountain overlooking Osoyoos. When you're tired of watching the view, try birdwatching; many rare species live in or pass through these desert hills, including the white-headed woodpecker. Two bedrooms have private baths; there's a VCR and movie library in the common area. ~ Deerfoot Road, one kilometer west of Route 3 (just east of Osoyoos); 250-495-5334, fax 250-495-5314. MODERATE.

The town of Osoyoos (an Indian word meaning "narrows of the lake") has Canada's only true desert, located on the northern tip of the Sonoran Desert.

Night skies are dependably clear on Anarchist Mountain east of Osoyoos, so that's where Jack Newton set up a small inn devoted to stargazing. **The Observatory** has three self-contained suites, a small theatre/observatory, and a huge expanse of sky for guests to peruse. The three suites include kitchens. ~ Located 5 miles (8 km) east of Osoyoos on Route 3; 250-495-6745; www.jacknewton.com. MODERATE.

HIDDEN ►

The country lane heading south from Route 3 outside Keremeos looks like it leads into nowhere. Chopaka Road follows this beautiful valley, tracing the Similkameen River's path toward the U.S. border, until you think it'll wind down to nothing. That's where **Sentux't Brushy Bottom B&B** is, in a wooded creek bottom on Indian Reserve land. The Victorian-style home is furnished with antiques; the two guest bedrooms are small but comfortable; and the surrounding yard and gardens are peaceful. Breakfast includes Native foods, if guests wish. ~ Located 4 miles (7 km) southwest of Route 3 along Chopaka Road, 12 miles (20 km) south of Keremeos; 250-499-5560. BUDGET.

HIDDEN ►

You could never build **Cathedral Lakes Lodge** today. Its location inside a wilderness provincial park would be off-limits to construction, but in this case the lodge predates the park, which is one of B.C.'s finest hiking destinations. The lodge fits its special locale admirably. The two dozen or so units (the number varies according to demand) range from comfortable lodge rooms to fairly funky cabins; the resort's capacity is 48, and it often fills in the summer. You'll find a hot tub as well as lake and mountain views. Borrow a canoe for a tranquil spin on the lake, or ask lodge operator Richard Padmos for suggestions. Closed in winter. ~ Cathedral Provincial Park, 18 miles (29 km) west of Keremeos; access to lodge is by foot or special lodge shuttle only; 250-492-1606, 800-255-4453; www.cathedral-lakes-lodge.com, e-mail info@cathedral-lakes-lodge.com. BUDGET TO MODERATE.

DINING

The indoor courtyard at **Theo's** is stucco-walled and quiet; the Greek and Mediterranean food relies on Okanagan ingredients and wine for its hearty elegance with traditional chicken and lamb dishes and Northwest variations such as salmon in phyllo dough. ~ 687 Main Street, Penticton; 250-492-4019. MODERATE TO DELUXE.

◄ HIDDEN

The vast array of delicatessen shelf items at **Il Vecchio** is augmented by a lunchtime array of scrumptious, very large and economical handmade sandwiches. Turkey, roast beef, sausages, cheeses, salami—you name it. It's piled on bread with condiments and pickles for about C$3. Travelers on a budget can't beat it; it's just east of the main drag in downtown Penticton. ~ 317 Robinson Street, Penticton; 250-492-7610. BUDGET.

Never mind the purported New Orleans slant to the menu at **Joe's on the Lake**. Order a hamburger or sandwich, sit back and watch the passing parade along Lakeshore Drive, and enjoy the breeze off the beach just across the street. Be sure to order fries with a unique Canadian delicacy—a dish of brown gravy to dip them in. ~ 950 West Lakeshore Drive, Penticton; 250-492-4092. BUDGET.

There's more than coffee at **Hog's Breath Coffee Company**—they restock the shelves each morning with a vast array of hefty and flavorful muffins and pastries—but most important, the coffee is the best in Penticton. Hog's Breath is also a sort of informal information clearinghouse for the biking/hiking/sailboarding set. ~ 202 Main Street, Penticton; 250-493-7800. BUDGET.

"No Grease—Lots of Spoons" is the claim at the **Falls Restaurant** in Okanagan Falls at the south end of Skaha Lake. Nevertheless, there's some grease; this economical little eatery serves up such steadfast heartland meals as meatloaf and casserole with succotash. It's all filling, the service is cheery as can be and the bill is quite modest. ~ 1032 Main Street, Okanagan Falls; 250-492-5847. BUDGET.

The working windmill atop the **Windmill Teahouse** in Osoyoos is a replica of one in Holland. Built here in the '50s, the unique restaurant has been reopened to put the windmill back to use; flour is ground almost every day, and the breads used in the restaurant's sandwiches are baked with that flour. It's hard to get anything fresher; patrons can also buy the flour for use at home. ~ Route 3 and 44th Street, on the east side of Osoyoos; 250-495-5006. BUDGET.

Campo Marina is an unprepossessing sight—a tiny café along motel row in Osoyoos. But its Italian food is perennially voted the most popular in the South Okanagan, and diners never leave hungry, or with empty wallets. You get a lot of food for your money here. ~ 7506 Main Street, Osoyoos; 250-495-7650. BUDGET TO MODERATE.

SHOPPING Downtown Penticton is a pleasant, two-by-six-block area of small shops, cafés and stores, including eight banks, a locksmith and an optician. Beach and resort wear is available at **The Bum Wrap**, a small but well-stocked store on the main drag. ~ 285 Main Street, Penticton; 250-493-1612. And that beach-blanket essential, a good book to read, can be found at **The Book Shop**, which spans over 5000 square feet and offers a gargantuan selection of used paperbacks and hardcover books. ~ 242 Main Street, Penticton; 250-492-6661.

Bruce and Kathy Harker have spent almost three decades perfecting the techniques of organic fruit and vegetable growing— and then the techniques of marketing their crops to the public. **Harker's Fruit Ranch**, 2 miles (3 km) south of Keremeos, is a thriving, expansive fruit and vegetable stand as a result of that dedication. Their produce is unfailingly good. It's worth a small detour south. ~ Route 3, Cawston; 250-499-2751.

BEACHES & PARKS **SKAHA LAKE PARK** The most obvious attraction at this Penticton city park is the beach: a long, well-maintained, clean stretch of golden sand, it has buoys marking deep water (and keeping boat traffic at a distance), offshore float platforms for kids to play on, and concession stands in case you just have to have a hot dog or cotton candy. Parking is ample; crowds cover the sand only on weekends. However, don't overlook the marvel at the east end of the park, beyond the concession stand: the **Rotary Children's Playground**, one of the finest such facilities you'll find anywhere. Along with swing sets, climbing gyms and

AUTHOR FAVORITE

The outdoor patio at Penticton's **Villa Rosa** borders Westminster Street. With grapevine-covered arbors and generously spaced tables, it's a charming spot on a warm Okanagan evening; unfortunately the cedar fence doesn't keep out all the traffic noise. It's still more than worth a visit for the best gourmet Italian food in town—and the menu almost always features Mama Rosa's homemade lemon ice cream for dessert. ~ 795 Westminster Avenue, Penticton; 250-490-9595. MODERATE.

other contraptions, it includes a water-play area where kids can joust with firehose nozzles or run through spray showers. A nearby marina offers many kinds of watercraft for rent. ~ Elm Avenue and Cypress Street in south Penticton.

OKANAGAN LAKE PARK This city park is a bit removed from the main drag, and thus slightly less crowded on weekends than Skaha Lake Park. The almost constant north breeze keeps the beach cool; the yacht club and marina, with boat rentals, are nearby. ~ On Front Street, in the northeast corner of Penticton.

KALEDEN BEACH PARK On weekdays you can ◄ HIDDEN
park your car *by itself* in the lot at this beach in Kaleden, the quiet orchard town off Route 97 on the west side of Skaha Lake. Although the beach isn't as pristinely sandy as those in Penticton's city parks, it's clean and quiet, and there's plenty of grassy ground to spread out a blanket. There's a float platform offshore about 30 yards, too. ~ A block west of Lake Hill Road on Ponderosa Avenue, Kaleden.

CAMP-ALONG RESORT Campsites are literally in an orchard at this private campground, which hugs a high bench above Skaha Lake in Kaleden. A heated swimming pool; full shower and toilet facilities; a laundromat and store; a playground and badminton, horseshoe and basketball courts offer recreational opportunity, and quiet beaches are just a few minutes' drive away. ~ Located at Site 2 Comp. 12 RR1, Kaleden; 250-497-5584, fax 250-497-6652.

▲ There are 27 tent sites and 35 vehicle/RV sites, offering 15- or 30-amp hookups; C$20 to C$32 per night. Most sites are beneath pear and apricot trees.

VASEUX LAKE PROVINCIAL PARK This important wildlife preserve harbors extensive wetlands that draw migratory waterfowl, woods that attract songbirds and desert slopes that are home to bighorn sheep. ~ Located 10 miles (16 km) south of Penticton on Route 97; 250-497-6810.

▲ Rather near the highway are 12 vehicle/tent sites in a small, wooded campground; C$14 per night.

INKAMEEP CAMPGROUND Two distinctions make this spot ◄ HIDDEN
outside Osoyoos notable. It's the only local campsite operated by an Indian band, and it's the best access to the Pocket Desert, which is in the hills above the lakeshore campground. Campground keepers regularly catch and pen rattlesnakes from the desert to show skeptical visitors; the campsites, along the lake, are not prone to viper visits. ~ 45th Street, one mile northeast of Osoyoos; 250-495-7279; www.campingosoyoos.com.

Text continued on page 314.

The Wine Frontier

The bounty of the Okanagan has extended beyond fruit baskets and vegetable stands. In this most northerly series of West Coast valleys, the fruit of the vine has developed into a burgeoning new industry. Since 1990, Okanagan wines have gained notice outside the region, and some of the appellation district's pinot noirs, rieslings, gewürztraminers and merlots—varieties that do best in northern climes—are earning favorable ratings from connoisseurs. The valley also has its own novelty—ice wine, made from grapes deliberately allowed to freeze on the vine, then picked and crushed. Popular among consumers who prefer sweeter wines, each year's ice-wine releases attract ever greater interest across the Pacific and in Hawaii.

With two dozen established wineries, and more opening every year, the valley is becoming the latest "wine country" attraction, with its own winery tour, including tasting rooms and wine-related events. Most of the wineries are within a ten-minute drive of the main road through the valley, Route 97. Tasting rooms are generally open daily April through October. October is the best time to visit, when production is in full swing and the valley in beautiful fall color.

Driving from winery to winery in private cars, of course, presents challenges—one driver has to pass up tastings (Canada is strict on drunk driving), finding your way takes time, the driver misses much of the scenery.

Okanagan Wine Country Tours offers half-day and all-day journeys through the wine country, with expert commentary, visits to several wineries, lunch and, most of all, convenience. Possible itineraries embrace both North and South Okanagan districts; tours use luxury vans, and pickup can be arranged at hotels throughout the valley. ~ 1789 Harvey Avenue #200, Kelowna; 250-868-9463.

Located in the Shuswap Lake area, **Larch Hills Winery** specializes in cool-climate varietal wines, such as Ortega, Madelaine Angevin and Siegerrebe. The winery is in the vineyard, which is on a south-facing slope serving up a spectacular view. ~ 110 Timms Road, Salmon Arm; 250-832-0155; www.larchhillswinery.bc.ca.

The **British Columbia Wine Institute** not only certifies its members with a VQA (Vintner Quality Alliance) seal, it produces a pamphlet describing the province's wineries. Maps to each winery and descriptions of its products are included. Not all the Okanagan wineries are members, however. ~ 1864 Spall Road, Suite 5, Kelowna; 800-661-2294.

For wines aged in a pyramid, stop by **Summerhill Estate Winery**, where owner Steven Cipes produces fine Rieslings and other table wines as well as fruity sparkling wines—production is organic and the wines are additive-free. The winery offers a limited food menu and a fabulous view of Okanagan Lake. ~ 4870 Chute Lake Road, Kelowna; 250-764-8000, 800-667-3538; www.summerhill.bc.ca.

Also in Kelowna, **Quail's Gate** is a top-notch estate winery specializing in red and white varietals such as merlot, pinot noir and chardonnay; the winery is in a 125-year-old heritage log home. Tastings and tours are free and run year-round. The winery has a budget-priced, bistro-style restaurant, which is closed in winter. ~ 3303 Boucherie Road, Kelowna; 250-769-4451, 800-420-9463; www.quailsgate.com.

Mission Hill is a very good, mainstream producer of classic reds and whites—merlot, chardonnay—with exceedingly ambitious plans. More than $30 million has been spent toward the winery's goal of becoming one of the top ten in the world. Visitors will find an extensive visitor facility, a theater, a 1200-seat outdoor amphitheater, tasting rooms, dining rooms, and underground cellars reminiscent of centuries-old European wineries. ~ 1730 Mission Hill Road, Westbank; 250-768-7611; www.missionhillwinery.com.

In the Oliver area, one of the valley's lushest orchard regions, **Gehringer Brothers** produces high-quality chardonnay, merlot and other fine table wines. The tasting room overlooks Osoyoos Lake. ~ RR1, Road 8 (just off Route 97), Oliver; 250-498-3537, fax 250-498-3510.

Burrowing Owl is a small, low-key winery whose wines have begun to regularly win prizes in international competitions, especially for its fruity reds. The winery is next to the preserve devoted to restoring B.C.'s small population of its namesake desert owls. ~ 100 Burrowing Owl Place, Oliver; 250-498-0620, 877-498-0620.

The view itself is intoxicating at **Lang Vineyards**. Situated in Naramata at the south end of Okanagan Mountain Park, the Lang family concentrates on limited quantities of natural table wines. ~ 2493 Gammon Road, Naramata (15 minutes north of Penticton on the east side of Okanagan Lake); 250-496-5987, fax 250-496-5706.

▲ The best of the 310 sites, down at the quietest end of the facility, are numbered 200 and above; C$21 to C$29 per night.

HAYNES POINT PROVINCIAL PARK

Yet another in the string of big, popular Okanagan Valley provincial parks, this one is literally in the town of Osoyoos, occupying a narrow spit of land that almost divides the lake. During low water, there's a point where you can walk across Lake Osoyoos. A very nice path leads into a wetland marsh, good for birdwatching. The winds can be troublesome in the afternoon on hot days. The warm lake waters are a major attraction; this is one of the most in-demand campgrounds in Canada, with most sites in summer reserved months ahead. ~ Located on a narrow point that juts into Lake Osoyoos in the town of Osoyoos, just south of downtown off Route 3; 250-495-2120.

The world's largest sundial occupies the east end of the beach at Skaha Lake Park.

▲ The 41 vehicle/tent sites have decent visual separation. Sites located on the north side are more exposed to the wind; C$22 per night.

KETTLE RIVER PROVINCIAL PARK

Set in a pine and cottonwood forest in the pastoral Kettle River valley, this park offers camping, picnicking, a playground, and general peace and quiet. Since it's a bit off the main roads, the summer crowd pressure is less than the Okanagan's main parks. ~ Route 33, 3 miles (5 km) north of Route 3, outside Rock Creek; 250-760-1835.

▲ There are 87 vehicle/tent sites with good visual separation; the best sites are closest to the river, but they go first; C$17 per night.

CATHEDRAL PROVINCIAL PARK

Cathedral Park is one of the hidden highlights of British Columbia's provincial parks system. This high-country terrain is a hiker's paradise, with trails leading along timberline ridges, past gemlike lakes, through fantastic rock formations and up to pinnacles that offer stunning vistas for hundreds of miles. The Cathedral Lakes Lodge serves visitors who use it, European-style, as a base for dozens of day hikes. Access to the lodge is by private shuttle only. ~ Located 20 miles (32 km) southwest of Keremeos on the well-maintained gravel Cathedral Park Road; 604-795-6169.

▲ There are two wilderness campgrounds, 70 developed hike-in sites; C$5 per night. It's a long, steep hike up to the lakes and campgrounds from the road below. There's also a small vehicle campground with ten sites at the very end of the Ashnola River Road; unlike most provincial park campgrounds, there is no water or firewood provided.

Despite some of the local place-names (Salmon Arm, for example) and a few spectacular occasions (the quadrennial return of millions of spawning coho salmon to the Adams River), this region doesn't compare to other parts of the province in terms of its fishing opportunities. Yes, there are fish in the big lakes—including the Kamloops rainbow trout, known for its unusual size and great fighting power. But overall, the runs (especially of kokanee salmon) have been declining severely in recent years.

Outdoor Adventures

FISHING

Kamloops Lake is the obvious place to try for the Kamloops trout. Shuswap and Okanagan lakes provide numerous spots for angling, but prospects here aren't likely to be spectacular. Dedicated anglers will want to head to the more remote locales such as the Douglas Lake area and Cathedral Provincial Park.

Make sure to check on local fishing regulations and equip yourself with the appropriate licenses. For more information, see Fishing in Chapter One.

In Kamloops, check with **The Kamloops Fly Shop** about all fishing-related matters and to stock up on tackle. ~ 1366 Hugh Allen Drive, Unit 104, Kamloops; 250-377-8461. Some of the region's lodges can also provide guidance to good fishing spots. Near Kamloops, try **Roche Lake Resort**. ~ Off Route 5A, 20 miles (32 km) southeast of Kamloops; phone/fax 250-828-2007; www.rochelake.com.

In the Douglas Lake Ranch area, **Stoney Lake Lodge** is an excellent resource. ~ Located 10 miles (16 km) east of Quilchena; 250-350-3344, 800-663-4838, fax 250-350-3336; www.douglas lake.com.

Cathedral Lakes Lodge can direct you to remote backcountry sites in Cathedral Provincial Park. ~ Cathedral Provincial Park, 18 miles (29 km) west of Keremeos; 250-492-1606, 800-255-4453; www.cathedral-lakes-lodge.com.

The best way to see Lake Osoyoos is by boat; among other things, it's almost the only way to see the lake's elusive painted turtles that inhabit a quiet back bay. **Suncatcher Lake Cruises** offers daily tours with knowledgeable guides in a pleasant, open-air boat. ~ The Holiday Inn Sunspree Resort, 7906 Main Street, Osoyoos; 250-495-2345.

HOUSE-BOATING

SHUSWAP LAKE   Shuswap Lake is the unchallenged houseboating capital of Canada, for four very good reasons: the summer weather is warm and mostly sunny, the lake itself gets quite warm as a result, the scenery is magnificent and many of the back arms of the lake are largely undeveloped. Although it's possible to chug from Sicamous, the usual departure point, to the farthest end of the lake in nine hours, more leisurely journeys are usual and advisable. Boaters can fish, swim, hike up lakeside trails, or just plain relax and enjoy the quiet.

Not so many years ago the lake's tranquility was losing ground to the party-boat syndrome; even in the most distant sections of Shuswap, an evening on a seemingly quiet beach might wind up more like a night next to a fraternity house. Houseboat operators and provincial park officials have curbed this trend considerably by banning portable stereos, enforcing noise and behavior regulations, and ceasing the practice of renting to college tour operators. Now, although the lake can seem a bit crowded during the July–August peak season, it's still reasonably peaceful, and boaters can find an unoccupied piece of beach for themselves. Whatever season you're interested in, advance reservations are advisable.

Boats range from compact and economical to huge and luxurious—three bedrooms, two baths, a hot tub on the top deck. A week's rental ranges from US$1000 to almost $3000, depending on the boat and the season. As with so many other B.C. locales, September is a choice month to visit; crowds dwindle, the weather is still good, and prices drop.

Three Buoys Houseboats, one of the oldest operators on the lake, has the newest and finest fleet on Shuswap as well as the greatest depth of experience. Their well-appointed boats are spruce and their prices are fair and their onshore facilities are the best. ~ 710 Riverside, Sicamous; 250-836-2403, 800-663-2333; www.threebuoys.com.

Twin Anchors is another major houseboat fleet operator in Sicamous; they have a sister operation departing from Salmon Arm. ~ 250-836-2450, 800-663-4026; www.twinanchors.com.

HOPE TO KAMLOOPS Lakefront Sports Center carries paddleboats, canoes and kayaks. ~ 1310 Water Street, Kelowna; 250-862-2469.

PARKPLACE

Provincial declaration of 49 new or expanded parks in the Okanagan in early 2001 makes the area one of the premier conservation preserves in North America. The centerpiece, Snowy Park, is adjacent to Cathedral Provincial Park and, combined with parks and wilderness areas in the United States, creates the largest contiguous park area across the 49th Parallel international border. Other new parks include desert grassland preserves near Osoyoos, and several new preserves in the Monashee Mountains northeast of Kelowna. For more information, contact the Provincial Parks regional office in Kamloops. ~ 250-371-6200.

KELOWNA AND NORTH OKANAGAN   Sports Rent has canoes, paddleboats and rubber rafts. ~ 3000 Pandosy Street, Kelowna; 250-861-5699. To explore the 76 miles of Okanagan Lake, **Kelowna Marina** rents cruise and ski boats. Closed mid-October to mid-April. ~ On Okanagan Lake, Kelowna; 250-861-8001.

GOLF

Canadians are nuts about golf. There's no other way to put it; one result has been a proliferation of golf courses in the B.C. interior that means almost every town and valley has a links or two, and golf vacation packages are offered by almost every major hotel and tour operator. In the Thompson–Okanagan region there are more than 50 golf courses, ranging from modest par-3s to world-class championship courses.

In Kamloops, **Rivershore Golf Links** winds along the South Thompson River east of town, next to the South Thompson Inn. This Robert Trent Jones course earns four stars from *Golf Digest*; the design melds to the landscape rather than dominates it. ~ East Shuswap Road, 5 miles (8 km) east of Kamloops; 250-573-4622. The **Dunes at Kamloops** takes advantage of its desert location with a championship course offering the Canadian version of target golf. ~ 652 Dunes Drive, Kamloops; 250-579-3300, 888-881-4653.

Salmon Arm Golf Club, set amid the rolling hills above the city, overlooks Shuswap Lake. ~ 3641 Route 97B, Salmon Arm; 250-832-4727.

The profusion of courses in the Kelowna area is amazing; the Okanagan Valley seems to have as many golf developments as Scottsdale or Palm Springs.

The **Harvest Golf Club** is probably the premier course in the area. Critics have observed that golf development is pushing out agriculture; this championship 18-hole design by Graham Cooke winds the course through an established apple orchard, offering an interesting coexistence for golfing and farming. The views of Okanagan Lake and Kelowna are magnificent. ~ 2725 K.L.O. Road, Kelowna; 250-862-3101, 800-257-8577. Nearby **Orchard Greens**, a friendly nine-hole course, is also set amid an orchard. The view from the ninth tee is one of the best in the Okanagan. ~ 2777 K.L.O. Road, Kelowna; 250-763-2447.

Two more championship courses in the Kelowna area are worthy visitor destinations. **Gallagher's Canyon**'s two courses are set amid a ponderosa pine forest. One of the courses, the Pinnacles, offers a two-for-one deal on Monday. ~ 4320 Gallagher's Drive West, Kelowna; 250-861-4240. **Predator Ridge Golf Resort** is high on a plateau, and is the area's only true links-style course. ~ Route 97, 4 miles (6 km) south of Vernon; 250-542-3436.

SKIING

The mountains ringing the Okanagan area provide the ideal climatic conditions for ski areas—reliable snow from Pacific storms, coupled with sunnier weather and drier snow than skiers find at the big coastal resorts. Some of the Okanagan's high slopes receive 24 feet of snow in a winter, and the season runs from late November to late April. Some of the smaller of the region's half-dozen areas are within a half-hour's drive of Penticton or Kelowna.

The biggest and best known is **Big White Ski Resort**. Second in British Columbia only to Whistler in size, Big White offers 92 runs, 21 bowls, 2075 acres of skiing, and accommodations for 5000 visitors. A high-speed quad lift whisks skiers up the mountain; lift lines are rare. Cross-country trails are also available. The lift-served tubing park is one of the largest in North America. Big White is about a 45-minute drive from Kelowna. ~ Route 33, 35 miles east of Kelowna; 250-765-3101, 800-663-2772.

Silver Star Mountain is known as the area's family resort. The Victorian-style ski village is compact; the mountain offers 84 runs with a 1500-foot vertical drop. An extensive cross-country ski trail network includes a 30-mile (49-km) track at the nearby Sovereign Lake area. Night skiing, tobogganing and snowboarding facilities are available. There's a shuttle from the Kelowna airport. ~ At the end of Silver Star Road, 10 miles (16 km) northeast of Vernon; 250-542-0224, 800-663-4431.

BIKING

HIDDEN ►

The **Kettle Valley Railway** is truly one of the finest secrets in the B.C. interior. An incredible engineering feat built in 1910 in a rush to ensure that B.C. products would be shipped to Vancouver, not south to Washington state, the railroad was abandoned in 1963. And turned, with incredible community vision, into a hiking/biking trail in the mid-'80s. Now it is simply one of the most spectacular spots anywhere to go for a bike ride. The most thrilling stretch of the Kettle Valley Railway is high above Kelowna at Myra Canyon, where the route crosses 16 major trestles and two bridges and passes through two tunnels, simply to cover five miles. The railbed itself is 350 miles long, but not all that has been converted to trail.

GUIDED ADVENTURE

The idea behind the **Canadian Adventure and Education Centre** is simple: Get people out in the Shuswap's beautiful natural surroundings and they will learn confidence, relax and bit—and have fun. Tours and adventures are usually custom-designed ("survival training for the family," they call it), but frequently include water-borne activities on area lakes and streams. ~ Salmon Arm; 250-679-5433, 866-226-2332; www.canadec.com.

Unfortunately, the huge forest fire that swept Okanagan Mountain in 2003 destroyed many of the trestles that once afforded passage along the trail—and offered spectacular views into the lake valley 3800 feet below. A national campaign is under way to raise money to reconstruct the trestles and restore the trail; meanwhile, various portions of it remain open; check in Kelowna for the latest information on what's been restored. Also, a major stretch of the old railbed farther east in the Christina Lake area is open to bikers and hikers. ~ Located 6 miles (10 km) south of Kelowna; access is from Myra Canyon or McCullough roads; both are difficult to find, so maps are necessary for visitors. They're available at tourist Info Centres, bike shops and bookstores.

Bike Rentals & Tours   A number of bicycle touring companies offer excursions to KVR trails. In Summerland, on the west side of Okanagan Lake, **Sunoka Adventure Tours** reaches several of the more recently opened stretches of the KVR. ~ Dale Meadows Road, Summerland; 250-494-8346.

Great Explorations, a Vancouver-based company, offers full two-week bike tours that traverse the entire passable length of the KVR Trail from Nelson to Hope. Options may include lodging or camping along the way. ~ 604-730-1247, 800-242-1825; www.great-explorations.com.

The Okanagan contains some of the very best hiking in all British Columbia—considerably enhanced by the province's brand-new parks along the U.S. border, expanding the area preserved in Cathedral Provincial Park. Hikes often consist of stiff climbs up mountain shoulders from low-lying valleys so they are guaranteed to test your fitness. The terrain, once you make it above timberline, affords vistas of hundreds of miles. All distances for hiking trails are one way unless otherwise indicated.

HIKING

HOPE TO KAMLOOPS   **Manning Provincial Park** encompasses some of the most beautiful alpine scenery reachable by car in southern British Columbia. Although it's quite crowded in summer, several hikes afford the opportunity to escape the crowds and experience the high country. The **Lightning Lakes Chain** (7 miles/12 km) is a trek along a high valley that holds four pretty lakes; the trailhead is at Lightning Lake Campground, 3 miles (5 km) from the Manning Park visitor center on Route 3. The **Monument 83** (9 miles/15 km) trail takes experienced hikers up a creek valley to the U.S. border. The trailhead is on Route 3, 2.5 miles (4 km) east of the visitors center. ~ 250-840-8836.

The **Lac du Bois Grasslands** are a patchwork of lowland bunch grass, highland meadow, and ponderosa and aspen forest, in the low range of mountains north of Kamloops Lake. In early summer, rare wildflowers such as the mariposa lily bloom in the

◀ *HIDDEN*

grasslands; the aspen forests harbor migratory songbirds. Numerous hiking trails crisscross the area; one of the best hikes is up **Wheeler Mountain** (3 miles/5 km), which offers the opportunity to cross several different ecological zones. ~ Follow 8th Street north out of west Kamloops; it becomes the Wheeler Mountain/ Pass Lake Road. The trailhead is approximately 6 miles (10 km) out of Kamloops. Grasslands maps are available from the Kamloops Forest District Office, 250-371-6500.

KELOWNA AND NORTH OKANAGAN Summertime brings alpine flowers, migratory birds and bright sunny days to **Silver Star Mountain** ski resort area east of Vernon, so the resort offers visitors chairlift rides to the mountaintop; from there you can walk down on two trails reserved for hikers. The **Silver Queen– Water Rustler Trail** (2 miles/4.5 km) wanders down through pretty subalpine forest and flower meadows; the **Attridge Scenic Loop** (3 miles/5 km) offers spectacular views west to the Okanagan Valley. A resort naturalist offers wildflower walks on Sunday; reservations are recommended. ~ Silver Star Road, 12 miles (20 km) east of Vernon; 250-542-0224.

SOUTH OKANAGAN Surrounded by mountains as they are, the Okanagan and Thompson valleys offer numerous opportunities for hikers to venture into the hills. With the exception of Cathedral Park, there are no major wilderness parks in the area; even so, the mountains are mostly quite wild, and bears and cougars regularly venture to the edge of the region's towns.

Cathedral Provincial Park is one of the premier hiking destinations in Canada. With two wilderness campgrounds and a full-fledged wilderness lodge (see Lodging, above) in the park center, visitors come from across Canada and Europe to spend several days hiking the spectacular landscape in this alpine basin. With six shimmering lakes and a dozen developed trails, a week or more of hiking is possible. Among the best hikes are the **Rim Trail** (6 miles/10 km), which leads visitors above timberline to Stone City, a fantastic rock formation; and the trail to **Ladyslipper Lake** (3 miles/5 km), a pretty walk through subalpine forest to a beautiful lake. For hardy individuals, a loop up **Lakeview Mountain** and back down past **Goat Lakes** (9 miles/15 km roundtrip) affords exceptional views and is uncrowded. ~ Cathedral Provincial Park is 10 miles (16 km) southwest of Keremeos on the Ashnola River Road; 604-795-6169.

▼▼▼▼▼▼▼▼▼▼▼

Transportation

CAR

The main routes into the Okanagan are **Route 1** from Vancouver, **Route 5** (the Coquihalla) from Hope (C$10 toll), Route 97C (the Okanagan Connector) from Merritt, **Route 6** from the Kootenays and **Route 3** from Hope to Osoyoos. Using the **Coquihalla and Okanagan Connector**, a multilane, mostly controlled-access route, it's a bit more than a four-hour drive from Vancouver to Kelowna.

From Seattle, the best route is to take **Route 90** east to **U.S. Route 97**, then follow that north; it's about a seven-hour drive.

A similar amount of travel time greets motorists coming from Calgary along Route 1.

From Spokane, in northeastern Washington, it's about five hours, following **U.S. Route 395** north into Canada, then Route 3 west, to Osoyoos.

All these roads traverse scenic landscapes, ranging from the deep forests of the Cascades' west slope, to the arid canyons of the inland empire, to the ponderosa pine highlands of the inland mountains. In fall, winter and spring, snow and ice are possible along the higher-elevation stretches. The provincial toll-free road conditions phone is 800-663-4997.

Kamloops, Kelowna and Penticton have scheduled air service from Vancouver and Calgary; Kelowna has direct service to Seattle as well. **Kelowna Airport** is served by Air Canada, Horizon Air and WestJet.   **AIR**

For ground transportation from the Kelowna Airport, call **Kelowna Transit** (250-860-8121).

Greyhound Bus Lines (800-661-8747; www.greyhound.com) serves Kamloops, Kelowna, Penticton and other points from Vancouver and Calgary. The Kelowna Bus Station is located at 2366 Leckie Road; 250-860-3835.   **BUS**

Most major chains offer car rentals in Kamloops and Kelowna, including **Avis Rent A Car** (800-879-2847), **Budget Rent A Car** (888-368-7368) and **National Car Rental** (800-387-4747).   **CAR RENTALS**

Passenger service into Kamloops is provided by **VIA Rail**. ~ 800-561-8630; www.viarail.ca.   **TRAIN**

The bigger towns are served, respectively, by **Kamloops Transit Systems** (250-376-1216), **Kelowna Transit Systems** (250-860-8121) and **Penticton City Transit** (250-492-5602).   **PUBLIC TRANSIT**

EIGHT

The Kootenays

On the map, the wedge-shaped southeastern corner of British Columbia that encompasses the Kootenay and Rocky Mountain regions is just a small fraction of the province—10 percent, perhaps. But many, residents and visitors alike, consider it their favorite part of B.C. Credit a unique landscape and society for attracting travelers and immigrants from all over North America. The Kootenays (the nickname generally used to describe the whole region) are like nowhere else.

At first glance that seems somewhat mysterious. It's a mountainous region, with settlement confined to low valleys cutting through towering snowy ranges—but this describes most of British Columbia. It has a large and successful community of artists and artisans—as do the Gulf Islands, Victoria and Vancouver. Its lifestyle is relaxed and friendly—likewise dozens of other places in B.C. Deep forests, fabulous lakes, unspoiled wilderness and big rivers—these commonplace B.C. attributes are found in full measure in the Kootenays.

What distinguishes these valleys and the mountains around them are the sheer magnificence of the landscape, the steadfast affection its residents hold for it and for their communities, and a strikingly independent, unfancy and unfettered approach to life. It's no mere happenstance that in Nelson, the region's de facto cultural capital, the downtown core is thriving, without a single empty storefront, while the modern, edge-of-town mall struggles—the reverse of almost every other small city in North America.

There's virtually no limit to the pleasures visitors can partake in here: skiing, fishing, boating, hiking, climbing, wildlife watching, bicycling, wilderness trekking and horseback riding—to name a few. With a half-dozen major developed hot springs, and many more developed only to the extent that users have built tubs and ponds, the Kootenays lead B.C. in thermal opportunities. To all that add exceptional local art and theater, good dining and an unreserved friendliness toward all, and B.C.'s Kootenays region is, in the opinion of many, the place to go.

322

That wasn't the attitude early European explorers held. Like the rest of B.C., this region was long inhabited by First Nations peoples who lived fairly serene lives dependent on salmon, abundant wild game and berries. The sheer difficulty of moving around, which helped keep this area peaceful among native groups, also hindered European exploration. David Thompson, the first British explorer, encountered this obstacle when he tried to fulfill what must have seemed a fairly simple assignment: survey the entire length of the Columbia. It took almost half a decade (twice as long as Alexander MacKenzie took to cross the whole continent).

It would be hard to say which is the most mountainous section of British Columbia, but the southeastern corner could certainly compete. It holds four major named ranges—the Rockies, the Purcells, the Selkirks and the Monashees—and some of the valleys between them are so narrow, the mountains so high, that midwinter sunlight barely reaches the valley floor. The Columbia River originates here, running first north and then southward between the Selkirks and Monashees to cross the U.S. border near the town of Trail. The Kootenay River, for its part, springs from the mountains above the Columbia, skirts within a mile of the bigger river's headwaters lake, then cuts an arc into the United States that reverses the Columbia's, returning to B.C. at Kootenay Lake before it jogs west to join the Columbia. Along the valleys, six major lakes further frustrate easy passage.

It's a confusing topography indeed—as Thompson found out. He wandered, and eloquently described, a region rich in natural beauty but not much else of interest to Western civilization. Although prospectors roamed the mountains, and several small strikes occurred, not much settlement took place until major finds of silver, copper and gold were discovered around Kootenay Lake in the 1880s. The discovery precipitated what turned out to be B.C.'s last significant treasure-seeking rush.

As with any such boom, cities suddenly sprang up: Sandon, Greenwood, Kaslo, Nelson, Kimberley, Fernie, Slocan, Fort Steele. At one point, Nelson was B.C.'s third-largest city, after Vancouver and Victoria; Kimberley remains the second-highest town in Canada. Both now pin their economic hopes on a more renewable resource—tourism—than ore extraction. But the past was illustrious: by the turn of the century, the region was producing much of Canada's silver and gold; and by World War I, most of the copper in the British Empire was being extracted from the "Boundary Country" between Trail and Grand Forks.

Although diehards still wander the mountains looking for one last undiscovered lode, mining slowly fizzled through the 20th century. Today the region depends on its surface assets—spectacular mountains, bountiful winter snows, sparkling blue lakes and B.C.'s omnipresent timber—for its livelihood. And a great many people simply get by, doing this or that—throwing pottery, raising llamas—so they can live here.

So visitors get to experience not only the landscape that drew the area's residents, but the easygoing, unabashedly libertarian lifestyle they have created. It's a unique blend, represented aptly by the confusing time situation: the eastern Kootenays (the Columbia Valley and Kimberley, Creston and Cranbrook areas) are on Mountain Time. However, one small area (Creston) does not switch to daylight saving time; so in summer, officials physically move the signs that warn travelers they have crossed time zones.

There are two major east–west highways—Route 1 and Route 3—that cross this region, and two major north–south ones, 23/6 and 93/95. Sound simple? It's not. Three of the most famous and forbidding of all North American passes, Rogers and Kicking Horse on Route 1 and Crowsnest on Route 3, are part of the road system—and three free ferries funnel traffic across deep lakes too expensive to bridge. Long, winding passages up and down narrow valleys are the norm here. The canyons require almost constant straining to look upward—a sunroof is a practical asset for sightseers here. It's a good idea to stop frequently and have a look around, considering how hard it is to watch the road when you're trying to peer straight up. And even though distances may look short on the map, be prepared for long drives. From Crowsnest Pass in the east to Vancouver in the west is about 300 miles (485 km) as the crow flies—and almost twice that, 600 miles (1000 km), along Route 3, which winds up and down through the mountains along B.C.'s southern border.

▼▼▼▼▼▼▼▼▼▼▼▼▼

Western Kootenays

Route 1 takes you east from Okanagan to Revelstoke, the crossroads of the western Kootenays. This is mountain country, a region bounded on the west by Lake Revelstoke and on the east by Kootenay Lake—bodies of water that stretch a hundred miles south, nearly to the U.S. border. Between the lakes are wilderness jewels as well as friendly, funky mountain towns like Kaslo and Nelson.

SIGHTS

As Route 1 heads east from the Shuswap Lake area it enters the Monashee Mountains; 14 miles (24 km) up the first valley from Sicamous, **Craigellachie** marks a spot Canadian railroad builders must have wondered if they would ever reach. Here the tracks from east and west finally met in November 1885 and railroad officials drove the last spike, cementing a bargain made 14 years earlier when British Columbia agreed to join Canada in exchange for a railroad. Today there's a rest stop made up to look like a railway station; while you're resting, the still ceaseless intercontinental train traffic roars by, attesting to the continuing significance of this rail route.

After another 30 windy mountain miles (48 km), you reach **Revelstoke**, the gateway to the Rockies and Kootenays for travelers coming in on the Trans-Canada Highway. Long an important railroad junction, it's assuming a growing role as a visitor center, with numerous small inns, cafés and adventure outfitters. This is the place to mount hiking, canoeing or skiing expeditions in nearby wildernesses—and to obtain essential local expertise.

For information on Revelstoke, contact the **Revelstoke Chamber of Commerce.** ~ 204 Campbell Avenue; 250-837-5345, 800-487-1493; www.revelstokecc.bc.ca.

The **Revelstoke Railway Museum** honors the town's past with exhibits depicting construction of the Trans-Canada rail-

Text continued on page 328.

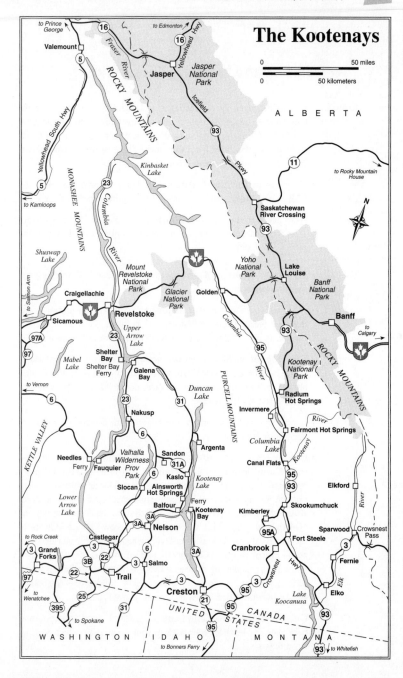

The Kootenays

Nelson and the Western Kootenays

Day 1
- From Vancouver, fly to Castlegar and pick up a car, or drive to Nelson from Seattle (7 hours) or Vancouver (6 hours) or Spokane (3 hours). All of those routes are scenic, traversing mountains and river valleys; the drive from Vancouver along Route 3 is the most spectacular, crossing three separate ranges.

- Check in to **Inn the Garden** (page 334), Nelson's exceptional B&B or the **Heritage Inn** (page 334), a century-old landmark.

- Head down to the **Glacier Gourmet** (page 335) for pizza, a look at all the local arts and crafts, and on Friday night, local jazz groups.

Day 2
- Make reservations for dinner tonight at All Seasons Cafe, Nelson's gourmet restaurant.

- Whether you had breakfast at your accommodation or not, start the day's walking tour of Nelson with coffee and a muffin at **Oso Negro** (page 335), the town's premier gourmet coffee shop.

- Get a copy of the Nelson heritage walking tour map, head uphill and check out the dozens of Victorian, Edwardian and Arts and Crafts homes lovingly preserved by local residents. It's a steep climb . . . but the last leg is downhill.

- Grab a bite to eat at one of the dozen small downtown cafés on Vernon or Baker streets.

- Take the rest of the afternoon to stroll downtown Nelson. The historic **Courthouse** and **City Hall** (page 331) were both designed by famed B.C. architect Francis Rattenbury. The downtown is also notable for the health of its commercial district; this is one place where the business core thrives and the suburban mall struggles. **Hempland** (page 336) and the several "grow" shops indicate a local cultural characteristic; several fine art and craft galleries, such as the **Hummingbird Gallery** (page 336) and **Craft Connection** (page 335), concentrate on area artists. The **Kootenay Co-op** (page 336) is not only a store, it's a social and political clearinghouse whose bulletin board is like a cultural Yellow Pages.

- Dine at **All Seasons Cafe** (page 335), just above downtown in a back alley. The leisurely walk back to your room is a perfect evening wind-down.

Day 3 • Into your car today, though it can't hurt to stop at Oso Negro again on your way out of town. Head up Route 6 to Slocan, a half-hour away, then along **Slocan Lake** (page 329). The spectacular mountain range across the lake holds Valhalla Wilderness Park, one of the most challenging hiking destinations in the Kootenays.

• At Nakusp, head east into the Selkirks for a late-morning visit to **Nakusp Hot Springs** (page 330), a genial, laidback resort run by the village of Nakusp.

• Back on Route 6, return south to New Denver and turn east into the Goat Range; halfway up, a short detour takes you to the ghost town of **Sandon** (page 329), the source of most of the silver that once made the region wealthy. Several restored buildings hold small shops and cafés; the hike to the top of nearby Idaho Peak affords a sensational view of the Kootenays.

• Head back down the road to **Kaslo** (page 329), a wonderfully scenic little town on the shores of Kootenay Lake. Down the tree-lined streets to the lakeshore is where you'll find the **SS Moyie** (page 330), a spectacular restored lake paddlewheeler.

• Stop for late lunch or early dinner at the **Rosewood Cafe** (page 335), Kaslo's famed soup-and-sandwich bistro.

IF YOU HAVE MORE TIME

If you have the time, finish up your Kootenays tour a half-hour south of Kaslo with a restful stop at **Ainsworth Hot Springs Resort** (page 333), where the view across the lake will hold your attention when the water makes you drowsy. Too tired for the drive back home? This is a low-key lodge, too.

road, especially railroad operations during the middle of this century. A restored steam engine is on site. Closed in winter. Admission. ~ 719 Track Street, Revelstoke; 250-837-6060; www.rail waymuseum.com.

Just outside of town is **Mount Revelstoke National Park**, founded in 1916 at the insistence of local residents. The park is an alpine fastness distinguished by Summit Road, a 15-mile highway to the top of the 5500-foot (1830-meter) mountain—one of the few places in B.C. you can drive to the top of a peak. Shuttle bus service from a picnic area one mile below the summit reduces traffic; the peak affords fabulous views of the Monashee and Selkirk mountains. ~ Route 1, 9 miles (15 km) east of Revelstoke; 250-837-7500.

An hour's drive east of Revelstoke, **Glacier National Park** is one of Canada's most heavily traveled, not just because Route 1 traverses its middle. It's also a stunning high-mountain fortress of barren peaks, alpine meadows and the glaciers that give the park its name. Prodigious annual snowfalls produce more than 400 active glaciers, including the **Illecillewaet**, once known as the Great Glacier. A century ago, this was a magnet for travelers who Canadian Pacific lured to B.C. for a stay at the now-defunct Glacier House Lodge and a trek up to the glacier itself. The park also includes several magnificent stands of old-growth cedar, vast alpine wildflower meadows and numerous wilderness lakes with almost 90 miles (140 km) of hiking trails.

Route 1 traverses the park, crossing **Rogers Pass**, a forbidding 4600-foot (1382-meter) crease through the mountains, first used by Canadian Pacific in 1885. Snowsheds shield the road from persistent avalanches; when CP used the pass the "white death" took the lives of 250 railroad workers in a 30-year period. That history is re-created at the **Rogers Pass Visitors Centre**, which also serves as information center for the surrounding park. ~ Located 42 miles (68 km) east of Revelstoke, 250-837-6274; Glacier Park administration and information, 250-837-7500.

You could continue down the other side of Rogers Pass into the eastern Kootenays (see below) or wind back down to Revelstoke and follow the water.

The Columbia River as it passes through Revelstoke is free-flowing; this is one of the few places the much-dammed waterway runs unrestrained. One of the major barriers is just north of town, at **Revelstoke Dam**, Canada's highest concrete gravity dam. Visitors can take free self-guided tours between May and October. ~ Located about two miles (4 km) north of Revelstoke on Route 23; 250-814-6697.

Just south of Revelstoke, two beautiful natural lakes were combined when another dam near Castlegar raised the water level 40 feet. Now the **Arrow Lakes** are just one, although maps preserve the fiction by marking "upper" and "lower" lakes. The valley that holds the water is a visually stunning, narrow passage between the Selkirk and Monashee mountains, with snowy peaks and hanging valleys looming mysteriously above. Route 23 traverses the Arrow Valley, one of B.C.'s most scenic drives. Halfway along, the free **Shelter Bay ferry** crosses the reservoir about once an hour. ~ The ferry is 30 miles (49 km) south of Revelstoke on Route 23.

For information on the southeast B.C. Rockies, contact Tourism Rockies. ~ 1905 Warren Avenue, Kimberley; 250-427-4838, 800-661-6603; www.bcrockies.com.

Halcyon Hot Springs, on the shore of Arrow Lake, is the most recent hot springs resort to be established in the Kootenays—reviving a historic destination to which Arrow Lake steamers once sailed. (See Lodging, below.) ~ Route 23, just north of Nakusp.

At Nakusp, Route 23 branches into Route 6, which heads west (actually south for a while) and southeast. After heading into the mountains again, the latter branch skirts **Slocan Lake** and at New Denver meets Route 31A, the road east to Kaslo.

In this steep, forbidding range above Kootenay Lake, prospectors found silver in 1892 in what might be the steepest, most forbidding valley of all. Here the sun barely reaches the valley floor, and access is along winding roads not for the height-fearing. Nonetheless, **Sandon** became one of B.C.'s most prosperous communities a century ago, with 5000 residents—and electric power before Vancouver or Victoria had it. There were 24 hotels, 23 saloons, an opera house and, of course, a legendary mine nearby, the Noble Five. Now it's a ghost town sprucing up to capture visitor gold, with a café, a few tidy houses occupied by diehard residents, and great day hikes to abandoned mine works and another nearby ghost town (Cody).

◀ HIDDEN

There's also a five-mile drive to the **Idaho Peak Lookout**, which offers a staggering view of the Kootenays and the vast wildflower meadows that abound here. ~ Sandon is located three miles south of Route 31A, between Nakusp and Kaslo; the Sandon Road is about five miles east of New Denver.

Follow Route 31A down the old railroad grade and you end up in **Kaslo**. Its site on the shores of Kootenay Lake is compelling enough, but Kaslo has more to offer than mere scenery. Tree-lined streets, small cafés, bakeries and B&Bs welcome visitors to this out-of-the-way hamlet; it has been called B.C.'s prettiest town, an eminently believable distinction.

The **Kaslo Library** is housed in the town's 1898 original city hall, a beautiful clapboard tower building. The 1893 **St. Andrews Anglican Church** across the street thrusts its own tall steeple toward the sky, lending the village a New England air. Across the lake, the **Purcell Wilderness** beckons adventurers. ~ For Kaslo visitor information, call 250-353-2525.

HIDDEN ▶

Kaslo was the terminus for the railway that brought silver down from Sandon, where it was loaded on paddlewheelers for shipment downlake. The oldest and last of those boats, the **SS Moyie**, is beached here; it stopped operating in 1957, and restoration began soon after, a testament to the vision and affection of local residents. Today it offers a good perspective on what life was like along the lake when this was the only transportation. Superbly restored, the *Moyie* still holds a hint of the exotic glamour that sternwheelers once provided Kootenay visitors, with mahogany trim, lots of brass, even a gold-leaf frieze. Put C$5 in the kitty and you get to blow the steamship whistle. Next to the ship, a relocated miner's shack suggests the far less glamorous back-country life prospectors endured. A replica of the *Moyie* plies the waters at Heritage Park in Calgary. Closed in winter. Admission. ~ Located on the beach off of Front Street, Kaslo; 250-353-2525.

Sixty miles (92 km) long, 1 to 4 miles wide, hemmed in by precipitous mountain ranges, **Kootenay Lake** is famed not only for its scenery but for its fish: anglers seek the world's largest rainbow trout, the Gerrard, which grows up to 30 pounds, and kokanee (landlocked) salmon. The lake rarely freezes, so fishing continues year-round.

South of Kaslo and east of Nelson, in Balfour, the only way to cross Kootenay Lake anywhere along its length is the **Kootenay ferry**, which advertises itself as the world's longest free ferry ride. It leaves about once an hour, taking 40 minutes to cross. ~ Junction of Routes 31 and 3A, Balfour.

Heading west again (this time on Route 3A from Balfour, along the west arm of Kootenay Lake) brings you to **Nelson**—just what you envision a well-restored former mining boom capital to be, a village of elegant homes and sturdy historic structures clinging to the slopes above the foot of Kootenay Lake. There are more than 350 heritage buildings here, reflecting not

sights

AUTHOR FAVORITE

The Kootenays are the hot springs capital of Canada, and hot springs devotees like me have a definite favorite in the Kootenays. Hidden in the mountains above Arrow Lake, **Nakusp Hot Springs** is a low-key, un-crowded spot where area residents and a small number of visitors gather to enjoy the clean pools fed from springs above Kuskanax Creek. Run by the village of Nakusp, the facilities include changing rooms, showers, a snack bar, and towels and swimsuits for rent. The water emerges from the spring at 130°F, and cools to 108°F (42°C) in the hottest section of the bathing pool. There are cabins and campsites nearby. Admission. ~ Off Route 23, 8 miles (13 km) east of Nakusp; 250-265-4528.

only residents' commitment to their town and its past, but the fact that the post-boom economy never became strong enough for the sort of commercial development that swept aside so many other towns' pasts in the middle of this century. Today, Nelson is enjoying a new boom, attracting ever more visitors and new residents. Looking for a certain omnipresent fast-food restaurant? Not here: townspeople blocked it. Want a well-made pasta bowl? Literally hundreds of artists, musicians and craftspeople live in this area. ~ Nelson visitor information, 250-352-3433, 877-663-5706; www.nelsonbc.com.

The best way to enjoy Nelson is by walking; guides to historic buildings downtown and heritage homes (ranging from Victorian to Craftsman) on the heights above are widely available. Especially notable are the **Courthouse** and **City Hall**, diagonally across from each other at Vernon and Ward streets, which were designed by Francis Rattenbury, the legendary architect responsible for the Parliament buildings and Fairmont Empress in Victoria. Like those edifices, the Nelson buildings, although smaller, are sturdy, imposing stone structures whose ornate Chateau-style touches bespeak the town's early-20th-century desire to create Edwardian grandeur in its remote mountain setting.

Nelson's 1927-vintage **Capitol Theatre** has seen highlights— the first "talkie" played here six decades ago—and lowlights: during a 1960s interregnum it served as a furniture warehouse. But it was never demolished entirely, and in 1983 the city bought it and began refurbishment. The organ lofts are now balconies; the gilt-edged murals, wall roses and art deco touches have been restored to their original brilliance. The Capitol now serves as a community auditorium—occasionally hosting, as it first did, silent movies with live musical accompaniment. ~ 421 Victoria Street, Nelson; 250-352-6363.

West and south of Nelson, a number of villages and a couple of mountain-crossroads towns hug the highways. After 25 miles (41 km), Route 3A enters Castlegar from the north; Route 22 takes you south another 15 miles (24 km) into the town of **Trail**, notable as a present-day reflection of the area's heritage: here Cominco, Ltd., operates the world's largest zinc and lead smelter, which employs 2500 people. Ore is shipped in from throughout the world now that most of the Kootenays' mines are played out. Former Cominco employees conduct tours for visitors; to arrange tours, and for more information on Trail, call the Chamber of Commerce, 250-368-3144.

The 42 rooms at Revelstoke's **Regent Inn** are large and commodious—especially the bathrooms, which dwarf those you'll find at many ultra-deluxe hotels. The Regent's downtown location is convenient to shops and cafés, and the hotel itself is home to

LODGING

one of Revelstoke's most active nightspots. Want a really economical room? There are several right over the bar. In the winter, this functions as a ski lodge, serving as a base for a local heli-skiing operation. Continental breakfast is included with the room. ~ 112 East 1st Street, Revelstoke; 250-837-2107, 888-245-5523, fax 250-837-9669; www.regentinn.com, e-mail regent@regent inn.com. BUDGET TO MODERATE.

Housed in a heritage home just off the main drag, the **Revelstoke Traveller's Hostel and Guest House** features 26 immaculate, private and semiprivate rooms with oak floors and trim. Guests enjoy a large kitchen, complimentary internet access and a free area shuttle bus. There are even a few tent sites. ~ 400 2nd Street, Revelstoke; 250-837-4050, fax 250-837-6410; www.host els.bc.ca, e-mail info@hostels.bc.ca. BUDGET.

Tucked away in a quiet, wooded residential area outside Revelstoke, **MacPherson Lodge B&B** affords a peaceful alternative to the town's tourist bustle. Sited on the slopes above the Revelstoke Valley, the log structure has two units with a common kitchen, balconies and views across the valley. Each room has a private bath. Hiking and cross-country skiing trails are close by. ~ 2135 Clough Road, Revelstoke; 250-837-7041, 888-875-4924, fax 250-837-7077; www.macphersonlodge.com, e-mail info@ macphersonlodge.com. BUDGET.

HIDDEN ►   With a 125-acre wooded peninsula all to itself, the **Mulvehill Creek Wilderness Retreat** is a bed and breakfast that also functions as a self-contained small country resort. Hiking trails lead to private beaches or along the creek to a 300-foot waterfall; guests can canoe or fish in the quiet bay, or picnic along Upper Arrow Lake. Rooms at the B&B range from two large suites to six cozy bedrooms (with shared bath) in the main house. The

---

THE VALLEY BETWEEN

The **Kettle Valley** is a gentle, pastoral passage between the Monashee Mountains and the Okanagan Highlands. No towering snowclad peaks in the distance; in a way, the low-key scenic beauty is a charming contrast to the ceaseless mountains east and west of here. Two notable museums depict the valley's past. The **Kettle Valley Railway Station** was the start-point for the famous rail line that connected southern B.C. to the Vancouver area. The handsome restored station building is now a railway museum. ~ Route 3, 1 mile (2 km) west of Midway. In town, the **Kettle River Museum** contains artifacts and exhibits depicting the early cattle-ranching industry and the region's law enforcement efforts to control cross-border outlawry. Admission. ~ For general information about Midway, call 250-449-2222.

large garden provides much of the produce used in Mulvehill's meals. ~ 19240 Route 23, 14 miles (23 km) south of Revelstoke; 250-837-8649, 877-837-8649; www.mulvehillcreek.com, e-mail mulvehil@revelstoke.net. BUDGET TO MODERATE.

The first resort at **Halcyon Hot Springs** was opened in 1888; by the turn of the 20th century it was a major B.C. destination, with Arrow Lakes sternwheelers stopping twice a day and the local water bottled for shipment throughout North America. The old resort burned down in 1955, and the ruins disappeared below water when hydrodams raised the level of Arrow Lakes in the 1960s. All this history bears on the current lodge and spa at Halcyon, which opened in late 1998. With hot, warm and cool pools, the full-service spring facilities should suit every taste; the modern log lodge and six chalets offer every convenience. ~ Route 23, just north of Nakusp; 250-265-3554, 888-689-4699, fax 250-265-3887; www.halcyon-hotsprings.com, e-mail info@halcyon-hotsprings.com. MODERATE TO DELUXE.

Opened in 1892, the **Leland Hotel** in Nakusp is the oldest operating hotel in B.C., barely beating out the Heritage Inn in Nelson. Its somewhat funky guest rooms are furnished with period antiques; a busy pub keeps things hopping downstairs. Ask for a room with a view of Arrow Lake, above which the hotel perches. ~ Located half a block west of Route 6, Nakusp; 250-265-4221. BUDGET.

Nakusp Hot Springs Cedar Chalets offers seven large, full ◄ *HIDDEN* house keeping units at the hot springs site 20 minutes from Nakusp. Units are carpeted, with electric heat, kitchens and private baths. Aside from the hot springs, hiking, fishing and cross-country skiing are nearby activities. ~ Nakusp Hot Springs, 8 miles (13 km) east of Nakusp off Route 23; 250-265-4505. BUDGET.

Ainsworth Hot Springs Resort is more low-key than its coun- ◄ *HIDDEN* terpart Fairmont across the mountains; makes sense, as it's just up the road from Nelson, capital of the laidback attitude in B.C. Perched on a small bench above Kootenay Lake between Nelson and Kaslo, Ainsworth has a 43-room lodge with comfy rooms, a restaurant and lounge and resort amenities such as massage services. The centerpiece, however, is the water. With a hot pool overlooking the lake and Purcell Mountains beyond, the vista while you soak is amazing—and if you tire of the view, you can explore steamy old mine passages behind the pool now filled with hot water. There's also a cold plunge pool next to the hot one. The entire resort is non-smoking. ~ Route 31, 12 miles (18 km) south of Kaslo, Ainsworth Hot Springs; 250-229-4212, 800-668-1171, fax 250-229-5600; www.hotnaturally.com, e-mail info@hotnaturally.com. BUDGET TO MODERATE.

Like its counterpart in Revelstoke, the **Dancing Bear Inn** is a member of Hostelling International. This restored heritage building offers private and semiprivate rooms. Wood trim abounds; the rooms feature beds with duvets. The lobby has a fireplace; kitchen, laundry and storage facilities are generous. The location is convenient to shopping (the Kootenay Co-op is practically next door), cafés and other in-town attractions. ~ 171 Baker Street, Nelson; 250-352-7573, fax 250-352-9818; www.dancingbearinn.com, e-mail info@dancingbearinn.com. BUDGET.

HIDDEN ▶ Perched on the hill just above downtown Nelson, **Inn the Garden** has an enviable location. But it's far more than that; this beautifully restored Victorian home offers three floors of superb guest accommodations, ranging from elegant single bedrooms to the lofty and expansive third-floor two-bedroom suite. Baths are shared and private; the decor is restrained, with wicker and other period furnishings and few of the excessive frills that often clutter Victorian B&Bs. The cottage next door can accommodate up to six people, with full kitchen facilities. Off-street parking is provided, and guests enjoy private entrances. The owners' knowledge of the Nelson area is exceptionally comprehensive. ~ 408 Victoria Street, Nelson; 250-352-3226, 800-596-2337, fax 250-352-3284; www.innthegarden.com, e-mail info@innthegarden.com. BUDGET TO MODERATE.

The **Heritage Inn** has served visitors to Nelson continuously since 1898, and its extensive dark wood trim and wandering hallways reflect its century-old heritage. All 43 guest rooms in the four-story hotel have been updated with comfortable beds, TVs and other modern conveniences; all have private baths with the sort of spacious tubs you don't find in modern hotels. The pub is Nelson's most popular after-work watering hole. Nelson's numerous heritage attractions are just steps away; the famed City Hall is across the street. ~ 422 Vernon Street, Nelson; 250-

AUTHOR FAVORITE

If I want to enjoy wilderness, helicopters aren't part of the agenda. They're not at **Mountain Trek Fitness Retreat**, either, where you walk to get where you're going. But just because Mountain Trek focuses on health and exercise doesn't mean guests have no opportunity to relax. With conditioning expeditions that include hikes through meadows filled with wildflowers and yoga classes on a sandy beach on Kootenay Lake, this lodge treats both body and soul. Its 12 private rooms are augmented by weight rooms, a sauna, an outdoor hot tub, and gourmet healthful cuisine. The pools at Ainsworth Hot Springs are just minutes away. ~ Route 31, Ainsworth Hot Springs; 250-229-5636, 800-661-5161, fax 250-229-5246; www.hiking.com. DELUXE.

352-5331, fax 250-352-5214; www.heritageinn.org, e-mail info@
heritageinn.org. BUDGET.

Overlooking Christina Lake, **Sunflower Inn** is a peaceful B&B
at the end of a quiet lane off the highway. The three-story log
home has three guest rooms furnished in pine, with earth tones
throughout—mustard, forest green, rust. The upstairs suite is incredibly spacious and features a soaking tub and woodstove.
Canoeing, fishing and swimming are available on the inn's beachfront. ~ 159 Alpine Road, Christina Lake; 250-447-6201, fax
250-447-6592; e-mail suninnbb@sunshinecable.com. MODERATE
TO DELUXE.

Housed in a nicely restored heritage home at the end of Kaslo's   **DINING**
main street, the **Rosewood Cafe** serves cuisine delectable enough
that travelers stop in from across B.C. It's not fancy, but the   ◄ HIDDEN
soups, sandwiches, pastas and daily specials are of gourmet quality, and the service is exceptionally friendly. ~ 213 5th Street,
Kaslo; 250-353-7673. BUDGET.

With a menu that features highly flavorful West Coast cuisine,
and a subdued, elegant atmosphere, the **All Seasons Cafe** represents gourmet dining in the Kootenays—and does a good job of
it. The daily menu features hearty soups, fish dishes and lamb entrées, and all are gracefully prepared. Naturally, it's located in a
restored heritage home. ~ 620 Herridge Lane, Nelson; 250-352-
0101. MODERATE.

There's barely enough room in **Oso Negro** for all the cus-   ◄ HIDDEN
tomers, especially when the weather closes the outdoor patio.
This coffeehouse expertly roasts its own beans every day—the
drip coffee and specialty drinks stand up to connoisseur scrutiny.
Housed in the same facility, the **Only Bakery** offers scrumptious
rolls, muffins and fresh breads for breakfast, lunch or dinner. ~
522 Victoria Street, Nelson; 250-352-7661. BUDGET.

The **Glacier Gourmet** is a renaissance establishment serving
coffee drinks, baked goods, pizza, sandwiches, burgers, nachos,
a juice bar, ice cream and daily soups and salads. There's also jazz
on Friday night. And it's a gallery exhibiting the work of local
artists. Have they left anything out? ~ Vernon and Hall streets,
Nelson; 250-354-4495. BUDGET.

The Nelson area claims more artists and craftspeople per capita   **SHOPPING**
than any other town in Canada; galleries are thus an integral part
of the community's lifestyle. The best is the local cooperative
gallery, **Craft Connection**, which exhibits about 20 local artists
and craftspeople. Styles range from classic to abstract; offerings
range from oil paintings to porcelain housewares. ~ 441 Baker
Street, Nelson; 250-352-3006. **Figments** focuses on crafts, rang-

ing from textile weaving to pottery and metal sculpting. ~ 458 Ward Street, Nelson; 250-354-4418. The **Hummingbird Gallery** concentrates on fine art, chiefly oils and watercolors and cast sculpture. ~ 515B Vernon Street, Nelson; 250-352-2083.

The **Kootenay Co-op** is not only the best place to shop for organic foods and supplies in Nelson, it functions as a community bulletin board and meeting place. The inventory is extensive, as is the opportunity to scout out local activities. ~ 295 Baker Street, Nelson; 250-354-4077.

The cultural agenda in operation at **Hempland** isn't much of a surprise—the Kootenay region is known for its socially liberal outlook. If you need something made of hemp, this is the place. Organic cotton clothing, soaps, candles and other natural stuff are also available. You can even acquire hemp chain oil for your chain saw. This was the first hemp store in B.C. ~ 557 Ward Street, Nelson; 250-352-3844.

NIGHTLIFE No matter how remote it is from major population centers, Nelson's fervent support for the artistic life means good music finds a good audience. That's why local and regional artists favor the

HIDDEN ► **Royal Blues Pub** for one-night stands. Music ranges from blues to reggae to bluegrass. ~ 330 Baker Street, Nelson; 250-354-4333. The most popular dance/music spot with the younger crowd is the **Civic Pub**, where house and hip-hop predominate. ~ 705 Vernon Street, Nelson; 250-352-5121.

Nelson's Heritage Inn offers two distinctly different places to socialize—**Mike's Place Pub** is a classic tavern with a fine selection of ales, beer and mixed drinks. **The Library Lounge** is a quiet wood-paneled enclave where locals gather by the fire for relaxed conversation. ~ 422 Vernon Street, Nelson; 250-352-5331.

BEACHES & PARKS **MOUNT REVELSTOKE NATIONAL PARK** 🚶 🚲 In a region where thousands of miles of wilderness are unmarred by roads or even marked trails, Revelstoke is an exception: it's a 65,000-acre park defined largely by its accessibility. In recent years, the volume of traffic has forced park authorities to close some areas to cars—now you park in a lot about a mile from the top of Mount Revelstoke and take a free shuttle bus to the summit. Still, it's one of the few places where you can get so close to the top of a major mountain without much exertion. Crowds aside, there are a few pleasant trails (including some strenuous climbs) as well as views of the Columbia Valley from the summit of Mount Revelstoke that make it well worth the trip. ~ Route 1, just east of the town of Revelstoke; 250-837-7500.

▲ Backcountry camping requires a permit; C$10 per night.

GLACIER NATIONAL PARK 🚶 🚲 🛶 ⚓ Glacier Park (not to be confused with a park of the same name in a country to the south) truly is dominated by snow, ice and—you guessed it—glaciers. Snow is possible any day of the year and nearly certain between September and June. As much as 15 percent of the park's 337,500 acres are covered by permanent icefields and more than 400 glaciers. The high Monashee Mountains offer excellent hiking through old-growth forests, alpine meadows, and back into hanging valleys with glaciers perched above and rushing rivers and waterfalls along the way. Though the summer here is exceedingly brief, it's a great time to see a profusion of wildflowers. Bears (both black and grizzly), mountain goats, moose and marmots are all frequently sighted in the park. ~ Route 1, 25 miles east of Revelstoke; the park information center is on Route 1 at Rogers Pass summit; 250-837-7500.

If the town of Nelson looks familiar to movie buffs, this is where Steve Martin filmed *Roxanne* in the early 1980s.

▲ Glacier's two campgrounds, both right off Route 1 in the subalpine zone, total 80 vehicle/tent sites. All sites are C$13 per night. Backcountry hikers must obtain permits at C$6 per night, up to a maximum of C$30.

MARTHA CREEK PROVINCIAL PARK

This small yet fully developed park, set on a slight bench above Lake Revelstoke, is designed for use by families. With volleyball and horseshoe courts, an adventure playground for kids, ample boating facilities and good fishing, the park serves as a laidback lakeside recreation area. ~ Route 23, 11 miles (18 km) north of Revelstoke; 250-837-5734.

▲ There's little privacy at the 25 sites; C$14 per night.

BLANKET CREEK PROVINCIAL PARK

Set on a quiet, somewhat remote peninsula in Upper Arrow Lake, this small park offers excellent access to water activities such as swimming, fishing, canoeing and wildlife watching. There's a warm-water swimming lagoon, and a short hike takes visitors to picturesque **Sutherland Falls**. The heights of the Selkirk Mountains are directly across the lake. The park is on the grounds of a heritage homestead, and remnants of the pioneer orchards still grace the grounds. ~ Route 23, 12 miles (19 km) south of Revelstoke; 250-837-5734.

▲ The 64 vehicle/tent sites set above the lakeshore give campers decent privacy; C$14 per night.

VALHALLA WILDERNESS PROVINCIAL PARK

Thrusting high into alpine country from the shores of Slocan Lake, Valhalla Park is a rugged, scenic and difficult backcountry paradise set amid sharp peaks. Here you'll find a dozen glacial alpine lakes, an equal number of high peaks, and abundant wildlife. There are just three established trails and no developed campsites. Old-growth stands of cedar and spruce line the valleys; huge expanses of above-timberline ridge await mountaineers.

Access into the 115,000-acre park is by boat or foot only. ~ The main hike-in access is from Little Slocan River Road, 12 miles (19 km) west of Slocan; 800-689-9025.

▲ There are five wilderness campgrounds and one backcountry shelter, but no developed sites; C$5 per night.

KOKANEE CREEK PROVINCIAL PARK
This quiet park is on the shores of Kootenay Lake; the creek originates in Kokanee Glacier Park high above. The 600-acre park has pleasant beaches and good access for canoeing and fishing; a playground and nature trails keep families occupied. ~ Route 3A, 7 miles (13 km) north of Nelson; 800-689-9025.

▲ There are 132 vehicle/tent sites above the lakeshore; C$22 per night.

KOKANEE GLACIER PROVINCIAL PARK
This 80,000-acre wilderness park in the mountains above Nelson offers a full range of backcountry experiences—wildlife watching, hiking, fishing and camping—with the added bonus of three backcountry cabins available on a first-come, first-served basis. The park contains 30 alpine lakes, its namesake glacier and ghost towns left from a mining boom a century ago. The established trail network is extensive, and a summer resident ranger staff helps keep order. Some trails may be closed in late summer due to bear activity. As with other high-mountain parks in the region, Kokanee is subject to snow during any time of the year. Call ahead to check on possible road or trail closures. ~ Located 9 miles (15 km) north of Kokanee Creek, on gravel road unsuitable for low-clearance vehicles.

▲ Cabins are C$15 to C$30 per night; plentiful wilderness camping is otherwise C$5 per night.

PURCELL WILDERNESS CONSERVANCY
Lying between Kootenay Lake and the Columbia Valley is the Purcell Mountain range, a half-million acres of which are set aside as the Purcell Wilderness Conservancy. There are no roads that enter this area and only a couple of established trails lie within. Experienced backpackers can take a 35-mile trek that crosses the park, climbing a 7400-foot pass in the process and traveling be-

WHAT A LOT OF ... FISH

The thriving fishery on Kootenay Lake represents the result of a determined effort to restore the lake's once-moribund health after years and years of environmental neglect; the key was the application of more than 5000 tons of fertilizer. (Yes, seriously—it boosted the phytoplankton in the lake.)

tween countless spruce trees, streams, rocky ravines and mead-
ows. ~ Trail access is four miles (6 km) east of Route 31 from
Argenta on Kootenay Lake, or about 25 miles (40 km) west of
Route 93/95 from Invermere.

▲ Wilderness camping only; no developed sites; C$5 per
night.

The Eastern Kootenays region is centered on the   ▼▼▼▼▼▼▼▼▼▼▼▼▼
Rocky Mountain Trench, an 850-mile (1400-km)   **Eastern Kootenays**
cleft in the earth's crust that is the longest such
valley in North America, running from Montana to the northernmost reaches of B.C. This is where the continent is slowly
stretching, with the Rockies forming one wall of the cleft and
various interior ranges forming the other. It spans from 2 to 25
miles (3 to 40 km) in width and is clearly distinguishable from
outer space.

The uniformity of this earth wrinkle leads to topographic
oddities: all three of the major rivers that flow through the cleft
(the Kootenay, Columbia and Fraser) have places where their
waters (or tributaries) come within mere miles of each other, and
then head off westward to cut narrow canyons through the
mountains. The trench is thus an obvious north–south travel
route; even so, it is blocked at one point by Kinbasket Lake, one
of the lakes along the Columbia formed by the erection of a hydroelectric dam in the '60s. This long narrow basin typifies the
region, a land where human development clusters in the few lowlands and a few roads are the only entries civilization makes into
the high country.

The east side of the cleft is bordered by numerous Rocky
Mountain peaks that surpass 10,000 feet (3400 meters) and on
the west by equally numerous 9000-foot (3100-meter) summits
in the Purcells, the Monashees and the Cariboos. Glaciers tumble
from high ridges and bowls; freshets pour over the sides of cliffs
into hanging valleys. The streams below are the distinctive milky
blue-green that signifies glacial origin. It's no wonder the Canadian Rockies are known worldwide for their scenic grandeur.

As Route 1 descends from Rogers Pass, it enters the Columbia   **SIGHTS**
Valley and follows the course of the river until, at Golden, it climbs
again into Yoho National Park.

Golden, the townsite built where the Kicking Horse River
emerges into the Columbia Valley, is the western gateway to the
vast parkland in the Rockies; thus it is an active visitor center,
drawing as many as two million guests a year. It's also a major
Canadian Pacific administrative center and supports a small but
thriving wood-products industry. Here, hang gliders launch from

Mount Seven above Golden for airborne jaunts that sometimes carry them as far as Montana.

The old railroad planners laid out the town on a grid to keep things simple; unfortunately, they used numbers in both directions: avenues run north–south, streets run east–west. "North" in an address means above the river, "south" means below. This being said, the town is small enough that you're likely to run into your destination sooner than you might expect. For information on lodging and outfitter services, call the **Golden Info Centre**. ~ 250-344-7125, 800-622-4653; www.rockies.net/columbia-valley.

HIDDEN ▶   Just outside Golden, **Rafter J Frontier Village** is a privately operated replication of an early mining and ranching camp. Longhorn cattle complete the heritage atmosphere. A cabin that sleeps eight is available for guests who wish to spend the night. Admission. ~ Blaeberry Valley Road, Golden; 250-344-6432.

Head east up Route 1 and before long you'll reach **Yoho** and **Kootenay national parks**, adjacent preserves on the B.C. side of the Rocky Mountains that, together with Banff and Jasper National Parks in Alberta and several smaller provincial parks, form a 300-mile unbroken chain of parkland along the Canadian Rockies. This is the largest such mountain preserve in the world, and thus has been designated a UNESCO World Heritage Site. It is a vast and compelling wilderness, penetrated only by three major highways and a few secondary access roads. Grizzlies, moose and caribou roam through spectacular alpine scenery. Wilderness trekking opportunities are unlimited.

Yoho embraces the high, wild Yoho Valley, a fastness in which grizzly bears outnumber humans. Kootenay holds the headwaters of the Kootenay River and is distinguished by its variety, climbing from lowland arid terrain with cactus and sage to timberline peaks and glaciers.

Both parks hold countless lakes, tumbling rivers and streams, breathtaking vistas and trackless wildernesses. Passes must be bought by all visitors, and additional permits are needed for camping and wilderness hiking. ~ Yoho National Park information, 250-343-6783; Kootenay National Park information, 250-347-9615, 250-347-9505.

Above Field, the small town between the Yoho park boundary and Kicking Horse Pass, lies a fossil deposit on the upper slopes of **Mount Field** that contains Cambrian specimens more than 500 million years old. The beds are not open to the general public, although guided tours are occasionally mounted. (Inquire at Yoho Park offices.) Extensive examination and evaluation of the fossil beds by paleontologists is underway.

About ten miles (16 km) east of Field, the turnoff to Yoho Valley Road leads into the heart of the park and two of its campgrounds as well as to the park's most famous sight, **Takakkaw**

Falls. At almost 1200 feet (384 meters), these are the second-highest falls in B.C., and typify the hanging valley falls so common in the Kootenays. *Please note: The last stretch of road leading to the falls viewpoint contains very narrow hairpin curves that cannot be negotiated by recreational vehicles or vehicles pulling trailers.*

Kicking Horse Pass in Yoho is the location of the Big Hill, the original Canadian Pacific railbed that, at a 4.5 percent grade, was the steepest rail climb (and descent) in North America. Though the trains used four extra engines, accidents were common on the line once it was built; the remains of one wrecked train can be seen near one of Yoho National Park's campgrounds. To solve the problem, engineers hit on a remarkable and ingenious solution: hairpin turns, which work fine on highways, don't work for trains, so instead Canadian Pacific crews bored two full-loop tunnels that climb within the mountain itself. The tunnels, built in 1911, added 6 miles (10 km) to the railbed's length, but decreased the grade to 2.2 percent. Halfway up the pass (10 miles/16 km east of Field, just after the Yoho Valley Road turnoff), travelers can witness this feat at the **Tunnels Rest Stop** along Route 1. A catwalk leads out over the mountainside to a viewing platform from which you can see both portals of the lower tunnel; if you time it right, it's possible to watch the lead engines emerge from the tunnel while the caboose is entering below (or above).

Down in the valley again, head south from Golden on Route 95 for a different sort of terrain. With more than 600,000 acres, the **Columbia Wetlands** form the largest intact marsh area in British Columbia, and thus are significant habitat for literally millions of migratory birds each spring and fall. In the summer, the wetlands provide nesting grounds to numerous eagles, ospreys and herons, some of whose nests can be seen piled atop power poles throughout the valley (and in the many riparian cottonwoods that line the river's channels and backwaters). Mostly overlooked as a visitor attraction until recently, the wetlands are a wonderful place for a peaceful, meditative cruise in a canoe,

◄ *HIDDEN*

AUTHOR FAVORITE

sights   A peaceful float down the **Columbia Wetlands** in late spring, with thousands of migrating birds on every side and glistening peaks above, is my idea of a serenity-inducing way to spend a day. This is one of the most important migratory-bird stopping points in Western Canada. See above for more information.

watching the plentiful wildlife. (See Tours, below.) The wetlands encompass much of the valley floor between Golden and Invermere, a 70-mile (114-km) stretch that's never very wide; in May and June, during spring runoff, the valley often fills almost completely with water.

At the lower end of the valley—also the southern boundary of Kootenay National Park—**Radium Hot Springs** are operated by Parks Canada. The 104°F (40°C) water is the most radioactive in North America—not enough to be harmful, but enough that some people believe it to be beneficial. (And enough that some dye-colorings in swimsuits will be transmogrified.) A concrete pool is set right against the walls of Sinclair Canyon; the water bubbles up from the source in a vent in the middle of the hot pool. There's also a cool pool, for swimming, and ample changing rooms, showers and other visitor facilities—including a massage clinic, in case the water doesn't soothe all your ills. (It's important to note, if booking accommodation, that the town Radium Hot Springs, which has many motels and hotels, is actually a couple of miles away from the springs themselves. Two lodgings right at the springs are listed under Lodging, below.) Although some find the water not hot enough, hot springs aficionados rate Radium Hot Springs as the most laidback among the Eastern Kootenays' commercial springs. Admission. ~ Route 93, about 1 mile (2 km) east of the Route 95 junction; 250-347-9485, 800-767-1611. Radium Hot Springs Visitor Info Centre, 250-347-9331, 800-347-9704; www.radiumhotsprings.com.

Continuing south on Route 95 will take you past Windermere Lake and then into **Fairmont Hot Springs Resort**, an internationally known resort built around its namesake springs that includes amenities such as golf and tennis, and much concomitant residential condominium development. Perched on a bench above the river on the east side of the Columbia Valley, the complex has an enviable site and is fairly attractive as such resorts go. ~ 250-345-6311, 800-663-4979; www.fairmontresort.com.

SHE'LL BE COMING 'ROUND THE MOUNTAIN

Discovery and survey of Kicking Horse Pass itself are famous moments in North American development. As Canadian Pacific chronicler Pierre Berton described in *The Great Railway*, one engineer had a heart-stopping introduction to the pass: "Shaw had one terrible moment when his horse ran into a nest of hornets and another when he met two men with a packhorse coming from the opposite direction. Since it was impossible to turn around, they simply pushed one of the wretched animals over the cliff."

Although it has small tributary streams feeding it from the Purcell Wilderness to the west, glacially green **Columbia Lake** (just below Fairmont Hot Springs) is considered by geographers to be the headwaters of the Columbia River; from here, the Northwest's mightiest stream winds north, then south, then west, to its mouth on the Pacific 1410 miles (2000 km) away.

Canal Flats is the odd patch of land between the upper end of Columbia Lake and the Kootenay River as that waterway roars by on its journey out of the Rockies southward. The Kootenay passes less than two miles from Columbia Lake here before heading south into the United States then turning back north to meet the Columbia 150 miles (243 km) later. This strange near-confluence inspired a bright idea in an early visionary who dug a canal across the land, planning to create a steamboat circuit from Nelson to Golden; however, the passage proved arduous and only two boats ever crossed Canal Flats. A scheme to reopen the canal, funneling Kootenay River water into the Columbia for hydroelectric power, was scuttled by intense environmental opposition in the '70s.

South of Columbia Lake, you cross from the fir and lodgepole into the ponderosa pine zone that typifies so much of the intermountain West.

Top of the World Provincial Park, at the end of a 30-mile ◀ *HIDDEN* gravel road much used by logging trucks, is an 18,000-acre walk-in alpine wilderness with good camping, fishing and hiking possibilities. Several semideveloped wilderness campsites, and one cabin with room for as many as 24 people, make it not quite as wild as other backcountry areas. But the scenery—glittering lakes ringed by spruce trees in high-mountain bowls—should be sufficiently sublime for just about any wilderness devotee. ~ Located 30 miles (54 km) east of Route 95 on the Lussier River Road, which begins in Skookumchuck; wlapwww.gov.bc.ca/bcparks.

Farther down 95A (95A splits from the main Route 95 branch just south of Skookumchuck and rejoins at Cranbrook, after about 20 miles), you come to **Kimberley**. Like so many other once-prosperous mining towns, Kimberley has latched onto a theme to attract visitors and their dollars. At 3710 feet (1113 meters) this is Canada's second-highest town; the surrounding Purcell Mountains could be mistaken for the German Alps; so, behold, a neo-Bavarian village. Shopkeepers have added gingerbread fronts and brightly colored shutters; an accordion player wanders the town square, which features the world's biggest cuckoo clock.

The Sullivan Mine, whose ore has been the foundation of the town's economy for almost a century, is scheduled to close early in the new millennium. Residents hope Kimberley's new identity will supplant the old, while maintaining the town's low-key way of life. The town's redevelopment has brought a pedestrian plaza (the **Platzl**)—two blocks lined with shops, cafés and other small businesses. ~ Kimberley visitor information, 250-427-3666; lodging information, 800-667-0871; www.kimberleyvacations.ca.

The chert mined from the Top of the World Provincial Park area was used to make tools and weapons.

The overall effect is admirably restrained and there isn't a hint of the chain-brand uniformity that has cropped up in other theme towns. There are no pizza or hamburger name-brands in Kimberley. There is a beautiful public garden, **Cominco Gardens**, whose history reflects that of the city. Created by the Cominco mining company in 1927 not only to benefit the community but to promote its fertilizer brands, the 12-acre garden was passed on to the city in 1986. Its theme sections include a rose garden, a Victorian gazebo, and a prairie garden. ~ 306 3rd Avenue, Kimberley; 250-427-2293.

The **Bavarian Mining Railway** puts to use a train that once hauled ore underground and now takes you on a 6-mile (10-km) scenic route that starts downtown. Fee. ~ Howard Street, two blocks northwest of the Platzl, Kimberley; 250-427-3666.

Kimberley Alpine Resort, just west of town, has been undergoing large-scale expansion to bring it in line with B.C.'s other ski resorts. It's a major mountain with a friendly feel. ~ 250-427-4881; www.skikimberley.com.

Over on the main branch of Route 95 is another interesting frontier town. Founded as a Kootenay River ferry crossing, **Fort Steele**'s ultimate hopes depended on the presumed arrival of the railroad. But the railroad never came this way, and the once-thriving trade center declined until the era of highway travel. Now, redeveloped by the provincial government as a rather large heritage town, Fort Steele comes alive each summer with actors portraying 1890s shopkeepers, café operators, printers, wagon-masters, even politicians available for heckling by visitors. More than 60 buildings and homes have been restored to their century-old luster, and bakeries, cafés and tearooms offer victuals. A lengthy boardwalk provides visitors today the same relief from mud and dust that it did back before concrete sidewalks became standard. The grounds include a reconstructed military post in which schoolkids often "bunk over" on overnight field trips, and archaeological digs take place even today. Operations are limited in winter. Admission to Heritage Town grounds. ~ Route 95, about 20 miles south of Skookumchuck; 250-489-3351.

Cranbrook is the regional center for B.C.'s southern Rocky Mountains; unlike so many other area towns, its development hinged on the railroad, not mining, when Canadian Pacific designated it a division center in 1898. ~ Cranbrook information, 250-489-5261, 800-222-6174.

Cranbrook's top attraction today reflects that past: the **Canadian Museum of Rail Travel** holds a nearly complete luxury train from the late 1920s, when rail travel was not only the fastest but the most elegant way across the continent. The nine cars on display include a dining car, a solarium car, three deluxe sleeping cars, and a superintendent's car, all featuring deluxe woodwork, brass and plush upholstery. The museum also holds a caboose and restored CPR station. Closed mornings in winter. Admission. ~ 1 Van Horne Street North, Cranbrook; 250-489-3918.

Creston, about an hour south and west of Cranbrook, lies near where the Kootenay River returns from Montana and Idaho to rejoin the Columbia farther north; it's at the edge of a broad valley whose warm climate and ample water make it important for both migratory birds and orchardists. ~ Creston information, 250-428-4342; www.crestonbc.com/chamber.

The 17,000-acre **Creston Valley Wildlife Management Area** ◄ *HIDDEN* displays the valley's lush wetlands habitat, which is home at some point during the year to 265 different species of birds. The area's interpretive center has a viewing tower, galleries explaining the wetlands ecology, a library and a gift shop; visitors are offered the opportunity to take a one-hour canoe journey into the marsh. Admission. ~ Route 3, 6 miles (10 km) west of Creston; 250-402-6900.

In town, the most notable feature at the **Creston Valley Museum** is a replica of the unique Kootenay canoe, the original Native transport, which points down at bow and stern. The museum itself was painstakingly constructed of local stone over a period of 15 years. Admission. ~ 219 Devon Street, Creston; 250-428-9262.

The **Columbia Brewery**'s heritage dates back to 1898; the modern company opened its doors in 1959, long before microbreweries became fashionable. Its brands, including Kokanee, Kootenay Ale and Kootenay Black Lager, are popular throughout the Northwest. Tours and tastings are available in summer at the brewery. ~ 1220 Erickson Street, Creston; 250-428-9344.

If you head the other direction from Cranbrook and Fort Steele, east on Route 3/93 instead of west to Creston, you'll end up in the **Elk Valley**. **Fernie** is the center of this picturesque vale in the south end of the Canadian Rockies. Sweeping scenery, excellent fishing and hunting, and wilderness hiking and camping opportunities abound here, and they're lower in profile than those farther north in the big parks. First developed in the early 20th century as a coal-mining center, the valley continues to provide coal to the steel mills of Asia. Lest you think of it as a coalblack-fouled strip, it is also rich in wildlife, holding major concentrations of bighorn sheep, mountain goats, grizzly bears and elk.

Sparwood, 20 miles (29 km) up Route 3 from Fernie, is the heart of coal country, and thus offers a unique claim to fame: the world's largest dump truck, the 250-ton Titan, is parked next to the Info Centre in the middle of town. Like several other small Northwest towns, Sparwood has turned over the walls of many downtown buildings to muralists. A walking tour of the dozen murals depicting the Elk Valley's past takes about 20 minutes, starting from the Chamber of Commerce Info Centre. ~ 250-425-2423.

The far north end of the valley—reached by secondary roads that may or may not be passable in passenger cars, depending on the weather and road maintenance—holds two of B.C.'s grandest wilderness parks, **Elk Lakes Provincial Park** and **Height of the Rockies Provincial Park**. Both are undeveloped and offer no facilities whatsoever—just untrammeled wilderness. For further information, visit wlapwww.gov.bc.ca/bcparks.

LODGING

HIDDEN ►

Nestled at the foot of the mountains west of Golden, **Alpine Meadows Lodge** offers easy access to high-country hiking—and since it's just above the Columbia, equally easy access to peaceful canoeing, birdwatching and fishing in the Columbia wetlands backwaters. The lodge itself is a custom-built three-story structure with beautiful fir floors milled from wood cut on site. Ten guest rooms all have private baths; the third-story loft room is especially commodious and quiet. Packages include all meals, and the host, Irv Graham, has an extensive knowledge of the Canadian Rockies. ~ 717 Elk Road, Golden; 250-344-5863, 888-700-4477, fax 250-344-5853; www.alpinemeadowslodge.com, e-mail info@alpinemeadowslodge.com. MODERATE.

A Quiet Corner Bed & Breakfast is indeed on a back corner in Golden, far from the main road but convenient to in-town shopping and dining. With just two shared-bath rooms and a private-bath suite decorated in subdued Victorian furnishings, the inn gives guests personalized attention. Home-cooked breakfasts are sumptuous. ~ 607 South 14th Street, Golden; 250-344-7869, 877-344-7869, fax 250-344-7868; www.aquietcorner.com, e-mail beryl@aquietcorner.com. BUDGET TO MODERATE.

HIDDEN ►

Local rancher, merchant and legislator H. G. Parson built a fine in-town house for himself in Golden in 1893. (Yes, he's the one for whom the community of Parson, 15 miles south, is named.) The very same **H. G. Parson House** is now a genuinely historic B&B in a quiet neighborhood. Decorated in period furnishings, the three rooms with private baths offer elegance today equal to that Parson enjoyed a century ago. The large veranda affords fine views of the surrounding mountains. ~ 815 12th Street South, Golden; 250-344-5001, 866-333-5001, fax 250-344-2821; www.hgparsonhousebb.com. BUDGET TO MODERATE.

Purcell Lodge is not only off the beaten track, it's off the track entirely. There are only two ways for visitors to reach this exclusive hiking and skiing lodge high above Golden—on foot, an arduous uphill trek, or by regularly scheduled helicopter. Nestled on a timberline bench at 6000 feet (2195 meters) this ten-room lodge offers peak comfort, with every modern convenience supplied by a small hydroelectric plant on a nearby stream. Accommodation packages include all meals; guests simply spend their time hiking, skiing and relaxing. Call for reservations and transportation information. ~ Box 1829, Golden, BC V0A 1H0; 250-344-2639, fax 250-344-5520; www.purcell.com. DELUXE.

Creston Valley's annual May Blossom Festival celebrates its bountiful fruit industry.

Nestled back in a mountain valley northwest of Golden, **Blaeberry Mountain Lodge** is remote but easily reached. The six units range from self-contained cabins to lodge rooms to a traditional tepee. Baths are shared or private; packages include meals. There's a common kitchen, and numerous adventure activities depart right from the lodge in any season. Closed November. ~ Moberly School Road, Golden; phone/fax 250-344-5296; www. blaeberrymountainlodge.bc.ca, e-mail info@blaeberrymountain lodge.bc.ca. BUDGET TO MODERATE.

◄ *HIDDEN*

Set back off the highway on Horse Creek Road south of Golden, **Kapristo Lodge** is in a quiet location but easily reached. Its 90-acre site at the foot of Kapristo Mountain affords a splendid view of the Purcell Range across the valley; the lodge itself is a light-filled wood structure with a big sunroom and adjoining dining room. Most of the six rooms have private baths; one is a deluxe suite with a kitchen, fireplace and hot tub. Breakfast is included, and guests can arrange other meals featuring the lodge's fine Austrian cuisine. ~ Horse Creek Road, 7 miles (12 km) south of Golden; 250-344-6048, fax 250-344-6755; www.kapristo lodge.com, e-mail kapristolodge@redshift.bc.ca. DELUXE.

◄ *HIDDEN*

Kicking Horse Lodge is right in Field, and Field is about as quiet and scenic a highway town as you'll find. The lodge is convenient to Yoho, Golden and Lake Louise. The modern wood-accented two-story lodge building contains 14 units, including kitchenettes and one large family unit that can accommodate up to six guests. A restaurant and lounge round out the amenities. ~ 100 Centre Street, Field; 250-343-6303, 800-659-4944, fax 250-343-6355; www.kickinghorselodge.net, e-mail khlodge@telus.net. BUDGET TO MODERATE.

Luxury is unstinting at **Emerald Lake Lodge**, located along a gorgeous lake in the lower end of Yoho Valley. Rooms are in handsome chalets, with balconies and fireplaces; the lodge offers every amenity, including a sauna and outdoor hot tubs. Hiking, horseback riding, fishing, canoeing and skiing are among the activities available. High-season prices are steep, but fees plunge almost by half in the off-season. ~ Emerald Lake Road, five miles north of Field; 250-343-6321, 800-663-6336, fax 403-609-6158; www.crmr.com. DELUXE TO ULTRA-DELUXE.

Guests at the 27-bed **Hostelling International–Whiskey Jack Wilderness Hostel,** in the heart of Yoho National Park, have their choice of how to enjoy the park's natural surroundings. You can step out the door and set off on adventures that range from hours to weeks, or you can simply sit back on the porch and try to measure Takakkaw Falls by eyeballing the water's plunge. ~ Yoho Valley Road, Yoho National Park; 403-762-4122, fax 403-762-3441; www.hihostels.ca. BUDGET.

HIDDEN ►   The road ends in the driveway at **Wells Landing B&B,** which overlooks the Columbia River outside Parson. This cozy log home offers guests three comfortable downstairs rooms with shared baths and acres of pastoral valley beauty just out the door. A major heron rookery is across the river. Be sure to check out host Ron van Vogt's rare, classic stereo system and LP collection. Open May through September; can be open other times by special request. ~ 4040 Sanborn Road (3 miles/5 km off Route 95), Parson; 250-348-2273, fax 250-348-2278. MODERATE.

Set high on a hill overlooking the springs, the **Radium Hot Springs Lodge** embraces all the virtues of this mountain canyon—scenery, fresh air, and the hot-springs water. The 66-room lodge has been refurbished; the rooms are furnished with modern amenities including satellite TV and balconies from which to enjoy the view. An elevator takes guests down to the springs, which are operated by Parks Canada. The extensive grounds are home to a herd of bighorn sheep. ~ Route 93, just off of Route 95; 250-347-9341, 888-222-9341, fax 250-347-9342; www.radiumhot springslodge.com, e-mail rockieshotspot@telus.net. DELUXE.

Although thousands of square feet of hot pools make **Fairmont Hot Springs Resort** Canada's largest, much more than hot water draws crowds of guests (half a million a year, in fact) to this complex in the Columbia River Valley south of Invermere. Golf—two 18-hole courses—and tennis in the summer, skiing in the winter and other outdoor activities ready guests for a good long soak. The resort has seven restaurants, fitness facilities, a health spa, and 360 guest rooms ranging from functional to deluxe. ~ Fairmont Hot Springs; 250-345-6311, 800-663-4979, fax 250-345-6616; www.fairmontresort.com. MODERATE TO DELUXE.

Mountain Edge and **Silver Birch** are a pair of sister condominium resorts at the Kimberley ski area just west of town. Silver Birch offers two- and three-bedroom townhouses with private driveways, full kitchens, dining and living rooms and wood-burning fireplaces. Mountain Edge has one-bedroom vacation condos with private entrances. For summer visitors, Trickle Creek Golf Club is nearby. ~ Located at Kimberley Alpine Resort, just west of Kimberley; 250-427-5381, 800-525-6622, fax 250-427-7167; www.kimberleycondos.com, e-mail info@kimberleycondos.com. MODERATE TO DELUXE.

Wood accents abound in the four guest rooms at **House Alpenglow**, a Bavarian-style B&B on the road between downtown Kimberley and the nearby ski area. Two rooms have private bath; another is spacious enough for a family of six. A hearty Bavarian breakfast prepares guests for a day on the slopes or strolling through town. ~ 3 Alpenglow Court, Kimberley; 250-427-0273, 877-257-3645, fax 250-427-0276; www.kimberley bc.net/alpenglow. MODERATE.

Boundary Street House is a peaceful cottage-style home just a block from downtown Kimberley. Its three guest rooms include two on the lower level with private bath; one features an old-fashioned clawfoot bathtub. ~ 89 Boundary Street, Kimberley; 250-427-3510, 888-427-7660, fax 250-427-3528; www.bound arystreet.com, e-mail info@boundarystreet.com. MODERATE.

As guest ranches go, the 210-acre **Wild Rose Ranch & Resort**   ◄ HIDDEN
is small—just four units for guests. That helps preserve the quality experience that's the focus of this ranch, which concentrates on riding and fishing from April through October. Housing is in a modern cedar log lodge or cabin (all rooms have private bath); meals are family style in the lodge dining room. Trail rides leave daily for lengthy excursions into the Crown land surrounding the ranch; flyfishing expeditions head for local lakes and streams, including a top-notch trout lake accessible by horseback from the ranch. Closed January. ~ Wolf Creek Road, Wasa Lake (east of Kimberley); 250-422-3403, 800-324-6188, fax 250-422-3149; www.wildrose-ranch.com, e-mail wildrose@cyberlink.bc.ca. DELUXE.

Wasa Lakeside B&B styles itself as a resort as much as a B&B—accommodations include suites with private entrances, and every

◆◆◆

BUNKING IN THE WOODS

Beaverfoot Lodge, at the foot of Kootenay National Park, is a cross between a guest ranch and a traditional mountain lodge. You can stay in the lodge itself (31 rooms with shared bath), a classic log structure at the edge of a spruce grove, or in Beaverfoot's wagon train "bunks." Trail rides head up into alpine wilderness and numerous other outdoor adventures are available, ranging from hayrides to peak scrambling. ~ Beaver Foot Forest Service Road, Golden; 250-344-7144, fax 250-344-7190; www.rockies.net/~beaverft, e-mail beaverft@rockies.net. BUDGET TO MODERATE.

unit has a view of the lake and the Rocky Mountains beyond. There's a sandy beach, with swimming, waterskiing, canoeing, sailing and biking available for guests. Despite all this, rates are surprisingly reasonable. ~ Box 122, Wasa Lake, BC V0B 2K0; 250-422-3636, 888-422-3636, fax 250-422-3551; www.wasa lakeresort.com, e-mail info@wasalakeresort.com. MODERATE TO DELUXE.

Six acres of private valley grounds surround **Mañana Farm B&B** outside Creston along Duck Creek. The B&B is close to the Creston Valley Wildlife Centre, and thus convenient for birders and hikers. Two rooms in the house share a bath; full country breakfasts are included. No credit cards. ~ 5429 Route 3A, Creston; 250-866-5453. BUDGET.

DINING

Located in a heritage house B&B right along Golden's main street, **Sisters & Beans** is operated by three siblings who offer the closest thing Golden has to gourmet dining, with an Austrian flavor. Lunch and dinner specials are the best bets, ranging from chicken to veal. ~ 1122 10th Avenue South, Golden; 250-344-2443. MODERATE.

With fresh-roasted coffee, **Jenny's Java Express** provides the quality that coffee lovers seek on the road. Muffins, breakfasts, lunch sandwiches, salads and pizza are also on the menu, and it's an internet café as well. No dinner. ~ 420B 9th Avenue North, Golden; 250-344-5057. BUDGET.

Kicking Horse Grill is a popular Golden supper house, with pastas, steaks, burgers, and chicken and seafood dishes. Family-style dining is the norm; the cabin housing the restaurant adds mountain atmosphere. ~ 1105 9th Street, Golden; 250-344-2330. MODERATE.

The **Timber Inn** is hard to miss, right along Route 95 in Parson, about a half-hour south of Golden. Diners here enjoy a wonderful westward view across the Columbia Valley and German and Austrian specialties, including veal, as well as a good beer selection. Outdoor dining is offered in good weather. ~ 3483 Route 95, Parson; 250-348-2228. MODERATE.

AUTHOR FAVORITE

I like to start my day at **Kimberley City Bakery**, on the Platzl in Kimberley. Creations include fresh-baked Swiss breads, pastries and desserts, as well as fresh-ground coffees and coffee specialty drinks. There are also light lunch offerings such as soup and sandwiches. Breakfast and lunch only. ~ 287 Spokane Street, Kimberley; 250-427-2131. BUDGET.

In keeping with the area's overall European theme, two restaurants in the Radium Hot Springs area offer fine dining Continental style, with decor and atmosphere to match. Because both are located in resort areas, reservations are recommended. The **Old Salzburg Restaurant** serves Austrian dishes, with schnitzels, lamb and roast beef, house-made pastas and fine desserts. ~ Junction of Routes 93 and 95, Radium Hot Springs (in town); 250-347-6553. MODERATE.   ◀ *HIDDEN*

The **Black Forest** is a steak and schnitzel house specializing in German menu items. Lamb, chicken and house-made desserts round out the fare. ~ Route 95 and Athalmer Road, Invermere; 250-342-9417. MODERATE.

Fresh, locally roasted Kicking Horse coffee is the key to breakfast at **Bobbie's Cafe**, where Bobbie herself whips up a mean (but not lean) stack of pancakes. Breakfast is buffet style. Lunches are home-cooked soups, salads and sandwiches. Fish and chips are the fare Friday and Saturday, when Bobbie's is open 24 hours. ~ Invermere Industrial Park, Road #2, Invermere; 250-342-0638. BUDGET.

Using wood-fired ovens, **Quality Bakery** prepares traditional European breads and modern adaptations such as sourdough multigrain. All breads are made by hand, and the bakery's Swiss pastry chef serves up daily delights such as strudels and tortes. At lunch you can order up huge sandwiches on fresh-baked bread. Breakfast and lunch only. ~ 7th Avenue, Invermere; 250-342-9913. BUDGET.

As you'd expect, dining in Kimberley hews to a Bavarian theme. But the **Old Bauernhaus** goes beyond simple conformance to a theme—it's a post-and-beam building that was first erected in southern Bavaria around 1750. Dismantled piecemeal and shipped to Canada, it was reassembled in Kimberley in the '80s. The cuisine is Bavarian and Austrian, with hearty meat dishes and splendid desserts. ~ 280 Norton Avenue, Kimberley; 250-427-5133. MODERATE.

Located right on the Platzl, **Gasthaus** is Kimberley's fine dining establishment. It, too, follows an Austrian theme, with other Continental and Canadian selections on the menu as well, including Northwest seafood. The wine list is the most extensive in town. ~ 240 Spokane Street, Kimberley; 250-427-4851. MODERATE.

When Kimberley residents want to go out for a family meal, **Alpenrose** is usually the choice. Nothing fancy here, just good pastas, pizza, sandwiches, chicken and seafood at sensible prices. Lunch only. ~ 136 Wallinger Avenue, Kimberley; 250-427-7461. BUDGET TO MODERATE.

Canyon Creek Pottery features a full line of work by local artisans, ranging from simple bowls to lamps and dinnerware sets.   **SHOPPING**

Most of the pottery is made on site. ~ 917 10th Avenue North, Golden; 250-344-5678.

With 11,000 square feet of retail space, the **Back Door** is a take-no-prisoners gift shop. You might not actually find anything you have to have among the assortment of candles, books, pictures, toys, kitchenware, ornaments, pottery, jewelry and innumerable other knickknacks, gewgaws and oddments. But poking your head in is almost an anthropological necessity. ~ 196 Spokane Street (main entrance on the Platzl), Kimberley; 250-427-7007.

Most of the meat products on display at **Kimberley Sausage & Meats** are handmade right in the store, including surprisingly hot Hungarian sausages. There's a great selection of cheeses as well. ~ 360 Wallinger Avenue, Kimberley; 250-427-7766.

As an outfitting center for the southern Canadian Rockies, Fernie is both an information post and a place to pick up supplies and equipment. **S.V. Ski Base** offers winter and summer recreation equipment for skiing, boarding, mountain biking and all sorts of other activities. ~ 432 2nd Avenue, Fernie; 250-423-6464. The **Kootenay Fly Shop** not only offers the best patterns for local rivers and lakes, it's a guiding and outfitting service and a repository of local knowledge about conditions. ~ 821 7th Avenue, Fernie; 250-423-4483.

PARKS

YOHO NATIONAL PARK 🚶 🚴 🐎 🛶 ⛵ 🛷 Yoho essentially consists of one high valley and its surrounding mountains—but what a valley! Snowy peaks loom seemingly straight overhead, waterfalls plunge from hanging side valleys; fauna ranges from marmots to grizzly bears. Yoho's backcountry is famous for the sheer splendor of its wilderness experience; within a reasonable half-day's hike in are the spectacular Hoodoos and glacier-encrusted Emerald Basin. Even travelers who wish to stay in their autos will encounter plenty of memorable sights, including Takakkaw Falls. Because Yoho is so popular—and the Trans-Canada Highway passes right through its southern edge—it's a good idea to arrive early in the day if you want a decent campsite. Day-use fee, C$10 per vehicle. ~ The Yoho Park Info Centre is located in Field; 250-343-6783; parkscanada.pch.gc.ca/yoho.

▲ Overall, four road-access campgrounds offer 262 sites. *Chancellor Peak* (58 sites; C$15/night) and *Hoodoo Creek* (106 sites; C$16/night) campgrounds are both quite close to the park's western entrance, and close to Route 1. *Monarch* (36 sites; C$15/night) and *Kicking Horse* (86 sites; C$20/night) campgrounds are at the beginning of the Yoho Valley Road, also just off Route 1.

In addition, *Takakkaw Falls* campground is a walk-in facility (it's a very short walk, and there are even carts you can use for hauling camp gear); sites are C$13 per night.

Firewood at all five campgrounds is an additional C$4 per night.

Backcountry hikers in Yoho must obtain permits at C$6, up to a maximum of C$30.

KOOTENAY NATIONAL PARK 🚶 🚲 🐎 🏠 ⛵ 🚤 ⛵ Embracing the Kootenay and Vermillion River canyons and much of their headwaters, this vast park is a diverse expanse of Rocky Mountain topography. The highlands include thousands of acres of alpine terrain, with sharp granite peaks, tumbling glaciers, emerald lakes and ice-blue streams. Then the park plunges down to lowland canyons that are practically desert, with cactus, sage and other arid climate representatives. Long used as a travel corridor by Native peoples, Kootenay now draws 2 million visitors a year. Activities include wilderness hiking and camping, cross-country skiing, fishing, climbing and wildlife watching. The river itself is a popular float. Day-use fee, C$10 per vehicle. ~ Kootenay National Park headquarters are at the West Gate, just outside the town of Radium Hot Springs; 250-347-9615 or 250-347-9505; parkscanada.pch.gc.ca/kootenay.

> The Takakkaw Falls in Yoho National Park are the second-highest falls in B.C.

▲ Three major developed road-access campgrounds lie within Kootenay National Park, all within close proximity of the region's major highways. *Redstreak Campground* is a massive facility, in the park but reached by a short road from Route 95 on the south edge of Radium Hot Springs. Its 242 sites include some with water, sewer and electric hookups for RVs; nightly fees range from C$17 to C$22 per night. *McLeod Meadows Campground* is along Route 93, the road through the park, in the Kootenay River Valley; 98 sites, C$15 per night. *Marble Canyon* campground is higher up in the park, in the Vermillion River drainage, along Route 93; 61 sites, C$15 per night.

Backcountry hikers in Kootenay must obtain permits at C$6, up to a maximum of C$30.

DRY GULCH PROVINCIAL PARK ▲ Basically just a campground located near, but well off, Route 95, this park offers 26 vehicle/tent sites in a shady gully in the Rocky Mountain foothills just outside Radium Hot Springs. The sites are well separated and mostly shaded by the park's pines. Sites are C$17 per night. ~ 250-422-3003.

CANAL FLATS PROVINCIAL PARK ⛵ 🎣 ⛵ 🚤 🚣 ◄ *HIDDEN* This small spit of land protrudes into the upper end of Columbia Lake, very near the official source of the Columbia River. It has pleasant, grassy picnic grounds, ample boating opportunities and great views of the Purcell Mountains across the lake. It's the top windsurfing site on the lake; breezes are fairly constant. This park is hard to find—keep your eyes peeled for the signs. ~ Located three miles (5 km) east of Route 95 at Canal Flats.

WHITESWAN LAKE PROVINCIAL PARK 🧍 🚲 🐴 ⛵ 🎣 🛶 🚤 🛥️

Boat-use restrictions help keep the atmosphere relatively peaceful at this well-used park east of Canal Flats. Three decades of quality management have yielded an exceptional fishery in Whiteswan and neighboring Alces Lake; and the Lussier Hot Springs near the entrance of the park round out the attractions. Heavy log and mine-truck traffic on the road demands great driver caution. ~ Whiteswan Park Road, 10 miles (16 km) east of Route 95; 250-422-3003.

▲ Four separate campgrounds hold a total of 88 vehicle/tent sites, all near one of the lakes; C$12 per night.

WASA LAKE PROVINCIAL PARK 🧍 🚲 🐴 ⛵ 🎣 🛶 🚤 🛥️

Wasa Lake vies with Osoyoos for the title of warmest in Canada, so naturally water play is the focus at this bustling summer park. Recreation runs the gamut from biking to windsurfing; there's an adventure playground for kids, and interpretive programs during the height of the summer season. ~ Route 95, 23 miles (40 km) south of Canal Flats; 250-422-3003.

▲ There are 104 vehicle/tent sites around the lake; C$17 per night.

TOP OF THE WORLD PROVINCIAL PARK 🧍 🚲 🛶 ⛵

This alpine wilderness park occupies a small enclave of peaks above the upper end of the Kootenay River Valley. The area shows evidence of long use by First Nations people, who mined chert on the high ridges. Fish Lake, in the center of the park, is a two-hour hike from the end of the road. ~ Located 30 miles (54 km) east of Route 95 on the Lussier River Road, which begins in Skookumchuck.

▲ There are 24 wilderness campsites; C$5 per night. There's also one cabin that accommodates 24 people; first-come, first-served, C$15-$30.

SECRETS & LIES

Local legend says many disasters (the 1901 mine explosion that killed 128 people; the 1908 fire that leveled town; the 1916 flood that roared down the valley) visited Elk Valley after an early settler tricked a Native maiden into revealing the coal seam's location by promising to marry her—and reneging once she revealed the secret. Her subsequent curse was formally lifted in a First Nations ceremony in 1964.

HEIGHT OF THE ROCKIES PROVINCIAL PARK 🏃 🚵 ⛵ 🛶
This undeveloped wilderness park is one of B.C.'s newest, pre-
serving the southernmost flank of an unbroken chain of park-
land that stretches north several hundred miles. Height of the
Rockies includes untrammeled alpine territory, with tumbling
streams, wildlife and solitude. ~ Located along the Elk Lakes
Forestry Road, 20 miles (32 km) north of Elkford.
▲ Wilderness camping only; no developed sites.

ELK LAKES PROVINCIAL PARK 🏃 🚵 ⛵ 🛶 A series of alpine   ◄ HIDDEN
lakes strung along the spine of the Rockies distinguishes this remote, little-used park. Anglers can fish for whitefish, Dolly
Varden and cutthroat trout in the teeming lakes and streams. ~
Located along the Elk Lakes Forestry Road, about 35 miles (57
km) north of Elkford.
▲ There are 20 developed wilderness sites; C$5 per night.

Outdoor Adventures

▼▼▼▼▼▼▼▼▼▼▼▼▼

Both Kootenay Lake and Upper and Lower
Arrow Lake have long wilderness shorelines
suited for extended kayak or canoe trips. The
Valhalla Wilderness shoreline of Slocan Lake is also a good destination for paddlers. Some developed campsites exist along all
these lakes. As in all narrow valley bodies of water surrounded by
mountains, high winds are possible, especially in the afternoon.

CANOEING & KAYAKING

Kootenay Kayak Company offers guided tours, kayak and
canoe rentals and outfitting for the West Kootenay region. Closed
October through April. ~ Box 88, Proctor, BC V0G 1V0; 250-
354-2056, 877-229-2949; www.kootenaykayak.com.

In Golden, **Alpine Rafting** has a full line of kayaking and
paddling equipment, information and guiding services on both
the Kicking Horse River (whitewater) and the serene Columbia
River wetlands. ~ 1020 North Route 1, Golden; 250-344-6778,
888-599-5299.

RIVER RUNNING

Rafting season generally runs from May to mid-September. The
Kicking Horse River is the centerpiece of Yoho National Park,
and one of the best-known raft routes in Canada; **Glacier Raft
Company** specializes in Kicking Horse raft trips. ~ Golden; 250-
344-6521. **Wet 'n Wild Adventures** leads whitewater rafting as
well as more leisurely canoe and kayak journeys on Class I to VI
waters in the Columbia Valley. ~ Box 2586, Golden, BC V0A
1H0; 250-344-6546, 800-668-9119; www.wetnwild.bc.ca.

Rivers and Oceans is a Nelson-based adventure company
that offers rafting trips in the western Kootenays. ~ 250-354-
2056; www.riversandoceans.com

Kootenay River Runners has been specializing in family-oriented trips down the Kootenay River since 1976. These all-day

jaunts take advantage of the Kootenay's less-turbulent course to offer fun for those not interested in high-grade whitewater chills. More exciting trips down the Kicking Horse River are also available. ~ Radium Hot Springs; 250-347-9210, 800-599-4399; www.kootenayriverrunners.com.

BOATING   At 100 miles in length, Kootenay Lake provides plenty of territory for extended boating trips. **Kaslo Shipyard Company** offers Kootenay cruises on dependable steel-hulled craft (not houseboats) with comfortable staterooms, galleys, baths and full equipment for overnight or weeklong cruises. Constant radio contact with the base is maintained; fuel is included. ~ Kaslo; 250-353-2686, 800-554-1657.

Kinbasket Adventures also offers guided float trips through the Columbia Wetlands. Veteran area fishing guide and wildlife expert Wayne Houlbrook adds his knowledge of the area's rich ecosystem to the peaceful trips. ~ Golden; 250-344-6012.

GOLF   Because it's situated facing south in a protected valley, the summer climate at **Kokanee Springs Golf Resort** is surprisingly warm. That results in a lush landscape with grand cedar trees and numerous vistas of the Kokanee Glacier high above. Despite its virtues, the public course is not as well-known as many of the B.C. Rockies' others. ~ Route 3A, 5 miles (8 km) east of the ferry landing, Crawford Bay (east side of Kootenay Lake); 250-227-9226.

Of the two public courses within Fairmont Hot Springs Resort, the upper one, **Mountainside**, is the more notable, having been voted Canada's most unique. The 600-yard par-5 fourth hole is nicknamed the "Fairmonster"; no matter how challenging you find the course, the views over the Columbia Valley and above to the foothills of the Rockies will engage you. ~ Fairmont Hot Springs, Route 95 at the north end of Columbia Lake; 250-345-6311, 800-663-4979.

The privately owned nine-hole executive course at **Canal Flats** is open to the public and, obviously, on level ground, so there are no steep fairways to frustrate the duffer. There is an island green. Spikes are banned to keep the 2046-yard course from getting chewed up. ~ Dunn Street, central Canal Flats; 250-349-5266.

HIDDEN ▶   Designer Les Furber incorporated numerous elevated greens at the public **Trickle Creek Golf Resort**, not only enhancing the views but boosting the hang time tee shots enjoy. Folded into the foothills of the Purcell Range outside Kimberley, Trickle Creek has been rated among North America's top ten for value and quality by *Golf Digest*. ~ Trickle Creek Road, off Gerry Sorensin Way, west side of Kimberley; 250-427-5171, 800-667-0871.

Every vantage point embraces a spectacular mountain peak at **Fernie Golf & Country Club**. Established in 1918 during the

Fat as a Kootenay Trout

Famed worldwide as a fishing destination, the Canadian Rockies offer visiting anglers an unparalleled variety of fishing opportunities. The high-country lakes and streams abound with native species such as cut-throat and rainbow trout, as well as introduced brook trout. The lowland rivers and lakes not only hold trout, they contain kokanee (or landlocked sockeye salmon; "kokanee" means "red fish" in the Kutenai language) and some warmwater fish such as perch, bass and walleye, even catfish.

Visitors can profitably toss a line in almost any stream or lake—remember to get a B.C. license, and check the often-confusing regulations diligently—but as is true elsewhere, the best fishing is likely to be found in wilderness settings where the pressure is less intense. Taking advantage of the services of a local guide not only will aid the day's fishing, but you'll be able to store up tips for future trips. Lodge operators are also excellent sources of information.

Steve Legge of **High Alpine Fly Fishing Adventures** has years of experience guiding (and partaking in) fishing expeditions in the high country around Golden. He offers half- or full-day trips, on foot or afloat, angling for cutthroat, rainbow, brook or bull trout. ~ Box 2009, Golden; 250-344-7114.

Mike Labach of **East Kootenay Sporting Adventures** is an old hand at fishing the mountains on both sides of the Columbia Valley, including the Purcells and the Elk Valley. ~ 706 5th Avenue, Kimberley; 250-427-7210.

Kootenay Lake is a lowland destination known for its healthy population of sizeable (up to 30 pounds) Gerrard rainbow trout. Like several of the area's lakes, it's almost imperative to have a boat for fishing. Rentals and information for Kootenay Lake can be had at **Woodbury Resort and Marina**, which is uplake from Nelson—prime jumping-off territory. ~ Route 31, 2 miles (3 km) north of Ainsworth; 250-353-7717.

The two Arrow Lakes are noted for their F fishery; Slocan Lake is renowned for its large rainbow and bull trout. In the high country, the most popular fishing destinations are the lakes of Valhalla Wilderness Park; the many lakes and streams of the Purcells; and rarely visited fastnesses of the upper Elk River Valley, north of Fernie. Fishing the latter almost demands guidance from local experts; contact the Elkford Chamber of Commerce at 250-865-4614, or the Sparwood Chamber, 250-425-2423.

town's early mining boom, the course has a mature appearance embellished by a handsome clubhouse. ~ At the end of 6th Avenue, east side of Fernie; 250-423-7773.

SKIING

With exceptionally fine and deep powder snow, **Whitewater** near Nelson is renowned as a small but enticing ski area. The vertical drop is 1300 feet, encompassing high-valley groomed runs, chutes, glades and open bowls; there are three lifts. There's a day lodge at the ski area base; accommodations are in Nelson, a half hour away. ~ Located off Route 6, 15 miles (24 km) southeast of Nelson; 250-354-4944, 800-663-9420; www.skiwhitewater.com.

With two developed mountains, a third in the works, 2900 vertical feet and five lifts, **Red Mountain** is by Kootenay standards a major ski area. The historic mining town of Rossland, just five minutes away, serves as the ski village, with numerous lodges, motels, small inns and restaurants. Red's inland location (45 miles/73 km southwest of Nelson) ensures the usual powder snow as well. ~ Located near the junction of Routes 3B and 224, Rossland; 250-362-7384, 800-663-0105; www.ski-red.com.

It's already a fine ski area on the western face of the Purcell Mountains, but a development in the works will transform **Whitetooth** into an international-class destination known as Golden Peaks Resort. A gondola, five chairlifts and considerable expansion of the skiing area will add more than 4000 feet of vertical drop. Two new hotels, a commercial center and condominiums will round out the new resort—and at the top of the mountain Whitetooth offers a very pricey but most exclusive suite in a new mountainside day lodge. ~ Whitetooth Road, west of Golden; 250-344-6114, 800-622-4653.

With a vertical drop of more than 4000 feet (1200 meters), **Panorama Mountain** offers skiers the opportunity to enjoy long, scenery-filled cruising runs. The base village is a ski-in/ski-out complex with its own gondola to help visitors get around while leaving their cars parked. Nearby Radium Hot Springs is a pop-

MUSH!

Winter visitors who'd like to save their ankles and their energy can avail themselves of one of Canada's most intriguing alternatives: dog sledding. **Kingmik Expeditions** offers dog-sled tours through Yoho and Banff national parks from its base in Golden. Short trips range from just over half an hour to a full day; longer tours can take up to five days. Guests rest on bunks and mattresses. The camps are good bases for snowshoeing and cross-country skiing. ~ 403-522-3525, 877-919-9779.

ular day trip. ~ West of Invermere on Toby Creek Road; 250-342-6941, 800-663-2929; www.panoramaresort.com.

You don't have to stay at an ultra-deluxe lodge to experience helicopter skiing. **Purcell Helicopter Skiing** operates from a base in Golden, lifting its customers high into the mountains west of town for some of the best wilderness skiing on earth. Daily or weekly excursions are possible. ~ Golden; 250-344-5410.

Kimberley Alpine Resort added 470 acres of advanced skiing terrain in 1998, and a resort village is underway at the foot of the mountain. At 2300 feet of vertical drop, it's a major mountain with a friendly feel; the Kimberley village is just minutes from the ski area base. There are seven lifts; lift pass rates are economical. ~ Kimberley Village; 250-427-4881; lodging reservations, 800-258-7669; www.skikimberley.com.

As if one alpine helicopter-access lodge weren't enough, **CMH (Canadian Mountain Holidays)** has six in the high terrain of eastern B.C.'s wilderness mountains—in the Cariboos, the Purcells, the Bugaboos and the Adamants. With all that territory, CMH is the largest employer of mountain guides on earth (110 guides). Each lodge offers accommodations for about 25 people, in comfortable rooms with private baths. Stone fireplaces, sundecks, hot tubs and saunas, and gourmet meals augment the lodge ambience. Daily skiing departs from the lodges to thousands of square miles of untracked wilderness powder. This is not cheap—weekly packages run up to US$3000—but the lodges are immensely popular, drawing customers from as far as Europe and Asia. ~ Box 1660, Banff, Alberta; 403-762-7100, 800-661-0252, fax 403-762-5879; www.cmhski.com.

Since almost all of southeastern B.C., except a few lowland valleys, experiences ample winter snowfall, **cross-country skiing** facilities abound. Most visitor areas have developed trail networks; many towns have hiking trail systems that become ski trails in winter, and most inns and lodges can offer guests skiing from their front doors. For specific information, consult the visitor information outlets in Revelstoke (800-487-1493), Nelson (250-352-3433), Kimberley (250-427-3666) and Golden (800-622-4653).

The **Dawn Mountain Nordic Trails** system outside Golden is one of the best examples of the region's commitment to cross-country skiing. Situated at 4265 feet (1300 meters) at the foot of the Whitetooth commercial alpine ski area, Dawn Mountain has groomed loops of varying difficulty ranging from 1 mile (2.5 km) to 4 miles (7 km). ~ Follow Canyon Creek Road, 7 miles (12 km) west of Golden; 250-344-7500.

You don't have to stay at a guest ranch to enjoy riding in the Rockies. **Triple C Trail Rides** operates out of Goat Mountain Lodge but is open to non-guests and drive-up visitors. Rides climb

RIDING STABLES

the beautiful Blaeberry Valley. ~ 2306 Blaeberry Road; 250-344-6579, 877-240-7433.

Owl Mountain Guest Ranch offers trail rides year-round along the Kettle River, on the Trans-Canada Trail and across the ranch itself near Christina Lake. Pack trips into many of the Western Kootenays wilderness areas are also available. ~ 250-447-9442.

BIKING

With a significant community of avid outdoorspeople, the Kootenays have a large established network of mountain-biking trails, many of which rely on old logging and railroad grades. Although the region's major highways are not ideal for biking, some of the backroads have less traffic and wind through beautiful country.

Mount Revelstoke National Park has a few opportunities for those who enjoy pedaling. The **Five Km Loop** (3 miles roundtrip) is a moderate mountain-biking path that cuts through old-growth forest. For more information on Mount Revelstoke and Revelstoke area trails, call 250-837-7502.

Though experienced cyclists clamor to Nelson's extremely steep and challenging rides (given names like The Paper Bag, Logjam and The Vein), novice riders can explore this mountain burg via its many abandoned railway grades and mining trails. The **Burlington Northern Railway** (50 km total) cuts through town.

Bike Rentals & Tours **Discovery Canada Tours** offers guided bike trips in the Western Kootenays in addition to canoeing and combination tours. Bike rentals are available as well. ~ Nelson; 250-353-7349.

If you want to cycle through Mount Revelstoke National Park, **High Country Cycle & Sports** is a full-service shop that will provide you with mountain bikes and maps. All rentals include helmets and water bottles. ~ 118 MacKenzie Avenue, Revelstoke; 250-814-0090.

In Nelson, **Gerick Cycle & Sports** sells, repairs and rents bikes as well as other outdoor equipment, including skis, canoes and kayaks. ~ 702 Baker Street, Nelson; 250-354-4622. **Summit Cycle** is the local base for outdoor recreation equipment in Golden, with biking and other supplies and trail information. ~ 1007 11th Avenue South, Golden; 250-344-6600.

Wild Ways is the adventure outfitter in Christina Lake, offering bike tours along many of the trails in the Western Kootenays, including the old Kettle Valley Railway and Columbia and Western railbeds. Half-day trips predominate; they also rent kayaks and canoes for use on the lake. ~ 250-447-6561; www.wildways.com.

HIKING

With a half-dozen major national parks and dozens of provincial parks—all featuring extensive trail networks—and hundreds of thousands of square miles of wilderness, there are literally thousands of miles of hiking trails in southeastern British Columbia. Some parks require permits for overnight wilderness hiking; many maintain developed wilderness campsites. Contact the regional administration offices for more information on B.C. parks in the area visit wlapwww.gov.bc.ca/bcparks, or call Kootenay Park Services at 250-422-3003. For hiking information in Glacier (250-837-7500), Yoho (250-343-6783) and Kootenay National Parks (250-347-9615), contact the park administration offices at the numbers listed.

All hiking trails listed are one way unless otherwise noted.

WESTERN KOOTENAYS Revelstoke's **Giant Cedars Trail** (.25 mile/.5 km) is a gentle boardwalk stroll through a valley grove of giant western red cedars. Interpretive signs identify plants of the ancient forest and explain the old-growth ecology. ~ Just off Route 1, approximately 12 miles (20 km) east of the town of Revelstoke; for information, call 250-837-7500.

The town of Kimberley was named after the South African diamond mine.

The **Great Glacier Trail** (3 miles/5 km), with a 1000-foot elevation gain, used to be one of the best-known in Canada, when access to the Glacier National Park high country was by rail and the Glacier House Lodge was nearby. Now the Illecillewaet Glacier has receded almost a mile, the lodge is in ruins, and hikers must climb a fairly steep path to the rock slope below the glacier. Allow two hours; an extra hour is required to scramble the next 1000 or so feet up to the glacier's snout. Or you could wait a century and see if it returns down the valley—Illecillewaet has been advancing somewhat once again. ~ Access is from the Illecillewaet Campground, just off Route 1; 250-837-7500.

Access roads—some fairly rough ones at that—reach only to the edge of **Valhalla Wilderness Park** on the west side of Slocan Lake. From there, you walk. Or you can use a boat to cross the lake and hike in from several shoreline landings. Whichever you choose, once you are inside Valhalla, spectacular wilderness awaits. Hikes for experienced backcountry travelers range up to five days, even though the park isn't all that large, because the terrain is so rugged. The climb from Slocan Lake to the Valhalla high country is more than 6000 feet (2000 meters)—for serious hikers only. ~ Access is from Slocan or New Denver.

◄ *HIDDEN*

On the other side of Slocan Lake, Kokanee Glacier Provincial Park occupies the high terrain of the Selkirks above Nelson. The most popular hike, a good choice for a day trip from Nelson, is a two-hour jaunt from the Gibson Lake parking lot to **Kokanee Lake** (2.5 miles/4 km), a pretty mountain valley lake with fishing opportunities and views of the Selkirk high country. You can continue on uphill another hour or two (roughly 1 mile, 1200-foot elevation gain) to the foot of the Kokanee Glacier. ~ Access is from Kokanee Landing, 7 miles (12 km) north of Nelson on Route 3A.

The Purcell Wilderness Conservancy is a huge roadless preserve in the Purcell Mountains east of Kootenay Lake. A lengthy, very difficult traverse of the wilderness is possible along a rugged trail that crosses the mountains between Kootenay Lake and the Columbia Valley. The **Earl Grey Pass Trail** (35 miles/57 km) is an arduous high-country trek only for experienced wilderness hikers; allow at least three days. Along the way, travelers pass through remote hanging valleys beneath sheer mountain peaks—a full-bore wild experience. ~ Trailhead access is from Argenta, on the east shore of Kootenay Lake, and Invermere, in the upper Columbia Valley. For more information, wlapwww.gov.bc.ca/bcparks.

EASTERN KOOTENAYS   How often wilderness trekkers have set down their packs, stretched stiffly and wished a hot tub was at hand. At the **Dewar Creek Hot Springs** trail (5.5 miles/9 km) in the Purcell Wilderness, that's exactly the scenario for hikers who reach this remote site. After a two-hour drive from Kimberley, the trail takes two to three hours and climbs about 600 feet (180 meters); thus attempts to reach here in a day hike will make it a long day indeed. An overnight or weekend trip is better. This is one of the largest and best hot-springs complexes in B.C. Some of the water is extremely hot (180°F/82°C) but numerous pools along the creek allow diversion of cool water to adjust the temperature. For directions, inquire in Kimberley, or consult *Hot Springs of Western Canada* by Glenn Woodsworth. (See Recommended Reading at the end of the book.)

HIDDEN ►

Hot springs dot the hillside along Dewar Creek (in the Purcell Wilderness in the Eastern Kootenays) for 500 feet.

The **Moonraker Trails** system is an extensive network in the foothills of the Purcell Mountains west of Golden, affording hikes that range from a couple of miles into subalpine meadows, to full-day treks that go above timberline. The **Gorman Lake Trail** (3 miles/5 km), part of the Moonraker system, leads to a high-country lake below timberline.

System maps are available in Golden at the Visitor Info Centre, or at recreation and sports stores. ~ Access is from the Canyon Creek Road.

Yoho National Park's trails give hikers access to backcountry destinations. The **Emerald Basin Trail** (5 miles/8 km) is a quick but steep climb from Emerald Lake into an alpine bowl with hanging glaciers and avalanche chutes. ~ The trailhead is on the east bank of Emerald Lake, 5 miles (8 km) north of Field at the end of Emerald Lake Road.

The **Wapta Falls Trail** (2 miles/5 km) leads through a quiet forest to the pounding 100-foot falls on the Kicking Horse River. ~ The trailhead is on Route 1 about two miles west of the Hoodoo Creek Campground.

Nearby, the **Hoodoos Trail** (5 miles/8 km) leads up Hoodoo Creek to one of the park's best-known sights, the spectacular rock spires (known as hoodoos) just above the creek. ~ The trailhead is on Route 1 at the Hoodoo Creek Campground, near the west entrance of the park.

A relatively quick day hike into the park's spectacular high country can be achieved on the **Yoho Pass Trail** (7 miles/12 km), which climbs a steep grade from Emerald Lake through the pass and back down to the Takakkaw Falls Campground. ~ The trailhead is at the east end of Emerald Lake.

Kootenay National Park, as you might expect, provides a good range of hiking opportunities. The **Stanley Glacier Trail** (5 miles/8 km) is a moderate ascent into the park's high country, climbing to Vermilion Pass and culminating below Stanley Glacier on the slopes of Stanley Peak. ~ The trailhead is on Route 93 about 6 miles (10 km) east of the Marble Canyon Campground.

The **Tokumm Creek Trail** (15 miles/24 km) leads into Prospectors Valley, a quiet alpine spot with a small lake and two wilderness camps. It's an overnight trip, but fairly gentle in elevation gain aside from the final mile to Kaufmann Lake.

Transportation

Route 1 and **Route 3** are the main east–west arteries through Southeastern British Columbia. Both are largely two-lane high-speed roads, with many passing lanes and occasional four-lane stretches. **Routes 93, 95** and **23** are mostly two-lane north–south roads with occasional passing lanes.

CAR

Free car ferries provide passage across Kootenay Lake and Upper and Lower Arrow Lake on a roughly hourly schedule; ferries run year-round, weather permitting. (The lakes rarely freeze entirely.)

AIR

Air Canada provides daily scheduled service to Castlegar Airport and **Cranbrook Airport** (near Kimberley) from Vancouver. (cranbrookairport.com).

BUS

Greyhound Bus Lines (800-661-8747; www.greyhound.com) provides service along Route 1 and Route 3. The station in Creston is located at 125 16th Avenue North. ~ 250-428-2767.

CAR RENTALS

Budget Rent A Car has a major operation at the Castlegar airport. ~ 250-365-5733.

TOURS

Midnight Sun Adventure Travel mounts extensive tours and adventures in the Rocky Mountain region of B.C., starting in Vancouver or Calgary and winding through Wells Gray, Mount Robson, Yoho, Kootenay, Banff and Lake Louise parks. These camping tours focus on hiking along the way; canoe and biking options are also available. ~ 843 Yates Street, Victoria; 250-480-9409, 800-255-5057; www.midnightsuntravel.com.

Pendragon Travel near Nelson is an experienced, versatile packager of adventure tours of all sorts—camping, biking, hiking, boating, with appropriate accommodations—in the Western Kootenays region. ~ Slocan; 250-354-4453; e-mail journey@netidea.com.

NINE

Cariboo–Chilcotin

When West Virginia outlaws Jerome and Thaddeus Harper decided in the early 1860s to hang up their black masks and retreat to the wildest, most remote ranch country they could find, they wound up in the heart of the B.C. interior, just west of the Fraser River, in the Chilcotin region. Here the country stretches from stark desert canyon along the Fraser Gorge, through rich grass plateaus, up to high-country meadows interspersed amid thick forests—all below the sheer peaks of the Coast Range.

It was here that they established what became the world's largest cattle ranch, at one point encompassing almost 4 million acres of deeded and leased land. Although often sold, now much smaller, and almost persistently in financial or political trouble, the legendary Gang Ranch is still here, typifying an area where almost everything seems a bit larger than real life. From Kamloops north, British Columbia assumes gargantuan proportions geographically, historically and psychologically.

The fact that the Cariboo–Chilcotin region is ringed by mountains creates a misimpression that fans of the region are not always inclined to correct: though mountains are on all sides, the interior is much gentler. Most of the area between the Coast Mountains and the Cariboos, once you get north of Kamloops, is beautiful, rolling highland in which rich grass hills are interspersed with open forest. Broken by the spectacular gorge of the Fraser River—so impassable that the region's major highway takes a route east of it—the Cariboo looks out over the Chilcotin, and vice versa, providing immense vistas and endless skies.

Here you can see vast meadows of clover and daisies with appaloosas and paints grazing. Every lake and pond seems to have its own pair of loons. This classic Western terrain is, not surprisingly, cattle, gold and timber country. Here sprawling ranch empires spread from lowland canyons to the meadows and forests of alpine terrain, on both sides of the Fraser River, and traditional cattle drives still take thousands of head from winter pastures to summer's high range and back again, an enduring annual cycle. Although Barkerville, the Cariboo gold rush town, is now a heritage site, gold is still drawn from B.C.'s interior mountains. There are even individuals, ranging from hobbyists to lifelong zealots, who still tramp the high country, panning or sluicing for the elusive ore. And on the high slopes that drain moisture from incoming Pacific storms, fir, spruce and pine feed the region's pulp and sawmills.

North of the Cariboo–Chilcotin—that is, north of Prince George, the region's major city—the terrain spreads out even more, turning into forested north country creased by mountains and swaddled with a million lakes. Here, along the river bottoms, are hay fields as large as small cities. Forests that would take weeks to walk spread between mountains few feet have trod. East of the mountains, in the Peace River country, the northern Great Plains send a spur into B.C.—the only part of the province that's truly flat.

At the edge of it all, the Coast Range sweeps northwesterly, a sheer wall of steep, almost impenetrable mountains that keeps the interior somewhat dry and both sides somewhat isolated. This coastline, cut by deep, long fjords, is one of the most convoluted in the world—when you reach the end of Gardener Canal at the start of the Kitlope Valley, you're almost 100 miles (161 km) from the open ocean. In all the expanse of this territory, there is just one road that reaches the coast, at Bella Coola. A legendary stretch of mountain highway, this was built by coastal residents tired of waiting for the provincial government to make good on old promises to connect them to the rest of Canada.

The vast territory, from Kamloops to Prince George, from the Rockies to the coast, is the land of moose, grizzly, cougar, wolf and wolverine. Some of B.C.'s biggest, wildest, most spectacular parks are here: Wells Gray, Tweedsmuir, Ts'ylos, Kitlope—each is larger than several U.S. states. Most have only a few roads penetrating partway into the park, with a lodge, a couple campgrounds and countless miles of wilderness next door. The 290-mile (470-km) Alexander Mackenzie Heritage Trail cuts through the Chilcotin wilderness, a modern revival of an ancient trail First Nations traders used to haul trade goods from the coast to the interior and back.

Natives had lived quietly along coastal inlets and inland along river valleys for thousands of years, depending on salmon, cedar and berries as they did throughout B.C.

Alexander Mackenzie is usually reckoned the first European to see this region when he trekked in from the Peace River in 1793, a remarkable journey that was mirrored farther south a decade later by Lewis and Clark. The Hudson's Bay Company established Fort St. James in the north Fraser country in 1806, shipping out millions of dollars in furs, but the region attracted little outside interest until 1860, when prospectors thrusting northward from the played-out Fraser Canyon gold deposits found the precious metal along the west slope of the Cariboo Mountains.

Some of the ground was fabulously rich—tales spread worldwide about early claim stakers who found 500 ounces of gold nuggets in one day of working. It set off the British Empire's most famous gold rush. By 1864 the central city of the gold fields, Barkerville, boasted it was the largest city north of San Francisco—after just two years in existence. Such was the draw of the Cariboo: Williams Creek east of Quesnel (not far from Barkerville) attracted 5000 people in the spring of 1862.

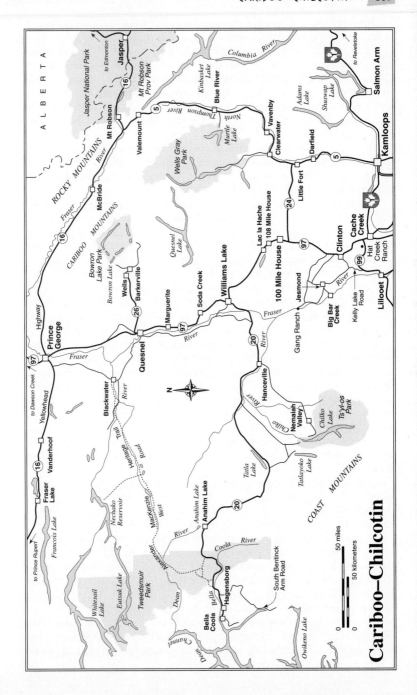

Cariboo–Chilcotin

That's the year B.C. colonial governor James Douglas decided a road was in order, an 18-foot passageway, sufficient for wagon traffic, stretching 400 miles (650 km) from Yale, at the foot of the Fraser Can yon, to Barkerville. This prodigious undertaking is one of the great developmental accomplishments of Canadian history. Road-builders faced stupendous obstacles cutting through some of the most rugged terrain in North America—fierce canyons, thick forests, testy weather. The Royal Engineers were called on to build two six-mile segments of the road, blasting it out of solid rock; the entire length was completed in two years, in 1864.

From 1858, when the first speck of gold was found in the interior, to 1930, when shaft mining overtook surface methods, the Cariboo yielded C$50 million in placer gold. That's a fortune, of course, but these days it's roughly what tourism is worth to the B.C. economy every two days.

When the gold was all claimed and the rush was over, most folk moved on. The ones who stayed had a look at the tall forests and waist-high grass and cast their lot with cattle or timber—both made possible by the Cariboo Road and, a few decades later, the arrival of rail. Ranching and wood products still dominate the area today. Williams Lake, the center of the Cariboo, is simultaneously a mill town and a cattle center—home of the Williams Lake Stampede, one of Canada's most popular small-town rodeos. On roads outside town, large signs still warn sternly of the penalties for rustling cattle or horses. But this is no longer just the land of the cowboy: many wranglers today are women, and a few, just as a century ago, are immigrants from Europe, drawn by the Cariboo mystique.

Most visitors who come to the Cariboo see only the obvious along the main roads: Wells Gray Park, Barkerville, Lac la Hache. Wonderful as these attractions are, and scenic as the highway may be, the region is also home to beautiful guest ranches, remote campgrounds, hundreds of marvelous fishing lakes, and wilderness canoe trips. Even fewer visitors see the Chilcotin at all; I'd say that's a shame, but the region's unspoiled nature depends on its uncrowded expanse. It truly is, as the old song goes, high, wide and lonesome.

Unlike most other pioneer tracks, such as the Oregon Trail and the Santa Fe Trail, the Cariboo Road lives today. It's Route 1 from Yale to Cache Creek; then it's Route 97 from there to Quesnel. It remains the major access route into central and north B.C. All major towns are along it, until you get to Prince George (which is reached by secondary roads); half the towns along it retain the names they acquired in gold rush days, when each way station was designated by its road distance from Lillooet—70 Mile House, 100 Mile House and so on.

Of course, things have changed a bit: at 108 Mile House, site of one of the major stage stations, there's now a pleasant summer/retirement community, with golf courses, resort hotels, even a health spa. However, it's not quite uptown yet— go hiking in the woods in back of 108 Mile House and you'd best wear a bear bell. And at Wells Gray Park, a recent golf tournament was interrupted by a bear stealing the golf balls as they came to rest on the green of the seventh hole.

Farther north, Tatshenshini–Alsek Park, a World Heritage site, holds what many consider the most spectacular wilderness canyon in North America. No roads reach here at all; the only way to see the park is by float trip or arduous

Three-day Getaway

Wells Gray Park

Day 1
• Fly or drive to Kamloops, the gateway to the eastern Cariboo. Head north on Route 5, driving up the **North Thompson River Valley**, a long vale of horse farms bordered by tall cottonwoods. When you reach **Clearwater**, stop at the Visitor Info Centre here at the junction of Route 5 and the Wells Gray Road.

• Head up the Clearwater River Valley toward Wells Gray; after about an hour, you'll reach **Helmcken Falls Lodge** (page 372), a charming log building overlooking a small valley. When you check in, be sure to check out the flotilla of hummingbirds at the lodge's feeders.

• After lunch, drive over to **Helmcken Falls** (page 371) about 15 minutes away. If you want to experience the falls away from the crowds, a half-hour hike along the canyon rim is a good choice.

• Have dinner at the lodge; if you're lucky, they'll make s'mores at an after-dinner campfire down by the stables.

Day 2
• After breakfast, grab a picnic lunch from the lodge kitchen and head into the park for some hiking. Start with the hour-long jaunt to **Ray Farm** (page 393), an old homestead, then on into the fir/cedar woods to **Mineral Springs**. The spring's naturally carbonated water is savory, but don't drink too much. (It's a laxative.)

• On to **Clearwater Lake** for a picnic. Watch for loons and grebes. Hop in a canoe supplied by **Clearwater Lake Tours** (page 390) for an afternoon paddle up this mountain lake. Pull in about an hour up the lake to view the old-growth cedar forest on the west shore.

• Dinner back at the lodge. Maybe afterward you'd want to do a quick nine holes at the **Wells Gray Golf Course** (page 392) next door. In summer, it's light 'til well after 10 p.m.

Day 3
• Don thick jeans for a half-day ride at **Wells Gray Ranch** (page 373), just down the road. Arrange a trip through the ranch's aspen woods to the rim of Clearwater Canyon, a deep, wide chasm in the Cariboo Mountains. Look for bear-claw marks on the trees along the way.

• Lunch at the ranch. If you have time, a game of horseshoes is always appropriate in ranch country—and if you really have time, the ranch's saloon is the area's most popular dinner and dancing spot.

• Drive back to Kamloops, about two hours.

backcountry trek. And even though road building has certainly put its stamp on this vast region, you can be sure no road will ever stretch into Tatshenshini Canyon.

Many roads—well, at least a dozen—do cross central and north British Columbia. But the land is so incomprehensibly vast that what lies next to and between those roads holds all the beauty, visitor interest and backcountry solitude anyone would ever need.

▼▼▼▼▼▼▼▼▼▼▼▼▼▼
Yellowhead Highway

There are just two roads north out of the southern, more developed section of British Columbia. Route 5, the Yellowhead Highway (of which this is just one section), cuts up the beautiful North Thompson River Valley to Wells Gray Park, then through the southern Cariboo Mountains, into the Rocky Mountain Trench and on to Mount Robson Park and Jasper. Except for the trip up the valley, this takes you through the mountainous fringe of the Cariboo, affording little opportunity to experience the region's high, rolling central plateau, but plenty of options for mountainous meandering.

Visitor information for the Cariboo–Chilcotin region is available from the **Cariboo Tourism Association**. ~ 800-663-5885, 250-392-2226; www.landwithoutlimits.com.

SIGHTS

The first major turnoff along the Yellowhead Highway north of Kamloops is for **Sun Peaks**, a recently renamed (it used to be Tod Mountain) and upgraded ski resort that is trying to give Whistler a run for its money. Despite its relatively newborn status, the resort offers a huge ski area (its 2894-foot/882-meter vertical drop is barely half Whistler's, though), cross-country ski facilities, hotels, condominiums, restaurants, golf courses, hiking trails—the works. With 3300 beds in the village's accommodations, it is second in size to Whistler in B.C. ~ Sun Peaks Road, 20 miles (32 km) east of Route 5; 250-578-7842, 800-807-3257; www.sunpeaksresort.com.

AUTHOR FAVORITE

There are bigger lakes, loftier peaks, deeper canyons and denser forests in B.C. than those in **Wells Gray Park**—but Wells Gray remains one of my favorite natural attractions in the province. Its beauty is more subtle and serene than sensational; the adventure opportunities are unlimited (especially for canoe fans) but sensible; and it has one of the best day hikes anywhere, to Ray's Farm. Nearby are splendid accommodations in a historic lodge and a user-friendly guest ranch. Overall, you just can't beat the breadth of what's available here. See page 371 for more information.

With towering cottonwoods along the river, mountain ridges pressing in on either side, and a road climbing up toward the highland lakes leading out of town, **Little Fort** (57 miles/93 km north of Kamloops) looks exactly like a place for, well, a little fort. There was a Hudson's Bay Company outpost here from 1850 to 1852 (nothing remains); today this is the gateway into the **Cariboo Lakes Country**, a highland plateau with more than 100 lakes known for their fishing. Along Route 24, the road west out of Little Fort, there are about two dozen fishing lodges that range from rustic to deluxe. Most of the lakes hold Kamloops rainbow trout.

Farther up, the Yellowhead follows the Thompson River around a wide bend to the east. From here (at Clearwater) the main access road for Wells Gray travels north into **Wells Gray Park**. Eighty years ago fire swept the valley around and in the park. The forest that has grown to replace it is a rich, marvelous woods that contains almost every Northwest tree—cottonwood, aspen, birch, maple, Douglas fir, ponderosa and white pine, Western red cedar, hemlock, spruce. It's as beautiful as the park itself, which holds four lakes, snowy peaks and glaciers along the spine of the Cariboo Range, waterfalls, a spectacular river canyon and vast expanses of untracked backcountry.

Since it's just off the main route between Jasper and Vancouver, this park is popular—probably B.C.'s best-known wilderness park aside from Garibaldi. Even so, it's large and unspoiled enough that superlative wilderness experiences await the backcountry trekker. **Helmcken Falls**, a 450-foot-high torrent of water not far from the park entrance, draws visitors from all over for good reason—B.C.'s fourth-highest falls are a spectacular sight, but visitors who dash into Wells Gray Park to see the falls, have a look at Clearwater Canyon from the lookout point and dip their toes in the waters of Clearwater Lake will be overlooking a wealth of other opportunities. ~ Off Route 5, about 100 miles (160 km) north of Kamloops.

Friends of Wells Gray Park is a Cariboo regional group dedicated to preserving the park's boundless natural wealth and educating visitors and residents about it. Each summer the group offers a series of natural-history field trips in the park, with topics ranging from mushroom and bird identification to the park's fascinating geology. For more information visit www.friendsof wellsgraypark.org.

Set in a spectacular bowl high in the Cariboo Mountains in the eastern part of Wells Gray Park, **Murtle Lake** is the largest North American lake restricted to non-motorized travel (mostly canoes). It offers weeklong paddles, sandy beaches, excellent fishing and wildlife viewing—and it's not even the most remote lake in Wells Gray. Access is from Blue River along Route 5, about 65 miles (105 km) northeast of Clearwater.

◄ *HIDDEN*

Valemount marks the northern tip of this region (a few miles farther north you enter the Fraser River watershed and northern British Columbia). This small high-valley town lies in a flat where the Cariboo, Monashee and Rocky mountains meet, and is the western portal to the Canadian Rockies.

Nearby, **Mount Robson Provincial Park** and **Mount Terry Fox Park** hold two peaks that loom above the valley. Robson, at 13,180 feet (3954 meters), is the highest peak in the Canadian Rockies; the surrounding park includes the headwaters of the Fraser River and a good network of trails (mostly for day hikes). ~ Mount Robson information, 250-566-4325.

Mount Terry Fox is a lower peak named to honor the Vancouver area one-legged runner whose attempt to cross Canada, electrifying the nation (and the world), was cut short by bone cancer. ~ Valemount Info Centre, 250-566-4846.

LODGING   Most of the accommodations at Sun Peaks ski resort are townhomes and condominiums, almost all available for rental through property-management firms. Two of the larger booking agencies are **Top of the Mountain Accommodations** (250-578-6939, 800-585-8834, fax 250-578-6935) and **Peak Accommodations** (250-578-2002, 800-337-3257, fax 250-578-8579; www.sunpeaks homes.com).

Nancy Greene's Cahilty Lodge was built by the famed Canadian skier and Olympic champion, and offers 192 units that range from standard hotel rooms to deluxe condominium apartments. Operated as a full-service hotel, the lodge's rooms feature light-colored wood trim and beige tones; there's also a fitness center, underground parking, bar and restaurant. ~ 3220 Village Way,

AUTHOR FAVORITE

Just as Helmcken Falls is the attraction most people associate with Wells Gray Park, **Helmcken Falls Lodge** is the accommodation people generally think of. This venerable wood structure at the foot of the park offers not only excellent accommodation but a good dose of history. The main cedar lodge was built in 1949 by two pioneer brothers; their original construction is still in use, along with several newer log buildings and facilities. There are 21 rooms with private baths. The food is much better than average for lodge fare, and activities abound: horseback riding, pack trips, canoeing, fishing and wilderness trekking. The setting, overlooking valley meadows in the shadow of Trophy Mountain, is spectacular. The namesake falls are about a 15-minute drive away. ~ At the entrance to Wells Gray Park (Box 239, Clearwater); 250-674-3657, fax 250-674-2971; www.helmckenfalls.com. MODERATE TO DELUXE.

Sun Peaks; 250-578-7454, 800-244-8424, fax 250-578-7451; www.cahiltylodge.com, e-mail info@cahiltylodge.com. DELUXE.

Sun Peaks International Hostel is operated by the same folks who run the International Hostel in Kelowna. In the center of the ski village, the hostel features a ski-in, ski-out location, laundry facilities, a TV lounge, Internet access and a full kitchen. The 31 beds are spread among private and semi-private rooms, a few with private bath. ~ 1140 Sun Peaks Road, Sun Peaks; 250-578-0057, fax 250-578-7490; www.sunpeakshostel.com, e-mail sun peakshostel@canada.com. BUDGET.

Tuloon Lake Fishing Lodge is in the heart of the Lakes ◀ HIDDEN Country fishing paradise, in the Cariboo west of Little Fort. You can't get there yourself; instead, lodge personnel pick you up in four-wheel drives for a one-and-a-half-hour trek to the lodge, which is on the plateau above Little Fort. There are seven lakes accessible from the lodge, all featuring Kamloops rainbow trout that grow up to five pounds. Four rustic cabins can accommodate a total of 12 people; meals and boats are supplied. Gas motors are prohibited, enhancing the peaceful atmosphere. ~ Box 53, Little Fort; 250-371-9926 or 250-828-2097. MODERATE.

Wells Gray Ranch is on the canyon-facing side of the road leading into Wells Gray Park, but most visitors never see the best aspect of the area's high-country fastness. You have to get on a horse to do that, and that's the attraction at Wells Gray Ranch. Its eight log cabins are comfy, spacious and well furnished, but what people come for are breathtaking rides through birch/fir/aspen forest to the canyon rim, where you can look down a half-mile into the Clearwater River. The ranch runs very popular pack trips into their camp along the river. You don't have to pony up the cost of a cabin, either; economical tent cabins and bunkhouses are available. ~ Located at Wells Gray Park (Box 1766, Clearwater); 250-674-2792 or 250-674-2774, fax 250-674-2197; www.canadian-adventures.com. MODERATE TO DELUXE.

There's nothing around **Clearwater River Chalet** but its name- ◀ HIDDEN sake river, the rich forests of the Wells Gray Park area—and peace and quiet. This custom log cabin on the banks of the river sleeps up to eight, and can be rented by just one party at a time. Hiking trails, river fishing and splendid views are right out the door. ~ Clearwater; 800-667-9552, fax 250-374-2711; www.river chalet.com, e-mail crc@riverchalet.com. BUDGET TO MODERATE.

The farmhouse that holds **McKirdy Creek B&B** outside ◀ HIDDEN Valemount is more than half a century old; the farm itself is even older and the setting is timeless, a beautiful birch-lined, mountainside meadow at the foot of the Rockies. The three rooms offer shared or private bath; there's also a separate cottage with housekeeping facilities. There's picnicking on the farm as well as plenty of biking and hiking. The country breakfasts feature farm-raised berries and other produce. ~ McKirdy Road, Valemount; 250-566-4542. BUDGET.

DINING   Just a nip and tuck off the main road in Valemount, **Coffee Logged** offers long-haul travelers exactly what they need—good strong specialty coffee drinks, savory muffins and snacks. Yes, it's housed in a log structure. ~ Route 1, Valemount; 250-566-0115. BUDGET.

SHOPPING   Set under the shade of the river valley's tall cottonwoods, the **Little Fort Fly Shop** offers a complete range of angling equipment, along with something even more important: information. This is the spot to find out where to fish, what flies and lures to use and how to get there, in addition to renting equipment or hiring a guide. Aside from the tavern and an ice cream stand, it's the busiest institution in Little Fort. ~ A half block west of Route 5, Little Fort; 250-677-4366.

BEACHES & PARKS   **BRIDGE LAKE PARK** 🏃 🚴 ⛵ 🛶 🚤 ⛴ Although this park is fairly small, it is the only one in the lakes district west of Little Fort, a fishing paradise with more than 100 bodies of water. Bridge Lake is one of the larger lakes; aside from fishing, the park offers swimming, canoeing and kayaking. ~ Route 24, about 30 miles (50 km) west of Little Fort; 250-397-2523.

▲ There are 20 large vehicle/tent sites set in the forest above the lake; C$14 per night. There are also seven walk-in sites.

WELLS GRAY PARK 🏃 🚴 🐴 🏕 ⛵ 🎣 🛶 🚣 🚤 ⛴ Once known as British Columbia's largest wilderness park (no longer true), Wells Gray is a magnificent expanse (more than a million acres) of mountain, forest and lakes in which just two small corners are accessible to carbound visitors. Both these access points are on a major lake, of which Wells Gray has five. The park offers visitors virtually every outdoor activity conceivable, ranging from quiet nature hikes to deep wilderness canoe treks. The principal visitor area, about 30 miles (49 km) north of Clearwater, has hiking, boating, sightseeing, camping and wildlife-viewing opportunities sufficient to keep you occupied for a week. This is where you'll find Wells Gray Park's most famous attraction, **Helmcken Falls**, a wide bowl where the Murtle River plunges 520 feet (130 meters) on its way down into Clearwater Canyon. ~ Wells Gray Park Road, 25 miles (40 km) north of Clearwater; 250-674-2194.

▲ There are four campgrounds with 128 vehicle/tent sites; two are on major lakes; C$14. The camps on Clearwater Lake are quite popular in summer and reservations are essential: 800-689-9025. Numerous wilderness campsites are scattered throughout the park; C$5.

MOUNT ROBSON PROVINCIAL PARK 🏃 🚲 🛶 ⛷ 🚂 ⛵
The centerpiece of this half-million-acre park is its namesake peak,
highest in the Rockies at almost 12,000 feet (3954 meters). The
surrounding valleys are the headwaters of the Fraser River. An extensive network of hiking trails affords access to wide (and high)
expanses of alpine terrain. ~ Along Route 16, 8 miles (13 km) east
of Tete Jaune Cache (north of Valemount); 250-566-4325.

▲ There are 176 vehicle/tent campsites in three highway
campgrounds; C$14 to C$17 per night. There are also 80 developed wilderness campsites; C$5 per night.

The Cariboo Road

Route 97, the old Cariboo Road, follows a small
valley north out of Cache Creek, then drives up
onto the high plateau, a beautiful land of pine and
fir, aspen and birch interspersed with meadows and tarns, before
rejoining the Fraser River at Marguerite. This 275-mile (441-km)
stretch of remote highway is the way to 108 Mile House, Barkerville, the Lac la Hache resort area, Bowron Lakes Park and
Prince George.

SIGHTS

When you head north out of Cache Creek along Route 97, you're
retracing the gold rushers' first steps out of the hot, cramped, difficult fastness of the Fraser and Thompson canyons. Not far up
the little valley, a cool creek plunges into a
peaceful meadow; it's no wonder the family
that homesteaded along Hat Creek established a way station for Cariboo Road travelers.

Today **Hat Creek Ranch** is one of British
Columbia's most evocative heritage sites, an attractive spot in which almost all the original buildings remain, ranging from barns and stables to the
roadhouse/hotel. (See Chapter Seven for more information.) Closed mid-October to mid-May. Admission. ~ Located 6 miles (11 km) north of Cache Creek, just
off of Route 97; 250-457-9722, 800-782-0922.

> Just up the creek from Hat Creek
> Ranch in a pretty glade, the local
> Bonaparte Shuswap Band has
> set up a traditional summer
> camp, where members will
> answer questions about
> their ancestors' peaceful
> lifestyle.

Clinton was one of the original stage stops along the Cariboo
Road; now it calls itself the "Guest Ranch Capital of B.C.," with
about a dozen such establishments within 100 miles of the town.
(See Lodging, below.) ~ Clinton Chamber of Commerce, 250-
459-2224.

The **South Cariboo Historical Museum**, housed in an 1894
brick schoolhouse, has gold rush and ranching exhibits and artifacts. Open summer only. Admission. ~ 1419 Cariboo Highway,
Clinton; 250-459-2442.

Before you head into the backcountry around Clinton, ask
about road conditions—these ranch roads are well maintained,

but wet weather can still make them treacherous. That's why ranchers use four-wheel drives. The opportunities to see wild animals—bears, deer, moose, small predators—along the road are considerable. This is the heart of the Cariboo ranch country.

HIDDEN ►

The **Big Bar Ferry** crosses the Fraser at a historic gold rush spot. Here Chinese labor was used to wash the river's gravel for gold more than a century ago; rock piles along the riverbank remain from this activity. The free ferry is a cable-drawn reaction ferry, which relies on the river's current for its power. The ferry runs, when river conditions allow, from 7 a.m. to 7 p.m., with breaks at lunch and dinner. ~ Located 3 miles west of the Jesmond Road, 35 miles northwest of Clinton.

HIDDEN ►

The road to the **Gang Ranch** is a long, scenic, winding gravel secondary road, well-maintained, that takes two to three hours from Clinton. Why go? It's an unmatched way to see what the Cariboo is like—rolling bunchgrass highlands bordered by beautiful aspen/fir forests, cut by deep desert canyons. When you cross the Gang Ranch bridge over the Fraser (a heart-stopping span built by the ranch, later sold to the province), you are in the Chilcotin and on the grounds of what was once the largest ranch in the world, an expanse comparable to the entire state of Maryland. Troubled by bankruptcy in the late '80s, the ranch is now owned by a Saudi Arabian prince who has actually spent just one afternoon there. Visitors will find a small store, ranch-hands to chat with, and a B&B that may or may not be open. (See Lodging, below.) ~ Located 60 to 90 miles (110 to 170 km) northwest of Clinton (depending on the route you take) off Big Bar Road; or 50 miles (90 km) west of Route 97 off Meadow Lake Road or Dog Creek Road; turn-offs are marked "Gang Ranch." It is highly advisable to stop at the Visitor Info Centres in 100 Mile House or Williams Lake for maps that can help guide you through the maze of logging and ranching roads west of Route 97. ~ Gang Ranch; 250-459-7923.

In the 19th century Barkerville was the capital of the gold rush, with a population that peaked at more than 5000.

HIDDEN ►

The only thing **Churn Creek Provincial Park** has to offer is a lot of something virtually no other B.C. park can—thousands of acres (more than 80,000) of unbroken Chilcotin rangeland, leading up into high-country meadow and forest; the only "attraction" is the creek. Access is time-consuming and difficult, with four-wheel drive a necessity; there are no facilities whatsoever. All that's part of the charm at this remote park, where uninterrupted hikes and trail rides are not only likely but certain. ~ South of Gang Ranch; on the west side of the Fraser River, access is from Big Bar Road, Meadow Lake Road or Dog Creek Road; information, wlapwww.gov.bc.ca/bcparks.

HIDDEN ►

Although the Cariboo is mostly flat and rolling highland, at **Chasm Provincial Park** a glacial flood cut through the underlying layers of lava, creating a 350-foot-deep (120-meter) canyon that reveals the multi-colored bedrock. The park is for picnickers and sightseers only; several excellent vantage points offer almost limitless views southeast into the heart of the Cariboo. ~ Turnoff is 12 miles (22 km) north of Clinton; park is 4 miles (7 km) east of Route 97; wlapwww.gov.bc.ca/bcparks.

The Route 97 rest stop just past 108 Mile Ranch, an hour farther up the road, is certainly conforming to its past—this roadhouse was one of the major stopping points along the Cariboo Road, and local historic preservation officials have done a superb job of restoring the site. The **108 Mile House** heritage site includes a museum, an original Cariboo Road hotel (just down the road at 105 Mile), a post office, a general store, several other original buildings and, most notable of all, a 1908 Clydesdale barn. This gargantuan log structure was built to be the largest wood barn in Canada; it was, and still is. It's still standing true, too, and hosts local barn dances and other gatherings. The nearby 108 Mile Ranch development is a tony golf-course resort. ~ Route 97, just past 108 Mile Ranch; 100 Mile House/108 Mile Ranch information, 250-395-5353.

Continuing on Route 97 past Lac la Hache and then another 50 miles or so north is **Williams Lake**, the capital of the Cariboo ranch country and the start of Bella Coola Road (Route 20), the only access into the Chilcotin. The rodeo arena just off Route 20 is the home of the Williams Lake Stampede, a late June event that's B.C.'s most famous rodeo. ~ Williams Lake Info Centre, 250-392-5025.

The **Museum of the Cariboo Chilcotin** offers excellent depictions of First Nations lifestyles, early ranching and rodeo history. Admission. ~ 113 North 4th Avenue, Williams Lake; 250-392-7404.

Soda Creek, located 15 miles (25 km) past Williams Lake on Route 97, marks an important point in the history of the Cariboo; this is where the Fraser River plunges into unnavigable canyon (the section of river from here downstream to Yale). The section of river upstream, however, was useable by paddlewheelers. No steamships run the river anymore, but a **reaction ferry**, using the power of the river current, crosses the Fraser not far upstream at Marguerite, affording access to the west-side ranchlands.

Following the Fraser River another 50 miles brings you to **Quesnel**, an erstwhile gold rush town turned into a forest products center. With three major mills and thousands of square miles of timberland to draw from, the town's gold is now wood fiber. Visitors are invited to view the bustle of the millyards at a viewing platform ("forestry observation tower") just north of the town center.

The **Quesnel Museum and Archives** is one of B.C.'s best storehouses of information about the Cariboo gold rush, with exhibits ranging from early mining equipment to a re-creation of a frontier bank. Several of the collections are from local pioneer families. The town's **Visitor Info Centre** is adjacent to the museum. ~ 250-992-8716, 800-992-4922.

HIDDEN ►

Anyone who's looked at the flimsy framing used in home construction today will be impressed by the foot-thick solid timbers used to build **Cottonwood House**, a verdant, bucolic heritage site on the road east to Barkerville. This roadhouse—its timbers are cottonwood, rather than fir—on the last leg of the Cariboo Road must have seemed like Eden to weary trekkers who had come hundreds of miles from Vancouver. Built in the early years of the Cariboo Road, it was acquired by John Boyd in 1874, and the Boyd family operated it until 1951. There are also a café, general store, barn and some RV camping space. Closed in winter. Admission. ~ Route 26, 18 miles (28 km) east of Quesnel; 250-994-3332.

Barkerville looks like a movie set—and it has been quite a few times. Unlike some of the West's other theme towns, this one is simply honoring its own past. Once it seemed destined to become a major city but when the gold petered out, so did the town. Restoration began in 1958, and it has slowly transmogrified into a living history site. It is a bit touristy—visitors can "pan" for preplanted gold, and an actor portraying the notorious Judge Begbie dispenses frontier justice. Even so, few places offer more in the way of genuine heritage, with 125 restored or reconstructed pioneer buildings. Visitors can buy period items at the stores, sample frontier cuisine (or modern cooking) at a half dozen restaurants and even stay in restored gold rush hotels. (See Lodging, below.) The townsite is open year-round, although many shops and demonstrations are shut during the winter. Admission in the summer. ~ Route 26, 50 miles (90 km) east of Quesnel; 250-994-3332. For information on the Wells/Barkerville/Bowron Lake area, contact the district Chamber of Commerce at 877-451-9355; www.wellsbc.com.

LODGING

When Norm Dove sold his high-tech business he and his wife Nan plowed much of the money into **Echo Valley Ranch**, and it shows. The facilities and programs here are first class throughout, ranging from the gourmet meals to the 15 fine rooms and three comfy cabins. All are superbly crafted out of native logs, as is the main lodge and the falconry where peregrines and gyrfalcons are kept. The riding territory around the ranch is gorgeous high Cariboo country, and the views from the lodge across the Fraser River Gorge to the Chilcotin Mountains are stunning. The honeymoon cabin, perched by itself above the nearby creek, is exquisitely private . . . save for ranch animals wandering by. Echo Valley has added a huge spa, featuring Thai-trained masseuses, to its menu of offerings. ~ Box 16, Jesmond; 250-459-2386, 800-253-8831, fax 250-459-0086; www.evranch.com, e-mail evranch@uniserve.com. DELUXE TO ULTRA-DELUXE.

Big Bar Ranch is one of the mainstays of the B.C. guest ranch industry, having plied its business in the Cariboo high country for decades now. Situated at the upper end of Big Bar Canyon, it straddles some of the region's most beautiful territory. Guests stay in the 12 lodge units (all have private bath) or in four private cabins; the most popular are the older ones farthest north and off by themselves. Also found here are teepees and tent cabins, horseback riding, pack trips, fishing, hiking, river rafting and general hanging about. ~ Kelly Lake, Jesmond (Box 27, Clinton); 250-459-2333, fax 250-459-2400; www.bigbarranch.com, e-mail info@bigbarranch.com. MODERATE TO DELUXE.

When things get old, they get quirky. You could easily say that of **Flying U Ranch**, the oldest guest ranch in Canada, one of the   ◄ HIDDEN
most esoteric, and an institution that engenders zealous loyalty from its long-established clientele. Founded in 1849 and converted to a guest ranch in 1923 by rodeo star Jack Boyd, the Flying U eschews many of the modern trappings of today's dude ranches—no massage therapists, swimming pools or New Age cuisine. (There is, however, a wood-fired sauna.) Guests stay in 23 small wood-stove-heated cabins, walk to the community shower/bath building, and tell tall tales in the Longhorn Saloon. The key to the experience is self-guided trail riding: Guests choose a horse at the start

AUTHOR FAVORITE

Some serious fitness regimens are offered to clients at the **Hills Health Ranch**—several long-stay guests have licked severe obesity and health problems. But the overall atmosphere is that of a fun guest ranch, with horseback riding, hiking, biking and wildlife watching in the beautiful wooded meadow behind the lodge. The 28 lodge rooms are attractive and modern; the ones facing east have the best views. There are also 16 spacious chalets that sleep up to six. The main lodge has full fitness facilities, plus whirlpool, pool and sauna, with extensive treatment rooms for everything from manicures to massage therapy. The Hills is equally popular in the winter, when the area's extensive network of hiking trails becomes a Nordic skiing trail system, much of it groomed. Be sure to try the handmade rose-hip body lotion, my favorite for soothing chore-sore hands. ~ Route 97, 108 Mile Ranch; 250-791-5225, fax 250-791-6384; www.spa bc.com, e-mail info@hillshealthranch.com. DELUXE TO ULTRA-DELUXE.

of their visit, saddle it up each morning, and head off where they wish through the ranch's 40,000 acres of aspen/fir parkland. ~ Green Lake, east of 70 Mile House; 250-456-7717; www.flyingu. com, e-mail flyingu@bcinternet.net. MODERATE TO DELUXE.

HIDDEN ▶

The **Log House B&B** is exactly that—a large modern log home with two guest accommodations. It's right on 108 Mile Lake, in a quiet residential area; there's a private beach, big yard, beautiful gardens and, in one of the units, space for kids. In fact, kids under eight are free. Need something to do? There's a wonderful trail around the lake; golf, sailing, horseback riding and other hiking areas are nearby. ~ 4785 Kitwanga Drive, 108 Mile Ranch; 250-791-5353, 800-610-1002, fax 250-791-5631; www.bbcan ada.com/theloghousebb. BUDGET.

HIDDEN ▶

Rowat's Waterside B&B is a large, comfy modern home set on the shore of Williams Lake. The five upstairs guest rooms all have a private bath and are furnished in homey floral fabrics; breakfasts are hearty affairs with waffles, big fruit plates, biscuits and eggs. Guests enjoy a private entrance. ~ 1397 Borland Road; phone/fax 250-392-7395, 866-392-7395; www.wlakebb.com. MODERATE TO DELUXE.

HIDDEN ▶

The main activity at **Black Creek Ranch,** a land conservancy preserve, is raising natural, range-fed beef. But there is one rustic cabin, right by a tree-shaded creek, that can house up to four family members who enjoy the pristine setting and recreation such as hiking, kayaking, horseback riding and fishing in the nearby Horsefly River. The ranch hosts only one party at a time, so solitude is assured. ~ Black Creek Road, 25 kilometers east of Horsefly; 250-620-3781; www.blackcreekranch.com, e-mail blackcreek@telus.net. MODERATE.

By gold rush standards the **Wells Hotel,** built in 1933, is a new accommodation. But its handcrafted furnishings—birch and Italian-slate floors, Douglas fir staircase—give it an antique flair that's augmented by the traditional flavor of the 16 rooms, which have furnishings that hint at the hotel's Craftsman-era heritage. There's a hot tub, fireplace lounge, dining room and tavern. The hotel is close to Barkerville and Bowron lakes. Some rooms share baths; breakfast is included in the rates. ~ 2341 Pooley Street, Wells; 250-994-3427, 800-860-2299, fax 250-994-3494; www. wellshotel.com, e-mail info@wellshotel.com. MODERATE.

When it was built in 1898, the **St. George Hotel Bed & Breakfast** was one of the finest private homes in Barkerville. Today it's a seven-room inn (three with private bath, one a suite) renovated with period furnishings and decor such as Victorian floral wallpaper and lace-edged quilts. The gourmet breakfast menu offers guests their choice of dishes, from pancakes to omelettes; guests enjoy a private dining room in the evening. Dinner is by reservation only. Closed in winter. ~ Box 4, Barker-

ville; phone/fax 250-994-0008, 888-246-7690; www.stgeorge
hotel.bc.ca, e-mail stgeorge@abccom.bc.ca. DELUXE.

Gourmet cuisine is hard to come by in the Cariboo. The closest **DINING**
approximation is at the area's resorts, and **108 Mile Ranch
Restaurant** offers fine dining that's worthy of the name, with fresh
seafood, pasta and chicken and lamb entrées that go beyond the
usual ranch-country cooking. The desserts
are up to snuff, too. ~ 108 Mile Ranch
Resort, 108 Mile Ranch; 250-791-5413.
MODERATE TO DELUXE.

Why is it spelled "Cariboo"? Early
prospectors had many attributes,
but extensive education was
not usually among them.
The name is considered
a misspelling of the once-
common caribou.

The decor and locale of **Cindy's Cafe** are
most unprepossessing—formica and strip-mall.
But the food is handmade, including fresh
Ukrainian sausage, pirogies, hamburgers and
scrumptious pies. Breakfast and lunch only. ~ 108
Mall (on Route 97 at the 108 airport); 250-791-5299.
BUDGET.

It's just pub food at the **Laughing Loon Pub,** but it's likely the
best in Williams Lake—great salads, salmon and halibut dinners,
even salmon fettuccini. The pub atmosphere is muted—it's a
family place. ~ 1730 Route 97, Williams Lake; 250-398-5666.
MODERATE.

Handsome hand-tooled saddles and bridles are to be expected at **SHOPPING**
a tack store; paintings of Cariboo scenes at a Western gallery.
Aside from some marvelous saddles, **Arrowstone Springs** also offers scratchboard prints by a regional artist who uses this rare
technique to produce evocative depictions of Western Canada. ~
Route 97, opposite Hat Creek Ranch heritage site, Hat Creek;
250-457-9580.

Not only is the **Station House Gallery** housed in a historic
1919 train station in Williams Lake—the train still rumbles by
on a regular basis, as it's by the BC Rail tracks. The gallery features work by local artists, with a gift shop that includes First
Nations crafts and scenes of the Cariboo. ~ 1 MacKenzie Avenue
North, Williams Lake; 250-392-6113.

DOWNING PROVINCIAL PARK 🏃 🚲 🛶 ⛴ ⚓ This **BEACHES
& PARKS**
pleasant little park encircles Kelly Lake, a small valley impound-
ment in the Cariboo at the foot of a high ridge, with views of
Mount Bowman to the north. The heart of B.C. ranch country ◀ *HIDDEN*
is nearby; the Gang Ranch is about a two-hour drive from here.
The park offers places to picnic or camp, and the lake provides
swimming, kayaking and canoeing. ~ Pavilion Mountain Road,
10 miles (16 km) southwest of Clinton; 250-397-2523.

▲ Along the lake are 25 vehicle/tent sites with poor visual separation; C$14 per night. About 20 walk-in sites are also dispersed around the lake.

GREEN LAKE PROVINCIAL PARK 🏃 🚲 🚤 🛶 ⛵ ⚓
Straddling one end of its namesake lake, this park offers visitors a chance to experience the Cariboo plateau country that so many nearby guest ranches occupy. Fishing, canoeing, swimming and water sports are the chief entertainments. ~ Located 10 miles (16 km) east of Route 97 at 70 Mile House; 250-397-2523.

▲ 121 sites in three lakeside campgrounds; C$14.

HORSEFLY LAKE PROVINCIAL PARK 🏃 🚲 🚤 🎣 🛶 ⛵ 🚣 ⚓ Nearby Horsefly River (the outlet of Horsefly Lake) was the actual site of the first gold discovery in the Cariboo, in 1859. The area was later named for one of its chief disadvantages, but by the lake itself, in the foothills of the Cariboo Mountains, a steady breeze helps keep insects down. Waterborne recreation abounds at the wonderfully scenic Horsefly Lake. A major sockeye run returns to the lake in autumn. Nearby Quesnel Lake is the deepest in B.C., at almost 1600 feet. ~ Located just east of Horsefly, about 40 miles (65 km) east of Williams Lake; 250-397-2523.

▲ There are 22 lakeside vehicle/tent sites; C$14 per night.

BOWRON LAKE PARK 🏃 🚲 🚤 🛶 ⛵ 🚣 🎣 ⚓ There are ample reasons for the continuing popularity of this wilderness series of lakes. It's not the only canoe circuit in B.C., but it's fabulously situated, in the high Cariboo Mountains, with stunning scenery, good fishing, excellent campsite facilities and marvelous wildlife viewing. The circuit includes six major lakes, two river runs and six portages for a total distance of about 60 miles (116 km). Most trekkers complete the trip in five to seven days. Reservations are required; the advance deposit is C$60 (about US$45) for a two-person party. Park officials limit daily departures to 50 people. For trip outfitting, see the Outdoor Adventures section at the end of this chapter. ~ Located about 75 miles (120 km) east of Quesnel; 250-992-2901.

◆◆

EARTHLY REQUEST

A sign in the middle of the Chilcotin's deepest fastness, the Nemaiah Valley, offers this exemplary message from the local First Nations band: *Greetings to travelers from the Nemaiah People—The Grass you walk on, the Streams you drink from and the Wood you burn are all gifts from the Creator and must be respected.*

▲ There are at least two dozen wilderness camps, some with shelters, and food caches at all campsites; reservations required. Aside from the wilderness camps, there is one vehicle/tent campground at the park headquarters with 25 sites on Bowron Lake; C$14 per night.

Route 97's biggest spur, Route 20, is the Bella Coola Road, which climbs west out of Williams Lake to a high ridge, only to drop into the precipitous Fraser Canyon then back up to the Chilcotin Plateau. It winds through this haunting land of meadows and open forest, into the Coast Range lakes country, across the mountains and down into the fjordland of the Discovery Coast, ending up at Bella Coola 260 miles (420 km) from Williams Lake.

Chilcotin

In many ways this is still B.C.'s wildest frontier, the land of pioneer ranches, wilderness lodges and First Nations people who continue to live as much as possible as their ancestors did. Bands of wild horses roam the plateau; moose, grizzlies, cougars and wolverines prowl the wildernesses of Tweedsmuir and Ts'yl-os parks; the Junction area herd of California bighorn sheep is the largest in the world. Salmon and rainbow trout thrive in its rivers and lakes.

For many years no road reached Bella Coola; the provincial and federal governments kept telling residents of this remote coastal enclave that it would simply be too expensive to penetrate the towering wall of the Coast Range. The interior highway reached to the Anahim Lake area about 70 miles from the town, and stopped. Finally local residents decided to take matters into their own hands, and in the early 1950s local contractors began cutting a road through the mountains. Three years later the effort was done—without any government help—and the same road grade, somewhat improved, is still used today. It's called the **Freedom Highway** because its completion finally offered coast residents the freedom to go where they wished by land.

SIGHTS

Driving it is a memorable experience, first across the unfettered expanse of the Chilcotin Plateau, then into the Coast Range and Tweedsmuir Park, then down the steep Bella Coola Grade—a five-mile stretch of switchbacks that descends from almost 5000 feet (1493 meters) to near sea level, with a few 18 percent grades—then along a coastal valley to Bella Coola. The journey takes a very long day from Williams Lake; it's imperative that drivers intending to drive this road make sure their vehicles—*especially their brakes*—are in good condition.

Farwell Canyon is one of those B.C. landscapes that surprise visitors so—it's desert, with sand dunes, cactus and arid vegetation. Hiking into the canyon, you'll notice how remarkably dif-

◄ HIDDEN

ferent it is from most of the Chilcotin; you might be in Arizona. ~ Turnoff is off Route 20 at Sheep Creek, then about 28 miles (44 km) south on gravel roads, usually passable to ordinary cars unless there's been rain. Pick up guide pamphlets in Williams Lake; wlapwww.gov.bc.ca/bcparks.

HIDDEN ▶

The turnoff to the **Nemaiah Valley** is at Hanceville, about 50 miles (82 km) west of Williams Lake; a long (50 miles/82 km) gravel road in active use by logging trucks lies ahead. Set amid the rugged peaks of the Coast Range, with rivers slashing through to drop into the vast fjord-like **Chilko Lake**, this is a spectacular area where visitors who heed the Nemaiah people's advice about respecting the land and its resources will be richly rewarded.

Ts'yl-os Park encompasses a large chunk of the area, including Chilko Lake, a major stretch of Chilko River and the surrounding mountains. This 600,000-acre park is almost entirely backcountry wilderness, without marked trails. Countless deer, bighorn sheep, mountain goats, cougar, lynx, wolves, moose and bears roam the meadows and forests, and three of the world's biggest salmon runs spawn their way up Chilko River every year between August and October—the sockeye run alone averages half a million fish. Eagles, herons and bears come out to feed on the dying fish. ~ Located 100 miles (160 km) southeast of Williams Lake off Route 20.

A circuit of the Nemaiah Valley (skirting Chilko Lake) is possible with four-wheel drive; you return to Route 20 at **Tatla Lake**. Several wilderness lodges offer visitor facilities (see Lodging, below).

Tweedsmuir Park, a couple of hours farther along Route 20, is another vast expanse of matchless wilderness in the Coast Range. With dozens of major lakes and hundreds of smaller ones, and thousands of square miles of mountains, forest and glaciers, this is one of B.C.'s most important parks. Route 20,

---

PANHANDLING—CARIBOO STYLE

You can't pan or sluice on already staked territory, and after 140 years of exploration much—but not all—of the Cariboo has been claimed. (However, many claims have lapsed, and the Chilcotin is far less thoroughly explored—some folks still disappear into the Coast Range each summer and reappear in September with a sack of gold.) You can contact the Gold Commissioner's Office (250-992-4313) in Quesnel for information and a map on places where one might find an unclaimed patch. Less adventurous souls can pan in the Quesnel River within the Quesnel city limits, at the juncture with the Fraser; this is set aside for public hand panning, like a stretch of the Fraser outside Yale.

which cuts through the southern quarter, is the only road. ~ 250-397-2523.

The adjoining **Kitlope Valley Park,** with no road access at all and no facilities, stretches over 790,000 acres from Tweedsmuir nearly to the coast, preserving the largest intact coastal rainforest in North America. Moose, black bears and grizzlies roam among 800-year-old trees that are nesting grounds for bald eagles and marbled murrelets. **Gardener Canal,** a long coastal fjord, meets the Kitlope River within park boundaries. The only way to visit the park is to take a boat up this fjord.

If you stick to the road, you'll reach the end of it at **Bella Coola,** 30 miles after leaving Tweedsmuir. The final 15 miles or so plunge down the steep face of the mountains ringing the valley; residents regularly drive it in passenger cars, and you can too, but be prepared to hold your breath at a couple of precipitous stretches. Bella Coola itself is a small fishing and logging village at the head of a coastal fjord, with small stores and a few motels and cafés. Abandoned canneries and unused docks mark the town's past; stunning scenery hints at its future as a remote visitor destination. Settled at the turn of the 20th century by Norwegian families who were lured there with promises of an agricultural paradise, it retains a strong Scandinavian flavor, with 1000 descendants of the original settlers still in the valley. The valley's setting, directly beneath glacier-capped peaks, is stunning. ~ The Bella Coola Info Centre can be reached at 250-392-2226, 800-663-5885.

The **Bella Coola Museum** in the town center gives visitors a glimpse of traditional First Nations life, the early logging and fishing history of this coast and the construction of the Freedom Highway. Closed September through May.

Nearby attractions include the **Big Cedar Recreation Site** south of town, where a giant Western red cedar 16 feet (five meters) in diameter attests to the richness of the temperate coastal rainforest. ~ Along the South Bentinck Arm, reached by boat tour only, 29 miles (47 km) south of Bella Coola.

A great way to see this coast is, predictably enough, by going over the water. BC Ferries' **Discovery Coast Passage** is a popular summertime service that takes visitors through the inside passage along the central coast from Port Hardy, on Vancouver Island, to Prince Rupert, with some trips stopping or starting in Bella Coola. Although it is used by area residents, it's basically a cruise that traverses North America's longest fjord coast, all of it wilderness, with the exception of Bella Coola and a few other remote outposts reached only by water.

This is the land of North America's largest remaining temperate rainforests, the home of eagles, orcas, grizzlies and the legendary Kermode bear (spirit bear), a rare white-coated black bear found along the coast north of Bella Coola.

Passage from Port Hardy to Prince Rupert takes about 15 hours. Numerous variations are available, including overnight voyages, stopovers in small island hamlets, and cruises to and from Bella Coola only. Sailings during the busiest months—July and August—book up as much as half a year in advance. Timely reservations are absolutely essential. Costs range from about US$100 (C$155) up to US$250 (C$388). Sailings are from May through September only. ~ 250-386-3431, 888-223-3779 in B.C.

LODGING

The **Chilcotin Lodge** is a historic (1940), renovated log roadhouse on the Bella Coola Road, not far from the best put-in points for Chilcotin River raft trips. It's also a popular restaurant and bar—and it's the only place for miles around. The ten refurbished upstairs rooms feature fir plank floors, simple original decor and shared baths. There's a comfortable sitting room with a stone fireplace; breakfast is included. If you were inclined to make a pilgrimage to the Gang Ranch, this would be a starting point. ~ Route 20 and Stack Valley Road, Riske Creek (about 25 miles/40 km west of Williams Lake); phone/fax 250-659-5646, 888-659-5688; www.chilcotinlodge.com, e-mail welcome@chilcotinlodge.com. BUDGET.

HIDDEN ►

The seven roomy, two-bedroom spruce log cabins of picture-perfect **Elkin Creek Ranch** are set among the aspens; the main lodge looks out over the hay meadows. Excellent fishing is available in Vedan Lake at the edge of the ranch. Trail rides follow the nearby hills into the Chilcotin wilderness. Have your own plane? You can fly in to the ranch's strip; those without planes can have the ranch owner, who operates a flying service, pick them up in Vancouver, turning an eight-hour drive into a one-hour flight. Closed October to mid-May. ~ Nemaiah Valley (about 100 miles/ 160 km west of Williams Lake); mail: 4462 Marion Road, North Vancouver; 604-573-5008, 877-870-0677, fax 604-573-0174; www.elkincreek.bc.ca, e-mail elkincrk@elkincreek.bc.ca. ULTRA-DELUXE.

HIDDEN ►

Puntzi Lake Resort enjoys a beautiful remote setting on the high Chilcotin plains, amid cottonwood and aspen groves along the sparkling sapphire lake. The resort's housekeeping cabins are rustic but comfy; fishing, boating and just relaxing pass the time. ~ 3846 Puntzi Lake Road; 250-481-1176; www.puntzilake.com. MODERATE.

HIDDEN ►

Chaunigan Lake Lodge has a beautiful setting on the shores of a high bench lake on the east slope of the Coast Range— plenty of territory for hiking, wildlife watching, mountain trekking. But there's really only one reason people come here: to catch the 18- to 24-inch rainbows in the lake. The lodge supplies boats and tackle if you need it, plus meals. The fishing is consistently good; Chaunigan Lake fans come from all over the world.

Horseback rides are also available. Guest cabins range from rustic (no bath facilities) to luxurious. ~ Chaunigan Lake, approximately 70 miles (114 km) southwest of Hanceville on the Nemaiah Valley Road; mailing address, 12682 Woolridge Road, Pitt Meadows; 604-465-5040, fax 604-465-9829; www.chauni gan.com, e-mail info@chaunigan.com. MODERATE TO DELUXE.

Chilko Lake is the centerpiece of Ts'yl-os Park, a jewel of Coast Range wilderness in the lee of Mount Waddington, B.C.'s highest peak. **Chilko River Lodge** is on the shore of the lake's major river, at the end of the road four hours from Williams Lake—it's a serene wilderness accommodation with full facilities that can be either a destination in itself or the jumping-off spot for a memorable wilderness trek. Six log cabins include baths, kitchenettes, outdoor firepit and woodstove for cool nights. Activities include fishing, boating, hiking, swimming, horseback riding and wildlife watching. ~ Chilko Lake Road (Box 43), Tatla Lake; 250-394-4105, 250-398-7744; www.bcadventure. com/chilkoriverlodge. MODERATE TO DELUXE.

Chilko Lake Resort & Guest Ranch is a luxury resort at the foot of Chilko Lake, with all the usual wilderness activities plus a heated swimming pool, a sauna, a hot tub, tennis courts, a game room and a dining room with a bar and lounge. Accommodations range from 14 deluxe waterfront suites and bungalows to 12 comfortable rooms in the main lodge, all built in the prototypical Chilcotin spruce log scheme. The setting on a lake promontory is magnificent. ~ Chilko Lake Road (Box 17), Tatla Lake; 250-481-3333, fax 250-481-3334; www.chilkolake.com, e-mail holiday@chilkolake.com. DELUXE.

Brockton Place is a small lodge in Hagensborg just east of Bella Coola; its 12 units are housekeeping rooms with kitchens, TV and free movies. Continental breakfast is included, and the scenery is remarkable. ~ Route 20, Hagensborg; 250-982-2298, fax 250-982-2145; e-mail leskoroluk@hotmail.com. BUDGET TO MODERATE.

Eagle Lodge is a most welcoming large B&B outside Bella   ◀ HIDDEN
Coola. With warm, spacious rooms, an ever-ready woodstove, a

AUTHOR FAVORITE

If you pictured in your mind the ideal setting for a guest ranch, **Elkin Creek Ranch** would probably come pretty close. Set in a remote Chilcotin Valley, with snowy mountains in the distance, green pastures in the foreground, a willow-lined creek at the valley bottom, and aspen woods edging the meadow, the ranch looks like a picture postcard. See page 386 for more information.

hot tub and beautiful grounds—plus homemade culinary delights such as raspberry jam—it's an unexpected pleasure in this remote valley. All the rooms have private baths; dinner, by arrangement, is a good idea. ~ Hagensborg; 877-799-5587; www.eaglelodgebc.com, e-mail eaglelodge@telus.net. MODERATE TO DELUXE.

Tweedsmuir Lodge was originally built back in 1930, long before the road reached the valley. It's a classic rustic park lodge, with log buildings, stone fireplaces and bear rugs. The lush meadow setting along the Bella Coola River is sublime, and snowcapped peaks hover overhead. Trailheads into the park's backcountry are just a few miles away. ~ Route 20, Stuie; 250-982-2402; www.tweeds muirlodge.com. MODERATE TO DELUXE.

The **Bella Coola Valley Inn** is not only Bella Coola's nicest motel, it's closest to the ferry dock for travelers getting on or off the BC Ferries Discovery Coast run. Its 20 rooms feature cable TV and refrigerators, and pets are welcome. There's a restaurant and pub, too. ~ MacKenzie Street (Box 183), Bella Coola; 250-799-5316, fax 250-799-5610; www.bellacoolavalleyinn.com, e-mail valleyinn@belco.bc.ca. MODERATE.

BEACHES & PARKS

TS'YL-OS PARK 🚶 🚲 🐎 🏕 🛶 🎣 ⚓ 🚤 ⛴ Just one road winds through the northeast corner of this rugged expanse surrounding the long, turquoise waters of Chilko Lake. Pronounced TSIGH-loss, the rest of the park is a high-country wilderness encompassing mountains, glaciers, wildflower meadows, fossil beds, open plateau and deep forests, accessible to adventurous canoe, kayak, horseback and foot trekkers. Those without considerable wilderness experience are best advised to avail themselves of local guides (See Outdoor Adventures; lodges along Chilko Lake are also a good resource). It's hard to muster enough superlatives to cover B.C.'s natural scenic wealth; this park is one of its true gems. ~ Located 30 miles (49 km) south of Route 20; 250-397-2523.

A number of fishing outfitters and lodge operators maintain secluded outpost cabins on fly-in wilderness lakes—guests will often have the entire lake to themselves, providing an unparalleled fishing experience.

▲ Two small lakeside campgrounds have 24 vehicle/tent sites. The one at the north end of the lake is one of the nicest in all B.C.; C$10 per night.

TWEEDSMUIR PARK 🚶 🚲 🐎 🏕 🛶 🎣 ⚓ 🚤 ⛴ Like its neighbor, Ts'yl-os, Tweedsmuir is an immense (almost 2 million acres), incomparably beautiful stretch of Coast Range wilderness with shimmering mountain lakes, plunging rivers and waterfalls, glacier-clad mountain peaks and dense coastal rainforest. Hunlen Falls, at almost 800 feet (259 meters), are the second-highest falls in B.C. The only road access is Route 20, which cuts through the southern fringe of the park. Several lodges provide visitor services; the rest of the park is for seasoned wilderness trekkers. The northern part of the park, reached from the Prince Rupert highway, offers a lengthy and uncrowded wilderness canoe circuit beginning at Ootsa Lake. ~ Along Route 20 about 180 miles (290 km) west of Williams Lake; 250-397-2523.

▲ There are 42 vehicle/tent sites; C$14 per night. There are also 11 developed wilderness campsites; C$5.

Outdoor Adventures

The high plateau country north of Kamloops, between Wells Gray Park and Quesnel, is famed for its myriad lakes holding Kamloops rainbow trout, as well as Dolly Varden, bull and some cutthroat. These are **FISHING** classic highland fly-fishing waters; anglers must obtain a B.C. fishing license and scrutinize the often-confusing specific regulations.

In the fall, huge salmon and steelhead runs throng some of the rivers and lakes, although by the time these anadromous fish have traveled hundreds of miles up the Fraser River to their spawning grounds they are not in the best condition.

The best general source of information for this area is the **Little Fort Fly Shop**. ~ A half block west of Route 5 in Little Fort; 250-677-4366.

Most of the lodges and guest ranches listed in the Lodging section are located on prime fishing waters, or can arrange transportation to nearby lakes and streams. Further, most of the pack trips guided by these ranches and outfitters (see Guides & Outfitters, below) include the opportunity for fishing. In the Chilcotin, Elkin Creek Guest Ranch, Chaunigan Lake Lodge, and the several lodges on Chilko Lake are all known for their fishing.

Big Creek is a tiny hamlet in the heart of the wild Chilcotin; from **GUIDES &** this base, Richard Dillabaugh and Walter Weigelman of **Anvil OUTFITTERS Mountain Guiding** have been leading fishing and wilderness expeditions into the untracked territory of the south Chilcotin for years. ~ Box 22, Big Creek; 250-394-4831.

Ts'yl-os Lodge is at the edge of the Chilko Lake wilderness, and offers outfitting and guide services for all area adventures, ranging from canoe trips to horseback treks into the depths of Ts'yl-os Park. The lodge maintains outpost camps inside the park. ~ North Chilko Lake; Box 2560, Williams Lake; 800-487-9567, fax 250-398-7738; www.tsylos.com.

Gary Shelton has spent a lifetime in the Bella Coola Valley and can guide visitors to the very best natural attractions in the area, from untouched rainforest to grizzly bear feeding grounds. He is a naturalist and bear safety expert. ~ 250-982-2316.

RIVER RUNNING

The Chilcotin River isn't the biggest around, but it is wild and unfettered, as is the fabulous territory it passes through. Farwell Canyon and Big John Canyon are legendary for their rock formations and rapids. **Chilko River Expeditions** offers one- and multiday floats down the Chilcotin, using the venerable Chilcotin Lodge as a base, and winding up at Gang Ranch. ~ Box 4723, Williams Lake; 250-398-6711, 800-967-7238.

CANOEING

Kanata Wilderness Adventures is headquartered in Clearwater, the gateway to Wells Gray Park, but mounts guided expeditions into Bowron Lakes, Tweedsmuir Park and the Dease River area as well—all wilderness canoeing meccas. Trips range from one week to a 12-day trek down the Dease River. ~ Box 1766, Clearwater; 250-674-2774; www.canadian-adventures.com.

Those wishing guides in the deep wilderness of Wells Gray Park—a good idea for nonexperts—can avail themselves of the seasoned knowledge of **Wells Gray Backcountry Chalets**, which offers equipment, gear, guidance and meals on multiday trips. ~ 250-374-0831.

Murtle Lake, a beautiful lake high in the Cariboo Mountains in Wells Gray Park, claims the distinction of being the largest lake in North America restricted to non-motorized boats, with commercial tour operators barred. With more than 50 miles of shoreline, it's a great canoe lake offering 19 developed shoreline campsites, spectacular scenery and wildlife, and solitude. Access is from Blue River; for information on canoe and gear rentals call the Wells Gray Info Centre, 250-674-2646. **Blazing Paddles Adventure Company** is a Blue River outfitter specializing in supplies for Murtle Lake trips, including canoe and portage cart rentals. ~ Box 11, Blue River; 250-673-2388.

HIDDEN ►

Hobson Lake is even more remote than Murtle; access is only by foot along an eight-mile (15-km) trail from the end of Clearwater Lake in Wells Gray Park. Each summer **Clearwater Lake Tours** stashes a few canoes at the foot of Hobson for truly adventurous trekkers to rent for a journey into the north Wells Gray wilderness, one of B.C.'s most remote lake trips. (Unlike many other North Country lakes, Hobson has no floatplane access.) This is for serious, experienced wilderness trekkers only! ~ Box 27, Clearwater; 250-674-2121.

Bowron Lake Park is known worldwide for the canoe circuit within it, a wilderness journey offering both splendid scenery and exceptional wildlife viewing. **Bowron Lake Lodge** provides not only outfitting—canoe and gear rentals, as well as supplies— but expertise: how to prepare for weather on the lakes (on some lakes, early morning canoe work avoids the worst of the wind, for instance), what fishing gear works best, which campsites are most desirable. The lodge also offers accommodation in modern

Git Along . . .

The Cariboo–Chilcotin is cattle country. The open rangeland and expansive ranches have defined the region at least as much as gold mining. And while even here the methods of raising cattle are changing, it's possible to get a taste of the old cowboy ways by hopping on a horse and heading down the trail—with or without accompanying herds.

The annual **Kamloops Cattle Drive** isn't quite the real thing. There are several hundred cattle along, and they're headed down a high country trail in the Cariboo, but there are also several hundred guest riders and the route is selected to allow fairly inexperienced riders to participate. For most participants it's as close as they'll ever get to the real thing, and it is far more genuine than many similar events. For one thing, it covers mostly open ground; no clumping along at the side of highways. The route shifts from year to year, but each drive is about five days, meals are supplied, and horse and gear rentals are available for the steed-less. ~ Kamloops Cattle Drive, 250-372-7075, 800-288-5850.

The **Great Cariboo Ride** is a less jazzy version trail ride, minus cattle. This annual wilderness country riding event takes place in the Williams Lake area, and features daily rides plus other activities such as hikes and swimming. Locale and cost vary from year to year. ~ 250-395-2753.

Dozens of ranches in the Cariboo–Chilcotin offer trail rides. Almost all are guest ranches, but they can also accommodate visitors not staying at the ranch. See the Lodging sections for specific listings for Wells Gray Ranch, Douglas Lake Ranch, Big Bar Guest Ranch and Elkin Creek Ranch. In the Wells Gray Park area, **Nakiska Ranch** also offers half-day and full-day rides. ~ At Trout Creek Road and Wells Gray Park Road, 19 miles (30 km) north of Clearwater; 250-674-3655.

Ts'yl-os Lodge mounts trail rides of various lengths into the depths of Ts'yl-os Park, which is among the most spectacular riding territories in North America. The lodge maintains outpost camps inside the park. ~ North Chilko Lake (Box 2560), Williams Lake; 800-487-9567, fax 250-398-7738; www.tsylos.com.

Canadian Outback Adventures, a Vancouver-based operator, offers pack trips into the north Chilcotin wilderness along the Alexander Mackenzie Trail. Guests fly in to Gatcho Lake and depart from there on horseback to indulge in wilderness flyfishing, hiking and wildlife viewing. ~ 1110 Hamilton Street #206, Vancouver; 604-921-7250, 800-565-8735; www.canadianoutback.com.

cabins before and after your journey. ~ Route 26, Bowron Lake; 250-992-2733; www.bowronlakelodge.com. The other outfitter at Bowron Lake, with much the same array of equipment and services, is **Becker's Lodge**. ~ Route 26, Bowron Lake; 250-992-8864; www.beckers.bc.ca.

GOLF

HIDDEN ►

Of all the beautifully situated golf courses in British Columbia, **Wells Gray Golf Course** may offer the most spectacular setting— and most interesting potential hazard: this is the course where a tournament was once interrupted by a bear engaging in ball theft. It's tucked in a valley beneath Trophy Mountain; golfers play along pretty Hemp Creek amid tall cottonwoods. ~ Wells Gray Park Road, one mile south of park entrance; 250-374-7853, 250-674-0009.

Many unlikely things await the traveler along the Cariboo Road; today that includes a full-fledged summer resort, 108 Mile Ranch, that offers one of B.C.'s best golf courses. The **108 Resort Golf Club** is an 18-hole championship course that makes full use of the beautiful, rolling woods-and-meadows topography of the Cariboo, including 108-Mile Lake. ~ Route 97, 108 Mile Ranch; 250-791-5465.

SKIING

Wells Gray Park is the perfect place for wilderness ski trips. **Wells Gray Backcountry Chalets** make such treks safer and more comfortable with its series of chalets and cabins in the park. Guests can simply ski to one chalet and enjoy daily jaunts from there, or undertake a challenging hut-to-hut journey over Trophy and Table Mountains—a true wilderness ski trek. ~ Box 188B, Clearwater; 250-374-0831.

Although there are downhill ski areas scattered throughout the Cariboo and North B.C., the region's most enticing attraction to dedicated skiers is **heli-skiing**, the no-pain-big-gain method of backcountry ski access that devotees swear is an unmatched experience. Heli-skiers are lifted each morning from a base lodge to a wilderness peak where they can ski untracked deep powder for miles.

There are two major operators in this region. The **Mike Wiegele Heli-Ski Village** is at Blue River, at the edge of Wells Gray Park, right off Route 5 about halfway between Kamloops and Jasper. Guests here are lifted either into the high Cariboos in Wells Gray or into the Monashee Mountains to the south. Snowfall here is deep and reliable; the extensive lodge facilities offer numerous activities aside from skiing, including a full fitness center. ~ Route 5 (Box 159), Blue River; 250-675-8381, 800-661-9170; www.wiegele.com.

TLH Heliskiing operates out of Tyax Mountain Lodge northwest of Lillooet, at the foot of the southern Chilcotin. Skiers are lifted into the east side of the range, high above the Fraser Plateau, where snowfall is deep (an annual average of 45 to 60 *feet*) and dependable and the weather is consistently good. Guests pay handsomely for packages (as much as US$3000 during peak periods) and are guaranteed a certain amount of vertical feet of skiing—100,000 feet for a seven-day package, for instance. The lodge itself is a handsome log structure, with a hot tub, massage, games room and gourmet meals. ~ TLH Heliskiing (Box 1118), Vernon; 250-558-5379, 800-667-4854; www.tlhheliskiing.com.

There are literally thousands of hikes in the Cariboo–Chilcotin region, ranging from quiet strolls along nature trails to heroic treks over long wilderness routes. Information on individual hikes is available in pamphlets describing each provincial park; BC Forest Service district guide maps also describe area hiking trails.

HIKING

It is essential that you be an experienced wilderness hiker before heading into the backcountry—even just for a day hike—or that you go with a knowledgeable guide.

All distances given for hiking trails are one way unless otherwise noted.

YELLOWHEAD HIGHWAY   Several hikes in Wells Gray Park are especially worthwhile. The **Ray Farm/Mineral Springs walk** (1.5 miles/3 km) is a short loop that takes you first to a Clearwater Valley homestead, with an intact cabin, orchard and cemetery beside a pretty meadow; then on to a carbonated mineral spring bubbling from a spout in the ground. Be sure to taste the water; it's very flavorful. But don't drink too much! (It has laxative properties.)

At **Helmcken Falls**, a path leads westward from the parking lot about a half mile (1 km) to a promontory overlooking the spectacular depths of Clearwater Canyon.

The **Murtle River trail** (7 miles/12 km) leads along this pretty river; it's fairly flat, but a mile-long spur leads to the top of Pyramid Mountain, affording an exceptional view of the park and Clearwater Valley.

CARIBOO ROAD   The **Alexander Mackenzie/Nuxalk Carrier Grease Trail** (290 miles/470 km) follows the route used by First Nations peoples to trade between coastal and inland bands; "grease" refers to the eulachon (a type of small anchovy) that coastal people caught and rendered to make their most important trade good. This same trail was followed by Alexander Mackenzie in 1793 when he became the first European to cross Canada. Today the trail starts near Quesnel, traverses the Chilcotin Plateau, then crosses the Coast Range and drops down to end near Bella Coola. This is an arduous, wild, rugged and lengthy wilderness trip that requires hikers to be in good shape, have considerable experience and arrange for supplies to be flown in to pick-up points. Journey length is 18 to 25 days; this is inarguably one of North America's most fantastic wilderness treks. Since the trail passes

◀ HIDDEN

through several First Nations reserves, it's best to contact their tribal offices beforehand for permission to cross their land. Several guidebooks to the trail have been published; for information, call the Quesnel Info Centre, 250-992-8716, 800-992-4922.

CHILCOTIN In Tweedsmuir Park, a fairly easy overnight trip leads to the **Rainbow Range** (destinations are between 6 miles/10 km and more than 20 miles/32 km), a multicolored chain of high ridges much loved by photographers. Although a long day hike is possible (especially in midsummer), it's best to pack overnight and enjoy the morning and evening light on the range. ~ The trailhead is off Route 20 at Heckman Pass, near the eastern boundary of Tweedsmuir Park; take a short access road to Octopus Lake to reach the trailhead.

Also in Tweedsmuir, **Hunlen Falls** is a favorite of many—a challenging destination best accomplished in a two- or three-day trip skirting Turner Lake. The falls spill out of the northwest end of the lake. ~ The trailhead is at Young Creek Picnic Ground on the Atnarko River Road, about 12 miles (20 km) west of Heckman Pass off Route 20.

▼▼▼▼▼▼▼▼▼▼
Transportation

CAR

Route 97 is one of two major north–south routes into the Cariboo–Chilcotin, starting in Cache Creek, continuing north through Williams Lake and Prince George, then on to Dawson Creek, where it retains the same numerical designation but becomes the Alaska Highway. **Route 5** runs from Kamloops north along the North Thompson River, then crosses the Monashee and Rocky Mountains into Jasper. Both are mostly two-lane national-class highways, with occasional four-lane sections and many passing lanes. **Route 16** is the major east–west road, running from the Rocky Mountains to Prince Rupert. Routes 5 and 16 together comprise the Yellowhead Highway.

Route 20 is an improved secondary road, paved most of its length, with many winding mountainous stretches. Be alert to the need for a full gas tank, good tires and adequate towing capabilities for the Coast Range crossing.

It is imperative, before traveling on side roads, that you inquire locally about road conditions. Most secondary roads are well maintained, and plowed regularly in winter, but wet conditions and potholes can make them hazardous for passenger cars.

AIR

Major access points into the Cariboo–Chilcotin are Kamloops, Cache Creek and Lillooet in the south and Prince George in the north. It is also possible to enter the region from Jasper in the east. Travelers wishing to fly into the region can utilize airports in Prince George, Kamloops or Williams Lake, with scheduled service, rental cars and other visitor services at all three. (See

Chapter Seven and Chapter Eleven for information on Kamloops and Prince George airports.)

Air Canada offers scheduled daily service into Williams Lake and Quesnel. ~ 604-273-2464, 800-663-3721; www.aircanada. ca. **Pacific Coastal Airlines** flies from Vancouver to Bella Coola and other coastal locales. ~ 604-273-8666, 800-883-2872; www.pacific-coastal.com.

Many charter air services have scheduled and on-demand flights, most by floatplane, into numerous regional destinations. Among the major operators are **Pacific Coastal Airlines** (604-273-8666) and **AvNorth** (250-742-3303).

FERRY

BC Ferries offers scheduled service to Bella Coola from Port Hardy roughly three times a week during summer. The Discovery Coast Passage route varies with different sailings; some trips are 15-hour direct passages to Bella Coola, some stop at various other small villages along the way. Fares range from about C$20 for single passengers up to as much as C$200 for a recreational vehicle. Travelers can make a round trip or disembark in Bella Coola and continue their journey elsewhere in the province. The reverse is also possible, although space is at a premium. Reservations are strongly advised, and are absolutely essential during the peak summer travel months. ~ 250-386-3431, 888-223-3779 in B.C.; www.bcferries.bc.ca.

BUS

Greyhound Bus Lines provides bus service to Williams Lake. ~ 800-661-1145 (in Canada), 800-231-2222 (in the U.S.); www.greyhound.com.

Gold Pan City Stage Lines offers service from Quesnel to Wells and Barkerville. ~ 250-992-6168.

CAR RENTALS

National Tilden Interrent (250-989-4261) is the car agency at the Williams Lake airport.

TEN

Queen Charlotte Islands

The Queen Charlotte Islands' mystic allure depends, superficially, on mist: This is a foggy, breezy, showery archipelago in which any given minute's weather is determined by the North Pacific air flow. Mist, rain, gusts of wind, patches of sunshine, rainbows and brief glimpses of an infinite horizon— "That's the weather, every day," says a resident, explaining why the well-dressed islander combines shorts with a rainsuit and reliable hat. One stays covered while the showers pass by, doffing hat and coat when the sun slants through and a rainbow arcs from the sea's surface to the top of one of the many island hills.

This misty mystique just scratches the surface, however. The islands hold equal measures of breathtaking scenery, bountiful wildlife and unsurpassed peace and quiet. Long, clean pebbly beaches welcome Pacific breakers; slope-shouldered hills clad in deep spruce forests rise up into the clouds; bears, deer, salmon and birds abound.

More than 200 islands and islets comprise the Queen Charlottes; but with development confined to the eastern parts of Graham and Moresby, the two biggest islands, much of the region qualifies as wilderness. The inland portions of the main islands are dominated by otherworldly muskeg, stunted spruce groves and an infinity of bog ponds; it's a landscape suited for science-fiction movies. Undergirding all is a rich First Nations heritage that is experiencing a profound rebirth. In the settled sections of Haida Gwaii (the Haida name for the islands), First Nations (Haida) and Canadian cultures intermingle to an extent rare elsewhere in B.C. And Gwaii Haanas National Park is perhaps Canada's finest attraction that features First Nations heritage.

Part of the draw also depends on its sheer remoteness. It's not easy getting to the Queen Charlotte Islands, about 60 miles (97 km) from the mainland; ferry service from Prince Rupert is the only way, aside from private boat and limited air service. The passage is a more-than-seven-hour jaunt across notoriously temperamental Hecate Strait, whose relatively shallow waters magnify wind-driven swells. In summer, the passage is usually smooth; in fall, spring and winter anything goes, and the 7000 residents are quite accustomed to the fact that frequently the ferries simply don't run—or do run, but hours or even days off schedule.

As a result, the islands' character is somewhat immune to the elements of modern life that seem so difficult to escape elsewhere. Sawmills and sawyers outnumber stockbrokers in the phone book. (The islands' economy is still quite dependent on its timber.) While visitors are welcome, dining, lodging and entertainment options are quite limited. There are no major hotels, no fast-food outlets, no shopping malls, no multiscreen cineplexes and only one traffic light, which maintains order at the main ferry landing in Skidegate. If traffic stops, it's likely to be on the smaller ferry connecting the north (Graham) and south (Moresby) islands when it encounters a pod of gray whales at play in Skidegate Channel. At such moments, with tiny islands appearing from the mist up-channel and a rainbow lifting its colors above Queen Charlotte City, the islands' appeal is perfectly clear.

Queen Charlotte City is the largest town in the islands, and thus the administrative center—such as it is. The town consists of one street (the main north island road, Route 16), and a two-block parallel side street in the "downtown" section. Here are a cluster of small cafés, inns and shops—mostly utilitarian—looking out on the narrow Skidegate Channel to the south.

SIGHTS

The main **Visitor Information Centre** for the islands is in Queen Charlotte City; here one can learn about the Queen Charlottes' unique natural history and select among the small number of tourist services. This is also one of the two places to receive the mandatory orientation necessary before visiting Gwaii Haanas. Closed October through April. ~ 3220 Wharf Street, Queen Charlotte City; 250-559-8316; www.qcinfo.com.

Skidegate is a small Haida settlement a mile east of the ferry dock, also along Route 16, where a number of Haida carvers have set up shop; visitors are asked to please drive carefully through town.

The **Haida Gwaii Museum** holds the world's largest collection of argillite carvings by Haida artists; argillite is a black stone found only at one secret location in the islands. There are also two exquisite totems carved by Haida masters Luke Watson and the late Bill Reid, and a concise but excellent evocation of traditional Haida culture and the islands' unique ecosystem. Admission. ~ Route 16, just east of the ferry terminal, Skidegate; 250-559-4643.

Next door, the **Skidegate Canoe House** holds Loo Taas ("Wave Eater"), a 50-foot canoe carved by Haida craftsmen for Vancouver's Expo '86. ~ Museum Road, Skidegate.

Even though it's right by the road, **St. Mary's Spring** would be easy to miss; keep your eyes peeled on the inland side of Route 16 about a mile (2 km) north of Skidegate. Island legend says

◄ **HIDDEN**

that if you drink from the spring, you will return to the Queen Charlottes.

Tlell, 20 miles (33 km) north on Route 16, is a small settlement of artists and back-to-nature types, situated between a river and a beach; the Richardson Ranch here is the oldest operating ranch in the islands.

Continuing north another 40 miles (65 km) brings you to **Masset,** the major town on the north end of the islands, with a few stores, gas stations and cafés. Old Masset, a mile north of the newer town, is a Haida settlement with a few nice totems decorating front yards; eagles and ravens flock to the shoreline trees here as if to signify their kinship with the descendants of the original human inhabitants of these islands. ~ Masset information, 250-626-3982, fax 250-626-3956; www.massetbc.com, e-mail visitorinfo@massetbc.com.

Delkatla Marsh, along the Tow Hill Road at the east edge of Masset, is a vital stopping point for migratory birds; a short hiking trail leads to viewing points.

If you keep going on Tow Road, you'll reach **Naikoon Provincial Park,** which embraces a spectacular expanse of shoreline and a vast inland terrain of muskeg on the northeast corner of Haida Gwaii's northernmost island. This is an unmatched place for the ordinary visitor to experience the special character of the Queen Charlotte Islands. Wilderness hiking, beachcombing, fishing and biking are among the many activities available here. Wildlife includes dozens of bird species, bear and deer, and small herds of wild cattle. **Tow Hill** is an unusual basalt tower right along the northmost shore of Graham Island, within the park; hikers to the top are rewarded with expansive views of the ocean and Graham Island. ~ Located off of Tow Hill Road, 16 miles (26 km) east of Masset; 250-557-4390.

Heading the other direction, south across Skidgate Channel, is **Sandspit,** the only town on the south (Moresby) island. It is the site of the islands' airport—a wind-tossed strip where planes often make several passes before actually landing—and the other major departure point for Gwaii Haanas. Several cafés, small inns and shops offer visitor services here. ~ Sandspit Visitor Information Centre, airport terminal, Alliford Bay Road; 250-559-8316; www.qcinfo.com.

LODGING   The **Hecate Inn** is a small lodge near the ferry landing in Queen Charlotte City. Its 16 units feature handmade cedar and oak furniture and cable TV; some suites have kitchenettes. ~ 321 3rd Avenue, Queen Charlotte City; 250-559-4543, 800-665-3350, fax 250-559-8788; www.qcislands.net/hecatein, e-mail hecatein@qcislands.net. BUDGET.

Gracie's Place has just five units (three with kitchens) and its friendly charm is as appealing as its eclectic, country antique decor. All of the guest rooms face out on Bearskin Bay and harbor; Gracie herself is a fountain of knowledge about the islands. ~ 3113 3rd Avenue, Queen Charlotte City; 250-559-4262, 888-244-4262, fax 250-559-4622; www.graciesplace.ca, e-mail gracie@qcislands.net. BUDGET TO MODERATE.

◄ HIDDEN

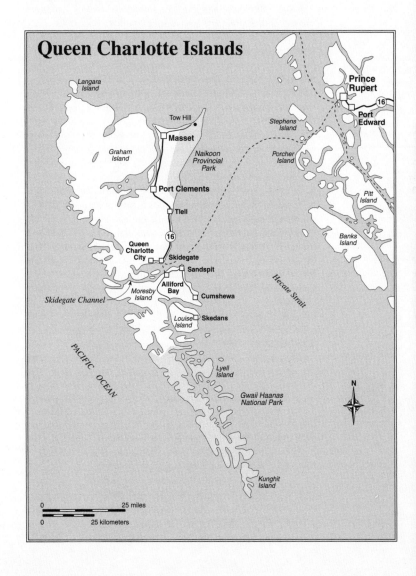

Queen Charlotte Islands

With its 12 rooms in a 1910 heritage building, the two-story **Premier Creek Lodging** is one of the larger accommodations on Graham Island. More like a small inn than a motel, four of the units are kitchenettes with views of the waterfront. Situated in the middle of Queen Charlotte City, it's convenient to the town's shops and cafés. Phones and cable TV bring the rooms up to modern standards. ~ 3101 3rd Avenue, Queen Charlotte City; 250-559-8415, 888-322-3388, fax 250-559-8198; www.qcislands.net/premier, e-mail premier@qcislands.net. BUDGET TO MODERATE.

Moonglow B&B is at the edge of Queen Charlotte City, convenient to the ferry dock but set back off the main road. Its one private room is decorated in country style; the grounds include a creekside walk and small waterfall, with a salmon hatchery. ~ 3611 Route 33, Queen Charlotte City; phone/fax 250-559-8845; www.qcislands.net/moonglow, e-mail sandra@qcislands.net. BUDGET.

HIDDEN ▶ The **Riverside B&B** is located right along the picturesque Tlell River in the artsy enclave of Tlell. The four comfortable rooms, all with private bath, are in a separate house with a shared kitchen. All the rooms have balconies overlooking the river. ~ Richardson Road, Tlell; 250-557-4418, 888-553-5522, fax 250-557-4412; www.qcislands.net/margaret, e-mail margaret@qcislands.net. BUDGET TO MODERATE.

The rustic log home that houses **Cacilia's Bed & Breakfast** is protected from the storms of Hecate Strait by its location back in the spruce forest, but the beach is just a minute away. The seven rooms range from doubles with baths to singles with a shared bath; bargain travelers can put down a sleeping bag in the common area. There's also one rustic cabin available. Kayak and bike rentals are available, and the host offers tour arrangements. ~ Route 16, Tlell; phone/fax 250-557-4664; www.qcislands.net/ceebysea, e-mail ceebysea@qcislands.net. BUDGET.

HIDDEN ▶ **Heron Lane Cottages** are just about as secluded as you can get, set back off a side road east of Masset on the way to Tow

AUTHOR FAVORITE

I marvel at the setting of **Jean's Beach House Bed & Breakfast**, which fronts on miles of unspoiled north shore beach and is backed by old-growth spruce forest. To this Jean adds a sumptuous breakfast and island hospitality. Two in-house rooms with ensuite baths and a small cottage with three more rooms help make the atmosphere cozy and welcoming. ~ Tow Hill Road, 7 miles (12 km) east of Masset; phone/fax 250-626-5662, 888-273-4444. BUDGET TO MODERATE.

Hill. The three cottages sit in a pretty grove of trees along a small creek; the biggest cottage has a loft with two double beds, a full kitchen and full bathroom. The "medium" cabin boasts two bedrooms, a kitchenette and full bath, while the smallest cottage has a double bed and ensuite bath. ~ 285 Heron Road, Masset; 250-626-5640; www.haidagwaiibc.com. BUDGET.

Alaska View Lodge B&B is so-named because, when the weather clears along its McIntyre Bay beach frontage, you can see the islands of Southeast Alaska in the dim distance. Three of the four rooms in the cedar lodge house look out on the ocean; the Swiss proprietors provide a hearty country breakfast to prepare their guests for a day of beachcombing or hiking in nearby Naikoon Provincial Park. ~ Tow Hill Road, seven miles (12 km) east of Masset; 250-626-3333, 800-661-0019, fax 250-626-3303; www.alaskaviewlodge.com, e-mail info@alaskaviewlodge.com. MODERATE.

With cable TV and breakfast included, **Moresby Island Guest House** is not exactly a hostel, but it serves much the same function in the Sandspit area. The ten units range from modest singles and doubles to three family-sized rooms; there's a laundry facility as well. ~ 385 Alliford Bay Road, Sandspit; 250-637-5300; www.moresbyisland-bnb.com, e-mail bnb@whistlerweb.com. BUDGET TO MODERATE.

If the islands have anything you'd call a hotel, the **Sandspit Inn** is it. Located at the airport, with 20 rooms, a gift shop, a dining room and lounge, it's the largest accommodation in the Queen Charlotte Islands. The inn specializes in arranging hunting and fishing packages for guests. ~ 469 Airport Road, Sandspit; 250-637-5334, 800-666-1107, fax 250-637-5340. BUDGET TO MODERATE.

Aside from world-class fishing, luxury is the lure at **Langara Lodge**, an outpost on the far northwest tip of the Queen Charlotte Islands that draws travelers to its exclusive, sumptuous accommodations. Here, anglers enjoy dependable fishing, gourmet meals and comfy amenities such as hot tubs and satellite TV in a wilderness setting. Access is by plane or boat only. ~ 4440 Cowley Crescent #201, Richmond; 604-232-5532, 800-668-7544, fax 604-232-5500; www.langara.com, e-mail info@langara.com. ULTRA-DELUXE.

Queen Charlotte Lodge is in the same general vicinity as Langara, offering similar opportunities in terms of scenery, fishing and accommodations, at a slightly more affordable scale. Gourmet cooking and amenities are still plentiful, and access is by plane or boat only. ~ 7069 Winston Street, Burnaby; 604-420-7197, 800-688-8959, fax 604-420-9194; www.queencharlotte lodge.com. DELUXE.

DINING

HIDDEN ▶

With its scenic location along the winding river, **Tlell River House** is as close as it comes to upscale dining on Graham Island. The seafood-oriented menu is apropos of the waterfront locale; the menu also includes salads, steaks and pastas. Diners can enjoy the outdoor patio in good weather. ~ Beitush Road (about .5 mile/1 km off Route 16), Tlell; 250-557-4211. MODERATE.

In Canada, as in Great Britain, local pubs are often the best places to eat. That's certainly the case at the **Yakoun River Inn**, the tavern in Port Clements (between Tlell and Masset) where residents gather in the evening. The fare is hearty—pizzas, grilled meat and fish, simple salads—and the atmosphere is relaxed. ~ 117 Bayview Street, Port Clements; 250-557-4440. BUDGET.

The setting and the food are equally unfancy at **Marj's Cafe** in Masset; what you get is hearty, unadorned, dependable café food in sizeable portions at economical prices. Breakfasts are suit able for ravenous loggers, so hungry travelers will be sure to leave well-filled. ~ 1645 Main Street, Masset; 250-626-9344. BUDGET.

Haidabucks Café not only offers a good cup of coffee and filling baked goods, it achieved international reknown when it won a lawsuit against Starbucks, which had demanded it change its name, so it was briefly the most prominent institution in the Queen Charlottes. The four young men who opened the café refer to themselves as "bucks," hence the name. ~ 1675 Main Street, Masset; 250-626-5548. BUDGET.

The best place to eat in Sandspit, according to many locals, is the country club. **Willows Golf Course & Clubhouse Restaurant** offers a variety of dishes from ribs to burgers. This is where residents go for dinner, but call ahead for hours. ~ 342 Copper Bay Road, Sandspit; 250-637-2388. MODERATE.

SHOPPING

Isabel Creek Store, across from the Queen Charlotte City Visitor Information Centre, is an excellent place to outfit yourself for a trip into the nether reaches of the islands. Offering natural foods such as organic cheeses, breads and seasonal produce, the store

TRADITIONAL MASTERS

Although there are several stores and galleries in the islands featuring the exquisite work of Haida artists, it's also possible to visit the artists, see and learn about their work and buy directly from them. The best starting place would be the **Skidegate Band Office**, on Front Street in Skidegate; 250-559-4496. Or inquire at the Queen Charlotte City Visitor Information Centre or the Haida Gwaii Museum; the latter carries a very limited selection of Haida jewelry.

is also a local bulletin board/information clearinghouse. ~ 3219 Wharf Street, Queen Charlotte City; 250-559-8623.

With interest in Haida and Northwest Coast First Nations culture growing, **Bill Ellis Books** is an important cultural resource in Haida Gwaii. The store also stocks titles on British Columbia history and natural history; a catalog is available. Closed weekends. ~ 720 Route 33, Queen Charlotte City; 250-559-4681.

Coffee and clothing are the fare at **Dress for Les** (250-557-2023), a unique establishment in Tlell housed in a large pink building. This is the best place on Graham Island to get a cup of coffee or cappuccino, as well as muffins, ice cream and consignment apparel. ~ Route 16, Tlell.

Jade, argillite, gold and silver are the focus at **Crystal Cabin Gallery**, a gift shop just off the main road in Tlell. Apparel featuring Haida designs is also available. Everything here is made by local artists. ~ Richardson Road, Tlell; 250-557-4383.

Aside from designer labels, **Joby's Wear** has apparel by Dorothy Grant, a Haida artist in Vancouver whose clothing incorporates traditional Northwest Coast motifs. Closed Sunday. ~ Skidegate Commercial Centre, Route 16, Skidegate; 250-559-7788.

Eagle Fugitive is the name of the small Skidegate shop that carries the work of Haida craftsman Nelson Cross. Offerings here range from gold and silver jewelry to small totems, original paintings and prints. ~ 225 Skidegate Crossroads, Skidegate; 250-559-0005.

Longhouse Gift Shop has Haida art and jewelry as well as more ordinary souvenirs such as T-shirts and books. ~ 107A Front Street, Skidegate; 250-559-8013.

NAIKOON PROVINCIAL PARK 🚶 🚲 ⛵ ⌣ Spreading across a vast, mysterious and little-traveled expanse of shoreline and muskeg on the northeast tip of Graham Island, this park is the major piece of public land aside from Gwaii Haanas open to Queen Charlotte visitors. Facilities are extremely limited, but Naikoon's otherworldly character demands a visit. ~ Route 16, 24 miles (38 km) from the Skidegate ferry terminal; 250-557-4390.

BEACHES & PARKS

▲ Two developed campgrounds along the main road offer vehicle-borne visitors a spot for the night on Graham Island. Nightly fee at both is C$14; space is very hard to come by during the summer, and visitors are well advised to grab a spot early in the day since it's first-come, first-served only. ~ 250-557-4390.

Misty Meadows, by the park entrance just past Tlell, has 40 spaces in the spruce fringe set back from the beachfront; the meadows are nearby. Privacy is moderate. *Agate Beach*, at the park's north end, has 32 sites that look directly out on the ocean. There's little privacy, but it's a great place to keep your eyes peeled for migrating gray whales and walk the beach looking for agates.

Text continued on page 406.

Islands of Wonder

The islands here overflow with life: lush woods crowd rocky beaches and headlands that lean into clear, fish-filled ocean waters. More than a million seabirds nest in the southern portion of Haida Gwaii (which means "islands of the people"), with many more migratory ones arriving in the spring and fall.

Though windswept and potentially stormy, the climate is surprisingly mild (in summer a temperate 70°F/21°C is normal and in winter it rarely freezes). And though it feels distant from anywhere else on earth, Haida Gwaii has been settled by people for at least 1500 years, possibly as long as 10,000 years.

The Haida made their homes here, fishing the abundant waters and relying on the forest for building materials and just about everything else. They developed woodcarving into a fine art: the totems, canoes and cedar longhouses that in many ways define Haida culture are adorned with intricate animal motifs and mythical beings that represent the personal and collective stories of their makers.

When Europeans began arriving at the end of the 18th century, the delicate balance of traditional life was disrupted. The Europeans brought trade goods in exchange for otter furs supplied by Haida hunters, and after a brief period of increased wealth for select villages, smallpox and other diseases decimated the population. Some villages were wiped out.

During the height of the fur trade, the village at Sgan Gwaii (Anthony Island) erected scores of totem and mortuary poles, reflecting the wealth and importance of the village. Waves of epidemics in the middle of the 19th century wreaked havoc, and by 1884 Sgan Gwaii was empty. Between 1892 and 1957 the village was plundered by successive groups—including curio dealers, ethnologists and museum collectors (in some cases with permission from nearby Haida bands). Yet despite the ravages of the years, this site continues to be the world's best display of Haida totem and mortuary poles, with more than two dozen examples. Remains of massive cedar longhouses also grace the island.

The village of Sgan Gwaii is now a UNESCO World Heritage site, part of **Gwaii Haanas National Park**, which encompasses the southern half of Moresby Island and 137 smaller islands. Gwaii Haanas means "islands of wonder," an appropriate name given the setting. Besides Sgan Gwaii, other ancient Haida villages, many with totems, dot the islands. Among the more notable locales are Skedans, Cumshewa and Hot

Springs Island—the last is a place where visitors can lounge in rock springs near stands of giant spruce as the mist drifts up from the ocean.

Conservation efforts in Gwaii Haanas focus on keeping the remaining totem poles standing. No intrusive measures are used to maintain the poles, which means no preservatives are applied. It is important for visitors to understand that the slow decay of the poles is culturally appropriate to the Haida. The idea is to let nature take its course, only slightly less quickly (fallen poles decompose more rapidly than standing ones). These sites are guarded by the Haida Watch men, a voluntary organization of Haida Nation members who reside at many of the abandoned sites, especially in summer. Visitor protocol demands that absolutely nothing be removed.

Gwaii Haanas is accessible only by private boat or through licensed tours. For private boaters, attention to tides, currents and the ever-changing North Pacific weather is absolutely necessary while traveling among the many passages, inlets and bays of Haida Gwaii.

Visitors not experienced in wilderness boating can reach the remote islands with a licensed tour operator. By traveling on a "mother ship," you can make day trips, returning to the cruise boat at night or when the weather worsens. **Mothership Adventures** is one of the originators of this mode of travel; guests berth on the *Columbia*, a 65-foot former Anglican mission boat, and make day trips into bays and inlets, including First Nations heritage sites. ~ P.O. Box 130, Victoria, BC V8W 2M6; 250-384-8422, 888-833-8887; www.islandnet.com/~momship.

Moresby Explorers ferry kayakers from a houseboat base right to the islands, reducing days of preliminary travel. Ranging from day trips to week-long adventures, you can reach the most out-of-the-way portions of Gwaii Haanas—or simply cruise to a nearby heritage site. ~ 469 Alliford Bay Road, Sandspit; 250-637-2215; www.sandspitqci.com/morex.

Queen Charlotte Adventures offers both luxury cruising and guided kayak adventures in the islands, emphasizing culturally focused trips to the heritage sites in Gwaii Haanas. Fishing charters into the highlands are also available. Packages range from one up to sixteen days. ~ P.O. Box 196, Queen Charlotte City, BC V0T 1S8; 250-559-8990, 800-668-4288, fax 250-559-8983; www.qcislands.net/qciadven.

Because of the sensitive nature of the setting, all visitors to Gwaii Haanas National Park must make reservations and participate in a mandatory orientation session prior to entering the reserve, and keep their visitor permits with them at all times. ~ Park administration, 250-559-8818.

Naikoon also has three wilderness shelters along the park's 30 miles (48 km) of east-facing beachfront. Wilderness camping is possible throughout the park, but Naikoon's inland muskeg environment offers special challenges to hikers and backcountry campers.

PURE LAKE PROVINCIAL PARK This is a pleasant spot for a picnic, or a dip on a hot day. The beach and lake surrounded by spruce muskeg are a two-minute walk from the parking lot. ~ Located just off Route 16 halfway between Port Clements and Masset.

GRAY BAY FOREST SERVICE CAMPGROUND ▲ Basically the only camping option on the south island, this semiprimitive site offers relatively uncrowded camping and miles of unspoiled sandy beach for strolling. Visitors must obtain a B.C. Forest Service campground pass to use the 20 campsites. ~ Located 13 miles (21 km) south of Sandspit along sometimes rough Gray Bay Road; watch for logging traffic.

▼▼▼▼▼▼▼▼▼▼▼▼▼▼

Outdoor Adventures

FISHING

The Queen Charlottes are known worldwide for their salmon and halibut fishing. Two fly-in lodges are situated in remote locations on Graham Island; geared to luxury adventurers with ample budgets, they are not designed to serve the casual traveler. They do offer, because of their remoteness and the sheer number of fish in the area, excellent fishing. **Langara Lodge** offers packages that include air travel from Vancouver, all meals, tackle, boat use and rain gear. The lodge is on its own island at the northwest tip of the Queen Charlottes. ~ 604-232-5532, 800-668-7544, fax 604-232-5500; www.langara.com. **Queen Charlotte Lodge** is slightly more rustic, but serves up similar fare. ~ 604-420-7197.

Island visitors simply wishing to sample a day or two of fishing can make arrangements with a number of local charter operators. During peak months (August and September, when salmon runs are at their height) it's best to reserve ahead if possible. **Cartwright Sound Fishing Charters** specializes in the wild west coast of the islands. ~ 250-637-2276.

GOLF

Windswept, temperamental weather; sandy open shoreline expanses; tricky conditions—that's what golf is like in its Scottish homeland. Island visitors can enjoy a similar environment at the two courses in the Queen Charlottes. Masset's links, the nine-hole **Dixon Entrance Golf & Country Club**, abut a decommissioned Canadian Forces base. ~ Golf Course Road (east of Masset on Tow Hill Road); 250-626-3500. Sandspit's course, **Willows Golf Course**, is a bit more refined than Masset's, with a full clubhouse. ~ 342 Copper Bay Road, Sandspit; 250-637-2388.

Because most travel within the islands is on water and much of the inland area is active timber-cutting territory, hiking options are limited in the Queen Charlottes. Drivers on back roads are cautioned to be alert for log trucks.

HIKING

Distances for hiking trails are one way unless otherwise noted.

Several hikes within **Naikoon Provincial Park** offer the chance for day trips or extended multiday journeys. The trail to **Pesuta Shipwreck** (6 miles/10 km roundtrip) begins at the Tlell River Bridge and winds through forest to the spot where a log barge wrecked in 1928; the bow of the barge is embedded in the sand. Hikers can return along the beach.

The **Tow Hill Trail** (.5 mile/1 km) at the north end of the park leads through magnificent old-growth spruce forest to the top of this basalt monolith, with splendid views of the surrounding ocean and island shore. ~ Located off of Tow Hill Road.

Naikoon's **East Beach** is a 50-mile (82-km) expanse of sand, all wilderness, with three established shelters and numerous other undesignated campsites. Park officials recommend hiking from south to north to avoid catching the prevailing winds in your face. Hikers who reach the north end can return to the road by following the **Cape Fife Trail** (6 miles/10 km) to the Tow Hill Road; this also makes a nice two-day loop hike for backpackers.

The short hike to **Spirit Lake** (1 mile/2 km) brings visitors to a small group of pretty lakes in the foothills above Skidegate. ~ The trailhead is along Route 16 about a mile east of the ferry landing.

▾ ▾ ▾ ▾ ▾ ▾ ▾ ▾ ▾ ▾

Transportation

There are basically just two main roads in the islands, **Route 16** from Queen Charlotte City up Graham Island to Masset; and **Airport Road/Alliford Bay Road** from Alliford Bay to Sandspit on Moresby Island. All other roads are used and maintained largely by the islands' forest products companies, and it's essential that before using them visitors check road conditions locally—preferably with the timber company. Check with the Visitor Info Centre in Sandspit or Queen Charlotte City for further information.

CAR

When driving off the main roads, it's imperative that visitors be alert for log trucks; the island's timber concerns operate larger-than-standard rigs, 16 feet wide. Drivers are careful, but they do have the right of way.

Sandspit Airport is the major airport for the Queen Charlotte Islands, with daily scheduled service year-round (though highly variable during the islands' stormy winter—October through May). Seasonal service is also available to Masset, former home of a Canadian Forces base. **Harbour Air** provides scheduled daily service from Prince Rupert to Sandspit and Masset. (Frequency depends on the season.) Charters and flightseeing trips are also

AIR

available. ~ 250-637-5350, 250-627-1341 (in Prince Rupert), 800-689-4234; www.harbour-air.com.

FERRY

BC Ferries offers scheduled service to Skidegate from Prince Rupert three times a week from October through June, weather permitting, and six days a week in summer. Some crossings are overnight; crossing time is approximately eight hours. Fares range from about C$20 for single passengers up to as much as C$200 for a recreational vehicle. Cabins and staterooms are available at extra charge. Meal service is provided, and passengers can watch a movie in the lounge during the crossing. Reservations are strongly advised, and are absolutely essential during the peak summer travel months. It's best to arrive early to claim your spot; even though the ferry often leaves late, pressure from those trying to get standby passage can be considerable, and it is possible to lose your place on the boat. ~ 250-386-3431, 888-223-3779 (within B.C.); www.bcferries.bc.ca.

The ferry between Alliford Bay and Skidegate (Moresby and Graham Islands) makes 12 crossings a day; fares range from C$4.50 to C$16.

CAR RENTALS

Car rentals are available at the Sandspit airport and in Queen Charlotte City. **Thrifty Car Rental** operates at the airport. ~ 250-637-2299. **Budget Rent A Car** operates at the Sandspit airport and in Queen Charlotte City. ~ 250-637-5688. **Rustic Car Rentals** is a local operation, offering economical rates for cars, trucks and vans. ~ Charlotte Island Tire, 605 Route 33, Queen Charlotte City; 250-559-4641.

ELEVEN

North B.C.

There are more major mountain ranges than there are major roads in North B.C.—more square miles of land than there are people. With just two north–south highways and only one east–west route, this is a vast area—California-size—that's virtually undeveloped and still wild. Region-wide expanses of mountain and forest await the visitor here, along with mammoth parks, lakes and rivers. One of B.C.'s three UNESCO World Heritage sites, Tatshenshini–Alsek, forms the remote northwest corner of this area. The northmost arm of the Rocky Mountains runs up the east side of the region, and the Coast Range on the west side is an imposing, spectacular barrier. The Peace River plain in the northeast corner is B.C.'s major flat expanse, a grain-growing and oil-producing region that's the most distant stretch of the North American Great Plains. This is the land for those who like things big and grand.

Here are thousands of square miles of untouched forest; major river valleys, such as the Stikine, with no roads; entire mountain ranges in which access is limited to foot, horseback, helicopter or floatplane. This is the land of the bears—grizzly and black. Visitors may often see them by the road when driving through on the region's few highways, especially in spring and early summer when the bears savor the young plant shoots that spring up along the roadsides. Moose, caribou, mountain sheep and goats are also common; the woods in summer are a cacophony of birdsongs. The rivers and streams teem with fish.

At Fort St. James, the exceptional national historic park that holds the original 1806 Hudson's Bay Company outpost, the fur barn is filled with a million dollars worth of pelts—beaver, lynx, fox, wolf, bear, marten, cougar, coyote. Restored fur trading outposts throughout North America offer similar sights—but here, living brethren of all those animals still roam free just beyond road's edge. Driving through the North Country, you'd best take seriously the highway signs that depict the dangers of moose crossing the road, and, on the Liard Highway, the wild buffalo that roam the region. And please don't stop in the middle of the Alaska Highway to gawk at all the bears you'll see by the side of the road.

The region's economy is based on the resources that surround human settlements. Prince George, with a dozen major forest-products mills, is the timber industry capital of Canada—sometimes called the last true mill town left in the world. Large-scale gold mines still extract precious metal from the Coast Range highlands; one of these mines is reputedly the most profitable on earth. The oil and gas extracted from the Peace River country has brought a share of Alberta's prosperity to this corner of B.C., as well as the classic downtown "busts" so common in oil country. The much-argued, C$20 billion proposal to build a gas pipeline following the Alaska Highway would bring both jobs and environmental challenges to the region if it bears fruit—although it is competing with a similar plan that would follow the Mackenzie River from the Beaufort Sea to northern Alberta.

The event that formed British Columbia in the mid-19th century was creation of the Cariboo Road from Hope to Barkerville, one of the great engineering accomplishments of the day. It's an achievement that was duplicated 80 years later when military crews forged the Alaska Highway from Dawson Creek to Fairbanks, 1520 miles (2450 km) through frozen wilderness, in an unbelievably quick eight months. The highway, and the ensuing oil development, opened the region up to development and later to travel. Modern highways make this remarkable wilderness accessible to almost all—but the region's character hasn't changed much.

▼▼▼▼▼▼▼▼▼▼▼▼▼

Prince George to Prince Rupert

The southern half of North B.C. is a belt of settlement along Route 16, basically hugging the lowlands of the upper Fraser River and Skeena River drainages. Surrounding this strip of habitation are unspoiled wildernesses containing uncounted lakes and streams—the homeland of the grizzly bear, moose, caribou and world-class salmon and trout fisheries. Forest products have long been the economic mainstay of this region; the industry's prolonged decline has begun to shift cultural and business attention to more renewable industries such as tourism and recreation. In that sense, although Prince George is the largest city in the region, Smithers may be the North B.C. capital of the future.

SIGHTS

Prince George is the capital of North B.C., a city of 80,000 with a university, airport, symphony, theater company and playhouse, art gallery, shopping and visitor facilities and 120 parks. The city's economy is the last major bastion of the timber industry in the province; with 13 major mills, it is Canada's timber capital. Information on the Prince George region is available from **Tourism Prince George.** ~ 1198 Victoria Street; 250-562-3700, 800-668-7646, fax 250-563-3584; www.tourismpg.com.

The **Fraser–Fort George Regional Museum** in Fort George Park includes a comprehensive delineation of the region's colorful history. Closed Monday and Tuesday from mid-October through April. Admission. ~ End of 20th Avenue, Prince George; 250-562-1612; www.museum.princegeorge.com.

Text continued on page 414.

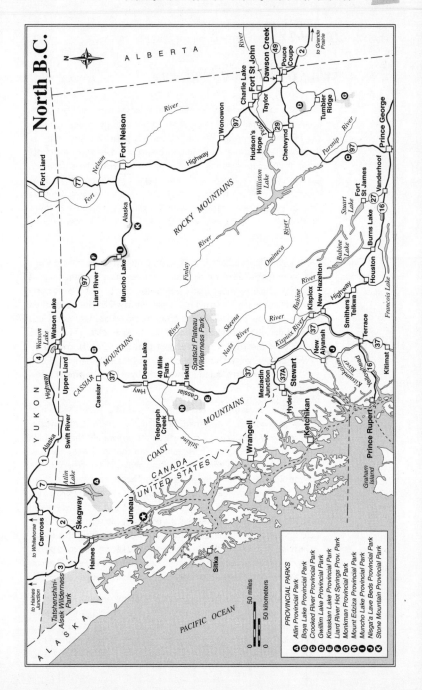

North B.C.

ALBERTA

to Grande Prairie

Fort Liard

Fort Nelson

Fort St John
Charlie Lake
Dawson Creek
Pouce Coupe
Taylor
Hudson's Hope
Chetwynd
Tumbler Ridge

ROCKY MOUNTAINS

Williston Lake

Parsnip River

Prince George

Vanderhoof

Fort St James
Stuart Lake

Burns Lake

Houston

Francois Lake

Smithers
Telkwa

New Hazelton
Kispiox
Kispiox River

Kisgegas

Terrace

Kitimat

Kitsumkalum River

Skeena River

Nass River

New Aiyansh

Meziadin Junction

Stewart
Hyder

Ketchikan

Wrangell

Graham Island

Prince Rupert

PACIFIC OCEAN

Fort Liard

77

Alaska Highway

Watson Lake

4

YUKON

Alaska Highway

1

7

Atlin Lake

to Whitehorse
Carcross

2

Skagway

Haines

3

Tatshenshini-Alsek Wilderness Park

to Haines Junction

ALASKA

Juneau

Sitka

UNITED STATES
CANADA

COAST MOUNTAINS

CASSIAR MOUNTAINS

Telegraph Creek
Stikine River

Dease Lake
40 Mile Flats
Iskut

Cassiar

37 Hwy

Upper Liard

Swift River

Watson Lake

Liard River

97

Muncho Lake

Nelson River

Fort Nelson

Finlay River

Omineca River

Spatsizi Plateau Wilderness Park

Stikine River

Bell-Irving

37

37A

Nass River

Babine River
Babine Lake

Babine Lake

16

27

97

29

49

2

PROVINCIAL PARKS

Atlin Provincial Park
Boya Lake Provincial Park
Crooked River Provincial Park
Gwillim Lake Provincial Park
Kinaskan Lake Provincial Park
Liard River Hot Springs Prov. Park
Monkman Provincial Park
Mount Edziza Provincial Park
Muncho Lake Provincial Park
Nisga'a Lave Beds Provincial Park
Stone Mountain Provincial Park

0   50 miles

0   50 kilometers

Driving the Alaska Highway

Everyone should drive this famed road at least once—and that's sufficient, unless you're like me and do so periodically simply to reach
Liard River Hot Springs. Before you set out, please be sure your car
(including tires) is in good condition; be prepared for snow in almost
any month except July; and bring along a healthy supply of patience.
Construction on the highway is a permanent condition—that's how
it became a modern road. Although there are a few decent lodges
(and one good one), camping is by far the best choice. For more
information on the highway, see pages 431–38 and Chapter Twelve.

Day 1
- Although Milepost Zero is in Dawson Creek, you can start in **Fort
  St. John** (page 433), save two hours and not miss anything (except
  the Mile Zero signpost that seven zillion tourists have previously
  taken pictures of). The road heads past pretty **Charlie Lake**, then
  climbs into low boreal foothills. All those side roads leading off into
  the wilderness access gas and oil facilities; at Mile 271/Km 435
  you'll pass the largest **natural gas plant** in Canada, owned by
  West Coast Energy. This is the economic base in Northeast B.C. If
  you didn't have breakfast in town, stop by **The Shepherd's Inn**
  (page 436) at Mile 72.

- After **Fort Nelson**, the road heads into the4 prettiest stretch of
  aspen parkland you'll see, then climbs up **Steamboat Mountain**,
  the first truly spectacular viewpoint on the highway. At the top (Mile
  333/Km 533) the Rocky Mountains climb the southwest horizon,
  with a vast valley between you and the peaks. The northern fringe
  of the Rockies is the highway's goal; you begin climbing into them
  after Steamboat, winding up at **Summit Lake** at Mile 373/Km 597.
  This sere, windswept spot is the highest point on the highway; if you
  like wind-buffeted campsites, this is a place you can stop for the night.
  Otherwise, I recommend another hour's drive to **Muncho Lake**,
  a high hanging valley in the Rockies, with a glacial lake, towering peaks,
  two campgrounds and an excellent inn (the best between Dawson
  and Whitehorse) called the **Northern Rockies Lodge** (page 436).

- But if you started early enough, and your stamina holds, another 45
  minutes will bring you to **Liard River Hot Springs Provincial
  Park** (page 438) at Mile 477/Km 765. You did call and reserve a
  campsite two weeks ago, didn't you? If so, a dandy spot awaits; if not,
  you're probably out of luck—try Trapper Ray's across the road. Liard's

is the most popular overnight stop on the highway; lounging in the exquisite lower hot pool, you'll converse with folks from all over North America, some of whom are tourists, some truckers, some Alaskans moving south or southerners moving to the Last Frontier.

Day 2 • Yes, you should have another dip in the hot spring before you leave; early morning is exceptionally nice. This is the finest visitor attraction on the highway, and when will you be back? A half hour up the road, take a short sidetrip to see **Smith River Falls** (page 435), an impressive double cataract of booming water. About 16 miles (27 km) after that, at Mile 519/Km 831, **Whirlpool Canyon** is a good spot to have a look at the **Liard River**, which winds through the Rockies and thrusts its way into the subarctic to meet the MacKenzie 800 miles away.

• The highway winds along the Liard, through an immense old burn, climbing a plateau to **Watson Lake** (page 446)—a good lunch stop (Mile 634/Km 1021). If it's hot, have a dip in the cool waters of Lucky Lake two miles east of town. Then have a hamburger at **Archie's** (page 450), spend ten minutes gawking at the famed **Signpost Forest** (page 447)—and head back out on the road.

• The highway dips in and out of the Yukon for hundreds of miles, crossing the last arm of the Rockies, traversing the **Continental Divide** (Mile 722/Km 1162). At Teslin (Mile 804/Km 1282), the **George Johnston Museum** (page 451) has a fine collection of Native artifacts and photos by Johnston documenting early-20th-century T'lingit life in the area. Just past town, the **Teslin Lake viewpoint** (Mile 806/Km 1297) affords an expansive vantage on the southern Yukon terrain—tall barren peaks shadowing ice-blue lakes, with lowland pine forest fringing the highway.

• **Marsh Lake** (page 452) is a couple hours farther on. Here's the place to stop for the night at **Inn on the Lake** (page 454) or **Marsh Lake Campground** (page 456), one of the Yukon government's better such facilities. Whitehorse is just a half-hour farther on—and that's the place to start a Yukon trek. (See Chapter Twelve.)

The **Prince George Native Friendship Centre** includes a gallery devoted to First Nations art, carving and crafts. ~ 1600 3rd Avenue, Prince George; 250-614-7726; www.pgnfc.com.

An hour traveling west along Route 16 brings you to Vanderhoof. The **Vanderhoof Museum** and adjoining heritage complex summarize the area's fairly brief history—although early trappers operated out of Fort St. James, real settlement didn't reach North B.C. until this century. A walkway leads among a series of restored historic buildings, including a bank, early jail, church, hotel/café, barn and telegraph cabin. Open summer only. Admission. ~ Route 16, at the west end of Vanderhoof in the small heritage park.

Even today it's possible to get a hint of the isolation early trappers faced at **Fort St. James**, 35 miles (56 km) north of Vanderhoof. By modern standards this is fairly remote; by 1806 standards it was brutally distant—hundreds of miles from the coast, thousands of miles from any major city. The restored fur barn at **Fort St. James National Historic Park** holds the reason this was here—a fortune (literally) in lynx, wolf, beaver, cougar, buffalo, bobcat, fox and other pelts. Most of the fort's buildings have been refurbished, and local role players depict and explain wilderness life on the shores of massive Stuart Lake. Enter the kitchen of the commandant's house at midday and a redolent pot of beans will be on the fire. This is one of Canada's best heritage sites; it holds the country's second largest collection of historic artifacts. Closed October through April. Admission. ~ Route 27, 35 miles (56 km) north of Vanderhoof; 250-996-7191.

Heading west from Vanderhoof, the road hugs several wide river valleys, a pastoral scene of small farms and homesteads, with occasional small towns and, in the distance, the flanks of the Coast Range. As you near Smithers, the valleys deepen a bit, the mountains crowd closer, and the countryside becomes a bit more alpine in appearance—even though in fact you are losing elevation as you wind down into the Bulkley River valley.

Smithers is an artistic center, a skiing and recreation capital, and an agricultural and commercial hub all in one. Situated in a narrow angle of the Bulkley River Valley, the town sits directly beneath Hudson Bay Mountain, a stunning 8125-foot (2621-meter) snow-draped peak. With many regional government offices and direct air service to Vancouver, Smithers is Northwest B.C.'s most important city after Prince George. The town has adopted a Bavarian village theme, and many downtown buildings are decorated—but not, thankfully, over-decorated—accordingly. ~ Smithers information, 1411 Court Street; 250-847-5072, 800-542-6673; www.tourismsmithers.com.

Just outside Smithers, **Driftwood Canyon Provincial Park** holds one of the most significant fossil beds in North America.

Ranging from 20 million to more than 50 million years old, the shale beds hold plant, animal and insect fossils; the main beds are a ten-minute hike in from the parking area. Fossils may not be removed from the beds. ~ On the Driftwood Canyon Road, six miles (11 km) northeast of Smithers.

About 5 miles (8 km) past Smithers along Route 16 is the Glacier Gulch trailhead that leads to **Twin Falls**, an easy quarter-mile up the trail to a tumbling cascade. The trail continues past the falls a steep three-and-a-half miles to the foot of **Kathlyn Glacier**. ~ The trailhead is located 5 miles (8 km) north of Smithers, just off of Route 16 on Lake Kathlyn Road.

Farther west on Route 16, 20 miles (32 km) from Smithers, park and walk to the viewpoint overlooking **Moricetown Falls**, a narrow chasm in the rocks through which the wide Bulkley River plunges into a deep pool. This has long been a traditional First Nations fishing site, and local Gitksan tribal members still take salmon at the falls during the runs in late summer and fall.

Overall tourism help for the region is available from Northern British Columbia Tourism Association. ~ P.O. Box 2373, Prince George, BC V2N 2S6; 250-561-0432, 800-663-8843, fax 250-561-0450; www.nbctourism.com.

The Skeena River Valley has been the home of the Gitksan people for millennia; like so many B.C. First Nations, they traditionally depended on cedar, salmon and berries for their livelihoods. The Gitksan word *'Ksan* means "between the banks"; the **'Ksan Historical Village** is set right on the banks of the upper Skeena River amid towering cotton-woods and re-creates the Native villages that have stood on this site for centuries. Visitors watch Gitksan artisans at work, and wander among massive totems and longhouses that exemplify the band's craftsmanship. A compact but well-designed museum explains Gitksan culture and lifestyle. With the snowy ramparts of the Skeena Range looming in the southern sky, the site is idyllic. The longhouses at 'Ksan are open to the public only during the frequent tours. Admission for tours. ~ Route 16, near Hazelton; 250-842-5544, 877-842-5518, fax 250-842-6533; www.ksan.org.

Old Hazelton, located just past 'Ksan, is a historic trading post (founded in 1866) with many renovated buildings, including a century-old Anglican church; the two-block downtown now holds several small cafés and shops.

The road north out of Hazelton leads up into the beautiful **Kispiox Valley**, a remote, pastoral area where grizzly bears wander through head-high grass, and salmon and steelhead swarm the river in late summer and fall. Famed for its fishing, the valley is also a friendly, distinctive rural community known for the independent nature of its inhabitants. Near the town of Kispiox, at the foot of the valley, is an enclosure holding 15 superlative

◄ HIDDEN

totems representing the three Gitksan clans—Frog, Wolf and Fireweed—that have lived here for centuries. ~ On the Kispiox Valley Road, 7 miles (12 km) north of Hazelton; 250-842-5248; www.kispiox.com.

Heading southwest from New Hazelton, Route 16 picks up the **Skeena River**, one of the largest in British Columbia and one of just three rivers that cut their way entirely through the Coast Range. The geographic difficulty of that feat is illustrated by the **Seven Sisters**, a jagged, stunning series of sawtooth peaks that rear up from the Skeena Valley southeast of the highway.

Terrace is a regional commercial and industrial center that occupies a wide bench where the Kitsumkalum River joins the Skeena 83 miles (134 km) southwest of Hazelton. The rest of Route 16 from Terrace along the Skeena River to Prince Rupert traverses one of the most awe-inspiring landscapes you're likely to see. Known as the **Rainbow Valley**, it is a narrow passage the river carves through the Coast Range, with shoulders and peaks that thrust up from the valley bottom literally at the edge of the river. As it widens, the Skeena River encompasses ever more of the valley until the road is simply a ribbon squeezed between the flowing water and the toe of the slopes. Each bend in the road brings a new vista into the high country above, where glaciers spill down and freshets of meltwater dangle from cliffs. The showers that skip across the valley leave rainbows behind; the Skeena becomes a mile-wide tidal tongue of water in which floating trees torn from the ground by floods are mere twigs. The cliffs above the road are the province of mountain goats.

Prince Rupert, 90 miles (146 km) west of Terrace, is not only the ferry departure point for the Queen Charlotte Islands, it's a visitor destination in its own right, and the capital of the north coast. The city's claim to fame (and the reason it was founded as a railroad terminus in 1910) is that it's Canada's closest port to

AUTHOR FAVORITE

In downtown Prince Rupert, the **Museum of Northern British Columbia** holds one of Canada's best, if brief, collections of coastal First Nations art, focusing on the totems and carvings that display the distinctively graceful Tsimshian (Skeena) designs. There's a one-of-a-kind cedar mortuary box; and the building itself, made of massive cedar pillars, is quite impressive. The gift gallery presents local artists and carvers; ask about the astounding work of Ron Telleck. Native artisans can usually be found working in the museum's carving shed, a half-block away. Admission. ~ 100 1st Avenue West, Prince Rupert; 250-624-3207, fax 250-627-8009; www.museumofnorthernbc.com.

Asia. Today, timber and mining products, and large cargoes of grain, head out on the Pacific from the port terminal south of the city. ~ Prince Rupert visitor information is 250-624-5637, 800-667-1994; www.tourismprincerupert.com.

Prince Rupert's 15,400 residents play host to an annual influx of 300,000 tourists. Nearby are practically numberless inlets, fjords, rainforest valleys and isolated islands. Southern Alaska is just a few miles away by boat. The downtown section lies along two streets that parallel the waterfront; the B.C. and Alaska Ferries docks are south of town about a mile.

Along the Ridley Island Road, leading to the grain-shipping terminal south of Prince Rupert, is a populist marvel, the **Secret Garden Trail**. A simple path that winds into the woods, it is decorated along the way with dozens of shrines and talismans area residents have placed in honor of loved ones, ranging from beaded bracelets to elaborate tableaus. ~ Located 2 miles (3.5 km) west of Route 16, on the north side of the Ridley Island Road.

Just north of downtown is **Cow Bay**, a rejuvenated historic section so named because long ago it was the home of a dairy. Later it became a maritime center and fell into decay; it's now been revived as a section of small shops, galleries, cafés and restaurants. Travelers who arrive in Prince Rupert well ahead of scheduled ferry departures—which is a good idea—will enjoy a couple hours strolling through Cow Bay, shopping and eating.

◄ HIDDEN

Once the North Coast of B.C. was the salmon cannery capital of the world. Today economic conditions and declining fisheries have shuttered most of the canneries. But, just south of Prince Rupert, Port Edward's **North Pacific Cannery Village Museum** affords visitors a chance to see how cannery life and work were; touring the plant buildings, village store, manager's house, mess hall and company office opens a window on the past. The complex has added a First Nations heritage exhibit, and offers overnight lodging in its old bunkhouse. (See Lodging, below.) Located near the broad mouth of the Skeena River, Port Edward is the oldest surviving North Coast cannery village. Admission. ~ Route 599, 12 miles (20 km) south of Prince Rupert; 250-628-3538.

The **Prince George B&B Association** is a confederation of local bed-and-breakfast inns, all with budget to moderate rates. ~ 250-561-2337, 888-266-5555. The **Bed & Breakfast Hotline** provides a similar service. ~ 877-562-2626; www.princegeorgebnb.com.

LODGING

Guests at **Hawthorne B&B** in Prince George enjoy a library, outdoor hot tub, laundry facilities and off-street parking. The two guest rooms are furnished with antiques and share baths. Gay-friendly. ~ 829 Prince George Pulp Mill Road, Prince George; 250-563-8299. BUDGET.

Chalet Sans Soucie is a large A-frame house set amid 40 quiet acres in southeast Prince George, not far from Route 97. The two units feature down quilts, private and shared bath, a TV lounge and laundry facilities. Golf and tennis are available nearby. ~ 10350 Pooley Road, Prince George; 250-963-7202, fax 250-963-5634; www.princegeorge.com/bnb/chalet.html, e-mail chalet@mag-net.com. BUDGET.

Vindsdalur is an Icelandic word referring to that island nation's unique horses. That's why Lisi and Marcus Ohm chose the name for their riverside guest house near Fort St. James; they breed Icelandic horses on the farm. The house is a handsome two-story log structure, fully equipped, that can sleep up to six. The Ohms also offer summer and winter backcountry tours in the area. ~ Box 1713, Fort St. James; 250-996-6129, fax 250-996-7079; www.vindsdalur.com, e-mail ohm@vindsdalur.com. MODERATE.

The **New Caledonia Motel** is Fort St. James' nicest motel, with fairly quiet rooms toward the back of the motel, some with kitchenettes. Guests enjoy complimentary VCR and movies. The national historic park is about a five-minute walk away. ~ 167 Douglas Avenue, Fort St. James; 250-996-8051, fax 250-996-8061. BUDGET.

The **Stuart Lodge** is a small lakeside resort just outside Fort St. James. Six lakeside cottages have baths, kitchens, TV, barbecue facilities. Boat rentals are available. ~ Stones Bay Road, Fort St. James; 250-996-7917; www.stuartlodge.com. BUDGET.

HIDDEN ► The enormous lake system created to supply hydropower to the aluminum smelter at Kitimat is also an incomparable wilderness gateway. **Nechako Lodge** occupies a dandy toehold at the end of the eastmost lake, Knewstubb, right by Kenney Dam. Comfortable lodge rooms and cabins are set amid a lodgepole forest above the shore; sailing, boating, hiking, fishing and wilderness trekking are among the recreation opportunities. Nechako also maintains a fly-in cabin on a peaceful lake nearby, with excellent trout fishing. ~ At the end of Kenney Dam Road, south of Vanderhoof; P.O. Box 2413, Vanderhoof; 250-690-7740, 877-560-0875; www.rainbowtroutfishing.com. MODERATE.

HIDDEN ► **Tyhee Lake Lodge** is really just one suite in a handsome wood home on the shores of a popular lake outside Smithers. Guests enjoy a private deck, a separate entrance, a kitchen, and a sunny exposure with a spectacular view. There's a canoe for poking along the lakeshore as well as accommodation for horses. ~ Tyhee Lake, just outside Telkwa; 250-846-9636. MODERATE.

HIDDEN ► Aside from being a comfortable, quiet and friendly B&B in a pleasant residential Smithers neighborhood, **Berg's Bed & Breakfast** has one incomparable asset: host David Berg. His background as a school bus driver and Bulkley Valley tour guide means he really knows the territory and can ensure that guests enjoy a top-notch visit to this beautiful area. Two of the three rooms here have views of Hudson Bay Mountain; one has a private bath and a separate entrance, and is just steps away from access to Smithers' excellent valley trail system. ~ 3924 13th Avenue, Smithers; 250-847-5925, 888-847-5925, fax 250-847-5945; www.bbcanada.com/2125.html, e-mail bvtbb@mail.bulkley.net. BUDGET.

For a small motel, the **Stork Nest Inn** has a lot to offer—clean, quiet rooms set back from the highway, with a steam room, cable TV and movies, even a honeymoon suite. All overnight guests get a full continental breakfast. The town's museum and information center are just a block away. ~ 1485 Main Street, Smithers; 250-847-3831, fax 250-847-3852; www.storknestinn.com, e-mail stork nest@telus.net. BUDGET TO MODERATE.

There's only one way to get to **Babine Norlakes Lodge**—over the water (by boat or floatplane). Situated right on the shores of Babine Lake, a well-known fishing and boating area, the lodge offers comfortable amenities in a beautiful setting, with expert fishing guidance. Guests stay in two housekeeping cabins or in the main lodge. Boat rentals and fishing tackle sales are available. ~ Located 70 miles (114 km) north of Smithers; 250-847-6160, fax 250-847-3444; www.babinenorlakes.com, e-mail clegg@babine norlakes.com. MODERATE.

Anglers worldwide know, at least by reputation, the Kispiox River—it's one of the most famous steelhead streams on earth. The **Sportsman's Kispiox Lodge**, right on the banks of the river, naturally caters to anglers, but many other adventures are avail-

AUTHOR FAVORITE

Of all the fly-in wilderness resorts in Western Canada, **King Pacific Lodge** stands out for a variety of distinctions. Its location, in a sheltered bay on spectacular Princess Royal Island, is sublime. The wildlife viewing is exceptional—orcas, humpback and gray whales, sea lions and seals, thousands of birds, and the chance to see the rare, white-phase Kermode bear. Though the lodge downplays consumptive sport, those interested in fishing will find exceptional saltwater and freshwater opportunities. Guest rooms are very comfortable and spacious; a full spa includes sauna, steam and whirlpool; and the cuisine is remarkably good considering the lodge's remote location. Although helicopter and powerboat jaunts are readily available, a relaxing spin around the bay in a lodge kayak is an equally fine endeavor. A visit to KPL is pricey, but yields a lifetime memory. ~ Barnard Harbour, Princess Royal Island; 604-987-5452, 888-592-5464, fax 604-987-5472; www.kingpacificlodge.com. ULTRA-DELUXE.

able, ranging from river floats to wilderness hikes. The lodge's guest cabins (with kitchens and baths) can sleep up to five; rooms in the main lodge have private baths. Dining and lounge facilities provide meals and entertainment. ~ Kispiox Valley Road, 9 miles (15 km) north of Hazelton; 250-842-6455, 888-547-7469, fax 250-842-6458. BUDGET TO MODERATE.

HIDDEN ▶   The best vantage in Prince Rupert belongs to **Eagle Bluff Bed & Breakfast**, which occupies a rambling historic building on the waterfront in Cow Bay. Eagle Bluff's six rooms offer private or shared baths, with nautical-theme furnishings and cooked-to-order breakfasts. Cow Bay's shops and galleries are just steps away. Reservations are a good idea, as this is Prince Rupert's best B&B. ~ 201 Cow Bay Road, Prince Rupert; 250-627-4955, 800-833-1550, fax 250-627-7945; www.citytel.net/eaglebluff, e-mail eaglebed@citytel.net. BUDGET TO MODERATE.

Cow Bay B&B has a sensational location overlooking the tiny historic district in Prince Rupert. The three rooms are in a restored early-20th-century building, and a fireplace, sundeck and harbor views enhance the experience. ~ 20 Cow Bay Road, Prince Rupert; 250-627-1804, fax 250-627-1919; www.cowbay.bc.ca, e-mail info@cowbay.bc.ca. MODERATE.

Once upon a time every town had a rooming house. Prince Rupert still has—**Pioneer Rooms** is located in a historic house just up the street from Cow Bay, and offers inexpensive lodgings, with facilities for light cooking, a barbecue setup in the backyard, bike rentals and laundry services. Rooms are compact and simply furnished, but quiet and clean. ~ 167 3rd Avenue East, Prince Rupert; 250-624-2334, 888-794-9998; www.citytel.net/pioneer. BUDGET.

The **Coast Prince Rupert** is the top hotel in this coastal city, offering 95 clean, modern rooms with air conditioning, free parking, access to exercise facilities, fishing charters and other recreational activities. The ferry terminal is just five minutes away. ~ 118 6th Street, Prince Rupert; 250-624-6711, 800-663-1144, fax 250-624-3288; www.coasthotels.com. MODERATE.

The **North Pacific Fishing Village** was once a residential complex clinging to the banks of the Skeena River, so it makes sense that there is lodging there still. It's more of a dorm than an inn—in fact, the building was originally a bunkhouse—but guests in the 15 sparely furnished rooms get breakfast and the chance to wake up to the sounds of the river. ~ Located 3 miles (5 km) from Port Edward on Skeena Drive; 250-628-3538. BUDGET.

DINING   Prince George may be an old-line mill town, but it has embraced many aspects of modern existence—including brewpubs. **Buffalo Brewing** offers its own ales and lagers, as well as tasty pub food, including burgers and steaks cooked over a wood fire. A sizeable brunch is offered on weekends. ~ 611 Brunswick Street at 6th Avenue, Prince George; 250-564-7100. MODERATE.

Early each morning the local ladies who operate the **OK Cafe**   ◄ HIDDEN
arrive at the historic building they lease in the Vanderhoof Museum heritage complex, fire up the ovens and stoves and start baking pies and breads and making soups. By noon their restaurant is jammed full with local residents who've come for a sandwich, bowl of soup and slice of pie. If you're within 50 miles, you shouldn't pass up the chance to join them—this is real home cooking, such as is often advertised but rarely delivered. Ever had a slice of pie four inches deep? On Friday, the farmers' market next door features homemade and homegrown goodies. ~ Route 16, at the west end of Vanderhoof; 250-567-5252. BUDGET.

The sandwiches are big, the ingredients fresh and the deli items locally made at **Ohm's Gourmet Deli** in Fort St. James. Try the sausages and cheese for dinner; they're North B.C.–made and quite good. ~ 470 Stuart Drive, Fort St. James; 250-996-7522. BUDGET.

The **Logpile Lodge** not only has an enviable location—the   ◄ HIDDEN
restaurant and lodge are ultra-romantic. Set atop a pastoral hill over looking the Bulkley Valley, the views are incomparable; the nightly menu, featuring gourmet contemporary cuisine, matches the scenery. Tables are limited, and dinner is by reservation only. ~ McCabe Road, Smithers; 250-847-5152. DELUXE.

There's nothing fancy at **Louise's Kitchen**, just good, honest Ukrainian and Canadian food. Modest prices and ample portions assure that every diner here gets excellent value—and the homey atmosphere is a plus. ~ 1293 Main Street, Smithers; 250-847-2547. BUDGET.

Any town with as strong a skiing and artistic community as Smithers needs a good coffee shop. **Java's**, at the south edge of the town center, is a roastery that custom roasts the beans it sells

AUTHOR FAVORITE

Gourmet cooking in Prince Rupert? At **Cow Bay Cafe**, that's exactly what you get: delectable Caribbean-flavored dishes based on local seafood, meats and poultry. Chef/owner Adrienne Johnston's blackboard menu changes daily, depending on what she finds at the market that morning. Here you'll find seafood preparations available almost nowhere else—ever had a filet of short-spined thorny-head? The harbor-view setting adds to the ambience. Reservations are highly advisable, as the small café seats only 40 diners at a time. ~ 205 Cow Bay Road, Prince Rupert; 250-627-1212. BUDGET TO MODERATE.

and brews; this is one of the best places to get coffee in all of North B.C. Java's has muffins and pastries, along with the usual soup and sandwiches at lunch. ~ 3735 Alfred Street, Smithers; 250-847-5505. BUDGET.

Situated as it is overlooking the Prince Rupert Harbour, **Smiles Seafood Cafe**'s menu is just what it ought to be—fish, crab, oysters, scallops and shrimp served in almost every way imaginable. The standard seafood platter brings a heap of all the above, with trimmings—perfect for dinner before setting off an overnight passage to the Queen Charlottes. ~ 113 Cow Bay Road, Prince Rupert; 250-624-3072. BUDGET.

HIDDEN ►

With the North Coast's teeming waters just steps away, it's obvious where **Opa Japanese Sushi** gets its daily supply of fresh fish and shellfish. Tucked in a cozy attic overlooking the Cow Bay area, Opa offers made-to-order sushi as well as Japanese noodle and teriyaki dishes. ~ 34 Cow Bay Road, Prince Rupert; 250-627-4560. BUDGET TO MODERATE.

Customers at **Cowpuccino** think so highly of this gourmet coffee outpost that they've sent postcards and snapshots from around the world featuring, naturally, cows of every description. Not only is the coffee good here, the muffins and pastries make for a yummy breakfast, and the store of adventure magazines is unsurpassed. Lunch offerings include soup and sandwiches. No dinner. ~ 25 Cow Bay Road, Prince Rupert; 250-627-1395. BUDGET.

The menu at **Zorba's** is mainstream Greek—spanakopita and lamb shanks—plus pizza and Sri Lankan dishes. It's nothing fancy but very filling, and the service is efficient for those who need to catch a ferry or head to the airport. ~ 715 2nd Avenue West, Prince Rupert; 250-624-6999. BUDGET TO MODERATE.

Naturally coffee is an important part of the rain-spattered lifestyle in Prince Rupert. **Lambada's** is a popular gourmet coffee shop downtown, with gourmet roasts behind its drinks and brewed coffee, and a large selection of muffins and baked goods. ~ 515 3rd Avenue West, Prince Rupert; 250-624-6464. BUDGET.

SHOPPING

Most communities in B.C. embrace a tradition sadly disappearing in the States: the independent bookstore. In Prince George the selection and local emphasis offered at **Books & Company** distinguishes this store from chain outlets; check out the titles on history and lifestyle in North B.C. ~ 1685 3rd Avenue, Prince George; 250-563-6637.

Angelique Levac brings Native artworks from throughout the North Pacific to her store in Prince George, **Angelique's Native Arts**. The focus is on the Northwest Coast, but Inuit and other aboriginal peoples are represented as well. ~ 433 George Street, Prince George; 250-561-2339.

Like most such outlets, **Sportworld** in Smithers not only offers adventure gear for sale or rent—canoes, inline skates, skis, snowboards, snowshoes and such—but up-to-date local information about where to use the equipment. Golf equipment, outdoor apparel, footwear and almost anything else you'd need for fun outdoors is also available. Closed Sunday from mid-April to November. ~ 3711 South Alfred Street, Smithers; 250-847-9333.

Big Smiles focuses on a different sort of art—having fun. This kite, yo-yo and toy store has North B.C.'s largest selection of fun makers for both children and adults. ~ 1191 Main Street, Smithers; 250-847-4004.

The dense swirls and blocks of color of Northwest Coast First Nations art, executed by an expert, are instantly recognizable and much sought after. Gitksan Nation member Ronald A. Sebastian's works are in private collections and museums across North America, Japan and Europe; his studio, **R.A.S. Fine Arts**, is in New Hazelton, where he exhibits the work of other Native artists as well as his own. Gold and silver jewelry, masks, bowls, talking sticks, totems and bentboxes are among the pieces on display. ~ 3379 Fielding Street, just off Route 16, New Hazelton; 250-842-6754.

Prince Rupert's local bookstore is Star of the West, where the shelves hold regional titles as well as bestsellers. There's also a good selection of North Coast maps and guides. ~ 518 3rd Avenue West, Prince Rupert; 250-624-9053.

Prince Rupert's Cow Bay area holds a modest but interesting collection of shops and galleries. **Blue Heron Gallery** is one of the best, exhibiting local artwork, crafts and decorations, with many reasonably priced gifts and mementos. ~ 123 Cow Bay Road, Prince Rupert; 250-624-5700. **Lady Raven's Creative Arts** focuses on First Nations artwork, carving and crafts. ~ 413 3rd Avenue East, Prince Rupert; 250-622-2122.

With 93 inches of rain a year on average, it's obvious why **The Rain Store** does a thriving business. They're ready to outfit visitors who didn't realize that it rains almost every day on the North Coast. They also offer a psychological rain antidote: Belgian chocolate. ~ 28 Cow Bay Road, Prince Rupert; 250-627-1002.

PURDEN LAKE PROVINCIAL PARK

This pretty lake, set in the northern foothills of the Cariboo Mountains, is a half-hour drive east of Prince George. Although the hills around the lake have been logged, a stand of old-growth fir lines the lakeshore. Summer weekends bring crowds to the sandy beach and warm lake waters of this 345-acre park. ~ Route 16, 35 miles (57 km) east of Prince George; 250-964-3489.

BEACHES & PARKS

▲ On the slope above the lake are 78 vehicle/tent sites (12 with tent pads) with good visual separation; C$14 per night.

CROOKED RIVER PROVINCIAL PARK
This 2150-acre park north of Prince George offers a full range of family recreation facilities, including a playground and horseshoe pits. Fishing, swimming and canoeing are favorite activities; powerboats are prohibited. ~ Route 97, 35 miles (57 km) north of Prince George; 250-964-3489.

▲ There are 90 vehicle/tent sites set in a lodgepole pine forest; C$14 per night.

SOWCHEA BAY RECREATION AREA
This is the nicer of the two parks along the southern shore of Stuart Lake outside Fort St. James. Set in a pretty birch and fir forest, the sand-and-gravel beach affords an inspiring vista across the lake to Mount Pope. ~ Located 5 miles (8 km) west of Route 27, south of Fort St. James; 250-964-3489.

▲ There's moderate visual separation at the 30 lakeshore sites; C$10 per night.

TYHEE LAKE PROVINCIAL PARK
With ample sandy beaches, a beautiful aspen forest and generally good summer weather, this park near Smithers is a popular recreation site. Swimming and sunbathing lure many here; anglers have a sporting chance to catch rainbow trout. ~ Located 1 mile (2 km) north of Route 16, Telkwa; 250-847-7320.

▲ There are 59 vehicle/tent sites set back off the lakeshore; C$20 per night.

HIDDEN ▶   **MORICETOWN CAMPGROUND** Operated by the local First Nations band, this campground occupies a quiet site on a bench above the Bulkley River, with a fabulous view of Hudson Bay Mountain across the valley. The Moricetown Falls are situated just below the campground. ~ 162 Telkwa High Road (half-mile off Route 16), Telkwa; 250-847-1461.

▲ There's no privacy at the 56 sites; C$12 to C$20 per night.

A SHOE TREE?

Prince Rupert is the home of one of the most unusual sights in B.C.: the **Shoe Tree**—a dead tree trunk on which dozens of pairs of shoes, boots, sandals and other footwear have been hung. "Hope for Lost Soles," the sign advertises. This is actually version number two of the idea—the original is near Port Hardy, and the idea has now cropped up in locales as distant as California and Texas. You can find Prince Rupert's Shoe Tree on Route 16, 3 miles (5 km) southeast of town, on the east side of the road.

'KSAN CAMPGROUND The broad tongue of land where the Bulkley and Babine rivers meet is a grassy vale shaded by tall cottonwoods. Here the summer sun shines warm and the air is touched by the sound of the two rivers; for centuries the Gitksan people have lived here, and the Hazelton Band has made part of this spot into the campground, one of the nicest in North B.C. Located just a few yards from the 'Ksan Historical Village, it's a remarkably peaceful place. ~ Route 16, next to 'Ksan Historical Village, Hazelton; 250-842-5297; www.ksan.org.

▲ The 60 spaces—the best, for tents only—are right along the Babine River; C$15 to C$20 per night.

KLEANZA CREEK PROVINCIAL PARK Once this side canyon in the Skeena Valley lured gold-seekers; a trail from the park campground leads upstream to old placer mining works. Today it's a pleasant, secluded campground along rushing Kleanza Creek, which offers good fishing in spring and fall. ~ Located 11 miles (18 km) east of Terrace, just off Route 16; 250-847-7320.

▲ The 32 vehicle/tent sites are all fairly close to the access road and not well screened; C$14 per night.

EXCHAMSIKS RIVER PROVINCIAL PARK Set in a grove of lofty old growth spruce trees, this park is basically a campground along Route 16—one of B.C.'s more attractive roadside provincial parks. It is off the main road a few yards, next to its namesake river, and the spruce grove and mountain shoulders looming across the river lend it a welcome natural atmosphere. It's a popular spot for fishing and boating, too. ~ Located along Route 16, 33 miles (54 km) west of Terrace; 250-847-7320.

▲ All 18 vehicle/tent sites are well shaded; C$14 per night.

PRUDHOMME PROVINCIAL PARK It's on a lake, yes, but the utility of this park near Prince Rupert seems to be as a place to spend the night for camping travelers before boarding the ferry for the Queen Charlotte Islands. Even so, kayaking, canoeing and boating are possible here, and fishing for rainbow trout can be fruitful. ~ Located along Route 16, 9 miles (15 km) east of Prince Rupert; 250-847-7320.

▲ Some of the 24 vehicle/tent sites have moderate exposure to the highway; C$14 per night.

Cassiar Highway

The Cassiar Highway, Route 37, is a famous thread of road through the North B.C. wilderness that stretches more than 400 miles (645 km) from the Yellowhead Highway near Hazelton to the Alaska Highway in the Yukon. The route follows part of an ancient First Nations grease trail; today all but about 80 miles of the road are paved, although drivers will frequently encounter rough and broken road surfaces.

This isn't a journey to be rushed, anyhow; the road penetrates B.C.'s deepest wilderness, with thousands of square miles of untracked territory on either side. Sights along or near the highway include the Nass River, Stikine River, Mount Edziza and Spatsizi Plateau wilderness parks, Dease Lake and River, and the Cassiar Mountains.

SIGHTS

Halfway between New Hazelton and Prince Rupert on Route 16 is the junction town of Terrace. From here you can follow the Kitsumkalum River road 55 miles north to the Nass Valley, site of Nisga'a Lava Beds Provincial Park (see page 431 for more information).

Continuing north past New Aiyansh brings you back to Route 37 at Cranberry Junction. From here, Route 37 heads north, and at Meziadin Junction Route 37A branches off west to **Stewart**, diving down a narrow, mountain-ringed valley where glaciers reach the road. At the end is the Portland Canal, one of the longest Northwest Coast fjords and the basis of the town's existence. Once a booming mining town with 10,000 residents, Stewart is now a fishing and forest industry center and Canada's northernmost ice-free port. Rugged mountains and impassable wilderness on all sides have drawn several film crews to this location.

Hyder, Alaska, just across the border from Stewart, is a vivid example of how tacky American backwaters can be. With sagging, unpainted, decaying buildings, the town's claim to fame is the fact that it has no law enforcement—at one point, an enterprising resident set up shop, offering visitors the chance to fire machine guns at a makeshift shooting range. A short drive up the only other road leading out of Hyder, along the Salmon River, brings you to a spot where grizzlies come to feast on fall-run salmon. U.S. wildlife officials have built a boardwalk here, three miles northeast of the town, to try keeping bears and tourists separate and peaceable.

Back on the main trunk of the Cassiar Highway, the stretch from Meziadin Junction to Stikine reminds you why this journey is still an adventure. You climb into a series of high river valleys, winding up in the Iskut. Vast expanses of forest stretch off into the distance. Black bears appear along the road grubbing up green shoots. The peaks of the Coast Range and the Skeena Mountains flank you for much of the distance. The road shifts from blacktop to gravel again and again, and there's absolutely nothing to signify human development except the road, passing cars, and a few isolated way stations.

Route 37 only crosses the **Grand Canyon of the Stikine** at one spot—and that's the only place a road approaches one of North America's deepest and most spectacular gorges. An exotic and highly rigorous destination for river runners who have vast experience and little fear, the canyon is only for veteran wilderness trekkers. At one point near the Tanzilla River confluence, legend has it (few people have ever actually been there, as technical rock-climbing skills are needed to reach it) this vast river crashes through a gap the top of which is just seven feet (two meters) wide! BC Hydro floated a proposal to build one of the world's highest dams in this wilderness, but stiff environmental opposition scuttled the idea. A provincial recreation area now encompasses the canyon, preserving this haunt of mountain goats, eagles and adventurers.

Allow two days to drive the entire length of the Cassiar Highway (Route 37) with no sidetrips.

The canyon recreation area embraces the Stikine between Spatsizi Plateau Wilderness Park and Mount Edziza Provincial Park; however, the Grand Canyon itself begins approximately 15 miles (25 km) west of the Cassiar Highway. A put-in point for boats on the highway is at **40 Mile Flats**, 160 miles (257 km) north of Meziadin Junction. The sign provincial officials have placed here isn't kidding: *The canyon is only for world-class wilderness river experts.*

Another 40 miles (65 km) north of 40 Mile Flats, **Dease Lake** is a high-country center that's about halfway along the Cassiar Highway, providing full visitor services. Gas stations, motels and truckstop cafés line the highway; a very small residential area to the west of the main road attests to the remoteness of this region—there just aren't many people out here.

Once upon a time, for a brief shining moment, **Telegraph Creek** had reason to believe it would take its place on the world stage. The new gold camps in the Yukon needed communications to the outside world; a telegraph line was strung from this spot—the limit of navigation on the Stikine River—hundreds of miles northward into the Yukon. But the gold rush faded, shorter and easier routes were found into the interior, and Telegraph Creek today is probably the most remote spot in British Columbia reachable by road.

◄ HIDDEN

And what a road it is—almost 100 miles of gravel from Dease Lake, first crossing a high ridge with the peaks of Mount Edziza Provincial Park in the distance, then diving down into the lower Stikine River Canyon. At one point the grade is 20 percent; narrow passages along canyon walls have no guard rails; switchbacks angle sharply. It's not for nervous drivers in Winnebagos—a popular T-shirt says, "I wrote my will, then I drove the hill." It is well maintained, however, and an incomparably scenic drive into one of North America's most spectacular canyons. When you get there, Telegraph Creek itself is a friendly, quirky jumping-off point for wilderness adventure. There's one inn and a remote guest ranch. (See Lodging, below.)

From Dease Lake north, Route 37 winds another 150 miles (242 km) or so through the **Cassiar Mountains**, passing the now-closed asbestos mining site at Cassiar, and dropping down into taiga forest to cross into the Yukon. Once you're in the Yukon, Route 1 takes you west; a day's drive will bring you to Route 7, which follows Atlin Lake south, back into British Columbia. At the end of the road is **Atlin Provincial Park**, a wide roadless expanse of mountain peaks and glaciers surrounding the southern portion of Atlin Lake. (See Chapter Twelve.)

The 90-mile-long Portland Canal in Stewart is the world's fourth-largest fjord.

If, instead of taking Route 7 south you stay on Route 1 and continue west for another day, you can head south on Route 3 from Haines Junction. This way takes you back across the B.C. border and skirts the edge of **Tatshenshini–Alsek Wilderness Park**, the province's least developed, most inaccessible park. This is a craggy region of mountains, lakes and glaciers that includes 15,500-foot (4725-meter) Fairweather Mountain (the highest point in B.C.) and abuts Alaska's Glacier Bay National Park.

LODGING

HIDDEN ►

The raw material for the spacious, sturdy log home that houses **Miles Inn** came from the property surrounding it. This superbly made, exquisitely comfortable B&B is just past Nisga'a Lava Beds Park in the Nass Valley, and looks out on a spectacular vista embracing the valley and the Coast Range beyond. All four rooms have private baths; the lower-level hot tub has a view of the valley. ~ New Aiyansh; 250-633-2636, 800-553-1199, fax 250-633-2699; www.kermode.net/milesinn, e-mail milesinn@ kermode.net. BUDGET TO MODERATE.

Set above the Cassiar Highway on a lodgepole pine-covered bench, **Willow Ridge Resort** is a traveler's rest near Iskut, in the Skikine River area, with an intriguing mix of accommodations— three cottages, three larger cabins, six tent pads and 13 RV spaces. There's a store, showers and laundry—and the highway bustle is far below. ~ Iskut; 150 miles (260 km) north of Meziadin Junction; 250-786-5859, fax 250-786-5809, radio phone JJ37280, Bob Quinn Channel, Whitehorse operator. BUDGET.

Bear Paw Resort is a log lodge with 12 guest suites overlooking the foothills of Mount Edziza Park. There are also eight guest cabins of various descriptions, and recreational activities ranging from trail rides to fishing. The dining room and saloon entertain guests in the evening, and the hot tub and sauna soothe the day's ills afterward. ~ Iskut; 250-234-3005. BUDGET TO MODERATE.

Set along a bench lake in the high country on the Cassiar Highway approaching Dease Lake, **Tatogga Lake Resort** is a self-contained oasis in the spectacular north end of the Skeena

Mountains. With a main lodge, housekeeping cabins, showers, laundry facilities, gas and tackle sales, it's equally suited to be a destination or a staging point for trips into nearby Spatsizi, Mount Edziza and Stikine River wilderness parks. ~ Iskut; 250-234-3526. BUDGET TO MODERATE.

Of the several highway motels in Dease Lake, the **Northway Motor Inn** is the nicest, set back a bit from the highway to cut down on the noise. Its 46 units include kitchenettes, TVs and plug-ins for winter travelers. ~ Route 37 and Boulder Street, Dease Lake; 250-771-5341, fax 250-771-5342. BUDGET TO MODERATE.

Considering it's the only accommodation in a place as remote and unique as Telegraph Creek, **Stikine Riversong Lodge** should be equally distinctive—and it is. The main lodge is housed in a handsome century-old Hudson's Bay Company warehouse; the five guest rooms upstairs share a kitchen and guest lounge. Two more self-contained units are nearby in an old rooming house. The river is just a few steps below the lodge; ask for one of the rooms along the front so you can throw open a window and listen to the Stikine surge past. The lodge is Telegraph Creek's only restaurant. It's also a supply store, and owner Dan Pakula is a warehouse of knowledge about the Stikine River Valley, its ecology and its history. ~ Telegraph Creek; 250-235-3196; www.stikineriversong. com, e-mail info@stikineriversong.com. BUDGET.

◄ **HIDDEN**

Along the Cassiar Highway, the best places to eat—in fact, usually the only options—are the lodges that provide accommodation.

DINING

MEZIADIN LAKE PROVINCIAL PARK 🚶 🚴 ⛱ 🛶 🚤 ⚓
Along the shores of a cold, high-country lake just off the Cassiar Highway, this 830-acre park serves as much as a stopover as it does a recreational center. Frequent bear incursions have prompted park officials to leave a bear trap parked near a picnic shelter with a sign sternly warning visitors not to block access to the trap. The lake is an ice-blue body of water set up against a stone cliff. ~ Route 37, Meziadin Junction; 250-847-7320.

BEACHES & PARKS

▲ The 62 vehicle/tent sites have virtually no privacy; C$14 per night.

KINASKAN LAKE PROVINCIAL PARK 🚶 🚴 ⛱ 🛶 🚤 ⚓
Set against the flanks of Mount Edziza Provincial Park and providing trail access into the larger park (you walk 15 miles/24 km from here to the boundary of Mount Edziza Park), this 4500-acre roadside park draws both travelers and recreational visitors. Its blue glacial lake is famed for trout fishing; nearby trails offer excellent hiking and mountain biking. ~ Route 37, 132 miles (213 km) north of Meziadin Junction; 250-847-7320.

▲ There are 50 vehicle/tent sites with pretty good privacy; C$14 per night.

MOUNT EDZIZA PROVINCIAL PARK 🚶 🐎 ⛵ Volcanic eruptions over the past four million years have created an otherworldly landscape that includes uniquely colored mountains and a perfectly formed cinder cone. The park is famed for its iron-red dirt expanses above timberline; numerous pristine mountain lakes add to the attractions. There are no facilities in this wilderness park (and no fees) and hiking is only for the experienced. Access is by hiking from Kinaskan Lake or Telegraph Creek, or by chartering a floatplane from Dease Lake or Telegraph Creek and landing in one of the park's larger lakes. ~ Located 10 to 60 miles (16 to 100 km) west of the Cassiar Highway.

▲ Wilderness camping only; no fee.

SPATSIZI PLATEAU WILDERNESS PARK 🚶 🐎 🛶 ⛵ This 1.5-million-acre preserve east of the Cassiar Highway is known especially as a destination for backcountry canoe trips on wilderness lakes that are about as far as you'd ever expect to get from paved ground. You can take a chartered floatplane to Tuaton Lake, put in your canoe at the headwaters of the Stikine River and follow the Stikine 150 miles (243 km) downstream to a pull-out point where the river crosses the Cassiar Highway. Or, if you'd rather keep your feet on the ground, you can take a circuit hike through the park to the headwaters of the Stikine River and back, which encompasses roughly 120 miles (195 km) and takes at least a week, providing an unparalleled wilderness experience; the main trailhead is on the Klappan River Road (not for passenger cars) 25 miles east of Tatogga. This park, like Mount Edziza, is only for wilderness experts or clients of experienced guides. Access is by foot or floatplane only. Visitors are advised to contact BC Parks officials before entering Spatsizi Park. ~ Located 15 to 100 miles (25 to 162 km) east of Route 97; 250-847-7320.

▲ There are eight cabins at one of its lakes reserved for first-come, first-served use, plus a cookhouse; fees and permits range from C$20 to C$35 per night, depending on length of stay and cabins used.

BOYA LAKE PROVINCIAL PARK 🚶 🚴 🐎 🛶 ⛵ ⛵ 🚤 ⛵ Set in lodgepole/aspen forest at the toe of the Liard River Plain, this 11,500-acre park is the nicest provincial park along the Cassiar Highway—unfortunately, it's also the most distant. Wildlife abounds around the blue-green waters of the lake, which draws thousands of migratory birds each summer. Fishing and boating entertain visitors; the park is well off the highway, so it's blissfully peaceful. ~ Located 58 miles (94 km) south of the Alaska Highway junction along Route 37; 250-847-7320.

▲ There are 44 very nice vehicle/tent sites along the lake; C$14 per night.

TATSHENSHINI–ALSEK WILDERNESS PARK 🏃 🛶 🚗 The new crown jewel of the BC Parks system, Tatshenshini–Alsek is a two-million-acre preserve that, together with Alaska's Glacier Bay National Park and the Yukon's Kluane National Park, forms the largest international wilderness preserve on earth. The park encompasses most of the extreme northwest tips of B.C., an odd tongue of land that occupies a mountainous region north of Alaska's Glacier Bay. The park's centerpiece is the famed Tatshenshini Canyon, a vast gorge that was saved from a mining scheme by international conservation pressure in the early 1990s. There is no road access to Tatshenshini–Alsek; Route 3, from Haines, Alaska, to Dawson City, Yukon, forms its easternmost border. Raft trips down the Tatshenshini are the most common method of visiting; permits for river trips must be obtained from Glacier Bay National Park officials in Alaska. For information on visiting the park, and on tour operators who lead trips through it, contact BC Parks at 250-847-7320.

Alaska Highway

The North Country sends its thick forests down into B.C. from the Yukon in an intriguing land where the Great Plains of North America reach their last, northernmost extent. Here there are big rivers—the Peace and Liard—long, long roads (the Alaska Highway); endless forests; spectacular mountains; and enormous oil and gas fields that today provide the underpinnings of the northeast B.C. economy.

SIGHTS

Hundreds of miles from Tatshenshini–Alsek, across British Columbia near the eastern border of the province, is **Dawson**

AUTHOR FAVORITE

The last major volcanic eruption in B.C. took place in 1775 when Tseax Cone spewed lava in a wide fan along the Tseax and Nass River valleys. **Nisga'a Lava Beds Provincial Park**, jointly managed by the province and the Nisga'a First Nation, is a sparsely vegetated moonscape set in a scenic coastal valley; the only road leads right through the lava beds, with several roadside interpretive areas. Further development of campgrounds, an interpretive center and other visitor amenities is planned. ~ Located 55 miles (90 km) north of Route 16 from Terrace; or an equal distance west of Route 37 along Nass Valley Road; 250-847-7320.

Creek, the start—Mile Zero—of the **Alaska Highway,** one of the world's legendary engineering feats. When the outbreak of World War II made it imperative that Canadian and U.S. military forces have overland access to Canada, engineers began forging north from Dawson Creek through deep forest, limitless plain, frozen tundra and forbidding mountains, reaching Fairbanks in just eight months, an almost unimaginable accomplishment.

For information on the Alaska Highway and the region, call the **Northern Rockies Alaska Highway Tourism Association.** ~ 9923 96th Avenue, Fort St. John; 250-785-2544, 888-785-2544; www.northeasternbc.com, www.hellonorth.com.

The road wasn't opened to civilians until 1948, and was known for years for the terrors it presented to vehicles and drivers. Now it's a popular weeks-long vehicle trek, undertaken each summer by caravans of lumbering recreational vehicles that couldn't have made it ten miles on the old Alaska Highway. It's still not effortless freeway, however. (See Transportation, below.) Several comprehensive guidebooks to driving the route are available in travel bookstores; one, *The Milepost* (Alaska Research Company), is updated annually.

Before highway engineers ever cast eyes on the endless forests northward, Dawson Creek was a commercial and shipping center for the homestead farms of the Peace River plains. ~ For Dawson Creek visitor information, call 250-782-9595.

A number of heritage buildings from those days in the early 20th century have been moved to Dawson Creek's **Walter Wright Pioneer Village** at the northwest edge of town. Two old schools, several old homes, two churches and various other buildings make up a fairly complete "town" set on a prairie much like the one that drew early settlers. A small adjacent lake offers warmweather

ON THE ALASKA HIGHWAY

Be aware: The milepost numbers and kilometer distances are highly flexible things. In the first place, some establishments that have been on the highway for years keep their original designations, even though the actual distances have changed—a gas station known as "708" may actually be at Mile 675, for instance. Why? Highway improvement over the years has shortened things considerably; and the government distance measurements in Canada are in kilometers; so our theoretical gas station is actually at Km 1088. Secondly, distances are still changing as ongoing highway upgrades straighten out old curves. Although entertaining, this is not really a big problem—almost everything on the Alaska Highway is, indeed, right on the highway. The few significant things that are off the highway are well signed.

swimming. Admission. ~ Along Route 97, 2 miles (3 km) from the center of Dawson Creek; 250-782-7144.

From Dawson Creek it's a mere 45 miles (75 km) north to **Taylor,** a pretty town set down in the Peace River bottomland; a benign climate (by north country standards) allows farmers here to grow summer vegetables including corn. Late-summer visitors should duck off the highway on the southeast end of town to visit the many produce stands. Taylor's economy depends on a major timber mill and a gas processing plant. The **Taylor Info Centre** is a helpful resource. Closed mid-September to mid-May. ~ 250-789-9015 (summer), 250-789-3392 (winter).

Peace Island Regional Park is a small enclave on a wooded island in the Peace River. The island, connected to shore by a causeway, draws locals to its picnic and camping areas for summer weekend gatherings. During the week you might have the place to yourself. Fishing, swimming, strolling along the nature trails or simply staring at the water are pleasant possibilities here. ~ Off Route 97, just south of Taylor; 250-789-9295.

◀ HIDDEN

Fort St. John, situated about 5 miles (8 km) past Taylor, is an oil industry center; you'd guess that from the large derrick in front of the town's museum. Visitor services are minimal—this is a working town. The **Fort St. John & District Chamber of Commerce** has brochures, maps and advice. Closed Saturday and Sunday. ~ 9923 96th Avenue, a half-mile north of Route 97, Fort St. John; 250-785-6037, fax 250-785-7181; www.fortst johnchamber.com.

The **Fort St. John–North Peace Museum** provides a fascinating look at the area's history, including the evidence of habitation 10,500 years ago, early European exploration and settlement, and the first oil strike that brought the region its current economic base. Closed Sunday in winter. Admission. ~ 9323 100th Street, Fort St. John; 250-787-0430; collections.ic.gc.ca/ north_peace.

West of Fort St. John, in the foothills of the northern Rockies, two giant hydro dams supply almost 40 percent of B.C.'s electric power—some of which, in summer, is exported far south to California and Mexico. The **WAC Bennett Dam,** named after a former B.C. premier, is the largest in B.C.; the 235-mile (378-km) lake behind it is the ninth-largest such reservoir in the world. Even with the volumes of snowmelt in the mountains to the west, five years passed before it filled in 1973. The dam's visitor center explains its huge power production but hardly mentions the vast mountain valley that was lost forever beneath the water. Below the Bennett Dam, the **Peace Canyon Dam** is a "river-run" structure (no true reservoir behind it) that also produces significant amounts of power. ~ Dam Access Road, 14 miles (23 km) west of Hudson's Hope.

The road from the Peace River country to Fort Nelson offers a look at the true north country—and at what effect human activity has had on it. Here are endless miles of trees—birches, cottonwoods, spruce and lodgepole—stretching off across the broad high plain to the horizon. It seems trackless and impenetrable until you notice that survey lines have been literally cut through the forest at mile intervals, banding the wilderness for the convenience of oil and gas exploration. Look closer, and you'll notice dozens of wellheads, pipeline markers and even a few drilling rigs, extracting the wealth from beneath the surface.

By the time you reach **Fort Nelson** at Mile 300 of the Alaska Highway (255 miles/412 km north of Fort St. John), you wonder if there is a number large enough to count the spruce and lodgepole pine trees you've seen in the endless taiga along the Alaska Highway. Fort Nelson is a small commercial center, with several highway motels and nondescript cafés, and a staging point for visitors to Stone Mountain and Muncho Lake provincial parks, two gems of the Northern Rockies.

At Mile 393 of the Alaska Highway you reach **Stone Mountain Provincial Park**, in the northernmost section of the Rocky Mountains and a place where you're almost guaranteed to encounter animals—large herds of caribou, moose and Stone sheep roam the area. ~ Located 93 miles (150 km) west of Fort Nelson.

Muncho Lake Provincial Park is another ideal spot for seeing wildlife and walking into the mountains. Muncho Lake itself is a sparkling destination for boaters and north country anglers. ~ Mile 456 of the Alaska Highway.

The traveler's reward for the seemingly endless miles of the first leg of the Alaska Highway comes at **Liard River Hot Springs**, reachable in a very long day, or two shorter legs, from Dawson Creek. Here one of North America's finest hot springs beckons, with a provincial park campground, a couple of lodges, and utter relaxation. Beyond this spot the highway winds through the Liard River country, passing by one of the largest

AUTHOR FAVORITE—SIGHTS

I'm often asked what my favorite place is in British Columbia; as often as not, I say **Liard River Hot Springs**. The experience of a leisurely, long hot soak in the spring, surrounded by beautiful northern forest, is incomparable—and the chance to visit with other travelers along the Alaska Highway is unforgettable. The companion provincial park campground is one of the most popular in B.C. so advance reservations are crucial to get the most out of a stop here. See above for more information.

forest-fire burn areas in B.C.—a 1982 blaze consumed more than 400,000 acres. Nature's regenerative powers are evident in the new forest springing up. ~ Mile 496 of the Alaska Highway.

About 19 miles (30 km) past Liard River, a short road to the north leads to **Smith River Falls**, a spectacular 50-foot-tall double cataract reached by a short hike from the parking lot. If the campground at Liard Hot Springs is full, this could be an emergency overnight stop as well.

◀ *HIDDEN*

From the hot springs it's still about 100 miles (160 km) along the Liard River to the Yukon border and the town of **Watson Lake**. Just past Watson Lake, the Cassiar Highway meets the Alaska Highway for travelers wishing to return to B.C. down this scenic westernmost route.

The Alaska has been serving Alaska Highway travelers for decades; in fact, the building, originally the Dew Drop Inn, was built in 1930, pre-dating the highway. Its 18 renovated rooms are on the second and third floors above the bustling restaurant and pub; simply furnished, Hotel Alaska offers lodging just steps away from the Mile Zero marker of the highway. ~ 10209 10th Street, Dawson Creek; 250-782-7998, fax 250-782-6277; www.alaskahotel.com, e-mail info@alaskahotel.com. BUDGET.

LODGING

You know you're in the north country when a motel provides winter plug-ins for engine-block heaters. The **Northwinds Lodge** in Dawson Creek is set a block off the main highway and offers 20 clean, quiet units (some with kitchenettes), complimentary coffee and plenty of room for parking large rigs. ~ 632 103rd Avenue, Dawson Creek; 250-782-9181, 800-665-1759, fax 250-782-6733. BUDGET TO MODERATE.

Paradise Lane B&B is situated on a small bluff overlooking Charlie Lake, outside Fort St. John. Guests can choose from a self-contained cottage or a suite (both have private baths), or an in-house room with a shared bath; a fireplace, in-room coffee, and canoe and paddleboat rentals nearby are other amenities. ~ Paradise Lane, Charlie Lake; 250-785-7477; e-mail paradiseln_bb@awink.com. BUDGET TO MODERATE.

◀ *HIDDEN*

Crystal Springs Ranch enjoys a splendid location along the Halfway River in the Rocky Mountain foothills, 50 miles (80 km) north of Fort St. John. This working ranch welcomes small groups of guests to four cozy log cabins with showers, kitchen facilities and unlimited peace and quiet. Trail rides, fishing on the ranch, canoeing and kayaking keep guests occupied. ~ Road 117, 30 miles (49 km) from Route 97, Wonowon; 250-772-5018; e-mail csr@mail.pris.bc.ca. BUDGET TO MODERATE.

◀ *HIDDEN*

The **Bluebell Inn** is the nicest motel in Fort Nelson, right along the highway as you come into town from the south. Its 46 units offer air conditioning, phones, cable TV, and some kitchenettes, plus laundry facilities. There are also some RV sites. ~ 50th Avenue and Route 97, Fort Nelson; 250-774-6961, 800-663-5267, fax 250-774-6983. BUDGET.

Of the several lodges along Muncho Lake, the best is **Northern Rockies Lodge**, a handsome log structure set back from the highway, with quite upscale new lodge rooms and chalet units. There's a European-style dining room, a lodge bakery, laundry services, boat and canoe rentals and a gas station—and satellite TV for travelers who simply can't miss Stanley Cup games. The well-trained staff is efficient and very helpful. Guide services into the surrounding wilderness are available, as are float-plane tours. ~ Muncho Lake, Mile 462 of the Alaska Highway; 250-776-3481, 800-663-5269, fax 250-776-3482; www.northern-rockies-lodge.com, e-mail liardair@northern-rockies-lodge.com. BUDGET TO MODERATE.

> In summer don't miss Fort St. John's farmer's market held each Saturday in the arena behind the Visitor Info Centre.

Trapper Ray's Liard Hotsprings Lodge is a log structure just across from the entrance to the hot-springs park. Its 12 comfortable rooms are decorated with rustic furnishings and have private baths; the hot springs are just a ten-minute walk. The lodge also has 40 camp sites, some with electrical hookups. The restaurant offers the best food for hundreds of miles—literally. ~ Mile 497 of the Alaska Highway, Liard River; 250-776-7349. BUDGET TO MODERATE.

DINING

Along the Alaska Highway, as on the Cassiar, the best places to eat are often the various lodges that offer accommodation. You can also stop in at the following eateries.

The **Alaska Café** offers classic pub food—pizzas, burgers, soups and salads—along with an extensive selection of beer. It's handy to all of downtown Dawson Creek. ~ 10209 10th Street, Dawson Creek; 250-782-7998. BUDGET.

The **Shepherd's Inn** is famed as a rest stop along the Alaska Highway. Here travelers find good, wholesome food such as soups, sandwiches and pies, plus fruit drinks made from local raspberries and blueberries. ~ Mile 72, Route 97; 250-827-3676. BUDGET.

Mae's Kitchen marks the halfway point between Dawson Creek and Fort Nelson on the Alaska Highway. If you left either spot at the crack of dawn, it's a good time to stop for a piece of pie—the provender this café is known for. There's also soup, sandwiches and all the usual highway comestibles to chow down. ~ Pink Mountain, Mile 147, Route 97; 250-772-3215. BUDGET.

BEACHES & PARKS

MONKMAN PROVINCIAL PARK This beautiful park, mostly wilderness, straddles the transition zone between the rolling foothills of the Canadian prairie and the high, snowy peaks of the Northern Rockies. Crystal line lakes, rushing streams and scenic waterfalls lure trekkers into the backcountry. Several developed backcountry camp sites offer food caches and pit toilets. ~ Located 39 miles (60 km) south of Tumbler Ridge (which is about 70 miles/115 km southwest of Dawson Creek); 250-787-3407.

▲ Two small developed campgrounds near the entrance to the park offer 42 vehicle/tent sites; C$14 per night.

GWILLIM LAKE PROVINCIAL PARK

Set along a pretty lake in the high reaches of the Peace River plain, this park offers vast opportunities for recreation—boating, swimming, hiking, biking, wildlife watching, fishing and just plain lazing. The lake holds bull trout, grayling and northern pike. ~ Situated just off Route 29, 30 miles (49 km) south of Chetwynd (which is 60 miles/97 km west of Dawson Creek on the Peace River Highway); 250-787-3407.

▲ There are 49 vehicle/tent sites with moderate privacy; C$14 per night.

SWAN LAKE PROVINCIAL PARK

One of B.C.'s first provincial parks (it was established in 1918), this quiet spot is several miles off the main road on a calm lake surrounded by aspen woods. The campground surrounds the playground/recreation area so parents can easily keep an eye on their kids. Volleyball courts and horseshoe pits help keep adults occupied. Closed October through April. ~ Located four miles (6 km) east of Route 2, 22 miles (35 km) southeast of Dawson Creek; 250-964-2243.

▲ There are 42 vehicle/tent sites on the lake; not much privacy, but a pleasant spot nonetheless; C$14 per night.

PEACE ISLAND REGIONAL PARK   ◀ HIDDEN

Located on an island in the Peace River, the park's verdant cottonwood groves and lush landscaping make it a wonderful spot for picnics, family reunions (one family reunion brought more than 1000 participants) and weekend getaways. Playgrounds, nature trails and horseshoe pits keep campers occupied. Closed mid-September through April. ~ Located just off Route 97, a mile south of Taylor; 250-789-9295.

▲ There are 26 relatively private sites along the river, plus a small overflow area; C$12 per night.

CHARLIE LAKE PROVINCIAL PARK

This Peace River park hugs the shores of a beautiful lake just north of Fort St. John; a thriving resort community rings the lake. In summer, the lake offers water sports and fishing for walleye, northern pike and other prairie species. The park has playing fields, a playground, horseshoe pits and security patrols in the summer. ~ Located 6 miles (10 km) north of Fort St. John along Route 97; 250-787-3407.

▲ Just off the lake are 58 vehicle/tent sites; C$14 per night.

STONE MOUNTAIN PROVINCIAL PARK 🚶 🚴 🐎 🏕 🏊 ⛵

🛶 🚤 🛥 This stunning 63,500-acre park and its neighbor, Muncho Lake, encompass the most northerly reaches of the Rocky Mountain chain that begins thousands of miles south in Mexico. Its soaring granite peaks, glacial lakes and innumerable wild animals afford visitors almost unlimited mountain park opportunities. Stone Mountain is particularly noted for its sheep and caribou populations; drivers must beware of the proclivity of these animals to wander the roadsides. ~ Route 97, 93 miles (150 km) northwest of Fort Nelson; 250-787-3407.

▲ There are 28 vehicle/tent sites at Summit Lake, the highest point on the Alaska Highway; although this is a scenic spot, the campground is quite exposed to both the highway and the seemingly eternal wind; C$14 per night.

MUNCHO LAKE PROVINCIAL PARK 🚶 🚴 🐎 🏕 🏊 ⛵

🛶 🚤 🛥 This is North B.C.'s premier highway-access park, offering stunning vistas, thriving wildlife, camping and recreation opportunities that Alaska Highway travelers can easily avail themselves of. The road skirts the jade-colored waters of Muncho Lake because in 1942 the original engineers wanted to avoid the daunting Liard River Grand Canyon farther north. ~ Route 97, 125 miles (201 km) northwest of Fort Nelson; 250-787-3407.

▲ Two campgrounds along the lake each offer 15 vehicle/tent sites; the nicest one is MacDonald, near the northern boundary of the park; C$14 per night.

LIARD RIVER HOT SPRINGS PROVINCIAL PARK 🚶 🚴 🏊

This oasis along the Alaska Highway really has just one draw, but it's a doozy—a hot-spring pool big enough to hold dozens of people at a time. Boardwalks provide access; changing rooms are on site. Because it's a drive of hundreds of miles just to get here, reservations are imperative in the summer; unreserved sites fill up by 1 p.m. Unfortunately, the campground, while well designed, is not far from Route 97; if you can, get a site on the loop farthest from the road, or you'll listen to the long-haul trucks throttle down as they come into town. *Please observe the bear safety warnings—they're for real. Fatal attacks have occurred here.* ~ Mile 496 of the Alaska Highway, just north of Liard River; 250-787-3407.

▲ You'll find 53 vehicle/tent sites; C$17 per night.

Outdoor Adventures

RIVER RUNNING

The Babine River carves its way down through the Skeena Mountains to New Hazelton, most of that length traversing sheer wilderness. Five-day trips down the Babine are the specialty of **Suskwa Adventure Outfitters**, which also offers less intense day-long outings on the Bulkley River. Either trip gives rafters the chance at

Finding Your Way in the Woods

There are several advantages to employing a guide service for off-road adventures in North B.C. First and foremost, it is absolutely necessary: this region is so vast and untamed that simply figuring out how to get to the most desirable areas requires local expertise, as there is little or no developed road access. Secondly, the need to be prepared for wilderness exigencies is paramount; local guides will be knowledgeable about bear safety, weather and trail or river conditions.

Utilizing a guide or outfitting service doesn't mean they'll accompany you, necessarily; many outfitters supply their clients with equipment, directions and advice; load them in a plane, helicopter or off-road transport; take them to a jumping-off point and arrange a pickup a week later. You'll have a much better experience.

The **Adventure Smithers Group** manages eight separate enterprises whose activities range from helicopter tours to mountaineering and wilderness expeditions. Areas covered encompass virtually all of North B.C. ~ Box 4951, Smithers; 250-847-3499, 877-610-8075; www.adventuresmithers.com.

A number of Skeena country guides offer services to anglers wishing to try their luck in the Kispiox River and other area streams.

Hook & Line Guiding specializes in fly-fishing excursions into the Kispiox Valley. Owner Wilfred Lee is a Skeena Valley expert and welcomes inquiries about fishing in the area. ~ Box 455, Hazelton; 250-842-5337.

Stone Mountain Safaris provides similar excursions into Stone Mountain Park and Kwadacha Wilderness Park from its lodge along the Toad River. Scenic flights, boat tours, trail rides and wilderness hikes are among the options for clients. ~ Box 7870, Toad River; 250-232-5469.

A number of charter operators in Prince Rupert offer wildlife-watching tours into the spectacular fjords and islands of the nearby wilderness coast. **Rainforest Marine Charters** uses a custom-built boat and emphasizes family trips for sightseeing, fishing, crabbing, beachcombing and other water-borne adventures. The same family also operates a B&B in Prince Rupert. ~ 250-624-9742, 888-923-9993; www.citytel.net/rainforest.

world-class fishing, whitewater and wildlife watching. ~ Smithers; 250-847-2885; www.suskwa.bc.ca.

Aquabatics provides canoe and kayak rentals, instruction and outfitting, plus sailboards, rafting equipment and trip planning. ~ 1960 Hudson Bay Mountain Road, Smithers; 250-847-3678, 800-748-2333.

SKIING

Although the landscape is draped in snow half the year, North B.C.'s lack of population and difficult winter access means there are few developed ski resorts, the most notable being Ski Smithers on Hudson Bay Mountain. Cross-country skiing, snowshoeing and dog-sledding are popular pursuits among residents, and limited opportunities—chiefly around major towns such as Smithers and Prince George—exist for visitors to sample these activities. Check with local Visitor Info Centres for more information.

> The area around the Liard River Hot Springs was so lush with plant life that it was originally called the "Tropical Valley."

The Bavarian-village theme adopted by Smithers is utterly appropriate in one respect—few places in North America more resemble the northern Alps, where ski towns cluster in valley bottoms beneath sheer peaks that seem like they're directly above. **Ski Smithers**, on Hudson Bay Mountain south of town, offers just such an atmosphere. With its base at 3700 feet, just 20 minutes from downtown Smithers, skiers feel like they could run right into town. This isn't one of B.C.'s major resorts—it has only one chairlift and two T-bars—but its deep snow, unsurpassed scenery and small-town friendliness make it one of the best. ~ Hudson Bay Mountain Road, Smithers; 250-847-2058; www.skismithers.com.

The **Bulkley Valley Nordic Centre**, at the foot of Ski Smithers, offers 19 miles (35 km) of groomed trails set with a double track and a middle skating lane, from late November to the end of March. Lights allow night skiing on 3 kilometers of track; there's a day lodge open seven days a week; and the area is maintained and operated by the Bulkley Valley Cross Country Ski Club, so user fees go directly back into the ski area. ~ Hudson Bay Mountain Road, Smithers; snow phone 250-847-3828.

GOLF

Although golf courses, like towns and cities, are much more scattered in North B.C. than in the southern part of the province, the courses that do exist offer lush natural surroundings, scenic views and few crowds. In midsummer, the chance to play golf in the evening—after dinner, as light lasts well past 10 p.m.—adds to the exotic allure of the game at these high latitudes.

Prince Rupert Centennial Golf & Country Club has 18 holes winding through coastal forest. On the front nine the course heads toward the mountains, affording scenic view of the Coast

Range; in the other direction the view is of peaceful residential areas. A spacious layout assures golfer separation; only in two spots do players on different fairways encounter each other. ~ 523 9th Avenue West, Prince Rupert; 250-632-4653.

Carnoustie Golf & Country Club is set along the highway, halfway between Prince George and Smithers, with nine scenic holes in the rolling Babine Lake country. ~ Route 16, 10 miles (16 km) west of Burns Lake; 250-698-7677.

Smithers Golf & Country Club has a full-service clubhouse with a dining room and pro shop—and 18 incredibly scenic championship holes on a course laid out to take advantage of the views of Hudson Bay Mountain. Twilight rates are available in summer. ~ Route 16 and Scotia Road, a half mile (1 km) west of Smithers; 250-847-3591.

Pine Valley Golf Centre is a public course in Prince George, close to town and Route 16, set amid towering pine trees. Rates are very reasonable. ~ Route 16, 1 mile (2 km) west of town center, Prince George; 250-562-4811.

The **Dawson Creek Golf & Country Club** enjoys, for B.C., an unusual setting, spread out just past town on a flat plain amid rolling meadows and small lakes and ponds. This 18-hole championship course has a pro shop, a restaurant and a lot of wide open space. ~ Mile 2.5 (4 km) Alaska Highway, Dawson Creek; 250-782-7882.

Charlie Lake is a scenic natural body of water just outside Fort St. John, famed as a retreat area. **Lake Point Golf & Country Club** overlooks the lake and surrounding rolling countryside; its 18 challenging holes have well-treed fairways and tricky greens. A full-fledged clubhouse offers a coffee shop, dining room, lounge and pro shop. ~ Golf Course Road, northeast of Route 97, Charlie Lake; 250-785-5566.

The **Lone Wolf Golf Club** is marked by "the world's largest golf ball"—actually an old fuel tank, 38 feet in diameter—but that's not the reason to play here. The 18-hole championship course is laid along the foot of the bluff outside Taylor, and offers a pleasant, pastoral experience in the Peace River Valley bottom. ~ Just off Route 97, Taylor; 250-789-3711.

HIKING

North B.C. is arguably the premier wilderness destination in Canada, with vast roadless areas and a number of parks dedicated to preservation of spectacular scenery and plentiful wildlife. Since the wilderness areas are so big and remote, most visitors use floatplanes or horses to reach them. Among the parks with little or no road access are **Kwadacha Wilderness, Kakwa Recreation Area, Wokkpash Recreation Area** and **Monkman Park**; for information on hiking in these, call the **Peace Liard Parks District** at 250-787-3407.

Farther west, **Spatsizi Plateau** and **Mount Edziza** are wilderness parks along the Cassiar Highway; **Khutzeymateen** (a grizzly bear preserve) and **Gitnadoix Recreation Area** are in the Prince Rupert area; for more information contact the Skeena Parks District, 250-847-7320. These parks are for experienced wilderness trekkers only; interested travelers who lack experience should ask for references to licensed guides and outfitters.

▼▼▼▼▼▼▼▼▼▼▼▼
Transportation

CAR

The **Cassiar Highway** (Route 37) heads north from near New Hazelton to the Yukon; totaling 400 miles (646 km), it has three major unpaved gravel sections and several smaller ones. Open year-round, Route 37 should be driven carefully in wet weather. Plan your gas stops carefully; highway signs warn travelers of long stretches with no service stations. The highway is under almost constant improvement; summer travelers can expect to encounter delays at construction projects, and graders will be maintaining unpaved stretches. Slow down when you encounter gravel sections after miles of pavement! The recorded road conditions information number is 900-451-4997.

The **Alaska Highway** (Route 97) starts in downtown Dawson Creek and wends its way north through the Peace River country, into the Liard highlands, then on into the boreal forests of the north and the Yukon. The entire highway in B.C. is now paved, but, as with the Cassiar, road improvement is ongoing and some stretches may be gravel as the roadbed is widened and re-graded. Summertime delays at construction projects are common. Although the highway is no longer the wilderness journey it once was, it's still a good idea to make sure your spare tire and radiator are in good condition, and don't let your gas tank dip below a quarter-full. And, I beg you, not only DO NOT stop on the road to look at bears (or mountain sheep, moose, whatever), keep your eyes peeled in front of you for RVers who have done exactly that. It's a common phenomenon.

Throughout North B.C. it is imperative, before traveling on side roads, that you inquire locally about road conditions. Most secondary roads are well maintained and plowed regularly in winter, but wet conditions and potholes can make them hazardous for passenger cars.

AIR

Passengers departing the **Prince Rupert Airport** must pay a C$28 airport fee in order to board their plane; it is collected separately from the ticket charge. The airport is on an island reached only by ferry, which operates a schedule designed to meet the two to three flights a day; ferry cost is C$11 per adult. A bus provides service from the Rupert Square Mall to the airport approximately an hour before each flight. ~ www.ypr.ca.

Air Canada offers scheduled daily service into Prince George and Prince Rupert. ~ 604-273-2464, 800-663-3721; www.airca nada.ca.

Many charter air services offer scheduled and on-demand flights, most by floatplane, into numerous regional destinations. **Tsayta Aviation** is a North B.C. wilderness outfitter/floatplane operator with bases in Fort St. James, Tsayta Lake and Smithers; a wilderness lodge at Tsayta Lake; and outfitting capabilities throughout the region. ~ 250-996-8540, 800-506-9831; www.bc airadventures.com.

Harbour Air is the major floatplane operator in Prince Rupert, providing scheduled and charter service throughout the North and Central B.C. coast, and up into Alaska. Harbour's regular runs into remote coastal communities offer the only efficient access to most such spots. ~ Seal Cove, Prince Rupert; 250-627-1341, 800-689-4234; www.harbour-air.com. **Inland Air**, based in Prince Rupert, offers charters, flightseeing, fishing trips and business aviation. ~ Prince Rupert; 888-624-2577; www.inlandair.bc.ca.

TRAIN

VIA Rail, Canada's national passenger rail service, operates a route from Jasper to Prince George and on to Prince Rupert. ~ 800-561-8630; www.viarail.ca.

BUS

Greyhound Bus Lines provides bus service to Prince George, Prince Rupert and Dawson Creek. ~ 800-661-1145; www.grey hound.com.

CAR RENTALS

At Prince George, **Hertz Rent A Car** (250-963-7454) and **Thrifty Rent A Car** (250-564-3499) all rent cars at the city's airport.

Thrifty Rent A Car has an agency at the Smithers airport. ~ 250-847-3332 or 250-847-5569, 800-367-2277.

TWELVE

Yukon Territory

More than a century after it first drew thousands to the Yukon, the Klondike Gold Rush continues to attract hordes of pilgrims. Today they are mostly tourists fascinated by the Klondike mystique—many of them Alaska Highway travelers who have ventured north in motor homes to see what the midnight sun and can-can dances are all about—and if they're lucky a leftover gold nugget will appear while they're toeing the gravel in Bonanza Creek.

Although all these things (including the occasional chunk of gold) make thousands of visitors quite happy, in a way it's a shame: The Yukon is a vast, magnificent place wondrously rich in attractions that visitors who stick to the two main tourist destinations will miss.

Think big: This is a sprawling land with broad, rolling green rivers, wildernesses larger than U.S. states, world-class climate extremes and immense vistas. The midsummer sky is a 24-hour dome of light; in winter the aurora borealis shimmers and curls across the heavens like electronic brush-strokes.

Bears abound—it's almost impossible not to see them, including grizzlies, quite close to civilization. The Yukon is one of the few places where there are almost as many grizzlies (7000) as black bears (10,000). (The Yukon government even publishes a cautionary pamphlet, *Guide to Roadside Bear Viewing*. Don't stop in the middle of the Alaska Highway, folks—pull over!) Broad plains spread to horizon-shadowing mountain ranges across which no trail winds. For those who like adventure there is no better place—you can blend physical challenges with unsurpassed scenery and historic elements: floating the Yukon River itself, for instance. And yes, maybe even the wilderness adventurer will look down and notice a glint of gold in a remote creekbed.

That golden glint is what first brought the Yukon to outside notice. Sparsely inhabited for thousands of years by Inuit, Dene and T'lingit peoples who depended on salmon and caribou for their livelihoods, the territory offered nothing of interest to the outside world until, in August 1896, luck smiled on a prospector who had drifted north from earlier gold rushes. George Carmack, along with his First Nations relatives Dawson Charlie and Skookum Jim, found bonanza-grade gold deposits in Rabbit Creek, outside what became Dawson City. Low-grade deposits had been panned for years by scattered Yukon miners; now the rush was on. The news did not reach the outside world until the following summer, when a couple hundred gold-laden miners traveled down the Yukon on steamboats and booked passage to Seattle and San Francisco. When they docked with fortunes ranging up to $500,000 packed in bags and boxes, the news flashed around the world, precipitating the greatest gold rush in human history.

By the spring of 1898 thousands of adventurers from all corners of the globe were headed to the Yukon. Most toiled up Chilkoot Pass, braving fierce storms, and wended their way down to Dawson City, the epicenter of the Rush. Estimates place the stampede at 100,000 souls—largest of all the gold rushes—and although few found wealth, the sheer size of the dream created a mythic era whose echoes linger today. Klondike and Dawson City are names that evoke adventure more than a century later.

The most easily found gold petered out in a decade or so; the take was about $100 million all told. Once the largest city in Canada west of Winnipeg (numbering 30,000 around 1900), Dawson began to shrink, and the territory followed suit. By World War II the Yukon was once again a remote outpost of human habitation, home to a few industrial gold mines, smaller placer miners and little else.

The Japanese attack on Pearl Harbor changed that. American and Canadian authorities determined an overland road to Alaska was crucial to defend the continent, and in just nine months military crews built 1523 miles (2456 km) of road from Dawson Creek, BC, to Fairbanks, Alaska. It was one of the great civil engineering feats of the 20th century, requiring that crews traverse hundreds of miles of frozen (or seemingly bottomless) muskeg swamp, skirt impassable mountains, cross the Liard River and numerous Yukon tributaries, and battle clouds of insects, paralyzing cold and the long nights of the North. All in nine months!

When the war ended the Alaska Highway was turned over to civilian use, and it changed life in the Yukon. Whitehorse, a major way station, became the territory's capital in 1953, solidifying Dawson's decline. Slowly upgraded from a primitive track, the highway evolved into a major commercial route between Alaska and the lower 48 states, and became a popular trek for visitors. This is the avenue most Yukon visitors take to the territory that calls itself "Canada's True North."

Thus began Dawson's second boom. With just 3000 winter residents, the city more than doubles in summer, with travelers from the Alaska Highway and dozens of tour buses that come north from cruise-ship docks in Skagway, Alaska. Meanwhile, Whitehorse is a bustling commercial and government center of 18,000 people. The rest of the Yukon remains pretty much what it was a century ago, a vast wilderness with a few widely spaced settlements and two major thoroughfares. Back then the byways were rivers, today they are highways. The legacies of both periods—including the historic glitter of past glory—dominate the territory to this day. There are now fewer people in the whole Yukon territory than there were in the Dawson City area in the year 1900.

Although all the major mines have shut down, throwing thousands of miners out of work, some of the mines continue to spill toxic waste into Yukon rivers. And the highway that brings tourists to Dawson brings its only real economy— aside from small family placer miners, the visitor industry is the one real dollar generator in the Yukon.

In this mythical land, many Yukon legends are true. Tens of thousands of fortune-seekers did thrash their way here, braving catastrophic challenges such as blizzards, floods, grizzlies and subarctic cold. Thousands found wealth; a few, such as writers Robert Service and Jack London, found fame. Most headed on to other dreams after 1900.

But the Yukon was never the rowdy, no-holds-barred boom territory most imagine—the famed Northwest Mounted Police saw to that, imposing order on the goldfields and in Dawson City. Gunplay was virtually unheard of (in 1898, the peak year of the Rush, there was not a single murder in Dawson City!) and the dancehalls were Victorian-sedate. All pioneers were required to bring a year's worth of supplies, so relatively few gold-rushers perished.

It's easy to misconstrue what lies north of the 60th Parallel today. The Yukon, for instance, is not Arctic. Protected by mountains from the worst polar air, the treeline extends quite far north and little of the territory is tundra. In the summer, it's actually quite warm and dry—Mayo has recorded a temperature of 96°F.

Some popular impressions are true, though. Bugs and bears are plentiful— bring plenty of DEET-laced insect repellent (trust me: citronella and other "milder" concoctions do not deter northern bugs), and if you're headed into the bush, mesh clothing might be a good idea. And it's not unusual to walk into a suburban Dawson bakery, as I did one morning, and find a loaded 16-gauge shotgun on the table by the door. A black bear (which would like croissants as much as any hungry traveler) had been trying to break in the back door and the baker had wanted to be ready to fend him off.

"That's the Yukon," the proprietress shrugged, handing me a fresh, warm chicken pot pie for lunch. The rough-and-ready spirit of the frontier still pervades everyday life in the Yukon. This is a place where residents must know how to thaw propane in the winter, as it gels below -45°F. The same take-it-as-it-comes attitude vastly improves the experience for visitors who head toward the midnight sun, too.

Watson Lake Area

The Alaska Highway—Route 97 in British Columbia, Route 1 in the Yukon—crosses the 60th Parallel briefly about 300 miles northwest of Fort Nelson, BC, dips south a while, and then returns to the Yukon just before entering Watson Lake, a famed way station on the highway that's 326 miles (525 km) from Fort Nelson—a short day's drive from Fort Nelson, or a very long day from Dawson Creek, the start of the highway 1021 km southeast.

SIGHTS

Aside from gas stations and cheap motels, there's not much to see in Watson Lake. Its chief claim to fame derives from its highway pull-off status. During construction of the highway a homesick soldier posted a sign indicating the direction and distance to his hometown in Illinois; travelers have been adding theirs ever since that 1942 start. Today more than 30,000 signs crowd the poles at the **Signpost Forest** in the town's center. It's right by the **Visitor Reception Centre,** just off the highway, which is where you can learn more about the Yukon and the construction of the highway—and where you must ask permission if you want to add a sign to the posts. Standards have evidently slipped a bit, and what were once exclusively signs pointing to hometowns now include other esoterica, such as the occasional family motor-home crest. ~ At the junction of the Alaska and Campbell highways, Watson Lake; Visitor Reception Centre, 867-536-7469.

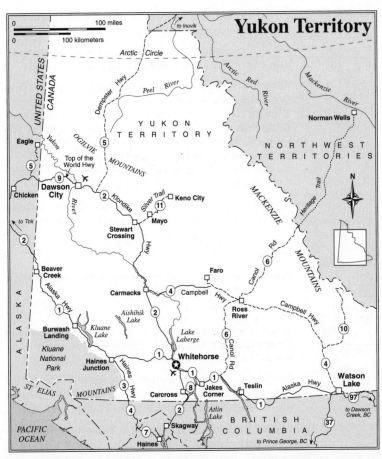

Text continued on page 450.

Four-day Getaway

Yukon Territory

Although the Yukon is vast and wild, a traveler can easily take in most of the more worthwhile visitor attractions in a four-day trip, starting in Whitehorse. A rental car will be necessary, but an ordinary passenger vehicle will do: The roads are built to modern standards and well-maintained. June is the best month—high summer crowds don't arrive until after Canada Day (July 1).

Day 1
- From the airport, it's a five-minute drive into **Whitehorse** (page 456), the territorial capital and only major town in the Yukon.

- First stop, right along the road (and the Yukon River): the **SS Klondike** (page 456). Be sure to take one of the narrated tours.

- Park at the **Yukon Visitor Reception Centre** (page 456) three blocks away (and pick up information and maps) and head off on foot to see the rest of downtown. Sights worth a stop include the **MacBride Museum** (page 457), a restored log cabin; the **Yukon Territorial Government building** (page 457), an impressive modern structure; and the **Old Log Church Museum** (page 457). Stop at the Westmark Whitehorse Hotel to get tickets for that night's Frantic Follies.

- A few blocks down 2nd Avenue is the **Law Courts Building** (page 457), home of the best collection of Yukon art in the region.

- Check in to the **High Country Inn** (page 458), downtown Whitehorse's best hotel.

- Have an early dinner, then see the **Frantic Follies** (page 461), the Yukon's hottest vaudeville show.

Day 2
- Before you hit the road, stop at the **Beringia Interpretive Centre** (page 458) for a half-hour, then spend a few minutes in the **Yukon Transportation Museum** next door.

- Head on up the **Klondike Highway** (page 465), following the footsteps of Klondike gold rushers. Have a late-morning cinnamon roll or man-sized hamburger at **Braeburn Lodge** (page 469).

- Stop just past Carmacks at **Five Finger Rapids** (page 466), a scenic overlook of the Yukon River and valley.

- When you reach Stewart Crossing, a sidetrip beckons: the **Silver Trail** (page 466). Turn up this improved gravel road to the **Keno City Mining Museum** (page 465).

- The rest of the drive to **Dawson City** (page 470) is down the **Klondike Valley**; just before you come into town you pass the leftover dredge tailings that bear witness to the fervor, and destruction, of gold mining.

- Arrive early evening at **Bombay Peggy's** (page 472), the finest inn in Dawson City.

Day 3
- Spend the morning walking through downtown Dawson City, in which a good half the buildings are gold rush–era holdovers. First stop: The **Visitor Reception Centre** (page 470) to pick up maps. Highlights are the **Palace Grand Theatre**; the **Commissioner's Residence**; the **Dawson City Museum**; and the **Robert Service Cabin** and **Jack London cabin**.

- In the afternoon, head up Bonanza Creek Road to see where it all started, stopping at **Dredge #4** (page 470) for a look at the huge machinery; **Discovery Claim**, where the first major strike was made; and **Claim #6**, where visitors can pan for gold.

- Back in town, dine at **Klondike Kate's** (page 474), then engage in after-dinner follies and gambling at the legendary **Diamond Tooth Gertie's** (page 474).

Day 4
- The drive back to Whitehorse is a full day through awesome scenery. Start with the free ferry across the Yukon at the foot of Front Street. Head up the **Top of the World Highway** (page 473), a winding byway across alpine ridges with views of the Ogilvie and Dawson ranges.

- Swing through Alaska, stopping at **Chicken** (page 473) to get a cinnamon roll, then into the Kluane Basin back in the Yukon. Along the shores of Kluane Lake is the **Kluane Museum** (page 462), which has excellent dioramas of local wildlife and First Nations life. At the **Sheep Mountain Visitor Centre** (page 462), brief exhibits explain the harsh yet beautiful terrain of Kluane National Park Reserve.

- It will be late afternoon by the time you make it back to Whitehorse, and your reward for a long day in the car is a soak at **Takhini Hot Springs** (page 458).

- Head past Whitehorse, along **Marsh Lake** (page 452), to check in and have dinner at **Inn on the Lake** (page 454), a lakeside lodge.

Across the road, the **Northern Lights Centre** is a big, blue barn-like building on a slight rise, much scorned by local residents for its cost. The hallways in the center hold a jumble of exhibits about Canada's participation in space programs; in the auditorium, about a half-dozen times a day, a somewhat quirky multimedia show attempts to describe and explain the aurora borealis to summer visitors who won't see the phenomenon in person. In winter, when the center's closed, the lights themselves provide a much better show. Admission. ~ Alaska Highway; 867-536-7827, fax 867-536-2823; www.northernlights centre.ca, e-mail nlc@yknet.ca.

An annual travel guide, available each spring from Tourism Yukon, lists just about every attraction, settlement, restaurant and lodging in the territory. ~ 867-667-5340, fax 867-667-3546; www.touryukon.com.

In the center of town, the **Robert Campbell Highway**, Route 4, heads into the Yukon wilderness. It's a reasonably well-maintained gravel road that leads through long river valleys and along the flanks of the Mackenzie Mountains; the only town on the Campbell Highway, Ross River, is 230 miles (370 km) from Watson Lake. Two miles (3 km) west of Watson Lake, the **Cassiar Highway** comes in from the south (see Chapter Eleven). The helpful folks at the Watson Lake Visitor Reception Centre have up-to-date information on road conditions for both of these highways.

LODGING

If you have to stay overnight in Watson Lake (not a good idea considering the lack of decent lodging) the **Watson Lake Hotel** has 48 rooms that are at least clean and moderately kept-up. Ask to be in one of the newer units, well away from the bar, and hopefully not too close to the Visitor Reception Centre parking lot. ~ Alaska Highway and Campbell Highway intersection; 867-536-7712, fax 867-536-7563; www.watsonlakehotels.com/wat son. BUDGET.

DINING

The dining situation along the Alaska Highway is dismal until you reach Whitehorse. The one place worth stopping in Watson Lake is, fortunately, eminently suitable for lunch: **Archie's** makes a mean hamburger, with french fries, onion rings, ice cream and all the other fixin's. The price is right, too. Grab a sack lunch and head to the park (see below) if neither the small seating area inside nor picnic tables outside sound appealing. It's also open for dinner. ~ Alaska Highway frontage, next to the Northern Lights Centre; 867-536-2400. BUDGET.

BEACHES & PARKS

LUCKY LAKE RECREATION AREA 🏃 🛶 ⚓ Right along the Alaska Highway, just before you reach Watson Lake, this gem of a park doesn't seem like it's north of the 60th Parallel. With sandy beaches, a water slide, and picnic grounds set beneath dusty pines on a dry hillside above the blue-green lake (good for rainbow trout), you might be 2000 miles farther south. On a warm day, it's worth a stop. ~ Alaska Highway, 1 mile (2 km) east of Watson Lake.

WYE LAKE PARK 🚶 🚲   This small community park encircles a shallow lake two blocks from the Alaska Highway, north of the commercial strip in Watson Lake. It's an exceedingly charming spot for a picnic lunch, and a stroll around the lake is a great way to stretch your legs. ~ Two blocks northeast of the Visitor Reception Centre.

◄ *HIDDEN*

WATSON LAKE CAMPGROUND 🚶 🚲 ⚓ ⛵ 🚤 🏊 🚿   One of a series of Yukon government campgrounds along the territory's highways, this is set in a copse of trees well above its namesake lake. Distance from the water doesn't keep the bugs at bay, but it's a fairly pleasant campground and a good place to stop for the night if your schedule puts you here at the end of the day. Fishing is good for Arctic grayling, trout and northern pike. ~ Located three miles (5 km) off the Alaska Highway, 2 miles (3 km) past Watson Lake; 867-667-5648.

▲ There are 55 sites; C$8 (prepaid ticket only).

The highway from Watson Lake to Whitehorse slants across the northernmost reaches of the Cassiar Mountains, dipping back into B.C. for a while before returning to the Yukon. This 283-mile (456 km) stretch takes six to eight hours to drive, and affords countless spectacular vistas but few specific attractions.

▼▼▼▼▼▼▼▼▼▼▼▼▼▼▼▼▼▼▼▼▼▼▼

Watson Lake to Whitehorse

Outside Watson Lake the Alaska Highway begins a slow climb along a superbly scenic stretch into the most northerly reach of the Cassiar Mountains, crossing the Continental Divide after about an hour. **Rancheria Falls** is a pretty picnic site with a boardwalk leading through forest to a gushing waterfall on the Rancheria River, 85 miles (137 km) west of Watson Lake, just before the Divide. Once on the Pacific slope you drop into the Teslin Valley, swinging down a steep hill to cross a long steel-grate bridge into **Teslin**.

SIGHTS

Situated on a small bay midway along icy-blue **Teslin Lake**, its namesake town is a small Tlingit settlement whose one attraction, the **George Johnston Museum**, is well worth a stop. Johnston was a Tlingit leader who collected Native artifacts and took thousands of photographs documenting Tlingit life in the early 20th century. The photos are intriguing and heartfelt depictions of village life before the arrival of the highway, which brought disease as well as commerce. Open in summer only. Admission. ~ Just off the Alaska Highway, Teslin; 867-390-2550.

The next stop on the highway is **Johnson's Crossing**, where Canol Road takes off northward toward Ross River and the Mackenzie Mountains. Huge signs warn darkly of the road's difficulties; it's not for passenger cars. The road, also dating to World War II, served a massive but short-lived pipeline project to bring oil down from the Mackenzie River fields in the Northwest Territories.

The Alaska Highway takes a short swing across low hills, bringing you to **Jake's Corner**, the turnoff for Atlin and Tagish/Carcross/Skagway. **Tagish** is a small settlement with a couple of lakeside lodges; **Carcross** is a junction town known for a small area of dry sand sometimes called the most northerly "desert." (A dubious claim—polar deserts are common in the Arctic.) **Skagway** is a major Alaska cruise-ship port; that's why all those tour buses are on the road headed to Whitehorse and Dawson City.

Atlin, which is actually in B.C. (but accessible only from the Yukon), is a former gold-rush town whose fortune-seeking glory was brief; in 1899 there were 19 hotels here. Today there is one; the town survives because it occupies a breathtaking site on Atlin Lake, across from the impenetrable wilderness of Atlin Provincial Park. It's a major departure point for wilderness adventures by canoe or kayak along the lake. ~ At the end of Route 7, 57 miles (92 km) from Jake's Corner. Visitor information is available at the Atlin Museum, 3rd and Trainor streets; 250-651-7522.

On the shores of Atlin Lake, the **MV Tarahne** is beached, an elegant 1916 sightseeing boat that harks back to Atlin's second heyday as a remote tourist destination. Travelers arrived after a complicated rail/road/boat journey brought 6000 passengers to the *Tarahne* in 1936. During the next year the depths of the Depression grounded the boat for good. Now in the process of restoration, it's open for occasional summer tours and other community events. ~ Atlin Lake; 250-651-7522.

Back on the Alaska Highway north of Jake's Corner, **Marsh Lake** is another scenic, glacially fed body of water around which a small residential community has sprung up; it's just a half-hour into Whitehorse. Several B&Bs, a campground, a coffee shop and an excellent lodge make this a good overnight stop.

LODGING Although the **Yukon Motel**'s "wildlife gallery" is a waste of time (and the admission fee), this roadside complex in Teslin has some very nice, wood-paneled rooms facing off the highway, toward the lake's backwater. It's the best lodging between Liard Hot Springs, BC, and Whitehorse for travelers who can't go any farther. ~ Alaska Highway, just past the Nisutlin Bay Bridge, Teslin; 867-390-2443, fax 867-390-2003; www.yukonmotel.com, e-mail yukonmotel@yknet.yk.ca. BUDGET TO MODERATE.

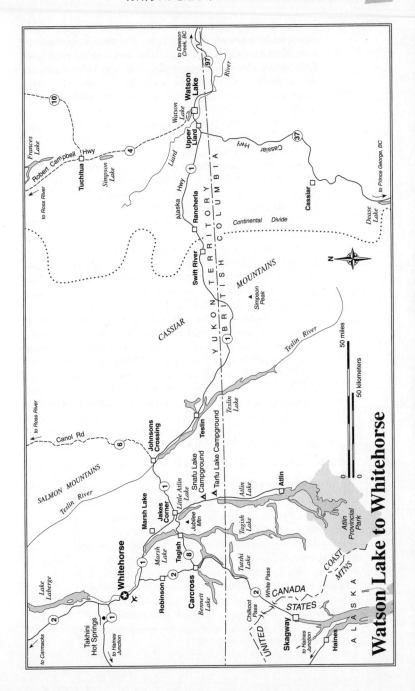

Watson Lake to Whitehorse

HIDDEN ►   **Tagish Lake Resort** is a small lakeside resort with three fully equipped log cabins (including baths) and ten lakefront campsites. Canoes and boats are available to cruise scenic Tagish Lake, and guided canoe trips on the Teslin and Yukon rivers are available. The isolated location is wonderfully peaceful. ~ Eight miles south of the Tagish-Carcross Road; phone/fax 867-667-1009. BUDGET TO MODERATE.

Tagish Wilderness Lodge, located on a remote arm of Tagish Lake at the foot of the Jubilee Mountains, is a fly-in-only small resort devoted to fishing, hiking, and peace and quiet. Guests stay in four cozy log cabins with bathrooms; meals are served in the main lodge nearby. Closed May, November and December. ~ Taku Arm, Tagish Lake; 867-393-4097; www.tagishwilderness-lodge.com, e-mail twlodge@polarcom.com. DELUXE.

HIDDEN ►   **Spirit Haven Bed & Breakfast** is a small guest facility in the Carcross Valley that enjoys a notable distinction: The hostess, Karon Danks, is one of the Yukon's elite pastry chefs. The two bedrooms in the main house share a bath; there's also a separate cabin. Breakfast includes pastries based on Yukon goodies such as huckleberries; evening meals can be arranged. ~ South Klondike Highway Km 115 (south of Carcross); 867-821-4722. BUDGET.

The **Atlin Inn** is a motel-style lodging overlooking the lake in central Atlin; rooms are small but clean, decorated in beige, pinks and blues. Try for rooms 10 or 12, which have a little more space and a view. The inn's café is a popular dining spot. ~ Atlin; 250-651-7546, fax 250-651-7500; www.atlinresort.com. BUDGET.

Marsh Lake is the shore **Inn on the Lake** occupies; facing south, it gathers in all the sun and scenery possible. This upscale, beautifully built modern log lodge offers five spacious, comfy rooms—including a marvelous top-floor suite with whirlpool tub. Guests enter through the kitchen, signifying the lodge's focus

AUTHOR FAVORITE

Encompassing the south end of Atlin Lake, the largest freshwater lake in B.C., **Atlin Provincial Park** has 677,000 acres of mountain peaks and glacier-filled valleys; a full third of the park is covered by glaciers. There's a small fishing and wilderness resort community, Atlin, at the end of the highway at the mid-section of the lake, about 10 miles (17 km) north of the actual park boundary. The lake offers boat access for experienced wilderness canoe and kayak travelers; however, there is no road access to the park and no developed facilities, neither trails nor campsites, within it. Permits are not needed. ~ For more information on Atlin Provincial Park, including references to outfitters who guide trips into the park, contact BC Parks; 250-847-7320.

on gourmet food with a German flair that reflects Yukon native
Carson Schiffkorn's heritage (and his clientele—German tour
groups frequent the Yukon). Amenities include kayaks, canoes,
sailboards, a sauna and outdoor hot tub and a small fitness center. Active outdoorsman Shiffkorn provides encyclopedic knowledge of the Yukon and its limitless recreation opportunities. The
inn also has a three-bedroom cottage. **Inn on the River**, a companion log lodge several miles away on the Teslin River, offers
similar accommodation in a serene wilderness setting (not accessible by passenger car). It's a good put-in point for canoe trips
down the Teslin. ~ Alaska Highway at Marsh Lake; www.excep
tionalplaces.com. MODERATE TO DELUXE.

DINING

The **Atlin Inn**'s café is a local dining hangout, as well as just
about the only dining room in town. It specializes in down-home
café food—turkey dinners, burgers and fries, and even old-time
favorites such as Swiss steak. ~ Atlin; 250-651-7546. BUDGET.

◀ HIDDEN

Tucked away in a rural subdivision off the Alaska Highway,
Judas Creek Commons represents a unique facet of Yukon life:
the country bakery. Each day hearty breads, pastries and muffins
come out of the oven at this coffeehouse; the pleasant sitting area
(with a cozy loft) is supplemented by a nice outdoor deck. If
you're around for one of Judas Creek's handmade gourmet pizza
nights (Thursday through Saturday), you're in for a treat. Open
for breakfast, lunch and dinner. ~ 34 Judas Creek Drive, Marsh
Lake; phone/fax 867-660-4744. BUDGET.

BEACHES & PARKS

TESLIN LAKE Perched in an aspen grove on a small
promontory above the lake, the small, two-acre campground here
has a dandy, sunny, somewhat bug-free site. The view across the
lake is grand, and the campsites are spaced well. A trail leads down
the slight bluff to the gravel shore of the lake. ~ Located 4 miles
(7 km) west of Teslin on the Alaska Highway; 867-667-5648.

▲ There are 27 sites; C$8 (prepaid ticket only).

◀ HIDDEN

SNAFU LAKE & TARFU LAKE CAMPGROUNDS
These two small campgrounds along the Atlin Road are tiny jewels in the scrub pine forest of the southern Yukon lowlands. Both
lakes are pretty, placid small bodies of water with excellent fishing
for lake trout and grayling; wildlife, including grizzly bears,
abounds. Peace and solitude are major virtues here. (Pay special
attention to bear safety, please.) ~ Located 16 and 20 miles (26 and
32 km) south of Jake's Corner on the Atlin Road; 867-667-5648.

▲ There are four sites at each campground; C$8 (prepaid
ticket only).

ATLIN PROVINCIAL PARK This half-million-acre
wilderness expanse encompasses large icefields and high peaks;
accessible only by plane or boat, it's for expert wilderness

trekkers only. Guide services are available in Atlin (see Outdoor Adventures at the end of this chapter). ~ 250-847-7320.

MARSH LAKE CAMPGROUND 🚶 🚴 ⛵ 🚤 ⚓ Set off the main road a few hundred yards, this campground is back in the trees away from the lakeshore on a small promontory in the lake. Hiking trails and a playground supplement the usual camping facilities; the nearby beaches are somewhat gravelly. Since it's close to Whitehorse, it's a popular weekend spot in the summer, one of the few campgrounds in the Yukon that may occasionally be full. ~ Located 21 miles (34 km) east of Whitehorse on the Alaska Highway; 867-667-5648.

▲ There are 37 sites; C$8 (prepaid ticket only).

Whitehorse

Whitehorse is a handsome town set on a flat bench straddling the upper reaches of the Yukon River. With 30,000 residents, this is the major city of the Yukon— and, in fact, the largest city west of Edmonton and north of Prince George. Although its history dates back to the Klondike Gold Rush (it was the major staging point for travelers headed down the Yukon to the Klondike) its size and prosperity today depend on the Alaska Highway. Once the military road became a civilian thoroughfare after World War II, Whitehorse assumed ever-greater commercial and official importance in Yukon life and was made the territorial capital in 1953.

SIGHTS

As you come into town from the south, signs indicate a small sidetrip to **Miles Canyon**, a famous cataract now tamed by a downstream dam. Numerous stampeders met their fates in the rapids of the canyon; a footbridge now affords a vantage on the still-narrow defile through which the Yukon River pours.

On down the Miles Canyon Road, the **MV Schwatka** cruise boat takes visitors through the canyon and up the Yukon; the two-hour cruise includes commentary on the surroundings and the history of the canyon. Admission. ~ Landair floatplane base on Schwatka Lake, 1 mile (2 km) east of Whitehorse on Miles Canyon Road; 867-668-4716.

As you come into downtown Whitehorse, the **SS Klondike** is the most prominent sight in town, beached along the Yukon. This Parks Canada historic site preserves the last paddlewheeler to run the Yukon. Beautifully restored, the boat can only be viewed by guided tours that depart regularly during the day. Be sure to ask about the amazing story of how it got here on dry land. Admission. ~ 2nd Avenue and Robert Service Way; 867-667-4511.

The **Yukon Visitor Reception Centre** in downtown Whitehorse is a huge, user-friendly facility whose expert staff is among the most professional you'll find anywhere. Although somewhat overwhelmed by crowds during the midsummer peak, they do their best to answer whatever questions visitors have—with comprehensive, truthful information. ~ 2nd Avenue and Hanson Street; 867-667-3084.

The **Yukon Territorial Government** building is a modern structure much admired for its design, which brings in available light, and for its Yukon art collection. ~ 2nd Avenue and Hawkins Street; 867-667-5811.

A much better, and lesser known, Yukon art collection is housed in the equally impressive **Law Courts Building** four blocks away. The sculptures and canvases here include works by native Yukon artists who have since achieved international fame; especially note the massive, vivid canvas by Ted Harrison, *The Great Land.* ~ 2nd Avenue between Wood and Jarvis streets.

◀ HIDDEN

Elsewhere downtown, the **MacBride Museum**, housed in a restored log cabin, contains exhibits on the gold rush and pioneer Yukon life. Admission. ~ 1st Avenue and Wood Street; 867-667-2709; www.macbridemuseum.com, e-mail info@macbride museum.com.

The **Old Log Church Museum** preserves an artifact of pioneer Yukon society. The small structure, once a Presbyterian church, houses a modest exhibit devoted to the affairs of the region's native peoples, plus the missionaries who arrived along with gold seekers. Admission. ~ 3rd Avenue and Elliott Street; 867-668-2555.

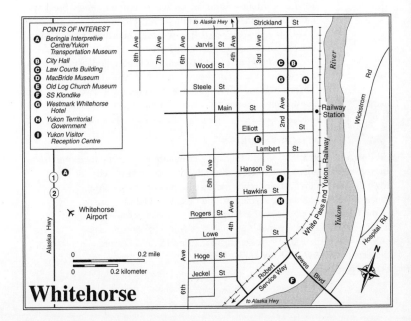

POINTS OF INTEREST

Ⓐ Beringia Interpretive Centre/Yukon Transportation Museum
Ⓑ City Hall
Ⓒ Law Courts Building
Ⓓ MacBride Museum
Ⓔ Old Log Church Museum
Ⓕ SS Klondike
Ⓖ Westmark Whitehorse Hotel
Ⓗ Yukon Territorial Government
Ⓘ Yukon Visitor Reception Centre

Whitehorse

The **Yukon Transportation Museum** explains just how people have long gotten around in this harsh environment, ranging from dogsleds to floatplanes. The room devoted to bush pilots is especially entertaining, with pictures depicting the hazardous practice of thawing engines out with kerosene heaters. Admission. ~ Alaska Highway, Mile 915/Km 1473, near the airport; 867-668-4792, fax 867-633-5547; e-mail ytranmus@yknet.yk.ca.

Takhini Hot Springs ought to be wonderfully alluring—thermal mineral water in the subarctic desert. Alas, the pools are rather desultory concrete affairs, and the bathhouse and other facilities need some sprucing up. The adjacent campground has almost 100 sites set in the woods across the parking lot. Admission. ~ Takhini Hot Springs Road, ten miles (18 km) northwest of Whitehorse; 867-633-2706, fax 867-668-2689; www.takhinihotsprings.yk.ca.

LODGING

The **High Country Inn** is the spiffiest hotel in Whitehorse, with luxuriously furnished rooms and suites, a small fitness center, and amenities such as in-room coffee and jacuzzi tubs, guest laundry and even secured parking. It's within easy walking distance of most of the town's attractions. ~ 4051 4th Avenue; 867-667-4471, 800-554-4471, fax 867-667-6457; www.highcountryinn.yk.ca, e-mail info@highcountryinn.ca. MODERATE TO DELUXE.

Located right along the Yukon riverfront, the **Edgewater Hotel** is an established Whitehorse lodge with 28 rooms and two suites, and a little bit of character in its comfortable decor. The service is attentive and an on-site restaurant serves breakfast, lunch and dinner. ~ 101 Main Street; 867-667-2572, 877-484-3334, fax 867-668-3014; www.edgewaterhotel.yk.ca, e-mail theedge@internorth.com. MODERATE.

Hawkins House Bed & Breakfast is a small deluxe inn set in a restored Victorian home furnished with period antiques. There's a grand foyer, parlor and balconies in two of the four guest rooms. Guests receive a complimentary welcome fruit bas-

AUTHOR FAVORITE

I felt a thrill when I touched a mammoth bone at the **Beringia Interpretive Centre**, a compact and wonderful museum at the edge of town devoted to the Yukon's prehistoric past. A film explains the significance of Ice Age comings and goings to the climate and human history of the Yukon, and well-displayed exhibits depict now-vanished wildlife. Closed mid-September to mid-May; open Sunday and by appointment only in winter. Admission. ~ Alaska Highway, Mile 915/Km 1473, near the airport; 867-667-8855, fax 867-667-8854; www.beringia.com, e-mail beringia@gov.yk.ca.

ket. ~ 303 Hawkins Street; 867-668-7638, fax 867-668-7632; www.hawkinshouse.yk.ca, e-mail cpitzel@internorth.com. MODERATE TO DELUXE.

The woodsy setting of **Country Cabins**, a set of half a dozen cozy, modern log cottages near Takhini Hot Springs, is peaceful, and the hot springs are a five-minute walk away. Breakfast includes home-made mueslix and muffins, set on the cottages' doorsteps. ~ Takhini Hot Springs Road; 867-633-2117; e-mail countrycabin@hypertech.yk.ca. BUDGET TO MODERATE.

◄ *HIDDEN*

DINING

The **Chocolate Claim** offers well-made coffee drinks, pastries and muffins, sandwiches and soups—and, of course, house-made chocolate goodies ranging from cakes to candies. Breakfast and lunch only. ~ 305 Strickland Street; 867-667-2202. BUDGET.

The Cellar is fine dining in Whitehorse proper. Steaks, ribs and seafood are the fare here, with an occasional sample of Northern cuisine such as caribou. The nightly soups and salads are quite tasty, and the ambience and service are relatively refined. ~ Edgewater Hotel, 101 Main Street; 867-667-2572. MODERATE.

Hugely popular with residents, **Sam 'n Andy's** offers a subarctic version of Mexican food that's filling if not thrilling. The evening crowds can be boisterous, but the fare is economical. ~ 506 Main Street; 867-668-6994. BUDGET.

Midnight Sun is the most popular coffeehouse in Whitehorse—even the local police stop in for their morning cup. The beans are freshly roasted and expertly blended; the muffins and pastries are tempting; and for lunch, soups, salads and light sandwiches are good. Breakfast and lunch only. ~ 4168 4th Avenue; 867-633-4563. BUDGET.

◄ *HIDDEN*

Alpine Bakery is a classic European bakery specializing in indulgent pastries, hearty breads and rich cakes. Considering the somewhat dismal dining situation in Whitehorse, a stop at the bakery's café makes as much sense as anything for lunch or dinner. The soups and sandwiches are dandy, or just grab some wholesome bread and make a picnic dinner by the river nearby at the SS *Klondike* park. ~ 411 Alexander Street; 867-668-6871. BUDGET.

SHOPPING

There's virtually nothing in print regarding the Yukon that you can't find at **Mac's Fireweed Books**—novels, guides, natural histories, maps, photo books. The store stocks all the editions of the legendary *Lost Moose Catalogue*, as well. ~ 203 Main Street; 867-668-2434.

Coast Mountain Sports started here as an outdoor supply store serving the specialized needs of Yukon adventurers. It has since grown into a chain spreading through Western Canada; needless to say, the gear is great, and the expertise is even better. ~ 208 Main Street; 867-667-4074.

Three Beans Natural Foods has organic fruits and vegetables, vitamins and natural remedies, plus a juice bar and a good handle on what's going on in the Whitehorse community. ~ 308 Wood Street; 867-668-4908.

Across from the MacBride Museum, the **North End Gallery** has the best selection of Yukon arts and crafts in Whitehorse, including coastal mask art, interior beadwork and Inuit carving. ~ 1116 1st Avenue; 867-393-3590.

NIGHTLIFE An institution in Whitehorse for 30 years, the **Frantic Follies** make a passable effort at adding a bit of modern intelligence (sly political jokes, for instance) to the mawkish vaudeville nonsense so many tourists expect when they come to the Yukon. Hugely popular—there are as many as three shows a night in the height of summer—the follies usually sell out ahead of time in July and August, so those wanting to see the show are best advised to grab tickets upon arrival in Whitehorse. The ticket office is at the Westmark Whitehorse Hotel, which is also where the follies are staged. Admission. ~ Westmark Whitehorse Hotel, Steele Street and 2nd Avenue; 867-668-2042; www.franticfollies.com.

▼▼▼▼▼▼▼▼▼▼▼▼▼▼▼

Alaska Highway
West of Whitehorse

The Yukon west of Whitehorse includes much of the territory's most spectacular scenery, a rugged landscape of towering mountains, icy lakes and milky glacial rivers through which the only road, the Alaska Highway, winds like a ribbon. Visitor facilities are few, however, so many travelers plan to make it all the way to Fairbanks in one leg.

SIGHTS The Alaska Highway climbs out of the Yukon valley to the northwest of Whitehorse, heading west toward the flanks of the spectacular Coast Ranges. At Haines Junction it abuts the edge of **Kluane National Park**, one of North America's most spectacular mountain fastnesses. This landscape of rock and glacier—often seen in automobile commercials made with the aid of helicopters—holds Canada's highest peak, Mount Logan. At 19,520 feet (5950 meters), this forbidding pinnacle ranks with Alaska's Mount McKinley as one of the most treacherous climbs in North America. Most of Kluane is a high province of snowfield and glacier, part of a UNESCO World Heritage Site that also includes Wrangell St. Elias National Park & Preserve in Alaska and Tatshenshini Alsek Provincial Park in British Columbia. There are no facilities within Kluane National Park, and only one campground (Kathleen Lake) at the edge of it. The interior of the park is for expert wilderness travelers only; a number of outfitters offer guided tours into the park, ranging from afternoon plane flights (not for the skittish) to weeklong treks.

Yukon Follies
Grin and Bare It

Although it's true that vaudeville and dancehall shows were mainstays of Yukon life in the gold-rush era, the modern-day versions to which visitors throng in Whitehorse and Dawson bear only superficial resemblance to those a century ago. The centerpiece that has gained international currency as prototypical of the Klondike, the famed can-can, may have never actually been performed in gold-rush days; historians find no evidence that the tame Victorian society of Dawson and Whitehorse countenanced such bawdy public exhibitions. Song-and-dance skits and burlesque satires are more likely what Klondike miners may have seen.

The Whitehorse version is the better of today's two shows. **Frantic Follies** plays nightly during the summer in the Westmark Whitehorse Hotel, offering a wry and fairly sophisticated look at the gold rush, leavened with modern perspectives. The short skit presenting Robert Service's "Cremation of Sam Magee" is uproarious. Shows run late May to mid-September. Admission. ~ Westmark Whitehorse Hotel, 2nd Avenue and Steele Street, Whitehorse; 867-668-2042; www.franticfollies.com.

The **Gaslight Follies** in Dawson City has a much better venue—the reconstructed Palace Grand Theatre—but a lowball script rather transparently aimed at the crowds of RV and tour-bus travelers who pay the bills in town. Expect lots of jokes about Viagra. Operated by the Klondike Visitors Association, proceeds support tourist services in Dawson City. Shows run May through September. Admission. ~ Palace Grand Theatre (the box office is across the street), King Street and 2nd Avenue, Dawson City; 867-993-5575.

Both follies frequently sell out a day or two ahead of time in July and August. And yes, both include the can-can—call it history in the making.

~ Visitor Reception Centre, Haines Junction; 867-634-7250; www.parkscanada.pch.gc.ca.

Past Haines Junction Route 1 dips down into the long, sandy valley that holds Kluane Lake. A long, milt-blue tongue of water butting up against the sere foothills of the Kluane ranges, the lake is subject to sudden windstorms. About halfway along the lake, at the toe of a spectacular glacial outwash valley, the **Sheep Mountain Visitor Centre** explains the nearby mountain habitat for the park's wild Dall sheep. ~ Alaska Highway Mile 1060/Km 1706.

At Burwash Landing, at the north end of Kluane Lake, the **Kluane Museum** offers a surprisingly top-notch set of dioramas depicting local wildlife and traditional First Nations life. Sponsored by the local Native band, it incorporates the recollections of many local elders. Admission. ~ Alaska Highway Mile 1093/Km 1759; 867-841-5561.

At Mile 1128/Km 1816 the highway drops into the **Donjek River** valley, a braided stream from whose banks the vistas embrace the Icefield Ranges, a sheer rampart of towering peaks and glaciers. From here the highway heads into a lengthy stretch of lowland marshes and plains, one of North America's most important waterfowl habitats, crossing the border into Alaska at Mile 1222/Km 1967. Unlike the one on the Top of the World Highway, this crossing is open 24 hours a day year-round.

LODGING   The **Raven Hotel**'s atmosphere is that of a small Austrian inn—suitably so, as it lies at the foot of the spectacular St. Elias Mountains in Haines Junction. The 12 tidy rooms all have private bath, telephone, TV and even room service. The entire hotel is non-smoking, and a gourmet German breakfast is included. ~ Haines Junction; 867-634-2500, fax 867-634-2517; e-mail kluaneraven@yknet.yk.ca. MODERATE.

The slogan, and expectations, at **Cottonwood RV Park** are both fairly low-key: "The place people come to stay for a day and stay another!" Maybe that's what makes this Kluane lakeside complex so charming. Most of the facility is devoted to campsites—the ones at the southeast end are best—but there are four nice, modern one-room cabins for rent as well, with kitchenettes and indoor baths. The complex also has a café, laundry, hot tubs, and a miniature golf course. Destruction Bay, incidentally, was so named because a maelstrom decimated a highway construction camp here in the 1940s. ~ Destruction Bay, Alaska Highway Mile 1067/Km 1717, 867-634-2739; radio phone 2M-3972, Destruction Bay channel; fax 867-634-2429. MODERATE.

HIDDEN ►   Housed in Quonset huts on the shore of Kluane Lake—and well off the Alaska Highway—**Kluane Bed & Breakfast** offers ten units with spectacular views. The lake is in the foreground, the soaring peaks of Kluane National Park in the distance. The

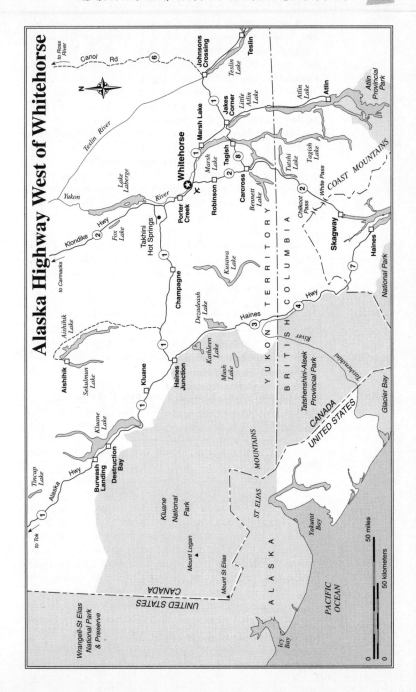

accommodations are comfortable: some A-frame, all small cabins. A full breakfast is included. ~ Two miles off the Alaska Highway (watch for signs) as you come down into Destruction Bay north of Haines Junction; radio phone 2M-3924, Destruction Bay channel. MODERATE.

Everything about **Tincup Wilderness Lodge** is fabulous. The lodge sits on a small bench in the middle of its namesake lake, nestled beneath tall Yukon mountains. The flight in to the lake, aboard owner Larry Nagy's Helio Courier floatplane, takes just a half-hour from the Alaska Highway pickup point (or four hours from Whitehorse), and affords a breathtaking view of the glacial rivers, towering ridges and indigo lake. Tincup Lake's grayling and trout are hale and willing; berry-picking, wildlife watching and Yukon tale-telling while away the rest of the time. Jose Janssen's gourmet cooking far exceeds the traditional wilderness lodge standard, and the six rooms in three nicely decorated, woodstove-warmed cedar cabins are spruce and cozy. After dinner, the wood-fired lakeshore sauna calls. ~ Tincup Lake (fly-in only); 604-762-0382, summer radio phone 600-700-0654; www.tincup.yk.ca. DELUXE.

DINING

The **Raven Hotel**'s dining room offers superior Continental cuisine featuring seafood and pasta. The overall theme is Austrian/Canadian, with such dishes as veal schnitzel and pork roasts. ~ Haines Junction; 867-634-2500, fax 867-634-2517. MODERATE.

PARKS

KLUANE NATIONAL PARK & PRESERVE 🏃 🚴 🚤 ⛵ This massive 13,000-square-mile park, more than 80 percent of which is composed of mountains and ice fields, is part of the much bigger UNESCO World Heritage Site that includes Glacier Bay National Park in the United States and the Tatshenshini Alsek Provincial Park complex in B.C. Aside from the Kathleen Lake day-use and camping area (see below), access is limited to experienced wilderness trekkers. Motorized boating is allowed on Kathleen and Mush lakes. The park includes two famed peaks, Mount Logan (Canada's highest) and Mount St. Elias, and draws climbers and mountaineers from around the world. Its weather is notoriously fickle, its scenery is indisputably spectacular, and its interior is forbidding. ~ Haines Junction is at Mile 1016/Km 1640. Kluane Park stretches along the length of the Alaska Highway from here to the Alaska border; however, there's no road access and no facilities aside from the Sheep Mountain Visitor Centre and the Kathleen Lake Campground. Visitor Reception Centre, Haines Junction; 867-634-7207; parkscan.harbour.com/kluane.

▲ *Kathleen Lake Campground* is the only established visitor facility in Kluane National Park. The lake is a pretty, sapphire body of water at the foot of the St. Elias Mountains, with hiking trails heading up the valley and into the wilderness. There are 41 sites; C$12.50. ~ Located 18 miles (29 km) south of Haines Junction on the Haines Highway; 867-634-7207.

Klondike Highway

The Klondike Highway (Yukon Route 2, although hardly anyone calls it that) encompasses the road from Whitehorse to Dawson City, once a wagon track through the Yukon, now a fine paved road. Figure a full day to cover the 333 miles (536 km) between Whitehorse and Dawson, with a few brief stops along the way, or a half-day detour along the Silver Trail. Several good campgrounds are available for those wanting more leisurely excursions.

SIGHTS

When you climb up out of Whitehorse and start crossing the Yukon plateau, the arid, sandy, aspen and pine-covered hills look ever so much like landscapes thousands of miles farther south. The turnoff to **Lake Laberge** is at Mile 140/Km 226, a short ten-minute sidetrip to look at this famously temperamental body of water, frequently whipped by fierce winds, along which gold-rushers dreaded passage. A small campground allows travelers to stand "on the marge of Lake Laberge," as in Robert Service's famous poem, "The Cremation of Sam Magee."

Back on the Klondike Highway, **Carmacks** is a major junction town; here the Campbell Highway comes in from the southeast. The **Tage Cho Hudan Interpretive Centre** offers exhibits on local First Nations life, including a depiction of the mammoth snares prehistoric Yukon residents used to bring down the shaggy beasts. ~ Carmacks; 867-863-5830.

AUTHOR FAVORITE

sights   With its massive equipment and dingy underground environment, mining is not much to look at—but it has been central to the development of the North. The **Keno City Mining Museum**, housed in an old dance-hall, holds two floors of artifacts and exhibits that detail the area's brief but rich history. Great attention is paid to everyday life as well as mining, and the highlight of the museum is the priceless collection of photos by Kenny Bradshaw. Bradshaw was a miner and self-taught photographer whose passion was documenting the lives of his community in the 1950s; his color portraits of mine families in their homes are remarkably genuine and constitute a Canadian national treasure. Closed September through May. Admission. ~ At the end of the Silver Trail, Keno City; 867-995-2792; www.kenocity.yk.ca/museum.htm.

Fifteen miles (23 km) up the road from Carmacks, **Five Finger Rapids** (Mile 236/Km 380) is a scenic overlook of a spot on the Yukon River where four basalt islands divide the now-massive stream. In gold rush days, winches were needed to haul steamboats up the river here.

HIDDEN ▶

At Stewart Crossing, the **Silver Trail** is a half-day, 140-mile sidetrip that leads into the heart of the Yukon wilderness and ends at a mining district now abandoned by all but a few hardy hangers-on. The highway first winds up the Stewart River valley to **Mayo**, a picturesque little town that once served as a steamboat landing for silver ore (which was shipped from here all the way to San Francisco) and now holds the distinction of registering one of the most extreme climates in the world: The record low temperature in Mayo is -82°F/-62°C and the record high is 96°F/36°C; the difference between the two is one of the greatest such disparities on earth.

Fittingly, the **Binet House Interpretive Centre** includes an exhibit on permafrost, as well as photos and artifacts documenting area life. ~ Center Street and 2nd Avenue, Mayo; 867-996-2926.

Past Mayo the road turns to oiled dirt (slick when it rains) and climbs into the foothills of the Nadaleen Range. Watch for survival shacks placed along the road, kept there for emergency winter car breakdowns. **Elsa**, a hamlet at Mile 60/Km 96, is a now-abandoned mine village on the flank of the mountain, with derelict buildings tumbling down toward the road.

Ten minutes farther lies **Keno City**, another once-thriving town that began to decline in the late 1930s and slumped further when the last nearby silver mine (at Elsa) closed in 1989. At one point Keno area mines accounted for 14 percent of all Canadian silver production. Today this is a virtual ghost town with a few residents (who spend their time fending off bears), a café, a hotel and bar, a scenic setting and an astoundingly good museum (see page 465).

Back on the Klondike Highway, the road traverses low plateaus, pausing on a hill overlooking the **Tintina Trench** (a vast geologic feature that illustrates plate tectonic), then dives down into the Klondike River valley.

At Mile 421/Km 678, the famed **Dempster Highway** leads off to the northeast. This is the only all-season road in North America that crosses the Arctic Circle, leading 460 miles (741 km) across spectacular tundra landscapes to Inuvik in the Mackenzie Delta, Northwest Territories. A set of eight interpretive panels describe the highway and the territory it traverses. ~ For information on traveling the Dempster Highway, including maps and highway guides, call 800-661-0788.

LODGING

Cranberry Point Bed & Breakfast occupies a quiet promontory on Fox Lake about an hour north of Whitehorse. The three one-

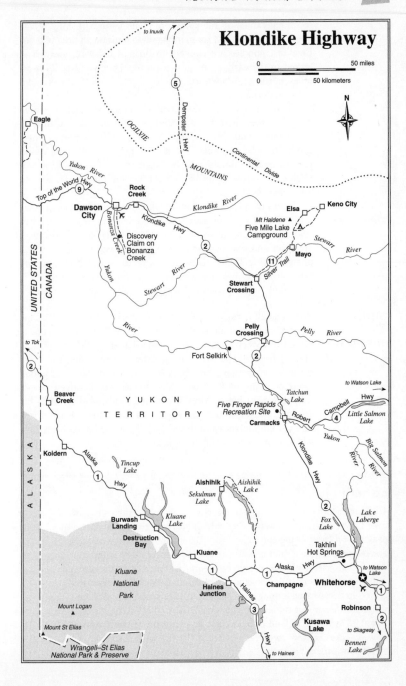

Klondike Highway

0   50 miles
0   50 kilometers

N

to Inuvik

5

OGILVIE

Dempster Hwy

MOUNTAINS

Continental Divide

Eagle

Yukon River

Top of the World Hwy

9

Rock Creek

Klondike River

Elsa

Keno City

Dawson City

Bonanza Creek

Klondike Hwy

2

Mt Haldene ▲

Five Mile Lake Campground

Discovery Claim on Bonanza Creek

Stewart River

Silver Trail

11

Mayo

Stewart River

UNITED STATES

CANADA

Yukon River

Stewart Crossing

River

Pelly Crossing

Pelly River

Fort Selkirk

2

to Tok

2

YUKON

TERRITORY

Tatchun Lake

to Watson Lake

Hwy

Beaver Creek

Five Finger Rapids Recreation Site

Robert

Campbell

4

Little Salmon Lake

Carmacks

Klondike Hwy

Yukon River

Big Salmon River

A L A S K A

Koidern

Alaska

Tincup Lake

Aishihik

Aishihik Lake

Sekulmun Lake

2

Fox Lake

Lake Laberge

Hwy

Burwash Landing

Kluane Lake

Destruction Bay

Kluane National Park

Kluane

Alaska Hwy

1

Champagne

Takhini Hot Springs

to Watson Lake

Whitehorse

1

Mount Logan ▲

Haines Junction

Haines

3

Robinson

2

Mount St Elias ▲

Kusawa Lake

to Skagway

Wrangell–St Elias National Park & Preserve

Hwy

to Haines

Bennett Lake

room log cabins on the lakeshore invite leisurely fishing or canoeing; there's a guest room in the main house with private bath. Breakfast goodies are cooked up on a woodstove, and tea is served in the early evening. ~ Klondike Highway Km 240, 30 miles north of Whitehorse; radio phone JJ3-9257, Fox Lake channel. BUDGET.

Accommodations at the **Carmacks Hotel** are basic—this facility has been here in one form or another since steamboat days—but include phones and color TVs. A few separate rental cabins are also available. The hotel arranges boat tours, canoe rentals, and a salmon/steak barbecue in the bush. ~ Klondike Highway, Carmacks; 867-863-5221, fax 867-863-5605. BUDGET TO MODERATE.

HIDDEN ▶

With just 30 residents in the whole surrounding village, visitors to **Keno City Cabins** are sure to feel they've really gotten away from the pressures of modern life. The two self-contained cabins are clean and spacious, with full kitchens, woodstoves, TVs and private baths. They're decorated with Yukon artifacts such as snowshoes, and pets are welcome. ~ Keno City; 867-995-2829, fax 867-995-2892; www.kenocity.yk.ca/cabins.htm. BUDGET.

DINING

HIDDEN ▶

With a small patio, an even smaller indoor seating area, and inconspicuous signs along the road, **Mom's Bakery** is an unexpected discovery on the way to Lake Laberge. "Mom" (Tracie Harris) fires up the oven and griddle each morning for sourdough pancakes, pies, breads, pastries and such; the baked goods are done in an outdoor oven. She also has good coffee to wash it all down. At lunch, Mom's soup and sandwiches certainly hit the spot. Breakfast and lunch only. ~ Lake Laberge Road, three miles (5 km) northeast of the Alaska Highway; radio phone 2M-4554, Whitehorse YJ channel. BUDGET.

BOOKING IT

The vast majority of Yukon accommodations are in the territory's two major towns, Whitehorse and Dawson City. In both locales the crush of visitors in peak season (roughly the end of June to mid-September) can create a fully booked situation, so it's not a wise idea to head that far north without reservations then. Although a room can usually be found in an emergency, it may not be the most desirable accommodation. **Select Reservations** is a Whitehorse-based lodging combine that handles properties of all descriptions throughout the Yukon. ~ 867-393-2420, 877-735-3281. Many Yukon B&Bs belong to **Bed & Breakfast Association of the Yukon** as well. ~ Box 5233, Whitehorse, YT, Canada Y1A 4Z1; www.yukon bandb.com. DELUXE.

· People half a continent away will tell you to stop at **Braeburn Lodge** on the road to Dawson City. And so you should, although I found the Sasquatch-size hamburgers here better than what it's famed for: equally huge cinnamon rolls. Suffice to say that there are crowds inside on summer afternoons, especially when the tour buses roll in to the vast parking lot. The servers won't let you leave without asking if you got enough to eat. ~ Klondike Highway Mile 55/Km 89; radio phone 2M-3987, Fox channel. BUDGET.

LAKE LABERGE CAMPGROUND Perched on a sandy, pine-covered knoll above the lake made famous by Robert Service, the small Lake Laberge Campground offers breezy and thus relatively bug-free camping. ~ Located 5 miles (8 km) off the Klondike Highway, at the end of the Lake Laberge Road; 867-667-5648.

▲ There are 22 sites; C$8 (prepaid ticket only).

TATCHUN CREEK CAMPGROUND This pleasant spot is next to the Klondike Highway but quiet enough to make a good stopping point for the night. Set along its namesake creek amid aspens and cottonwoods, it's pretty, and the sites are well separated. ~ Klondike Highway Mile 237/Km 383, right after you cross Tatchun Creek; 867-667-5648.

▲ There are 12 sites; C$8 (prepaid ticket only).

PELLY CROSSING CAMPGROUND This free compound consists of a scattering of primitive sites along the banks of the Pelly River, maintained by the Pelly Crossing First Nations community. There are a few shelters, picnic tables and firepits. ~ Turn left (west) just before the Pelly River bridge.

▲ There are roughly a dozen informal sites, spread among the cottonwoods on the river banks; no fee.

FIVE MILE LAKE CAMPGROUND Five Mile Lake, a three-acre finger of water in the pine scrublands north of Mayo, is shallow enough and out in the open enough that it warms substantially in summer. With a nice sandy beach, it's a popular spot on hot days. (And don't think it can't get hot—the record at nearby Mayo is 96°F/36°C.) There's a small playground for children, too. ~ Keno City Road, 5 miles (8 km) east of Mayo; 867-667-5648.

▲ There are 20 sites; C$8 (prepaid ticket only).

KENO CITY CAMPGROUND It's a bit raw and exposed (like the town itself) but this campground in Keno City hugs the banks of a pretty creek and offers a place to put up a tent or park a camper for the night. Wood and water are supplied. ~ Follow signs from the Keno City Café; 867-995-2792.

▲ There are 18 sites; C$5.

▼▼▼▼▼▼▼▼▼▼▼▼
Dawson City

Set on a flat expanse of gravel and sand along the Yukon, at its confluence with the Klondike beneath the steep flanks of the Ogilvie Mountains, Dawson City has a scenic location. That's not what brings visitors today, though—and it's not what brought stampeders more than a century ago. Back then this was the best spot for a steamboat landing near the Klondike gold fields, and Dawson's founder Joseph Ladue realized greater wealth than most prospectors. Ladue claimed the entire townsite just five days after the Bonanza Creek strike that started the rush; by 1898, two years later, house lots in Dawson went for $40,000 and the area was inhabited by 31,000 souls. The first boom was shortlived; a new strike in Nome, Alaska, drew thousands from Dawson City in 1900. Although dredging kept the gold pouring out until World War I, and placer mining continues today, Dawson declined slowly until it lost the territorial capital to Whitehorse in the 1950s. Just a decade later, though, Parks Canada began to rebuild and restore the town's historic sites. The memory of Dawson City's heyday is its draw today; it's an endearing mix of commercial razzmatazz and heritage preservation.

Life in the North is ably and colorfully described in the famous *Lost Moose Catalogue*, a collection of essays and artwork about Yukon people, places and events. Look for it in bookstores and other retail outlets, or ask the tourism folks to ship it to you (C$27).

SIGHTS

Dawson City's background is painfully evident as you approach up the Klondike Valley. Huge piles of gravel left behind by dredges line the riverbed; the devastation is a century old, but looks recent. A few miles before Dawson City, the turnoff to Bonanza Creek (Mile 444/Km 715) leads up the little valley that was the epicenter of the gold strike. Eight miles (13 km) up **Dredge #4** is a huge machine, the last of its kind and the largest in North America, that worked the creekbed until it was abandoned at this spot in 1959. At nine miles (15 km), the original **Discovery Claim** is where George Carmack, Dawson Charlie and Skookum Jim Mason found piles of gold in the creekbed on August 16, 1896, precipitating the rush. Just past there, the Klondike Visitors Association maintains a public area, **Claim #6**, where anyone who wishes may pan for gold, keeping whatever they find. Yes, visitors occasionally do come up with a few flakes.

Dawson itself occupies a small grid on the northeast side of the Yukon River. Front Street is the main through road; at Front and King Street, the **Visitor Reception Centre** is an ideal place to scope out the town and pick up maps for a walking tour. There's also lots of information about lodging and other visitor services in the area. Closed winter. ~ Front and King streets; 867-993-5575, 877-465-3006; www.dawsoncity.ca.

Most of the genuinely historic buildings in town have been acquired and restored by Parks Canada, which oversees Dawson City as a National Historic Park. Hotels, small stores and cafés are scattered throughout town; the whole town can be seen in a healthy half-day walk. Many of the buildings hold only window exhibits; those which have interior exhibits and/or activities are generally open daily May through September, and closed most or all the time in winter.

Among the more important sites (consult town maps for locations): The **Commissioner's Residence** (Government House), facing Front Street, is a beautifully restored 1906 mansion with porticoes and extensive gardens. This was the center of Dawson's social life, with receptions and teas regular affairs. (It was a *very* genteel gold-rush town.) Tours are available from June to late August. Also in the southeast section of town is the **Dawson City Museum**, housed in the old territorial administration building. It holds a thorough set of exhibits on the Klondike Gold Rush and mining days. Closed winter. Admission. ~ 5th Avenue; 867-993-5291.

Nearby, the **Robert Service Cabin** was the home of the "Bard of the Yukon" during his tenure in Dawson City—which came, ironically, well after the actual gold rush. Service interpreters give daily readings of his works here in summer. Closed September to mid-May. Admission. ~ 8th Avenue and Hanson Street.

Another famed writer who actually did participate in the gold rush was **Jack London**; the cabin he inhabited in the bush has been relocated to town and is now an interpretive center at which readings of his works are also offered daily. Closed mid-September to mid-May. Admission. ~ 8th Avenue and Firth Street; 867-993-5575.

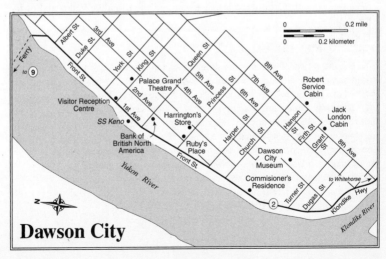

Dawson City

Right downtown, within a few blocks of the visitors center, a dozen or so historic buildings capture the flavor of the boom days. The **Canadian Imperial Bank of Commerce** is where Robert Service worked as a clerk until worldwide fame overtook him. ~Front Street, next to the SS *Keno*.

There's an original wood teller enclosure at the **Bank of British North America**. ~ 2nd Avenue and Queen Street. **Ruby's Place** is where Klondike gentlemen repaired of an evening for female companionship. ~ 2nd Avenue and Princess Street. **Harrington's Store** has been converted into a photo gallery in which the exhibit, *Dawson as They Saw It*, documents the heady days of the rush. Closed late August through May. ~ 3rd Avenue and Princess Street.

The **Palace Grand Theatre** is the centerpiece of central Dawson. This 1964 reconstruction of the original pine-plank venue was the first heritage project in Dawson; daytime tours give way to nightly shows of the Gaslight Follies (see Nightlife, below). The wooden structure is built entirely of lodgepole pine and spruce, and features an elaborate false front. The original was built in "Arizona Charlie" Meadows in 1899. Closed late August through May. ~ 2nd Avenue and King Street; 867-993-7200.

Right along Front Street, the **SS Keno** is one of the last remaining Yukon riverboats. Damaged in floods a decade ago, it was hauled behind a protective levee; restoration is underway. The levee itself is a pleasant stroll and a great place to gain a sense of the power and breadth of the Yukon River, one of North America's great waterways. ~ Front Street.

Just south of Dawson proper, the winding road to **Midnight Dome** climbs five miles (9 km) to a 2900-foot rounded pinnacle that affords superlative views of the Klondike Valley and of the

AUTHOR FAVORITE

The elegant, gilt-edged glamour that briefly shone in Dawson City is best captured today, in my opinion, at **Bombay Peggy's**, a glamorous small inn housed in a former brothel. Not long ago, the house was a 1900-vintage derelict slowly settling into a swamp downriver from central Dawson City. But its underlying beauty and historic nature appealed to a couple of highly enterprising young women who pooled their hard-earned savings, moved the house into town and set about restoring it. Today this is the finest lodging in Dawson, a two-story Victorian whose seven guest rooms, all different, are lavishly decorated in period furnishings such as clawfoot tubs, burgundy armchairs, gas-style lamps and armoires. ~ 2nd Avenue and Princess Street; 867-993-6969, fax 867-993-6199; www.bombaypeggys.com, e-mail info@bombaypeggys.com. DELUXE.

pillage done by dredges. To the north, the Ogilvie Mountains are visible. Atop Midnight Dome at midsummer, the midnight sun can be seen.

When you've seen all there is, a free, 24-hour on-demand ferry hauls cars across the Yukon to the foot of the Dawson Range mountains. The famed **Top of the World Highway** winds its way up out of Dawson City to the high ridges of the Dawson Range, with breathtaking perspectives on the Yukon River valley below and the pinnacles of the Ogilvie Mountains to the north. The road is above timberline most of the way. At 67 miles (108 km) it crosses the Alaska border; please note that U.S. Customs is open here only from 7 a.m. to 7 p.m.; the border is closed at night.

When you come down off the heights of the Top of the World Highway, what awaits is **Chicken, Alaska**—one of the quirkiest little hamlets in North America. There's not much here but a couple stores and a café, but the constant influx of tourist traffic has prompted the town to create two notable things: memorable cinnamon rolls and a sense of humor. You'll find both at the Chicken Café, where the rolls hit the counter most mornings by 8 a.m.; more humor can be found in a postcard that explains what life is really like in Chicken. Let me paraphrase: It's for the hardy.

Please note: Almost every lodging in Dawson City has a saloon on the ground floor. If you're not comfortable sleeping above boisterous nightlife, make sure you get a room away from the bar.

LODGING

Dawson's **Eldorado Hotel** is the cleanest and freshest of the half-dozen similar mainstream facilities in the city, with 52 rooms and suites. It's just a block to Diamond Tooth Gertie's and the Palace Grand. ~ 3rd Avenue and Princess Street; 867-993-5451, 800-764-3536, fax 867-993-5256; www.eldoradohotel. ca, e-mail eldorado@yknet.ca. MODERATE.

The Bunkhouse is a dorm-like guesthouse just off the main drag in Dawson. Rooms are clean and compact, and the location is handy to all the sights. There are both shared and private baths. ~ Front and Princess streets; 867-993-6164, fax 867-993-6051; www.bunkhouse.ca, e-mail bunkhouse@yknet.yk.ca. BUDGET TO MODERATE.

Dawson City River Hostel is perched on the slopes of the Yukon riverbank across from Dawson, reached by a free 24-hour ferry. It has 40 beds, eight family rooms, numerous tent sites, and a long list of facilities including a sauna, a store, firepits, free firewood and plenty of summertime daylight to make up for the lack of electricity. No credit cards. Closed October to mid-May. ~ Just east of the ferry landing, Top of the World Highway Mile 0; 867-993-6823; www.yukonhostels.com, e-mail yukonhostels@hotmail.com. BUDGET.

HIDDEN ▶ **Bear Creek Bed & Bannock** is owned and operated by a Yukon First Nations family, so the history here runs even deeper than in Dawson City. It's outside of Dawson, so the surroundings are more peaceful than accommodations in town. The four units are in a separate building, with kitchen, shower, laundry facilities and an outdoor barbecue. The continental breakfast features fresh-made bannock (Indian bread) daily. ~ Bear Creek Subdivision Road, 6 miles (10 km) south of Dawson City; 867-993-6765, fax 867-993-6532. BUDGET TO MODERATE.

DINING Set in the pastoral countryside along the Klondike Highway south of Dawson, **Tintina Bakery** offers dandy baked goods to

HIDDEN ▶ rural residents and alert travelers. Morning muffins and pastries are superb, lunch finds delights such as pot pies, and the breads are wholesome and fresh any time. Breakfast and lunch only. ~ Alaska Highway, 12 miles (19 km) south of Dawson City; 867-993-5558. BUDGET.

Klondike Kate's is Dawson's most reliable restaurant. It's not gourmet fare but the salads are good (greens, not iceberg lettuce), soups are hearty, and the pasta and meat dishes prepared well. Although Kate's is housed in a 1904 heritage building, the open-air roofed patio is more enjoyable—and protected from Dawson's occasional summer showers. Breakfast, lunch and dinner. ~ 1102 3rd Avenue; 867-993-6527; www.klondikekates.ca, e-mail info@klondikekates.ca. BUDGET TO MODERATE.

RiverWest Coffeehouse is the place to get coffee drinks (made with Yukon-roasted beans), muffins and pastries in the morning before you set out to explore Dawson City. Lunchtime brings a small selection of soups and sandwiches. ~ Front Street near King Street; 867-993-6339. BUDGET.

NIGHTLIFE Dawson City's **Gaslight Follies**—which take place in the Palace Grand Theatre—are supposedly an attempt to replicate the sort of vaudeville show the gold-rush miners would have patronized a century ago. The script is transparently geared to the Alaska Highway RV crowd. Operated by the Klondike Visitors Association, proceeds support tourist services in Dawson. Shows run May through September. Admission. ~ Palace Grand Theatre (box office is across the street), King Street and 2nd Avenue; 867-993-5575.

After the show at the Palace Grand Theatre, some of the cast and many of the tourists repair to **Diamond Tooth Gertie's** for late-night revelry that includes can-can dancing, cabaret acts, and low-key gambling. Admission. ~ 4th Avenue and Queen Street; 867-993-5575.

For drinks and tasty snacks, stop by the lounge at **Bombay Peggy's**. ~ 2nd Avenue and Princess Street; 867-993-6969.

KLONDIKE RIVER CAMPGROUND This is the more attractive—and more peaceful—of the two territorial campgrounds that serve Dawson City. Set in a pretty copse of cottonwood trees on riverbed gravel bars, the 38 campsites are fairly private. Downtown Dawson City is about 15 minutes away by car. ~ Klondike Highway, ten miles (16 km) south of Dawson City; 867-667-5648.

▲ There are 38 sites; C$8 (prepaid ticket only).

YUKON RIVER CAMPGROUND The chief advantage to this massive campground (largest in the Yukon) is its proximity to downtown Dawson City. A five-minute walk, then a five-minute ferry ride, and you're in Dawson. The campsites lie along a loop road that traces a big hook on the forested slope above the river. ~ At Mile 0, Top of the World Highway (just past the Yukon River ferry landing); 867-667-5648.

▲ There are 98 sites (the best ones are on the upper road); C$8 (prepaid ticket only).

Outdoor Adventures

GUIDES & OUTFITTERS

Atlin Quest is a multifaceted local guiding and wilderness outfitter—also offering art workshops and stand-alone cabins. Their ten-day adventures include hiking, camping and canoeing on Atlin Lake. ~ 800-651-8882; www.atlinquest.com.

Nahanni River Adventures & Whitewolf Expeditions offers guided wilderness tours of all sorts—on foot or by canoe or kayak, in its namesake river basin, as well as along the Tatshenshini, Sitkine, Coppermine and Yukon rivers. ~ 867-668-3180; www.nahanni.com.

CANOEING

Because it is a land of large, long rivers, many Yukon wilderness treks are done by canoe (or, less often, kayak) rather than on foot.

UNDER THE YUKON STARS

Travelers equipped to camp should take advantage of the Yukon's **Territorial Campgrounds**, 41 of which are located on or near roads. These are not parks; they are camping facilities that provide designated sites, picnic tables, fire rings, firewood and water. The $8 nightly fee must be paid with a ticket available for purchase at Visitor Info Centres, government offices and retail outlets. Cash is not accepted at the campgrounds; the government suggests (remember, things are quite laid-back up here) that campers who arrive without a permit go ahead and camp that night, then get a permit later and drop it in any campground permit box down the road. Unlike in B.C., there is no reservation system; however, YTG campgrounds rarely fill up. ~ Yukon Parks and Recreation, 867-667-5648.

More than two dozen major floats are possible, with sidetrips and excursions adding parameters to the point that a lifetime of river running would be needed to exhaust all the possibilities.

The **Yukon River** itself is a highly utilized route. Between Whitehorse and Dawson City the river is largely surrounded by wilderness; although it's large, there are few hazards, aside from the fairly mild whitewater at Five Finger Rapids. Halfway down the river, **Fort Selkirk** is a historic site that has been somewhat restored to its days as a frontier outpost, later steamboat landing. The entire trip from Whitehorse to Dawson takes up to 16 days.

Numerous other wilderness rivers call to more experienced paddlers, most famously the **Big Salmon**, a weeklong float, and the **Bonnet Plume**, an utterly untrammeled waterway in northeast Yukon that has no road access anywhere along its length.

Outfitters **Up North Wilderness Specialists** offers a full range of services for adventurous Yukon travelers, including canoe and kayak rentals, guided and unguided river trips, complete equipment outfitting, river maps, and transportation to embarkation points. Day trips are possible, too. ~ 103 Strickland Street, Whitehorse; 867-667-7905; www.upnorthadventures.yk.ca. **Kanoe People** is a Whitehorse adventure outfitter offering canoes and kayaks, along with advice and gear, transportation and guide services. ~ 867-668-4899; www.kanoepeople.com. In addition to canoe rentals, **Nature Tours of Yukon** provides guided trips on the Liard, Wind and Yukon rivers. ~ Whitehorse; 867-667-4868; www.naturetoursyukon.com.

Eagle Canoe Rentals offers canoes for floats down the middle Yukon, from Dawson to Eagle, Alaska. ~ Dawson City River Hostel; 867-993-6823.

FISHING   Lake trout, grayling and arctic char are the species that attract the most angling interest in the Yukon; each is represented by healthy populations. The Teslin River is famed for its grayling fishing; Kluane, Atlin, Tagish and Teslin lakes are renowned lake trout

AUTHOR FAVORITE

Among the dozens of wilderness rivers in the Yukon, the **Teslin River** is the most accessible and best-suited for intermediate paddlers who have not made such a trek before—yet completely appropriate for experts. The float begins at Johnson's Crossing on the Alaska Highway and ends eight days later at Carmacks on the Klondike Highway. There are no major cataracts, and the river is famed for grayling fishing. It's essential to use a local outfitters for any trips. See above for suggestions.

spots. But there are literally thousands of other options—local out-fitters can offer guidance to less-known places. Yukon Territorial fishing licenses are required for all anglers, plus a National Parks license for fishing in Kluane National Park. Regulations and fees vary, and change periodically; consult any outdoor supply store or government agent for up-to-date information.

2 Fly Fishing Adventures is a Whitehorse outfitter/guide service that specializes in exposing anglers to fly-fishing expeditions for all species of game fish, with instructors certified by fly-fishing federations. ~ 867-667-2359; e-mail fishyukon@polaris.ca.

Duffers who make it this far north won't have too many opportunities to swing a club. However, **Meadow Lakes Golf & Country Club** enjoys a sensational setting on the escarpment above the Yukon River just outside Whitehorse. A target-golf course, it has a full clubhouse, pro shop and rentals—and few crowds. ~ Alaska Highway, 3 miles (5 km) south of Whitehorse; 867-668-4653.

GOLF

Built in the 1940s to serve a short-lived oil pipeline project, the **Canol Road** north of Faro has deteriorated to the point that it's impassable to ordinary vehicles. Still used occasionally by mining exploration and wilderness outfitting operations, it has also become an exotic trek for mountain biking enthusiasts, who savor the rare opportunity to traverse virtually untouched wilderness on a roadbed. Crossing the heart of the MacKenzie Mountains into the Northwest Territories, this is a journey that can take up to a month, and exposes hardy travelers to unlimited scenery, wildlife and wilderness.

BIKING

In Kluane National Park, mountain bikers like tackling the old mining roads (for instance, Alsek Trail and Mush Lake Road) that wend through the area.

Bike Rentals Expert preparation is essential for biking the Canol Heritage Trail. **Kanoe People** rents bicycles for a half-day, full day or the week. ~ 867-668-4899; www.kanoepeople.com. **Fireweed Hikes and Bikes** offers rentals and day-trip advice in the Whitehorse area. Multiday biking and hiking excursions are also available. ~ 867-668-7313; www.yukonhikes.com.

In a land dominated by big rivers, hiking takes a back seat to canoeing and kayaking for wilderness exploration in the Yukon. With the exception of Kluane National Park, most developed trails are meant for day hikes and lead to spectacular views or alpine meadows. All distances listed for hiking trails are one way unless otherwise noted.

HIKING

The **Auriol Trail** (10 miles/16 km) is one of the few in Kluane National Park meant for day-use visitors. This six-hour climb into subalpine meadows exposes the visitor to the raw, semi-arid climate of the interior ranges of the southern Yukon, with their brief summer flowering in July. ~ At Haines Highway Mile 147/ Km 239, 4 miles (7 km) south of the Alaska Highway.

The **Chilkoot Trail** (32 miles/53 km), one of the most notorious treks in North America, was the path followed by Gold Rushers attempting to reach Dawson City in the early days of the Klondike. Canadian mounties required pioneers to bring along a ton of supplies to ensure they would survive the Yukon; today's trekkers don't have to bring that much, but it still is a major challenge. The trail wends its way from near Skagway, Alaska, to Bennett, B.C.; it's a two-day trek for seasoned hikers, three days or more for the rest of us. Even in summer, the weather can be temperamental, with snow showers possible on the higher portions of the trail. Aside from the Coast Range scenery, history still abides along the trail in the form of artifacts abandoned by Gold Rushers and left in place by the managers of what is now a historic park. Permits are required, and reservations are advised (only 50 hikers a day are allowed to cross the summit of Chilkoot Pass). ~ Yukon National Historic Sites Parks/Canada, 300 Main Street, Whitehorse; 867-667-3910.

Mount Haldene is a solitary mountain along the **Silver Trail** (4 miles/7 km) west of Stewart Crossing. The hike to the top is a six-hour trek on an improved trail, leading to one of the best vistas in the Yukon. Spread before you are literally thousands of square miles of wilderness; on clear days it's possible to see dozens of peaks. ~ Route 11, 18 miles (29 km) east of Mayo.

▼▼▼▼▼▼▼▼▼▼▼▼
Transportation

CAR

The major overland route—the only one—into the Yukon is the **Alaska Highway** (Route 97 in B.C., Route 1 in the Yukon) from Dawson Creek, BC, about a three-day drive (or two very long days) to Whitehorse. This famed road is now paved throughout its length, and upgraded to high-speed standards most of the way. Automotive services and facilities are found at regular intervals; it's a major trucking corridor.

The **Klondike Highway**, also a paved high-speed road, wends its way from Skagway, Alaska, to Whitehorse (a half-day drive); then across the central Yukon to Dawson City (a one-day, eight-to ten-hour drive).

The **Haines Highway** runs 108 miles (174 km) from Haines, Alaska, to Haines Junction; the only access to Skagway or Haines is from the Yukon interior, or the Alaska Ferry system.

The **Top of the World Highway** crosses the high country west of Dawson City; this is a winding, chip-seal route not meant for high-speed driving. Once it crosses into Alaska, it turns into a gravel road, the **Taylor Highway**, which can become impassable in persistent wet conditions. Allow a half-day, in good conditions, to drive from Dawson City to its return to the Alaska Highway at Tetlin Junction.

Whitehorse International Airport, just below the Alaska Highway on a bluff above the city, is the major air terminal for all of the Yukon. Yes, it is truly international—charter flights frequently arrive direct from Germany in the summer. **Air Canada** provides daily service to Whitehorse from Vancouver; 888-247-2262. **Canada 3000** offers summer service to Whitehorse; 877-359-2263.

Air North provides service between Dawson City and Whitehorse and Fairbanks, as well as to Old Crow, Inuvik and Juneau; 867-668-2228, 867-993-5110; 800-764-0407 (U.S.), 800-661-0407 (Canada); www.flyairnorth.com.

Alkan Air is the major flightseeing and charter operator in the Yukon. ~ 867-668-2107; www.alkanair.com.

Scheduled bus service to Whitehorse is provided from Fairbanks and Anchorage by **Alaskon Express/Gray Line Yukon.** ~ Westmark Whitehorse Hotel, 2nd Avenue and Steele Street, Whitehorse; 867-668-3225; www.graylinealaska.com.

Greyhound Canada provides scheduled service from Dawson Creek to Whitehorse. ~ 867-667-2223; www.greyhound.ca.

Budget Car Rentals offers a full range of vehicles in Whitehorse. ~ 867-667-6200; 800-268-8900. **National Car Rental** is represented by Norcan Leasing, with cars, trucks, vans and 4x4s available. ~ 867-668-2137.

Budget Car Rentals offers service in Dawson City; 867-993-5644.

Recommended Reading

The Canadian literary tradition is strong; within British Columbia are a healthy dozen or so publishers whose catalogs include a wide range of titles about the province and its people. Bookstores are commonplace in both big cities and smaller towns; I've spent many hours browsing the stacks in my favorite Vancouver, Victoria and Kelowna stores. Those looking for B.C. books who aren't actually in the province can check out the BCBooks website at www.bcbooks.com. It's by no means comprehensive, but it does have an interesting selection of titles about the province.

Here are a few of the best to look for:

The B.C. Fact Book. Mark Zuehlke. Whitecap Books, Vancouver, 1995. A miniature encyclopedia, from A to Z.

Bowering's B.C.: A Swashbuckling History. George Bowering. Penguin Books, Toronto/London, 1996. Bowering pulls no punches in his assessment of the tycoons, rogues and adventurers who settled the province. His perspective on the area's First Nations is particularly pointed.

Breaking Smith's Quarter Horse. Paul St. Pierre. Douglas & McIntyre, Vancouver, 1981. St. Pierre's gentle, evocative and thoughtful tales of ranch life in the Chilcotin are indelibly memorable. Also look for *Smith and Other Events* and *Boss of the Namko Drive.*

British Columbia: A Natural History. Richard and Sydney Cannings. Greystone Books, Vancouver/Toronto, 1996. Two scientist brothers, raised in the Okanagan, offer the definitive description of the province's geology, biology, weather, topography and wildlife. Beautifully illustrated.

The Chilcotin: British Columbia's Last Frontier. Chris Harris. Country Light Publishing, 108 Mile Ranch, 1996. Cariboo native Harris turns his camera lens and spare prose on this heartbreakingly beautiful corner of B.C. Harris is also the author of a companion volume about the Cariboo.

Food City: Vancouver. Angela Murrills. Polestar Press, Victoria, 2000. Murrills is the Georgia Strait's food critic; here she offers a fond but straightforward assessment of the city's distinctive West Coast cuisine, as well as its many other strains of cooking.

Hot Springs of Western Canada. Glenn Woodsworth. Gordon Soules Book Publishers, West Vancouver/Seattle, 1999. A geologist's admirably comprehensive compilation of every hot spring, big or small, known or suspected, in B.C., the Yukon, and parts of Alberta and Washington state. Includes maps and very exact directions.

Mighty River: A Portrait of the Fraser. Richard C. Bocking. Douglas & McIntyre, Vancouver/Toronto, 1997. A fond description of the continent's mightiest undammed river, and the threats that still face it.

Over Beautiful B.C. Beautiful British Columbia Magazine. Victoria, 1996. A companion to the fabulous hourlong video of the same name, this richly illustrated coffee table book offers an exceptionally informative text to accompany the photos.

Index

Lodging Index

HOSTELS

LODGING SERVICES

Dining Index

HIDDEN GUIDES

Adventure travel or a relaxing vacation?—"Hidden" guidebooks are the only travel books in the business to provide detailed information on both. Aimed at environmentally aware travelers, our motto is "Where Vacations Meet Adventures." These books combine details on unique hotels, restaurants and sightseeing with information on camping, sports and hiking for the outdoor enthusiast.

PARADISE FAMILY GUIDES

Ideal for families traveling with kids of any age—toddlers to teenagers— Paradise Family Guides offer a blend of travel information unlike any other guides to the Hawaiian islands. With vacation ideas and tropical adventures that are sure to satisfy both action-hungry youngsters and re-laxation-seeking parents, these guides meet the specific needs of each and every family member.

HIDDEN GUIDEBOOKS

____ Hidden Arizona, $16.95

____ Hidden Bahamas, $14.95

____ Hidden Baja, $14.95

____ Hidden Belize, $15.95

____ Hidden Big Island of Hawaii, $13.95

____ Hidden Boston & Cape Cod, $14.95

____ Hidden British Columbia, $18.95

____ Hidden Cancún & the Yucatán, $16.95

____ Hidden Carolinas, $17.95

____ Hidden Coast of California, $18.95

____ Hidden Colorado, $15.95

____ Hidden Disneyland, $13.95

____ Hidden Florida, $18.95

____ Hidden Florida Keys & Everglades, $13.95

____ Hidden Georgia, $16.95

____ Hidden Guatemala, $16.95

____ Hidden Hawaii, $18.95

____ Hidden Idaho, $14.95

____ Hidden Kauai, $13.95

____ Hidden Los Angeles, $14.95

____ Hidden Maui, $13.95

____ Hidden Miami, $14.95

____ Hidden Montana, $15.95

____ Hidden New England, $18.95

____ Hidden New Mexico, $15.95

____ Hidden New Orleans, $14.95

____ Hidden Oahu, $13.95

____ Hidden Oregon, $15.95

____ Hidden Pacific Northwest, $18.95

____ Hidden San Diego, $14.95

____ Hidden Salt Lake City, $14.95

____ Hidden San Francisco & Northern California, $18.95

____ Hidden Seattle, $13.95

____ Hidden Southern California, $18.95

____ Hidden Southwest, $19.95

____ Hidden Tahiti, $17.95

____ Hidden Tennessee, $16.95

____ Hidden Utah, $16.95

____ Hidden Walt Disney World, $13.95

____ Hidden Washington, $15.95

____ Hidden Wine Country, $13.95

____ Hidden Wyoming, $15.95

PARADISE FAMILY GUIDES

____ Paradise Family Guides: Kaua'i, $16.95

____ Paradise Family Guides: Maui, $16.95

____ Paradise Family Guides: Big Island of Hawai'i, $16.95

Mark the book(s) you're ordering and enter the total cost here ➥ [   ]

California residents add 8.25% sales tax here ➥ [   ]

Shipping, check box for your preferred method and enter cost here ➥ [   ]

❑ BOOK RATE   **FREE! FREE! FREE!**

❑ PRIORITY MAIL/UPS GROUND   cost of postage

❑ UPS OVERNIGHT OR 2-DAY AIR   cost of postage   [   ]

Billing, enter total amount due here and check method of payment ➥ [   ]

❑ CHECK   ❑ MONEY ORDER

❑ VISA/MASTERCARD _____ EXP. DATE _____

NAME _____ PHONE _____

ADDRESS _____

CITY _____ STATE _____ ZIP _____

MONEY-BACK GUARANTEE ON DIRECT ORDERS PLACED THROUGH ULYSSES PRESS.

ABOUT THE AUTHOR

ERIC LUCAS is a widely traveled writer who focuses on Western North America, natural history and business. He has been a newspaper editor and columnist and a magazine editor. His avocations include gardening, fishing, music and cooking. He lives in Seattle and Northern California.

ABOUT THE ILLUSTRATOR

DOUG McCARTHY, a native New Yorker, lives in the San Francisco Bay area with his family. His illustrations appear in a number of Ulysses Press guides, including *Hidden Wyoming*, *Hidden Tennessee*, *Hidden Bahamas* and *Hidden Kauai*.